ドットハック//たそがれのうでわでんせつ

.hack 3 //黄昏の腕輪伝説

漫画 IZUMI REI
依澄れい

原作 HAMAZAKI TATSUYA
浜崎達也

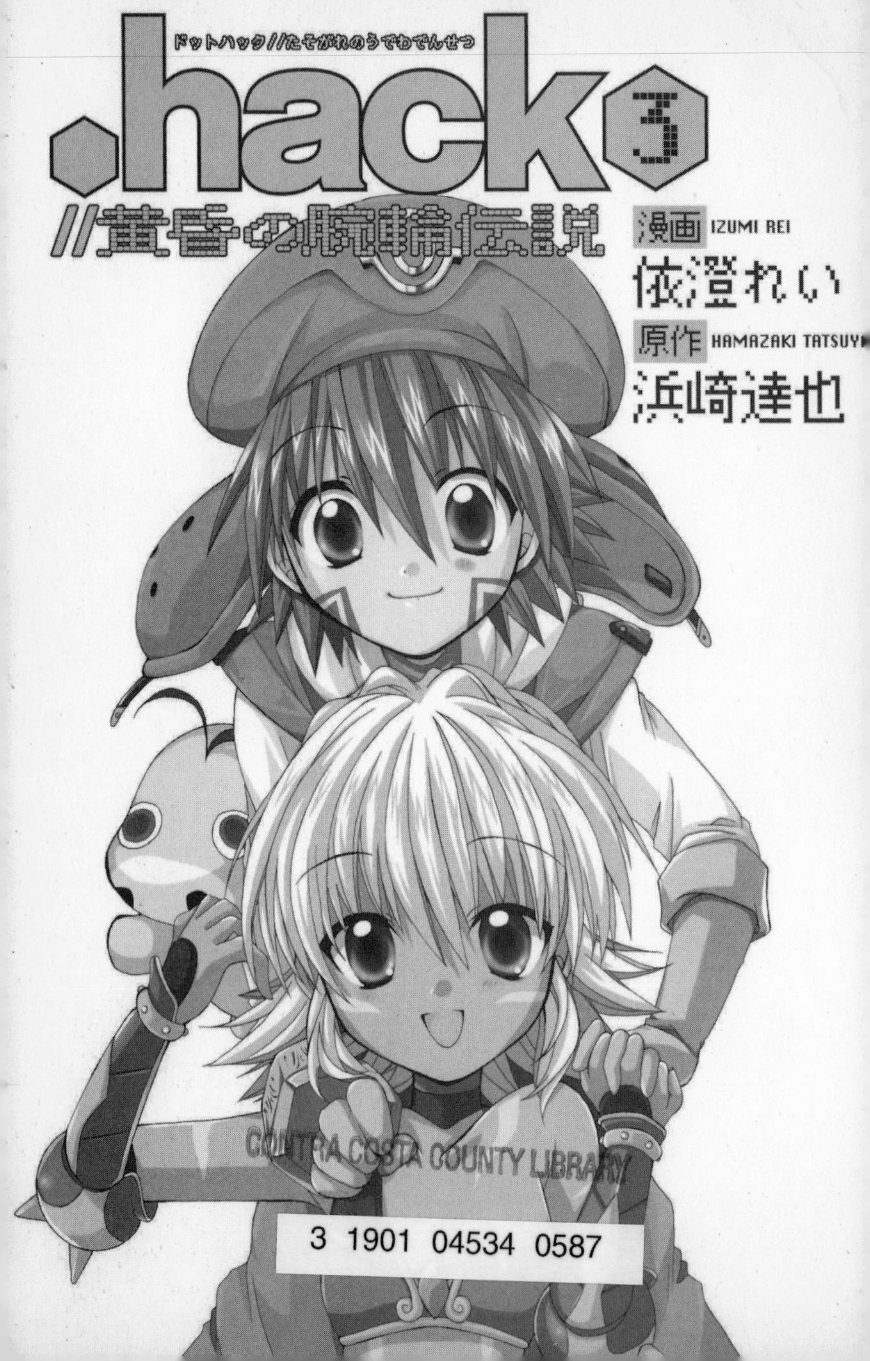

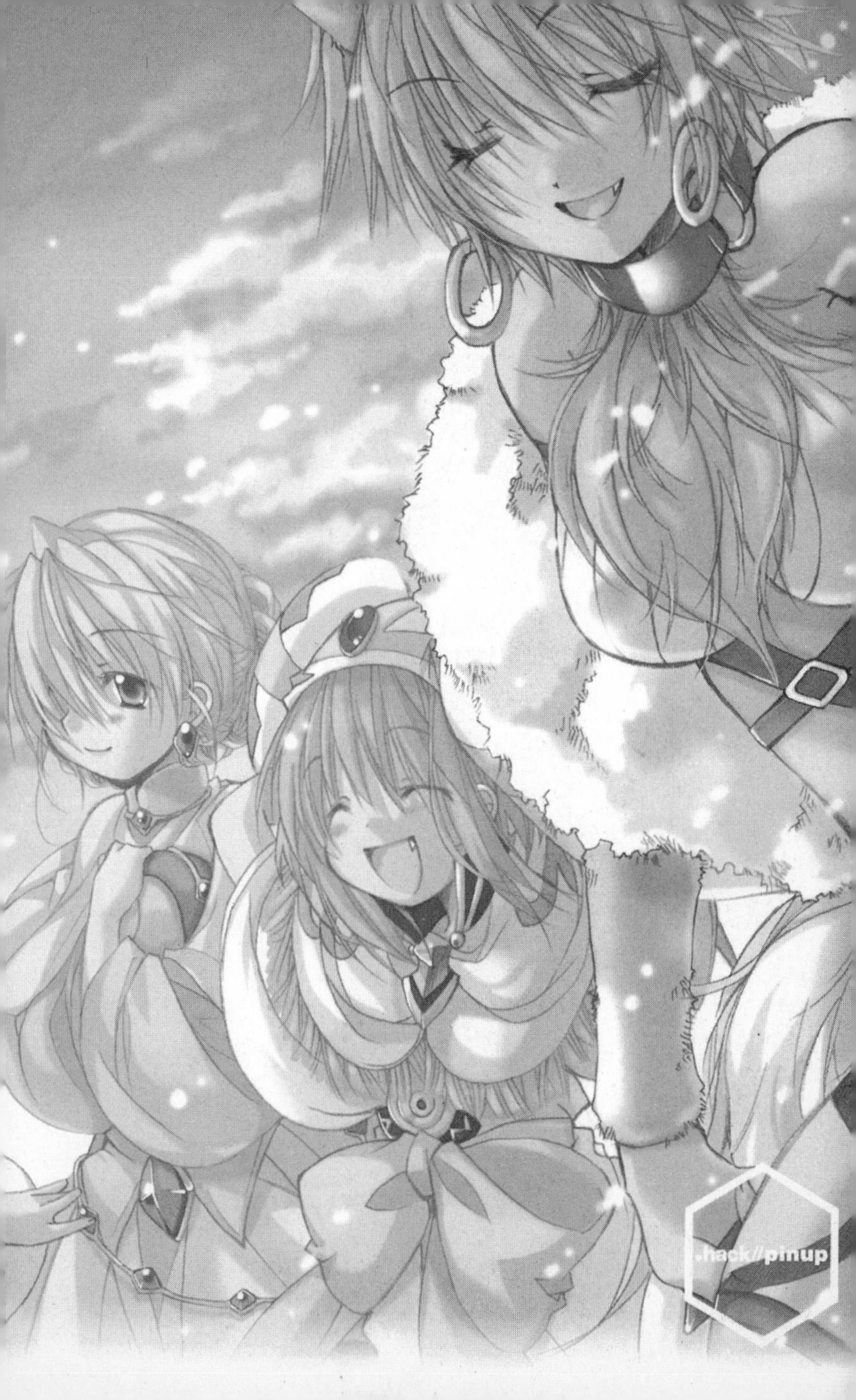
.hack//pinup

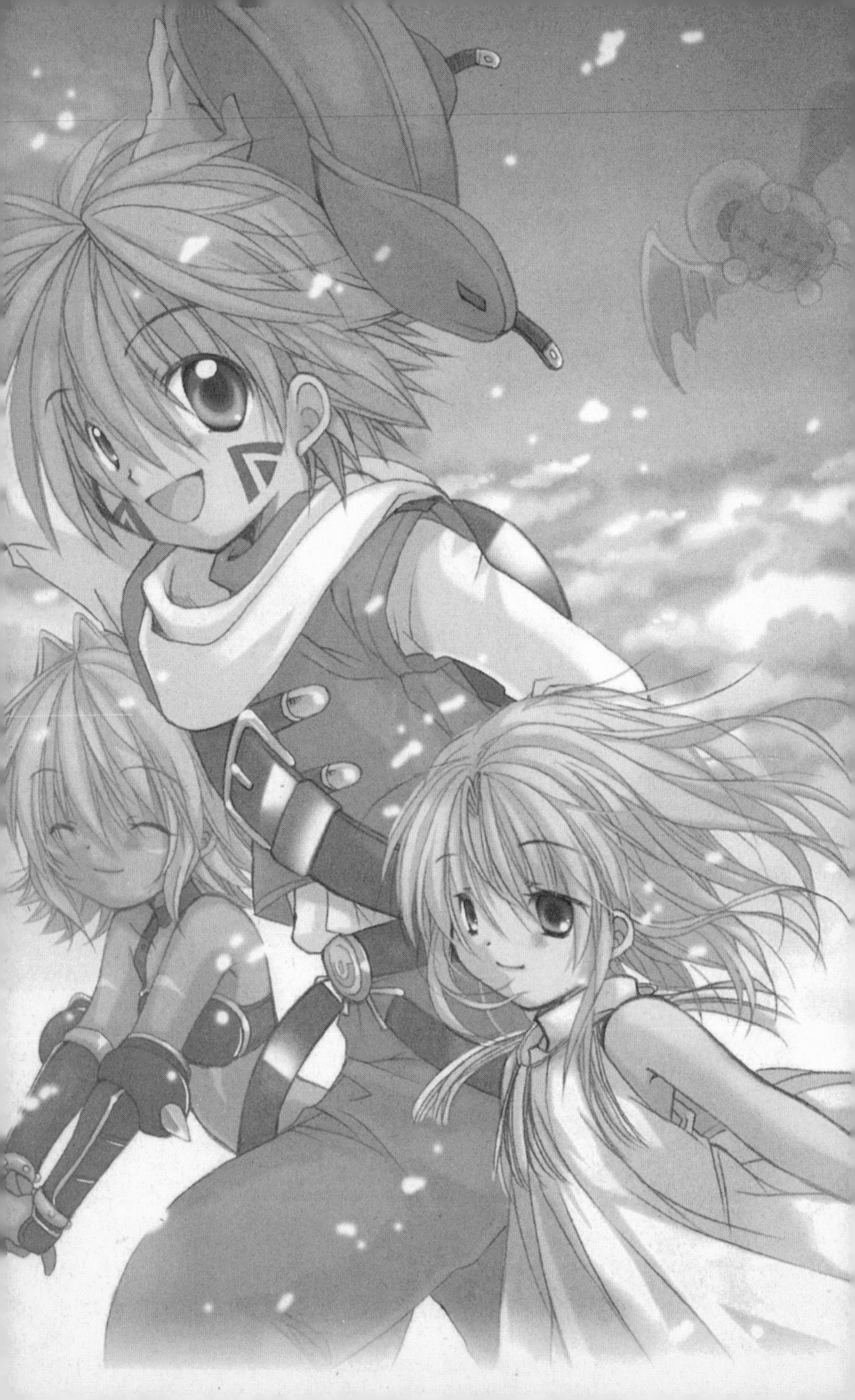

.hack//TABLE OF CONTENTS

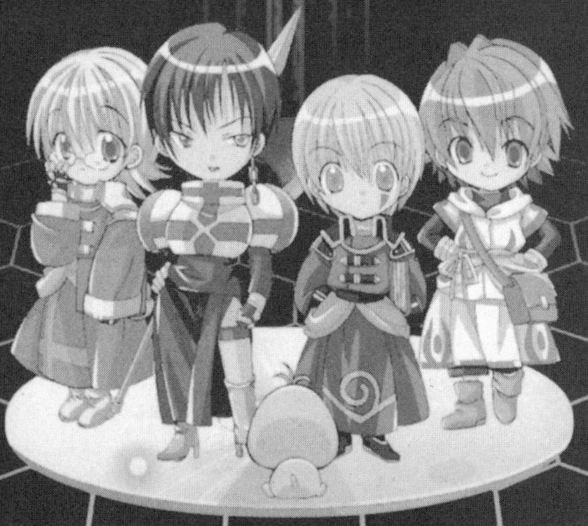

.hack//Legend of the Twilight Tales Vol. 3
Art by Rei Izumi
Story by Tatsuya Hamazaki

Translation - Naomi Kokuto
Retouch and Lettering - Peter Ahlstrom
Production Artist - James Dashiell
Production Assistant - Kathy Schilling
Cover Design - Patrick Hook

Editor - Jake Forbes
Digital Imaging Manager - Chris Buford
Pre-Press Manager - Antonio DePietro
Production Managers - Jennifer Miller and Mutsumi Miyazaki
Art Director - Matt Alford
Managing Editor - Jill Freshney
VP of Production - Ron Klamert
President and C.O.O. - John Parker
Publisher and C.E.O. - Stuart Levy

A 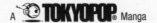 Manga

TOKYOPOP Inc.
5900 Wilshire Blvd. Suite 2000
Los Angeles, CA 90036

E-mail: info@TOKYOPOP.com
Come visit us online at www.TOKYOPOP.com

ISBN: 1-59532-369-4

First TOKYOPOP printing: November 2004
10 9 8 7 6 5
Printed in the USA

キャラクター紹介

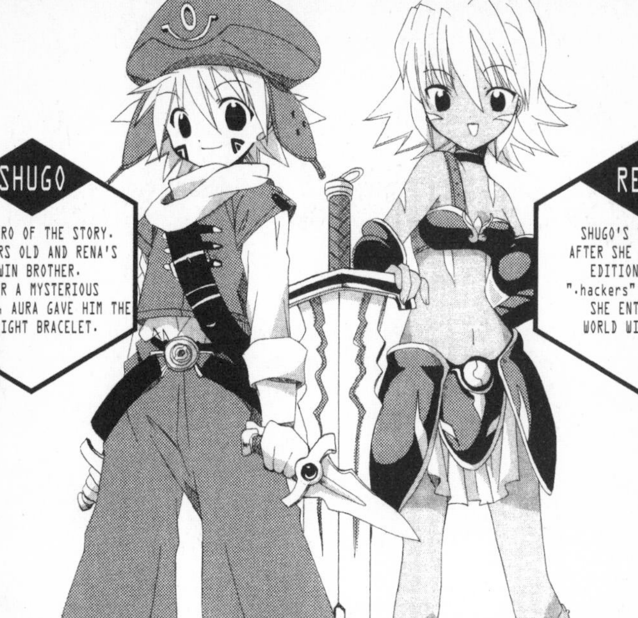

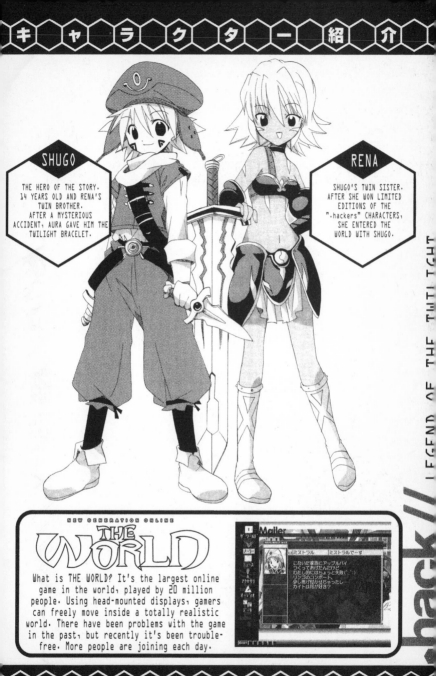

SHUGO

THE HERO OF THE STORY. 14 YEARS OLD AND RENA'S TWIN BROTHER. AFTER A MYSTERIOUS ACCIDENT, AURA GAVE HIM THE TWILIGHT BRACELET.

RENA

SHUGO'S TWIN SISTER. AFTER SHE WON LIMITED EDITIONS OF THE ".hackers" CHARACTERS, SHE ENTERED THE WORLD WITH SHUGO.

.hack//LEGEND OF THE TWILIGHT

NEW GENERATION ONLINE

THE WORLD

What is THE WORLD? It's the largest online game in the world, played by 20 million people. Using head-mounted displays, gamers can freely move inside a totally realistic world. There have been problems with the game in the past, but recently it's been trouble-free. More people are joining each day.

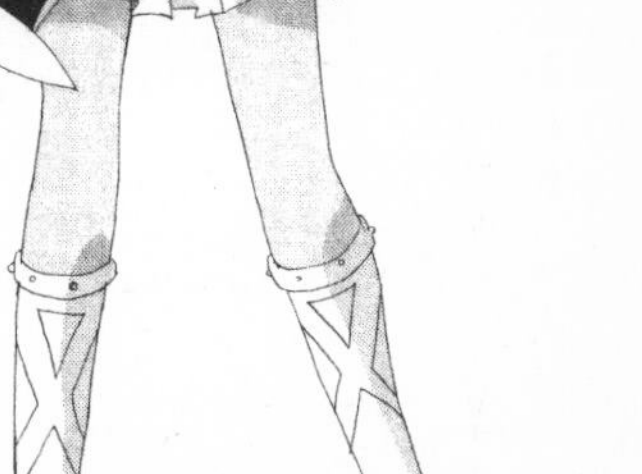
Mailer
ミストラル
ミストラルでーす
こないだ家族にアップルパイ
つくってあげたんだけど
わたし的にはちょっと失敗(^_^;)
リンゴのコンポート、
少し焦げ付かせちゃったし…
カイトは何が好き?

INTRODUCTION

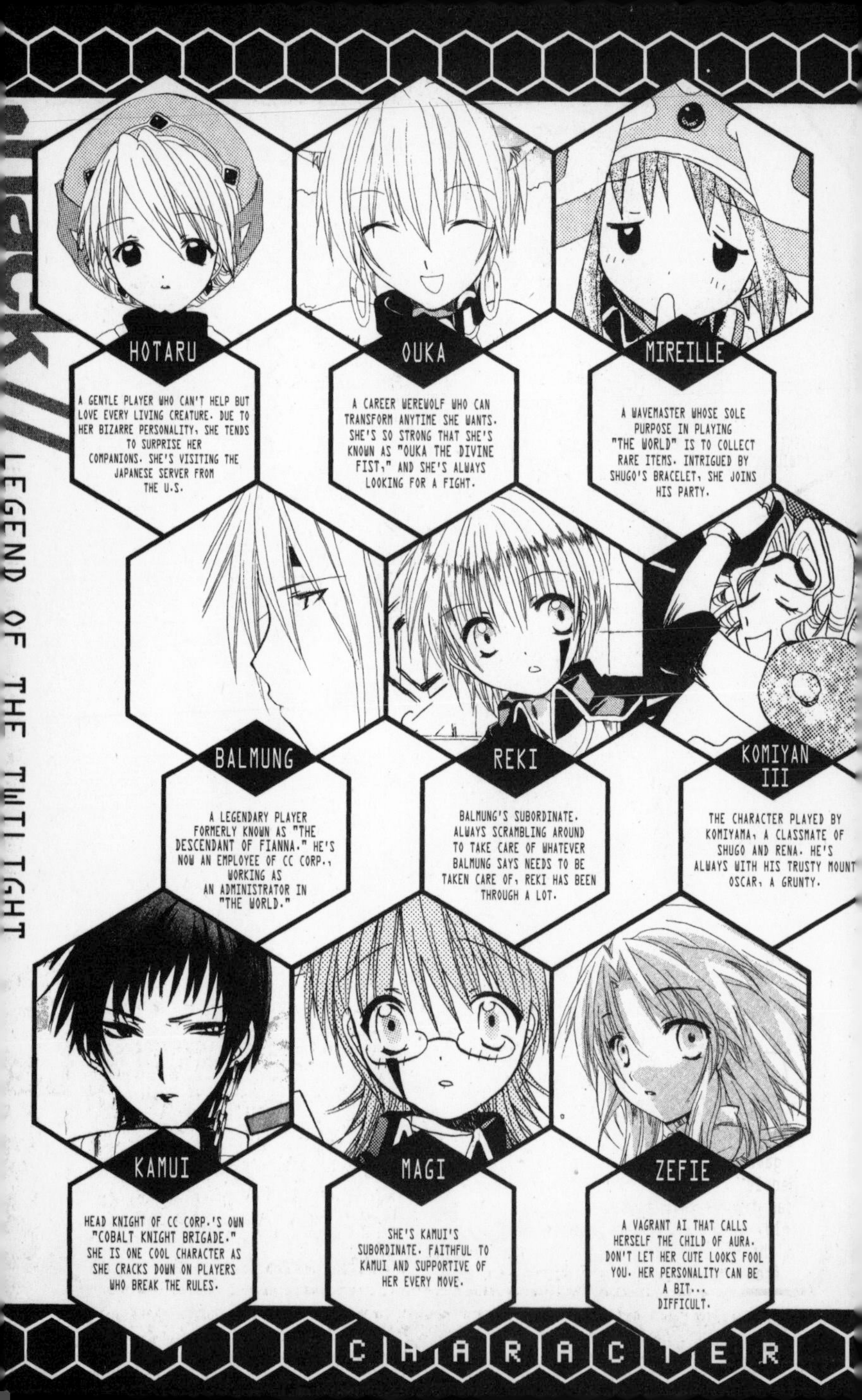
.hack// LEGEND OF THE TWILIGHT
HOTARU
A GENTLE PLAYER WHO CAN'T HELP BUT LOVE EVERY LIVING CREATURE. DUE TO HER BIZARRE PERSONALITY, SHE TENDS TO SURPRISE HER COMPANIONS. SHE'S VISITING THE JAPANESE SERVER FROM THE U.S.
OUKA
A CAREER WEREWOLF WHO CAN TRANSFORM ANYTIME SHE WANTS. SHE'S SO STRONG THAT SHE'S KNOWN AS "OUKA THE DIVINE FIST," AND SHE'S ALWAYS LOOKING FOR A FIGHT.
MIREILLE
A WAVEMASTER WHOSE SOLE PURPOSE IN PLAYING "THE WORLD" IS TO COLLECT RARE ITEMS. INTRIGUED BY SHUGO'S BRACELET, SHE JOINS HIS PARTY.
BALMUNG
A LEGENDARY PLAYER FORMERLY KNOWN AS "THE DESCENDANT OF FIANNA." HE'S NOW AN EMPLOYEE OF CC CORP., WORKING AS AN ADMINISTRATOR IN "THE WORLD."
REKI
BALMUNG'S SUBORDINATE. ALWAYS SCRAMBLING AROUND TO TAKE CARE OF WHATEVER BALMUNG SAYS NEEDS TO BE TAKEN CARE OF, REKI HAS BEEN THROUGH A LOT.
KOMIYAN III
THE CHARACTER PLAYED BY KOMIYAMA, A CLASSMATE OF SHUGO AND RENA. HE'S ALWAYS WITH HIS TRUSTY MOUNT OSCAR, A GRUNTY.
KAMUI
HEAD KNIGHT OF CC CORP.'S OWN "COBALT KNIGHT BRIGADE." SHE IS ONE COOL CHARACTER AS SHE CRACKS DOWN ON PLAYERS WHO BREAK THE RULES.
MAGI
SHE'S KAMUI'S SUBORDINATE. FAITHFUL TO KAMUI AND SUPPORTIVE OF HER EVERY MOVE.
ZEFIE
A VAGRANT AI THAT CALLS HERSELF THE CHILD OF AURA. DON'T LET HER CUTE LOOKS FOOL YOU. HER PERSONALITY CAN BE A BIT... DIFFICULT.
CHARACTER

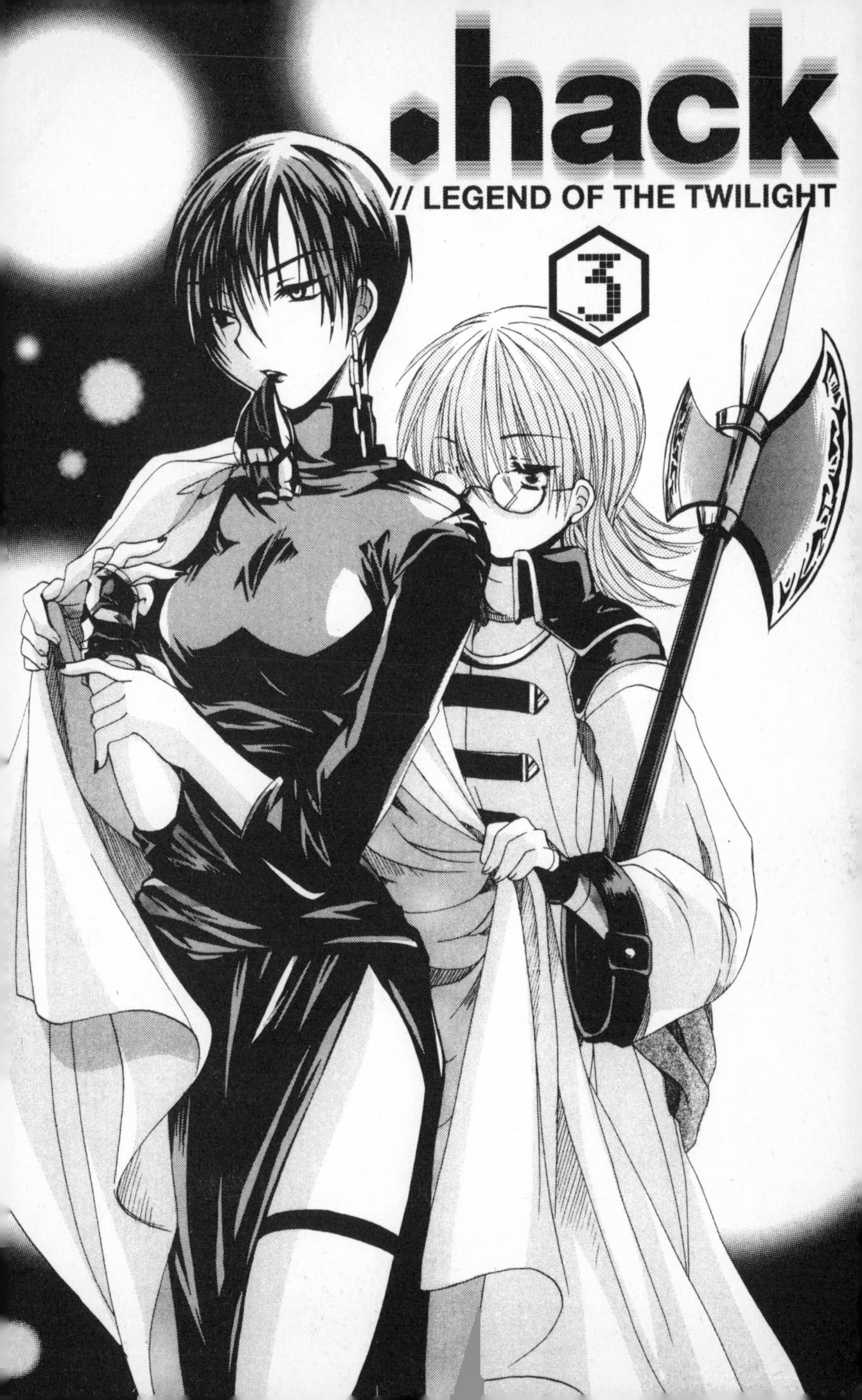
.hack
// LEGEND OF THE TWILIGHT
3

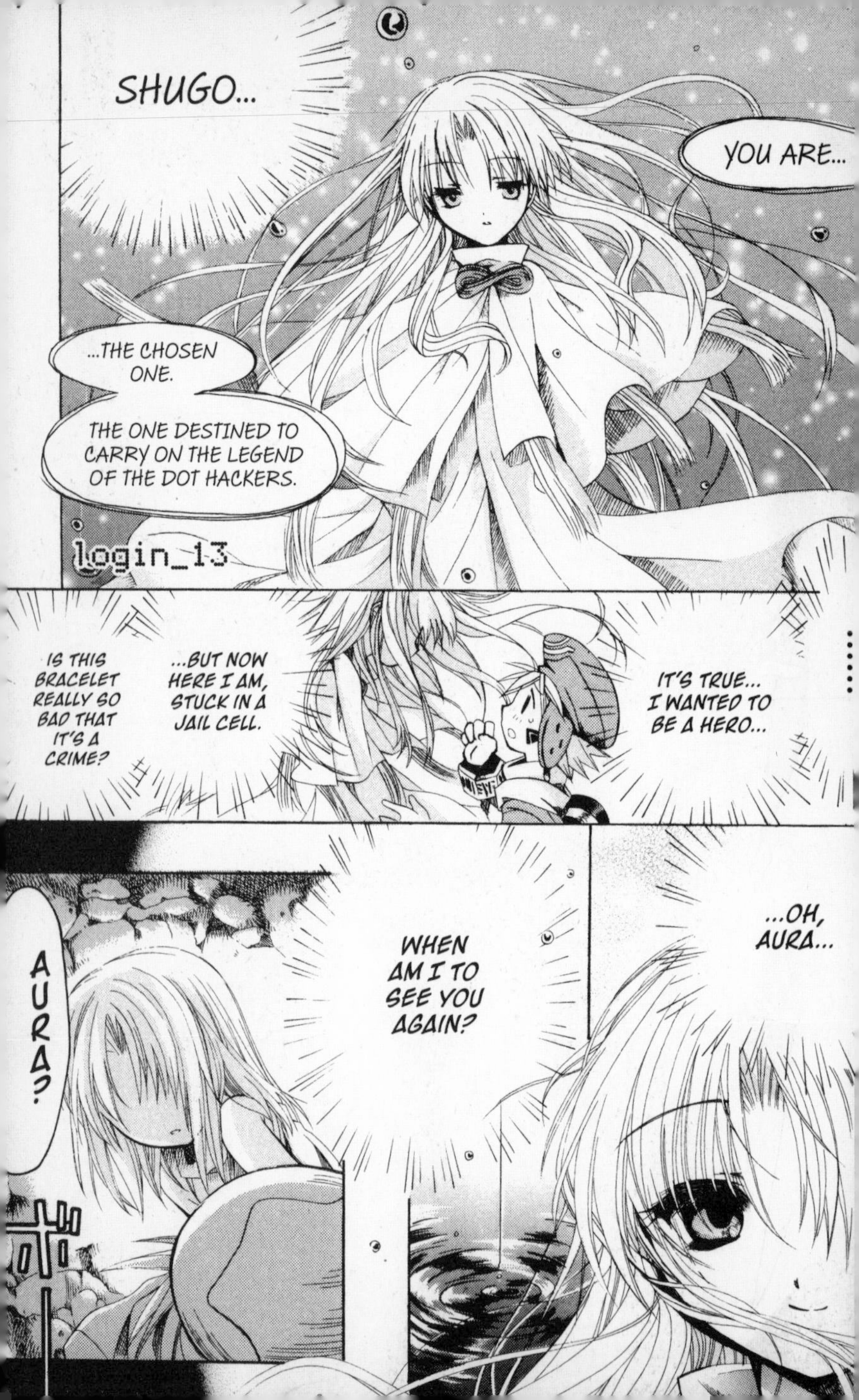
SHUGO...
YOU ARE...
...THE CHOSEN ONE.
THE ONE DESTINED TO CARRY ON THE LEGEND OF THE DOT HACKERS.
login_13
IT'S TRUE... I WANTED TO BE A HERO...
...BUT NOW HERE I AM, STUCK IN A JAIL CELL.
IS THIS BRACELET REALLY SO BAD THAT IT'S A CRIME?
...OH, AURA...
WHEN AM I TO SEE YOU AGAIN?
AURA?

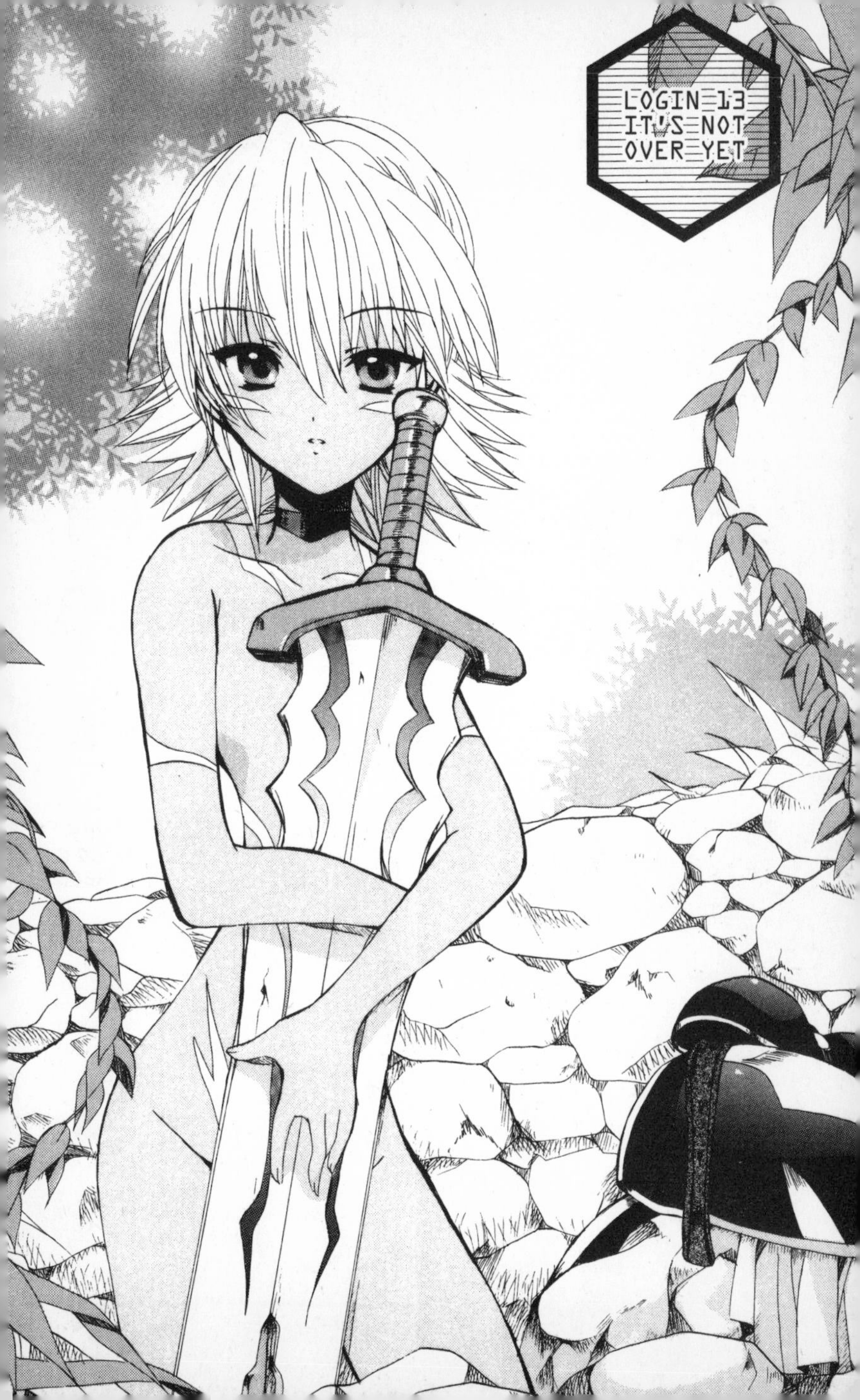
LOGIN 13
IT'S NOT
OVER YET

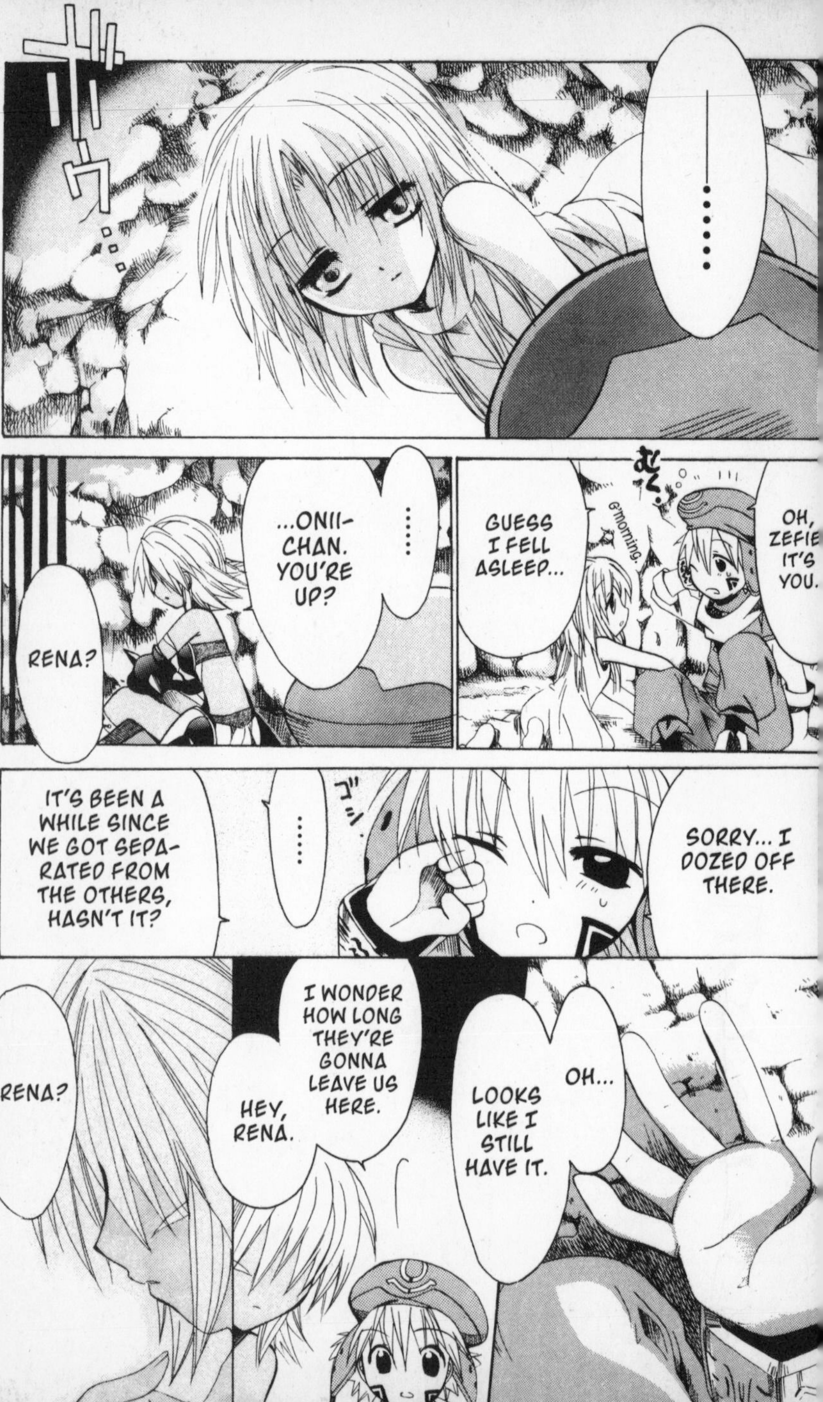

......
OH, ZEFIE IT'S YOU.
G'morning.
GUESS I FELL ASLEEP...
......
...ONII-CHAN. YOU'RE UP?
RENA?
SORRY... I DOZED OFF THERE.
......
IT'S BEEN A WHILE SINCE WE GOT SEPARATED FROM THE OTHERS, HASN'T IT?
OH...
LOOKS LIKE I STILL HAVE IT.
I WONDER HOW LONG THEY'RE GONNA LEAVE US HERE.
HEY, RENA.
...RENA?

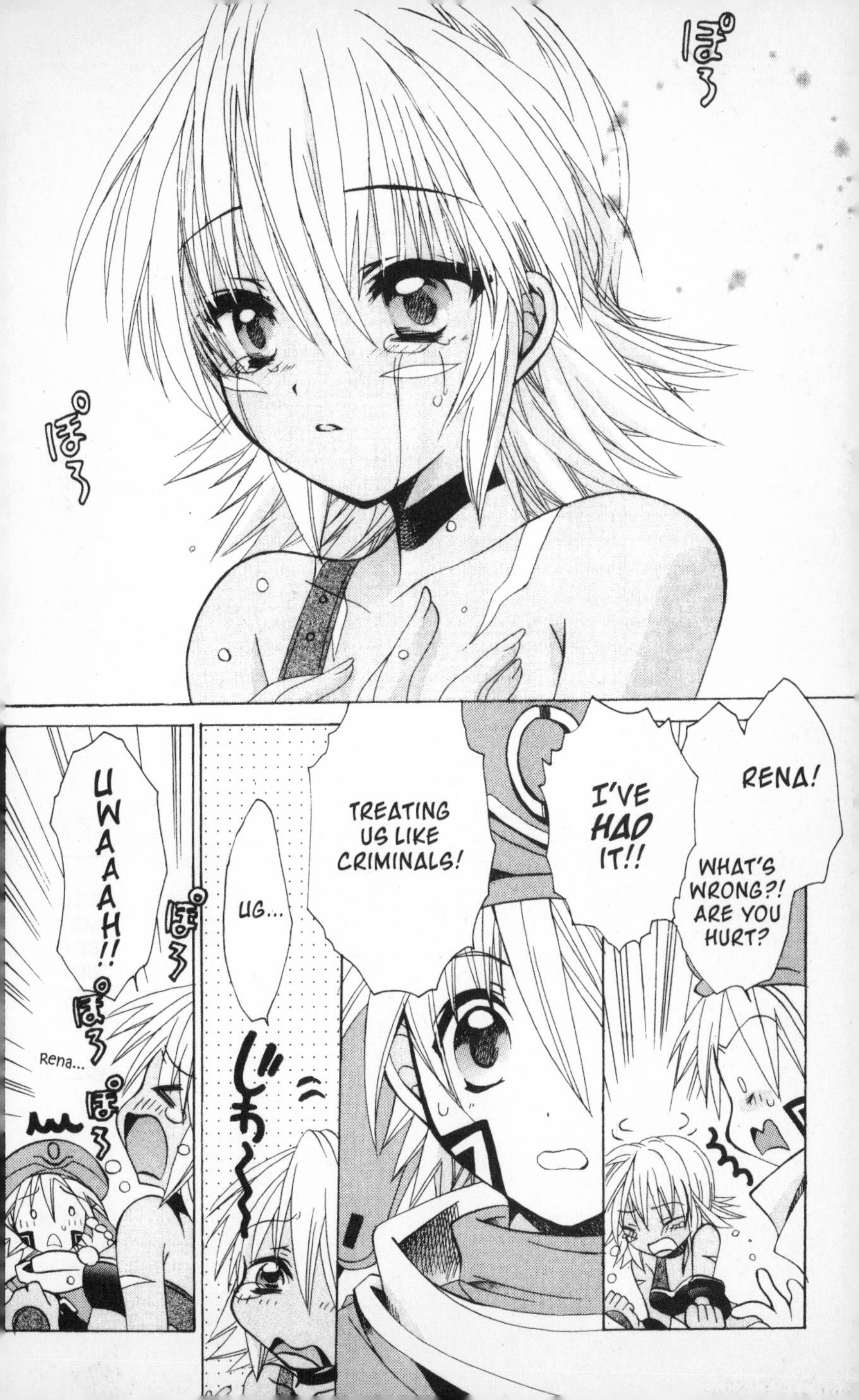
ぽろ〜
ぽろ〜
RENA!
WHAT'S WRONG?! ARE YOU HURT?
I'VE **HAD** IT!!
TREATING US LIKE CRIMINALS!
UG...
じわ〜〜
UWAAAAH!!
ぽろ
ぽろ
ぽろ
Rena...

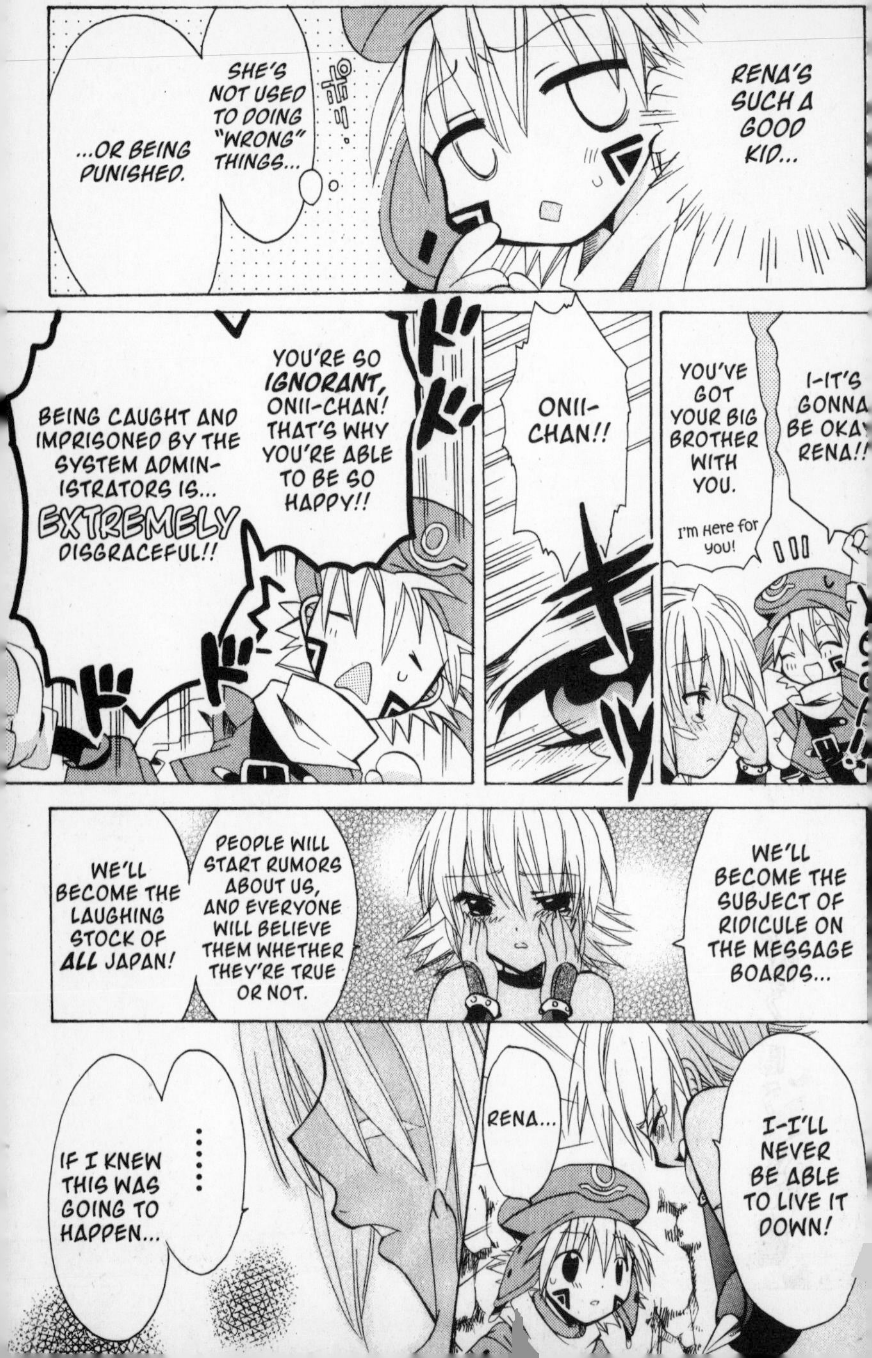
RENA'S SUCH A GOOD KID...
SHE'S NOT USED TO DOING "WRONG" THINGS...
...OR BEING PUNISHED.
I-IT'S GONNA BE OKA RENA!!
YOU'VE GOT YOUR BIG BROTHER WITH YOU.
I'm Here for you!
ONII-CHAN!!
YOU'RE SO IGNORANT, ONII-CHAN! THAT'S WHY YOU'RE ABLE TO BE SO HAPPY!!
BEING CAUGHT AND IMPRISONED BY THE SYSTEM ADMIN-ISTRATORS IS... EXTREMELY DISGRACEFUL!!
WE'LL BECOME THE SUBJECT OF RIDICULE ON THE MESSAGE BOARDS...
PEOPLE WILL START RUMORS ABOUT US, AND EVERYONE WILL BELIEVE THEM WHETHER THEY'RE TRUE OR NOT.
WE'LL BECOME THE LAUGHING STOCK OF ALL JAPAN!
I-I'LL NEVER BE ABLE TO LIVE IT DOWN!
RENA...
......
IF I KNEW THIS WAS GOING TO HAPPEN...

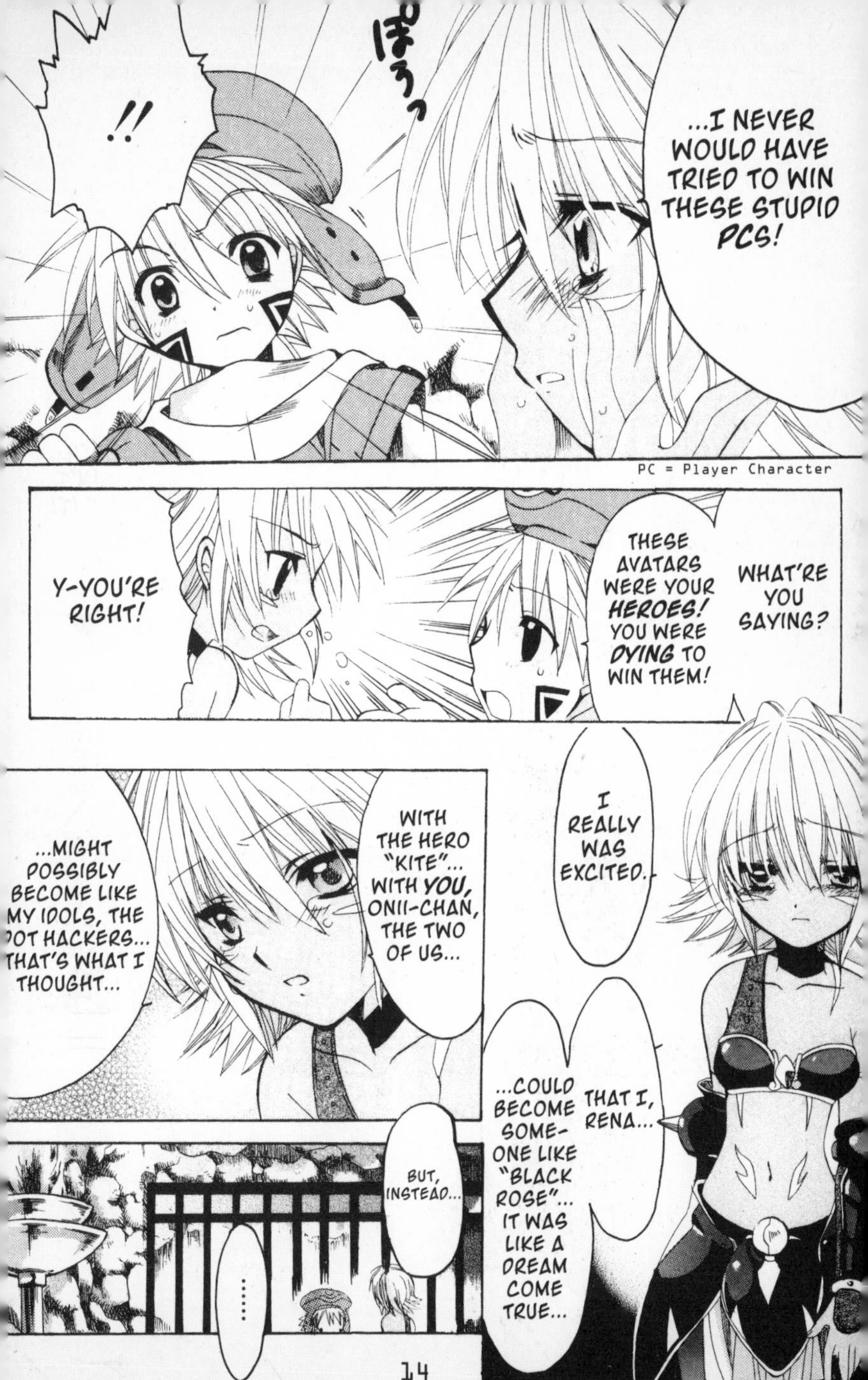
...I NEVER WOULD HAVE TRIED TO WIN THESE STUPID *PCS!*
!!
ぽろっ
WHAT'RE YOU SAYING?
THESE AVATARS WERE YOUR *HEROES!* YOU WERE *DYING* TO WIN THEM!
Y-YOU'RE RIGHT!
I REALLY WAS EXCITED.
THAT I, RENA...
...COULD BECOME SOME-ONE LIKE "BLACK ROSE"... IT WAS LIKE A DREAM COME TRUE...
WITH THE HERO "KITE"... WITH *YOU,* ONII-CHAN, THE TWO OF US...
...MIGHT POSSIBLY BECOME LIKE MY IDOLS, THE DOT HACKERS... THAT'S WHAT I THOUGHT...
BUT, INSTEAD...
......

PC = Player Character

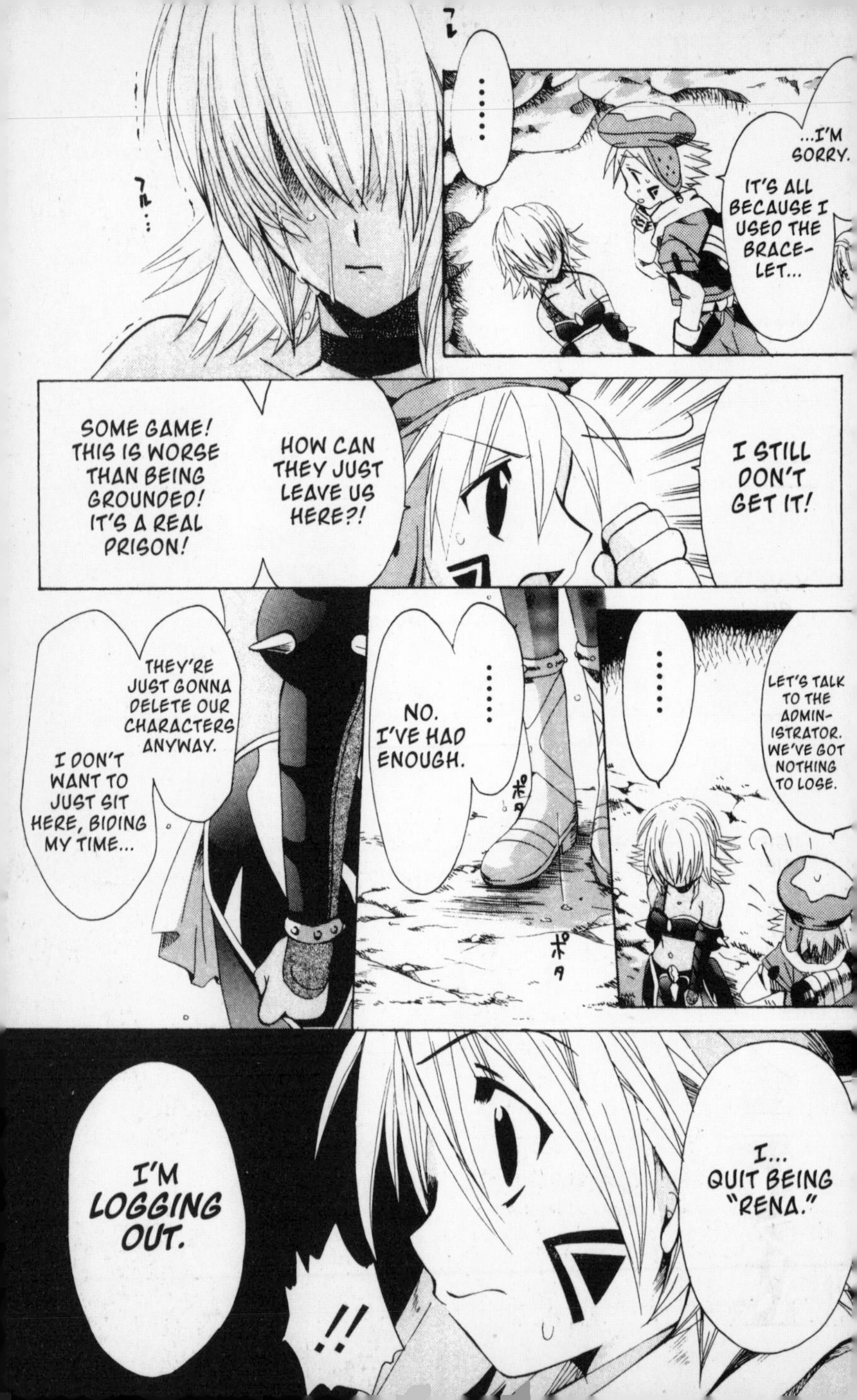
...I'M SORRY.
IT'S ALL BECAUSE I USED THE BRACE-LET...
......
I STILL DON'T GET IT!
HOW CAN THEY JUST LEAVE US HERE?!
SOME GAME! THIS IS WORSE THAN BEING GROUNDED! IT'S A REAL PRISON!
LET'S TALK TO THE ADMIN-ISTRATOR. WE'VE GOT NOTHING TO LOSE.
......
......
NO. I'VE HAD ENOUGH.
THEY'RE JUST GONNA DELETE OUR CHARACTERS ANYWAY.
I DON'T WANT TO JUST SIT HERE, BIDING MY TIME...
I... QUIT BEING "RENA."
!!
I'M LOGGING OUT.

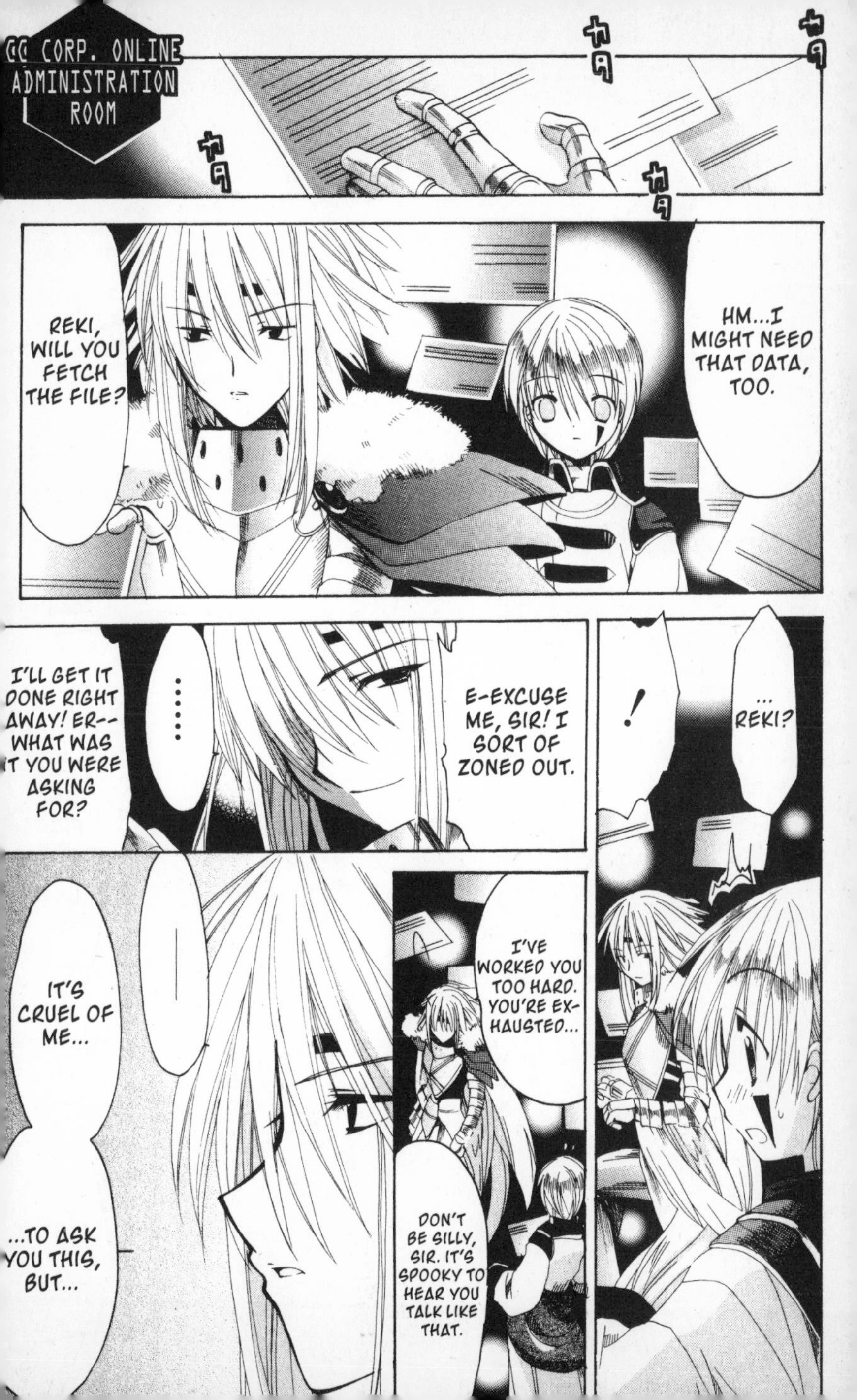
カタ
カタ
CC CORP. ONLINE ADMINISTRATION ROOM
カタ
カタ
HM...I MIGHT NEED THAT DATA, TOO.
REKI, WILL YOU FETCH THE FILE?
... REKI?
!
E-EXCUSE ME, SIR! I SORT OF ZONED OUT.
......
I'LL GET IT DONE RIGHT AWAY! ER--WHAT WAS IT YOU WERE ASKING FOR?
I'VE WORKED YOU TOO HARD. YOU'RE EX-HAUSTED...
DON'T BE SILLY, SIR. IT'S SPOOKY TO HEAR YOU TALK LIKE THAT.
—
IT'S CRUEL OF ME...
...TO ASK YOU THIS, BUT...

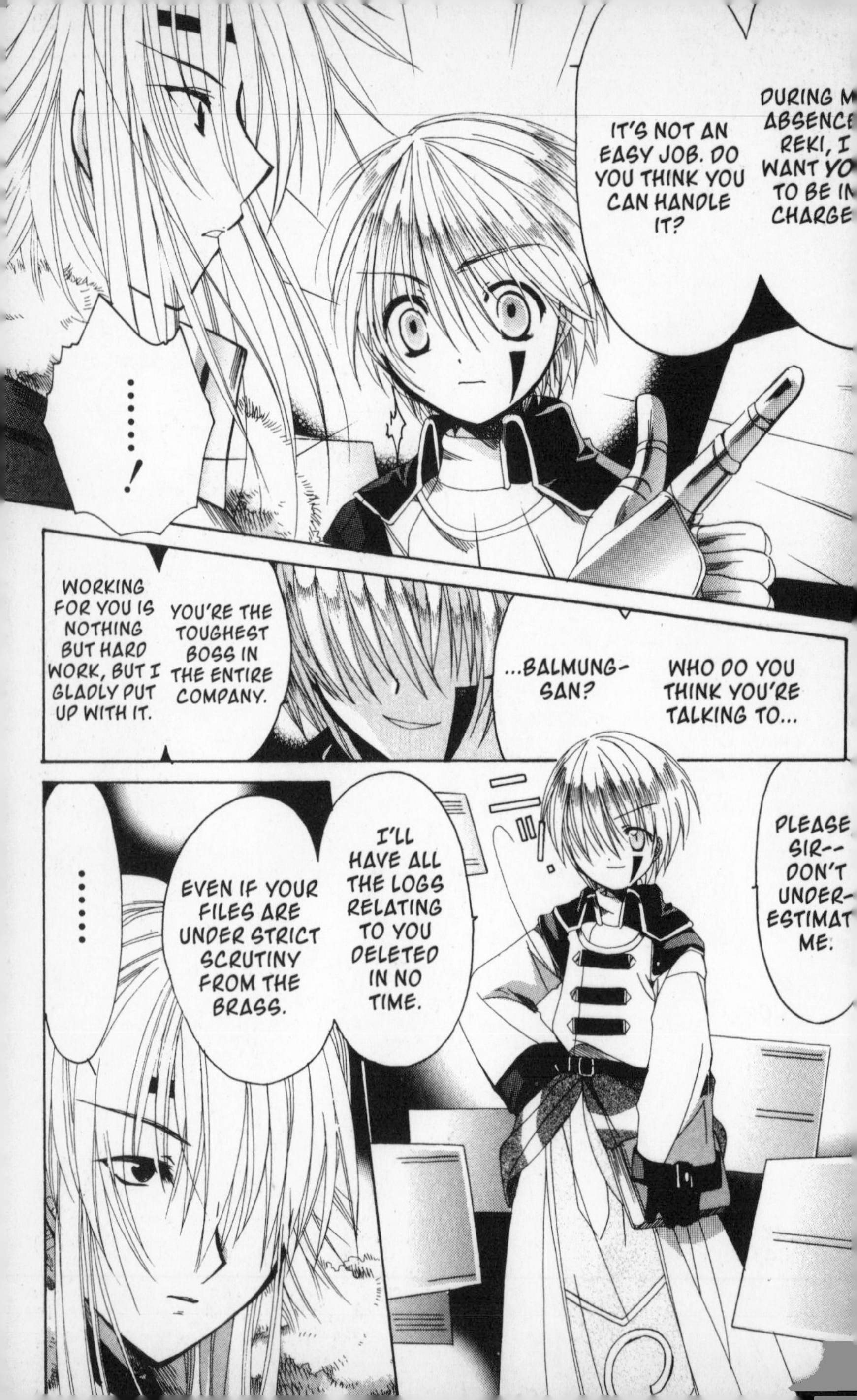
DURING M ABSENCE REKI, I WANT YO TO BE IN CHARGE
IT'S NOT AN EASY JOB. DO YOU THINK YOU CAN HANDLE IT?
......!
WHO DO YOU THINK YOU'RE TALKING TO...
...BALMUNG-SAN?
YOU'RE THE TOUGHEST BOSS IN THE ENTIRE COMPANY.
WORKING FOR YOU IS NOTHING BUT HARD WORK, BUT I GLADLY PUT UP WITH IT.
PLEASE SIR-- DON'T UNDER-ESTIMAT ME.
I'LL HAVE ALL THE LOGS RELATING TO YOU DELETED IN NO TIME.
EVEN IF YOUR FILES ARE UNDER STRICT SCRUTINY FROM THE BRASS.
......

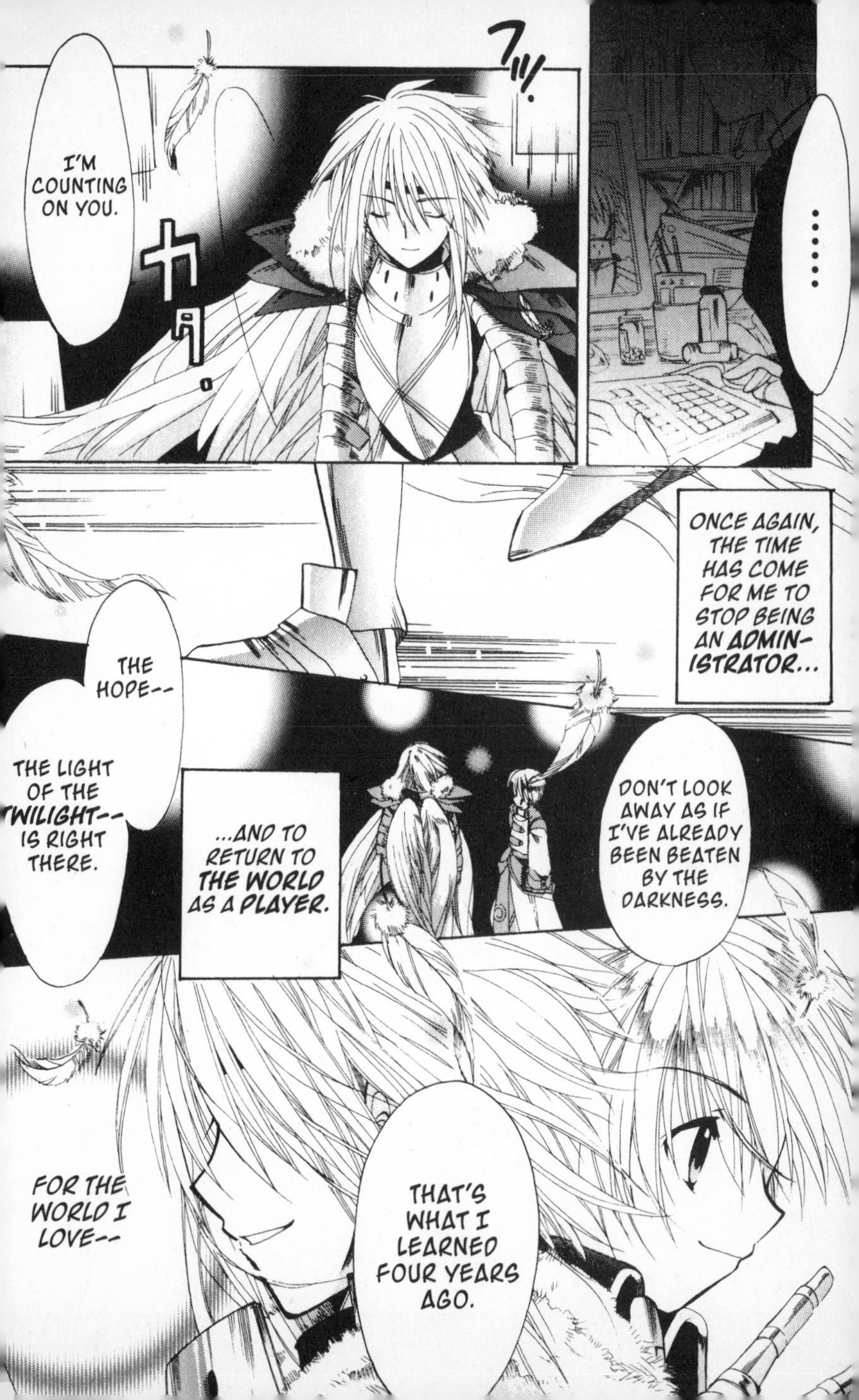

……
フッ!
I'M COUNTING ON YOU.
カタ。
ONCE AGAIN, THE TIME HAS COME FOR ME TO STOP BEING AN ADMINISTRATOR...
DON'T LOOK AWAY AS IF I'VE ALREADY BEEN BEATEN BY THE DARKNESS.
...AND TO RETURN TO THE WORLD AS A PLAYER.
THE HOPE-- THE LIGHT OF THE TWILIGHT-- IS RIGHT THERE.
THAT'S WHAT I LEARNED FOUR YEARS AGO.
FOR THE WORLD I LOVE--

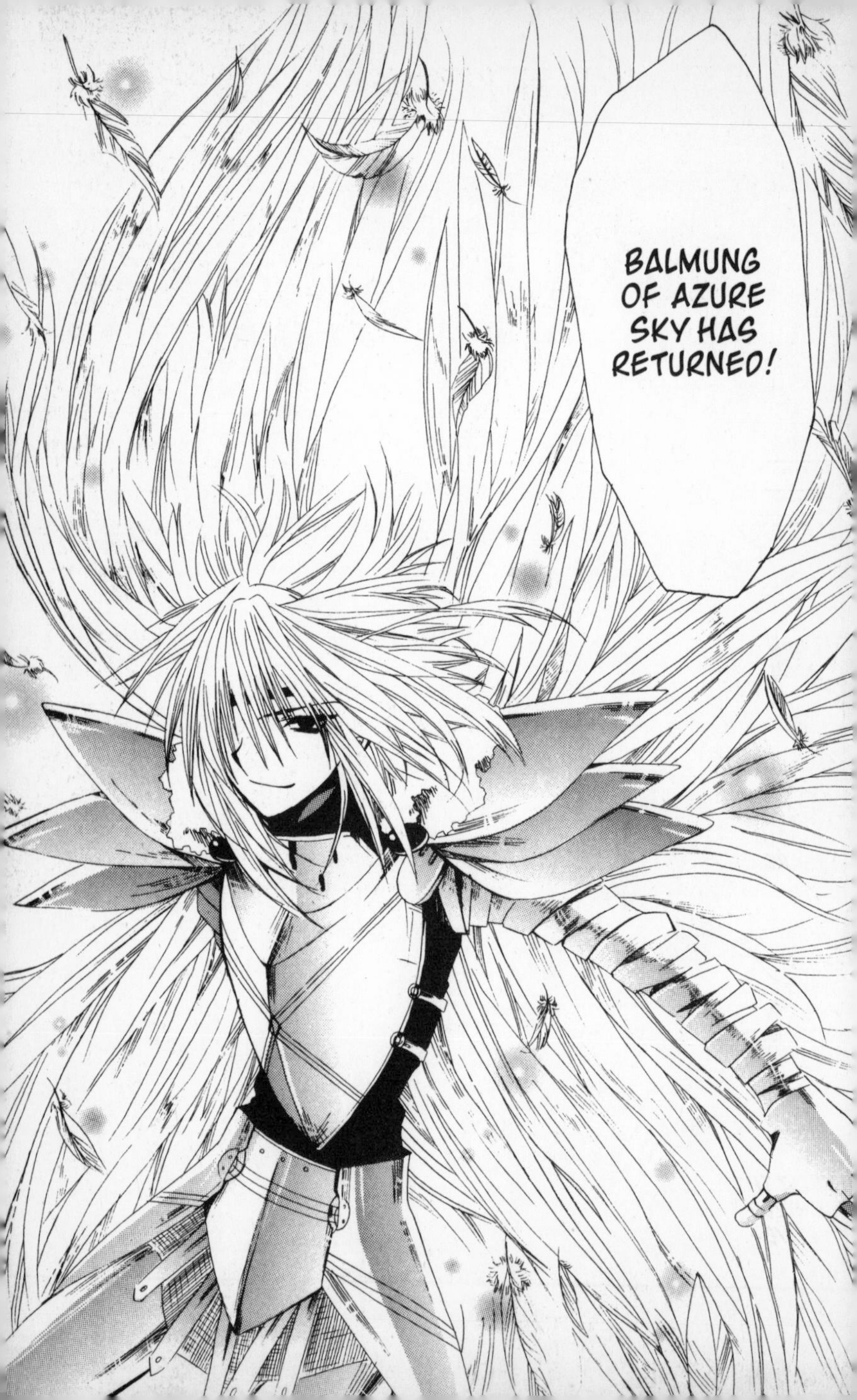
BALMUNG OF AZURE SKY HAS RETURNED!

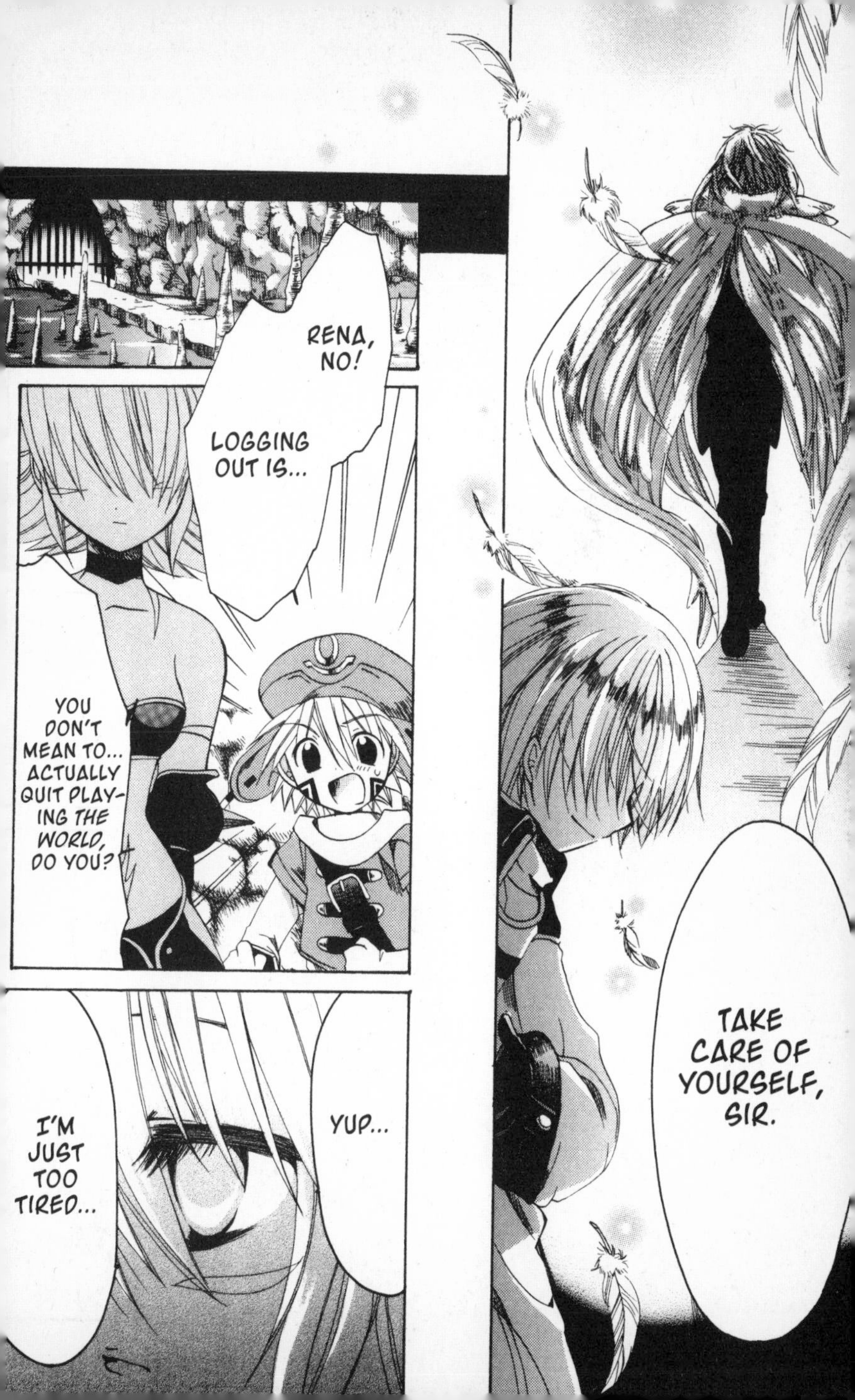
TAKE CARE OF YOURSELF, SIR.
RENA, NO!
LOGGING OUT IS...
YOU DON'T MEAN TO... ACTUALLY QUIT PLAYING THE WORLD, DO YOU?
YUP...
I'M JUST TOO TIRED...

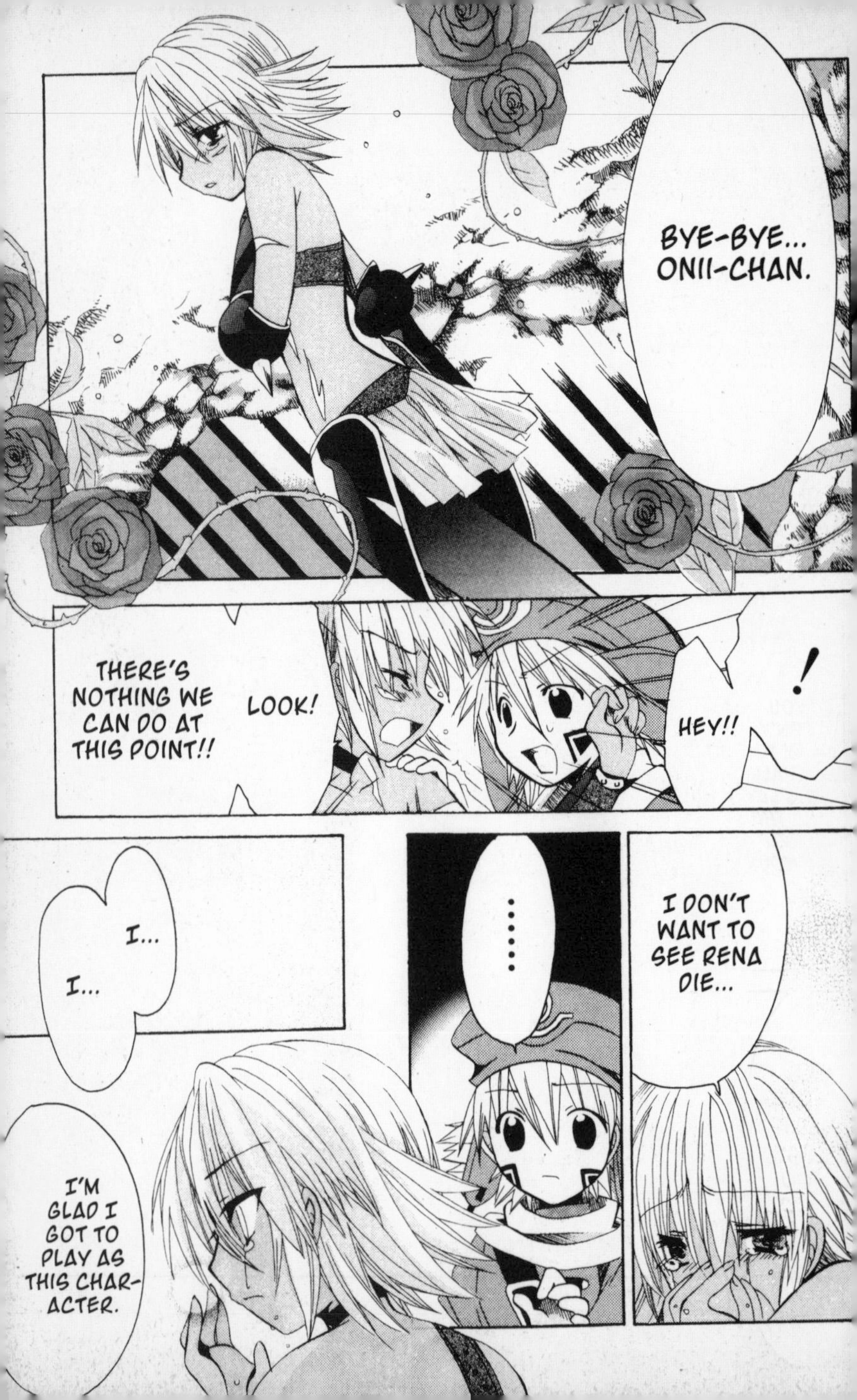
BYE-BYE... ONII-CHAN.
!
HEY!!
LOOK!
THERE'S NOTHING WE CAN DO AT THIS POINT!!
I DON'T WANT TO SEE RENA DIE...
......
I...
I...
I'M GLAD I GOT TO PLAY AS THIS CHAR-ACTER.

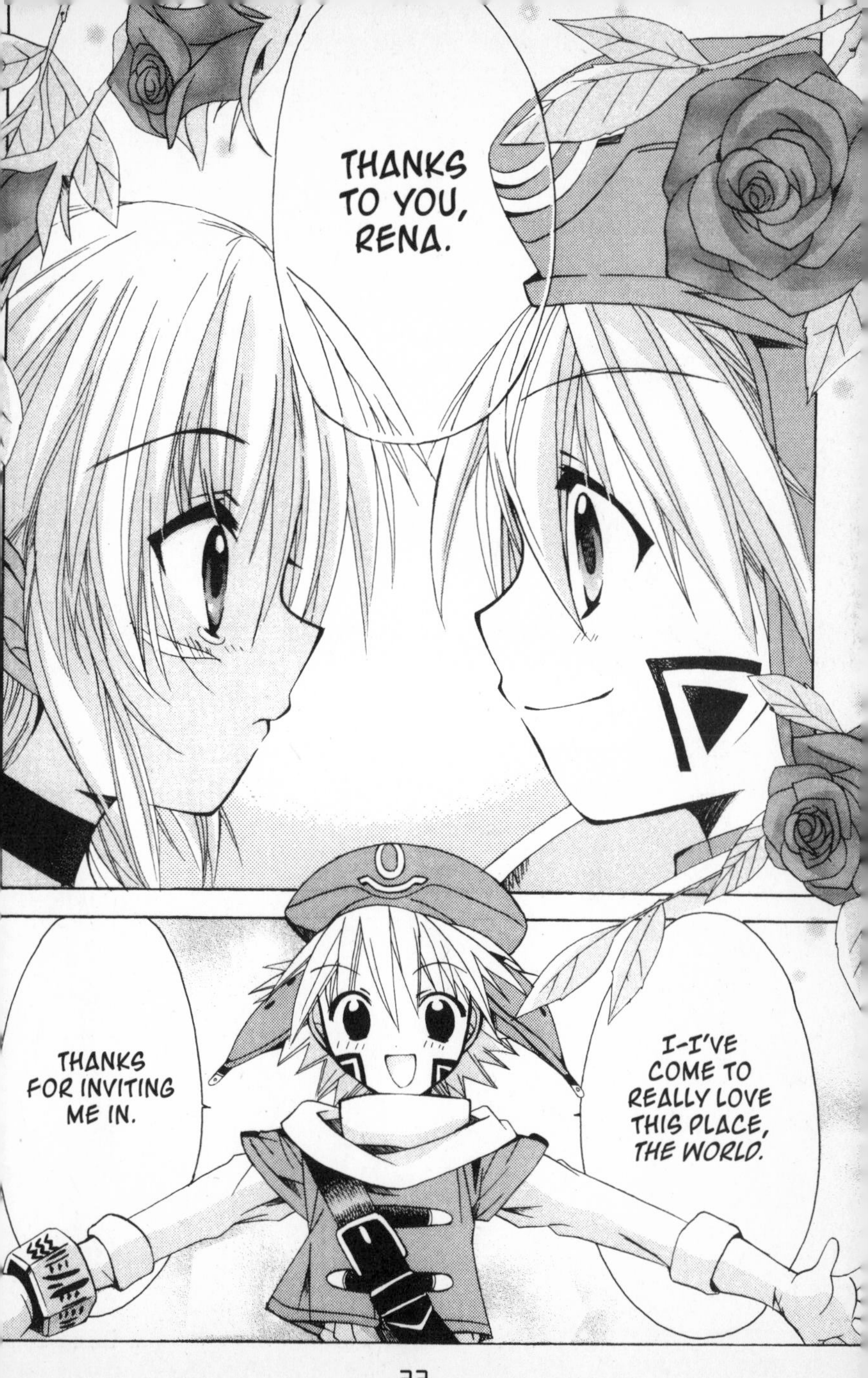
THANKS TO YOU, RENA.
I-I'VE COME TO REALLY LOVE THIS PLACE, THE WORLD.
THANKS FOR INVITING ME IN.

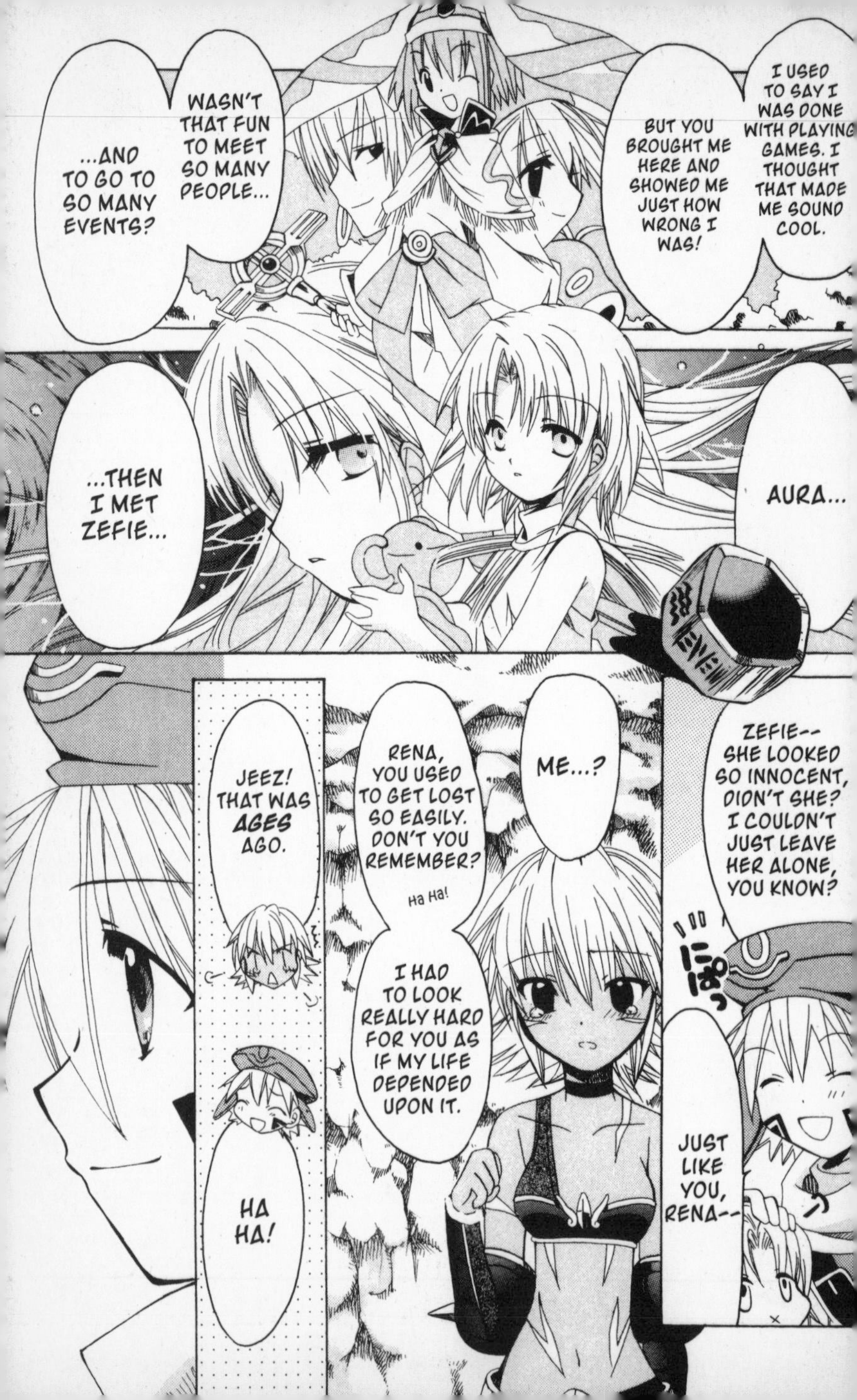
I USED TO SAY I WAS DONE WITH PLAYING GAMES. I THOUGHT THAT MADE ME SOUND COOL.
BUT YOU BROUGHT ME HERE AND SHOWED ME JUST HOW WRONG I WAS!
WASN'T THAT FUN TO MEET SO MANY PEOPLE...
...AND TO GO TO SO MANY EVENTS?
AURA...
...THEN I MET ZEFIE...
ZEFIE-- SHE LOOKED SO INNOCENT, DIDN'T SHE? I COULDN'T JUST LEAVE HER ALONE, YOU KNOW?
JUST LIKE YOU, RENA--
ME...?
RENA, YOU USED TO GET LOST SO EASILY. DON'T YOU REMEMBER?
Ha Ha!
I HAD TO LOOK REALLY HARD FOR YOU AS IF MY LIFE DEPENDED UPON IT.
JEEZ! THAT WAS **AGES** AGO.
HA HA!

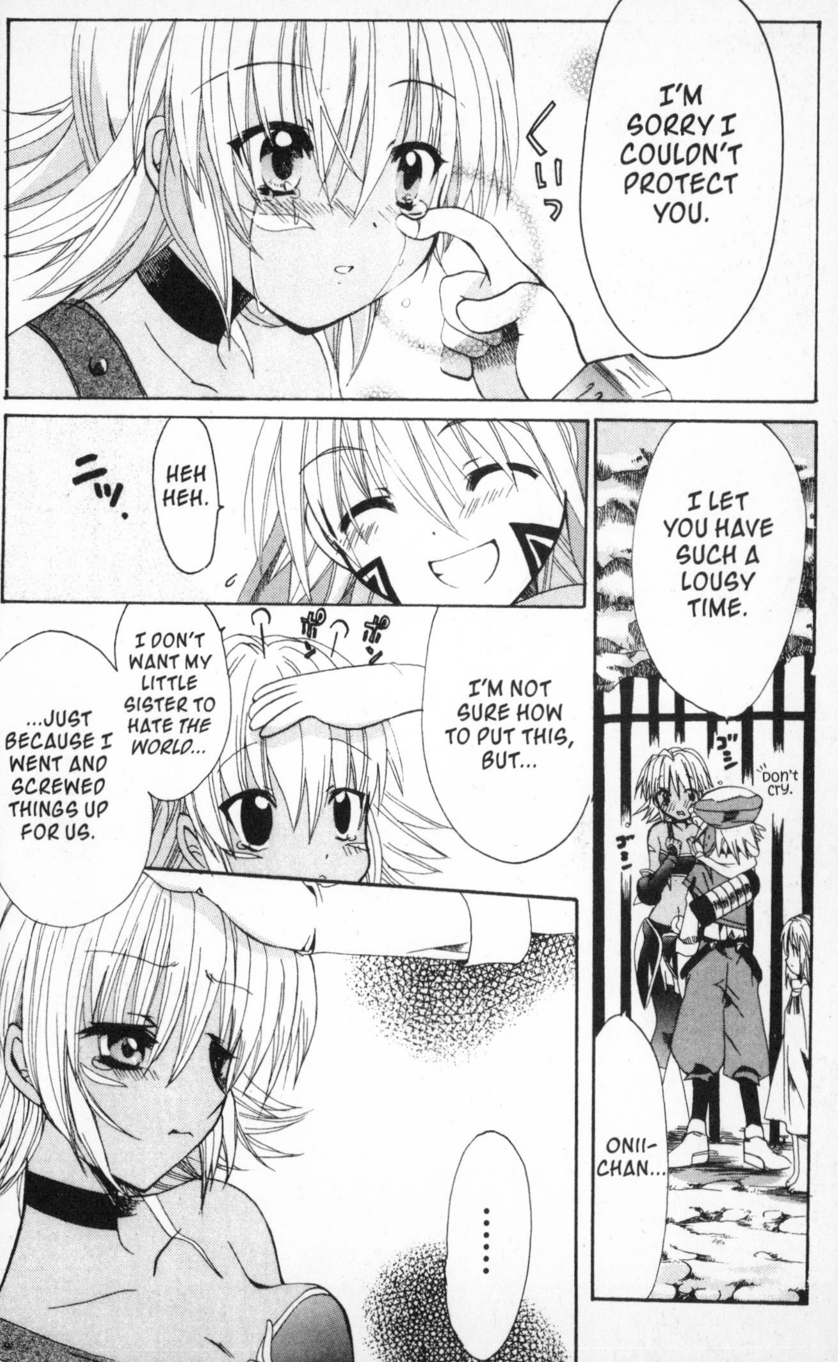
I'M SORRY I COULDN'T PROTECT YOU.
I LET YOU HAVE SUCH A LOUSY TIME.
Don't cry.
ONII-CHAN...
HEH HEH.
ニッ.
I'M NOT SURE HOW TO PUT THIS, BUT...
I DON'T WANT MY LITTLE SISTER TO HATE THE WORLD...
...JUST BECAUSE I WENT AND SCREWED THINGS UP FOR US.
......

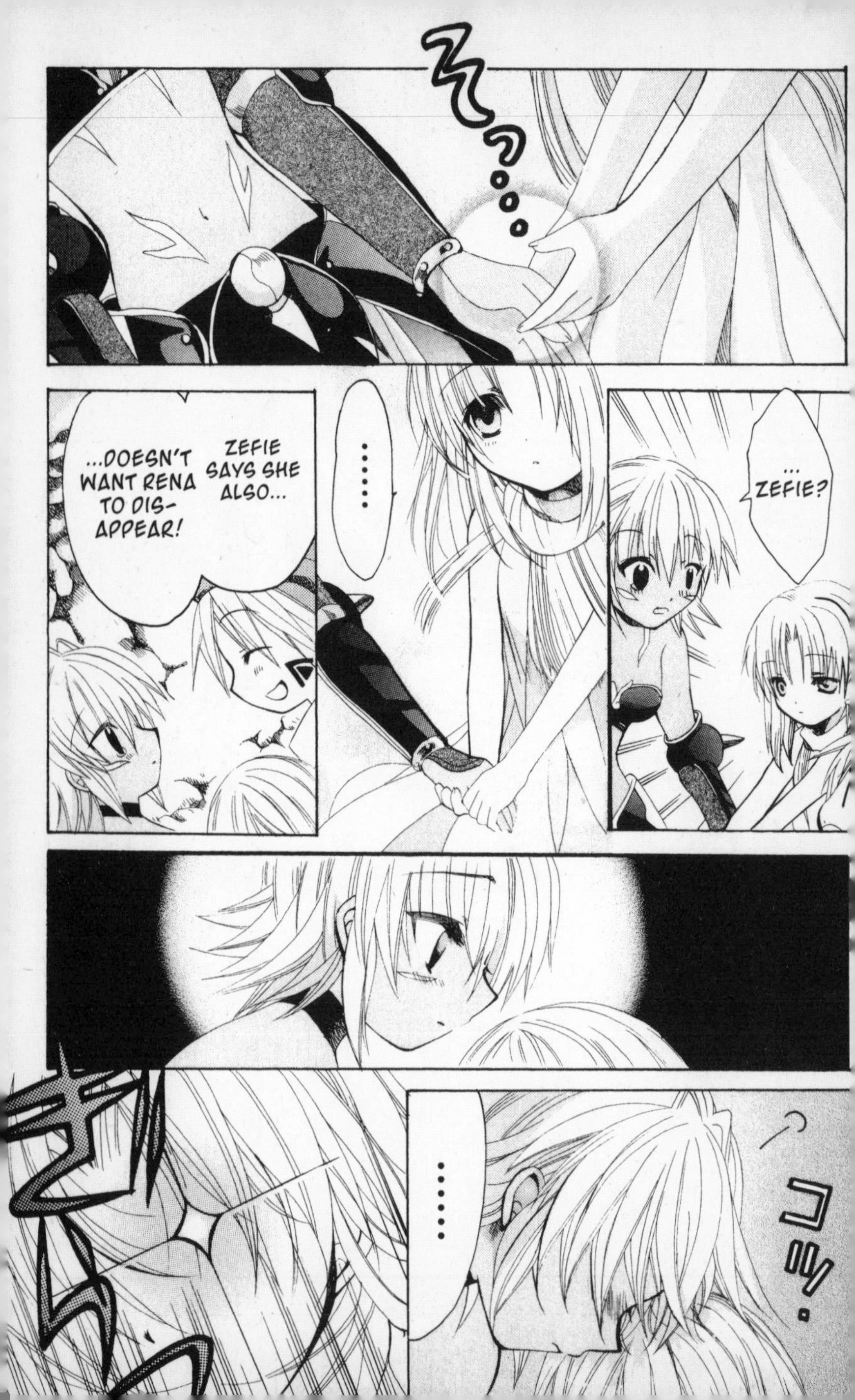

... ZEFIE?
......
ZEFIE SAYS SHE ALSO...
...DOESN'T WANT RENA TO DIS-APPEAR!
......

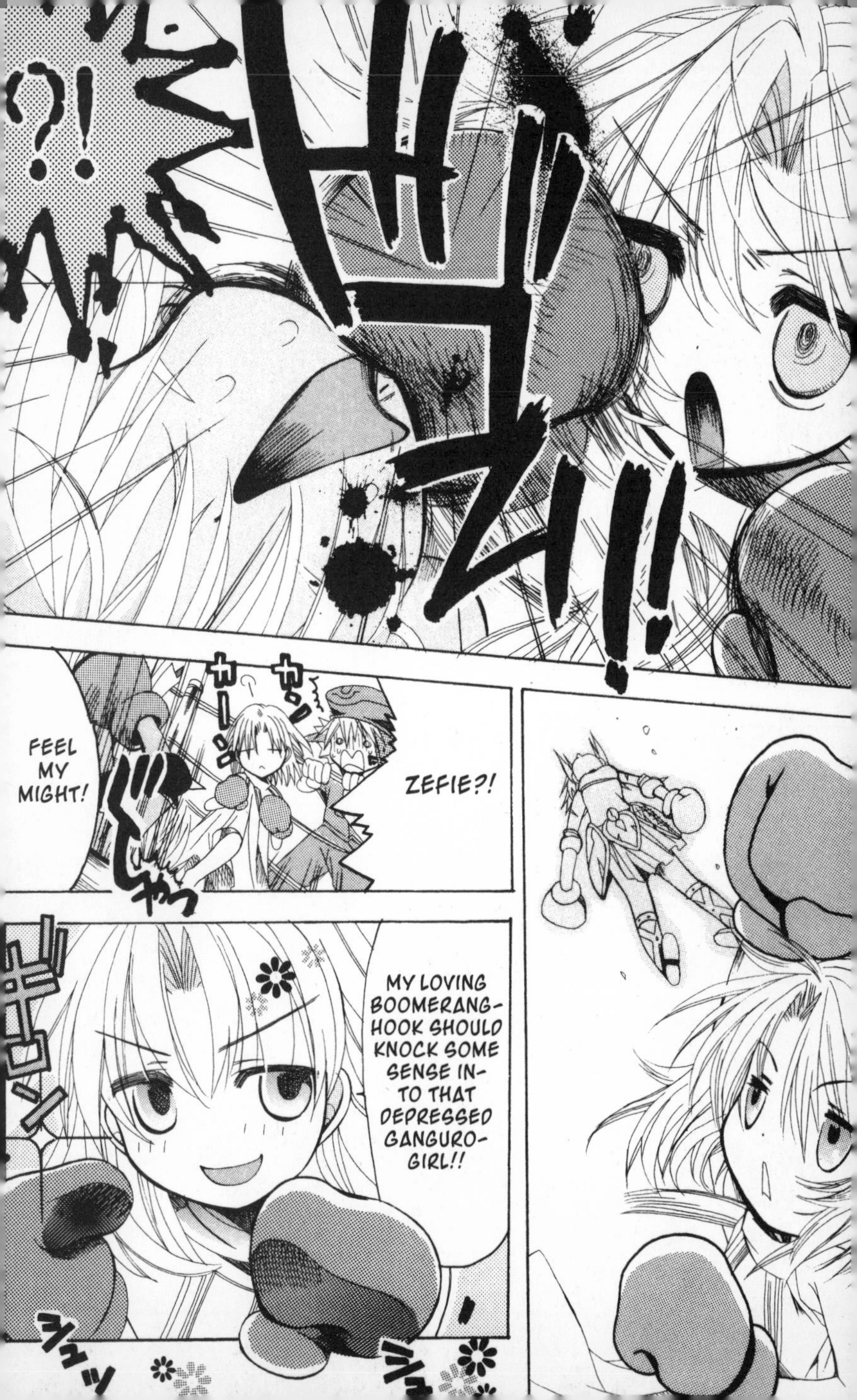
?!
ZEFIE?!
FEEL MY MIGHT!
MY LOVING BOOMERANG-HOOK SHOULD KNOCK SOME SENSE INTO THAT DEPRESSED GANGURO-GIRL!!

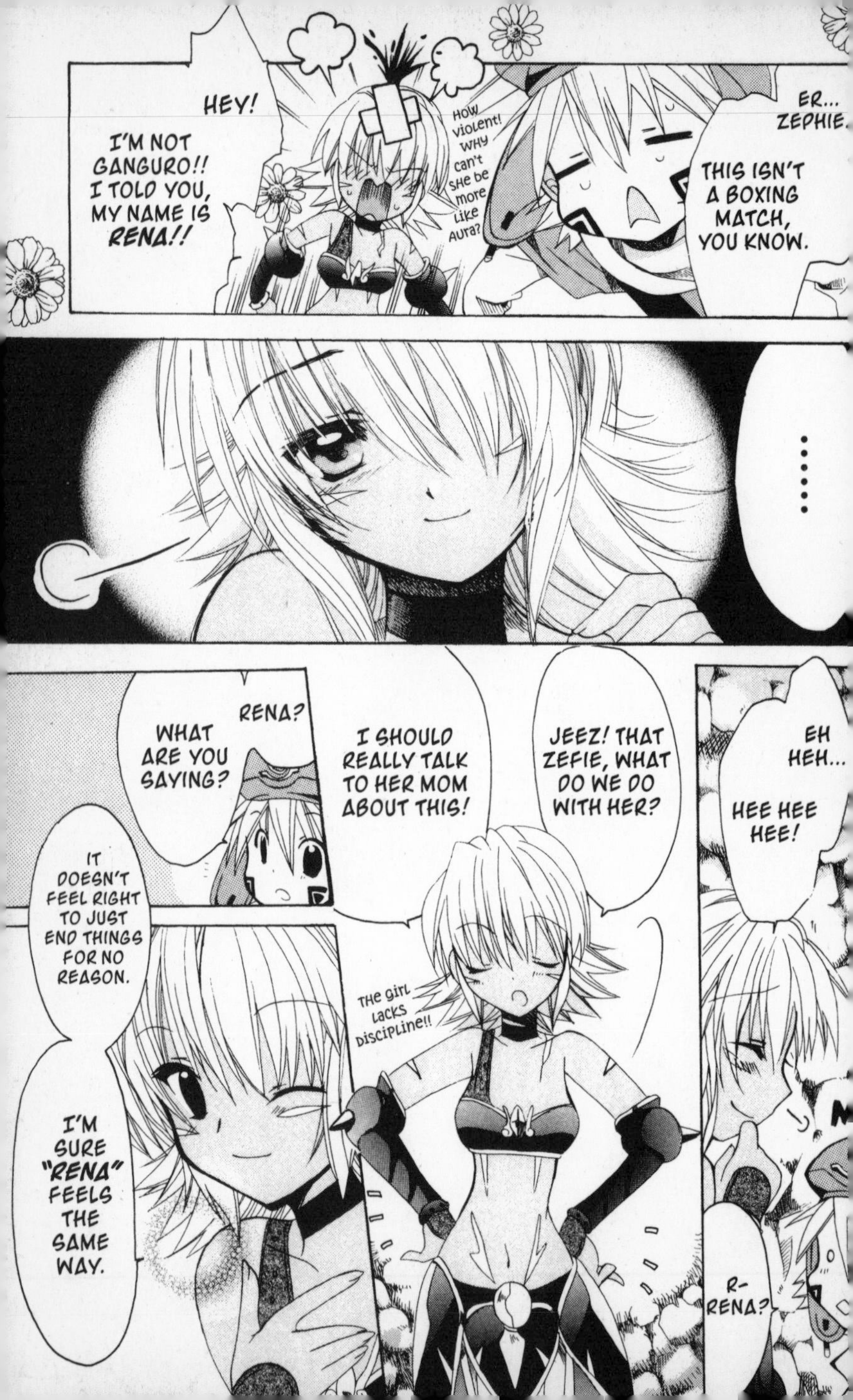
ER... ZEPHIE.
THIS ISN'T A BOXING MATCH, YOU KNOW.
How violent! WHY can't she be more like Aura?
HEY!
I'M NOT GANGURO!! I TOLD YOU, MY NAME IS *RENA!!*
......
EH HEH...
HEE HEE HEE!
R- RENA?
JEEZ! THAT ZEFIE, WHAT DO WE DO WITH HER?
I SHOULD REALLY TALK TO HER MOM ABOUT THIS!
The Girl lacks Discipline!!
RENA?
WHAT ARE YOU SAYING?
IT DOESN'T FEEL RIGHT TO JUST END THINGS FOR NO REASON.
I'M SURE *"RENA"* FEELS THE SAME WAY.

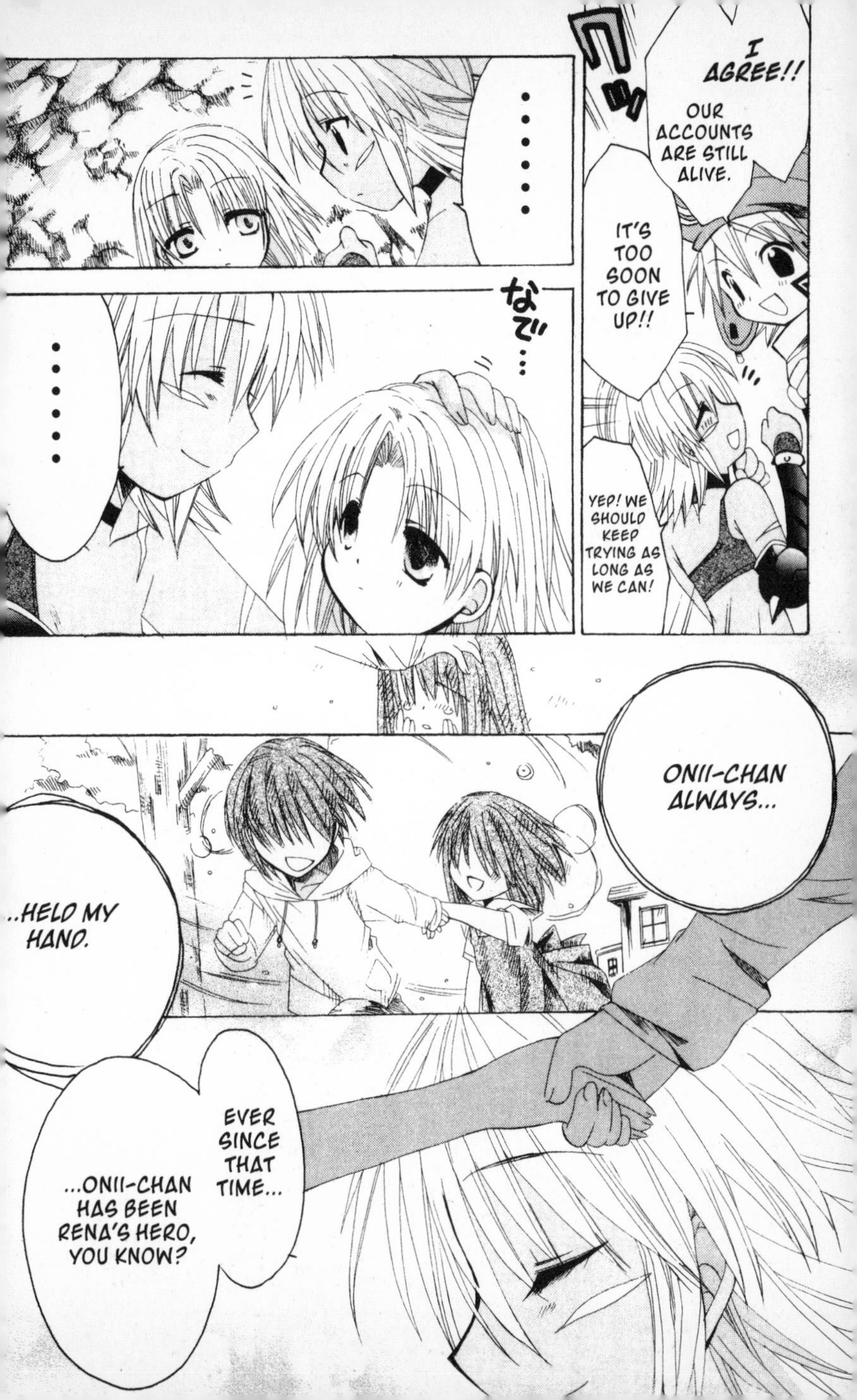
I AGREE!!
OUR ACCOUNTS ARE STILL ALIVE.
IT'S TOO SOON TO GIVE UP!!
YEP! WE SHOULD KEEP TRYING AS LONG AS WE CAN!
......
なで...
......
ONII-CHAN ALWAYS...
...HELD MY HAND.
EVER SINCE THAT TIME...
...ONII-CHAN HAS BEEN RENA'S HERO, YOU KNOW?

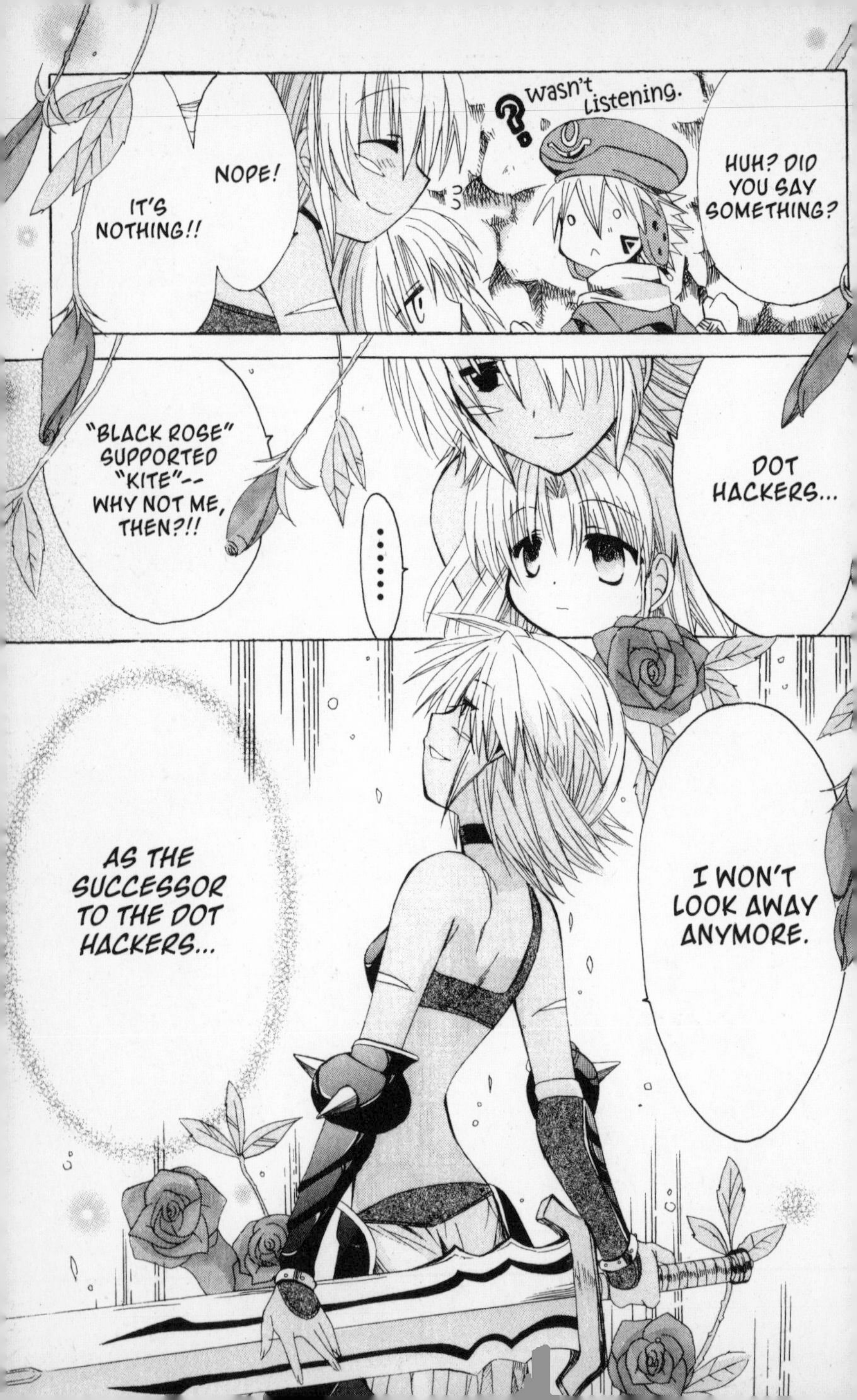
HUH? DID YOU SAY SOMETHING?
Wasn't listening.
NOPE! IT'S NOTHING!!
DOT HACKERS...
......
"BLACK ROSE" SUPPORTED "KITE"-- WHY NOT ME, THEN?!!
I WON'T LOOK AWAY ANYMORE.
AS THE SUCCESSOR TO THE DOT HACKERS...

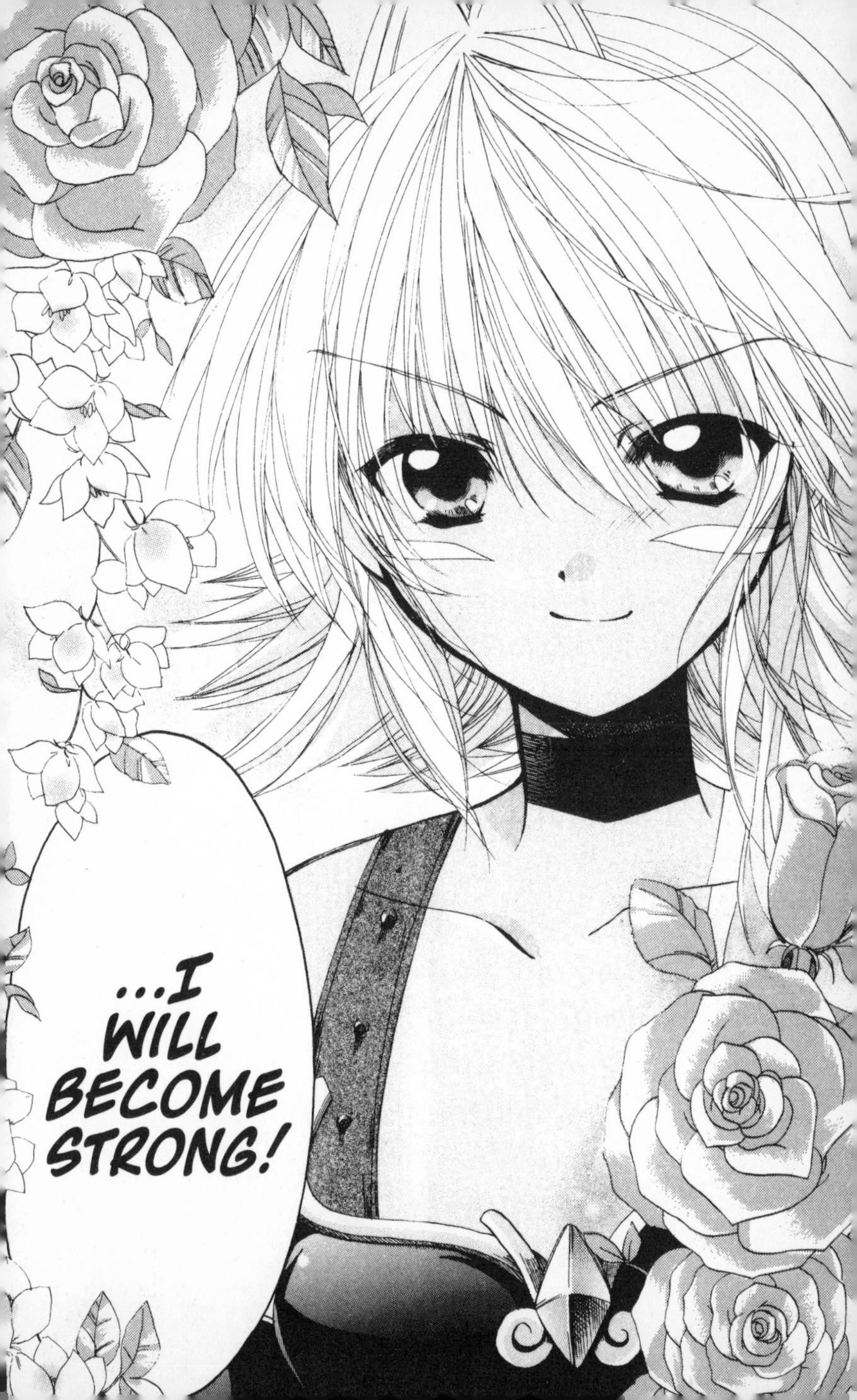
...I WILL BECOME STRONG!

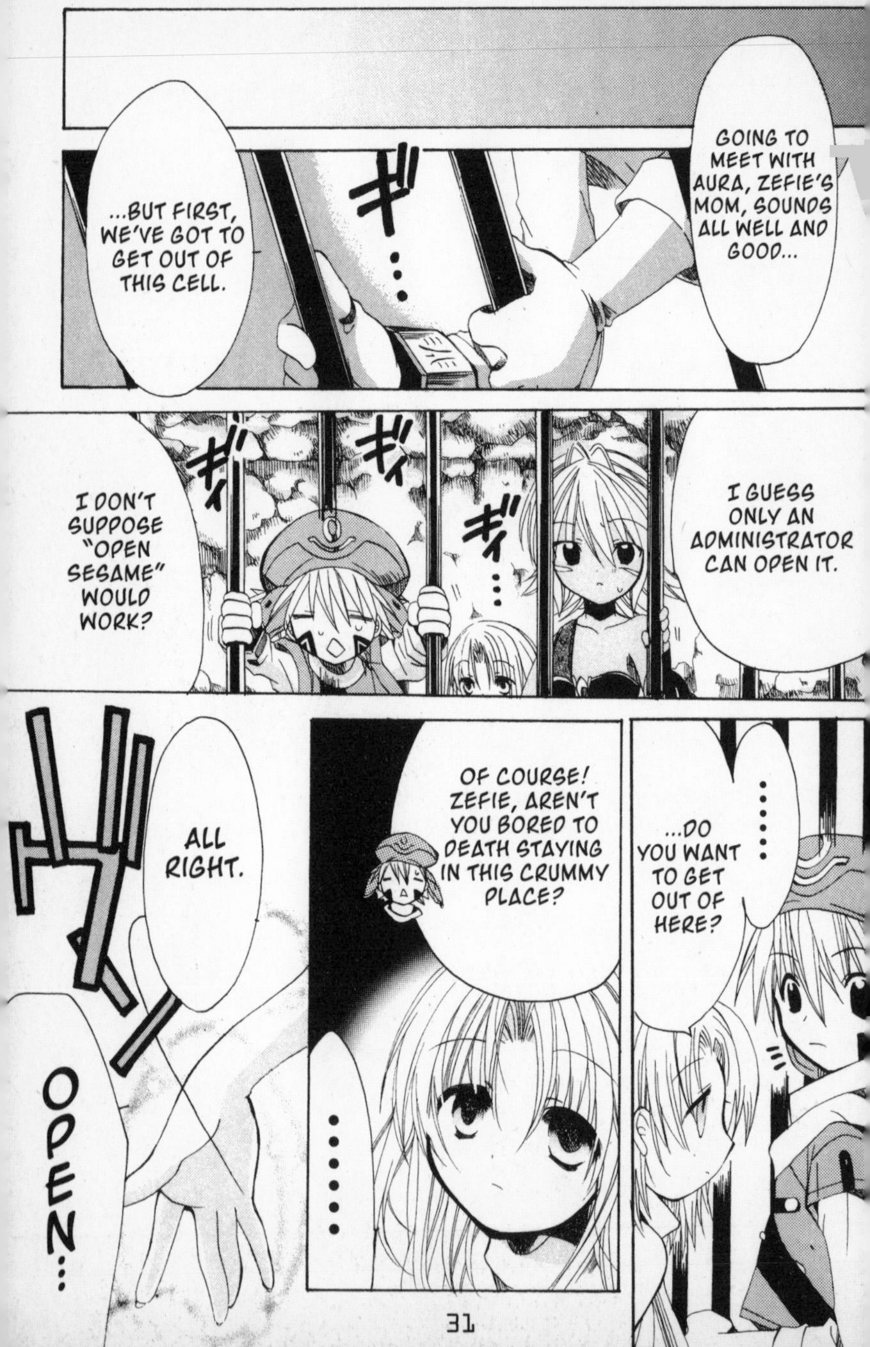
GOING TO MEET WITH AURA, ZEFIE'S MOM, SOUNDS ALL WELL AND GOOD...
...BUT FIRST, WE'VE GOT TO GET OUT OF THIS CELL.
I GUESS ONLY AN ADMINISTRATOR CAN OPEN IT.
I DON'T SUPPOSE "OPEN SESAME" WOULD WORK?
......
...DO YOU WANT TO GET OUT OF HERE?
OF COURSE! ZEFIE, AREN'T YOU BORED TO DEATH STAYING IN THIS CRUMMY PLACE?
......
ALL RIGHT.
OPEN...

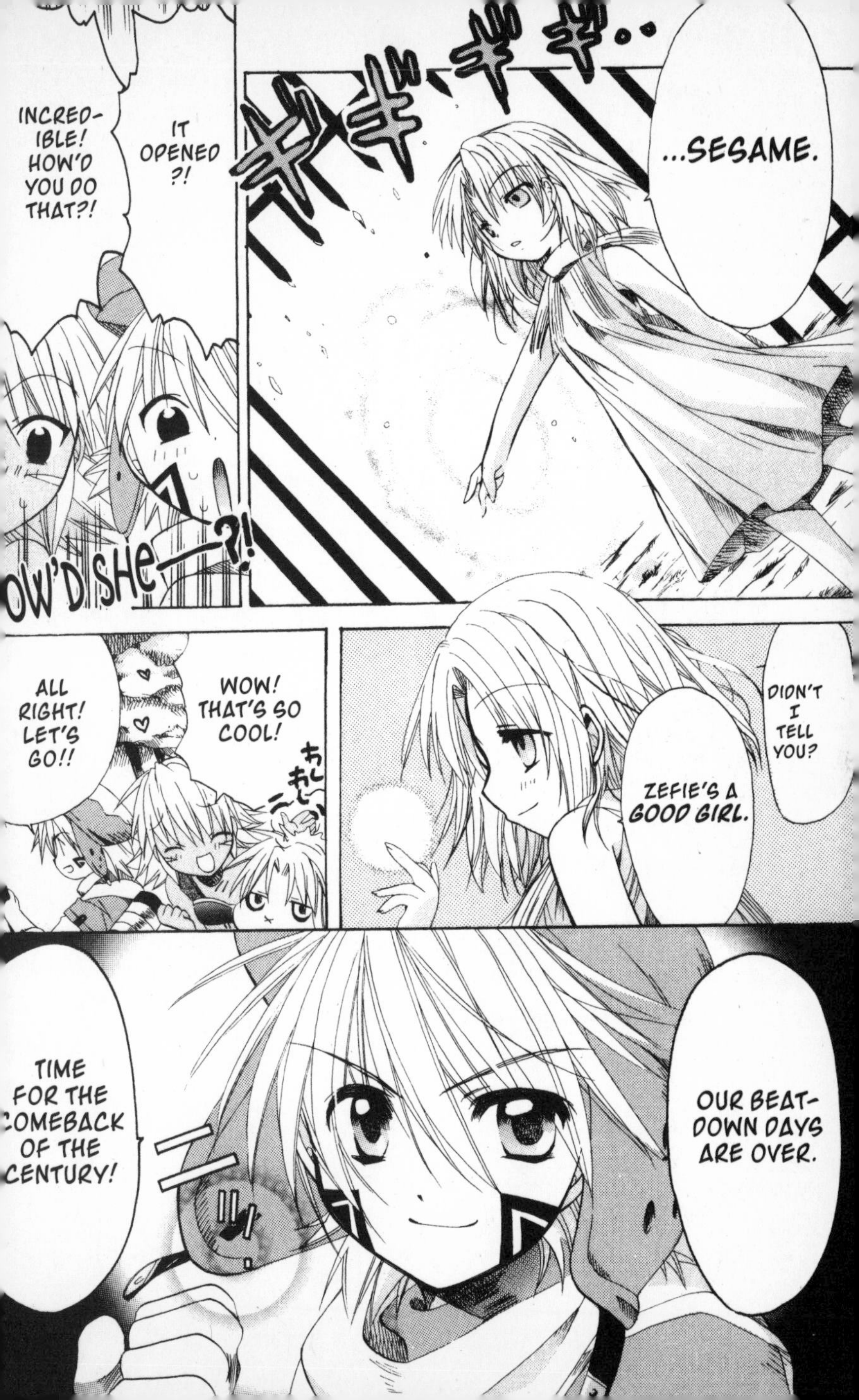
...SESAME.
IT OPENED?!
INCREDIBLE! HOW'D YOU DO THAT?!
OW'D SHE—?!
DIDN'T I TELL YOU?
ZEFIE'S A GOOD GIRL.
WOW! THAT'S SO COOL!
ALL RIGHT! LET'S GO!!
OUR BEAT-DOWN DAYS ARE OVER.
TIME FOR THE COMEBACK OF THE CENTURY!

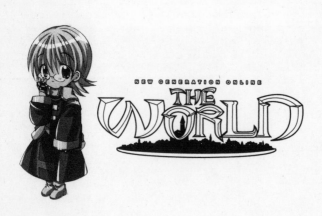

NEW GENERATION ONLINE
THE WORLD

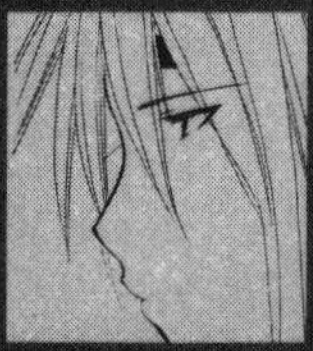

SUBJECT: FROM AZURE SKY

SENDER: BALMUNG

FRIENDS OF AURA,

BECAUSE YOU SEEM LIKE YOU'RE STILL LOGGED IN, I'M SENDING YOU AN E-MAIL. NOT AS A SYSTEM ADMINISTRATOR OR THE CC CORP., BUT AS BALMUNG OF AZURE SKY. THERE IS SOMETHING I MUST TELL YOU, THE DOT HACKERS.

PLEASE COME TO THE NET SLUMS TODAY AT XX:XX. I KNOW THIS IS SUDDEN, BUT IT IS OF GRAVE IMPORTANCE.

I ALSO CONTACTED OTHERS WHO MIGHT BE ABLE TO HELP VIA THEIR CELL PHONES.

I'LL LET YOU KNOW THE DETAILS LATER. IT COULD GET A BIT ROUGH. I SUGGEST YOU COME PREPARED FOR BATTLE.

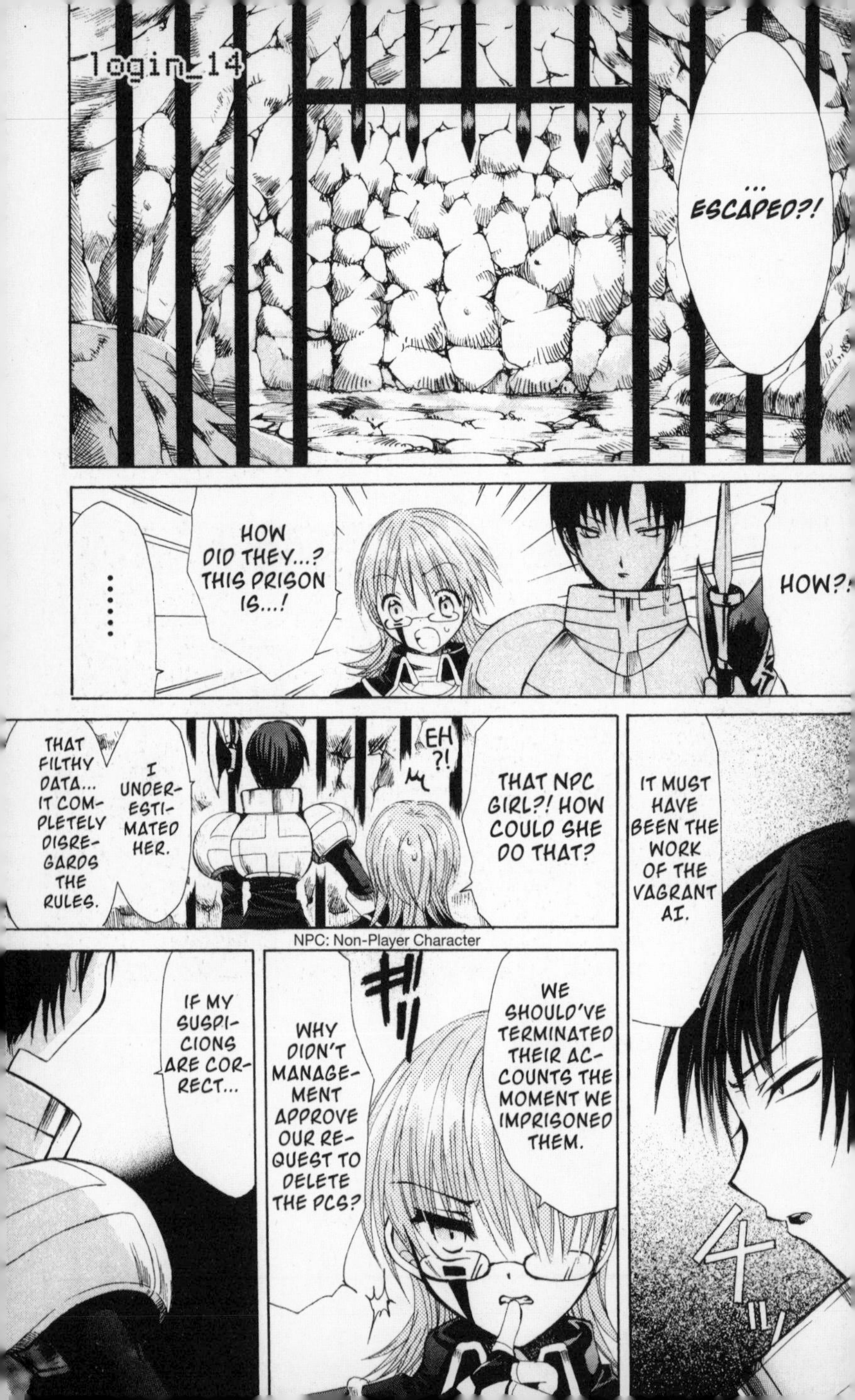
login_14
... ESCAPED?!
HOW?!
HOW DID THEY...? THIS PRISON IS...!
......
IT MUST HAVE BEEN THE WORK OF THE VAGRANT AI.
THAT NPC GIRL?! HOW COULD SHE DO THAT?
EH ?!
I UNDERESTIMATED HER.
THAT FILTHY DATA... IT COMPLETELY DISREGARDS THE RULES.
WE SHOULD'VE TERMINATED THEIR ACCOUNTS THE MOMENT WE IMPRISONED THEM.
WHY DIDN'T MANAGEMENT APPROVE OUR REQUEST TO DELETE THE PCS?
IF MY SUSPICIONS ARE CORRECT...

NPC: Non-Player Character

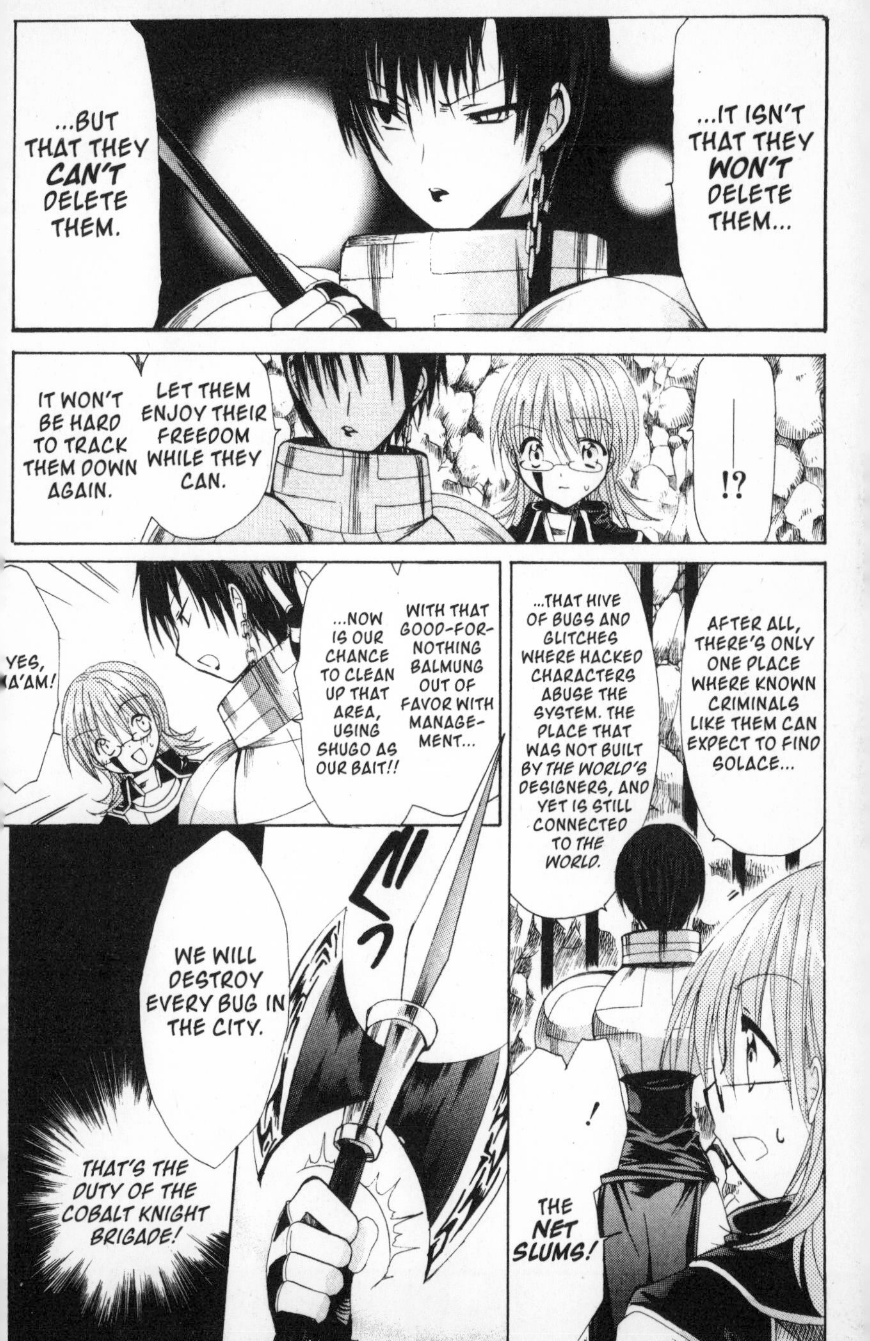
...IT ISN'T THAT THEY WON'T DELETE THEM...
...BUT THAT THEY CAN'T DELETE THEM.
—!?
LET THEM ENJOY THEIR FREEDOM WHILE THEY CAN.
IT WON'T BE HARD TO TRACK THEM DOWN AGAIN.
AFTER ALL, THERE'S ONLY ONE PLACE WHERE KNOWN CRIMINALS LIKE THEM CAN EXPECT TO FIND SOLACE...
...THAT HIVE OF BUGS AND GLITCHES WHERE HACKED CHARACTERS ABUSE THE SYSTEM. THE PLACE THAT WAS NOT BUILT BY THE WORLD'S DESIGNERS, AND YET IS STILL CONNECTED TO THE WORLD.
!?
!
THE NET SLUMS!
WITH THAT GOOD-FOR-NOTHING BALMUNG OUT OF FAVOR WITH MANAGEMENT...
...NOW IS OUR CHANCE TO CLEAN UP THAT AREA, USING SHUGO AS OUR BAIT!!
YES, A'AM!
WE WILL DESTROY EVERY BUG IN THE CITY.
THAT'S THE DUTY OF THE COBALT KNIGHT BRIGADE!

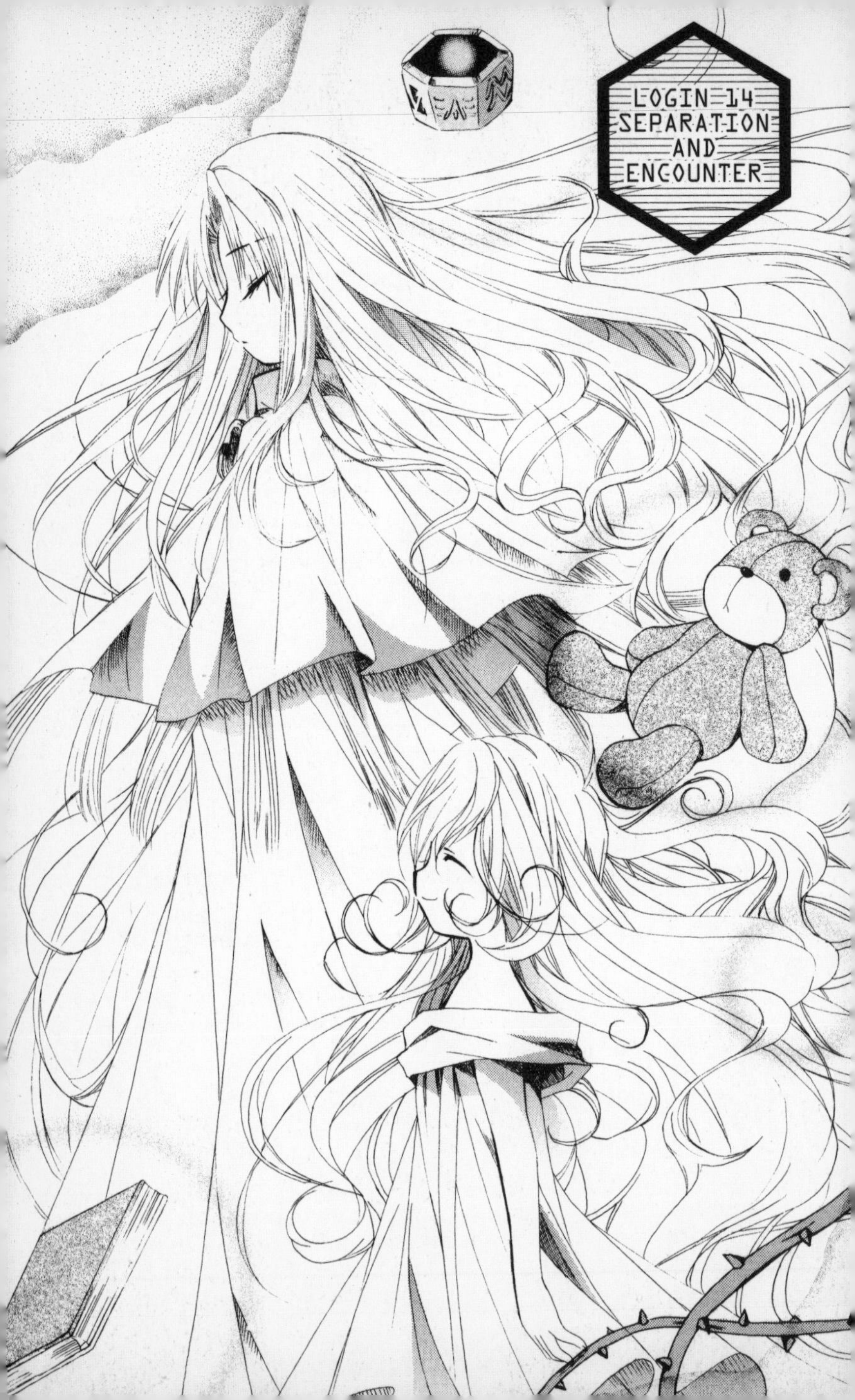
LOGIN 14
SEPARATION
AND
ENCOUNTER

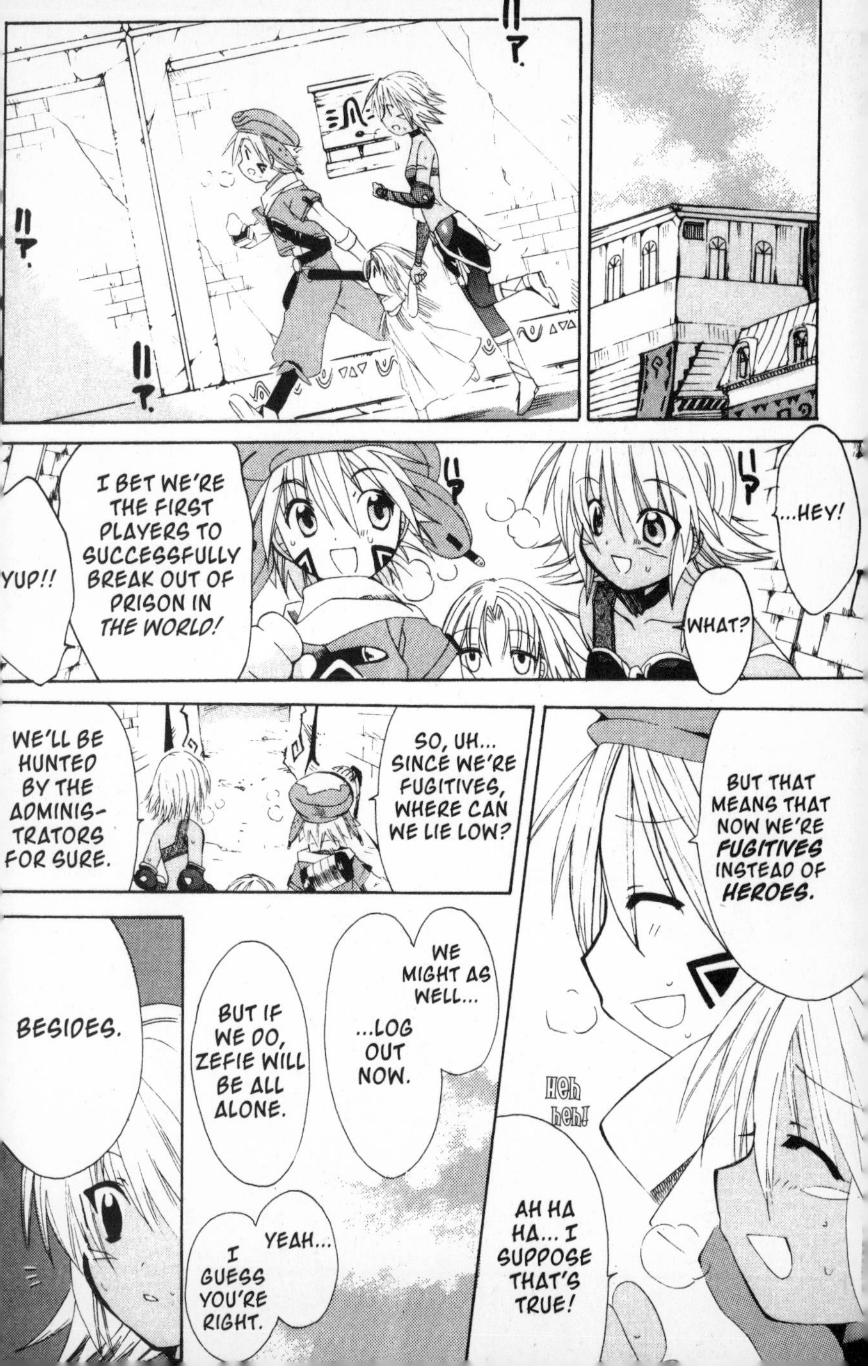
...HEY!
WHAT?
I BET WE'RE THE FIRST PLAYERS TO SUCCESSFULLY BREAK OUT OF PRISON IN *THE WORLD*!
YUP!!
BUT THAT MEANS THAT NOW WE'RE **FUGITIVES** INSTEAD OF **HEROES**.
HEH HEH!
AH HA HA... I SUPPOSE THAT'S TRUE!
SO, UH... SINCE WE'RE FUGITIVES, WHERE CAN WE LIE LOW?
WE'LL BE HUNTED BY THE ADMINIS-TRATORS FOR SURE.
WE MIGHT AS WELL...
...LOG OUT NOW.
BUT IF WE DO, ZEFIE WILL BE ALL ALONE.
BESIDES.
YEAH... I GUESS YOU'RE RIGHT.

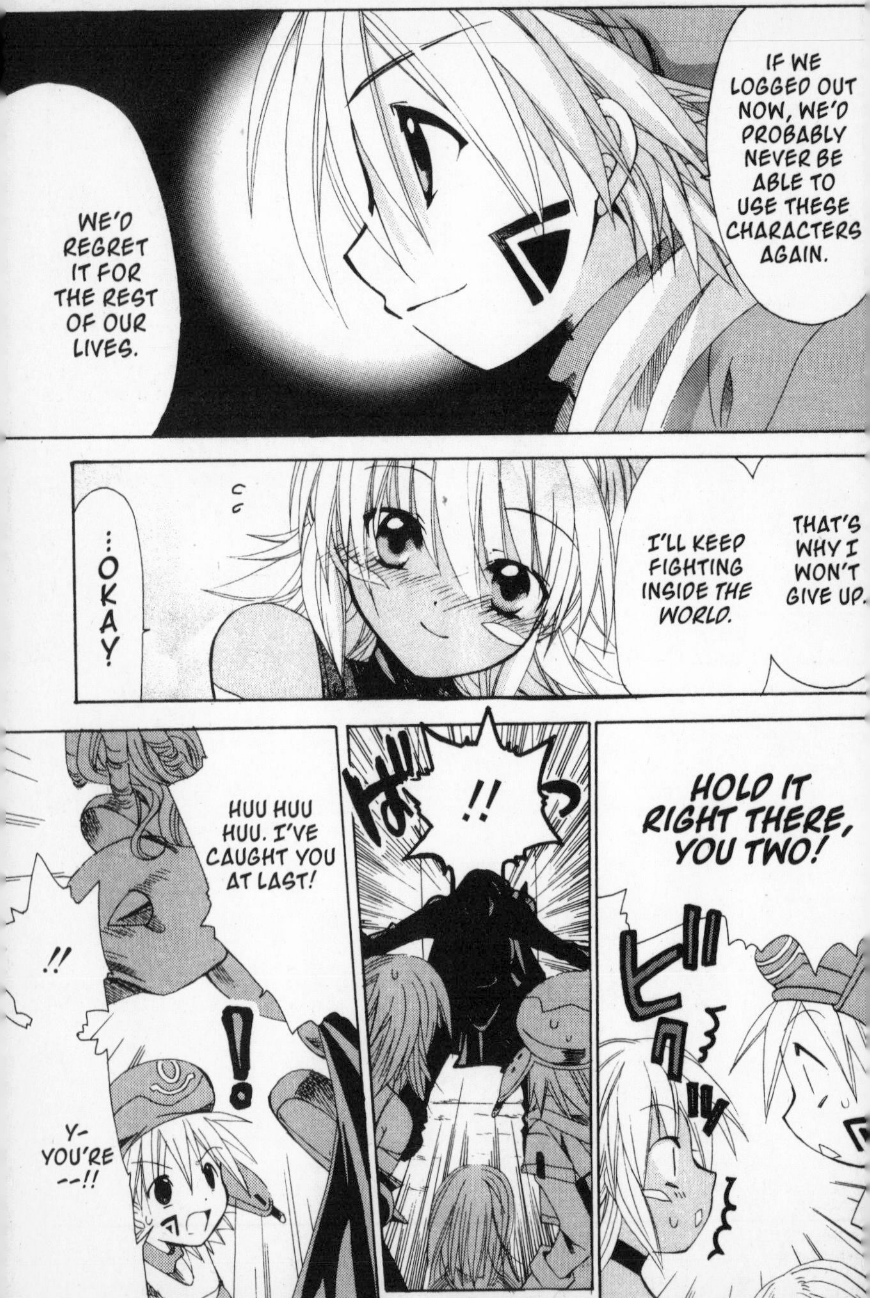

IF WE LOGGED OUT NOW, WE'D PROBABLY NEVER BE ABLE TO USE THESE CHARACTERS AGAIN.
WE'D REGRET IT FOR THE REST OF OUR LIVES.
THAT'S WHY I WON'T GIVE UP.
I'LL KEEP FIGHTING INSIDE THE WORLD.
...OKAY.
HOLD IT RIGHT THERE, YOU TWO!
!!
HUU HUU HUU. I'VE CAUGHT YOU AT LAST!
!!
!
Y-YOU'RE --!!

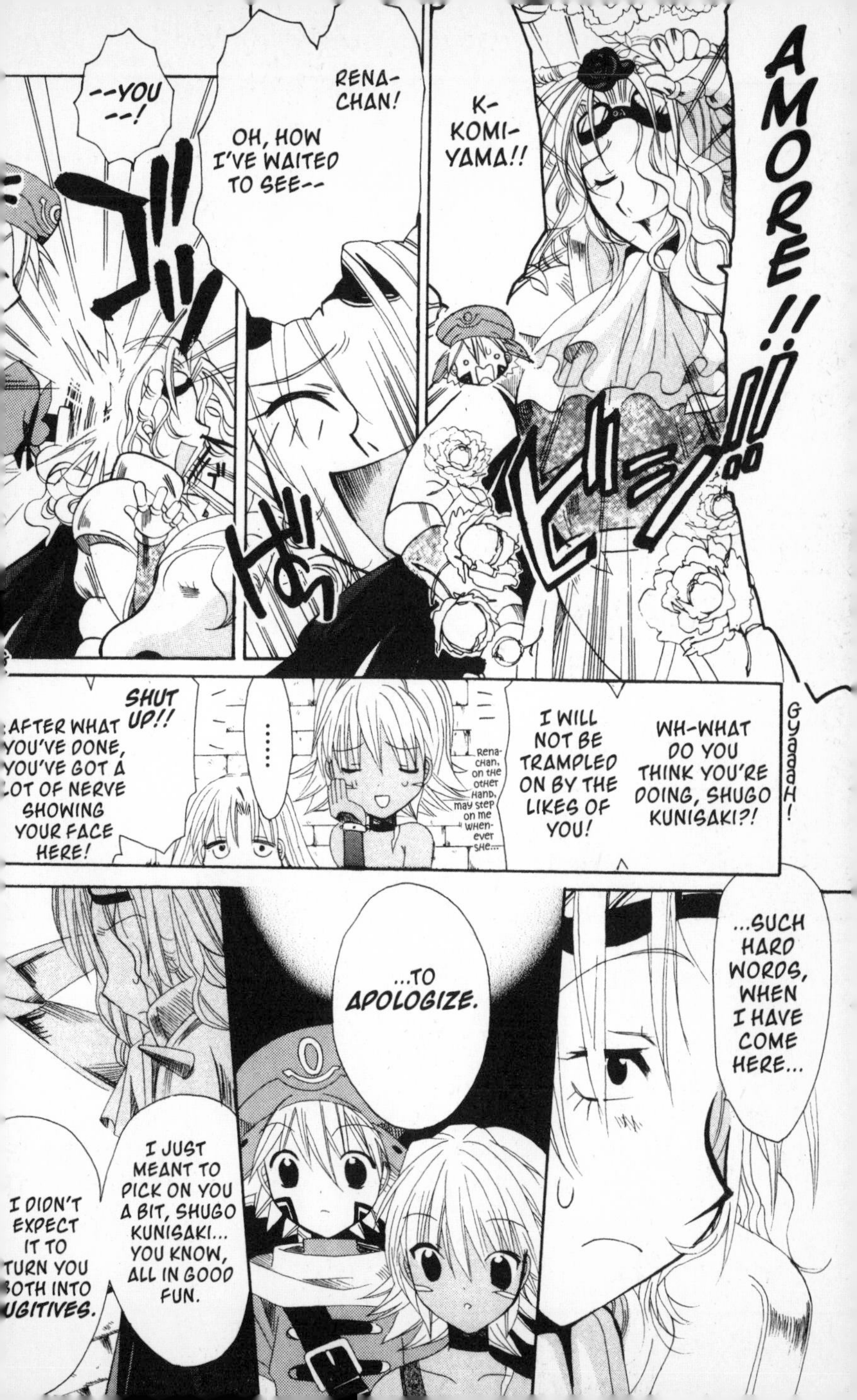
AMORE!!
K-KOMIYAMA!!
RENA-CHAN!
OH, HOW I'VE WAITED TO SEE--
--YOU--!
GYAAAAH!
WH-WHAT DO YOU THINK YOU'RE DOING, SHUGO KUNISAKI?!
I WILL NOT BE TRAMPLED ON BY THE LIKES OF YOU!
Rena-chan, on the other hand, may step on me whenever she...
......
SHUT UP!!
AFTER WHAT YOU'VE DONE, YOU'VE GOT A LOT OF NERVE SHOWING YOUR FACE HERE!
...SUCH HARD WORDS, WHEN I HAVE COME HERE...
...TO APOLOGIZE.
I JUST MEANT TO PICK ON YOU A BIT, SHUGO KUNISAKI... YOU KNOW, ALL IN GOOD FUN.
I DIDN'T EXPECT IT TO TURN YOU BOTH INTO FUGITIVES.

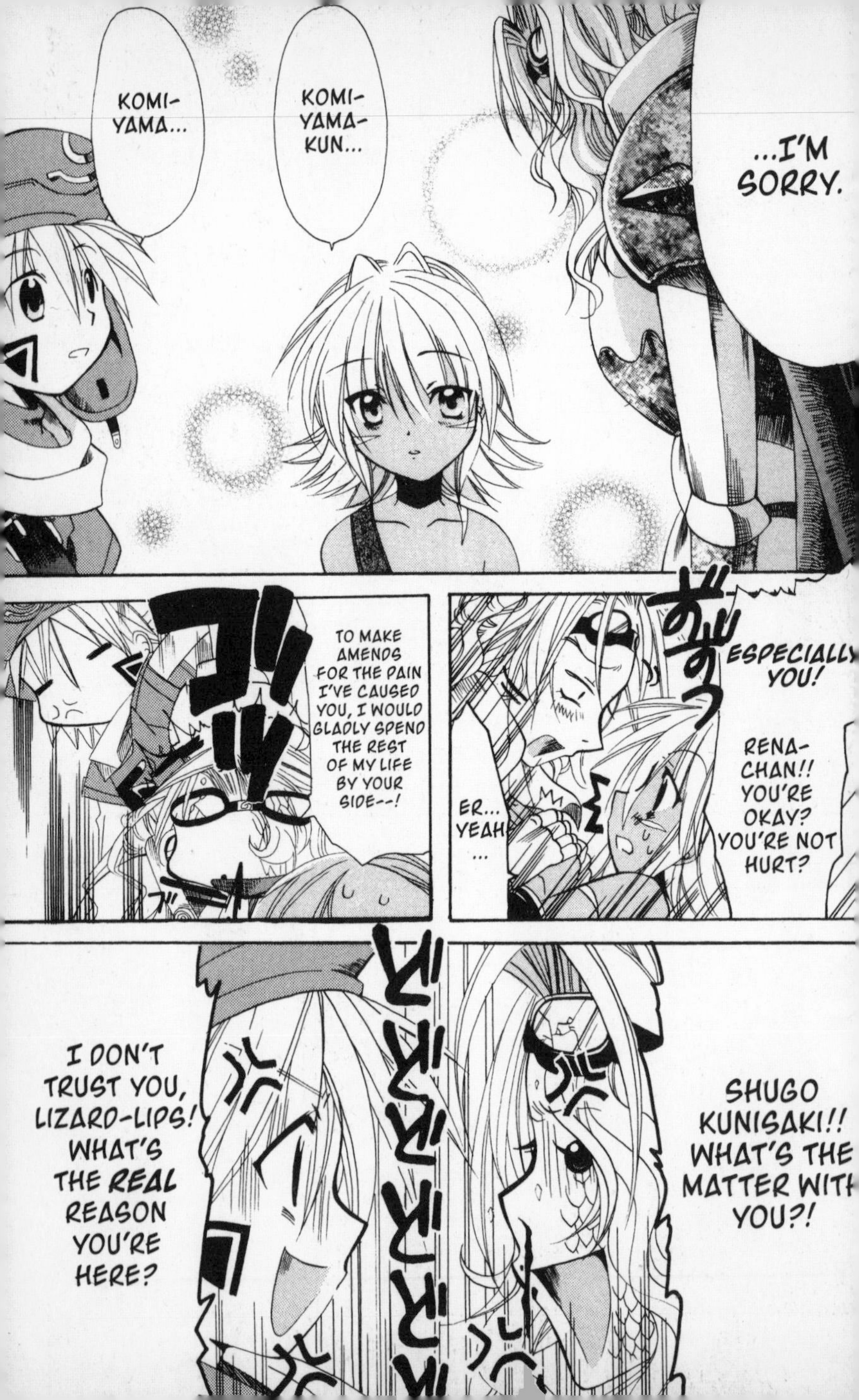
...I'M SORRY.
KOMI-YAMA-KUN...
KOMI-YAMA...
ESPECIALLY YOU!
RENA-CHAN!! YOU'RE OKAY? YOU'RE NOT HURT?
ER... YEAH ...
TO MAKE AMENDS FOR THE PAIN I'VE CAUSED YOU, I WOULD GLADLY SPEND THE REST OF MY LIFE BY YOUR SIDE--!
SHUGO KUNISAKI!! WHAT'S THE MATTER WITH YOU?!
I DON'T TRUST YOU, LIZARD-LIPS! WHAT'S THE *REAL* REASON YOU'RE HERE?

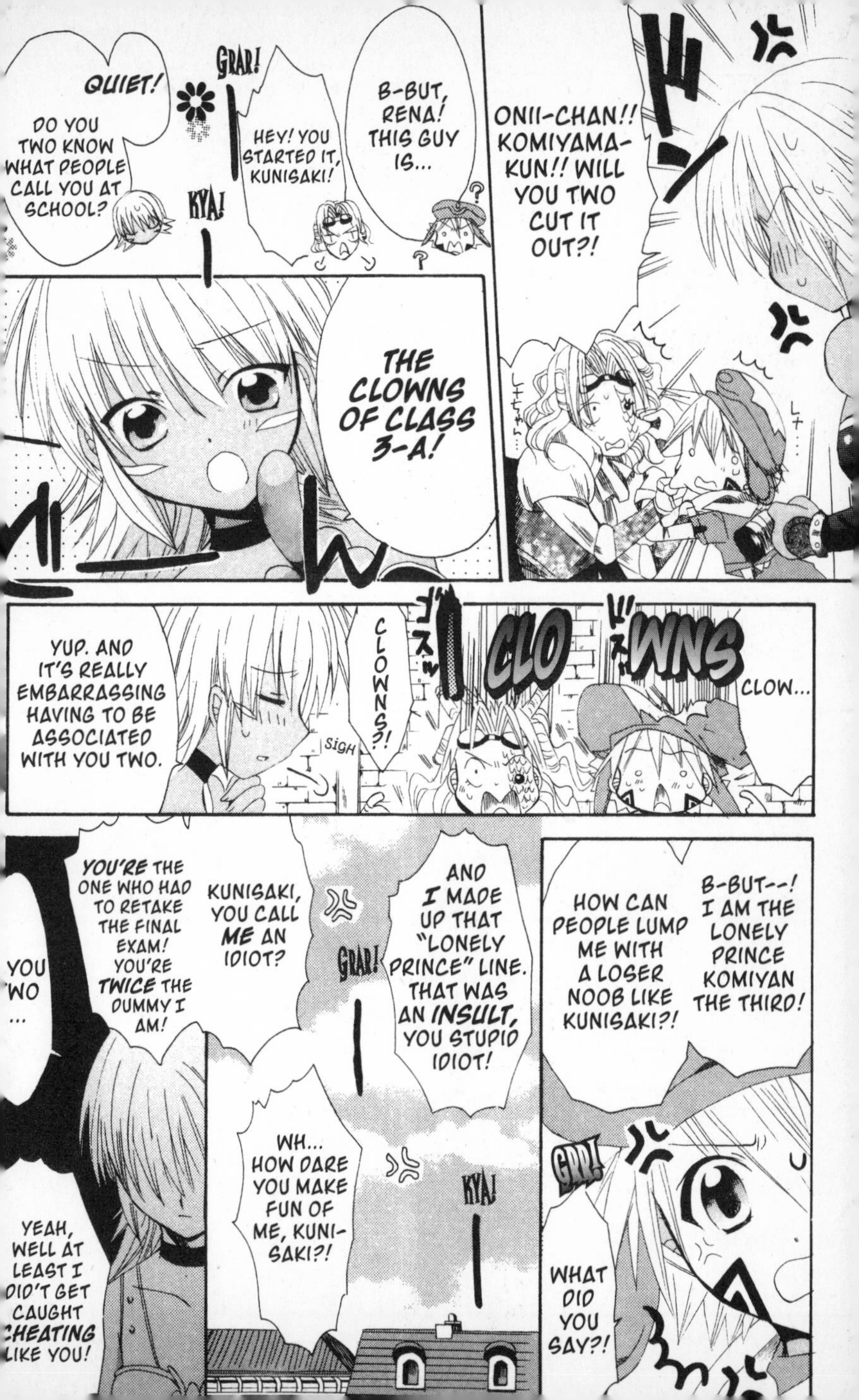
ONII-CHAN!! KOMIYAMA-KUN!! WILL YOU TWO CUT IT OUT?!
B-BUT, RENA! THIS GUY IS...
GRAR!
HEY! YOU STARTED IT, KUNISAKI!
KYA!
QUIET!
DO YOU TWO KNOW WHAT PEOPLE CALL YOU AT SCHOOL?
THE CLOWNS OF CLASS 3-A!
CLOW...
CLOWNS
CLOWNS?!
SIGH
YUP. AND IT'S REALLY EMBARRASSING HAVING TO BE ASSOCIATED WITH YOU TWO.
B-BUT--! I AM THE LONELY PRINCE KOMIYAN THE THIRD!
HOW CAN PEOPLE LUMP ME WITH A LOSER NOOB LIKE KUNISAKI?!
GRR!
WHAT DID YOU SAY?!
AND I MADE UP THAT "LONELY PRINCE" LINE. THAT WAS AN INSULT, YOU STUPID IDIOT!
GRAR!
KUNISAKI, YOU CALL ME AN IDIOT?
WH... HOW DARE YOU MAKE FUN OF ME, KUNI-SAKI?!
KYA!
YOU'RE THE ONE WHO HAD TO RETAKE THE FINAL EXAM! YOU'RE TWICE THE DUMMY I AM!
YOU TWO ...
YEAH, WELL AT LEAST I DIDN'T GET CAUGHT CHEATING LIKE YOU!

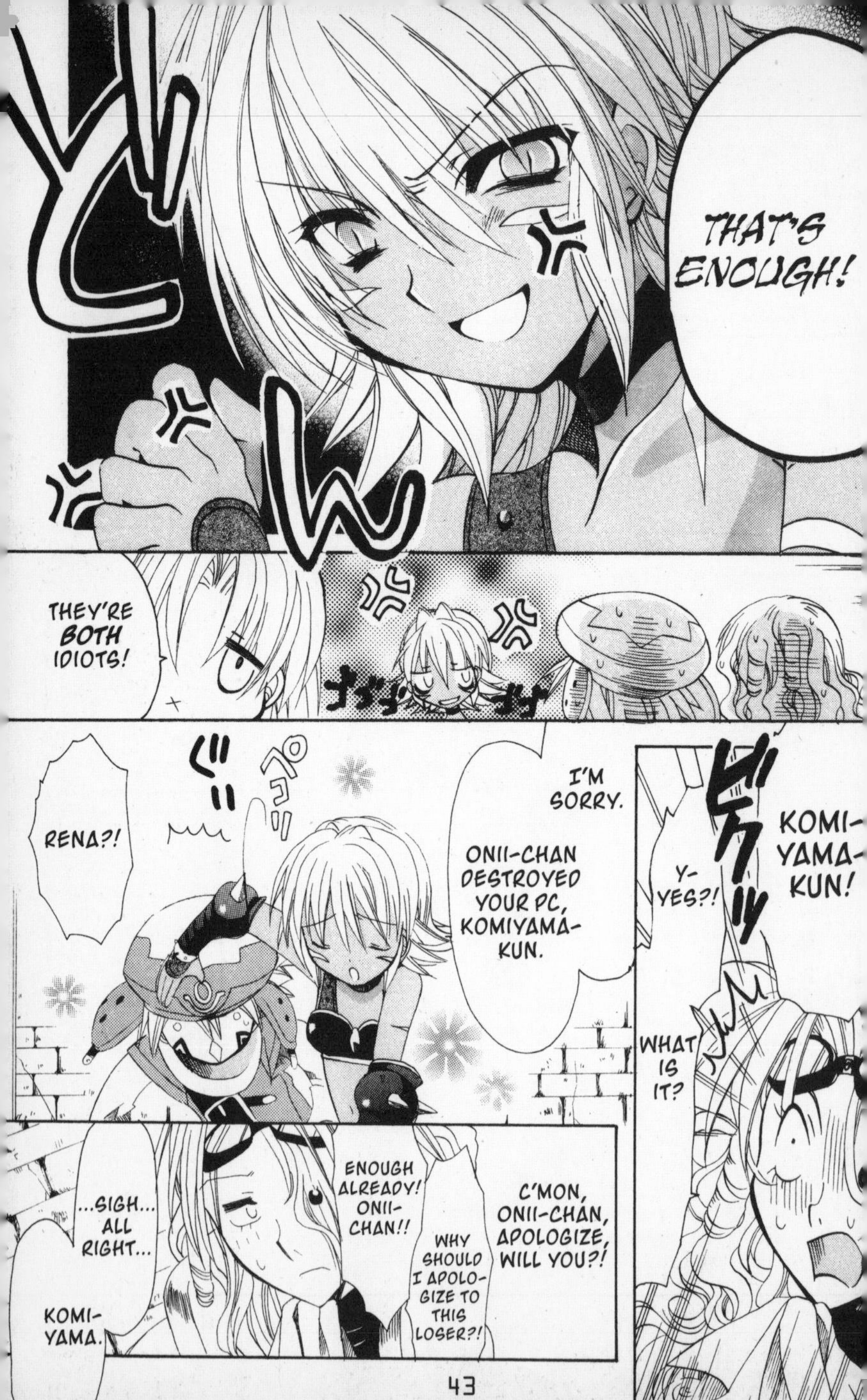
THAT'S ENOUGH!
THEY'RE BOTH IDIOTS!
KOMI-YAMA-KUN!
Y-YES?!
WHAT IS IT?
I'M SORRY.
ONII-CHAN DESTROYED YOUR PC, KOMIYAMA-KUN.
RENA?!
C'MON, ONII-CHAN, APOLOGIZE, WILL YOU?!
ENOUGH ALREADY! ONII-CHAN!!
WHY SHOULD I APOLOGIZE TO THIS LOSER?!
...SIGH... ALL RIGHT...
KOMI-YAMA.

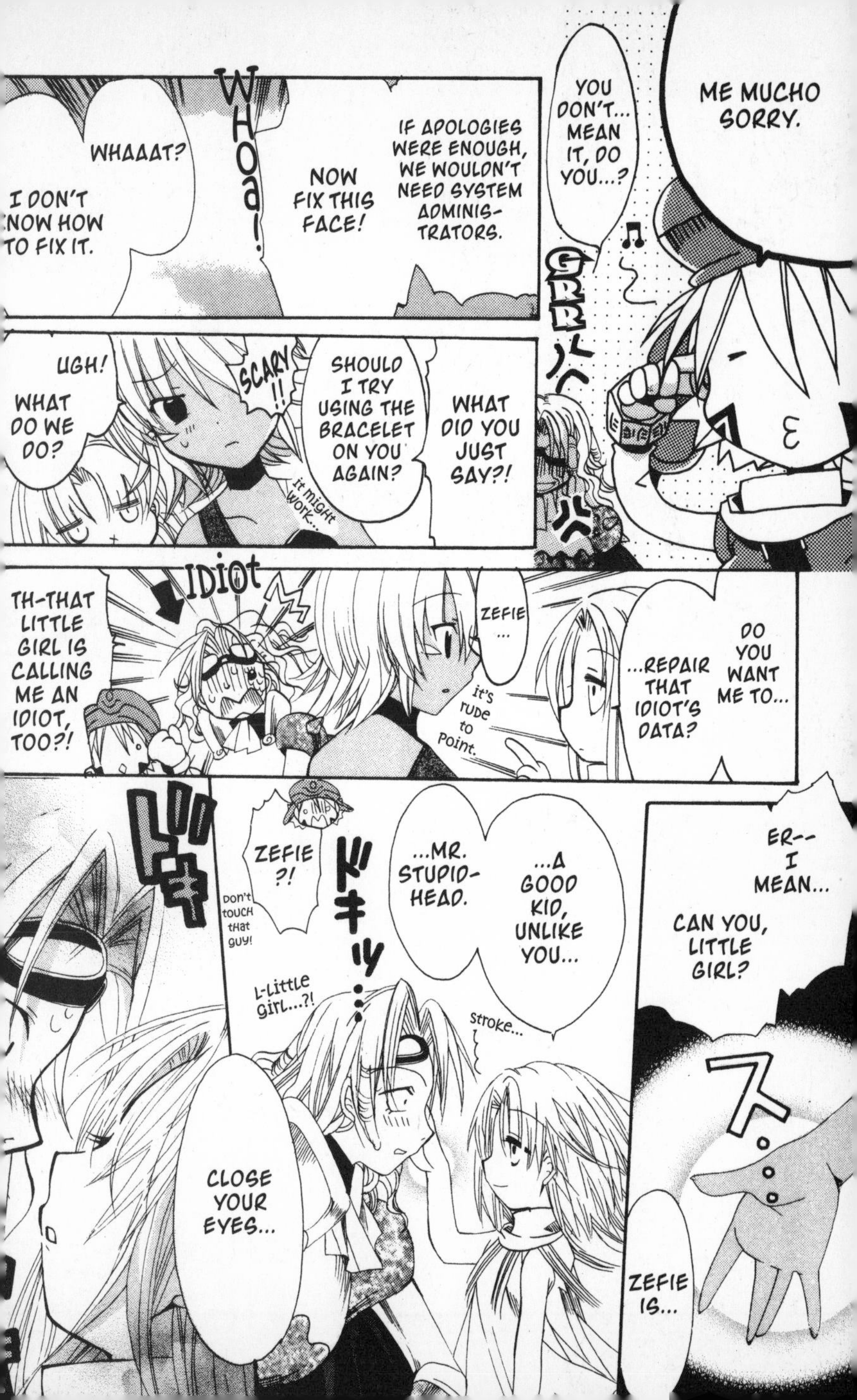
ME MUCHO SORRY.
YOU DON'T... MEAN IT, DO YOU...?
GRR
IF APOLOGIES WERE ENOUGH, WE WOULDN'T NEED SYSTEM ADMINIS-TRATORS.
NOW FIX THIS FACE!
WHOA!
WHAAAT?
I DON'T NOW HOW TO FIX IT.
WHAT DID YOU JUST SAY?!
SHOULD I TRY USING THE BRACELET ON YOU AGAIN?
SCARY!!
it might work...
UGH!
WHAT DO WE DO?
DO YOU WANT ME TO...
...REPAIR THAT IDIOT'S DATA?
ZEFIE...
it's rude to point.
IDIOT
TH-THAT LITTLE GIRL IS CALLING ME AN IDIOT, TOO?!
ER-- I MEAN...
CAN YOU, LITTLE GIRL?
ZEFIE IS...
...A GOOD KID, UNLIKE YOU...
...MR. STUPID-HEAD.
stroke...
ZEFIE?!
Don't touch that guy!
L-Little girl...?!
CLOSE YOUR EYES...

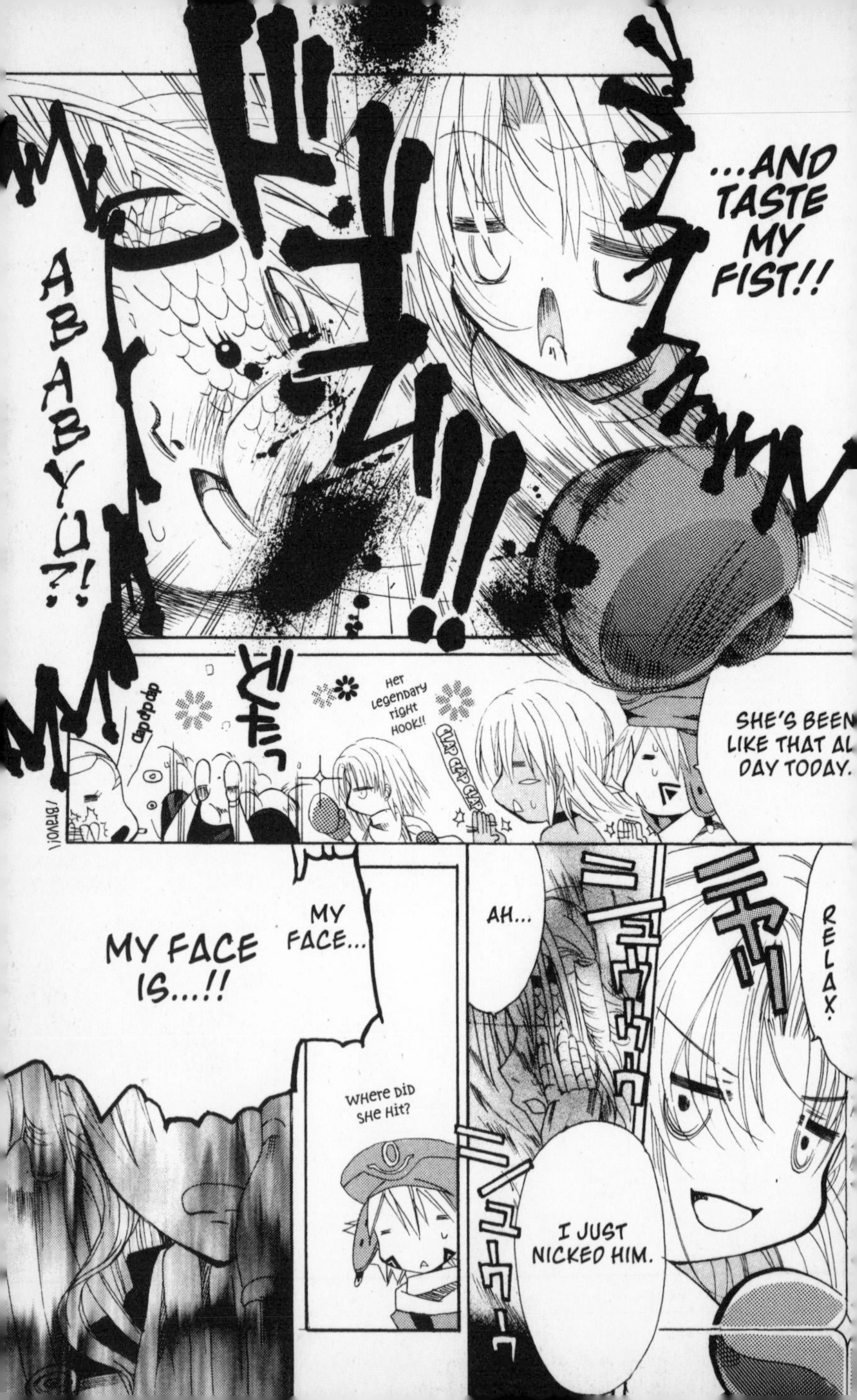
...AND TASTE MY FIST!!
ABABAYU?!
SHE'S BEEN LIKE THAT AL DAY TODAY.
Her legendary right HOOK!!
CLAP CLAP CLAP
clap clap clap
Bravo!!
RELAX.
I JUST NICKED HIM.
AH...
MY FACE...
Where did she hit?
MY FACE IS...!!

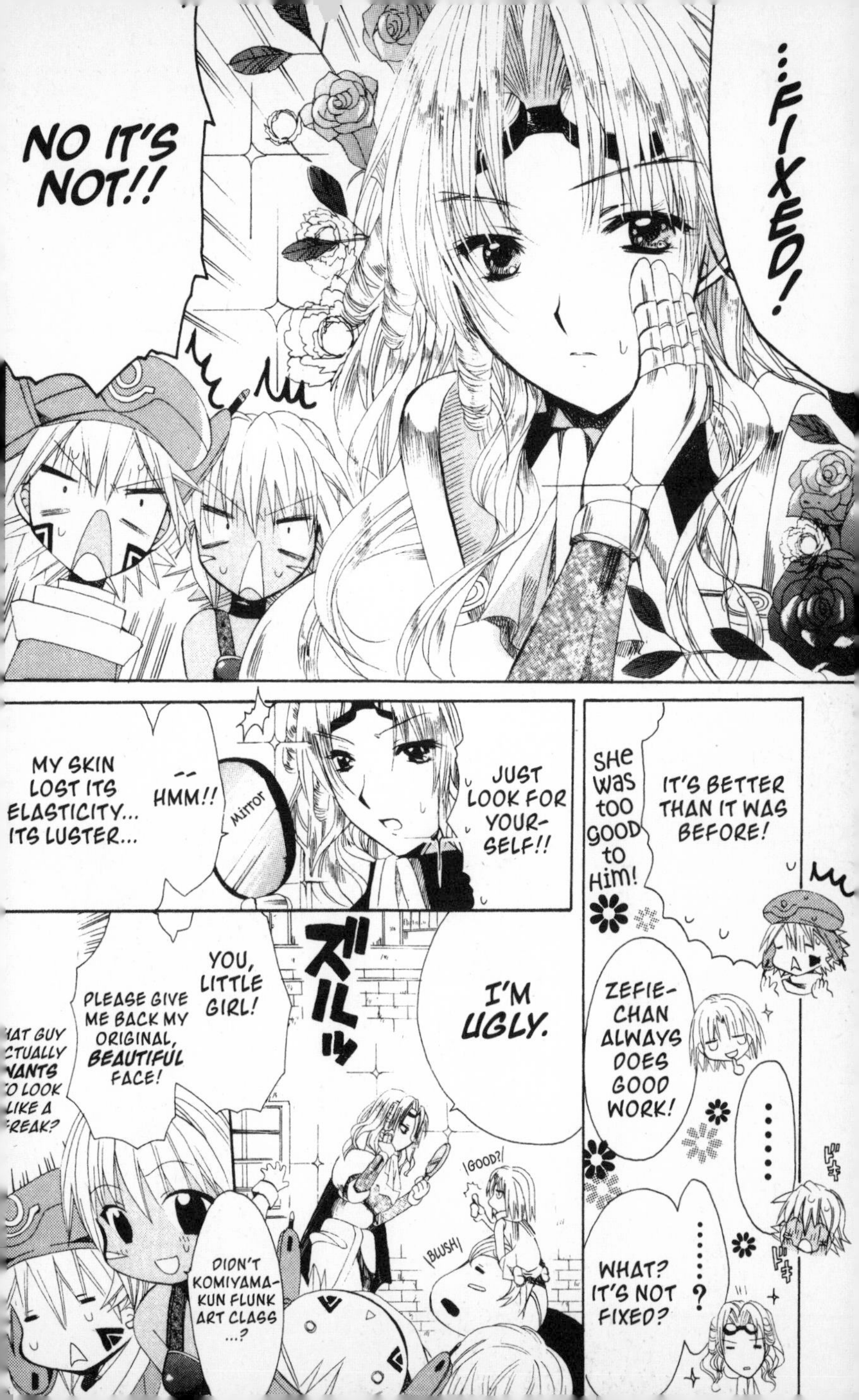
...FIXED!
MU
MU
NO IT'S NOT!!
SHE WAS TOO GOOD TO HIM!
IT'S BETTER THAN IT WAS BEFORE!
MU
JUST LOOK FOR YOURSELF!!
--HMM!!
Mirror
MY SKIN LOST ITS ELASTICITY... ITS LUSTER...
ZEFIE-CHAN ALWAYS DOES GOOD WORK!
......
......?
WHAT? IT'S NOT FIXED?
I'M UGLY.
YOU, LITTLE GIRL!
PLEASE GIVE ME BACK MY ORIGINAL, BEAUTIFUL FACE!
GOOD?
BLUSH
DIDN'T KOMIYAMA-KUN FLUNK ART CLASS ...?
HAT GUY CTUALLY WANTS O LOOK LIKE A REAK?

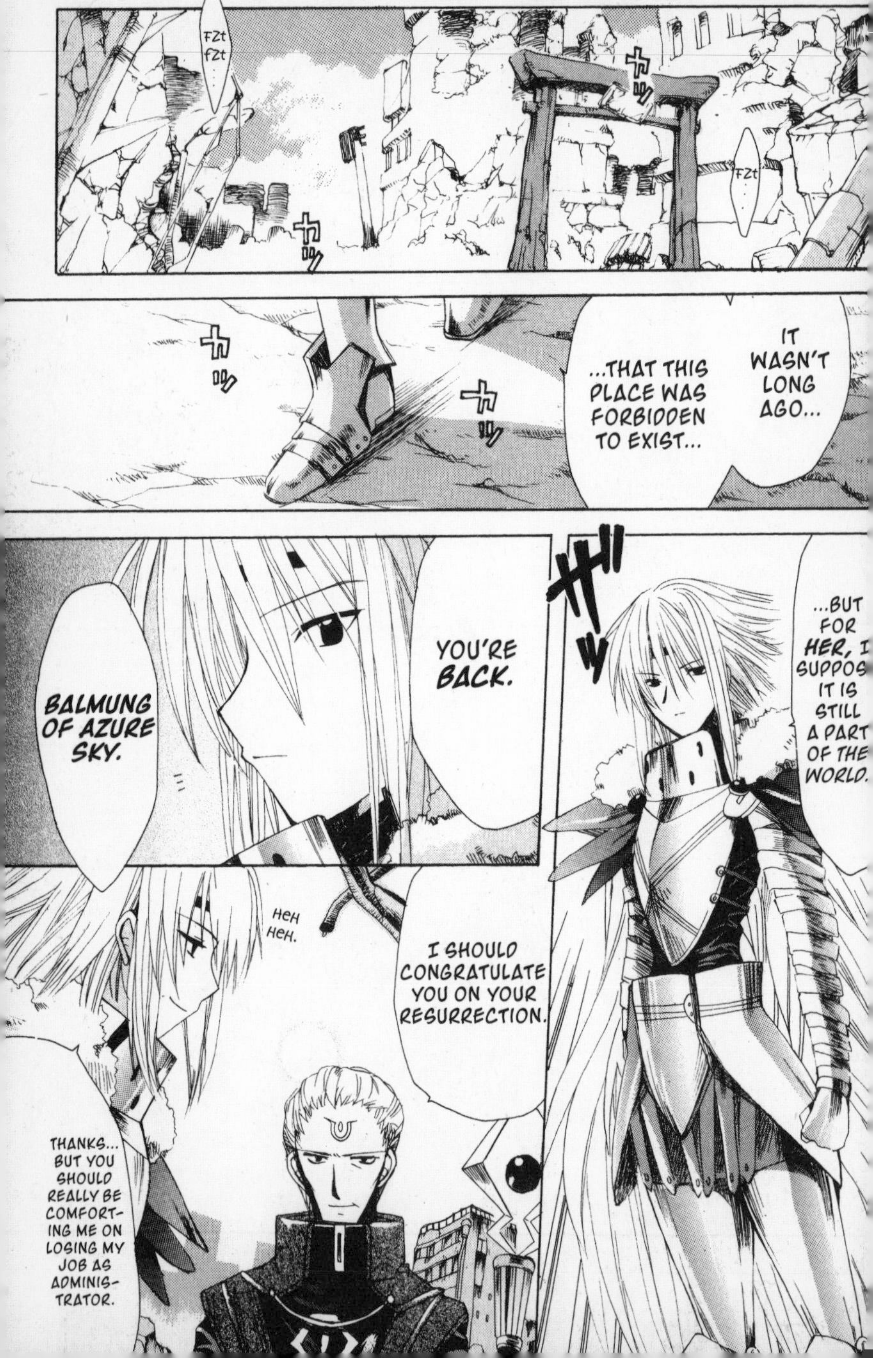
FZt . . .
カッ
FZt fZt . . .
カッ
IT WASN'T LONG AGO...
...THAT THIS PLACE WAS FORBIDDEN TO EXIST...
カッ
カッ
...BUT FOR HER, I SUPPOS IT IS STILL A PART OF THE WORLD.
YOU'RE BACK.
BALMUNG OF AZURE SKY.
I SHOULD CONGRATULATE YOU ON YOUR RESURRECTION.
HEH HEH.
THANKS... BUT YOU SHOULD REALLY BE COMFORTING ME ON LOSING MY JOB AS ADMINISTRATOR.

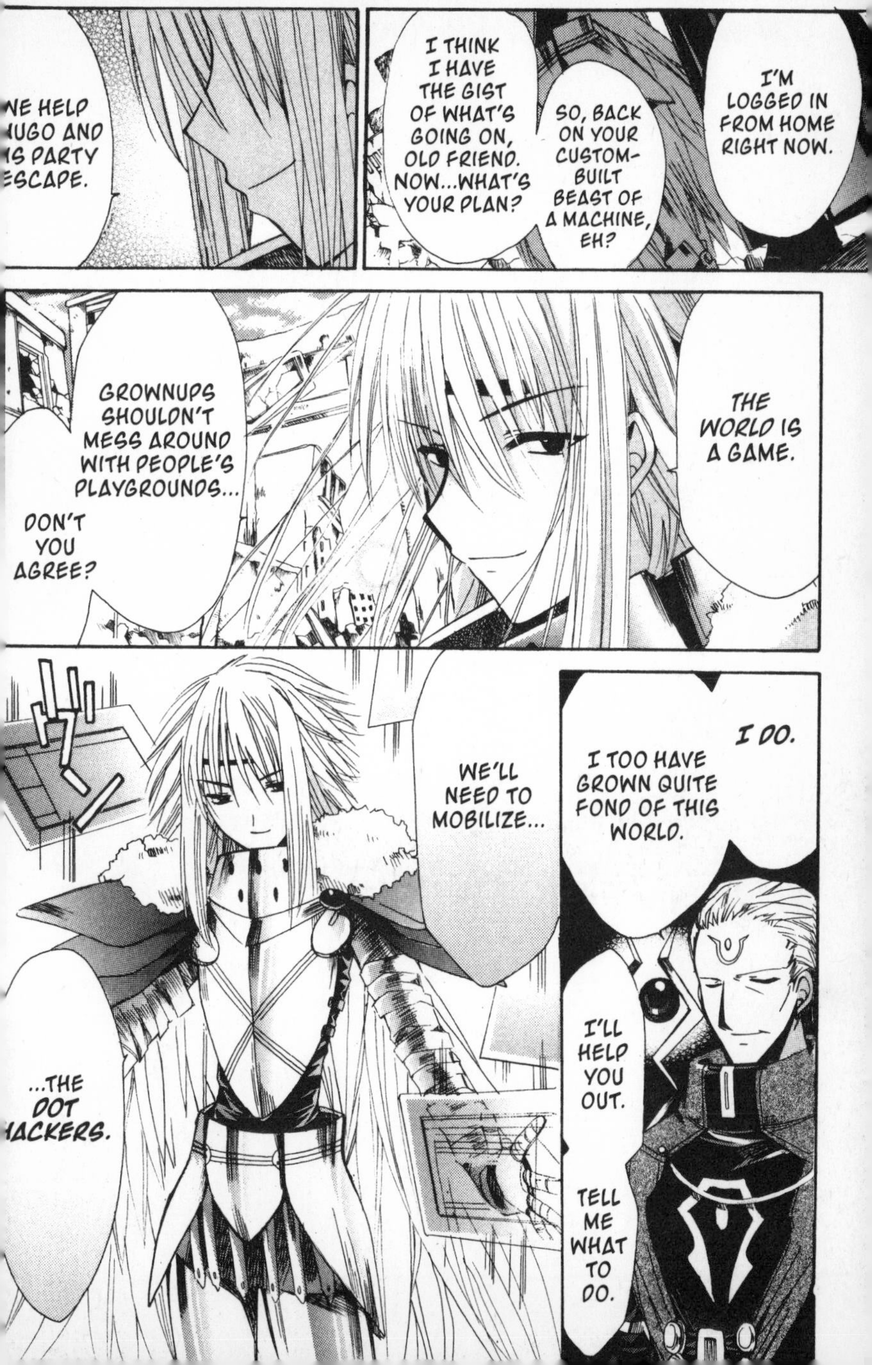

I'M LOGGED IN FROM HOME RIGHT NOW.
SO, BACK ON YOUR CUSTOM-BUILT BEAST OF A MACHINE, EH?
I THINK I HAVE THE GIST OF WHAT'S GOING ON, OLD FRIEND. NOW...WHAT'S YOUR PLAN?
NE HELP HUGO AND IS PARTY ESCAPE.
THE WORLD IS A GAME.
GROWNUPS SHOULDN'T MESS AROUND WITH PEOPLE'S PLAYGROUNDS...
DON'T YOU AGREE?
I DO.
I TOO HAVE GROWN QUITE FOND OF THIS WORLD.
I'LL HELP YOU OUT.
TELL ME WHAT TO DO.
WE'LL NEED TO MOBILIZE...
...THE DOT ACKERS.

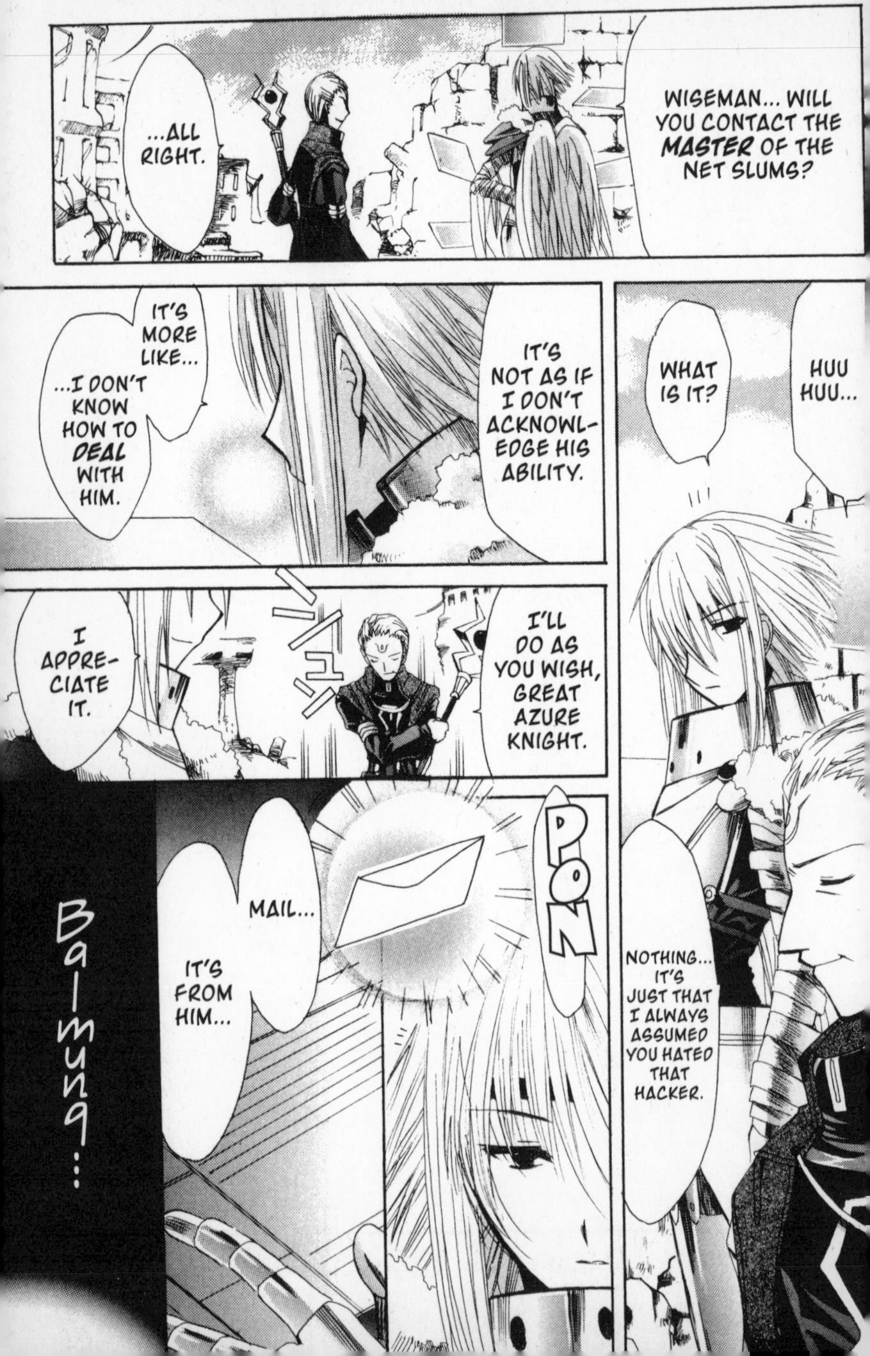
WISEMAN... WILL YOU CONTACT THE *MASTER* OF THE NET SLUMS?
...ALL RIGHT.
HUU HUU...
WHAT IS IT?
NOTHING... IT'S JUST THAT I ALWAYS ASSUMED YOU HATED THAT HACKER.
IT'S NOT AS IF I DON'T ACKNOWL-EDGE HIS ABILITY.
IT'S MORE LIKE...
...I DON'T KNOW HOW TO *DEAL* WITH HIM.
I'LL DO AS YOU WISH, GREAT AZURE KNIGHT.
I APPRE-CIATE IT.
PON
MAIL...
IT'S FROM HIM...
Balmung...

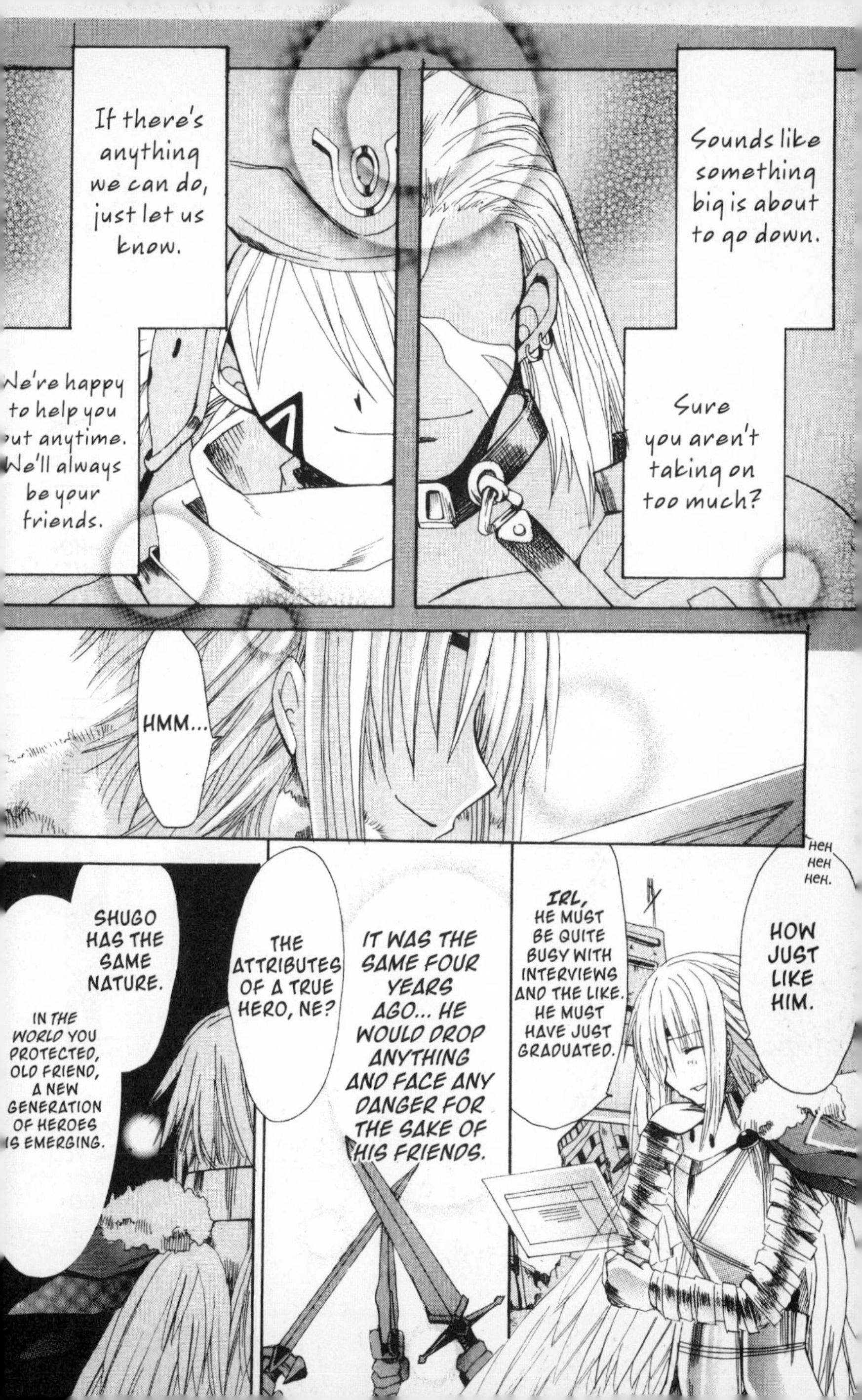
Sounds like something big is about to go down.
Sure you aren't taking on too much?
If there's anything we can do, just let us know.
We're happy to help you out anytime. We'll always be your friends.
HMM...
HEH HEH HEH.
HOW JUST LIKE HIM.
IRL, HE MUST BE QUITE BUSY WITH INTERVIEWS AND THE LIKE. HE MUST HAVE JUST GRADUATED.
IT WAS THE SAME FOUR YEARS AGO... HE WOULD DROP ANYTHING AND FACE ANY DANGER FOR THE SAKE OF HIS FRIENDS.
THE ATTRIBUTES OF A TRUE HERO, NE?
SHUGO HAS THE SAME NATURE.
IN THE WORLD YOU PROTECTED, OLD FRIEND, A NEW GENERATION OF HEROES IS EMERGING.

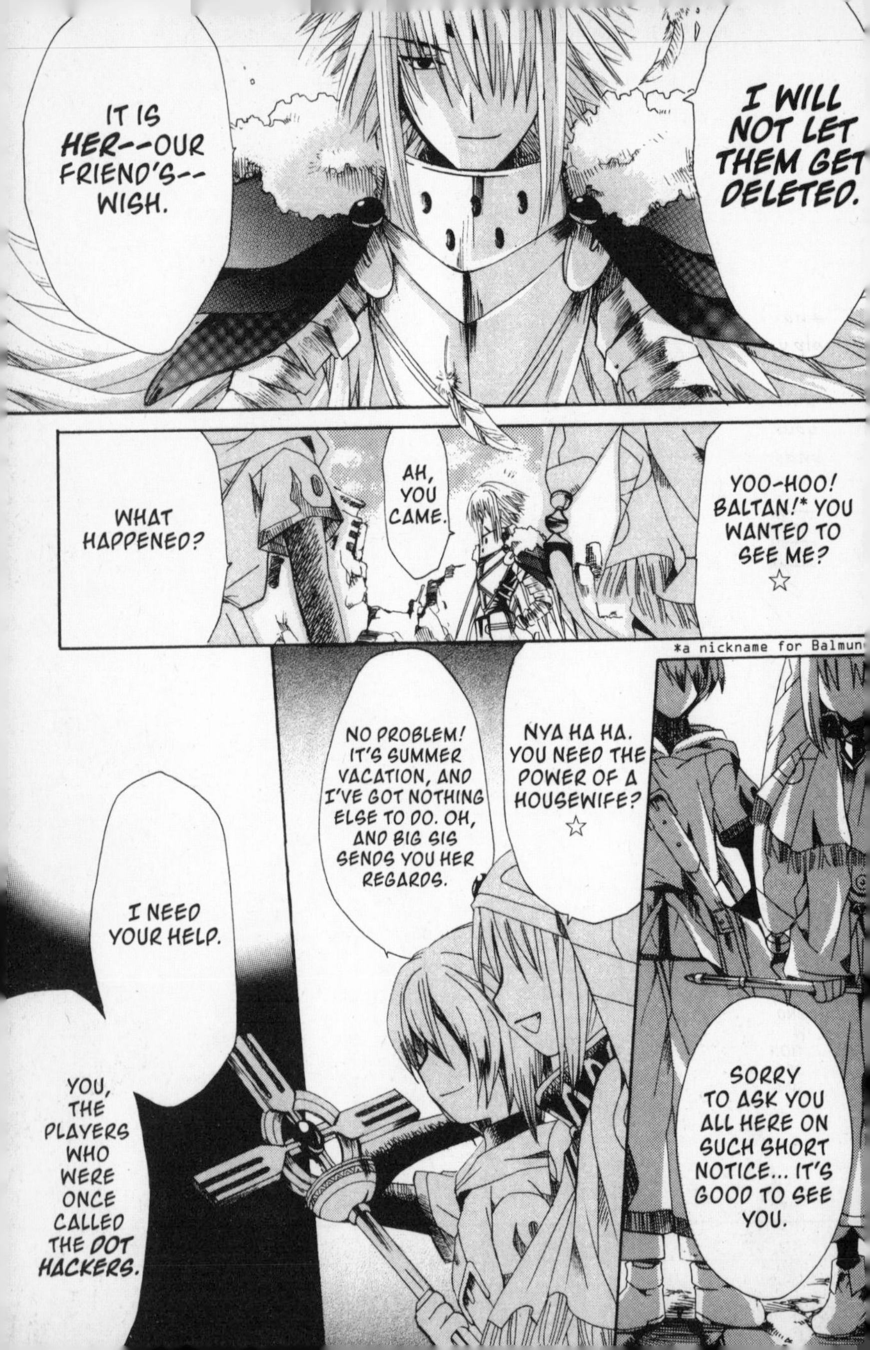
I WILL NOT LET THEM GET DELETED.
IT IS HER--OUR FRIEND'S--WISH.
YOO-HOO! BALTAN!* YOU WANTED TO SEE ME? ☆
AH, YOU CAME.
WHAT HAPPENED?
SORRY TO ASK YOU ALL HERE ON SUCH SHORT NOTICE... IT'S GOOD TO SEE YOU.
NYA HA HA. YOU NEED THE POWER OF A HOUSEWIFE? ☆
NO PROBLEM! IT'S SUMMER VACATION, AND I'VE GOT NOTHING ELSE TO DO. OH, AND BIG SIS SENDS YOU HER REGARDS.
I NEED YOUR HELP.
YOU, THE PLAYERS WHO WERE ONCE CALLED THE DOT HACKERS.

*a nickname for Balmun

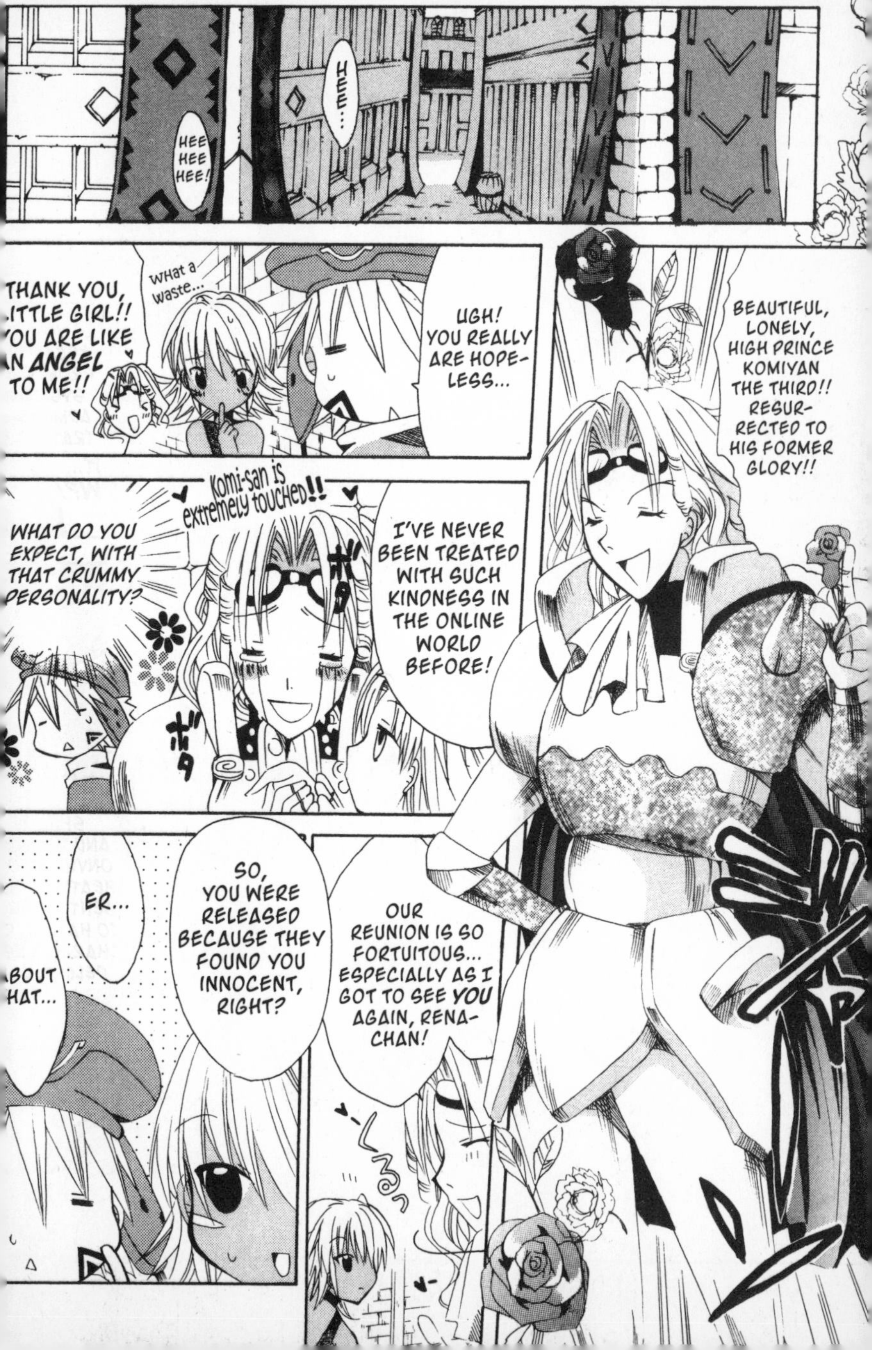
HEE...
HEE HEE HEE!
BEAUTIFUL, LONELY, HIGH PRINCE KOMIYAN THE THIRD!! RESURRECTED TO HIS FORMER GLORY!!
UGH! YOU REALLY ARE HOPELESS...
What a waste...
THANK YOU, LITTLE GIRL!! YOU ARE LIKE AN ANGEL TO ME!!
I'VE NEVER BEEN TREATED WITH SUCH KINDNESS IN THE ONLINE WORLD BEFORE!
Komi-san is extremely touched!!
WHAT DO YOU EXPECT, WITH THAT CRUMMY PERSONALITY?
OUR REUNION IS SO FORTUITOUS... ESPECIALLY AS I GOT TO SEE YOU AGAIN, RENA-CHAN!
SO, YOU WERE RELEASED BECAUSE THEY FOUND YOU INNOCENT, RIGHT?
ER...
ABOUT THAT...

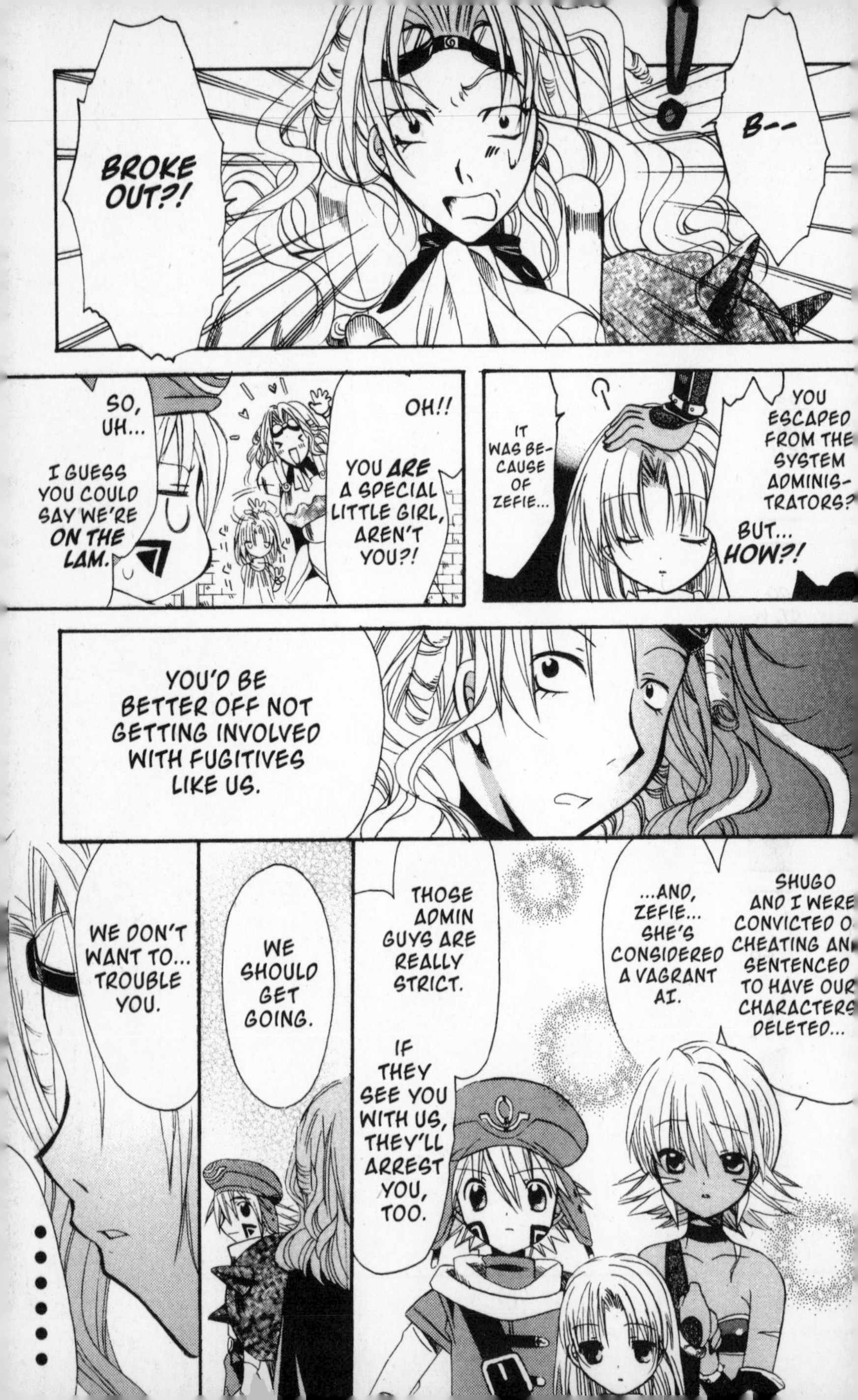
B--
BROKE OUT?!
YOU ESCAPED FROM THE SYSTEM ADMINISTRATORS?
BUT... HOW?!
IT WAS BECAUSE OF ZEFIE...
OH!!
YOU **ARE** A SPECIAL LITTLE GIRL, AREN'T YOU?!
SO, UH...
I GUESS YOU COULD SAY WE'RE **ON THE LAM.**
YOU'D BE BETTER OFF NOT GETTING INVOLVED WITH FUGITIVES LIKE US.
SHUGO AND I WERE CONVICTED O CHEATING AN SENTENCED TO HAVE OUR CHARACTERS DELETED...
...AND, ZEFIE... SHE'S CONSIDERED A VAGRANT AI.
THOSE ADMIN GUYS ARE REALLY STRICT.
IF THEY SEE YOU WITH US, THEY'LL ARREST YOU, TOO.
WE SHOULD GET GOING.
WE DON'T WANT TO... TROUBLE YOU.
......

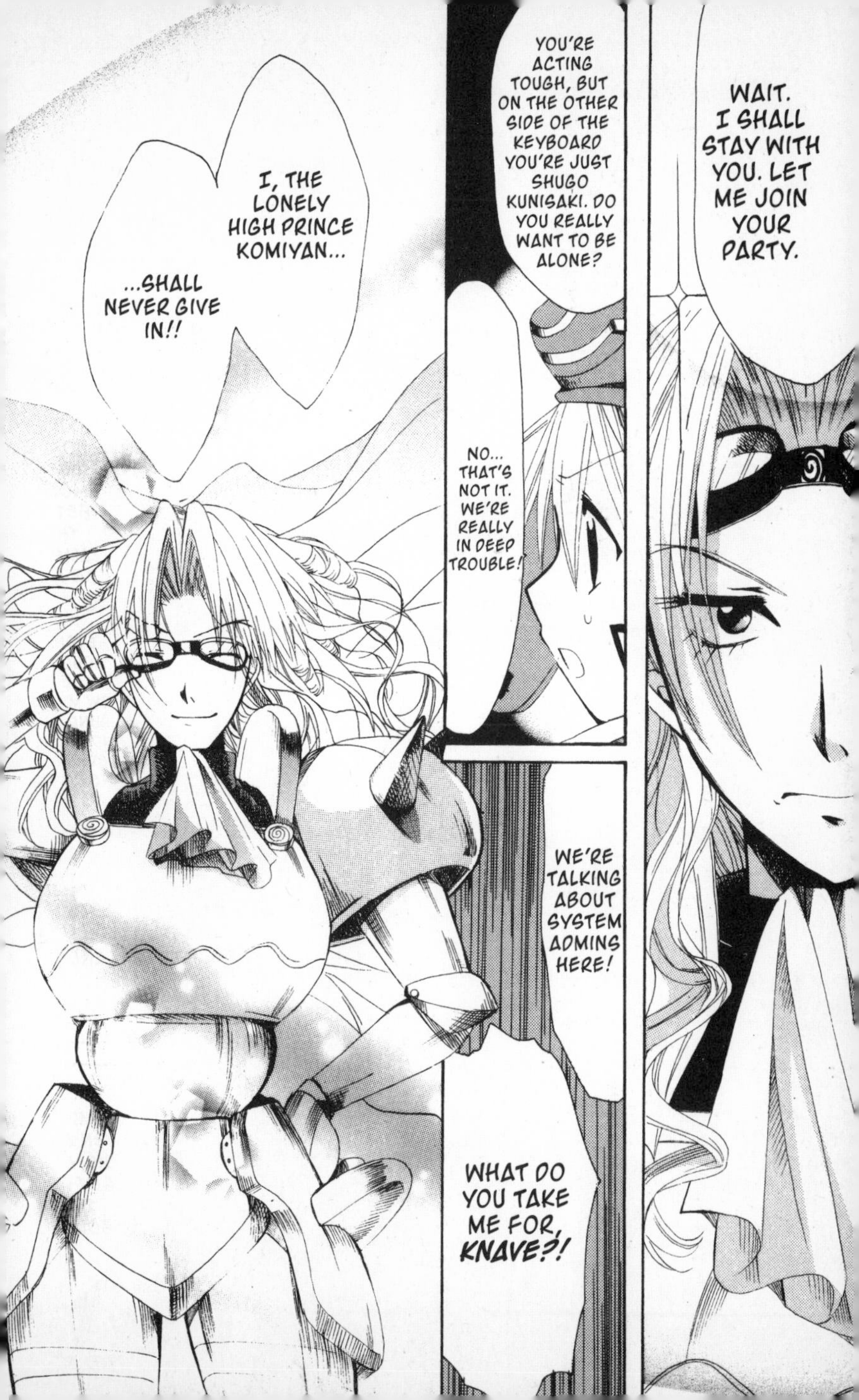

WAIT. I SHALL STAY WITH YOU. LET ME JOIN YOUR PARTY.
YOU'RE ACTING TOUGH, BUT ON THE OTHER SIDE OF THE KEYBOARD YOU'RE JUST SHUGO KUNISAKI. DO YOU REALLY WANT TO BE ALONE?
NO... THAT'S NOT IT. WE'RE REALLY IN DEEP TROUBLE!
WE'RE TALKING ABOUT SYSTEM ADMINS HERE!
WHAT DO YOU TAKE ME FOR, ***KNAVE?!***
I, THE LONELY HIGH PRINCE KOMIYAN...
...SHALL NEVER GIVE IN!!

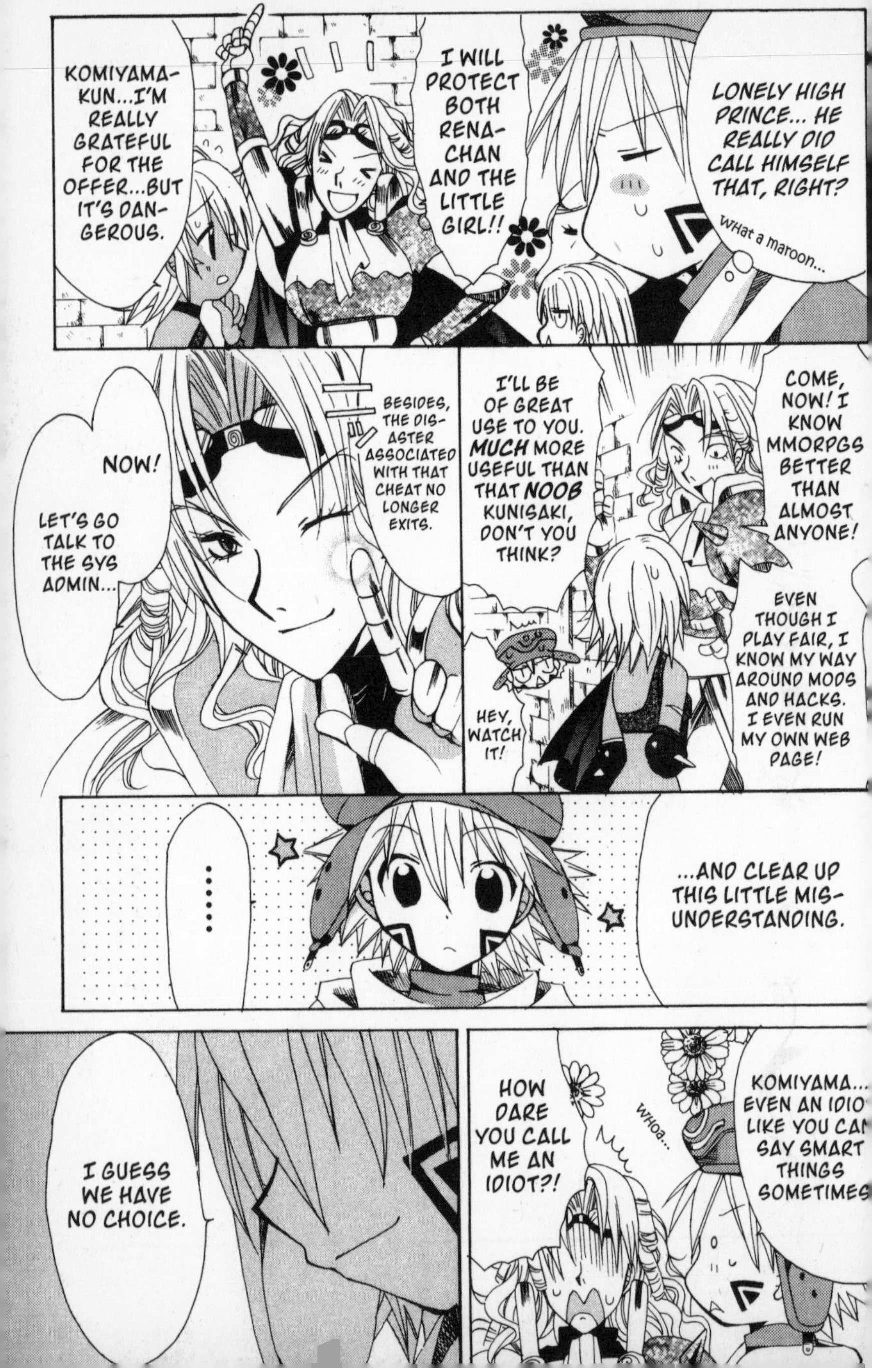
LONELY HIGH PRINCE... HE REALLY DID CALL HIMSELF THAT, RIGHT?
What a maroon...
I WILL PROTECT BOTH RENA-CHAN AND THE LITTLE GIRL!!
KOMIYAMA-KUN...I'M REALLY GRATEFUL FOR THE OFFER...BUT IT'S DANGEROUS.
COME, NOW! I KNOW MMORPGS BETTER THAN ALMOST ANYONE!
I'LL BE OF GREAT USE TO YOU. MUCH MORE USEFUL THAN THAT NOOB KUNISAKI, DON'T YOU THINK?
EVEN THOUGH I PLAY FAIR, I KNOW MY WAY AROUND MODS AND HACKS. I EVEN RUN MY OWN WEB PAGE!
HEY, WATCH IT!
BESIDES, THE DISASTER ASSOCIATED WITH THAT CHEAT NO LONGER EXITS.
NOW!
LET'S GO TALK TO THE SYS ADMIN...
...AND CLEAR UP THIS LITTLE MISUNDERSTANDING.
......
KOMIYAMA... EVEN AN IDIO LIKE YOU CA SAY SMART THINGS SOMETIMES
Whoa...
HOW DARE YOU CALL ME AN IDIOT?!
I GUESS WE HAVE NO CHOICE.

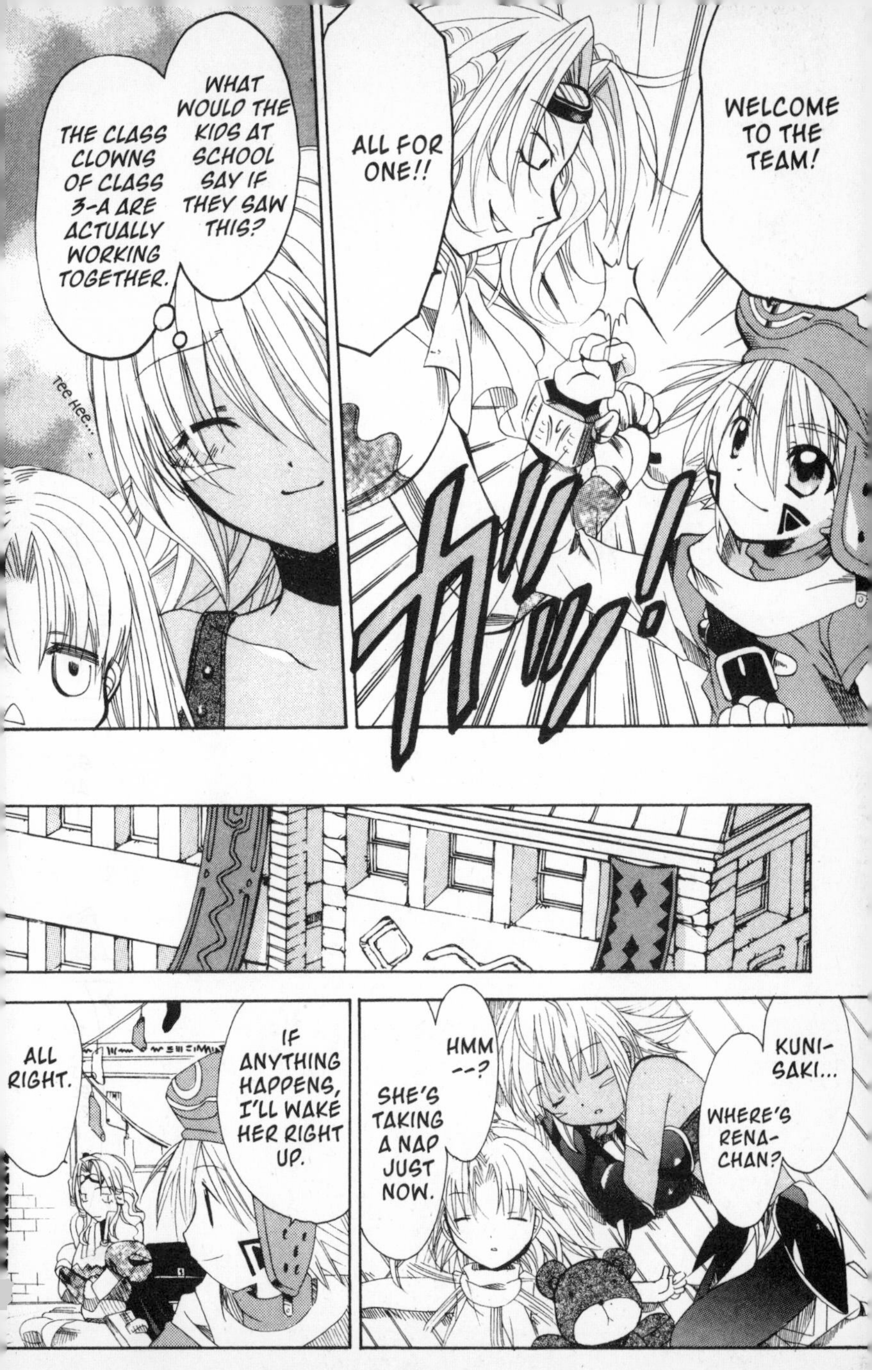
WELCOME TO THE TEAM!
ALL FOR ONE!!
THE CLASS CLOWNS OF CLASS 3-A ARE ACTUALLY WORKING TOGETHER.
WHAT WOULD THE KIDS AT SCHOOL SAY IF THEY SAW THIS?
Tee Hee...
KUNI-SAKI...
WHERE'S RENA-CHAN?
HMM--?
SHE'S TAKING A NAP JUST NOW.
IF ANYTHING HAPPENS, I'LL WAKE HER RIGHT UP.
ALL RIGHT.

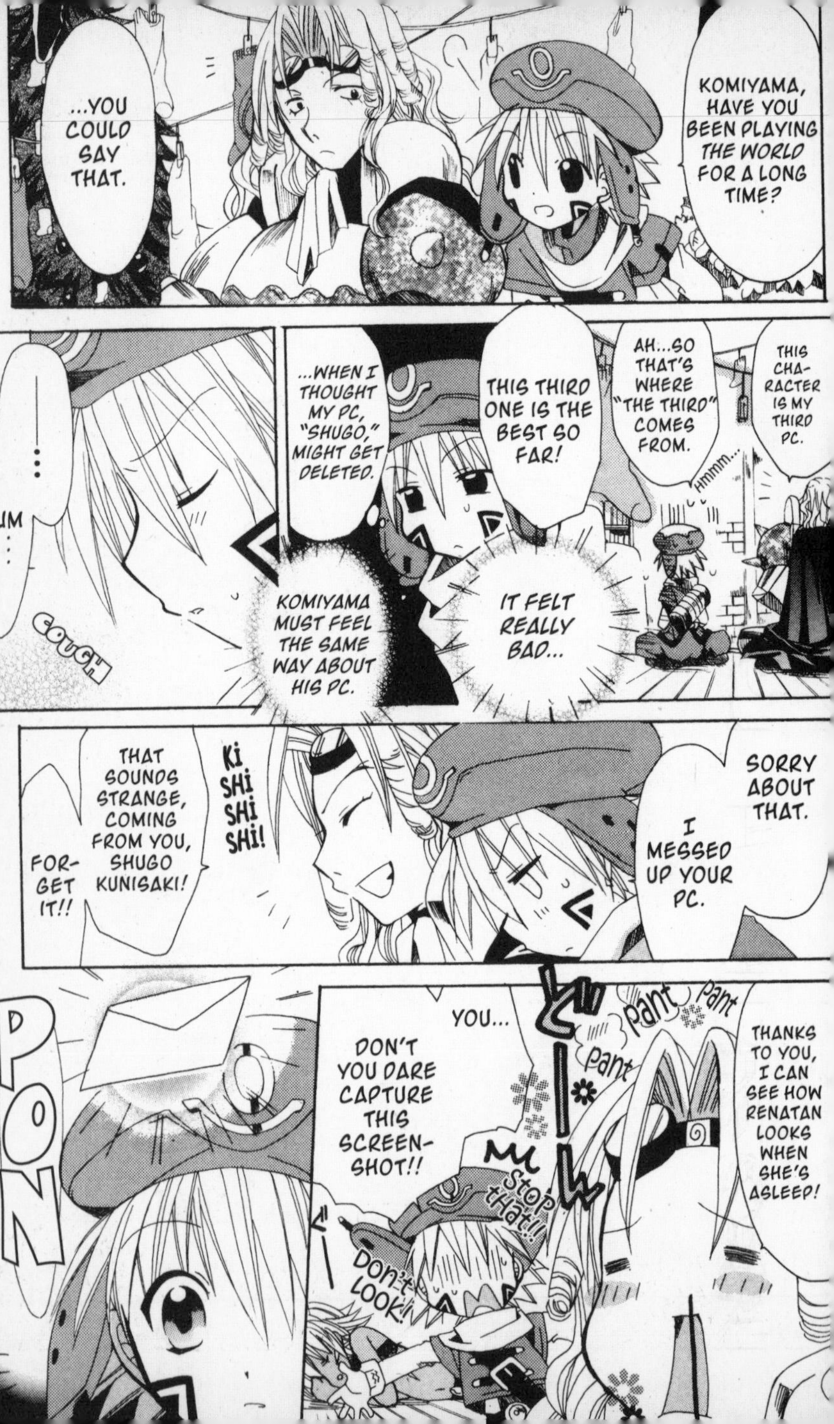
KOMIYAMA, HAVE YOU BEEN PLAYING THE WORLD FOR A LONG TIME?
...YOU COULD SAY THAT.
THIS CHARACTER IS MY THIRD PC.
AH...SO THAT'S WHERE "THE THIRD" COMES FROM.
Hmmm...
THIS THIRD ONE IS THE BEST SO FAR!
...WHEN I THOUGHT MY PC, "SHUGO," MIGHT GET DELETED.
IT FELT REALLY BAD...
KOMIYAMA MUST FEEL THE SAME WAY ABOUT HIS PC.
...UM...
COUGH
SORRY ABOUT THAT.
I MESSED UP YOUR PC.
KiSHiSHiSHi!
THAT SOUNDS STRANGE, COMING FROM YOU, SHUGO KUNISAKI!
FOR-GET IT!!
THANKS TO YOU, I CAN SEE HOW RENATAN LOOKS WHEN SHE'S ASLEEP!
pant pant
pant
YOU...
DON'T YOU DARE CAPTURE THIS SCREEN-SHOT!!
Stop that!!
Don't look!!
PON

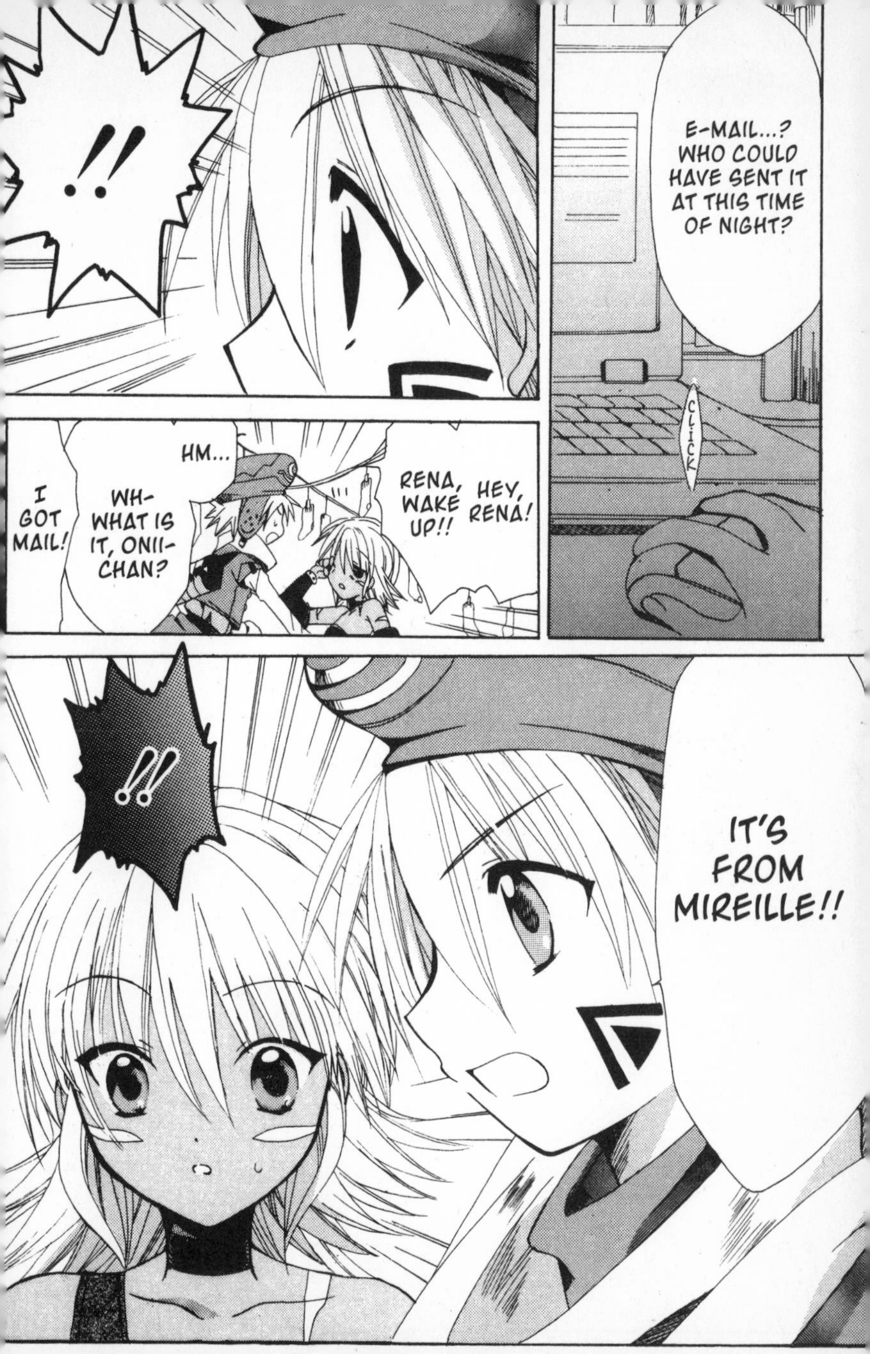
E-MAIL...? WHO COULD HAVE SENT IT AT THIS TIME OF NIGHT?
CLICK
!!
HEY, RENA!
RENA, WAKE UP!!
HM...
WH- WHAT IS IT, ONII-CHAN?
I GOT MAIL!
IT'S FROM MIREILLE!!
!!

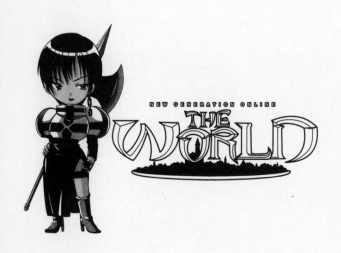

NEW GENERATION ONLINE
THE WORLD

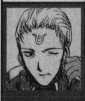

SUBJECT: THE BRACELET'S OWNER   SENDER: WISEMAN

TO THE MASTER OF THE NET SLUMS,

AS YOU ALREADY KNOW, CC CORP MANAGEMENT HAS MADE THEIR DECISION AS TO THE FATE OF THE TWO DOT HACKERS' AVATARS.

"WHAT CANNOT BE CONTROLLED MUST BE DELETED."

BALMUNG HIMSELF HAS ABANDONED HIS POST AS ADMINISTRATOR IN ORDER TO HELP THEM. NOW HE IS COUNTING ON YOU, THE HACKER, AND YOUR HOME THE NET SLUMS TO SEE THEM TO SAFETY. THE WORLD HAS INDEED FALLEN UPON HARD TIMES IF EVERY ADMINISTRATOR WITH A HEART MUST LEAVE THE CORPORATION.

TO ENSURE THAT AURA AND THE WORLD HAVE A FUTURE, PLEASE GRANT THE BEARER OF THE BRACELET ACCESS TO YOUR DOMAIN. MANY THANKS IN ADVANCE, OLD FRIEND.

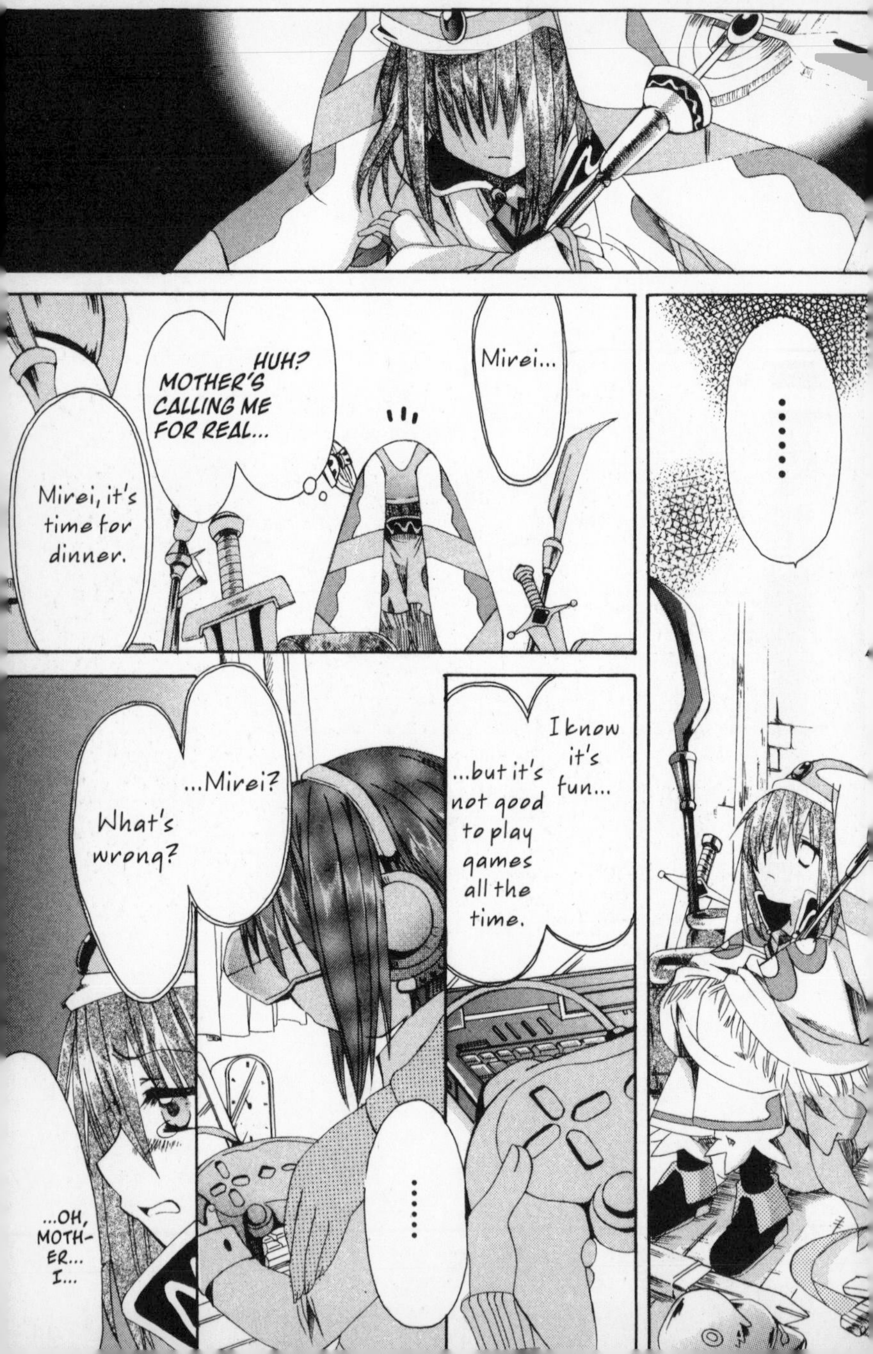
......
Mirei...
HUH? MOTHER'S CALLING ME FOR REAL...
Mirei, it's time for dinner.
I know it's fun...
...but it's not good to play games all the time.
......
...Mirei?
What's wrong?
...OH, MOTHER... I...

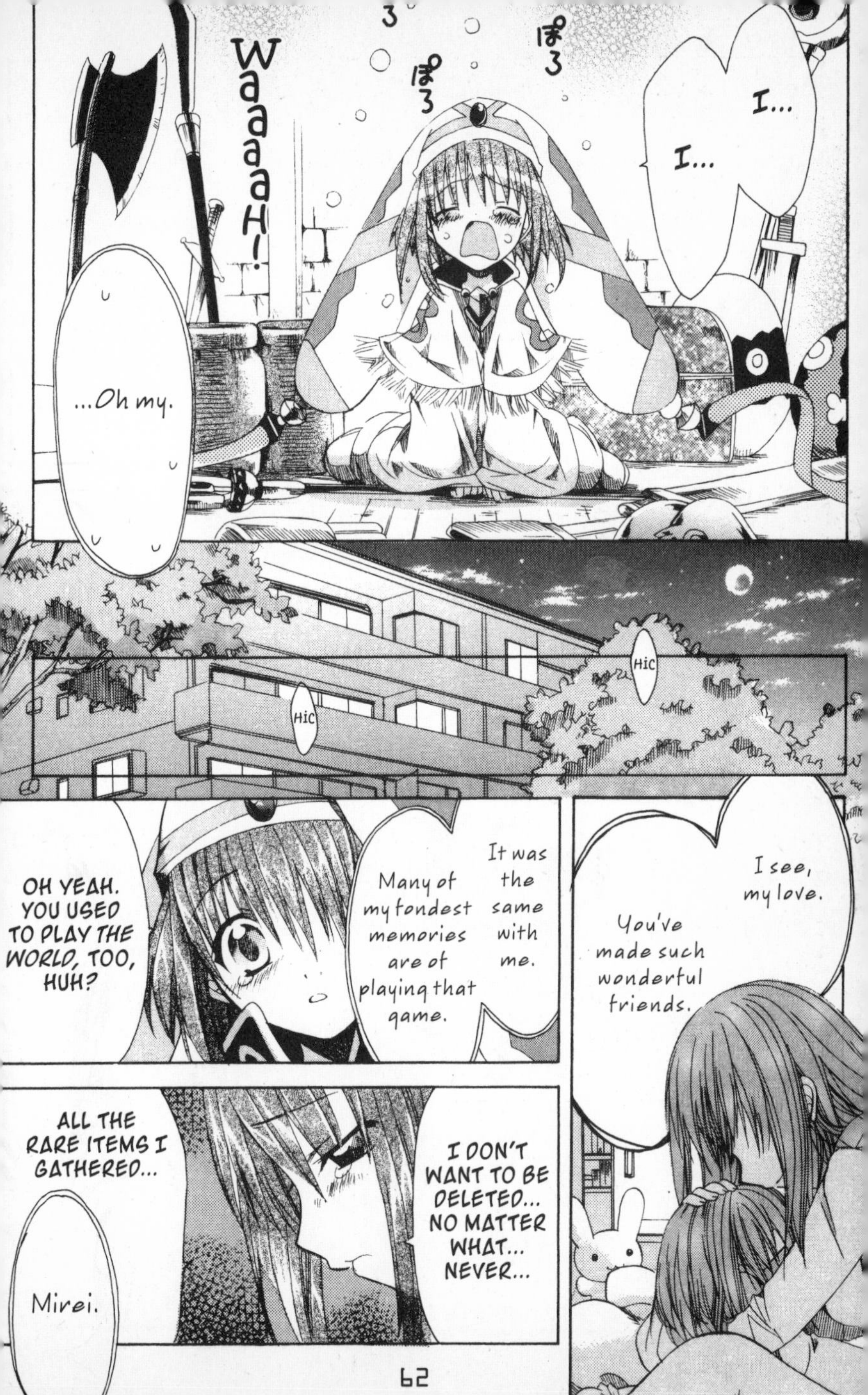

I...
I...
ぽろ
ぽろ
WaaaaaH!
...Oh my.
Hic
Hic
I see, my love.
You've made such wonderful friends.
It was the same with me.
Many of my fondest memories are of playing that game.
OH YEAH. YOU USED TO PLAY THE WORLD, TOO, HUH?
I DON'T WANT TO BE DELETED... NO MATTER WHAT... NEVER...
ALL THE RARE ITEMS I GATHERED...
Mirei.

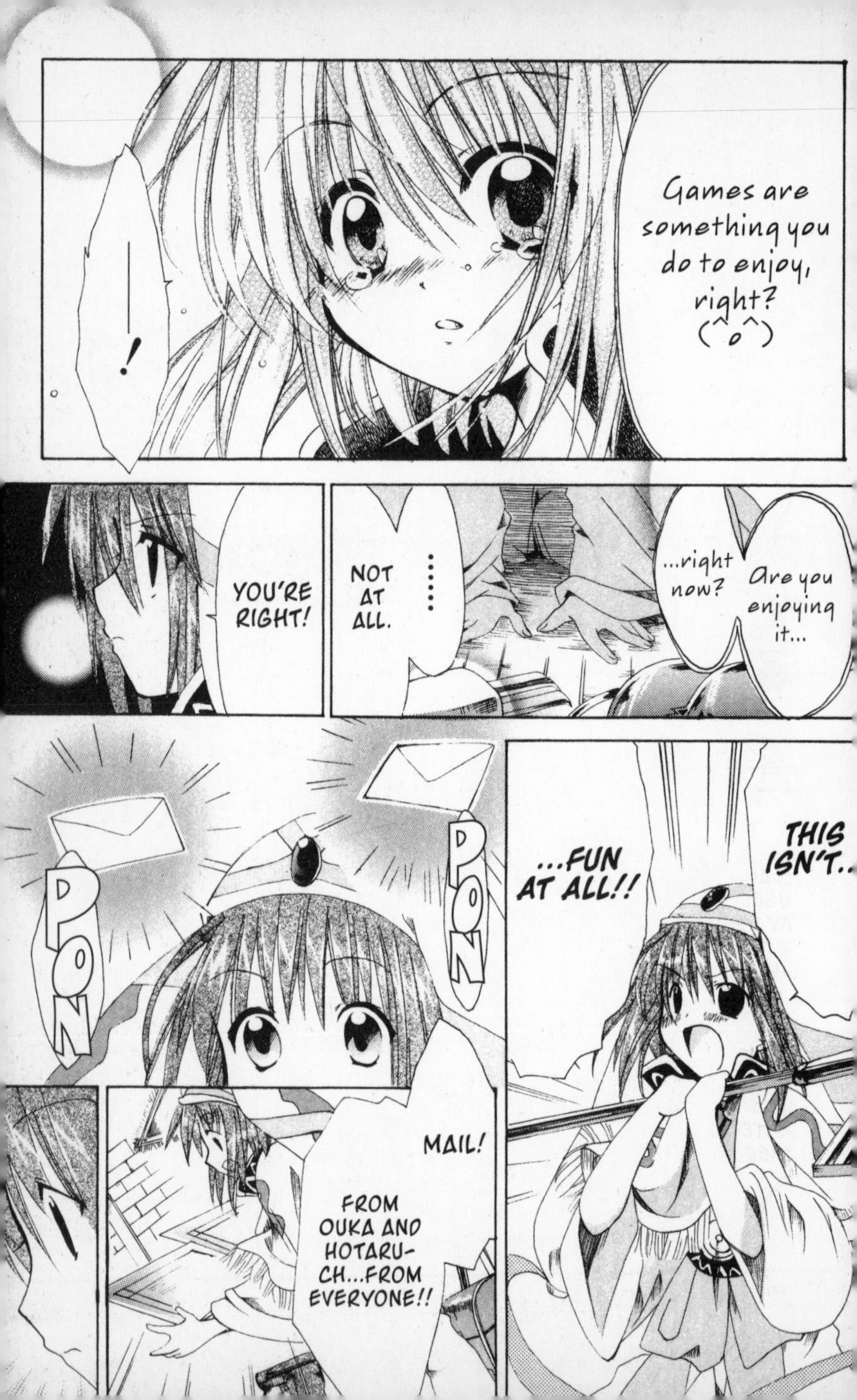
Games are something you do to enjoy, right? (^o^)
!
Are you enjoying it...
...right now?
......
NOT AT ALL.
YOU'RE RIGHT!
THIS ISN'T...
...FUN AT ALL!!
PON
PON
MAIL!
FROM OUKA AND HOTARU-CH...FROM EVERYONE!!

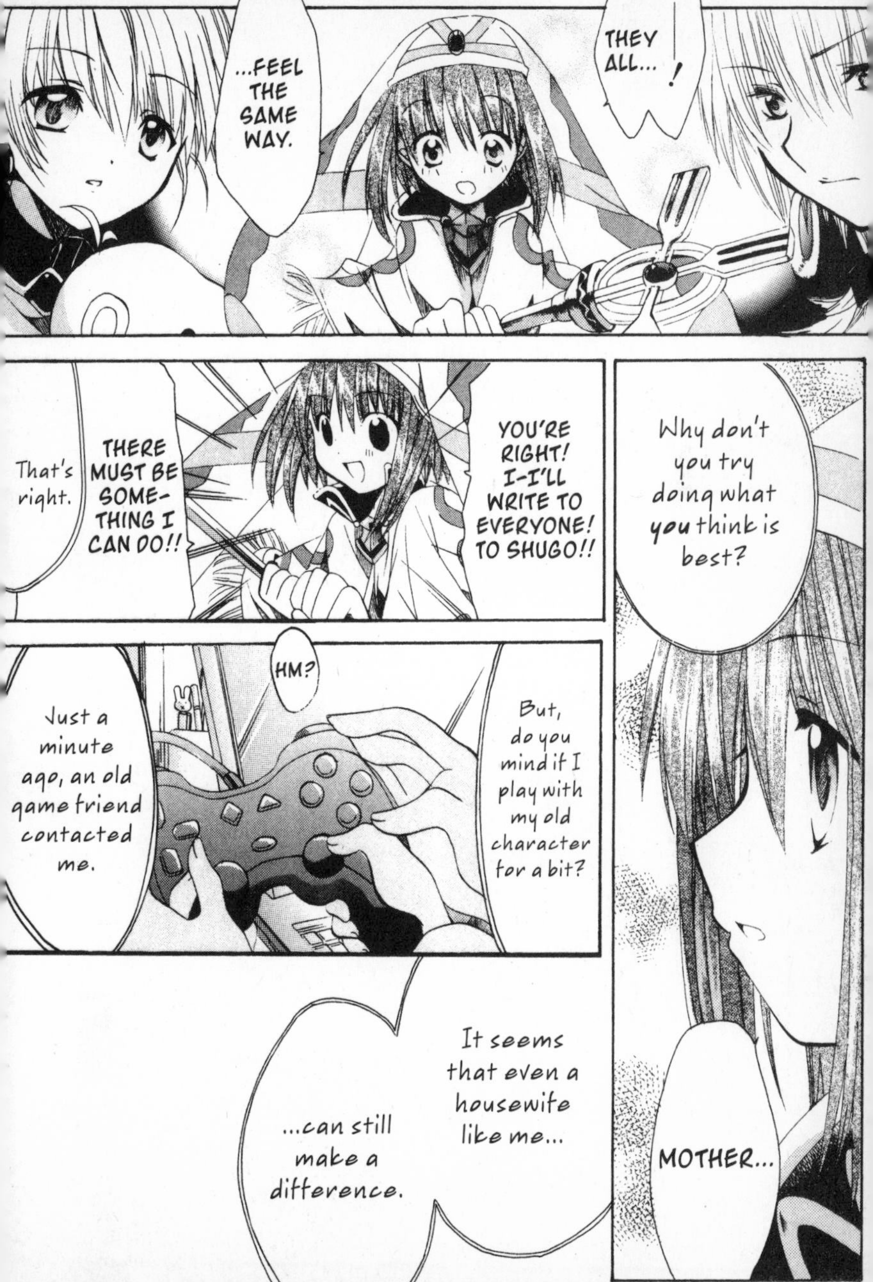
THEY ALL... !
...FEEL THE SAME WAY.
Why don't you try doing what you think is best?
MOTHER...
YOU'RE RIGHT! I-I'LL WRITE TO EVERYONE! TO SHUGO!!
THERE MUST BE SOME-THING I CAN DO!!
That's right.
HM?
But, do you mind if I play with my old character for a bit?
Just a minute ago, an old game friend contacted me.
It seems that even a housewife like me...
...can still make a difference.

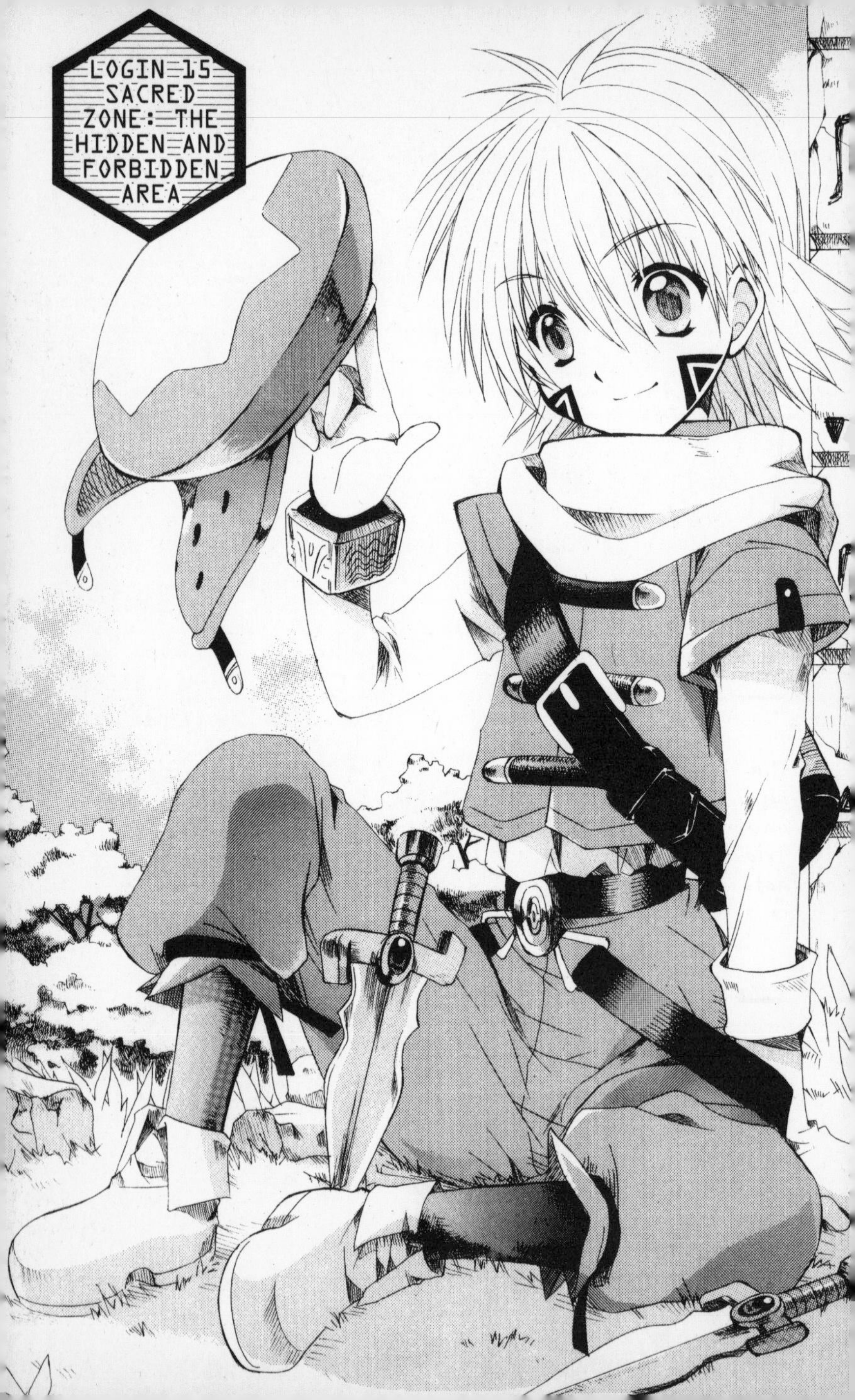
LOGIN 15
SACRED ZONE: THE HIDDEN AND FORBIDDEN AREA

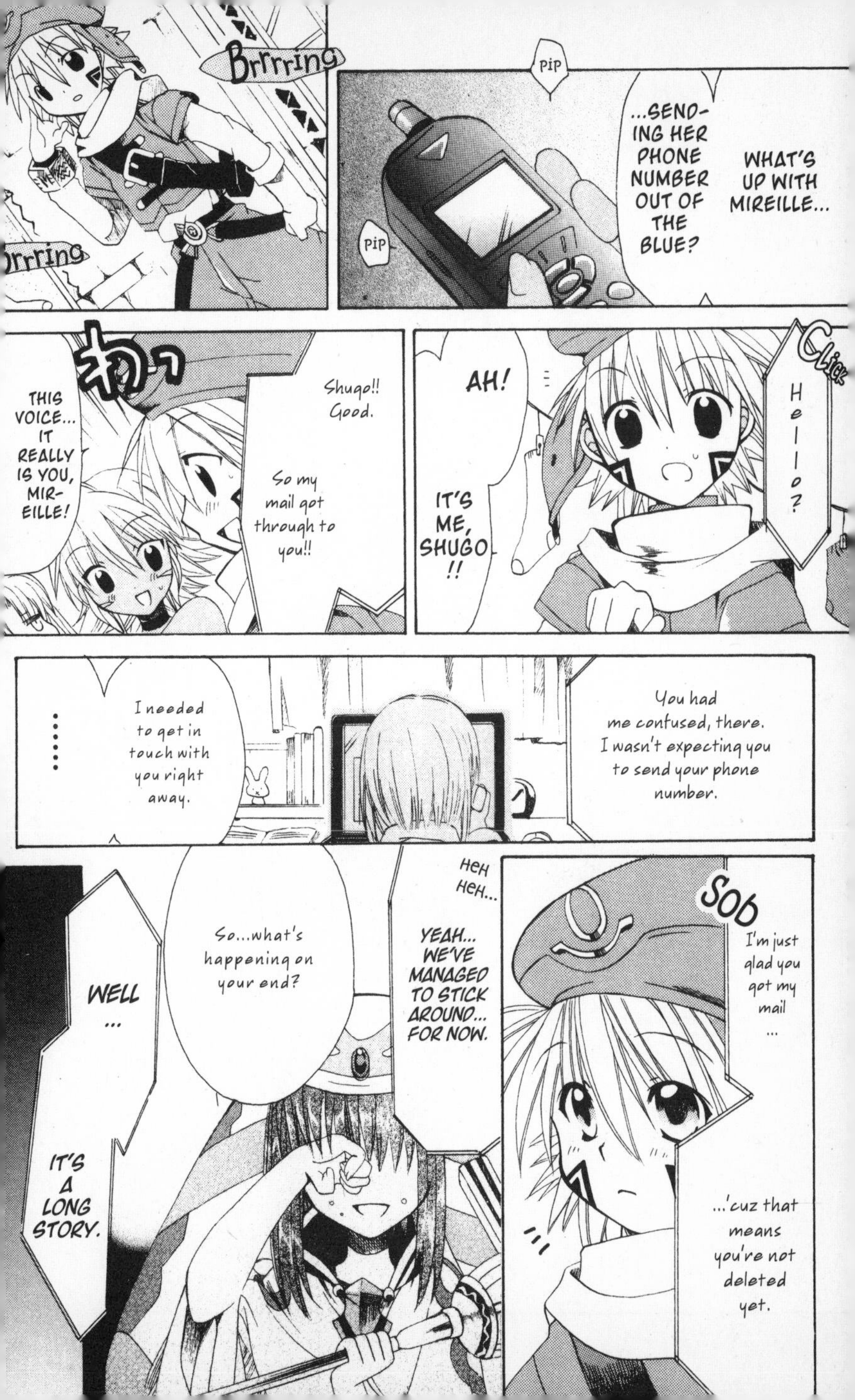
Pip
Pip
WHAT'S UP WITH MIREILLE...
...SENDING HER PHONE NUMBER OUT OF THE BLUE?
Brrrring
rrring
Click
Hello?
AH!
IT'S ME, SHUGO!!
Shugo!! Good.
So my mail got through to you!!
THIS VOICE... IT REALLY IS YOU, MIREILLE!
わっ
You had me confused, there. I wasn't expecting you to send your phone number.
I needed to get in touch with you right away.
......
Sob
I'm just glad you got my mail...
...'cuz that means you're not deleted yet.
Heh heh...
YEAH... WE'VE MANAGED TO STICK AROUND... FOR NOW.
So...what's happening on your end?
WELL...
IT'S A LONG STORY.

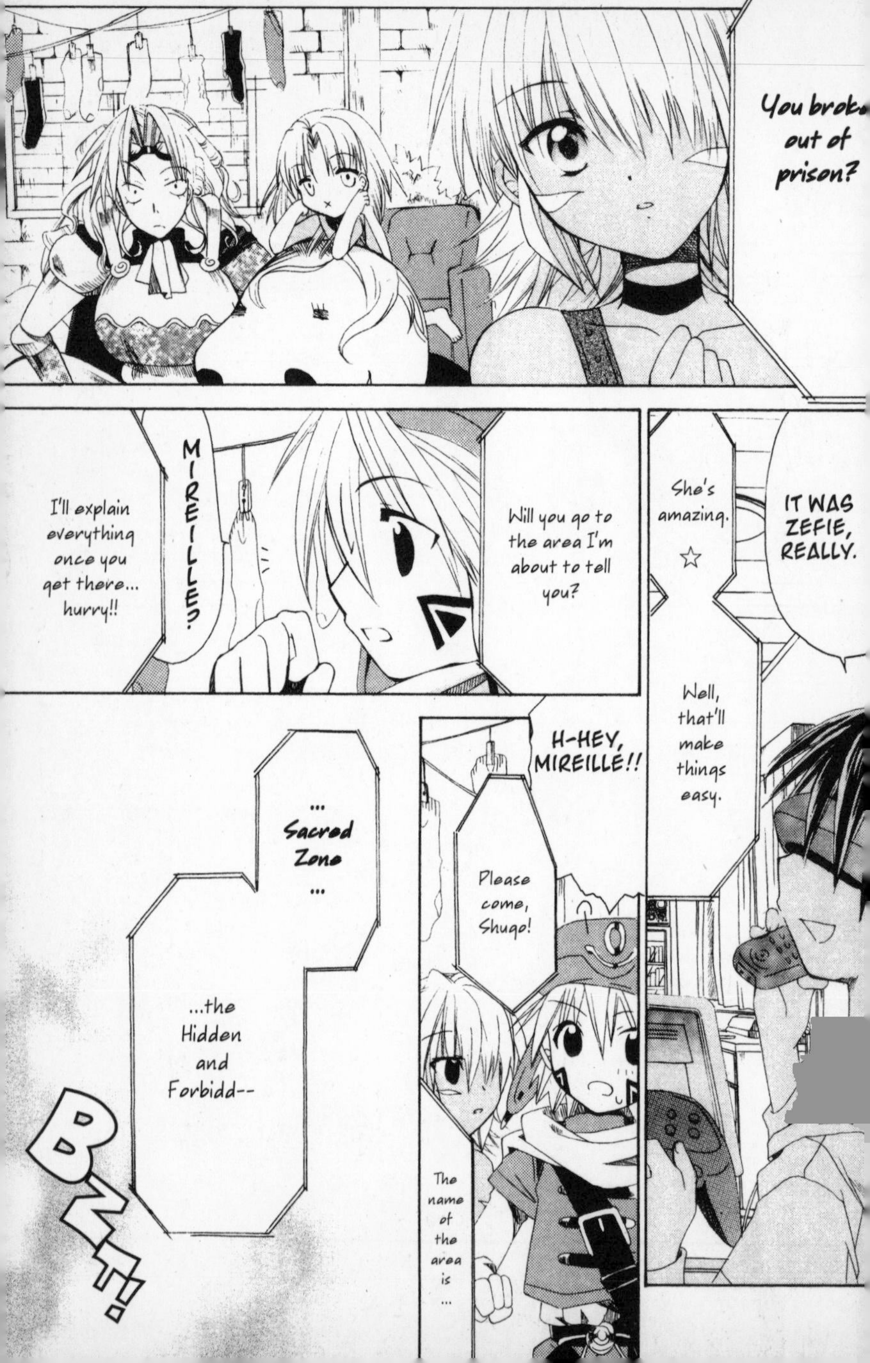
You broke out of prison?
IT WAS ZEFIE, REALLY.
She's amazing. ☆
Well, that'll make things easy.
Will you go to the area I'm about to tell you?
MIREILLE?
I'll explain everything once you get there... hurry!!
H-HEY, MIREILLE!!
Please come, Shugo!
The name of the area is ...
... Sacred Zone ...
...the Hidden and Forbidd--
BZZT!

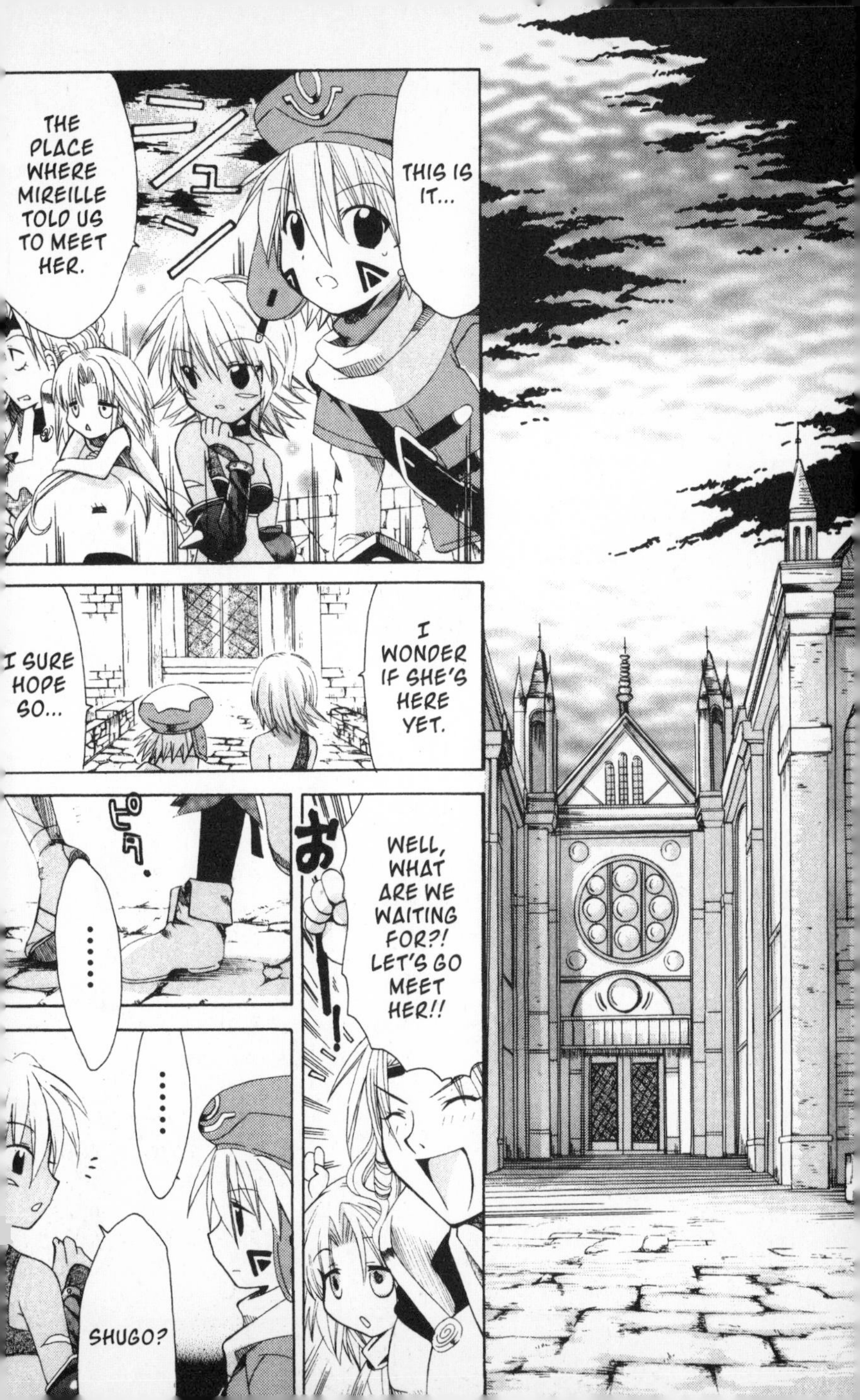
THIS IS IT...
THE PLACE WHERE MIREILLE TOLD US TO MEET HER.
I WONDER IF SHE'S HERE YET.
I SURE HOPE SO...
お
WELL, WHAT ARE WE WAITING FOR?! LET'S GO MEET HER!!
ピタ.
......
......
SHUGO?

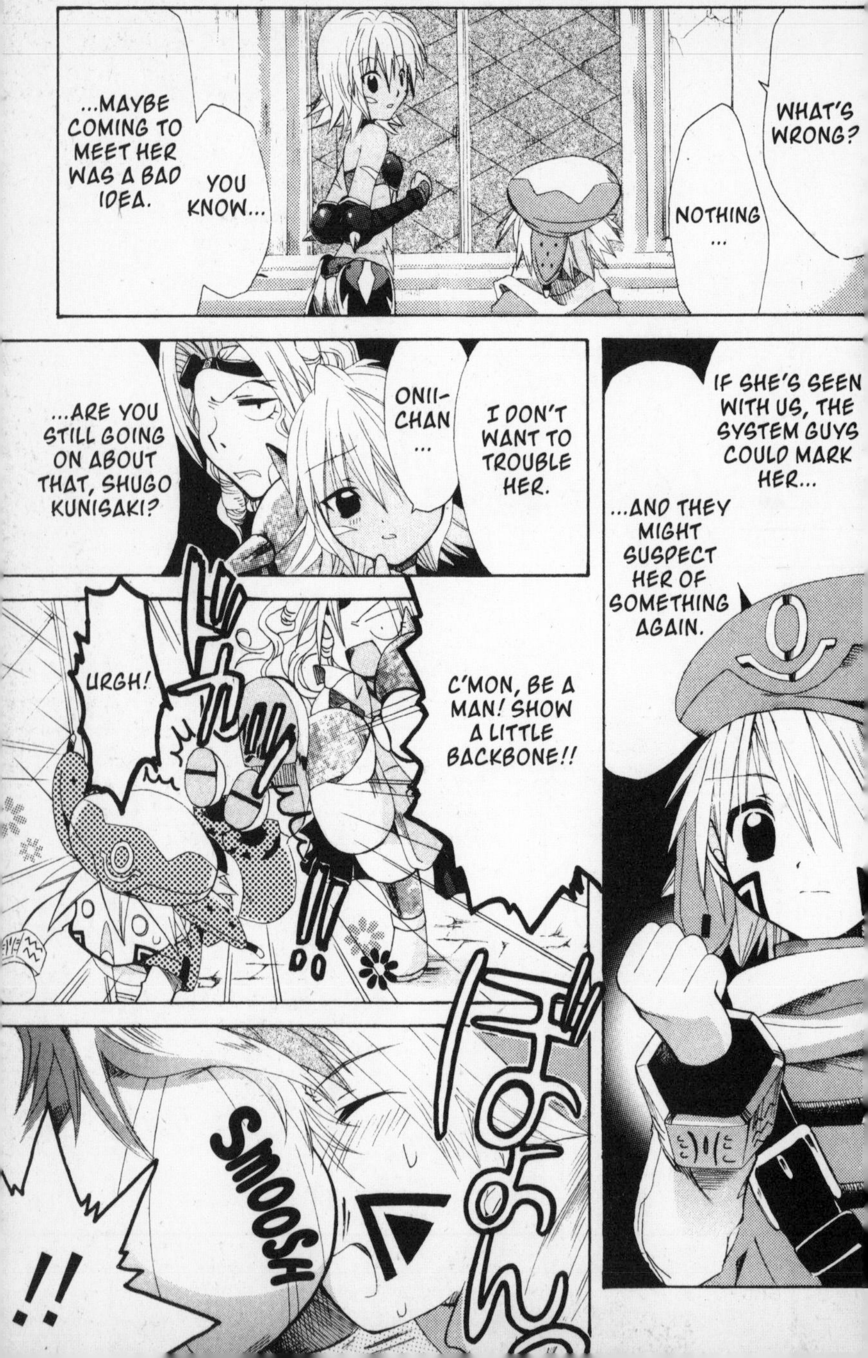
WHAT'S WRONG?
NOTHING...
YOU KNOW...
...MAYBE COMING TO MEET HER WAS A BAD IDEA.
IF SHE'S SEEN WITH US, THE SYSTEM GUYS COULD MARK HER...
...AND THEY MIGHT SUSPECT HER OF SOMETHING AGAIN.
I DON'T WANT TO TROUBLE HER.
ONII-CHAN...
...ARE YOU STILL GOING ON ABOUT THAT, SHUGO KUNISAKI?
C'MON, BE A MAN! SHOW A LITTLE BACKBONE!!
URGH!
SMOOSH
!!

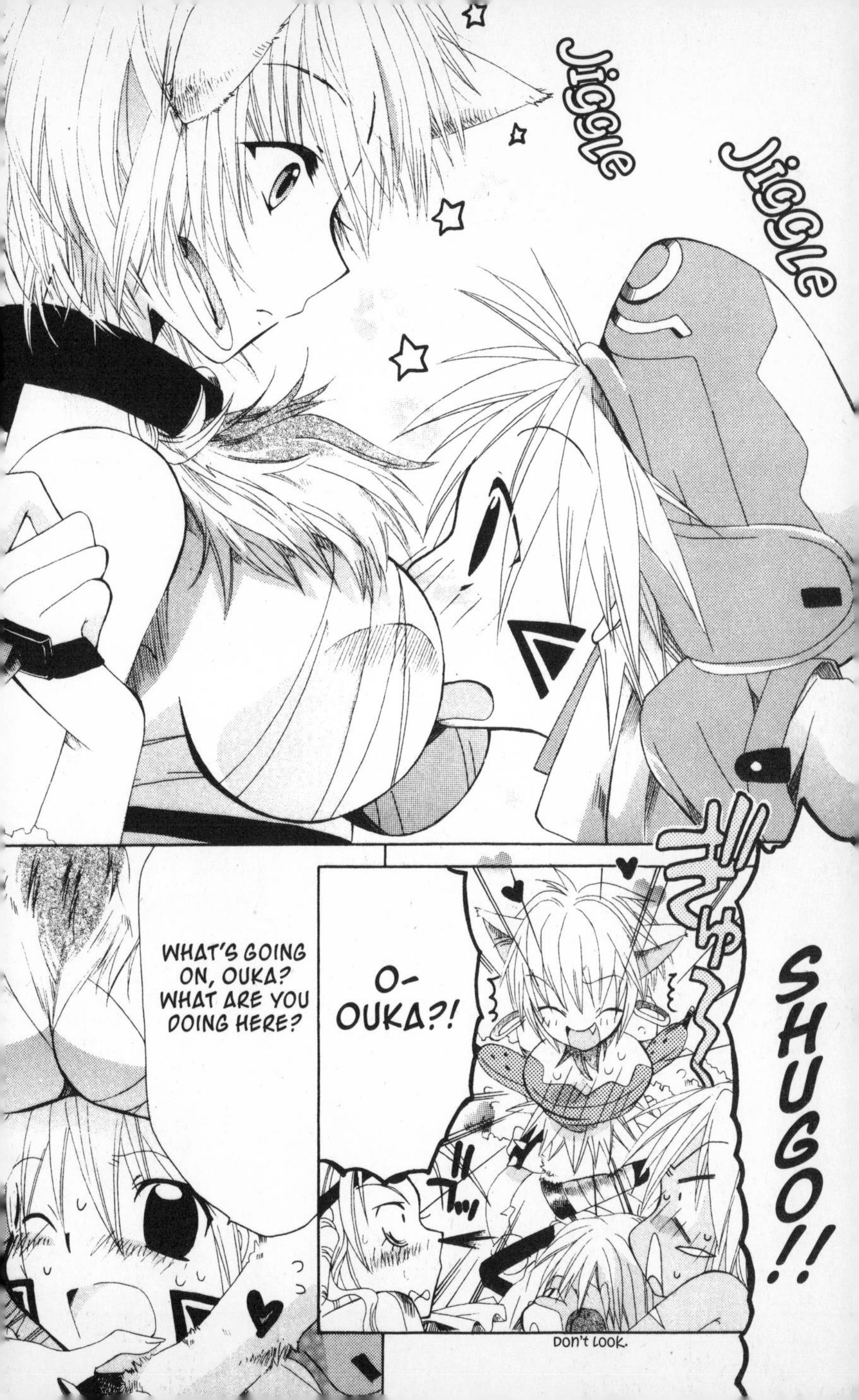

Jiggle
Jiggle
SHUGO!!
O-OUKA?!
WHAT'S GOING ON, OUKA? WHAT ARE YOU DOING HERE?
Don't look.

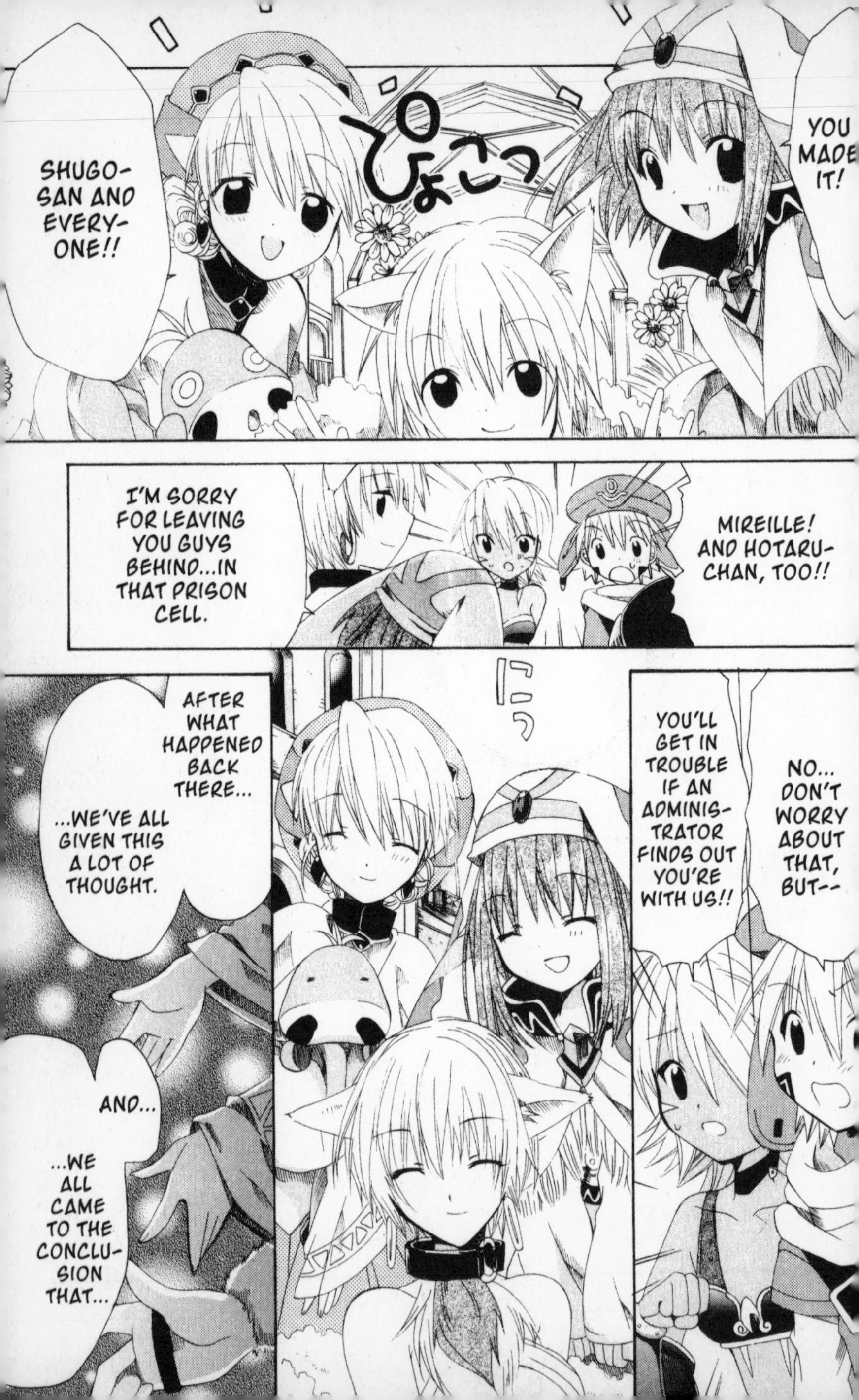
YOU MADE IT!
ぴょこっ
SHUGO-SAN AND EVERYONE!!
MIREILLE! AND HOTARU-CHAN, TOO!!
I'M SORRY FOR LEAVING YOU GUYS BEHIND...IN THAT PRISON CELL.
YOU'LL GET IN TROUBLE IF AN ADMINISTRATOR FINDS OUT YOU'RE WITH US!!
NO... DON'T WORRY ABOUT THAT, BUT--
にっ
AFTER WHAT HAPPENED BACK THERE...
...WE'VE ALL GIVEN THIS A LOT OF THOUGHT.
AND...
...WE ALL CAME TO THE CONCLUSION THAT...

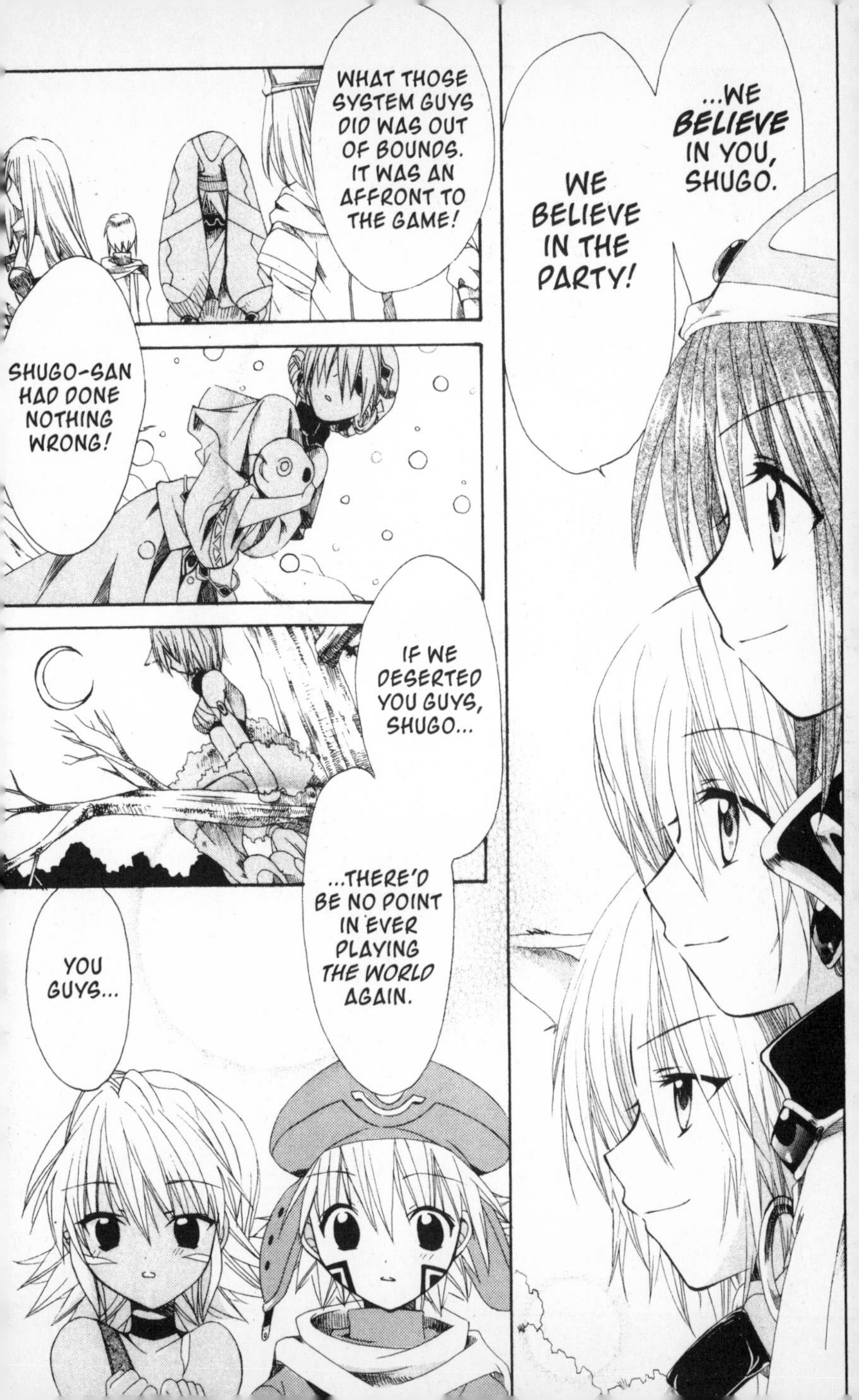
...WE BELIEVE IN YOU, SHUGO.
WE BELIEVE IN THE PARTY!
WHAT THOSE SYSTEM GUYS DID WAS OUT OF BOUNDS. IT WAS AN AFFRONT TO THE GAME!
SHUGO-SAN HAD DONE NOTHING WRONG!
IF WE DESERTED YOU GUYS, SHUGO...
...THERE'D BE NO POINT IN EVER PLAYING THE WORLD AGAIN.
YOU GUYS...

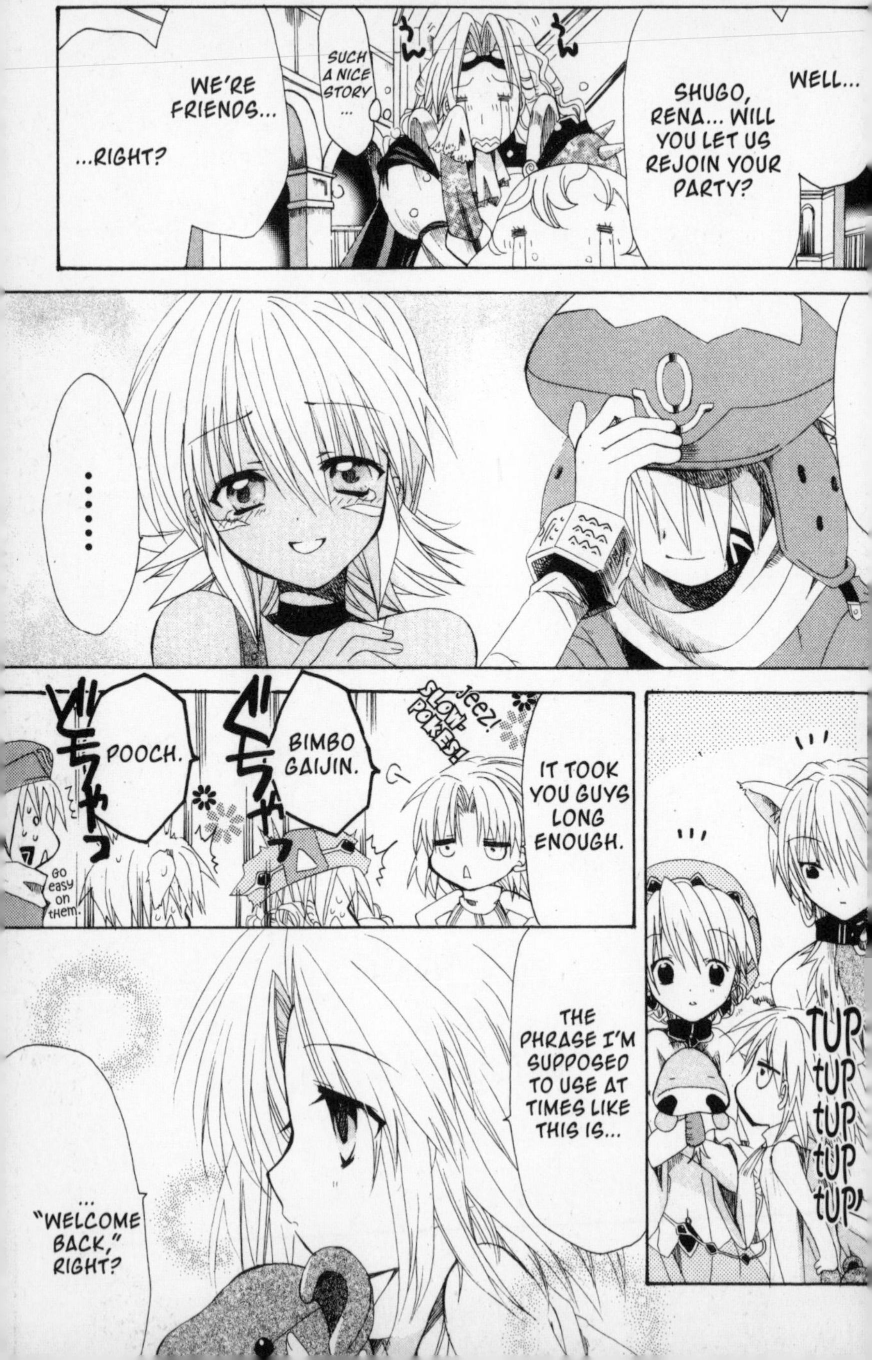

WELL...
SHUGO, RENA... WILL YOU LET US REJOIN YOUR PARTY?
SUCH A NICE STORY ...
WE'RE FRIENDS...
...RIGHT?
......
TUP tUP tUP tUP tUP
IT TOOK YOU GUYS LONG ENOUGH.
Jeez! SLOW-POKES!
BIMBO GAIJIN.
POOCH.
Go easy on them.
THE PHRASE I'M SUPPOSED TO USE AT TIMES LIKE THIS IS...
... "WELCOME BACK," RIGHT?

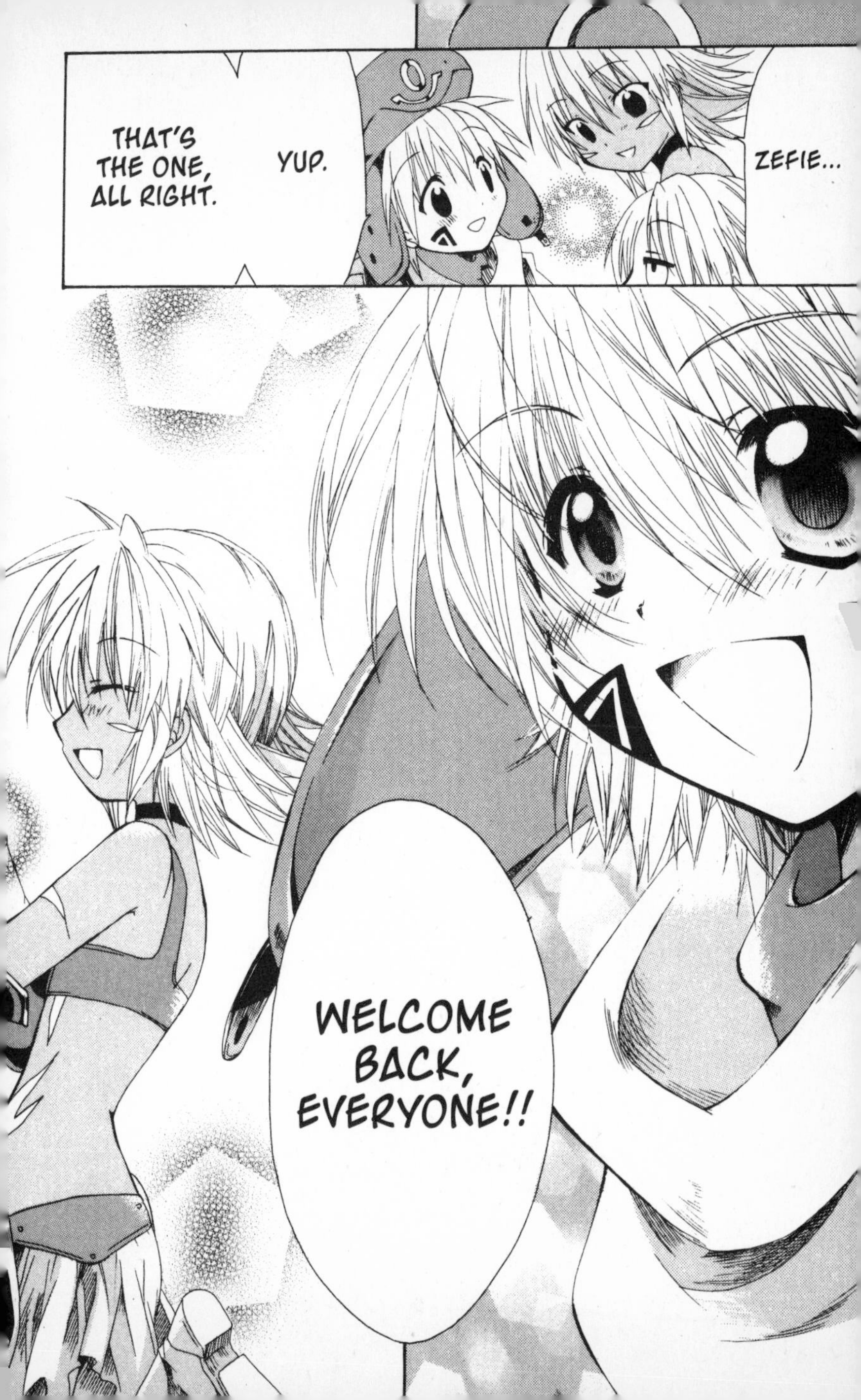
ZEFIE...
YUP.
THAT'S THE ONE, ALL RIGHT.
WELCOME BACK, EVERYONE!!

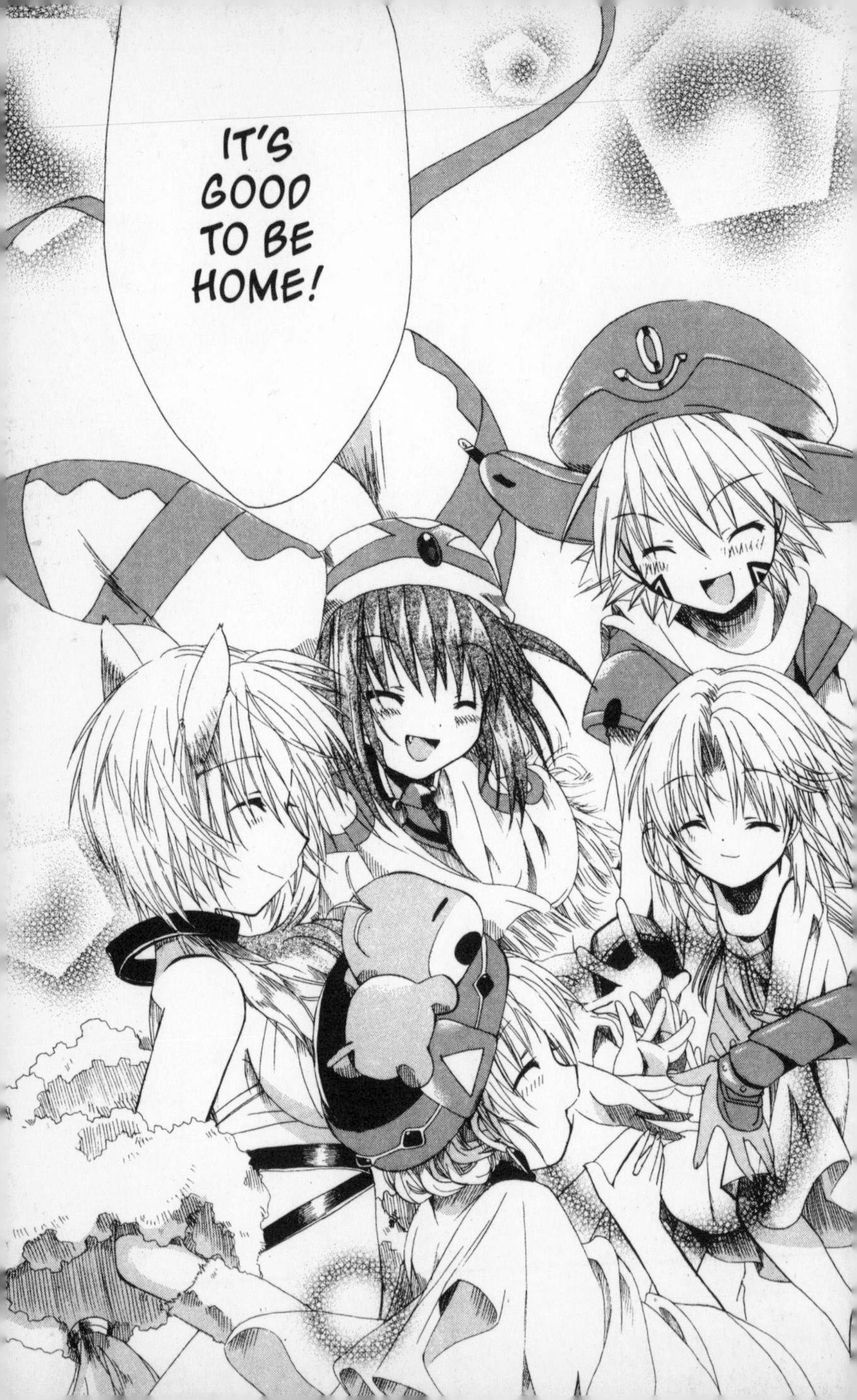
IT'S GOOD TO BE HOME!

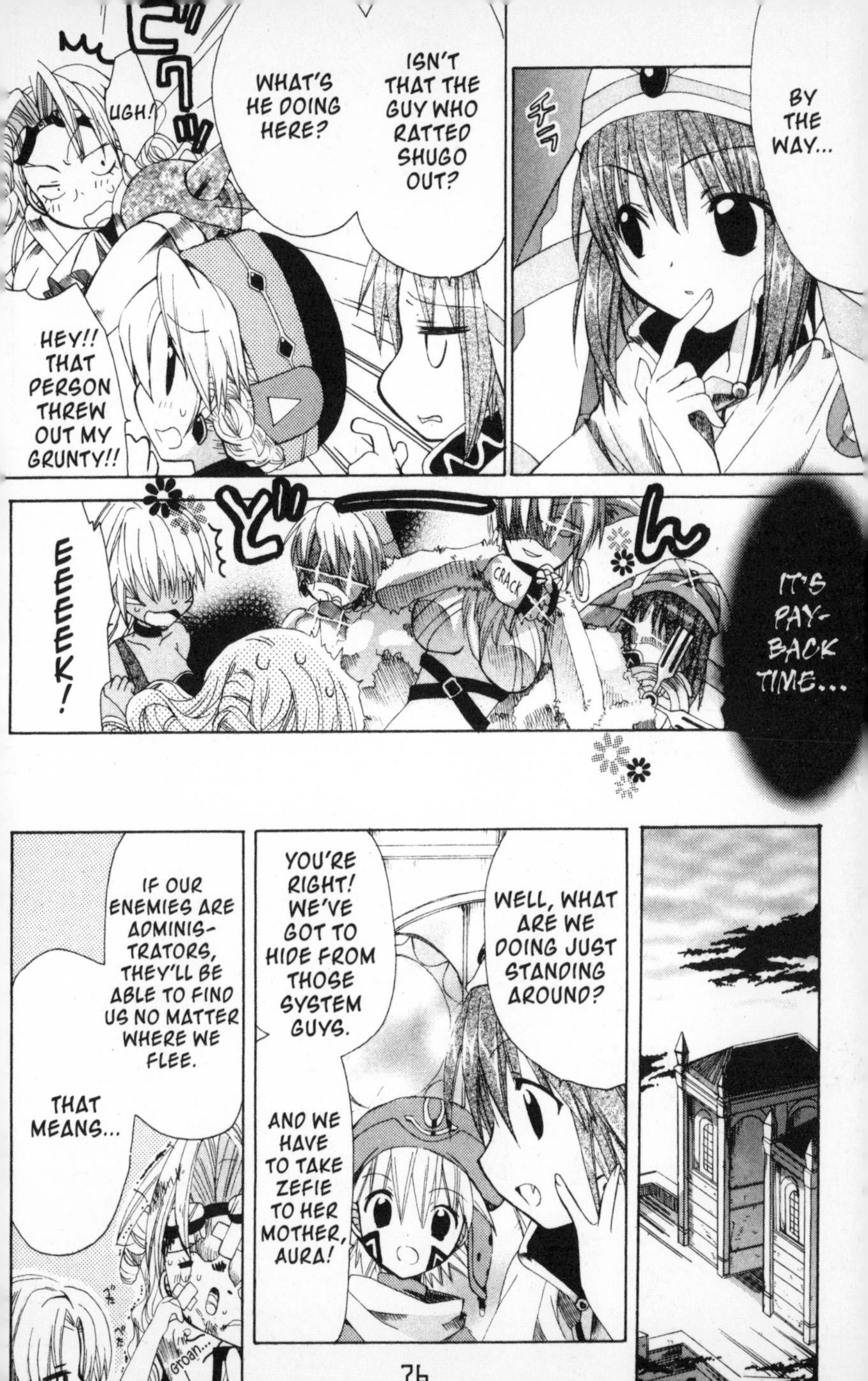
BY THE WAY...
ISN'T THAT THE GUY WHO RATTED SHUGO OUT?
WHAT'S HE DOING HERE?
UGH!
HEY!! THAT PERSON THREW OUT MY GRUNTY!!
IT'S PAY-BACK TIME...
CRACK
EEEEEK!
WELL, WHAT ARE WE DOING JUST STANDING AROUND?
YOU'RE RIGHT! WE'VE GOT TO HIDE FROM THOSE SYSTEM GUYS.
AND WE HAVE TO TAKE ZEFIE TO HER MOTHER, AURA!
IF OUR ENEMIES ARE ADMINIS-TRATORS, THEY'LL BE ABLE TO FIND US NO MATTER WHERE WE FLEE.
THAT MEANS...
Groan...

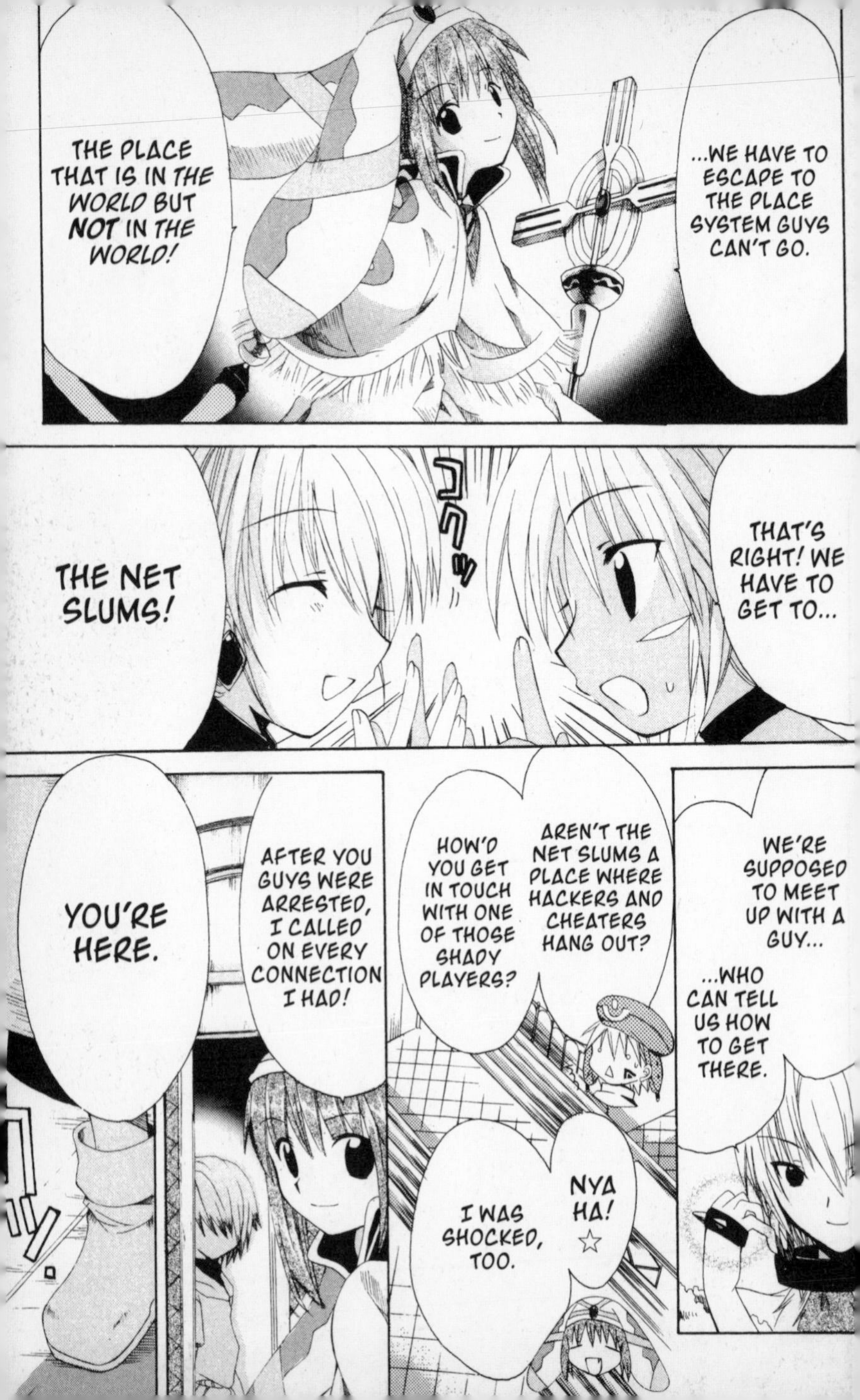
...WE HAVE TO ESCAPE TO THE PLACE SYSTEM GUYS CAN'T GO.
THE PLACE THAT IS IN THE WORLD BUT NOT IN THE WORLD!
THAT'S RIGHT! WE HAVE TO GET TO...
THE NET SLUMS!
WE'RE SUPPOSED TO MEET UP WITH A GUY...
...WHO CAN TELL US HOW TO GET THERE.
AREN'T THE NET SLUMS A PLACE WHERE HACKERS AND CHEATERS HANG OUT?
HOW'D YOU GET IN TOUCH WITH ONE OF THOSE SHADY PLAYERS?
NYA HA! ☆
I WAS SHOCKED, TOO.
AFTER YOU GUYS WERE ARRESTED, I CALLED ON EVERY CONNECTION I HAD!
YOU'RE HERE.

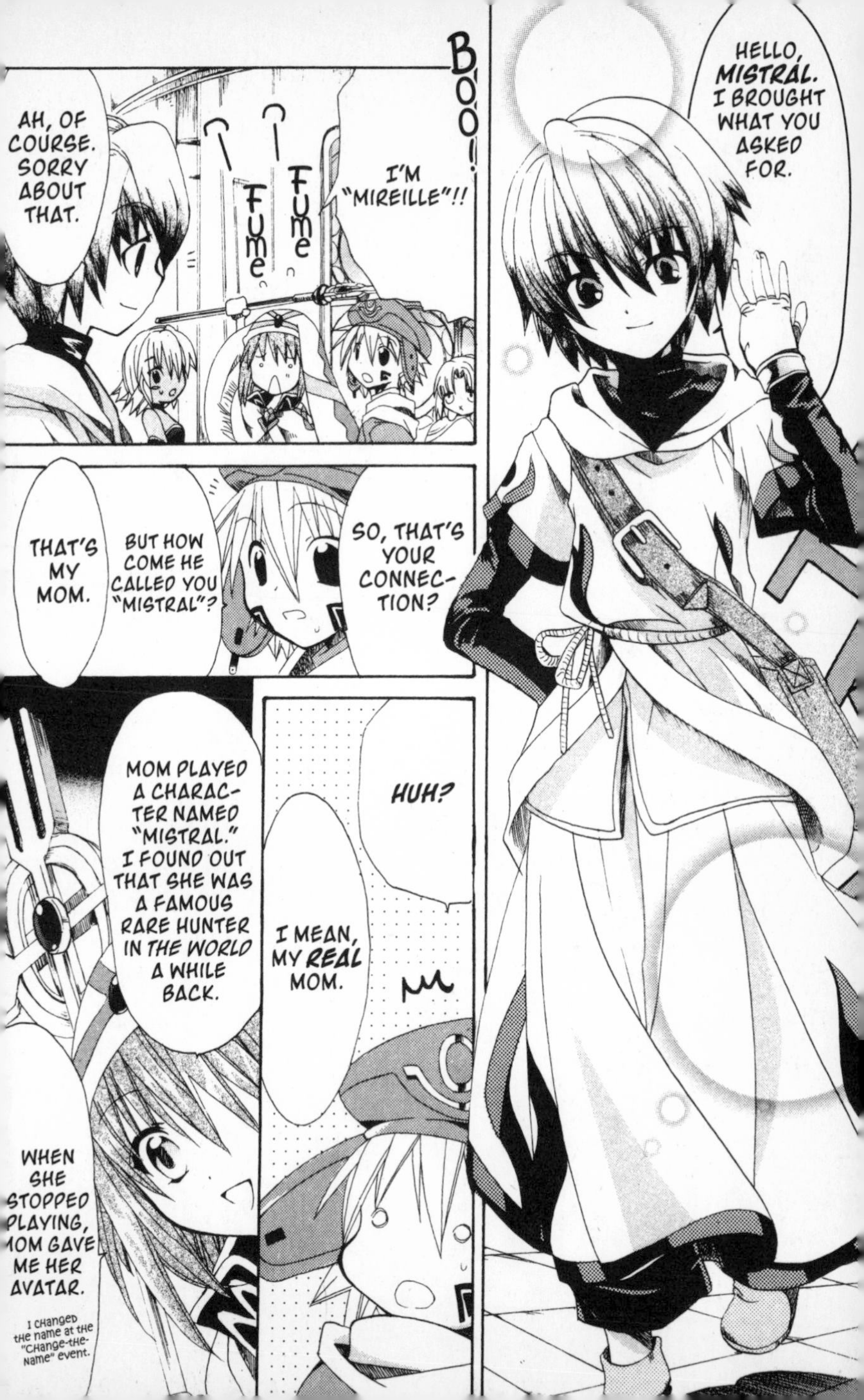
HELLO, MISTRAL. I BROUGHT WHAT YOU ASKED FOR.
BOOO!
I'M "MIREILLE"!!
Fume
Fume
AH, OF COURSE. SORRY ABOUT THAT.
SO, THAT'S YOUR CONNECTION?
BUT HOW COME HE CALLED YOU "MISTRAL"?
THAT'S MY MOM.
HUH?
I MEAN, MY REAL MOM.
MOM PLAYED A CHARACTER NAMED "MISTRAL." I FOUND OUT THAT SHE WAS A FAMOUS RARE HUNTER IN THE WORLD A WHILE BACK.
WHEN SHE STOPPED PLAYING, MOM GAVE ME HER AVATAR.
I CHANGED THE NAME AT THE "CHANGE-THE-NAME" EVENT.

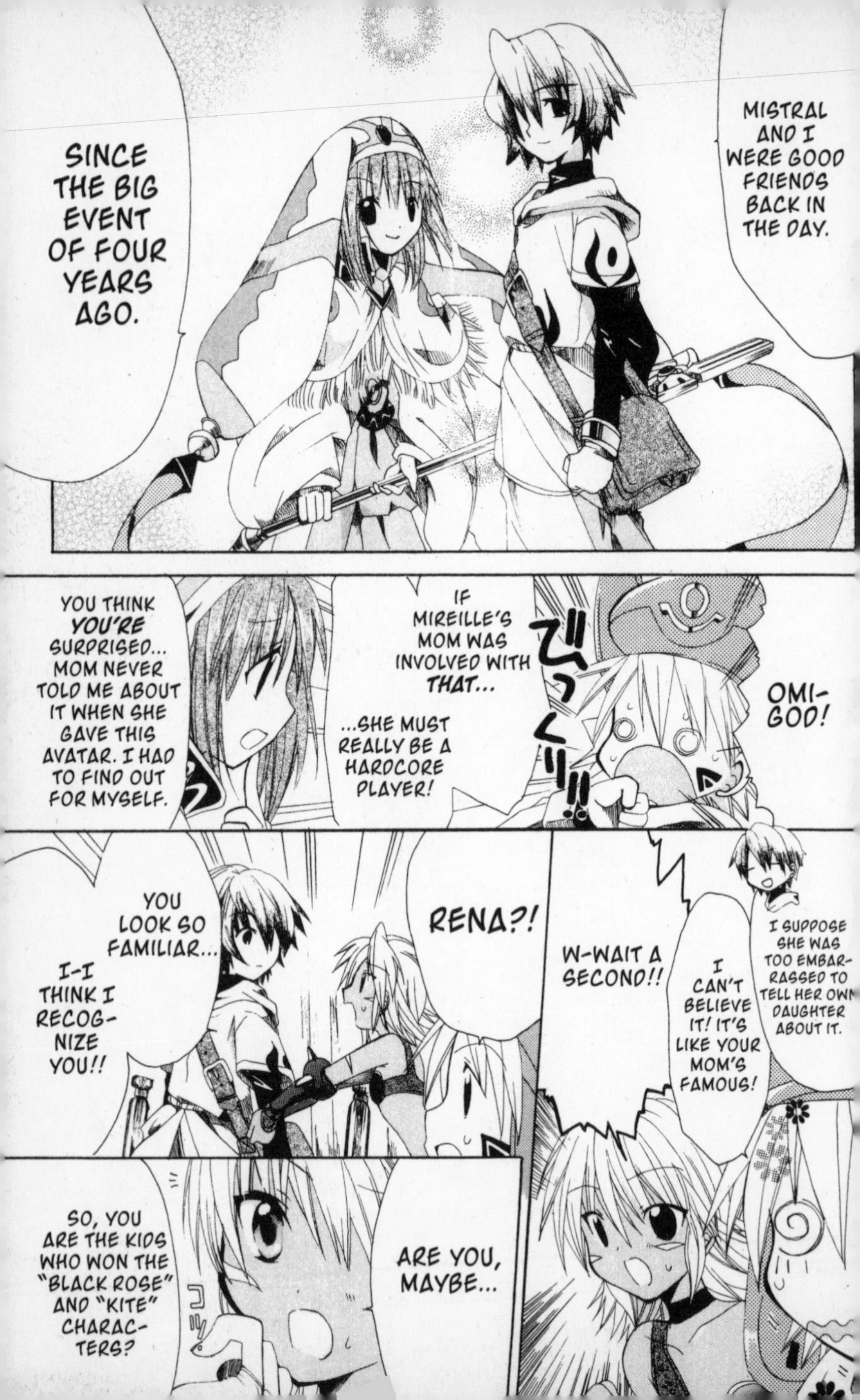
MISTRAL AND I WERE GOOD FRIENDS BACK IN THE DAY.
SINCE THE BIG EVENT OF FOUR YEARS AGO.
びっくり!!
OMI-GOD!
IF MIREILLE'S MOM WAS INVOLVED WITH *THAT*...
...SHE MUST REALLY BE A HARDCORE PLAYER!
YOU THINK *YOU'RE* SURPRISED... MOM NEVER TOLD ME ABOUT IT WHEN SHE GAVE THIS AVATAR. I HAD TO FIND OUT FOR MYSELF.
I SUPPOSE SHE WAS TOO EMBARRASSED TO TELL HER OWN DAUGHTER ABOUT IT.
I CAN'T BELIEVE IT! IT'S LIKE YOUR MOM'S FAMOUS!
W-WAIT A SECOND!!
RENA?!
YOU LOOK SO FAMILIAR...
I-I THINK I RECOGNIZE YOU!!
ARE YOU, MAYBE...
コツ
SO, YOU ARE THE KIDS WHO WON THE "BLACK ROSE" AND "KITE" CHARACTERS?

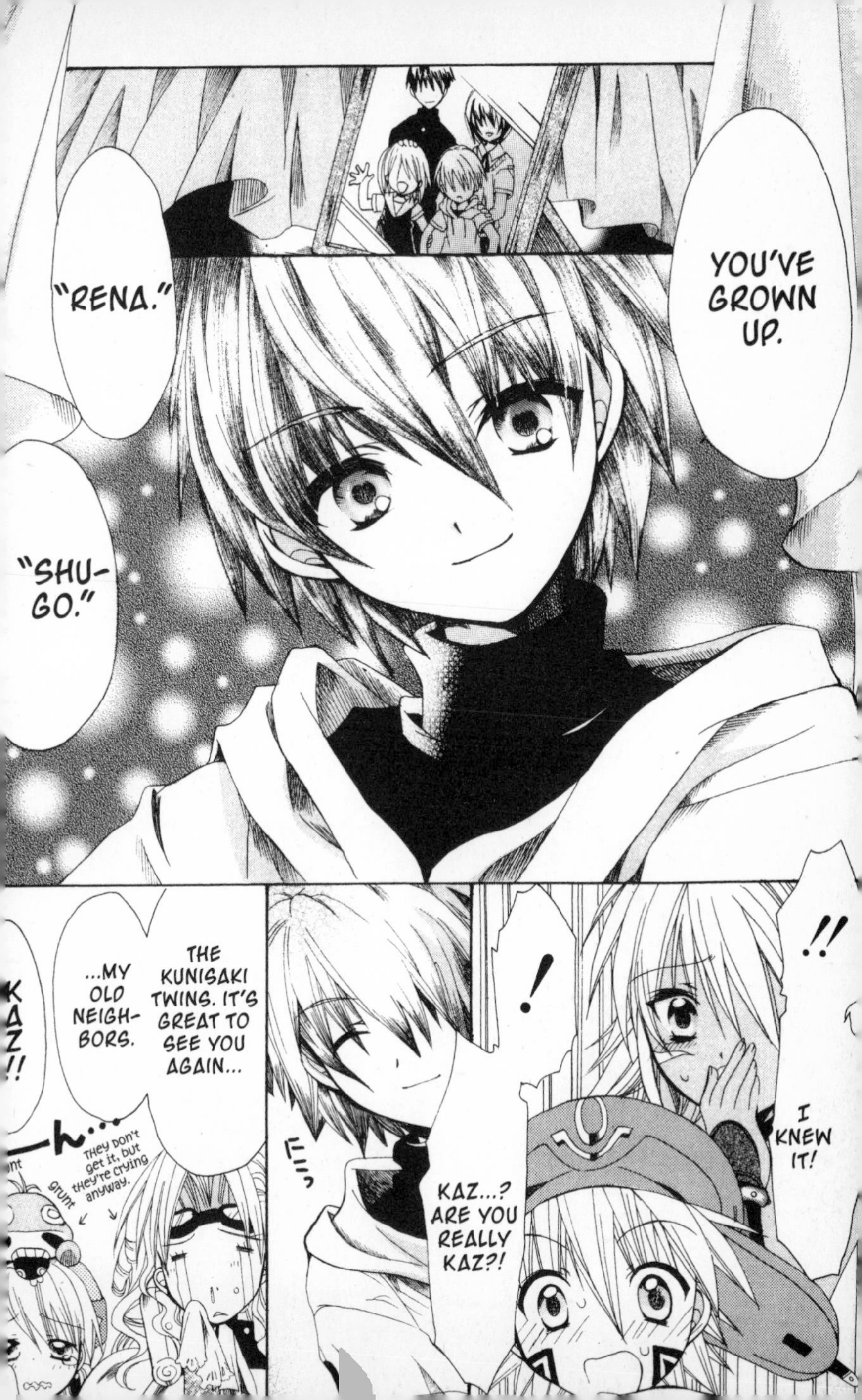
YOU'VE GROWN UP.
"RENA."
"SHU-GO."
!!
I KNEW IT!
!
KAZ...? ARE YOU REALLY KAZ?!
THE KUNISAKI TWINS. IT'S GREAT TO SEE YOU AGAIN...
...MY OLD NEIGHBORS.
KAZ!!
They don't get it, but they're crying anyway.
grunt

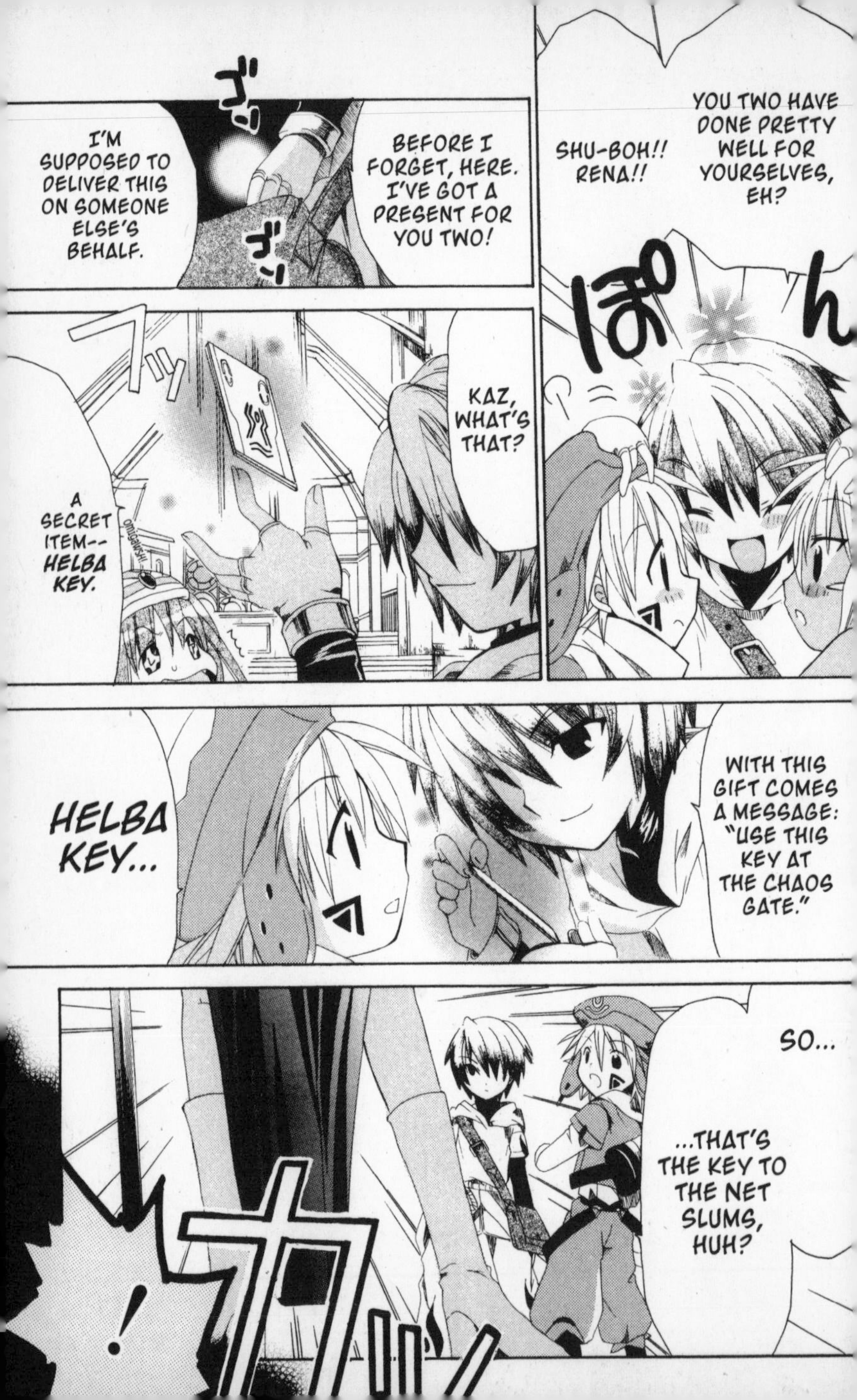
YOU TWO HAVE DONE PRETTY WELL FOR YOURSELVES, EH?
SHU-BOH!! RENA!!
ぽん
BEFORE I FORGET, HERE. I'VE GOT A PRESENT FOR YOU TWO!
I'M SUPPOSED TO DELIVER THIS ON SOMEONE ELSE'S BEHALF.
KAZ, WHAT'S THAT?
フッ
A SECRET ITEM-- HELBA KEY.
OMIGOSH!!
WITH THIS GIFT COMES A MESSAGE: "USE THIS KEY AT THE CHAOS GATE."
HELBA KEY...
SO...
...THAT'S THE KEY TO THE NET SLUMS, HUH?
!

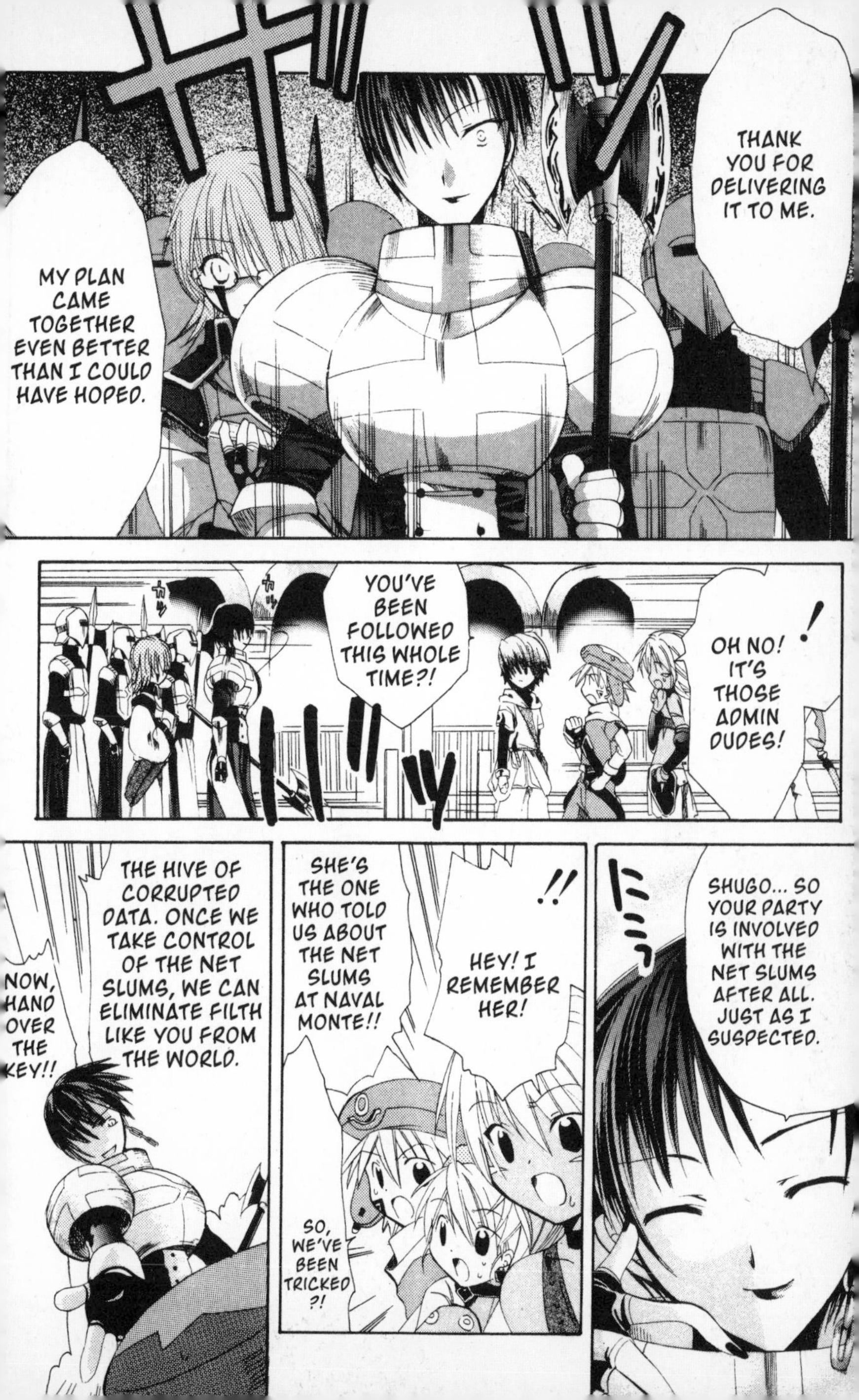
THANK YOU FOR DELIVERING IT TO ME.
MY PLAN CAME TOGETHER EVEN BETTER THAN I COULD HAVE HOPED.
!
OH NO! IT'S THOSE ADMIN DUDES!
YOU'VE BEEN FOLLOWED THIS WHOLE TIME?!
SHUGO... SO YOUR PARTY IS INVOLVED WITH THE NET SLUMS AFTER ALL. JUST AS I SUSPECTED.
!!
HEY! I REMEMBER HER!
SHE'S THE ONE WHO TOLD US ABOUT THE NET SLUMS AT NAVAL MONTE!!
SO, WE'VE BEEN TRICKED?!
THE HIVE OF CORRUPTED DATA. ONCE WE TAKE CONTROL OF THE NET SLUMS, WE CAN ELIMINATE FILTH LIKE YOU FROM THE WORLD.
NOW, HAND OVER THE KEY!!

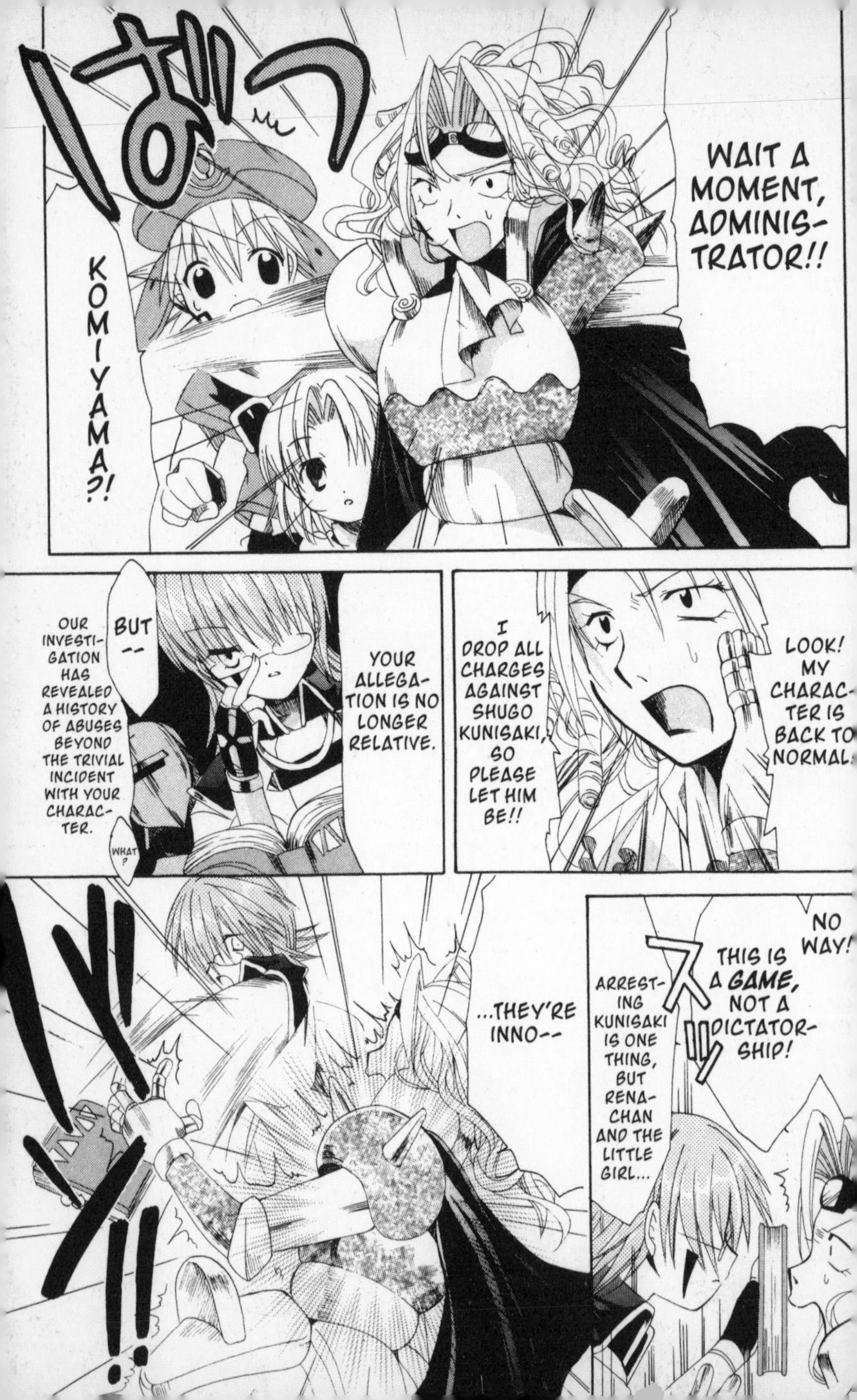
WAIT A MOMENT, ADMINISTRATOR!!
ばっ
KOMIYAMA?!
LOOK! MY CHARACTER IS BACK TO NORMAL.
I DROP ALL CHARGES AGAINST SHUGO KUNISAKI, SO PLEASE LET HIM BE!!
YOUR ALLEGATION IS NO LONGER RELATIVE.
BUT --
OUR INVESTIGATION HAS REVEALED A HISTORY OF ABUSES BEYOND THE TRIVIAL INCIDENT WITH YOUR CHARACTER.
WHAT?
NO WAY!
THIS IS A GAME, NOT A DICTATORSHIP!
ARRESTING KUNISAKI IS ONE THING, BUT RENA-CHAN AND THE LITTLE GIRL...
...THEY'RE INNO--

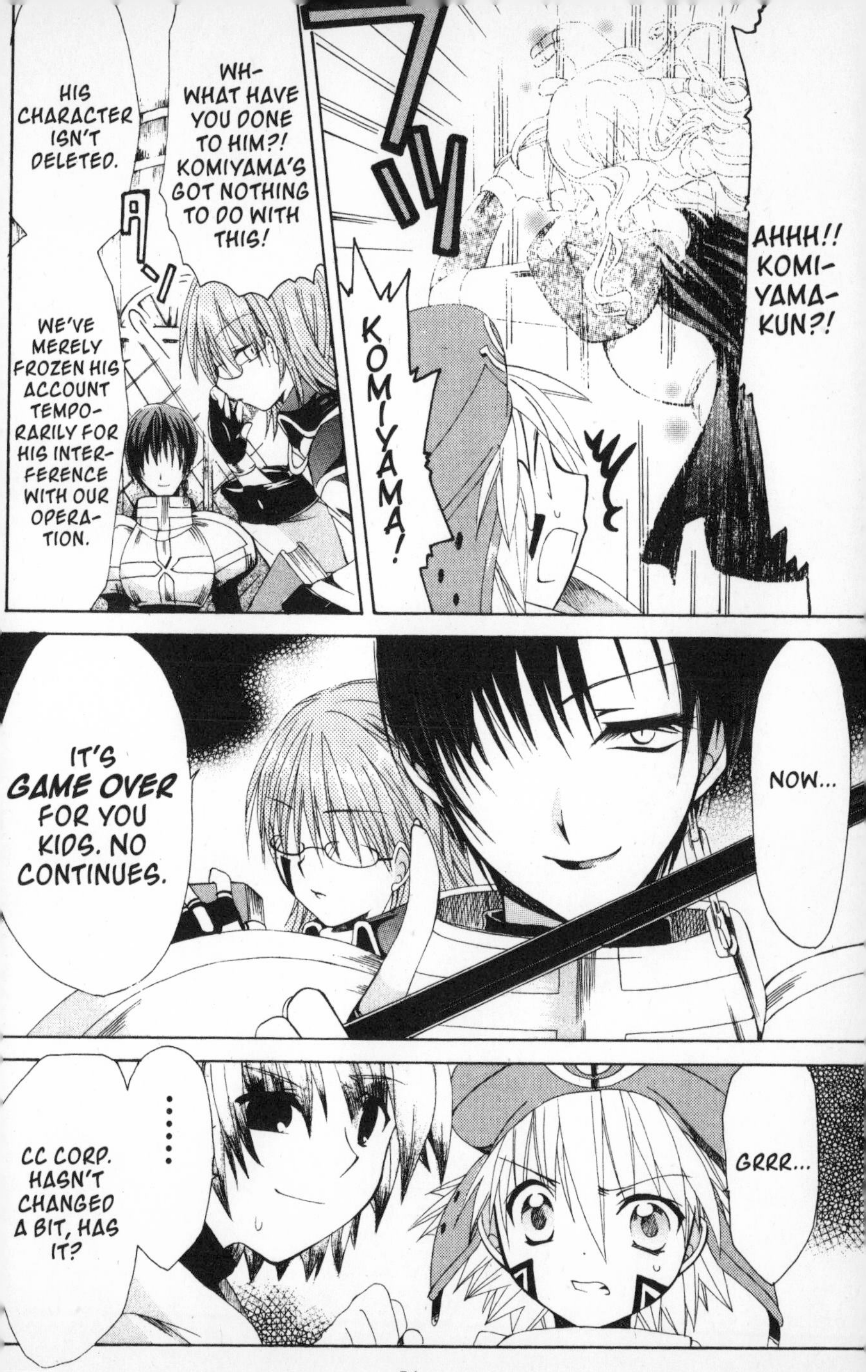
AHHH!! KOMI-YAMA-KUN?!
KOMIYAMA!
WH- WHAT HAVE YOU DONE TO HIM?! KOMIYAMA'S GOT NOTHING TO DO WITH THIS!
HIS CHARACTER ISN'T DELETED.
WE'VE MERELY FROZEN HIS ACCOUNT TEMPO-RARILY FOR HIS INTER-FERENCE WITH OUR OPERA-TION.
NOW...
IT'S GAME OVER FOR YOU KIDS. NO CONTINUES.
GRRR...
......
CC CORP. HASN'T CHANGED A BIT, HAS IT?

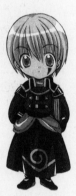
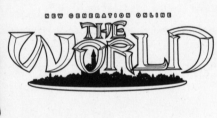

NEW GENERATION ONLINE
THE WORLD

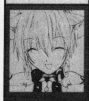

SUBJECT: RE: TO OUKA   SENDER: OUKA

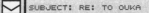

...WHAT IS "POWER?" THAT'S THE ANSWER I'VE BEEN
SEARCHING FOR SINCE JOINING THE WORLD, AND ALL ALONG
THE ANSWER WAS RIGHT IN FRONT OF ME!
IN THIS GAME, ABSOLUTE POWER LIES IN OUR USER
AGREEMENTS AND IN THE HANDS OF SYSTEM ADMINISTRATORS.
AFTER SHUGO WAS ARRESTED AND THE REST OF US THREATENED
WITH PUNISHMENT, IT ALL BECAME CLEAR.

AFTER READING THE MAIL FROM MIREILLE, I DIDN'T HESITATE
TO ANSWER. I FEEL THE SAME AS SHE DOES.

I DO NOT WANT TO LOSE THE FEW MONTHS I SPENT WITH
SHUGO. AS OUKA, I MIGHT PLAY TO TEST MY STRENGTH, BUT
A GAME WHERE I CAN'T PLAY WITH MY FRIENDS ISN'T WORTH
PLAYING.

INSTEAD OF REGRETTING IT LATER, I WANT TO DO WHAT I
CAN DO NOW. THAT WAY, NO MATTER HOW HARD IT IS, I WON'T
LOSE WHAT'S MOST IMPORTANT TO ME. WE ARE A TEAM, AFTER
ALL.

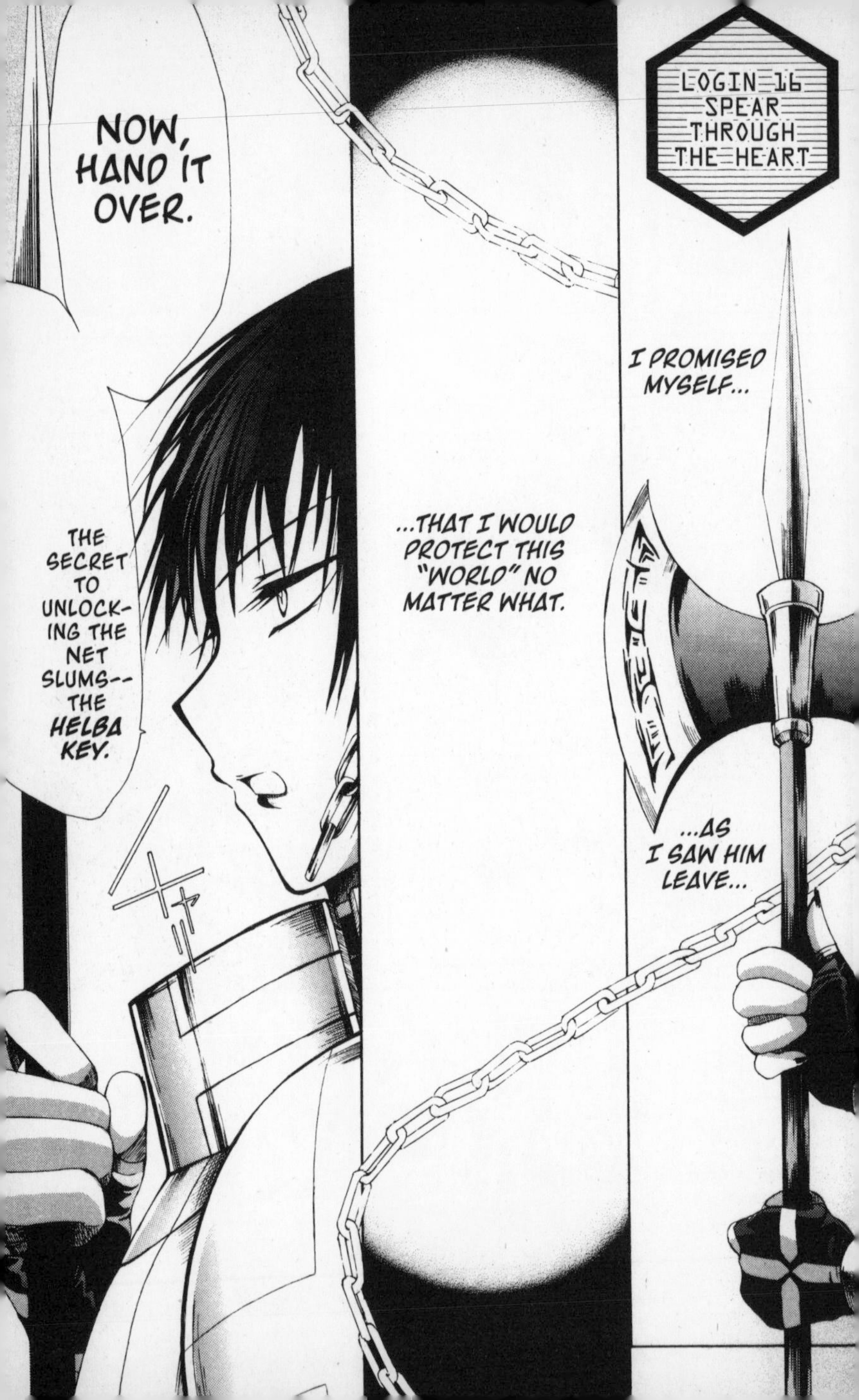
LOGIN 16 SPEAR THROUGH THE HEART
I PROMISED MYSELF...
...AS I SAW HIM LEAVE...
...THAT I WOULD PROTECT THIS "WORLD" NO MATTER WHAT.
NOW, HAND IT OVER.
THE SECRET TO UNLOCKING THE NET SLUMS--THE HELBA KEY.

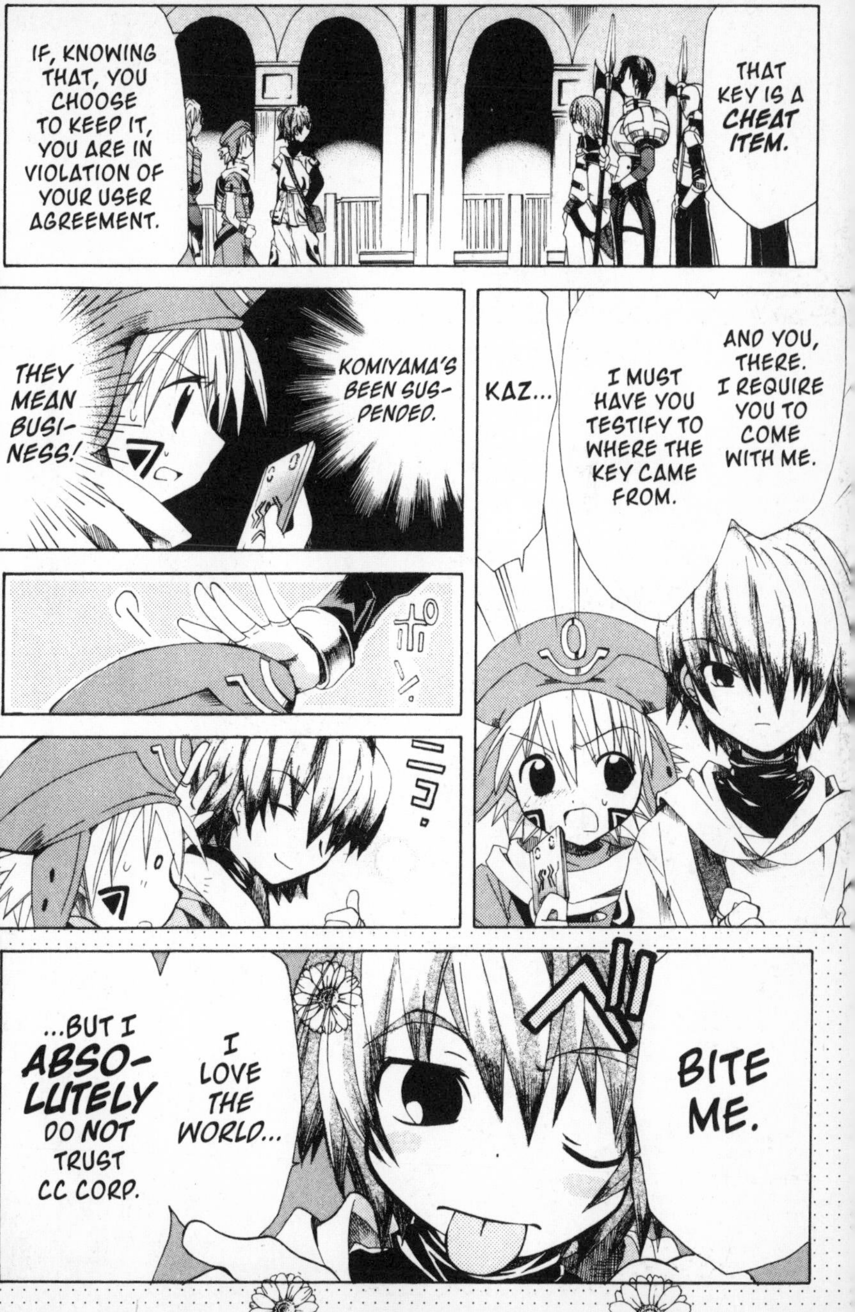
THAT KEY IS A **CHEAT ITEM.**
IF, KNOWING THAT, YOU CHOOSE TO KEEP IT, YOU ARE IN VIOLATION OF YOUR USER AGREEMENT.
AND YOU, THERE. I REQUIRE YOU TO COME WITH ME.
I MUST HAVE YOU TESTIFY TO WHERE THE KEY CAME FROM.
KAZ...
KOMIYAMA'S BEEN SUS-PENDED.
THEY MEAN BUSI-NESS!
ニコ。
BITE ME.
I LOVE THE WORLD...
...BUT I **ABSOLUTELY** DO **NOT** TRUST CC CORP.

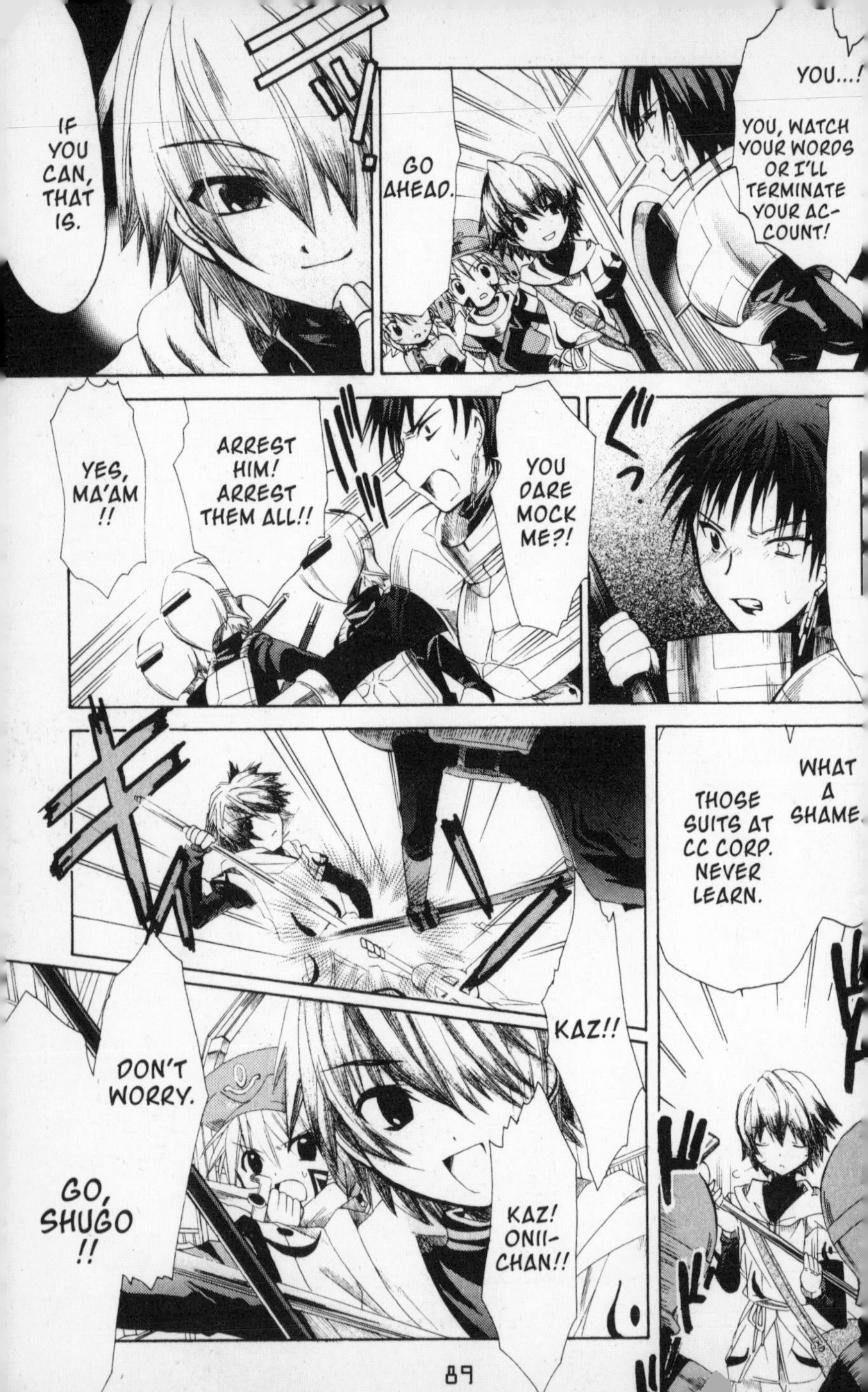

YOU...!
YOU, WATCH YOUR WORDS OR I'LL TERMINATE YOUR AC-COUNT!
GO AHEAD.
IF YOU CAN, THAT IS.
YOU DARE MOCK ME?!
ARREST HIM! ARREST THEM ALL!!
YES, MA'AM!!
WHAT A SHAME.
THOSE SUITS AT CC CORP. NEVER LEARN.
KAZ!!
KAZ! ONII-CHAN!!
DON'T WORRY.
GO, SHUGO!!

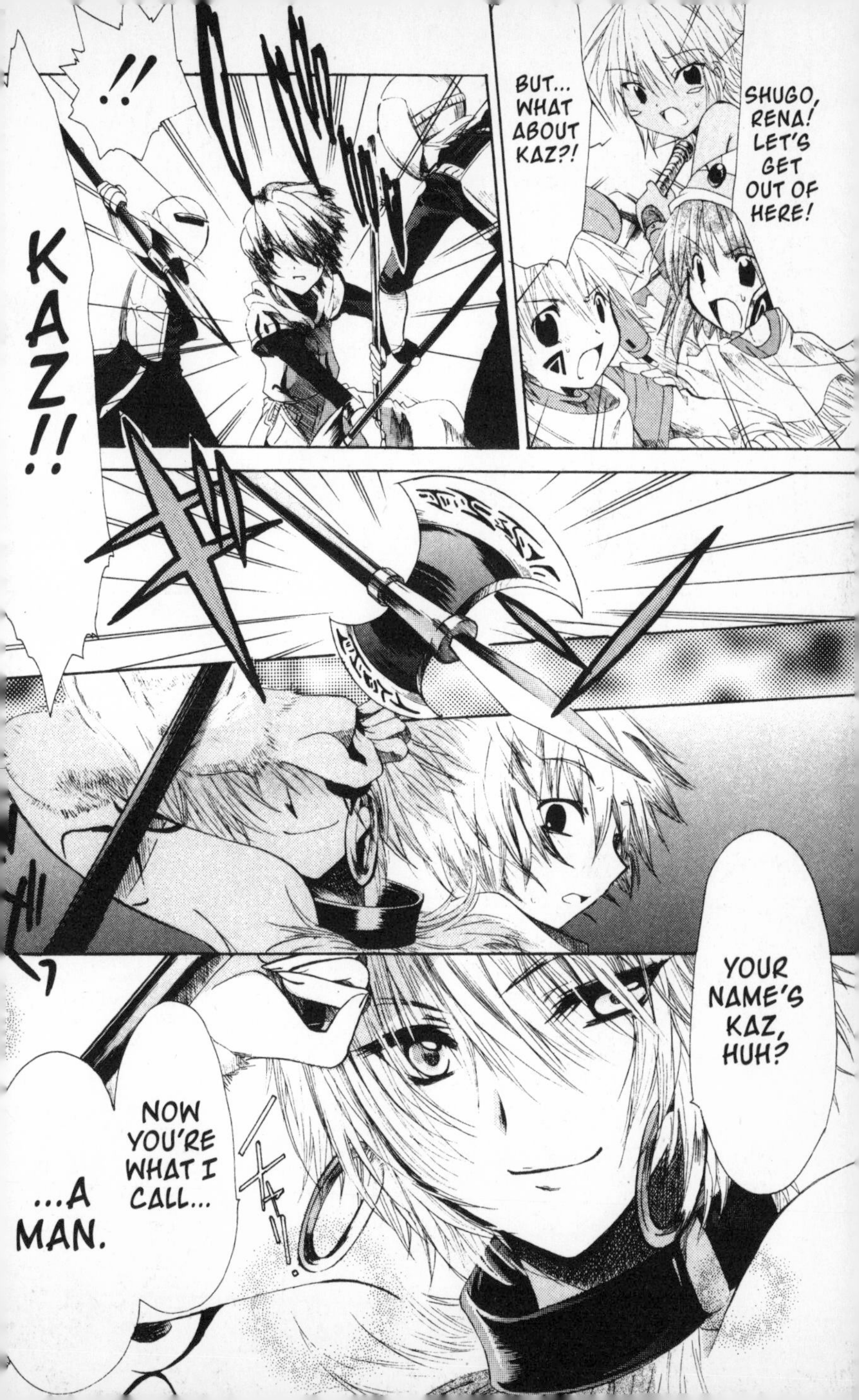
SHUGO, RENA! LET'S GET OUT OF HERE!
BUT... WHAT ABOUT KAZ?!
!!
KAZ!!
YOUR NAME'S KAZ, HUH?
NOW YOU'RE WHAT I CALL...
...A MAN.

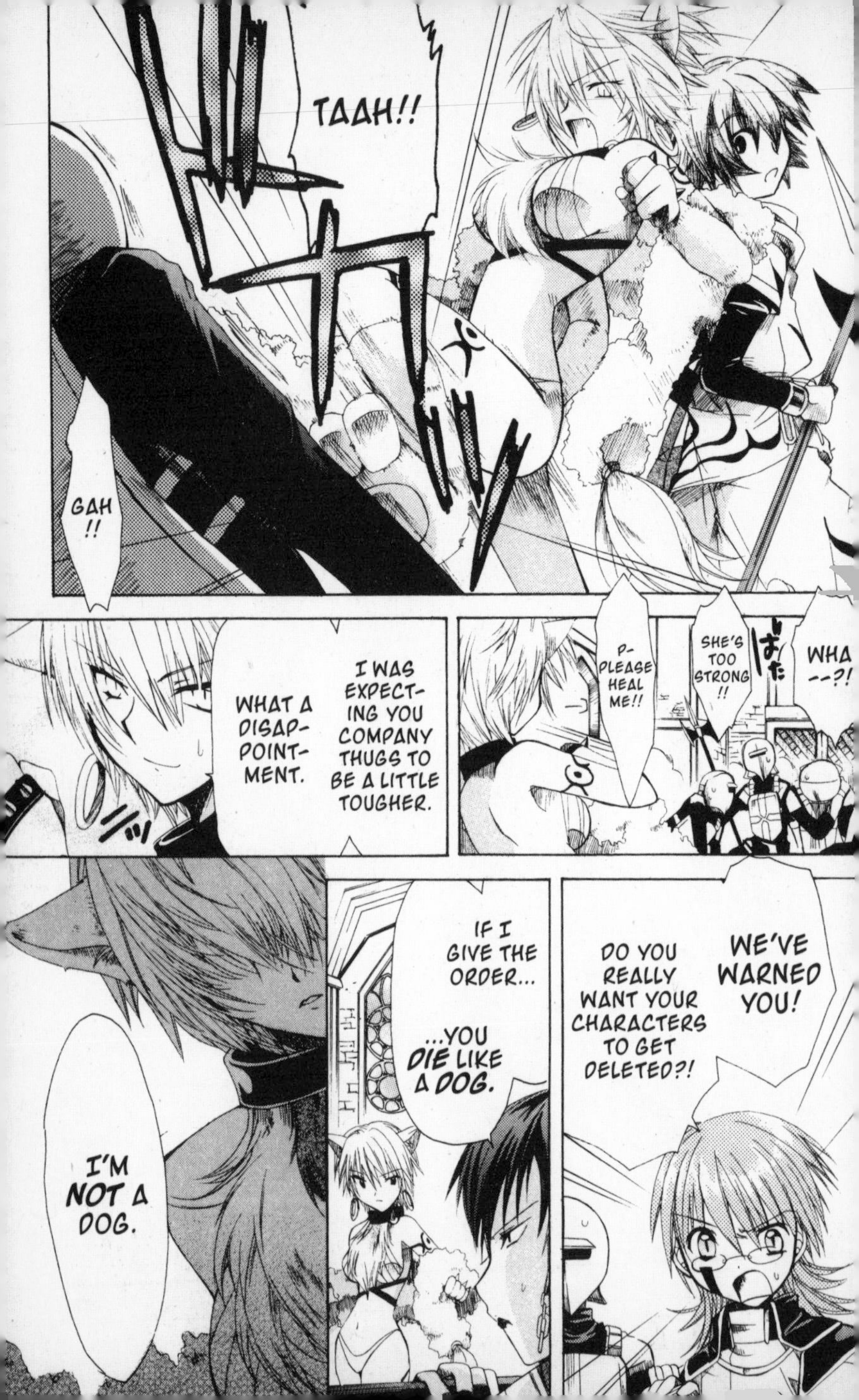
TAAH!!
GAH!!
WHA--?!
SHE'S TOO STRONG!!
ばた
P-PLEASE HEAL ME!!
I WAS EXPECTING YOU COMPANY THUGS TO BE A LITTLE TOUGHER.
WHAT A DISAPPOINTMENT.
WE'VE WARNED YOU!
DO YOU REALLY WANT YOUR CHARACTERS TO GET DELETED?!
IF I GIVE THE ORDER...
...YOU DIE LIKE A DOG.
I'M NOT A DOG.

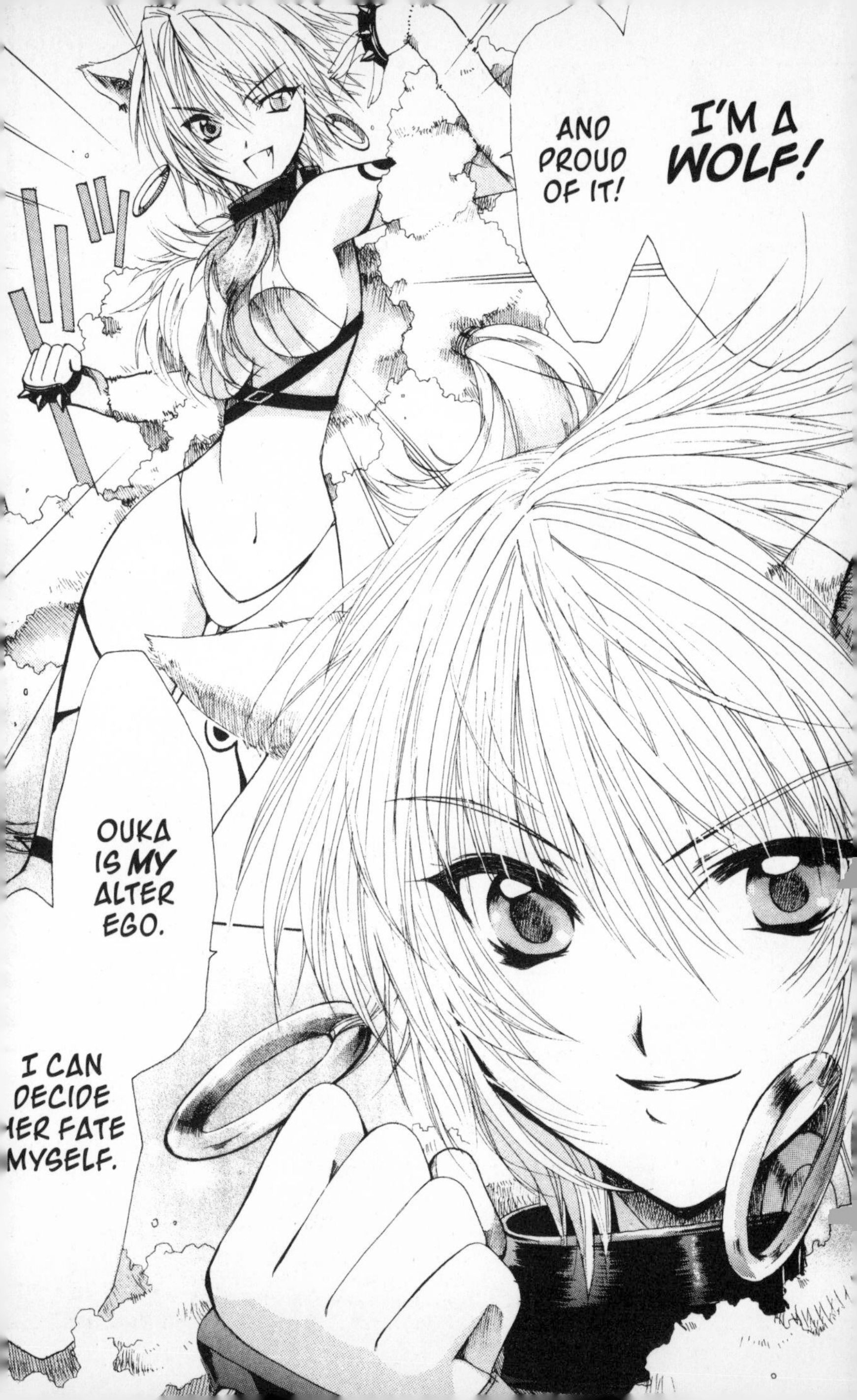

I'M A WOLF!
AND PROUD OF IT!
OUKA IS MY ALTER EGO.
I CAN DECIDE IER FATE MYSELF.

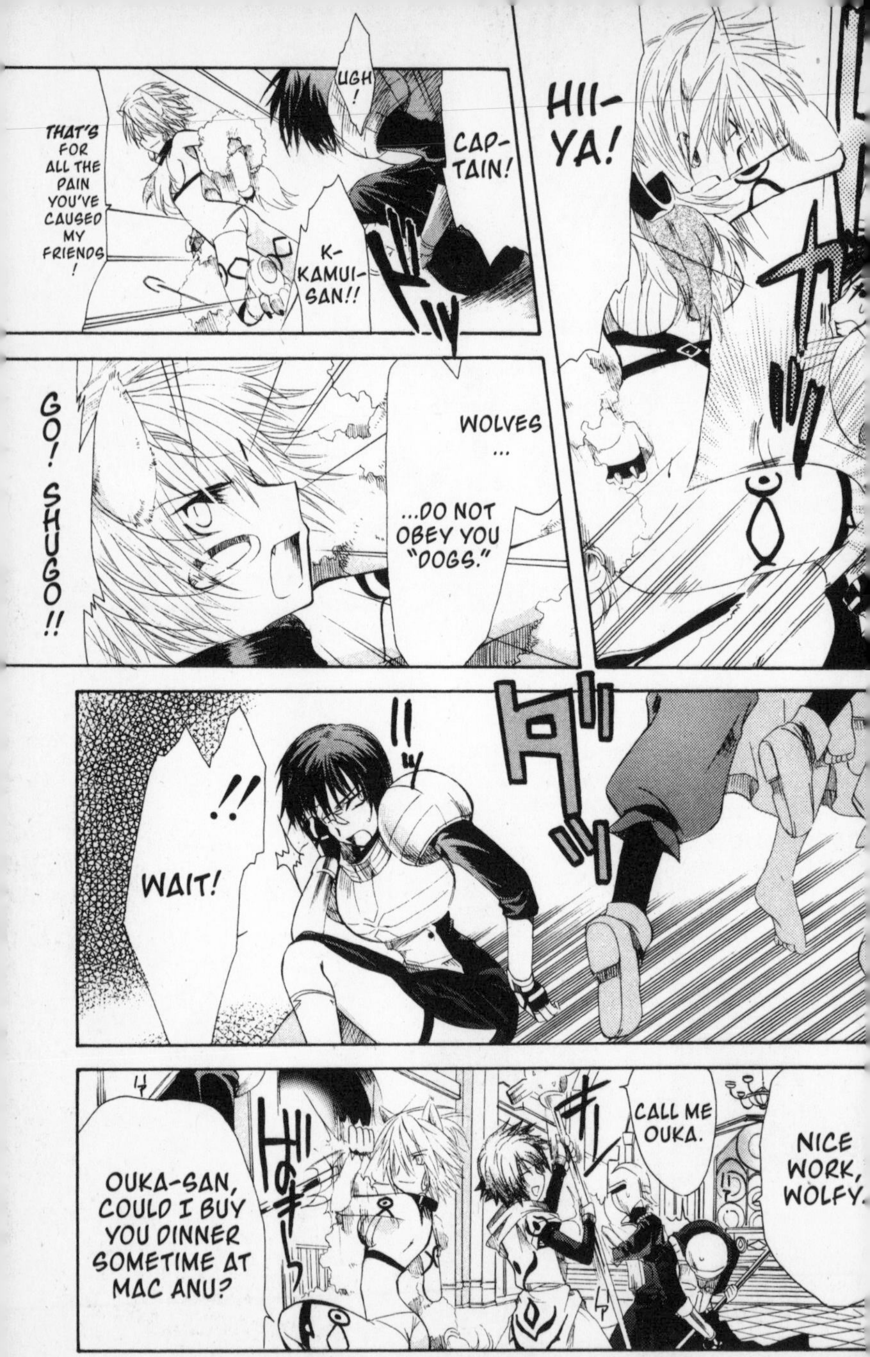
HII-YA!
UGH!
CAP-TAIN!
K-KAMUI-SAN!!
THAT'S FOR ALL THE PAIN YOU'VE CAUSED MY FRIENDS!
WOLVES...
...DO NOT OBEY YOU "DOGS."
GO! SHUGO!!
!!
WAIT!
NICE WORK, WOLFY.
CALL ME OUKA.
OUKA-SAN, COULD I BUY YOU DINNER SOMETIME AT MAC ANU?

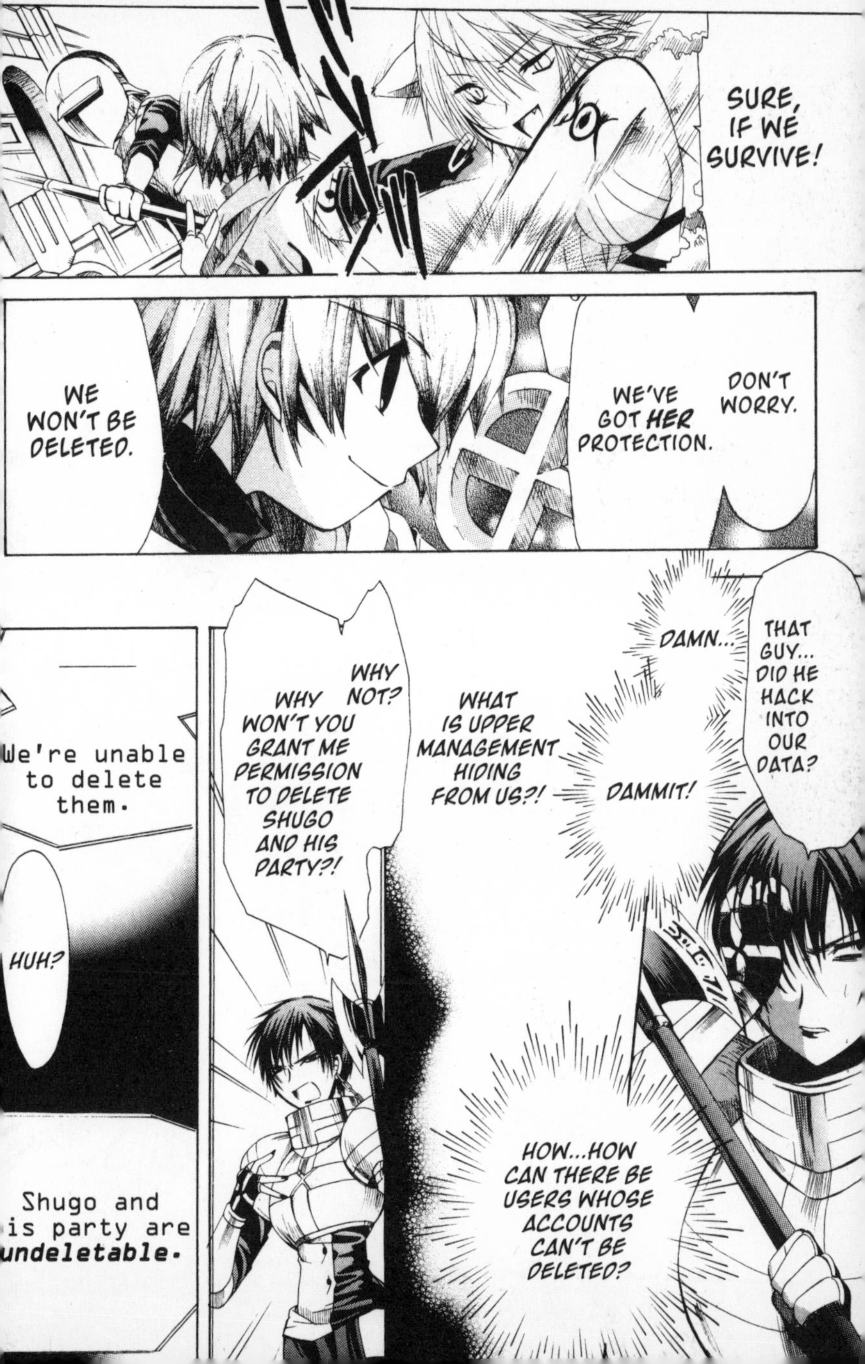
SURE, IF WE SURVIVE!
DON'T WORRY.
WE'VE GOT **HER** PROTECTION.
WE WON'T BE DELETED.
THAT GUY... DID HE HACK INTO OUR DATA?
DAMN...
DAMMIT!
WHAT IS UPPER MANAGEMENT HIDING FROM US?!
HOW...HOW CAN THERE BE USERS WHOSE ACCOUNTS CAN'T BE DELETED?
WHY NOT?
WHY WON'T YOU GRANT ME PERMISSION TO DELETE SHUGO AND HIS PARTY?!
We're unable to delete them.
HUH?
Shugo and is party are **undeletable.**

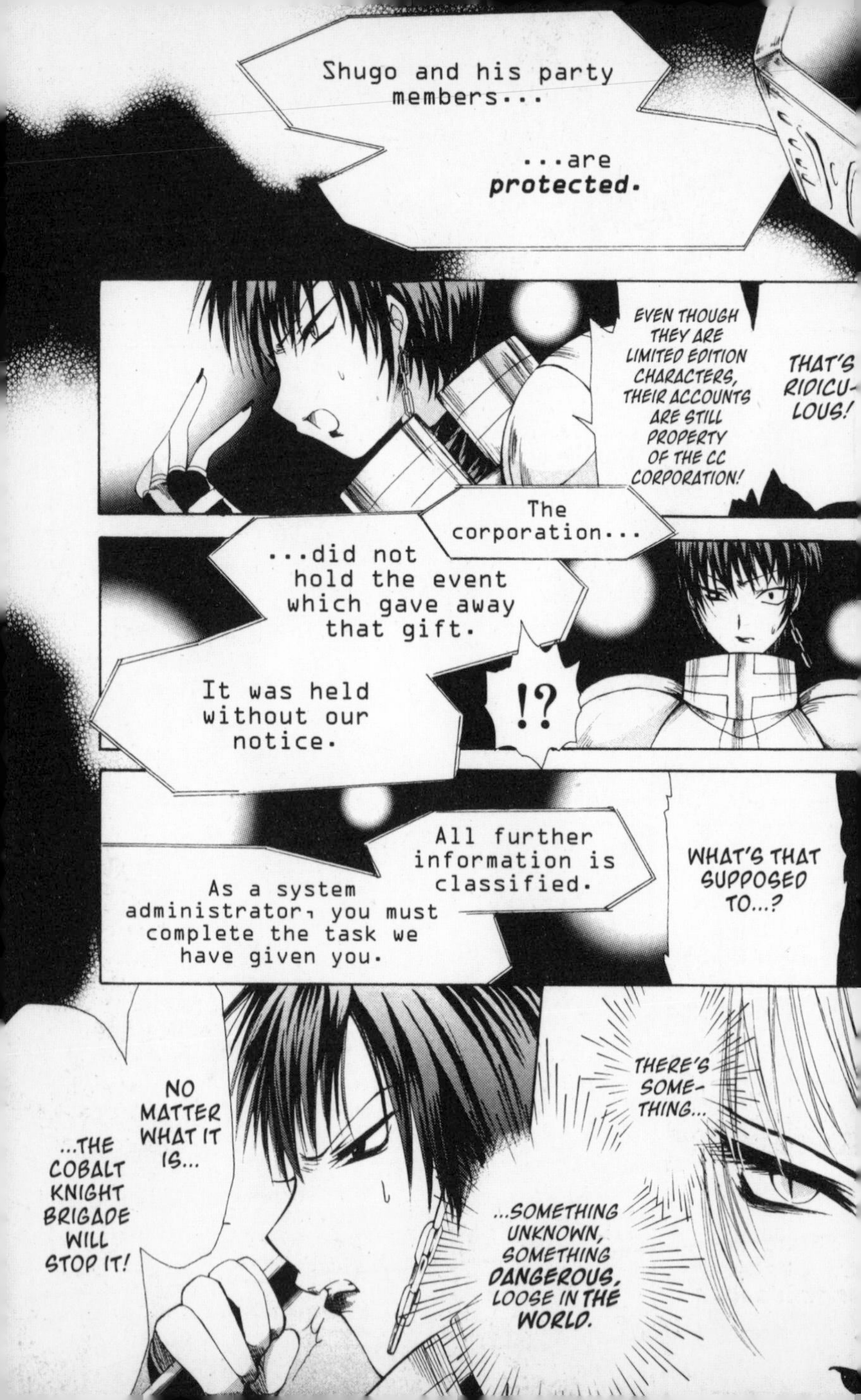
Shugo and his party members...
...are **protected**.
THAT'S RIDICULOUS!
EVEN THOUGH THEY ARE LIMITED EDITION CHARACTERS, THEIR ACCOUNTS ARE STILL PROPERTY OF THE CC CORPORATION!
The corporation...
...did not hold the event which gave away that gift.
!?
It was held without our notice.
WHAT'S THAT SUPPOSED TO...?
All further information is classified.
As a system administrator, you must complete the task we have given you.
THERE'S SOMETHING...
...SOMETHING UNKNOWN, SOMETHING **DANGEROUS**, LOOSE IN **THE WORLD**.
NO MATTER WHAT IT IS...
...THE COBALT KNIGHT BRIGADE WILL STOP IT!

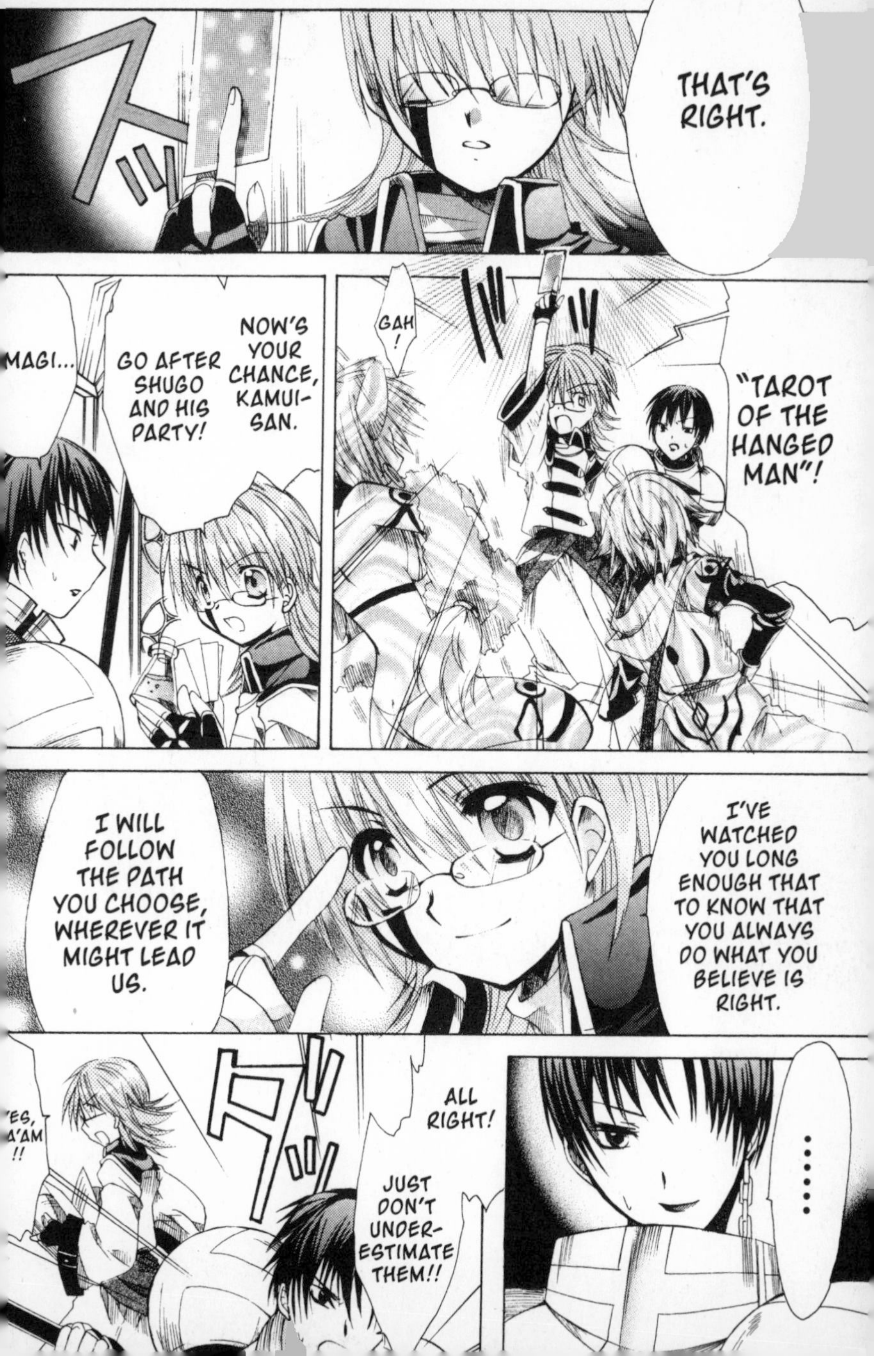
THAT'S RIGHT.
"TAROT OF THE HANGED MAN"!
GAH!
NOW'S YOUR CHANCE, KAMUI-SAN.
GO AFTER SHUGO AND HIS PARTY!
MAGI...
I'VE WATCHED YOU LONG ENOUGH THAT TO KNOW THAT YOU ALWAYS DO WHAT YOU BELIEVE IS RIGHT.
I WILL FOLLOW THE PATH YOU CHOOSE, WHEREVER IT MIGHT LEAD US.
......
ALL RIGHT!
JUST DON'T UNDER-ESTIMATE THEM!!
ES, A'AM!!

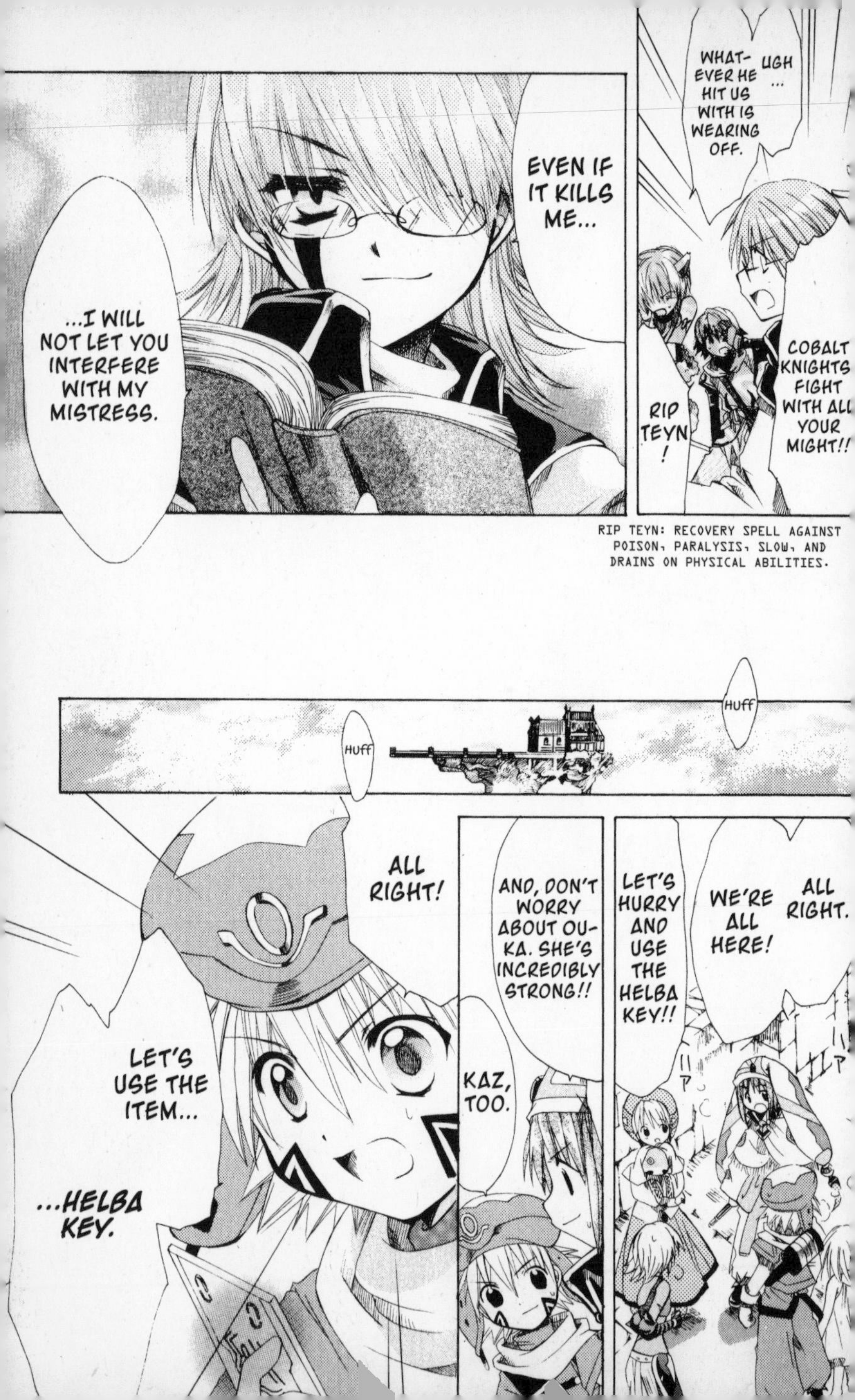
UGH ...
WHATEVER HE HIT US WITH IS WEARING OFF.
COBALT KNIGHTS FIGHT WITH ALL YOUR MIGHT!!
RIP TEYN!
EVEN IF IT KILLS ME...
...I WILL NOT LET YOU INTERFERE WITH MY MISTRESS.
RIP TEYN: RECOVERY SPELL AGAINST POISON, PARALYSIS, SLOW, AND DRAINS ON PHYSICAL ABILITIES.
HUFF
HUFF
ALL RIGHT.
WE'RE ALL HERE!
LET'S HURRY AND USE THE HELBA KEY!!
AND, DON'T WORRY ABOUT OU-KA. SHE'S INCREDIBLY STRONG!!
KAZ, TOO.
ALL RIGHT!
LET'S USE THE ITEM...
...HELBA KEY.

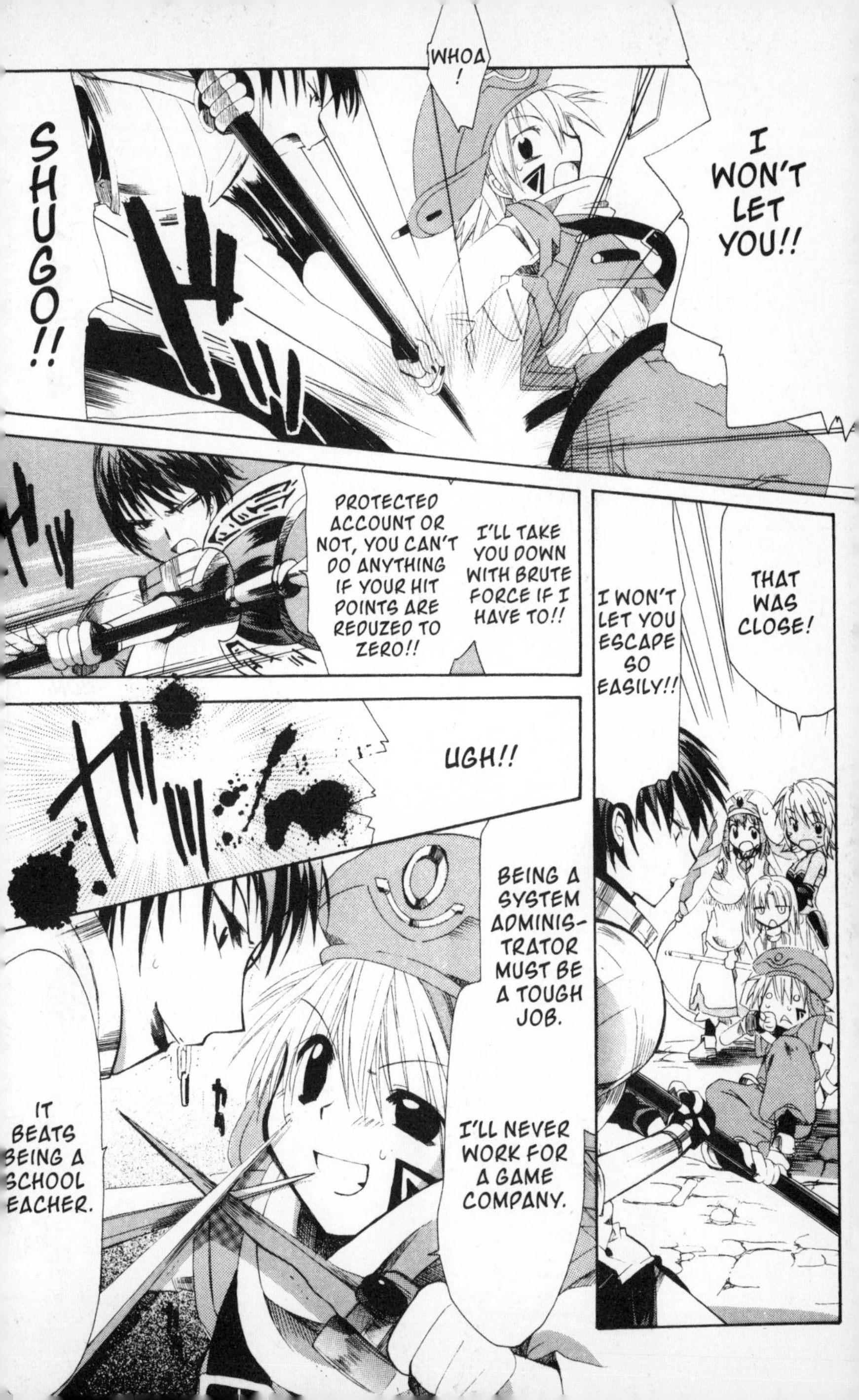
WHOA!
I WON'T LET YOU!!
SHUGO!!
THAT WAS CLOSE!
I WON'T LET YOU ESCAPE SO EASILY!!
I'LL TAKE YOU DOWN WITH BRUTE FORCE IF I HAVE TO!!
PROTECTED ACCOUNT OR NOT, YOU CAN'T DO ANYTHING IF YOUR HIT POINTS ARE REDUZED TO ZERO!!
UGH!!
BEING A SYSTEM ADMINIS-TRATOR MUST BE A TOUGH JOB.
I'LL NEVER WORK FOR A GAME COMPANY.
IT BEATS BEING A SCHOOL EACHER.

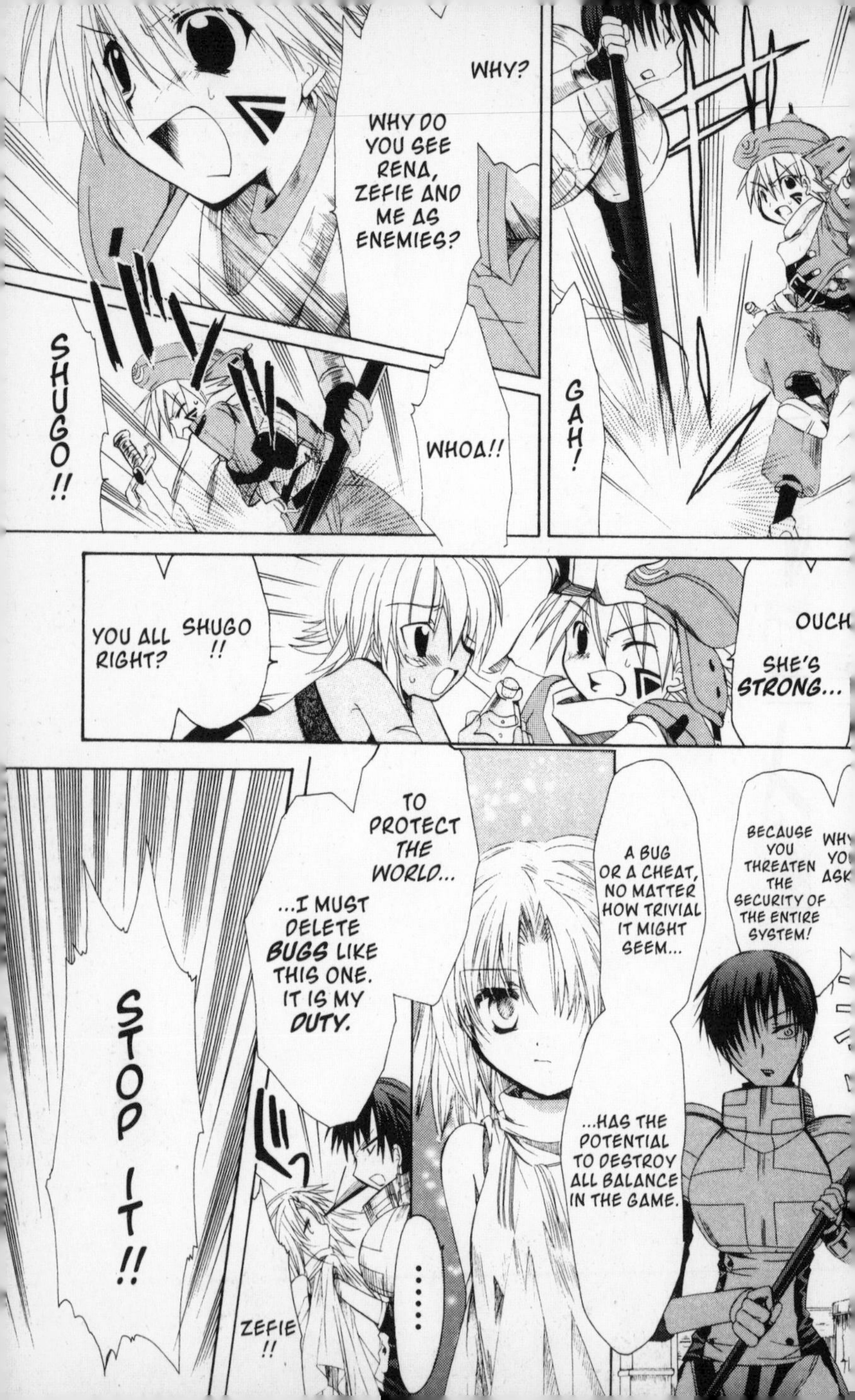
GAH!
WHY?
WHY DO YOU SEE RENA, ZEFIE AND ME AS ENEMIES?
WHOA!!
SHUGO!!
OUCH
SHE'S STRONG...
SHUGO!!
YOU ALL RIGHT?
WHY YO ASK
BECAUSE YOU THREATEN THE SECURITY OF THE ENTIRE SYSTEM!
A BUG OR A CHEAT, NO MATTER HOW TRIVIAL IT MIGHT SEEM...
...HAS THE POTENTIAL TO DESTROY ALL BALANCE IN THE GAME.
TO PROTECT THE WORLD...
...I MUST DELETE BUGS LIKE THIS ONE. IT IS MY DUTY.
......
ZEFIE!!
STOP IT!!

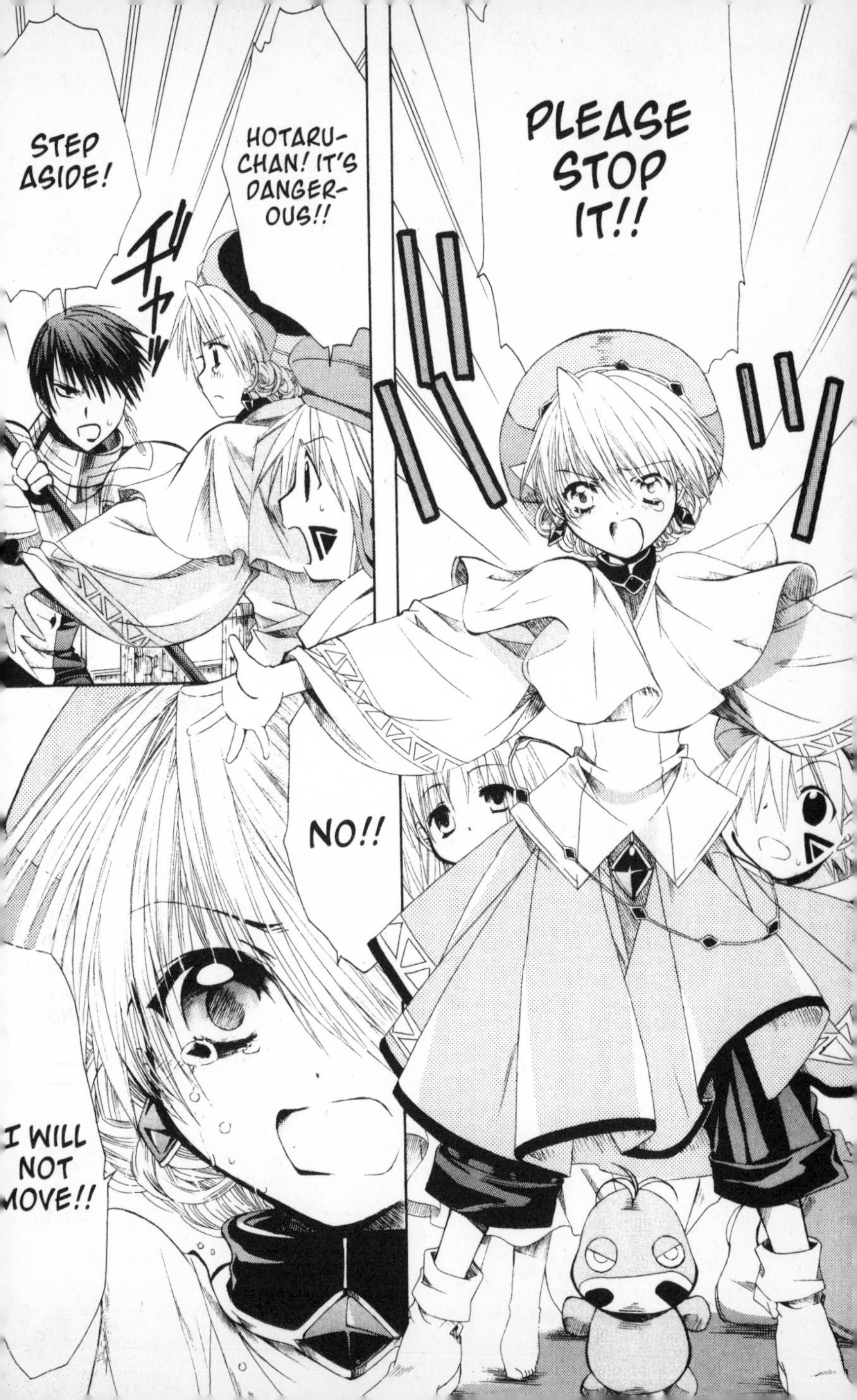
PLEASE STOP IT!!
HOTARU-CHAN! IT'S DANGER-OUS!!
STEP ASIDE!
NO!!
I WILL NOT MOVE!!

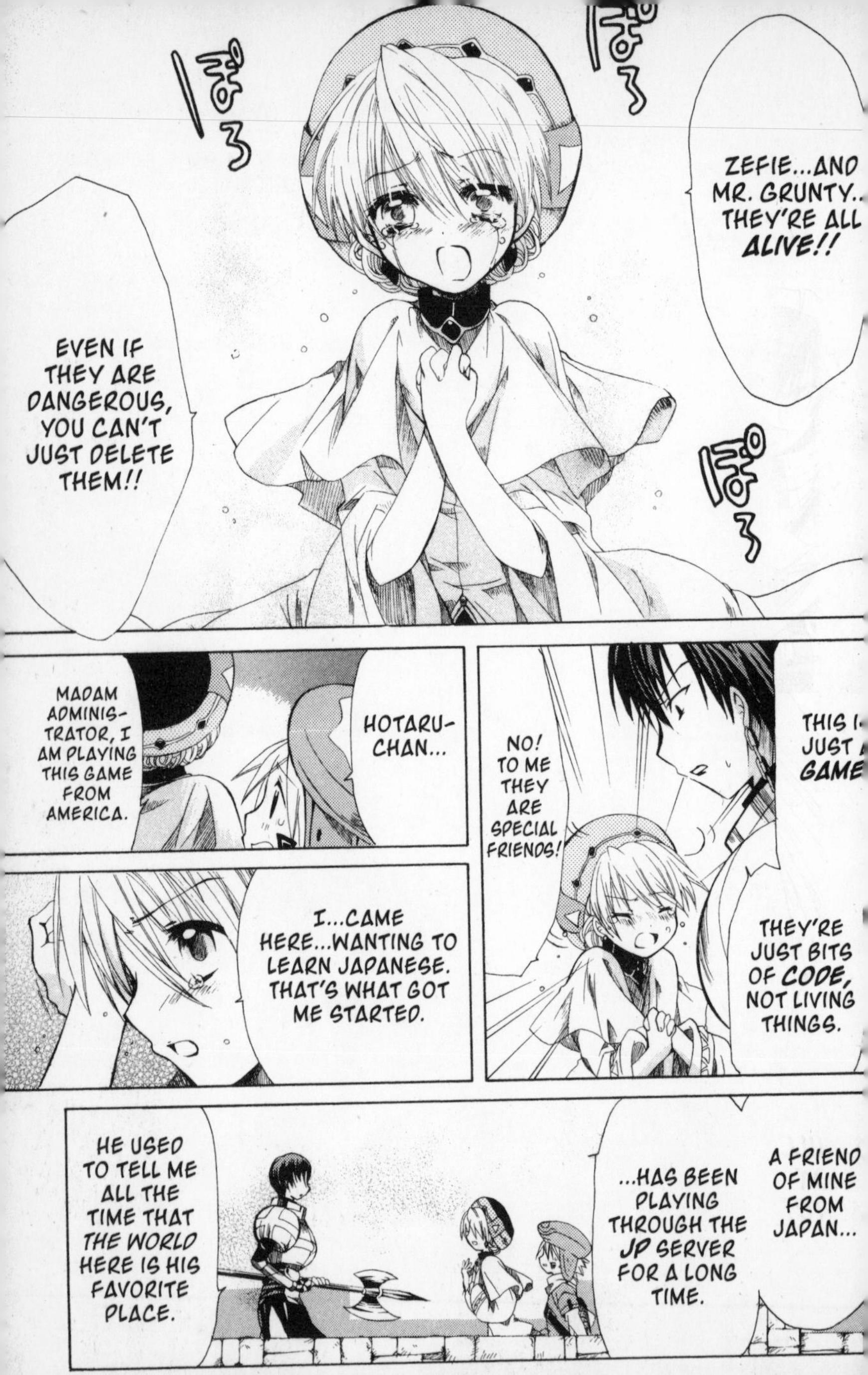
ぽろ
ZEFIE...AND MR. GRUNTY.. THEY'RE ALL ALIVE!!
ぽろ
ぽろ
EVEN IF THEY ARE DANGEROUS, YOU CAN'T JUST DELETE THEM!!
THIS I JUST GAME
THEY'RE JUST BITS OF CODE, NOT LIVING THINGS.
NO! TO ME THEY ARE SPECIAL FRIENDS!
HOTARU-CHAN...
MADAM ADMINIS-TRATOR, I AM PLAYING THIS GAME FROM AMERICA.
I...CAME HERE...WANTING TO LEARN JAPANESE. THAT'S WHAT GOT ME STARTED.
A FRIEND OF MINE FROM JAPAN...
...HAS BEEN PLAYING THROUGH THE JP SERVER FOR A LONG TIME.
HE USED TO TELL ME ALL THE TIME THAT THE WORLD HERE IS HIS FAVORITE PLACE.

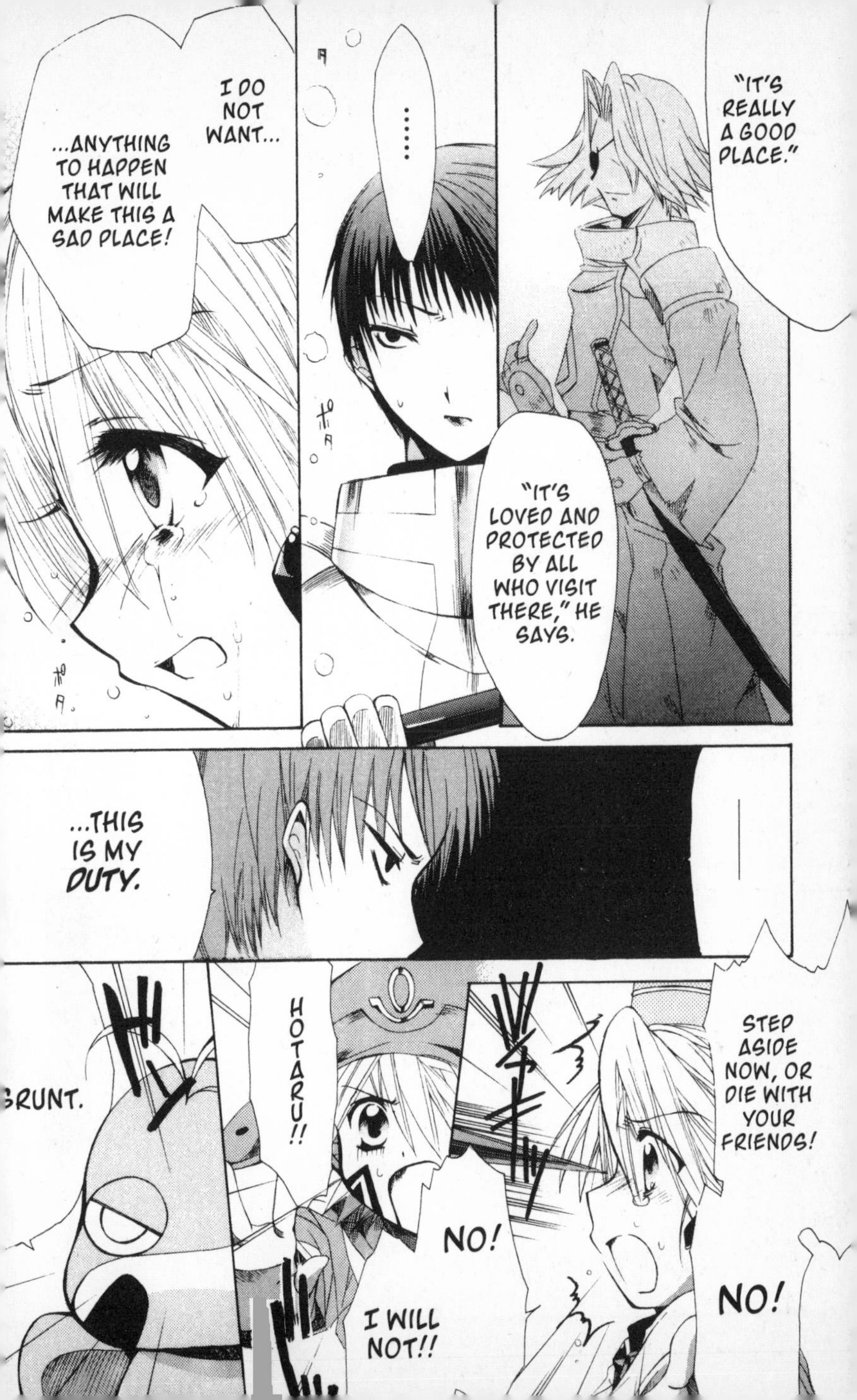
"IT'S REALLY A GOOD PLACE."
......
"IT'S LOVED AND PROTECTED BY ALL WHO VISIT THERE," HE SAYS.
I DO NOT WANT...
...ANYTHING TO HAPPEN THAT WILL MAKE THIS A SAD PLACE!
...THIS IS MY DUTY.
STEP ASIDE NOW, OR DIE WITH YOUR FRIENDS!
NO!
HOTARU!!
NO!
I WILL NOT!!
GRUNT.

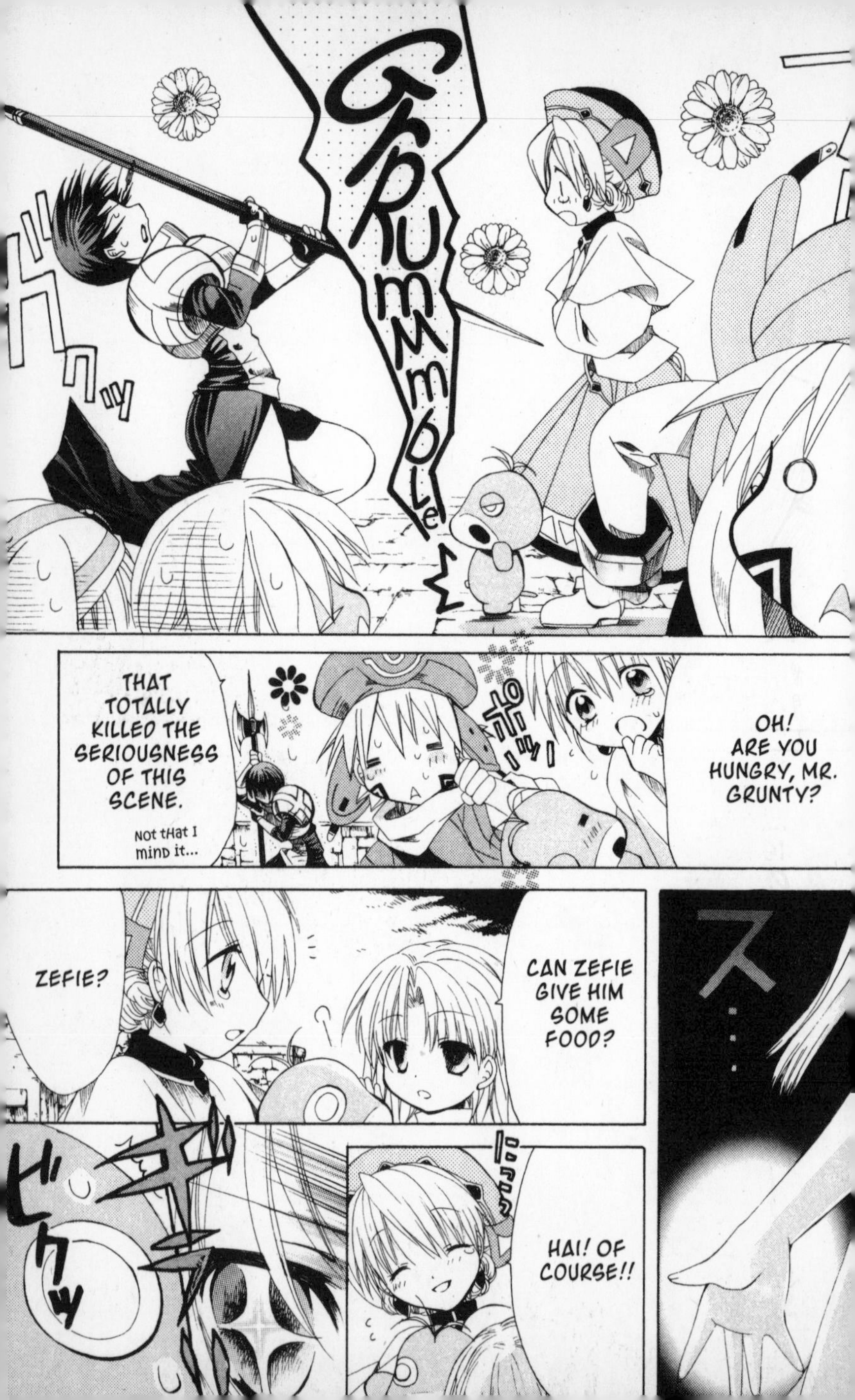
GRUMMMMBLE
OH! ARE YOU HUNGRY, MR. GRUNTY?
THAT TOTALLY KILLED THE SERIOUSNESS OF THIS SCENE.
Not that I mind it...
CAN ZEFIE GIVE HIM SOME FOOD?
ZEFIE?
HAI! OF COURSE!!

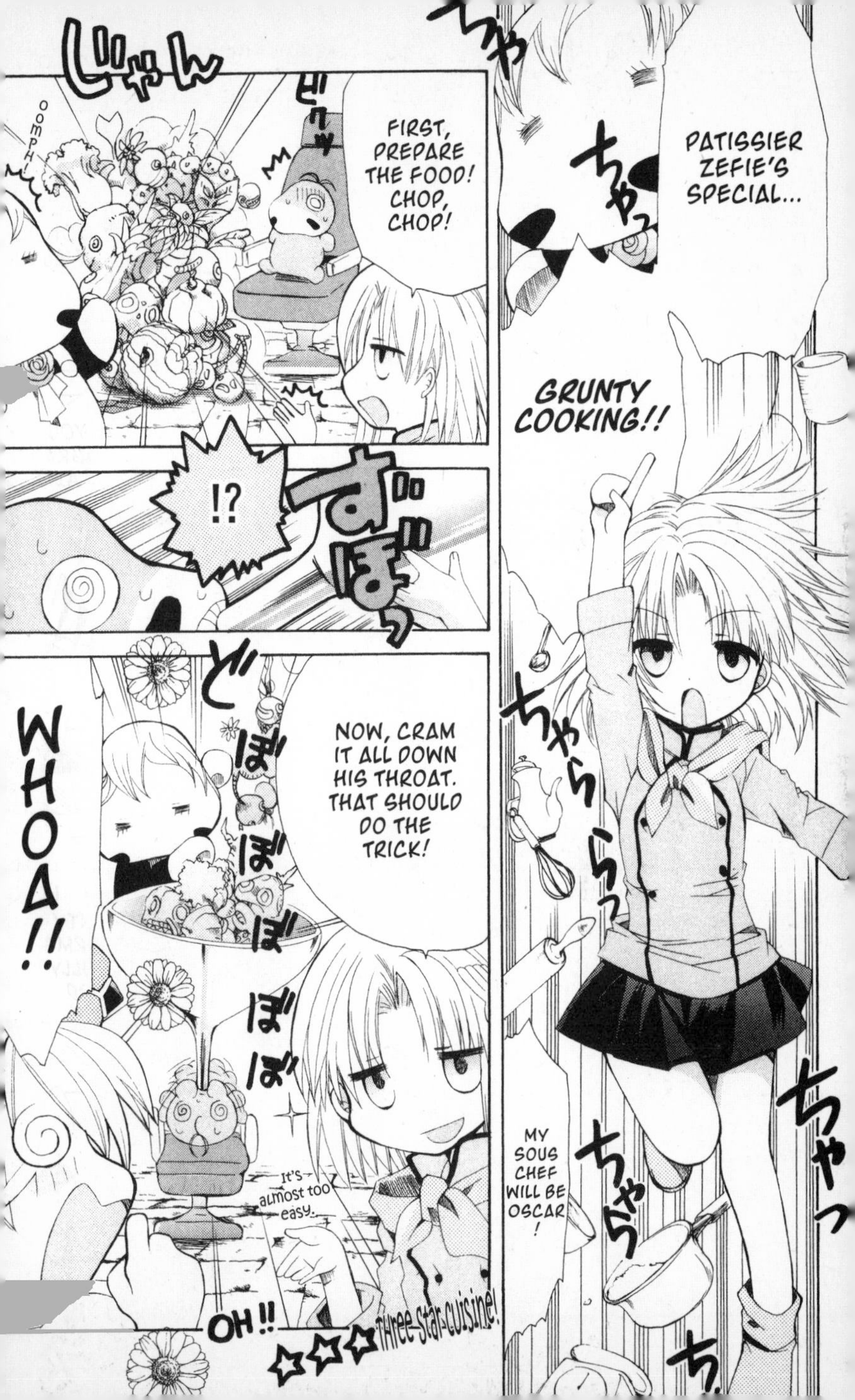

PATISSIER ZEFIE'S SPECIAL...
ちゃっ
GRUNTY COOKING!!
ちゃらららっ
MY SOUS CHEF WILL BE OSCAR!
ちゃっ
ちゃら
ち
じゃん
OOMPH!
ビクッ
FIRST, PREPARE THE FOOD! CHOP, CHOP!
!?
ずぼっ
どぼぼぼぼぼ
NOW, CRAM IT ALL DOWN HIS THROAT. THAT SHOULD DO THE TRICK!
WHOA!!
It's almost too easy.
OH!!
Three-star cuisine!

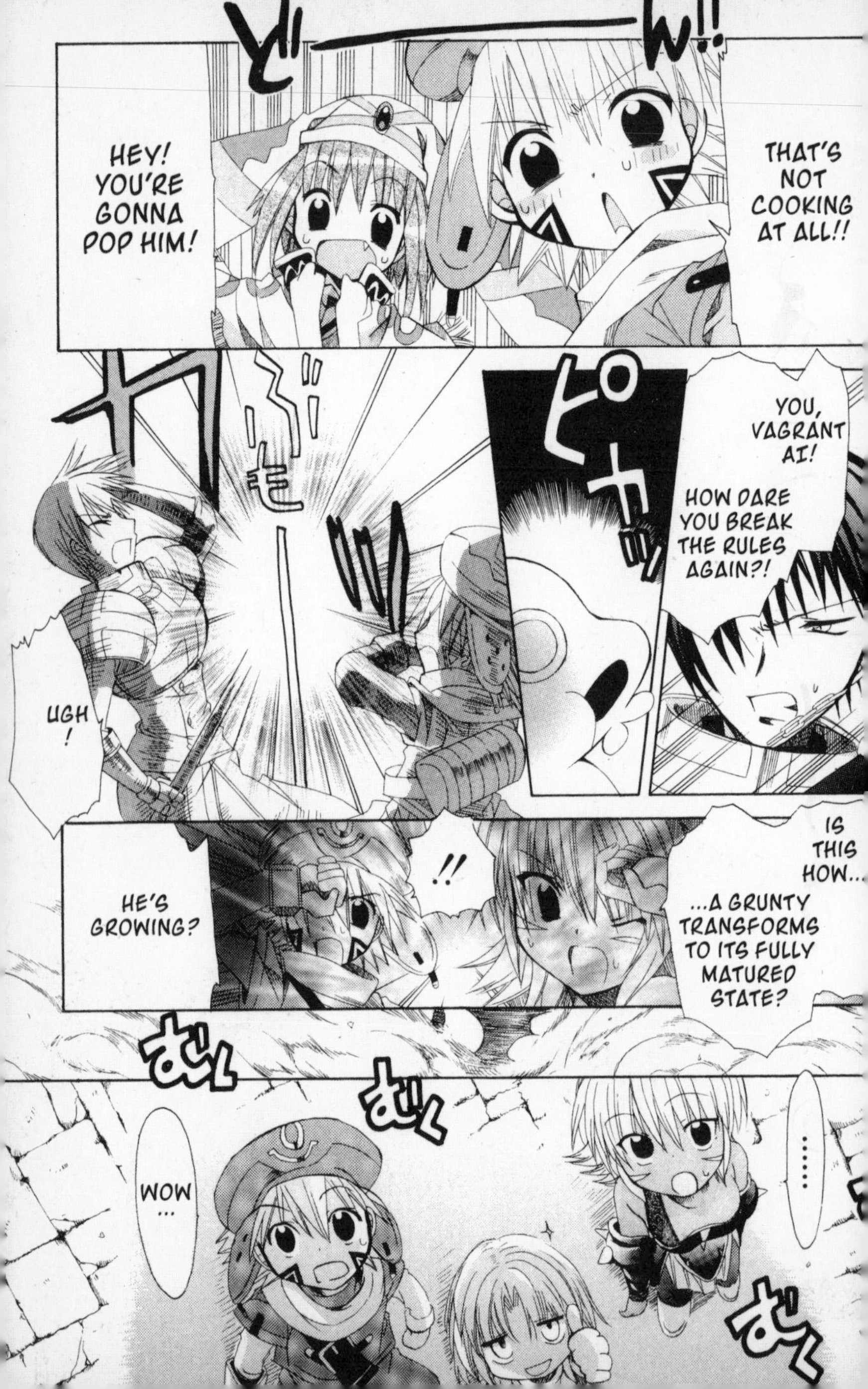
THAT'S NOT COOKING AT ALL!!
HEY! YOU'RE GONNA POP HIM!
YOU, VAGRANT AI!
HOW DARE YOU BREAK THE RULES AGAIN?!
UGH!
IS THIS HOW...
...A GRUNTY TRANSFORMS TO ITS FULLY MATURED STATE?
!!
HE'S GROWING?
......
WOW...

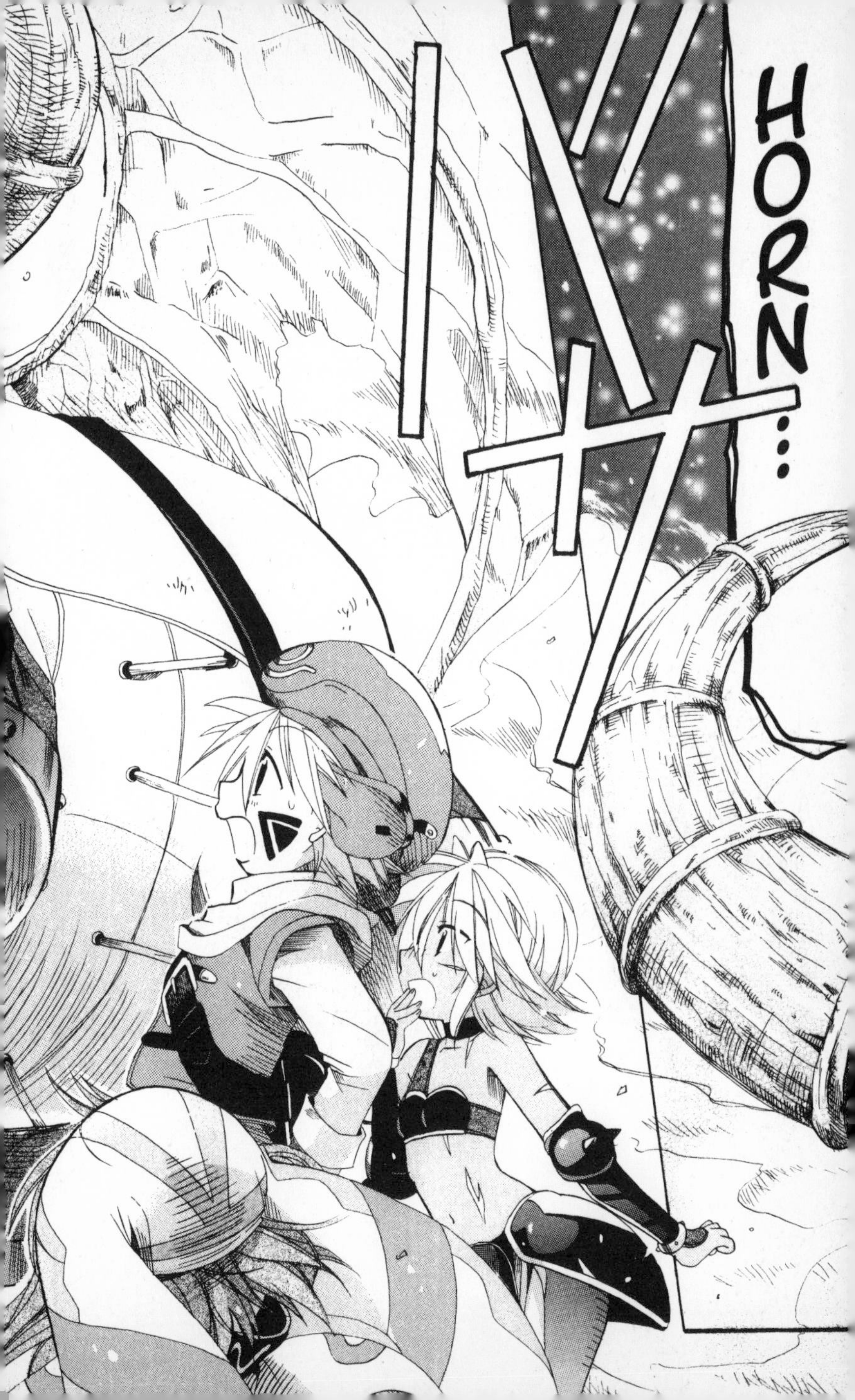
HORRN...

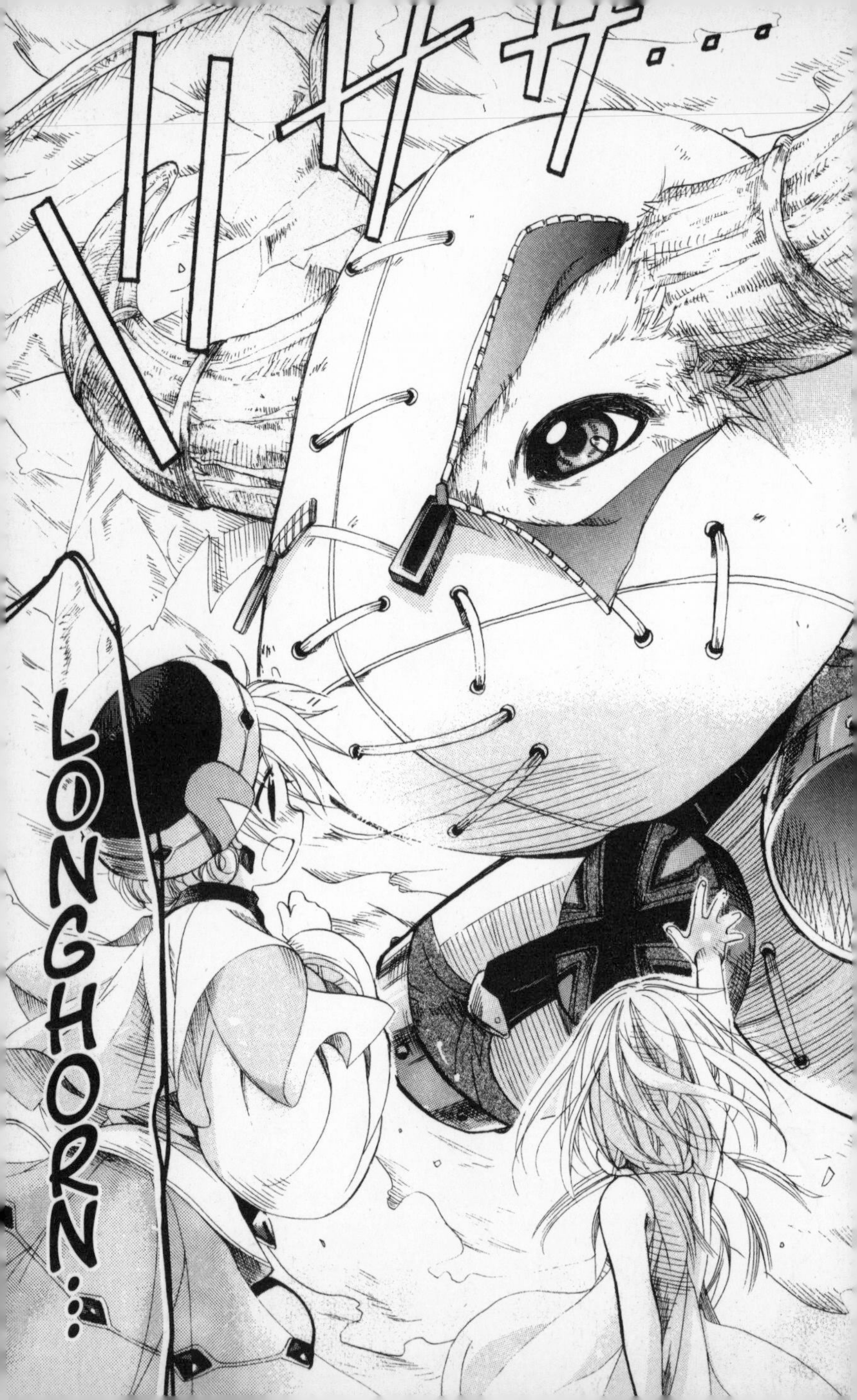
LONGHORN...

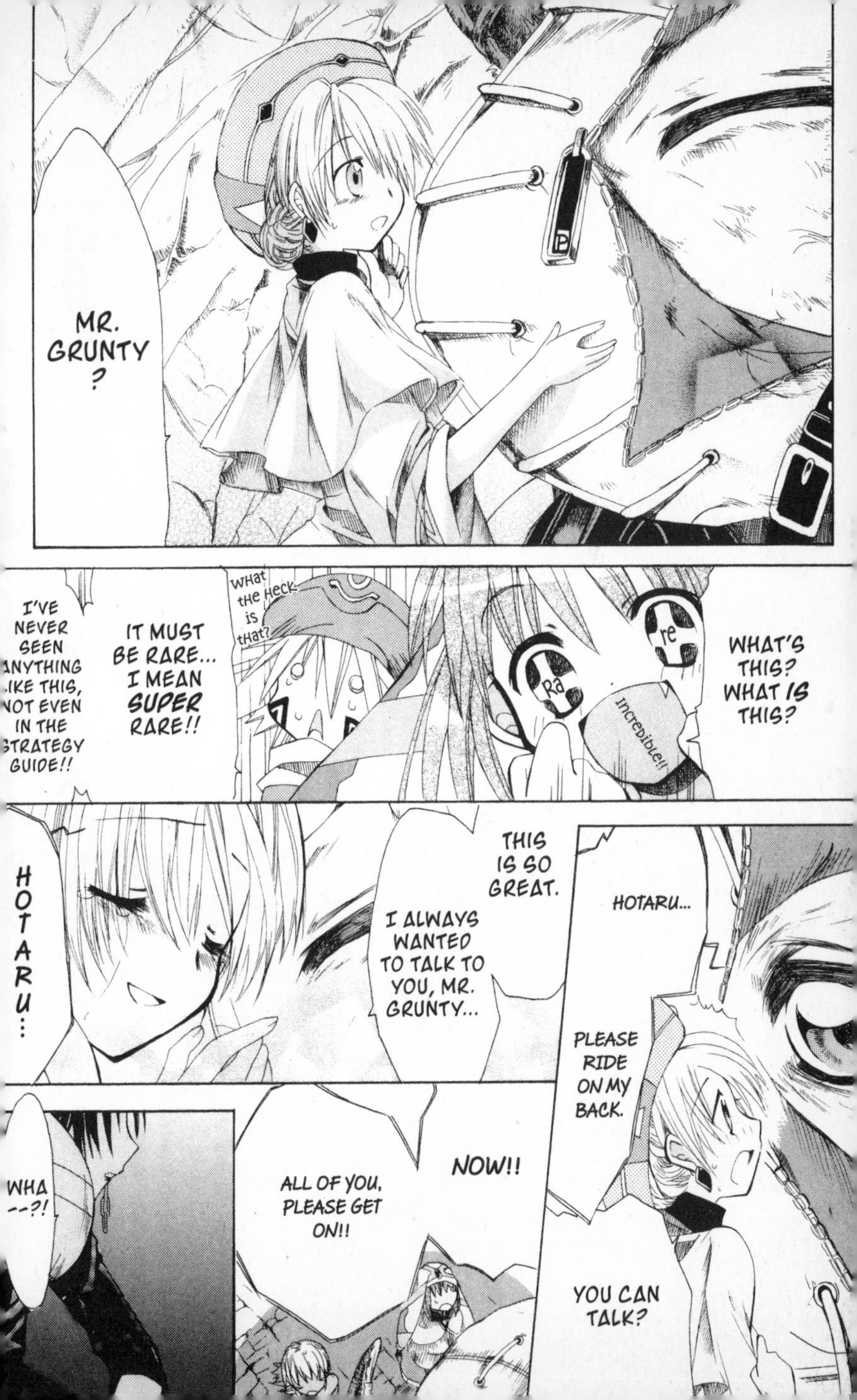
MR. GRUNTY?
WHAT'S THIS? WHAT IS THIS?
Rare
Incredible!!
What the Heck is that?
IT MUST BE RARE... I MEAN SUPER RARE!!
I'VE NEVER SEEN ANYTHING LIKE THIS, NOT EVEN IN THE STRATEGY GUIDE!!
HOTARU...
PLEASE RIDE ON MY BACK.
YOU CAN TALK?
THIS IS SO GREAT.
I ALWAYS WANTED TO TALK TO YOU, MR. GRUNTY...
HOTARU...
NOW!!
ALL OF YOU, PLEASE GET ON!!
WHA--?!

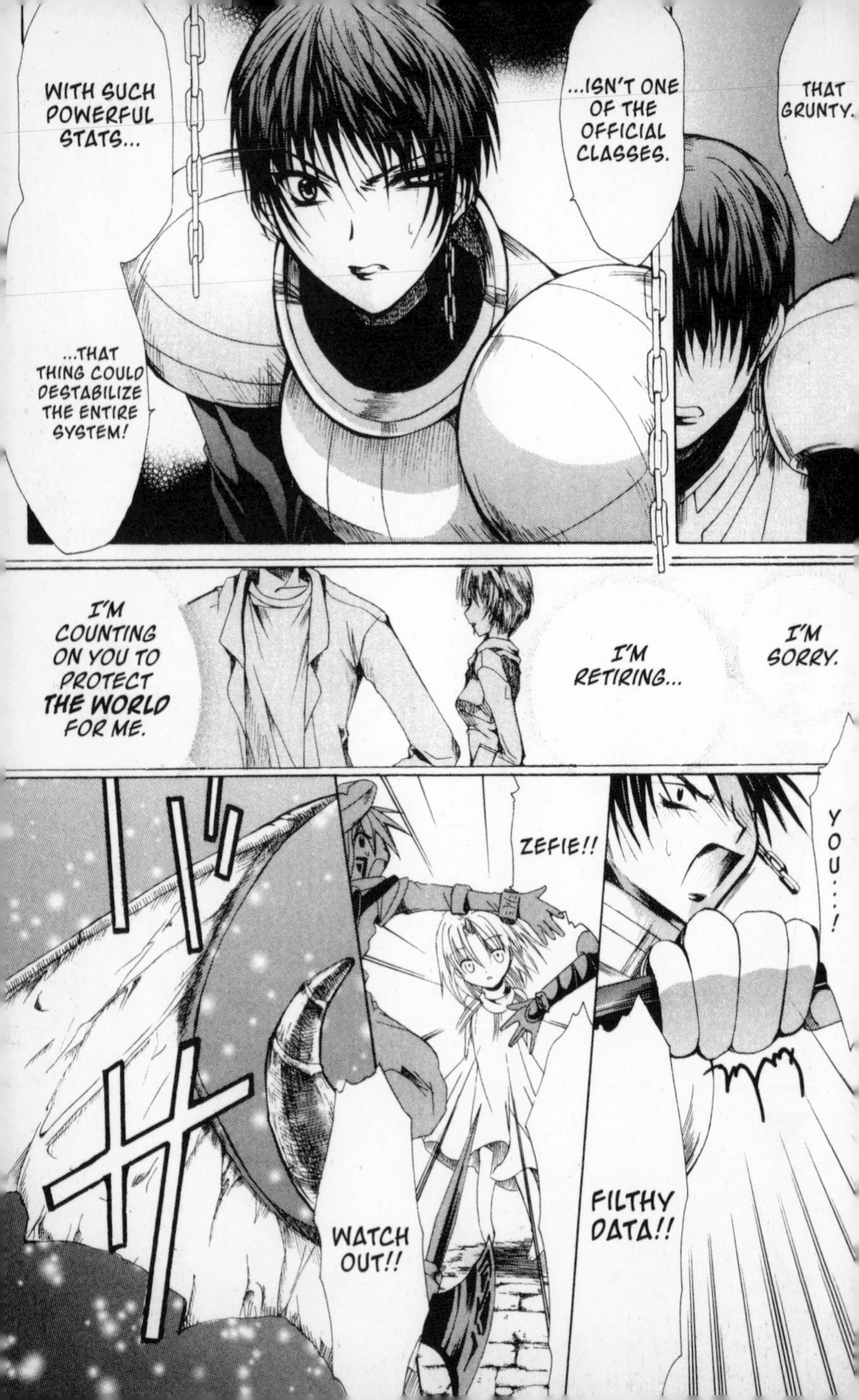
THAT GRUNTY.
...ISN'T ONE OF THE OFFICIAL CLASSES.
WITH SUCH POWERFUL STATS...
...THAT THING COULD DESTABILIZE THE ENTIRE SYSTEM!
I'M SORRY.
I'M RETIRING...
I'M COUNTING ON YOU TO PROTECT **THE WORLD** FOR ME.
YOU...!
FILTHY DATA!!
ZEFIE!!
WATCH OUT!!

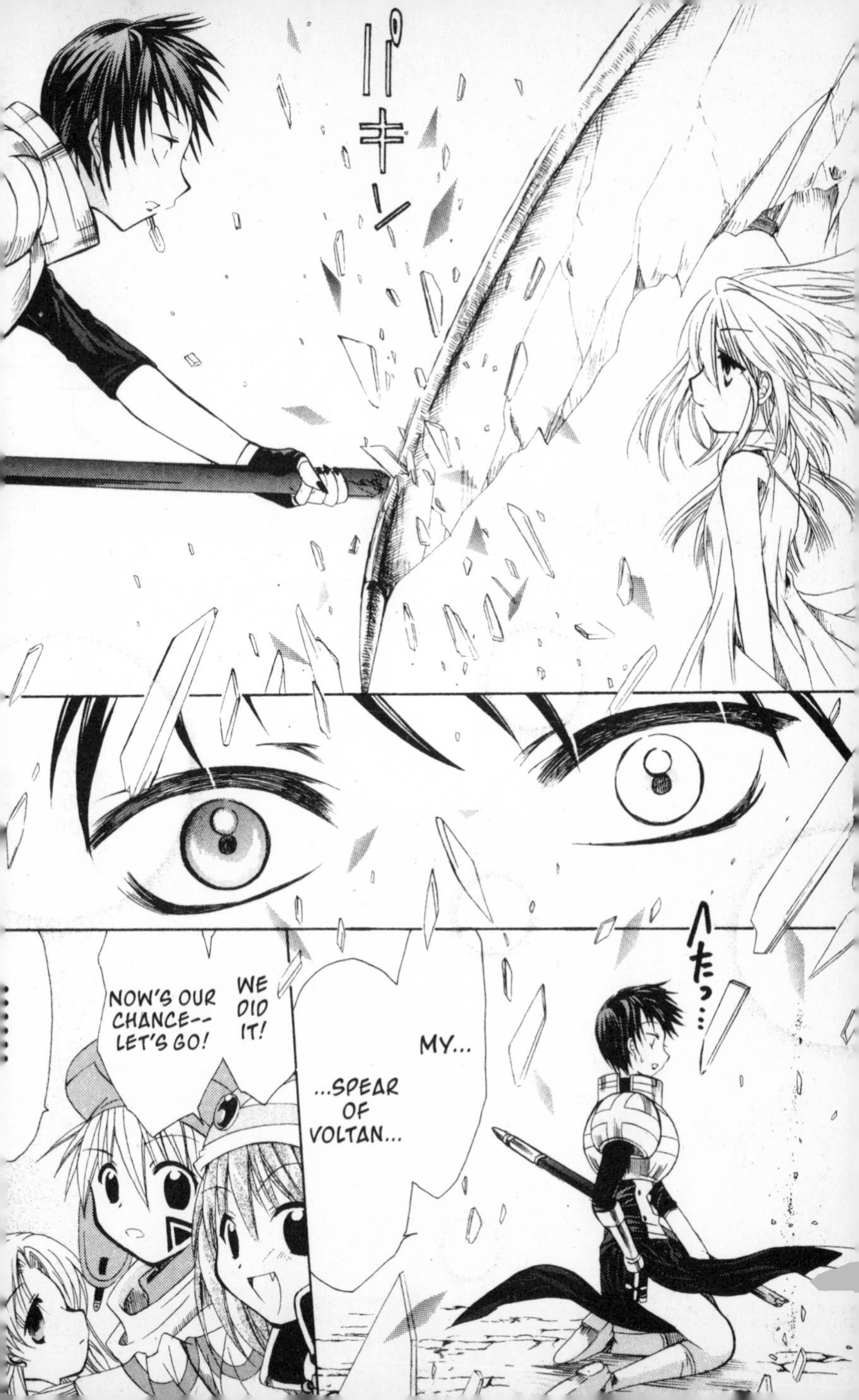
パキーン
へたっ…
MY...
...SPEAR OF VOLTAN...
WE DID IT!
NOW'S OUR CHANCE--LET'S GO!

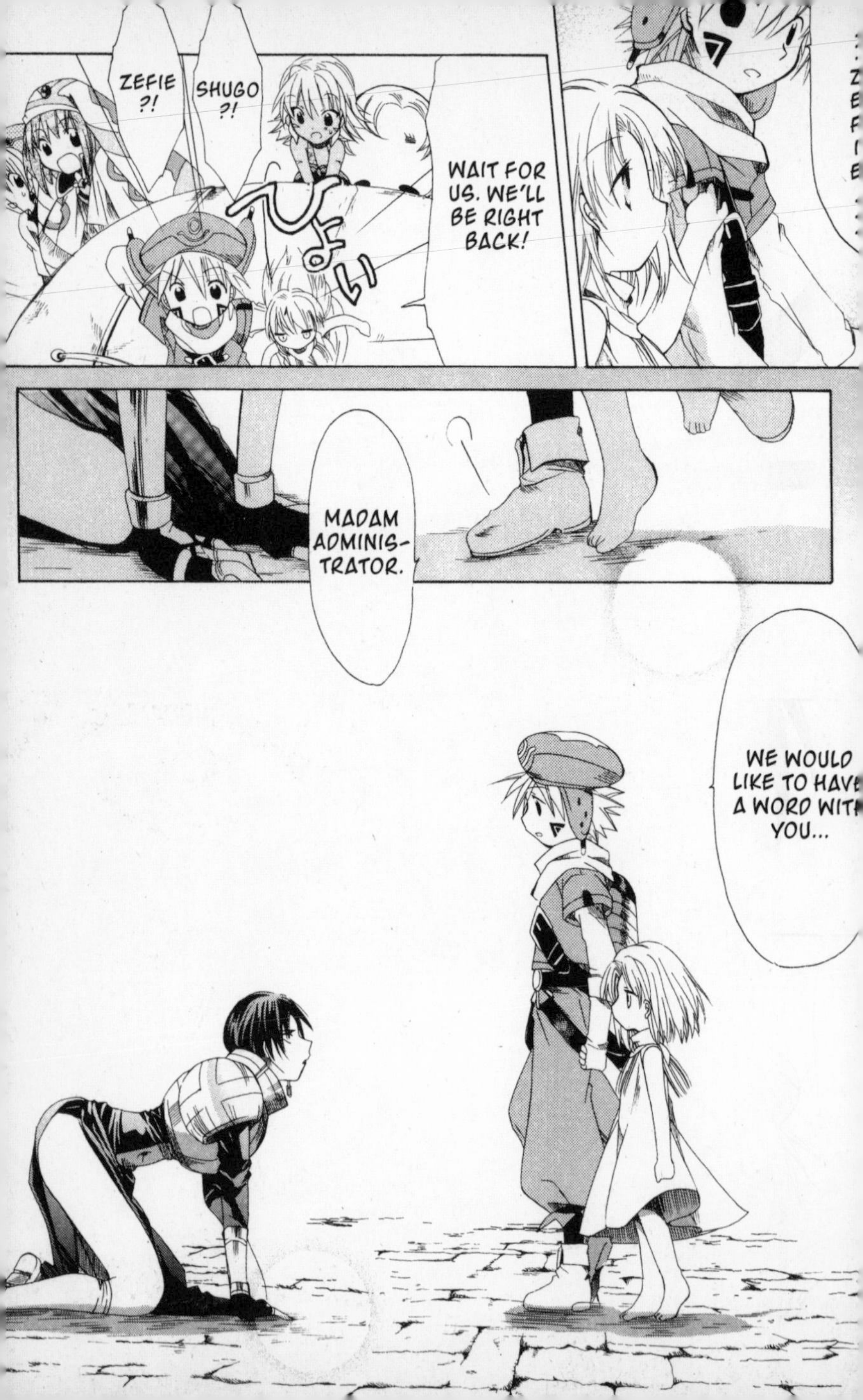
...ZEFIE...
WAIT FOR US. WE'LL BE RIGHT BACK!
SHUGO ?!
ZEFIE ?!
ひょい
MADAM ADMINIS-TRATOR.
WE WOULD LIKE TO HAVE A WORD WITH YOU...

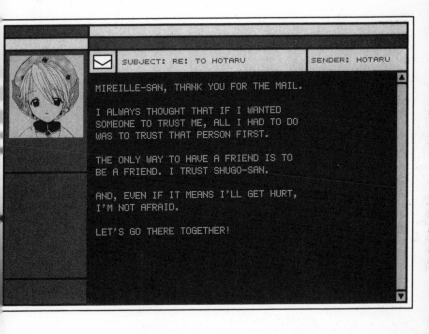

SUBJECT: RE: TO HOTARU   SENDER: HOTARU

MIREILLE-SAN, THANK YOU FOR THE MAIL.

I ALWAYS THOUGHT THAT IF I WANTED
SOMEONE TO TRUST ME, ALL I HAD TO DO
WAS TO TRUST THAT PERSON FIRST.

THE ONLY WAY TO HAVE A FRIEND IS TO
BE A FRIEND. I TRUST SHUGO-SAN.

AND, EVEN IF IT MEANS I'LL GET HURT,
I'M NOT AFRAID.

LET'S GO THERE TOGETHER!

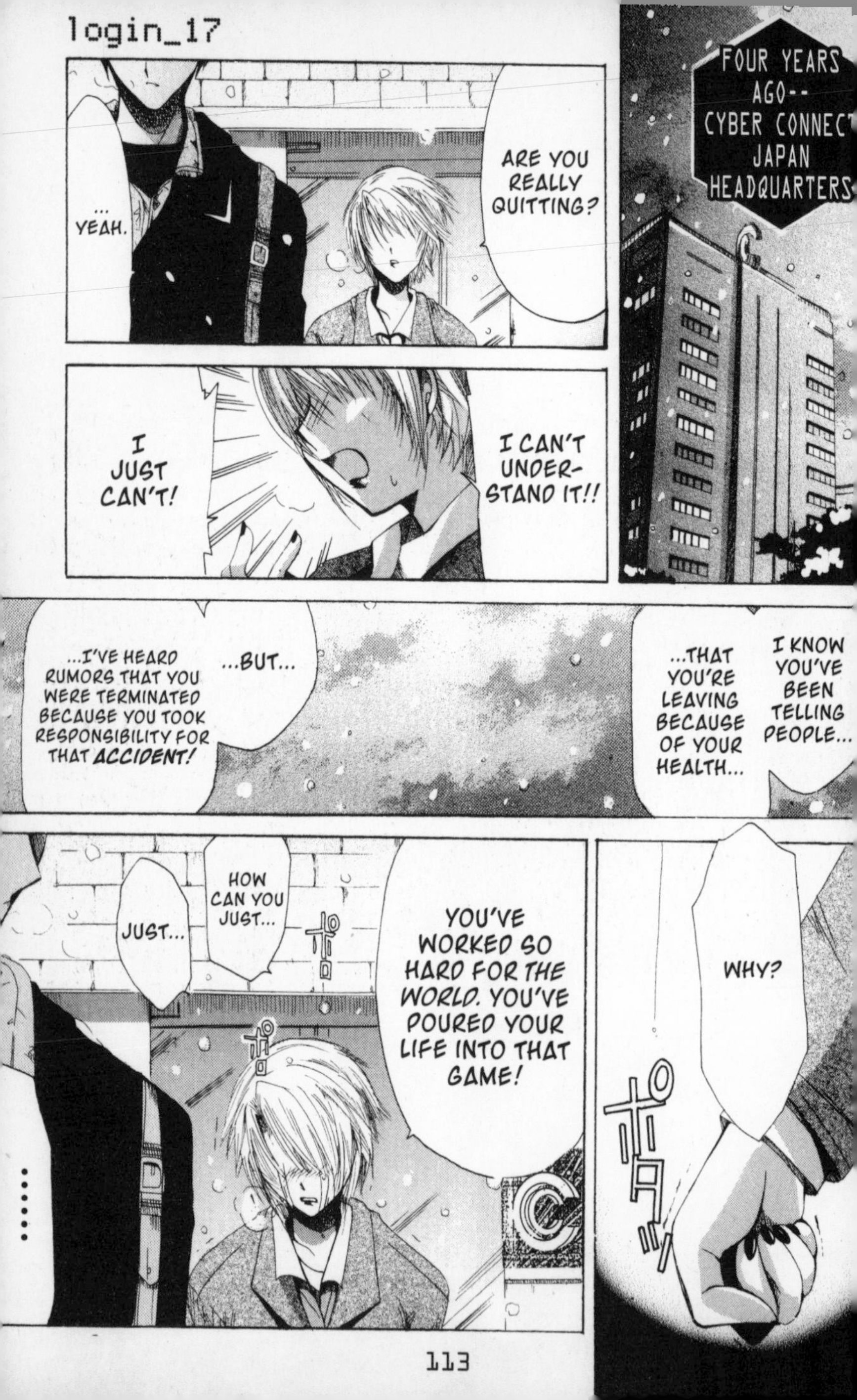
FOUR YEARS AGO-- CYBER CONNECT JAPAN HEADQUARTERS
ARE YOU REALLY QUITTING?
... YEAH.
I CAN'T UNDER-STAND IT!!
I JUST CAN'T!
I KNOW YOU'VE BEEN TELLING PEOPLE...
...THAT YOU'RE LEAVING BECAUSE OF YOUR HEALTH...
...BUT...
...I'VE HEARD RUMORS THAT YOU WERE TERMINATED BECAUSE YOU TOOK RESPONSIBILITY FOR THAT ACCIDENT!
WHY?
YOU'VE WORKED SO HARD FOR THE WORLD. YOU'VE POURED YOUR LIFE INTO THAT GAME!
HOW CAN YOU JUST...
JUST...
......

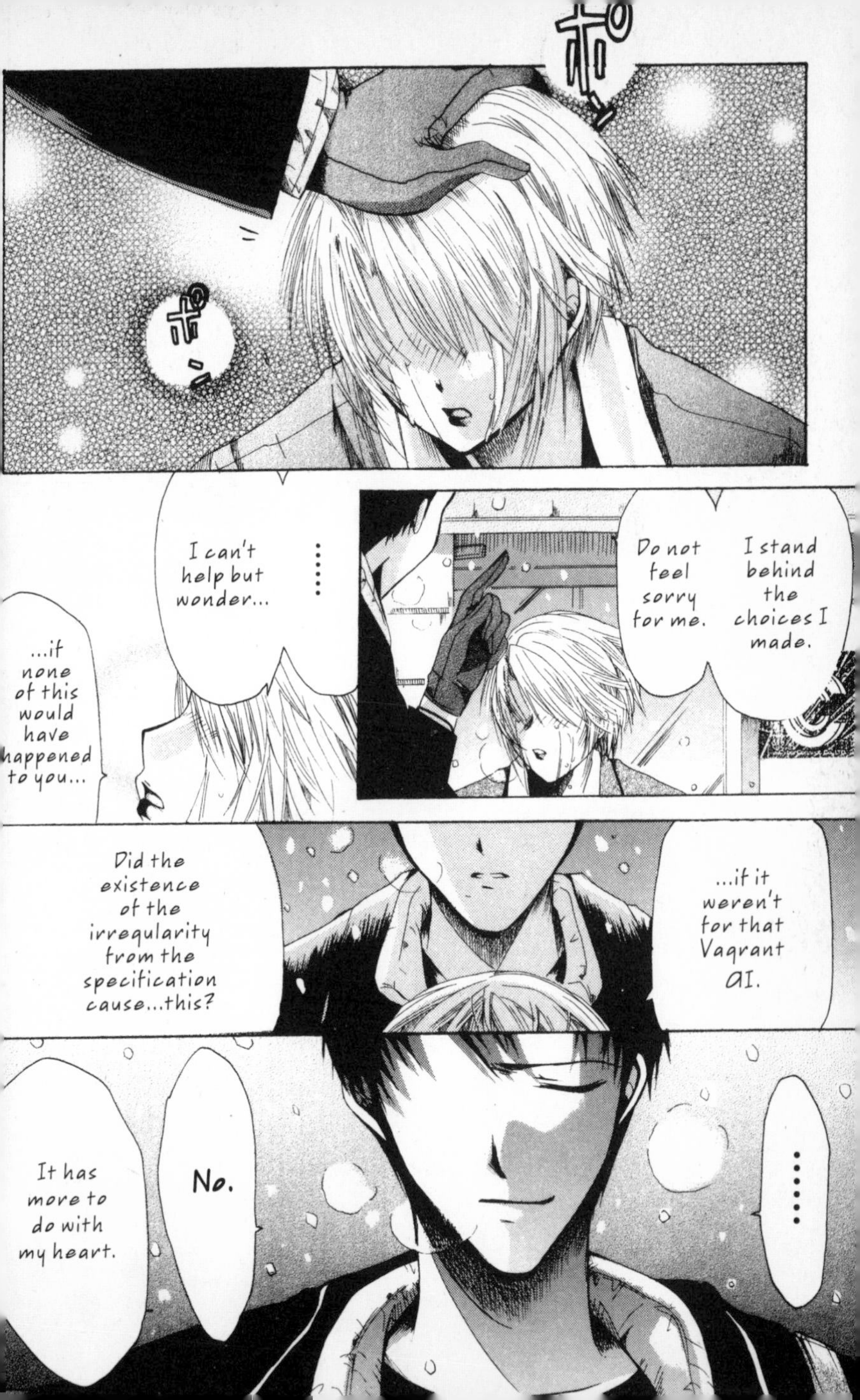
I stand behind the choices I made.
Do not feel sorry for me.
......
I can't help but wonder...
...if none of this would have happened to you...
...if it weren't for that Vagrant AI.
Did the existence of the irregularity from the specification cause...this?
......
No.
It has more to do with my heart.

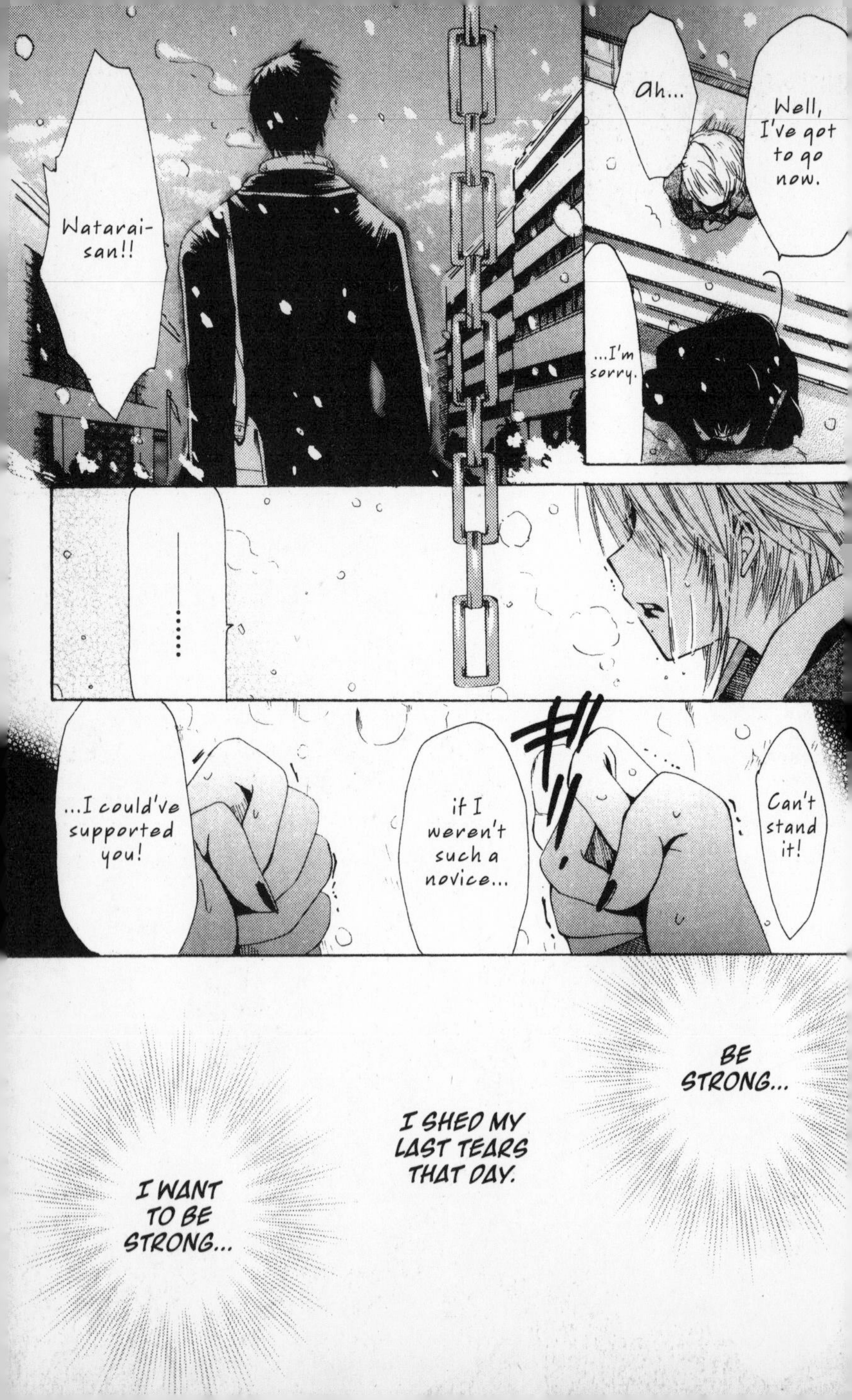
Well, I've got to go now.
Ah...
...I'm sorry.
Watarai-san!!
......
Can't stand it!
if I weren't such a novice...
...I could've supported you!
BE STRONG...
I SHED MY LAST TEARS THAT DAY.
I WANT TO BE STRONG...

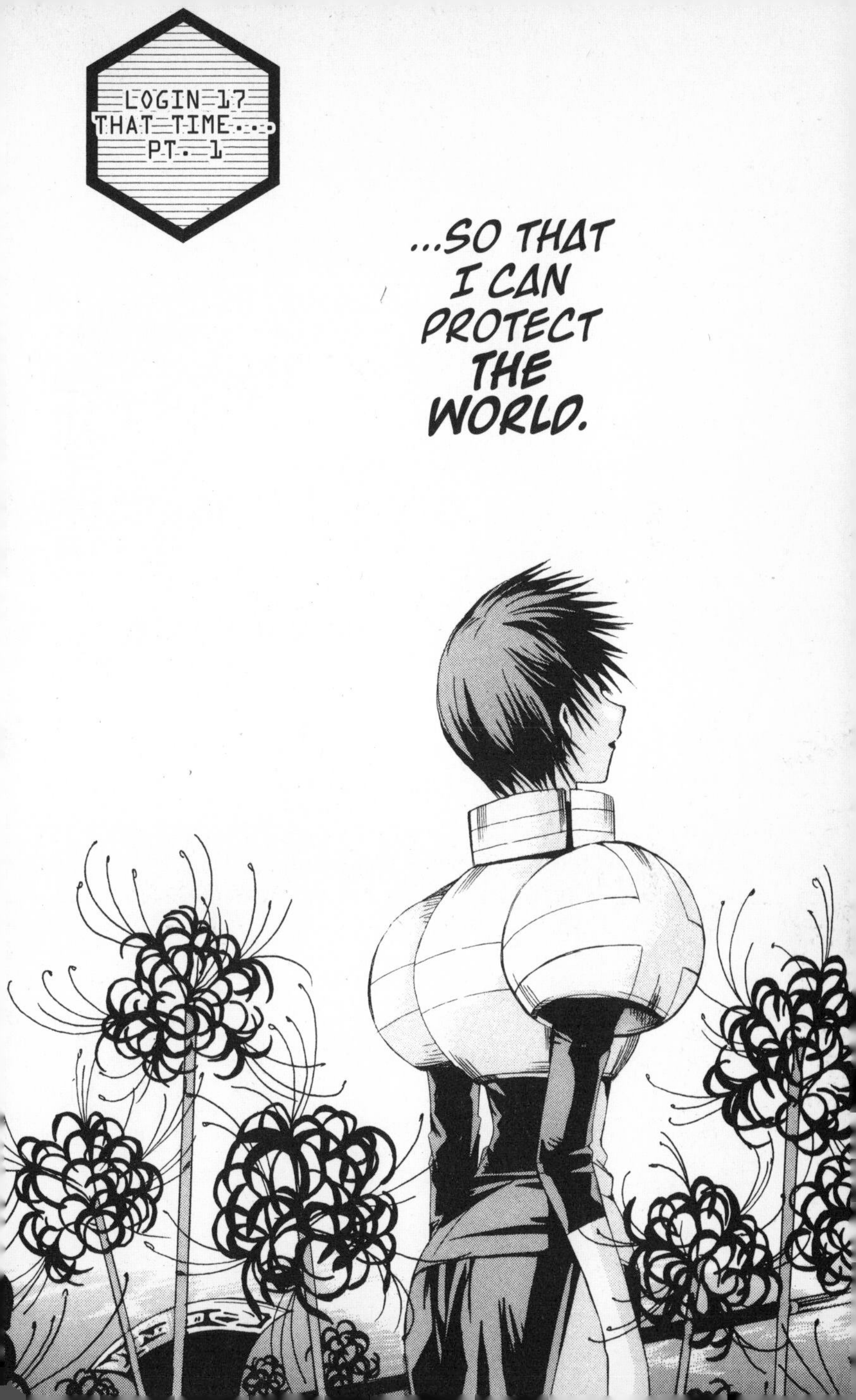
LOGIN 17
THAT TIME...
PT. 1
...SO THAT I CAN PROTECT THE WORLD.

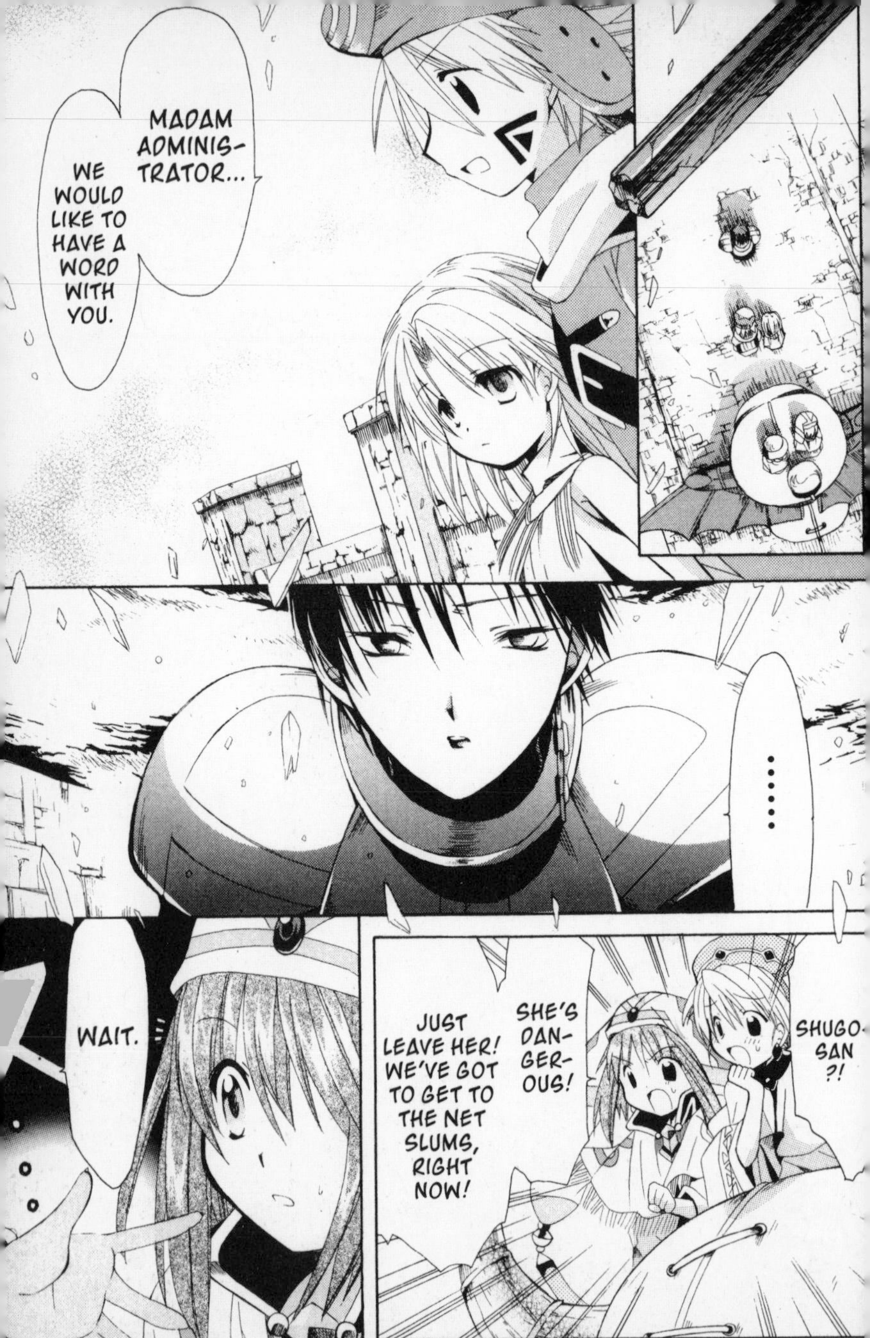
MADAM ADMINISTRATOR... WE WOULD LIKE TO HAVE A WORD WITH YOU.
......
SHUGO-SAN?!
SHE'S DANGEROUS!
JUST LEAVE HER! WE'VE GOT TO GET TO THE NET SLUMS, RIGHT NOW!
WAIT.

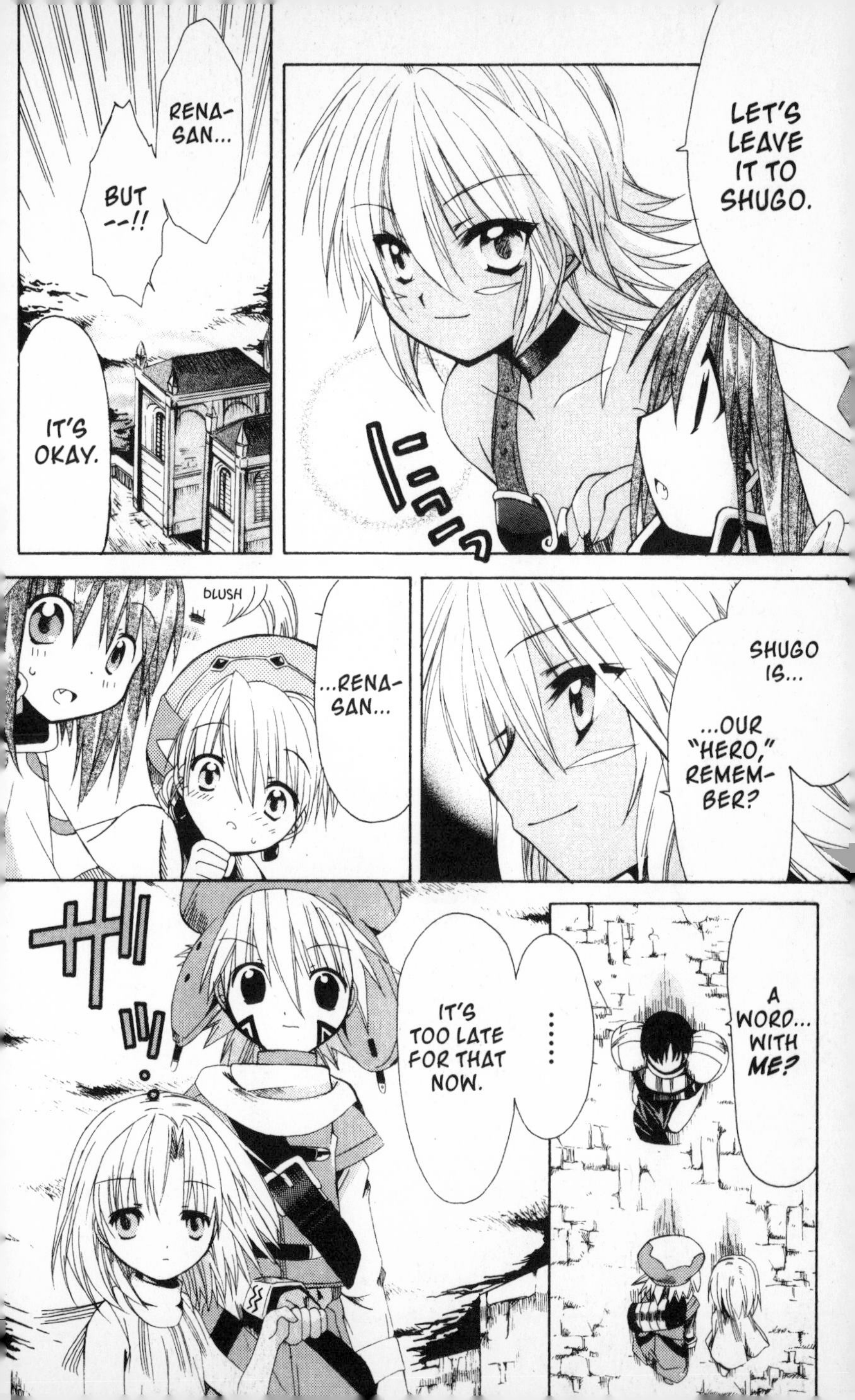
LET'S LEAVE IT TO SHUGO.
RENA-SAN...
BUT --!!
IT'S OKAY.
SHUGO IS...
...OUR "HERO," REMEMBER?
...RENA-SAN...
BLUSH
A WORD... WITH *ME*?
......
IT'S TOO LATE FOR THAT NOW.

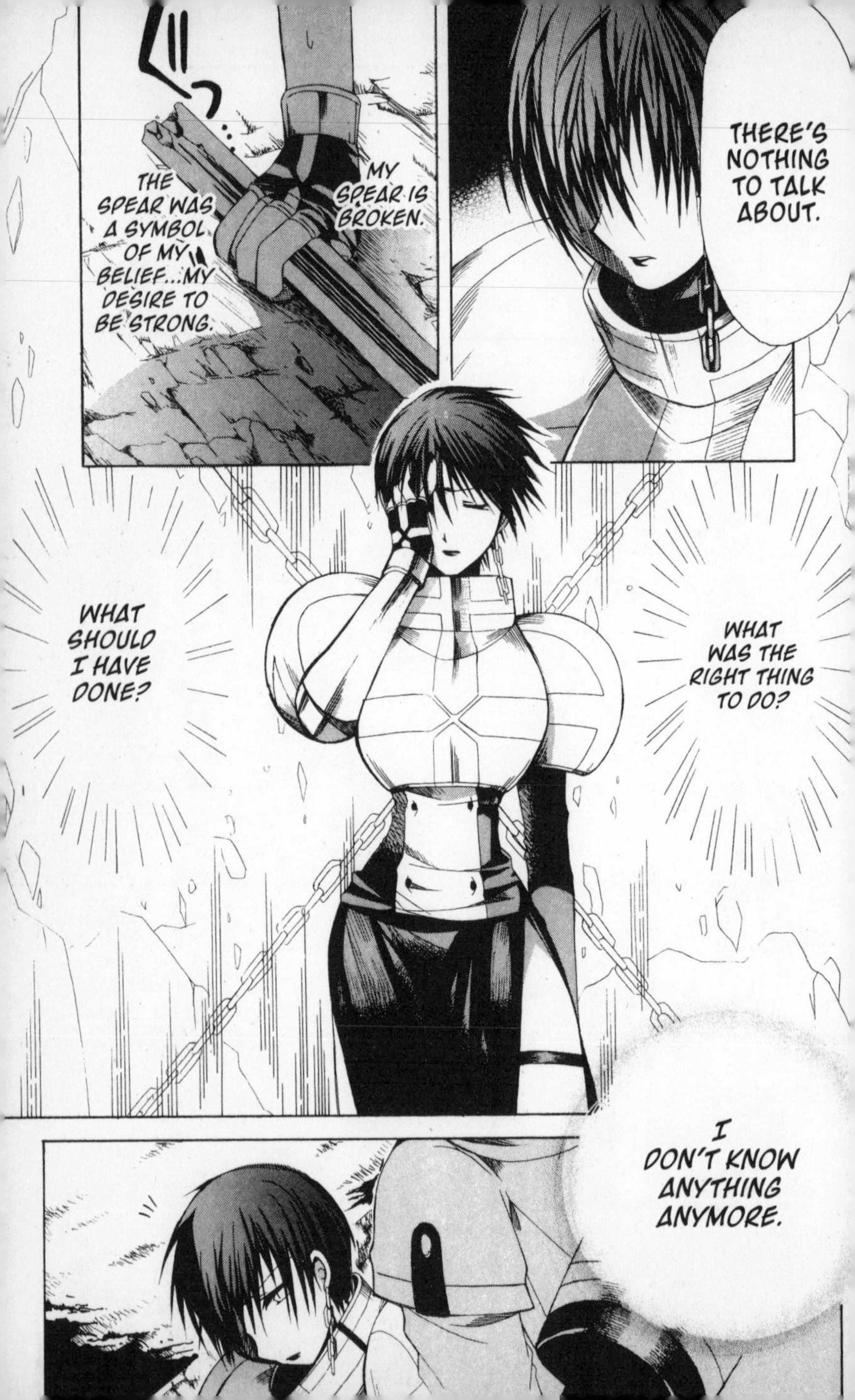
THERE'S NOTHING TO TALK ABOUT.
MY SPEAR IS BROKEN.
THE SPEAR WAS A SYMBOL OF MY BELIEF...MY DESIRE TO BE STRONG.
WHAT WAS THE RIGHT THING TO DO?
WHAT SHOULD I HAVE DONE?
I DON'T KNOW ANYTHING ANYMORE.

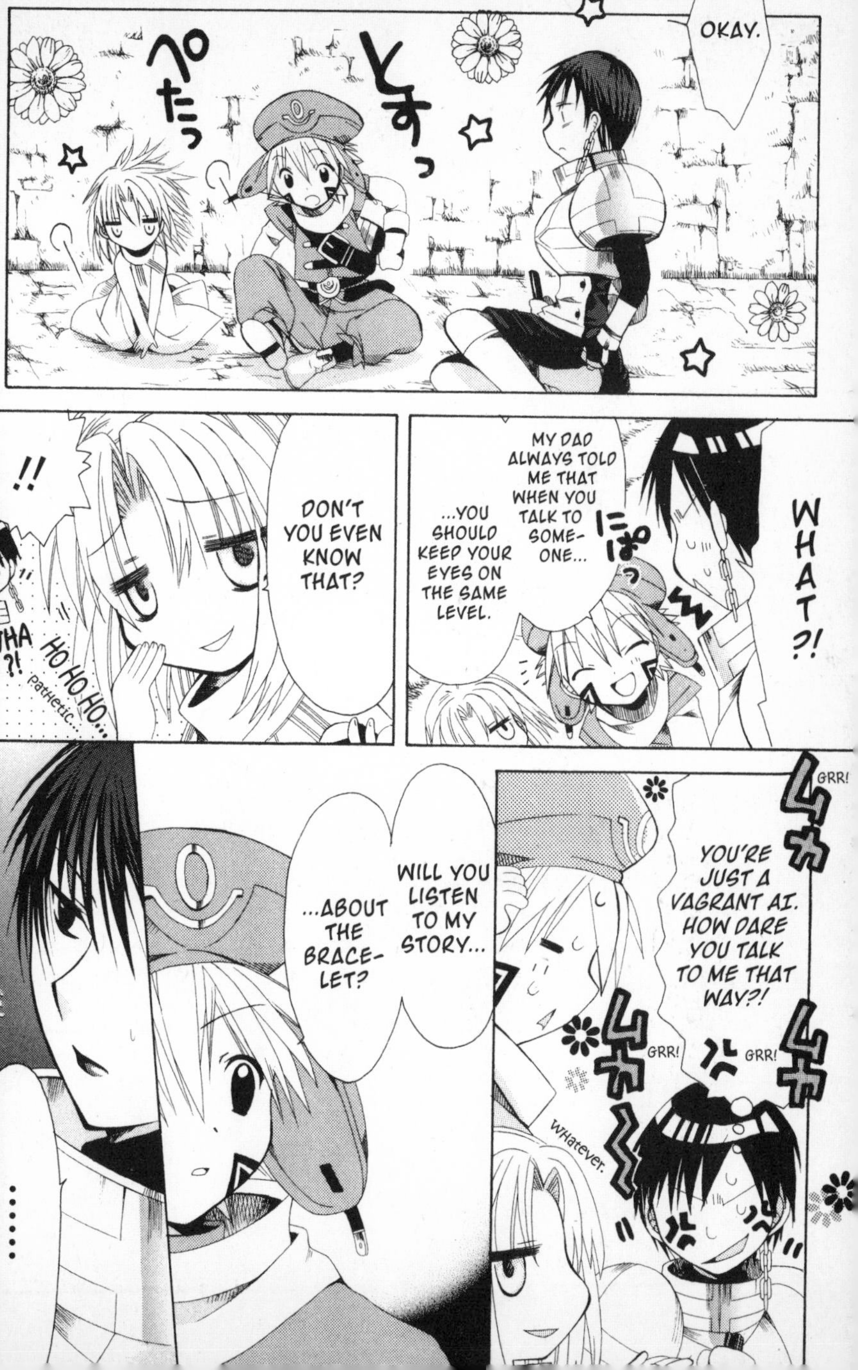
OKAY.
とすっ
ぺたっ
WHAT?!
にぱっ
MY DAD ALWAYS TOLD ME THAT WHEN YOU TALK TO SOME-ONE...
...YOU SHOULD KEEP YOUR EYES ON THE SAME LEVEL.
DON'T YOU EVEN KNOW THAT?
!!
WHA ?!
HO HO HO...
pathetic...
ムカ
GRR!
YOU'RE JUST A VAGRANT AI. HOW DARE YOU TALK TO ME THAT WAY?!
ムカ
GRR!
ムカ
GRR!
Whatever.
WILL YOU LISTEN TO MY STORY...
...ABOUT THE BRACE-LET?
......

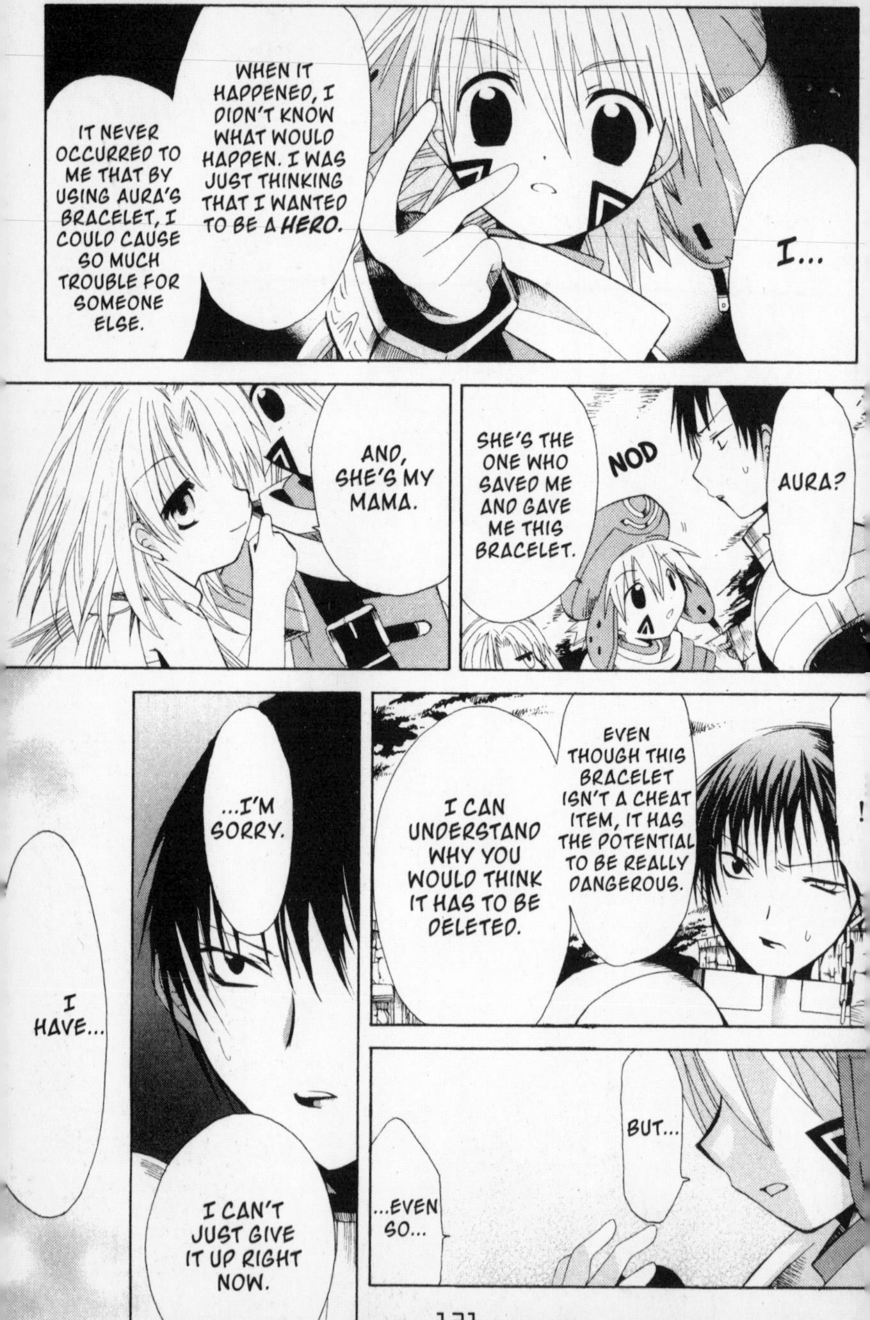
I...
WHEN IT HAPPENED, I DIDN'T KNOW WHAT WOULD HAPPEN. I WAS JUST THINKING THAT I WANTED TO BE A **HERO**.
IT NEVER OCCURRED TO ME THAT BY USING AURA'S BRACELET, I COULD CAUSE SO MUCH TROUBLE FOR SOMEONE ELSE.
AURA?
NOD
SHE'S THE ONE WHO SAVED ME AND GAVE ME THIS BRACELET.
AND, SHE'S MY MAMA.
!
EVEN THOUGH THIS BRACELET ISN'T A CHEAT ITEM, IT HAS THE POTENTIAL TO BE REALLY DANGEROUS.
I CAN UNDERSTAND WHY YOU WOULD THINK IT HAS TO BE DELETED.
BUT...
...EVEN SO...
...I'M SORRY.
I HAVE...
I CAN'T JUST GIVE IT UP RIGHT NOW.

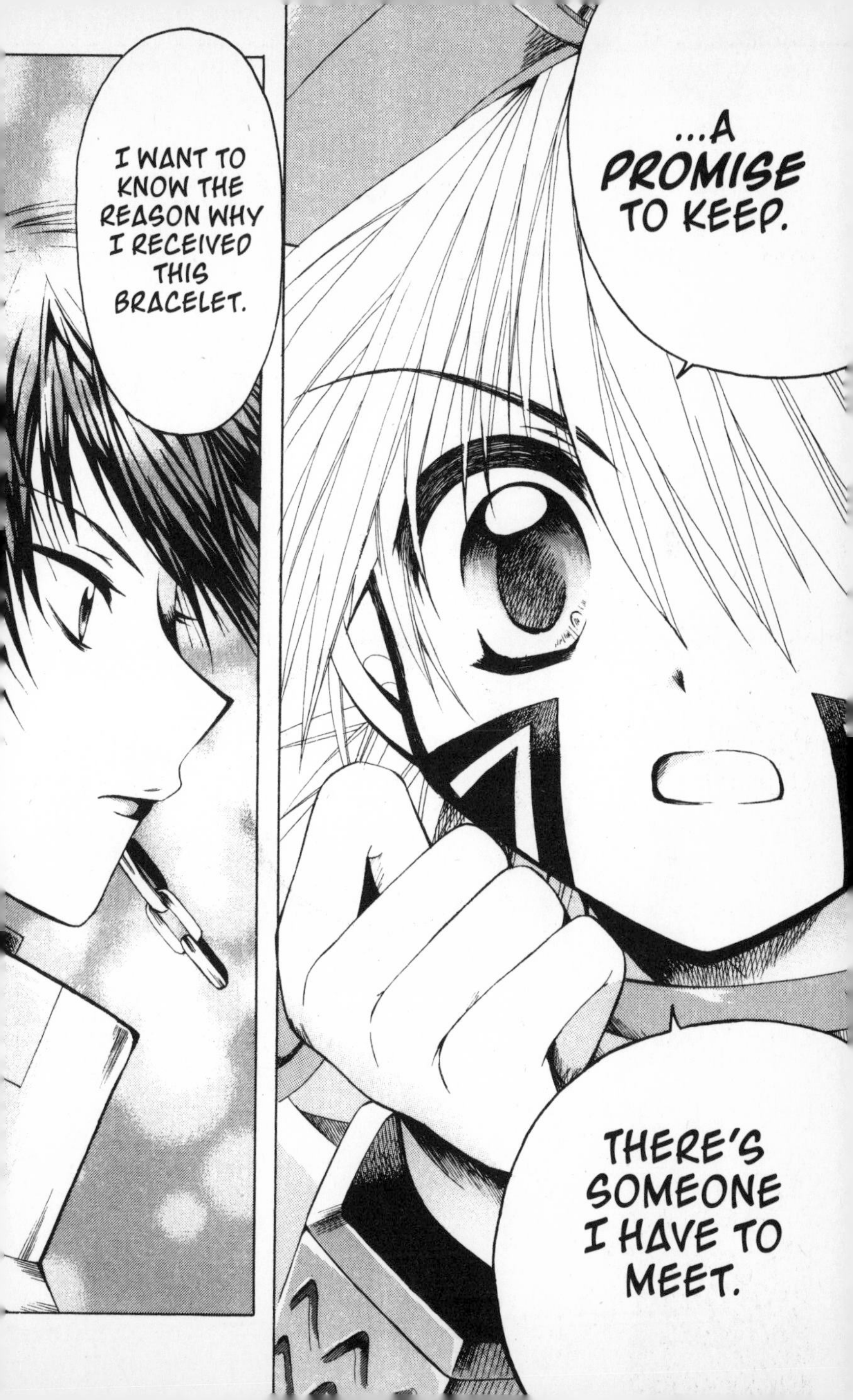
...A PROMISE TO KEEP.
THERE'S SOMEONE I HAVE TO MEET.
I WANT TO KNOW THE REASON WHY I RECEIVED THIS BRACELET.

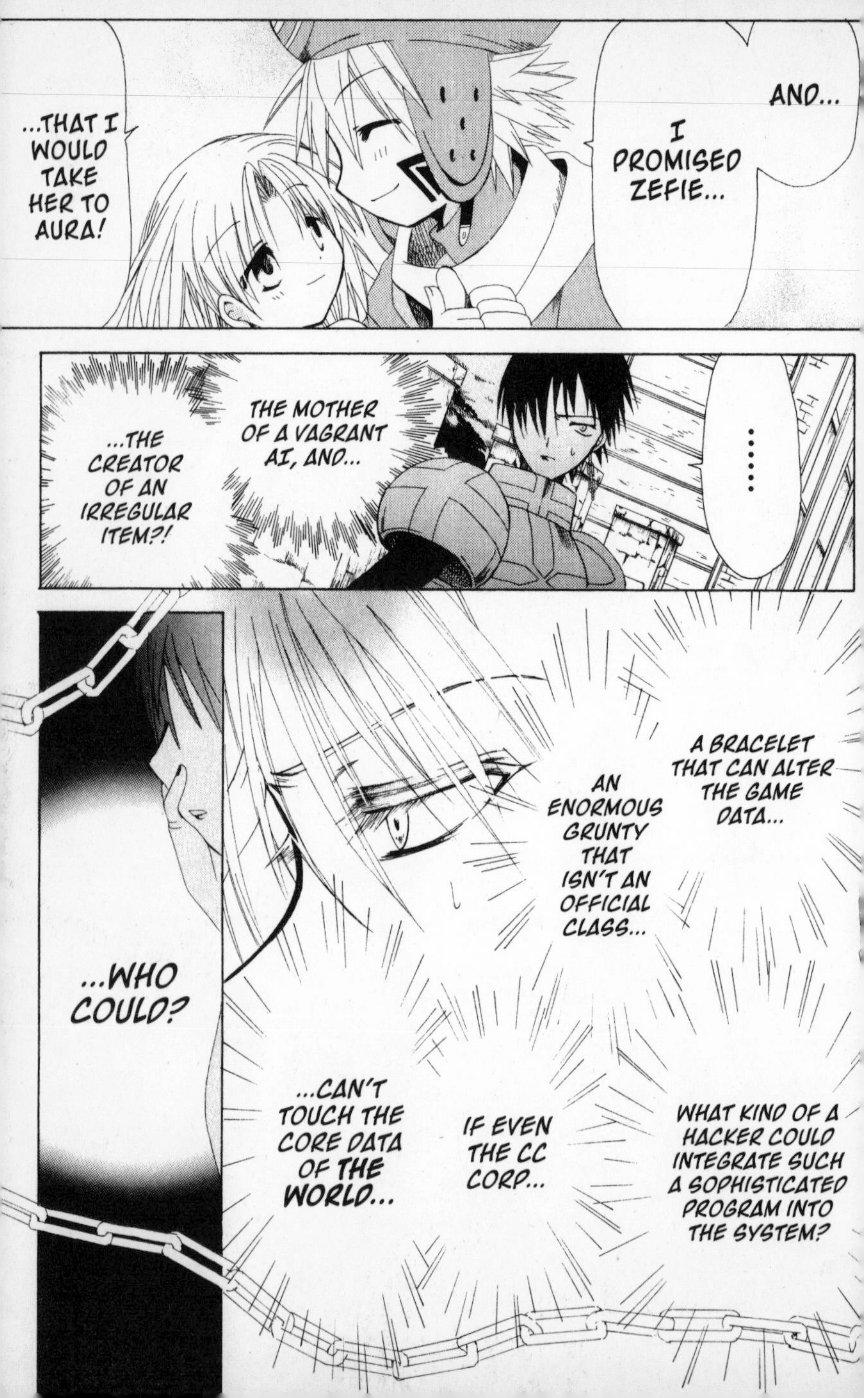
AND... I PROMISED ZEFIE...
...THAT I WOULD TAKE HER TO AURA!
......
THE MOTHER OF A VAGRANT AI, AND...
...THE CREATOR OF AN IRREGULAR ITEM?!
A BRACELET THAT CAN ALTER THE GAME DATA...
AN ENORMOUS GRUNTY THAT ISN'T AN OFFICIAL CLASS...
WHAT KIND OF A HACKER COULD INTEGRATE SUCH A SOPHISTICATED PROGRAM INTO THE SYSTEM?
IF EVEN THE CC CORP...
...CAN'T TOUCH THE CORE DATA OF THE WORLD...
...WHO COULD?

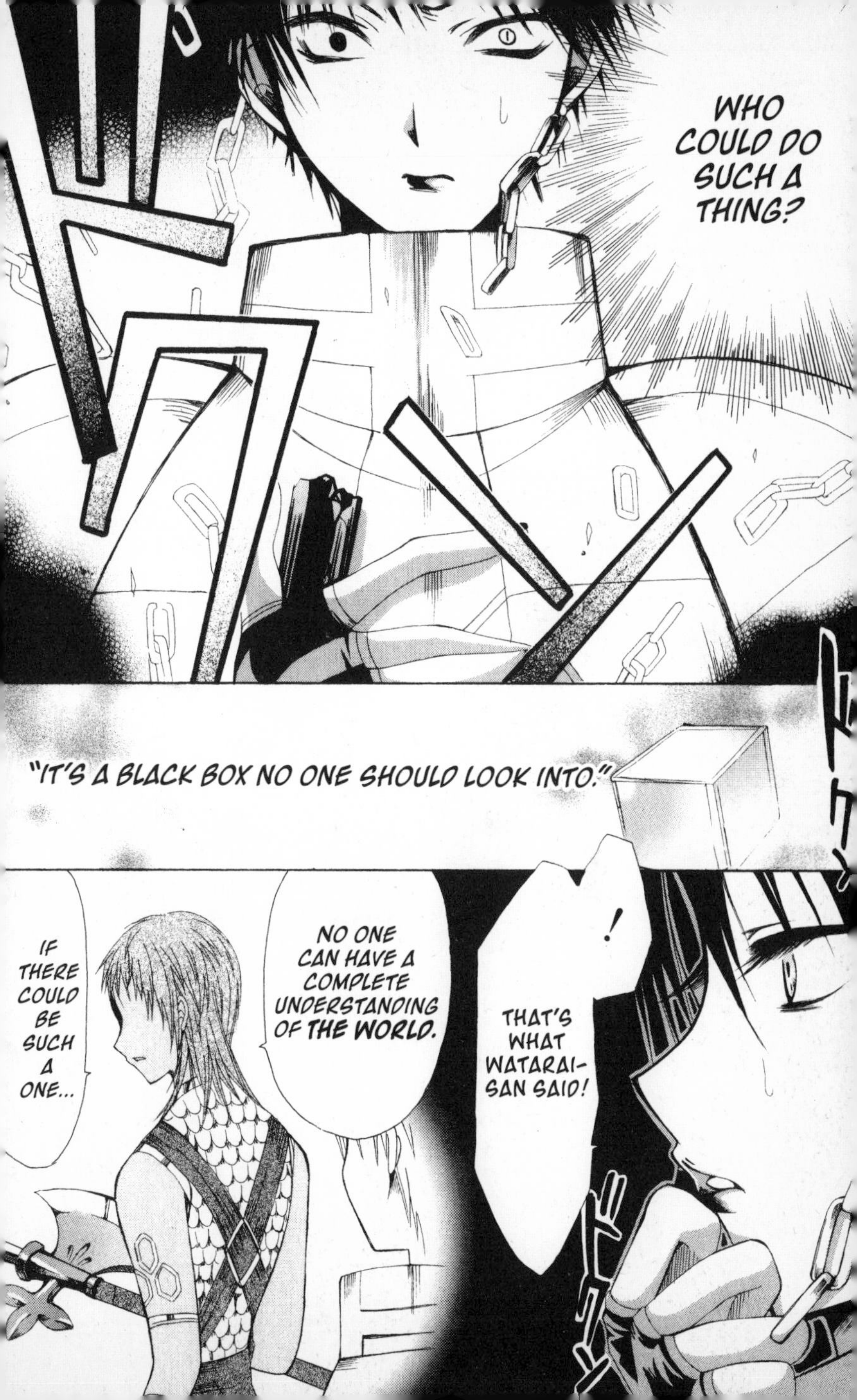
WHO COULD DO SUCH A THING?
"IT'S A BLACK BOX NO ONE SHOULD LOOK INTO."
!
THAT'S WHAT WATARAI-SAN SAID!
NO ONE CAN HAVE A COMPLETE UNDERSTANDING OF **THE WORLD.**
IF THERE COULD BE SUCH A ONE...

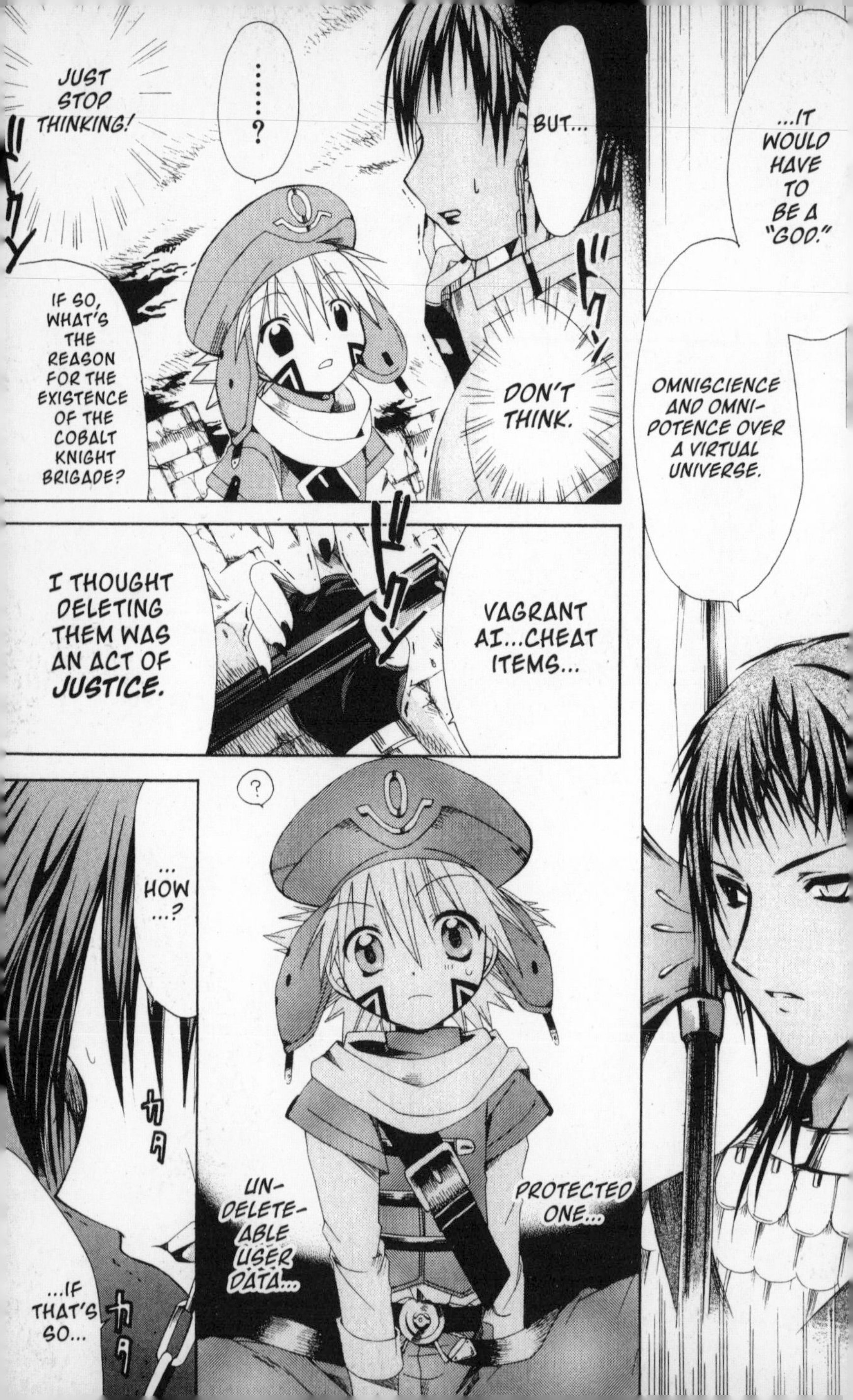
...IT WOULD HAVE TO BE A "GOD."
OMNISCIENCE AND OMNI-POTENCE OVER A VIRTUAL UNIVERSE.
BUT...
.....?
JUST STOP THINKING!
DON'T THINK.
IF SO, WHAT'S THE REASON FOR THE EXISTENCE OF THE COBALT KNIGHT BRIGADE?
VAGRANT AI...CHEAT ITEMS...
I THOUGHT DELETING THEM WAS AN ACT OF JUSTICE.
?
PROTECTED ONE...
UN-DELETE-ABLE USER DATA...
...HOW...?
...IF THAT'S SO...

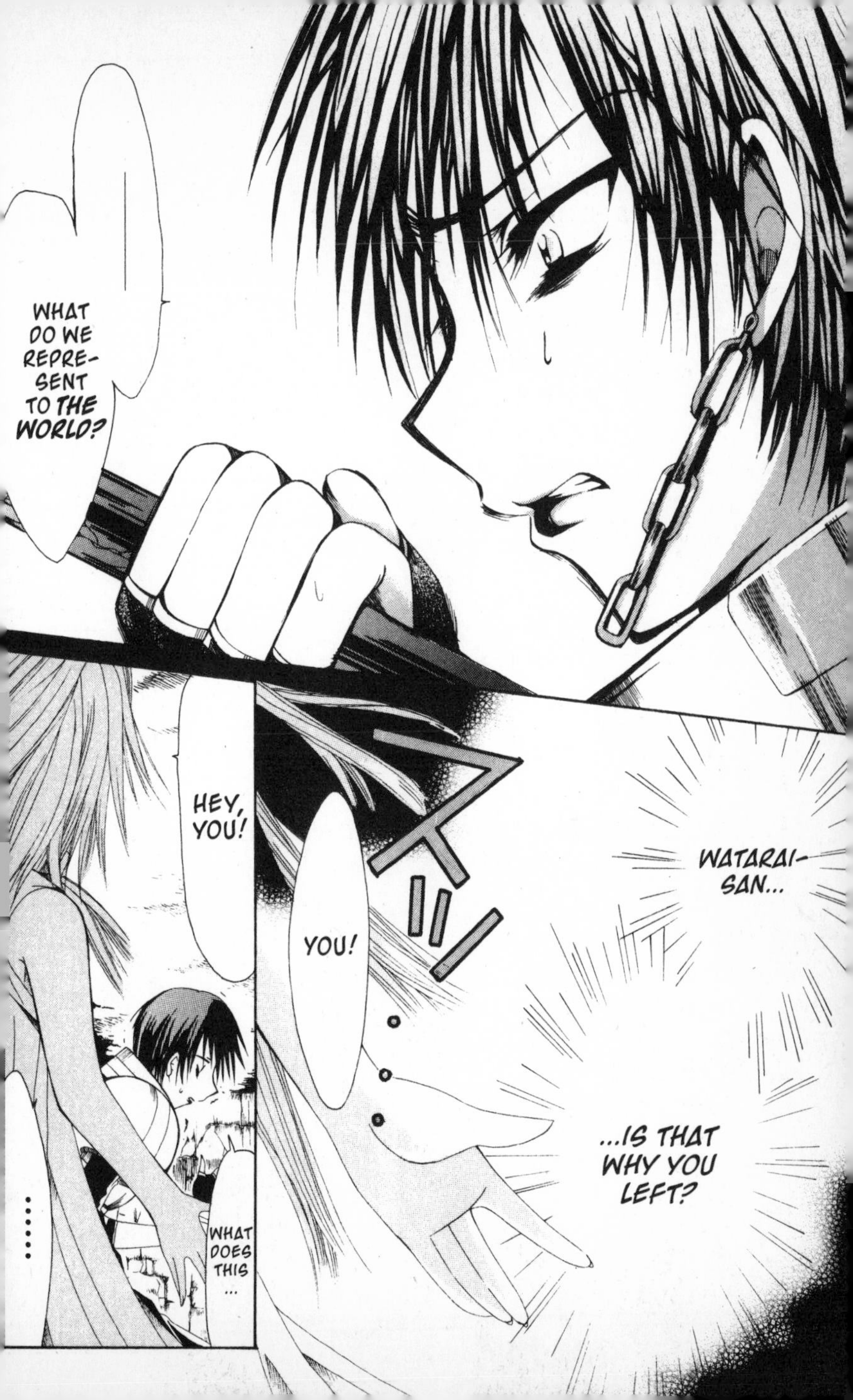
WHAT DO WE REPRESENT TO THE WORLD?
WATARAI-SAN...
YOU!
...IS THAT WHY YOU LEFT?
HEY, YOU!
WHAT DOES THIS ...
......

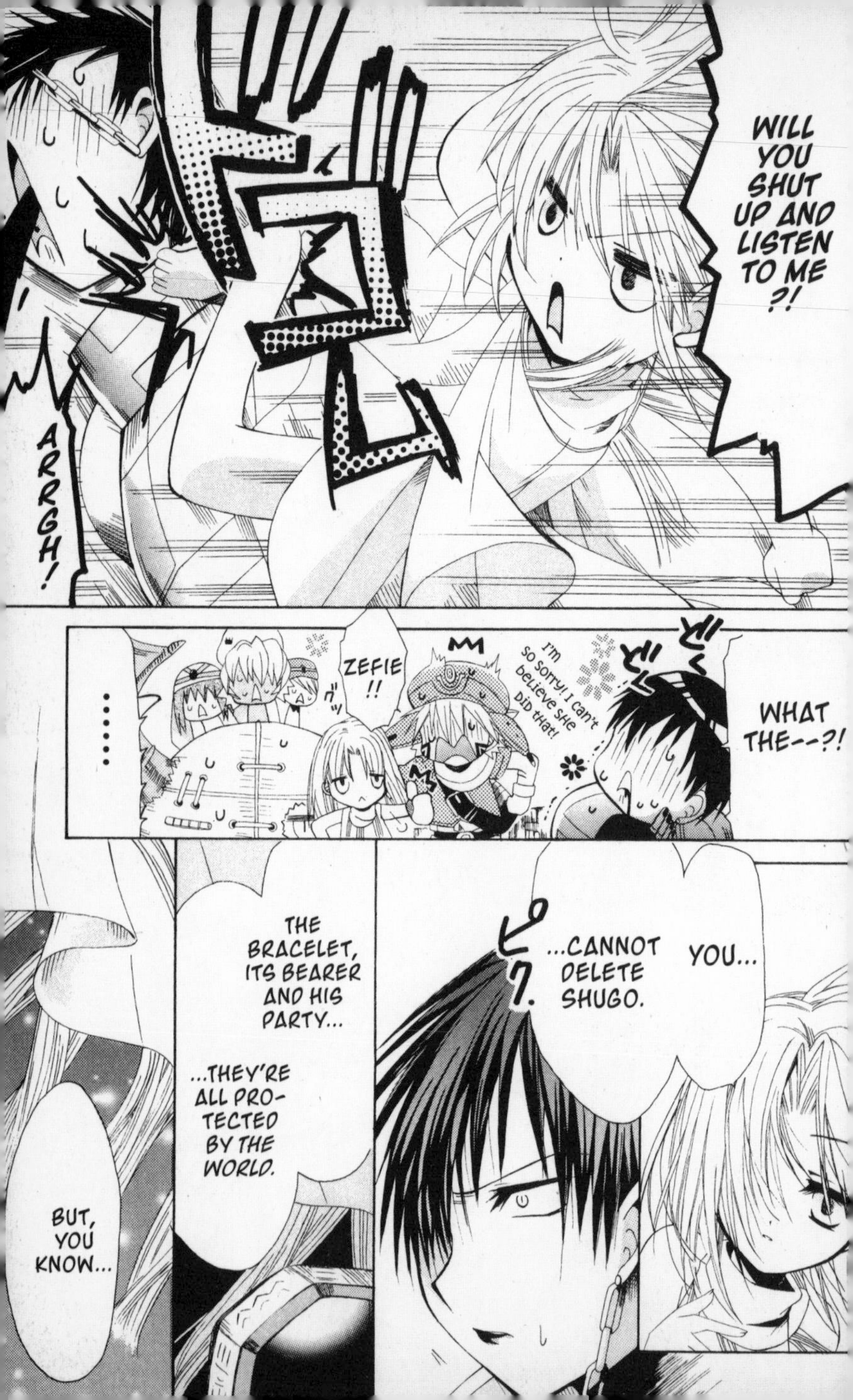
WILL YOU SHUT UP AND LISTEN TO ME?!
ARRGH!
WHAT THE--?!
I'm so sorry! I can't believe she did that!
ZEFIE!!
......
YOU...
...CANNOT DELETE SHUGO.
THE BRACELET, ITS BEARER AND HIS PARTY...
...THEY'RE ALL PROTECTED BY THE WORLD.
BUT, YOU KNOW...

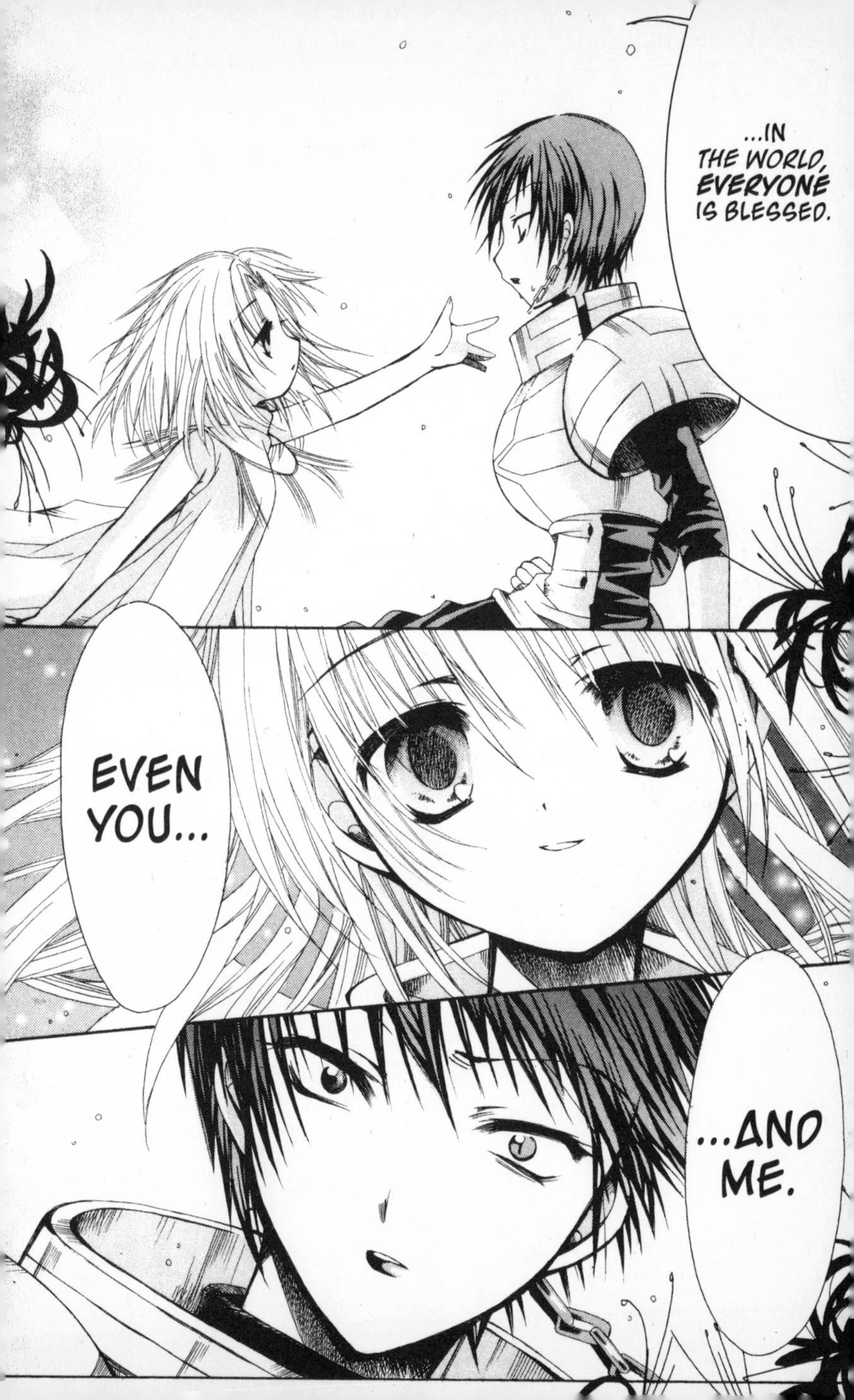
...IN THE WORLD, EVERYONE IS BLESSED.
EVEN YOU...
...AND ME.

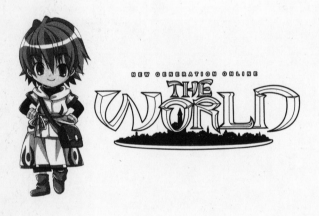

NEW GENERATION ONLINE

THE WORLD

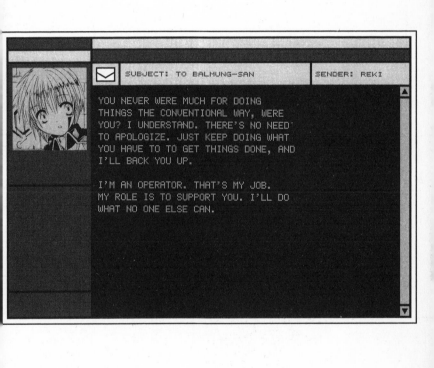

SUBJECT: TO BALMUNG-SAN   SENDER: REKI

YOU NEVER WERE MUCH FOR DOING
THINGS THE CONVENTIONAL WAY, WERE
YOU? I UNDERSTAND. THERE'S NO NEED
TO APOLOGIZE. JUST KEEP DOING WHAT
YOU HAVE TO TO GET THINGS DONE, AND
I'LL BACK YOU UP.

I'M AN OPERATOR. THAT'S MY JOB.
MY ROLE IS TO SUPPORT YOU. I'LL DO
WHAT NO ONE ELSE CAN.

login_18

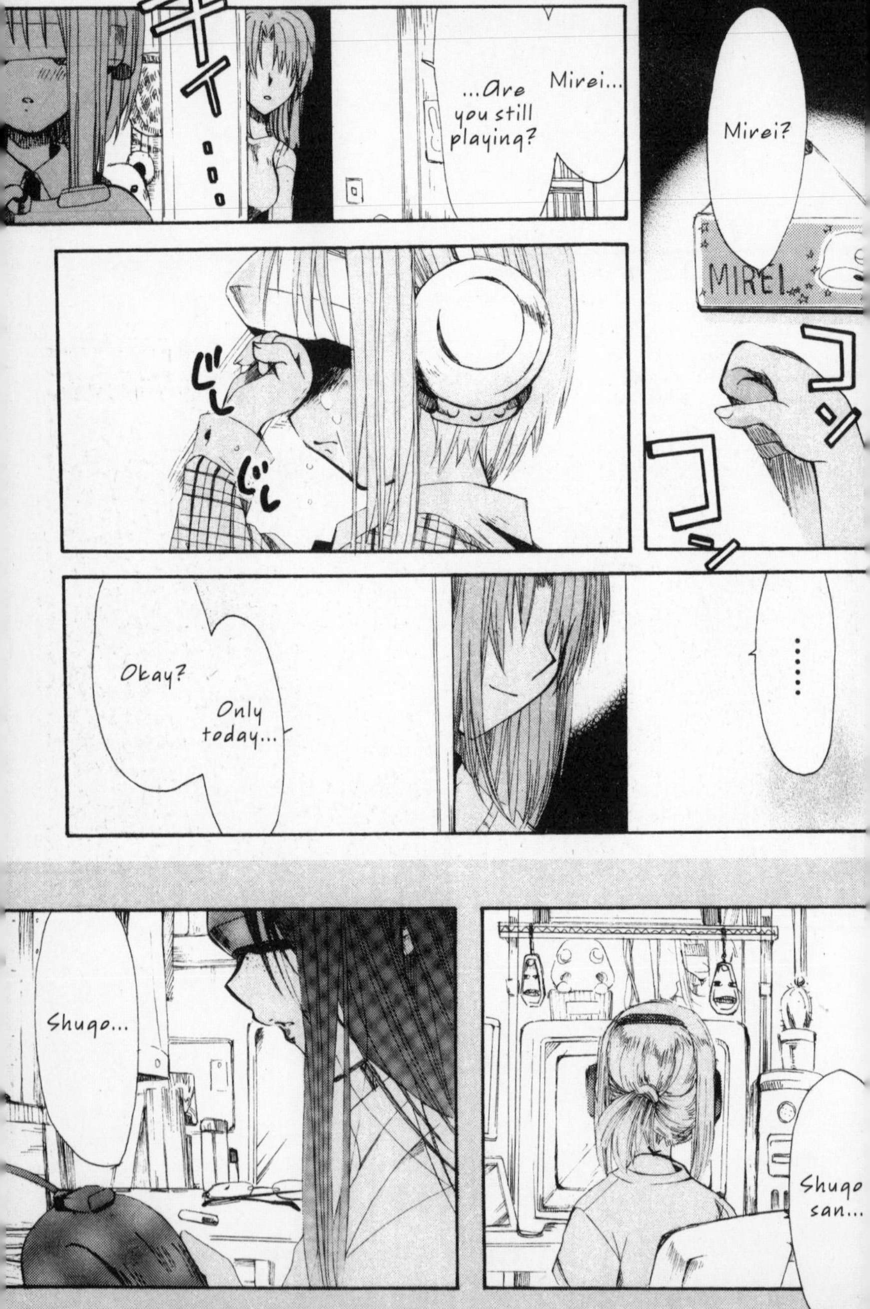
Mirei?
MIREI
コンッ
コンッ
Mirei...
...Are you still playing?
キィ…
じし
じし
……
Only today...
Okay?
Shugo san...
Shugo...

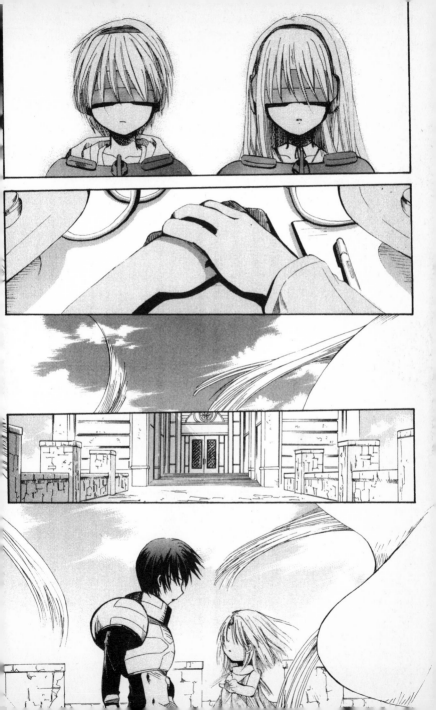

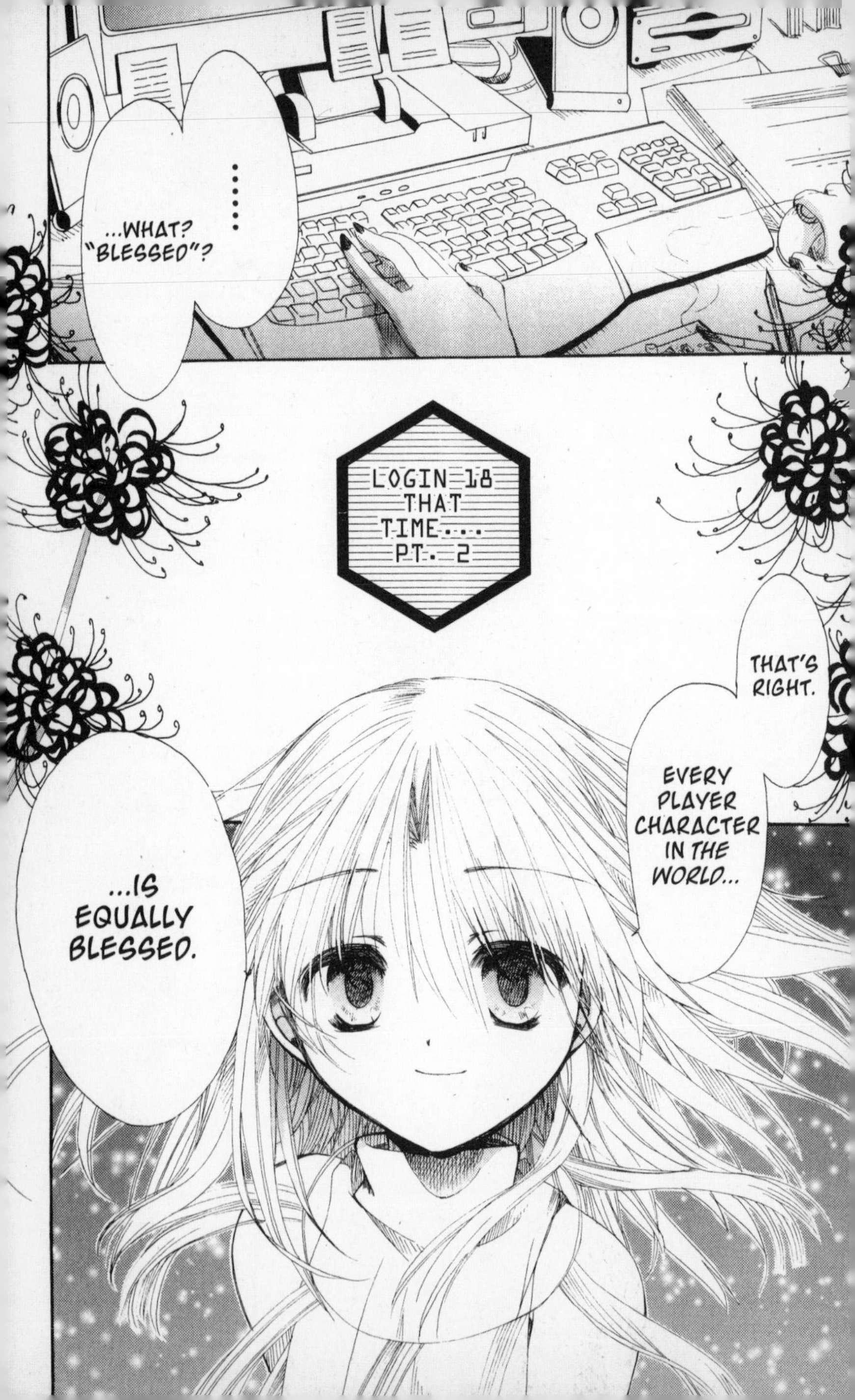
......
...WHAT? "BLESSED"?
LOGIN 18 THAT TIME.... PT. 2
THAT'S RIGHT.
EVERY PLAYER CHARACTER IN THE WORLD...
...IS EQUALLY BLESSED.

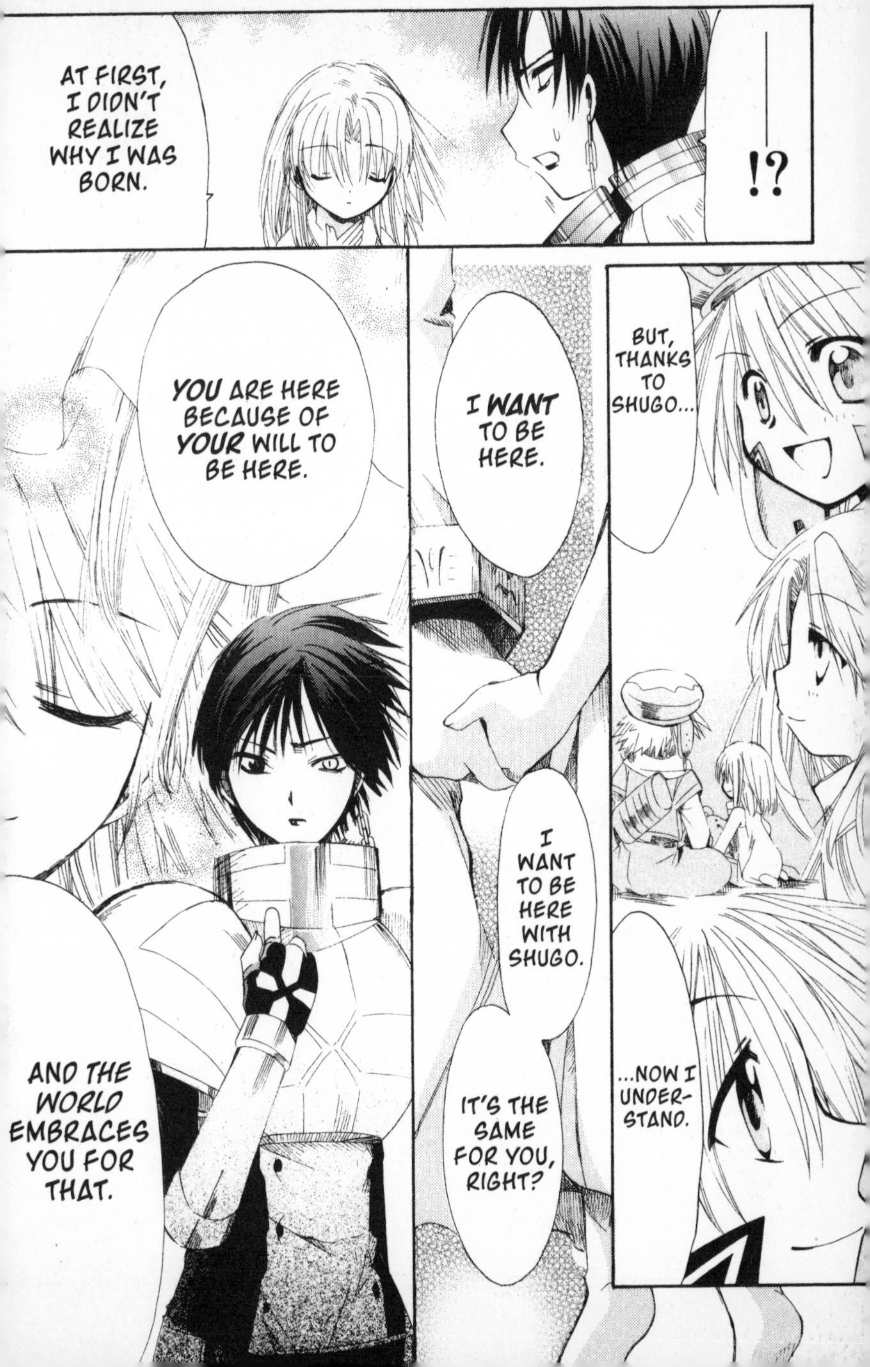
—!?
AT FIRST, I DIDN'T REALIZE WHY I WAS BORN.
BUT, THANKS TO SHUGO...
...NOW I UNDERSTAND.
I WANT TO BE HERE.
I WANT TO BE HERE WITH SHUGO.
IT'S THE SAME FOR YOU, RIGHT?
YOU ARE HERE BECAUSE OF YOUR WILL TO BE HERE.
AND THE WORLD EMBRACES YOU FOR THAT.

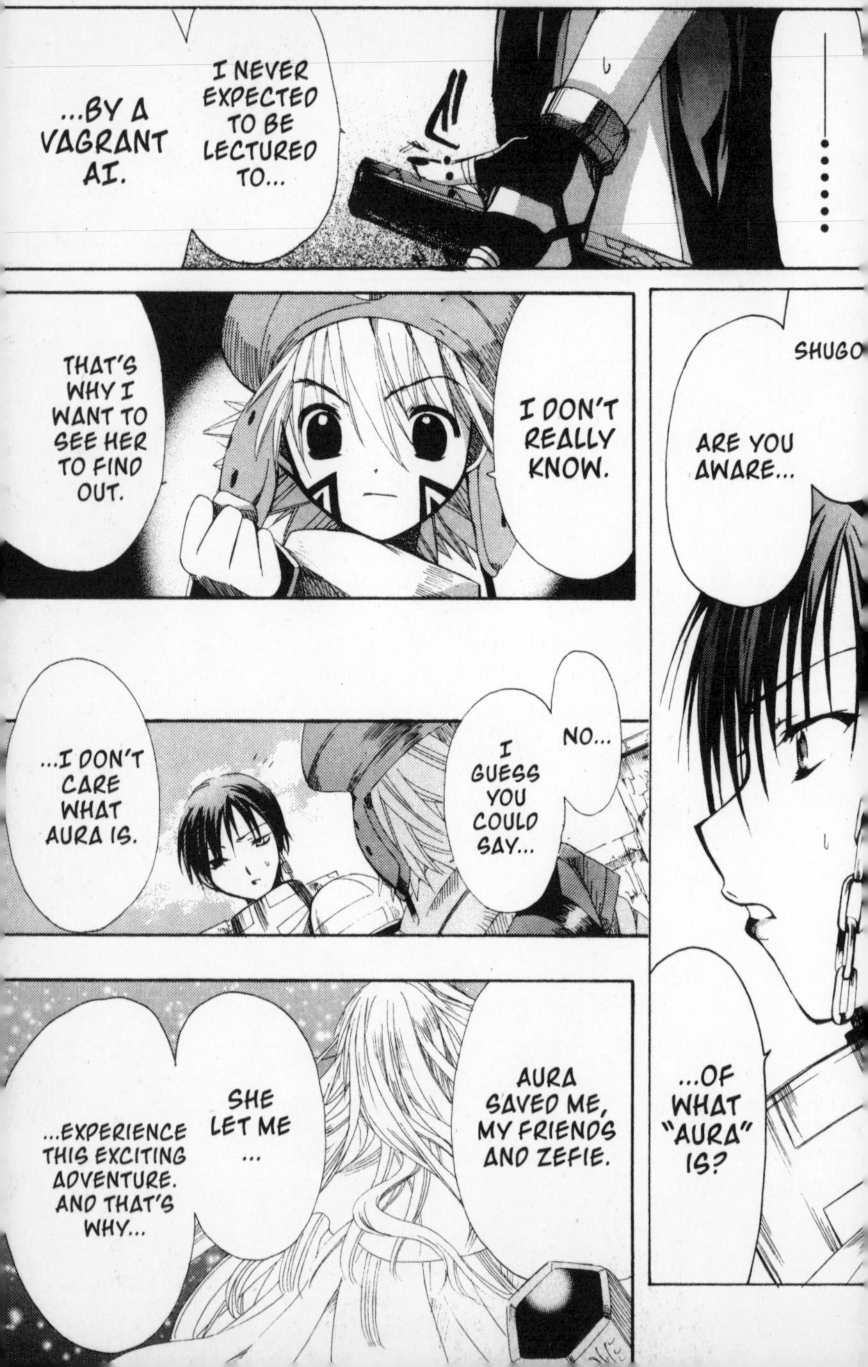
....
I NEVER EXPECTED TO BE LECTURED TO...
...BY A VAGRANT AI.
SHUGO
ARE YOU AWARE...
...OF WHAT "AURA" IS?
I DON'T REALLY KNOW.
THAT'S WHY I WANT TO SEE HER TO FIND OUT.
NO...
I GUESS YOU COULD SAY...
...I DON'T CARE WHAT AURA IS.
AURA SAVED ME, MY FRIENDS AND ZEFIE.
SHE LET ME ...
...EXPERIENCE THIS EXCITING ADVENTURE. AND THAT'S WHY...

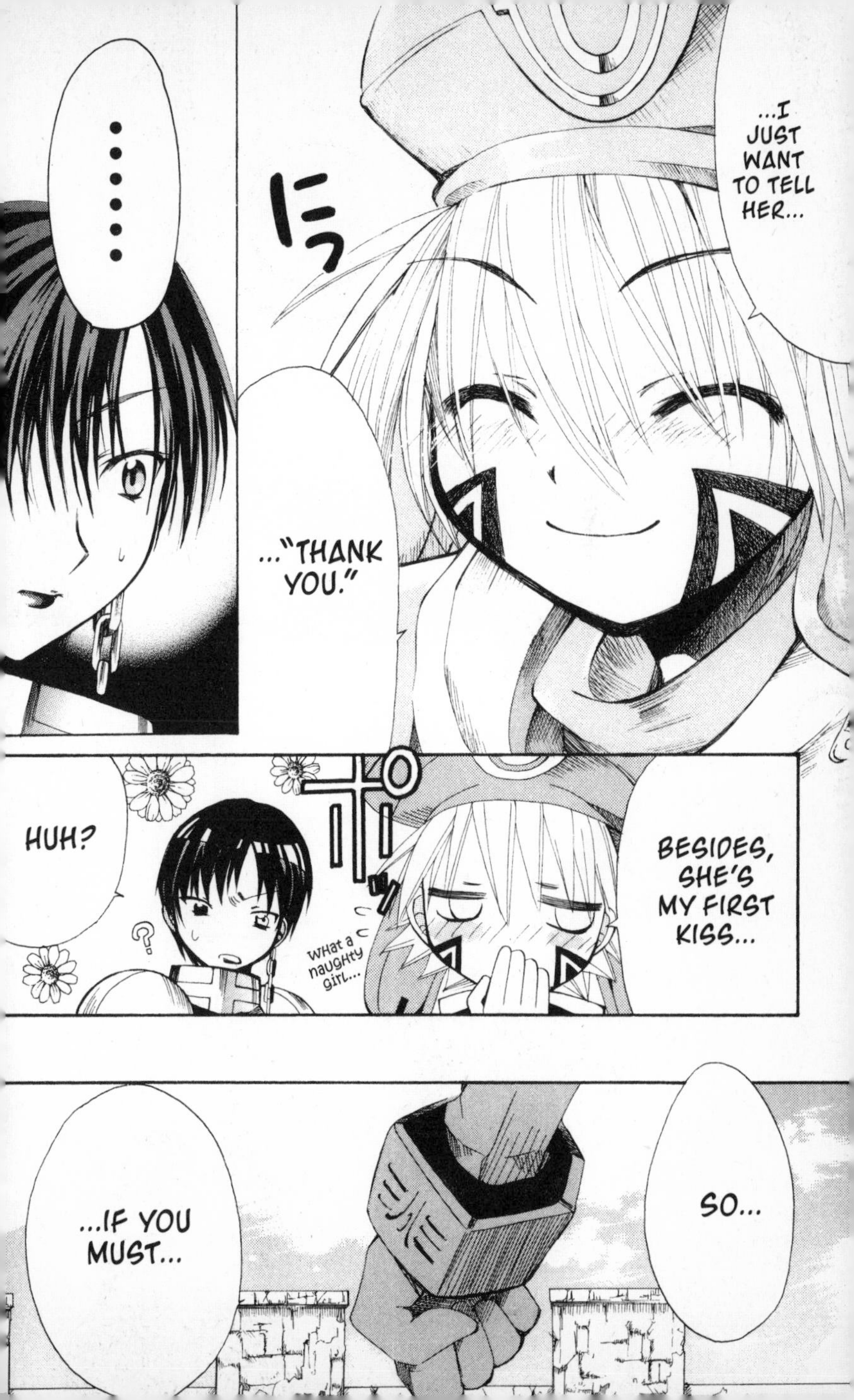
...I JUST WANT TO TELL HER...
にっ
..."THANK YOU."
......
BESIDES, SHE'S MY FIRST KISS...
What a naughty girl...
HUH?
SO...
...IF YOU MUST...

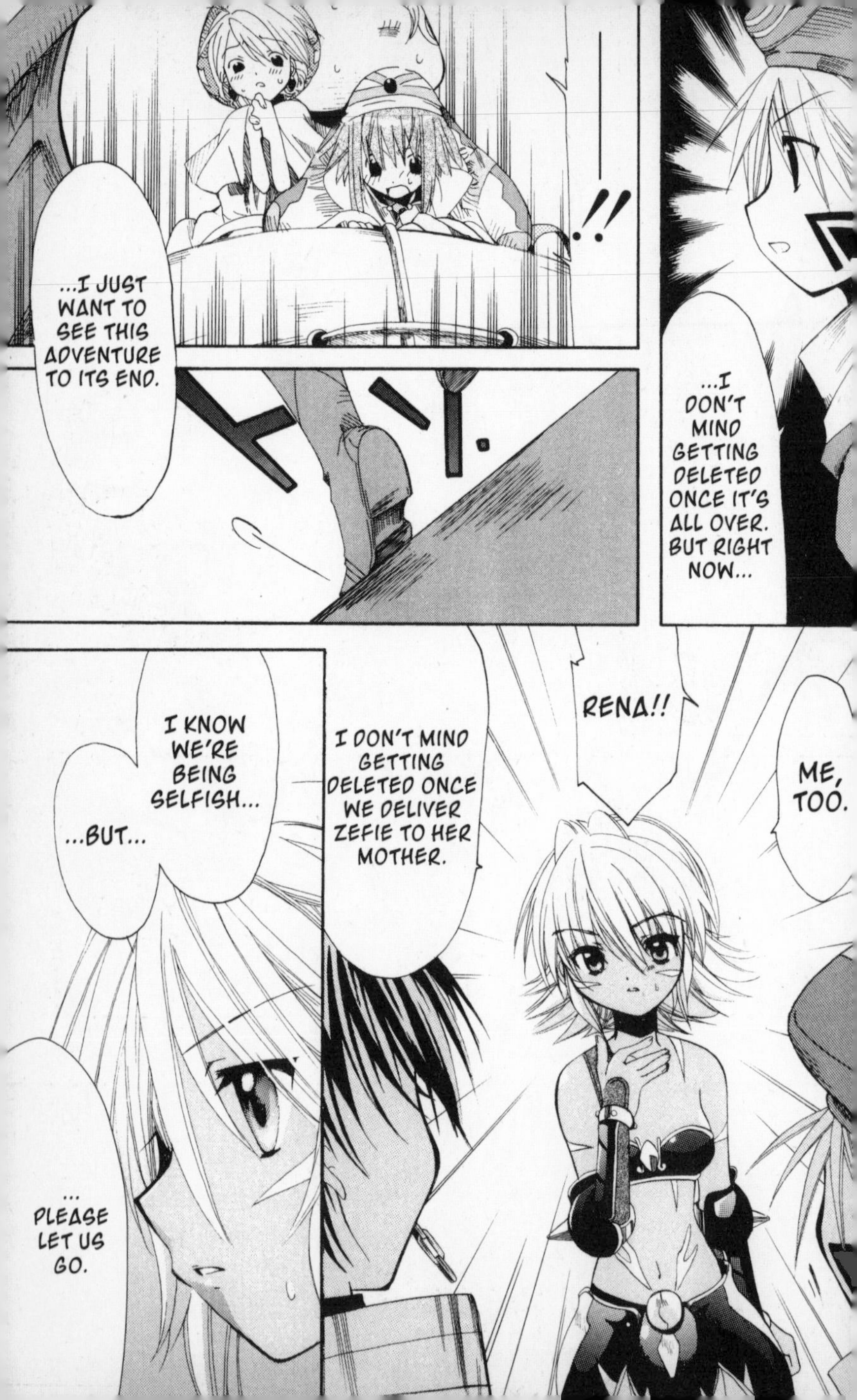
...I DON'T MIND GETTING DELETED ONCE IT'S ALL OVER. BUT RIGHT NOW...
!!
...I JUST WANT TO SEE THIS ADVENTURE TO ITS END.
ME, TOO.
RENA!!
I DON'T MIND GETTING DELETED ONCE WE DELIVER ZEFIE TO HER MOTHER.
I KNOW WE'RE BEING SELFISH...
...BUT...
... PLEASE LET US GO.

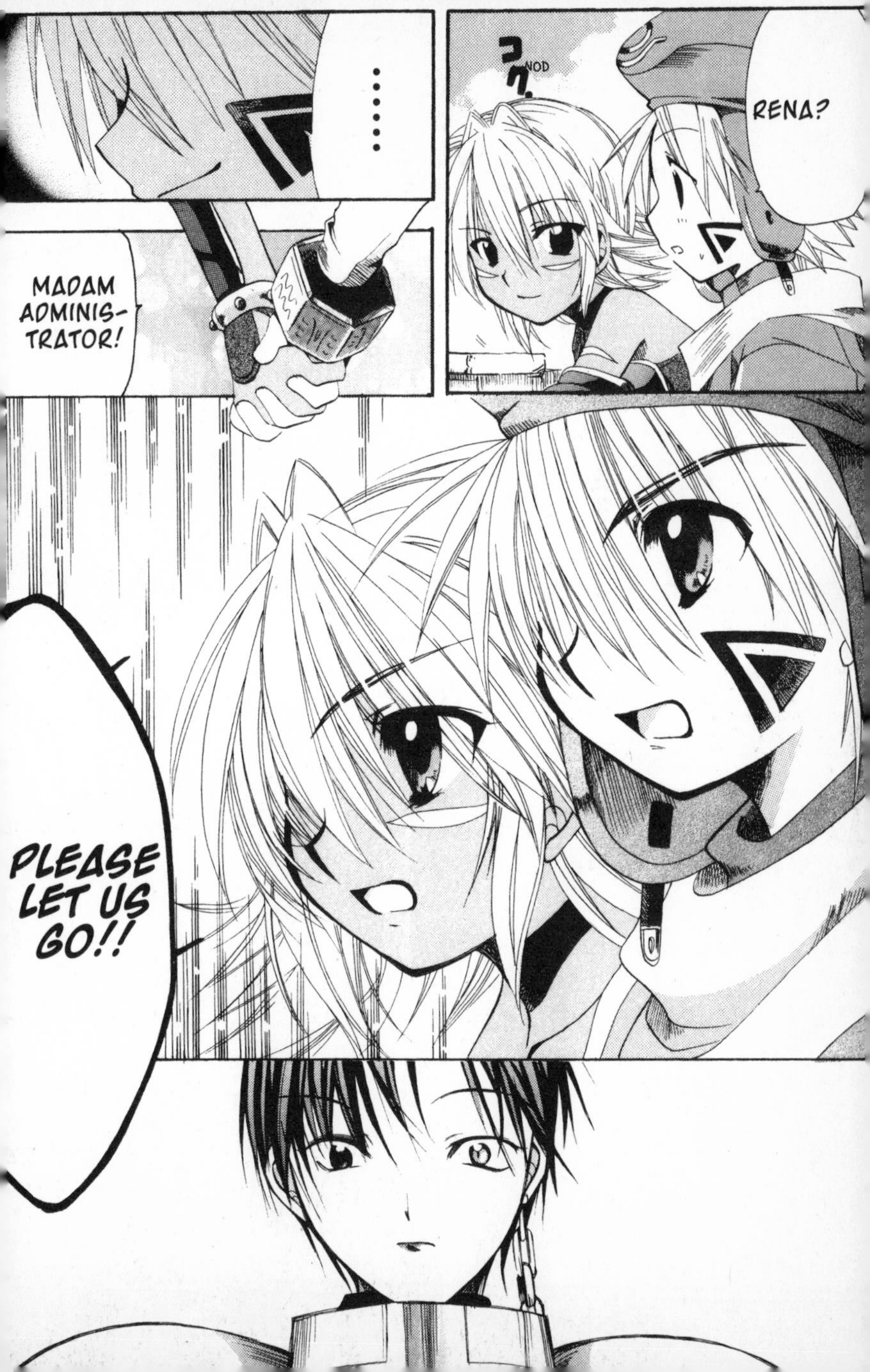
RENA?
コク NOD
......
MADAM ADMINIS-TRATOR!
PLEASE LET US GO!!

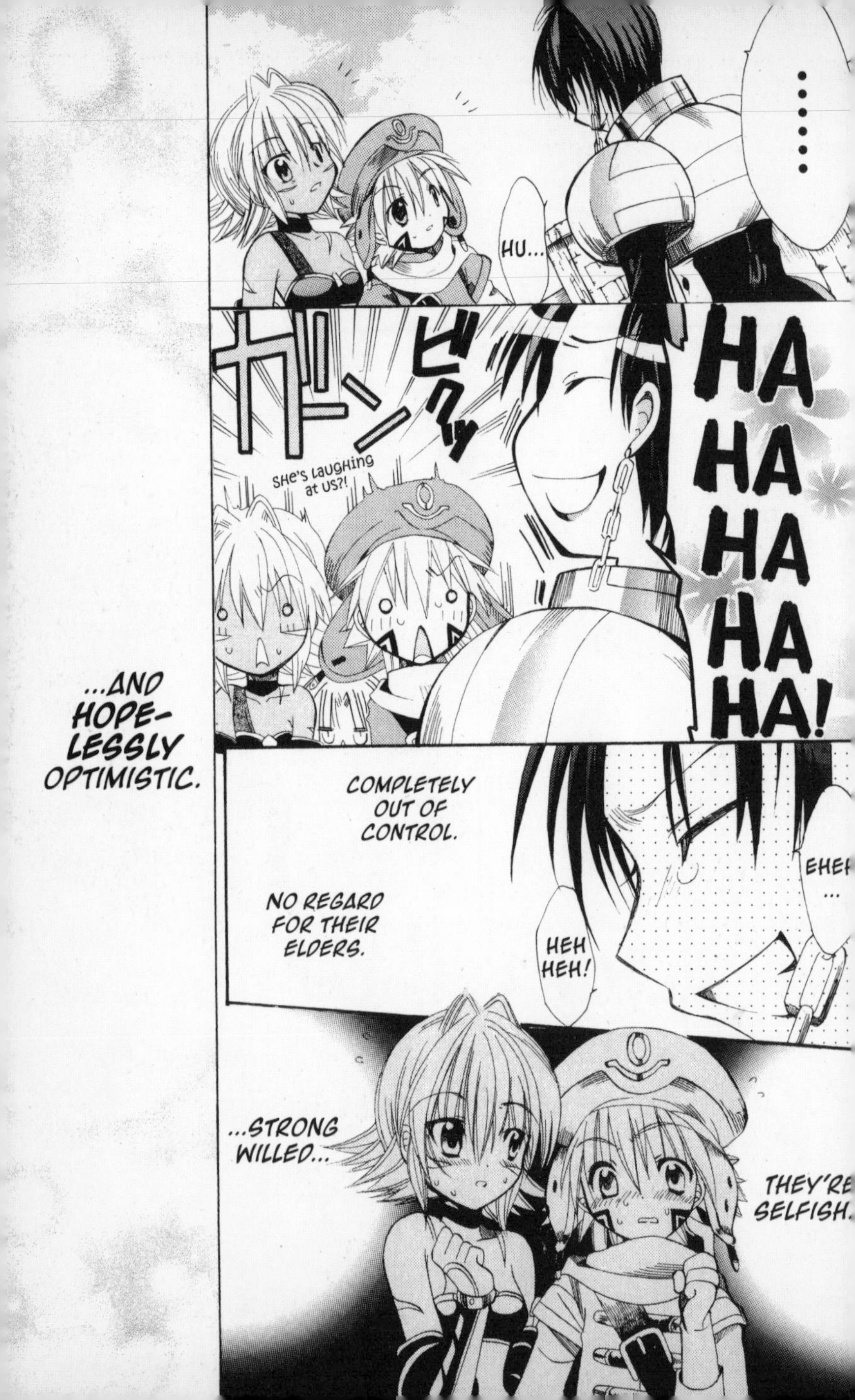
......
HU...
HA HA HA HA HA HA HA!
ビクッ
ガーン
SHE'S LAUGHING AT US?!
EHEH ...
HEH HEH!
COMPLETELY OUT OF CONTROL.
NO REGARD FOR THEIR ELDERS.
THEY'RE SELFISH.
...STRONG WILLED...
...AND HOPELESSLY OPTIMISTIC.

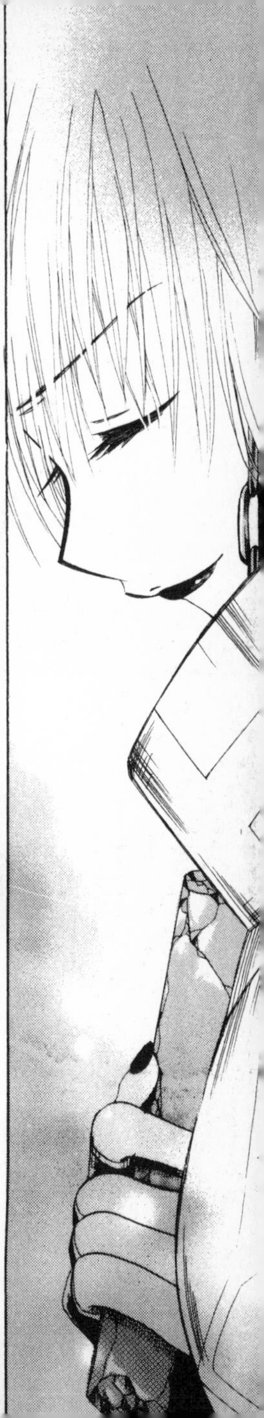

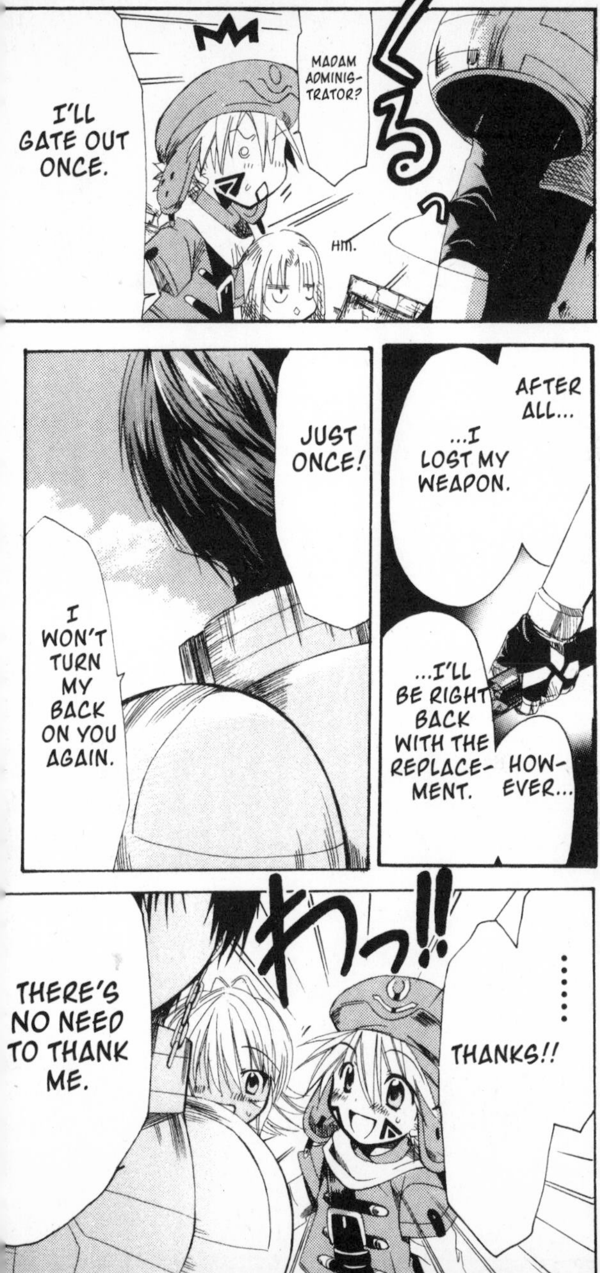
くる
MADAM ADMINIS-TRATOR?
I'LL GATE OUT ONCE.
HM.
AFTER ALL...
...I LOST MY WEAPON.
HOW-EVER...
...I'LL BE RIGHT BACK WITH THE REPLACE-MENT.
JUST ONCE!
I WON'T TURN MY BACK ON YOU AGAIN.
わっ!!
......
THANKS!!
THERE'S NO NEED TO THANK ME.

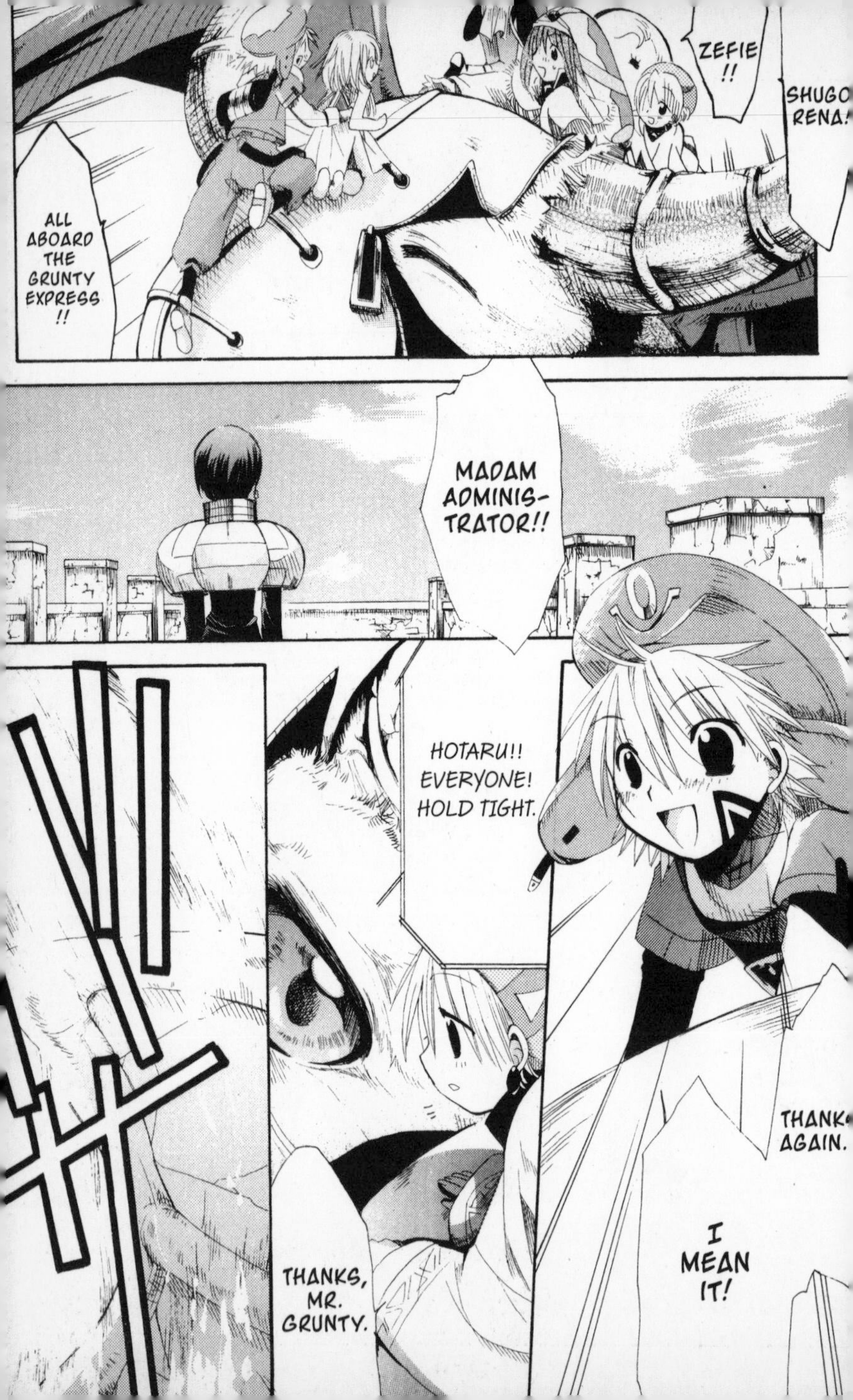
SHUGO RENA!
ZEFIE!!
ALL ABOARD THE GRUNTY EXPRESS!!
MADAM ADMINIS-TRATOR!!
THANKS AGAIN.
I MEAN IT!
HOTARU!! EVERYONE! HOLD TIGHT.
THANKS, MR. GRUNTY.

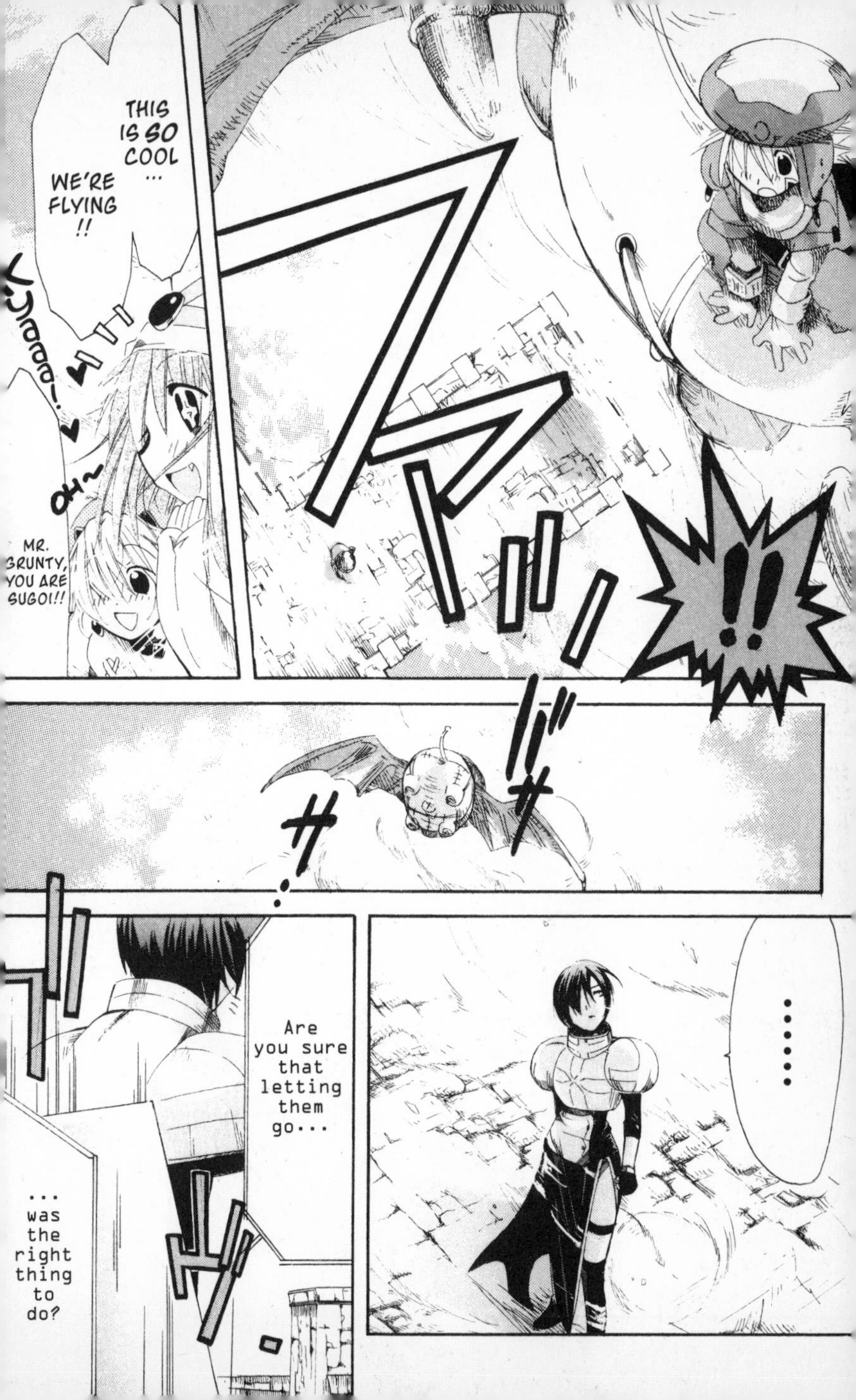
!!
THIS IS SO COOL ...
WE'RE FLYING !!
Uwaaaa!
Oh~
MR. GRUNTY, YOU ARE SUGOI!!
......
Are you sure that letting them go...
... was the right thing to do?

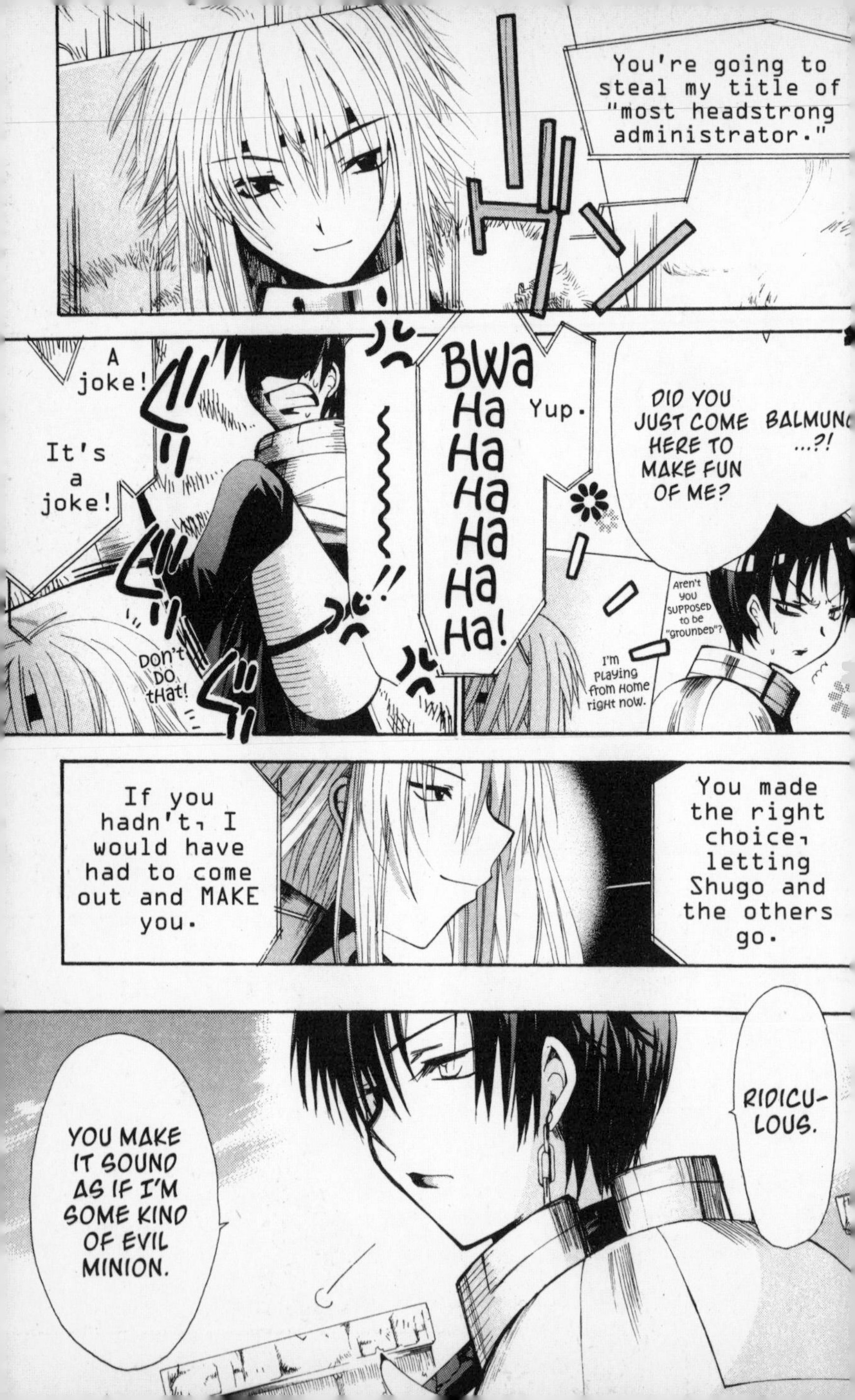
You're going to steal my title of "most headstrong administrator."
BALMUNG ...?!
DID YOU JUST COME HERE TO MAKE FUN OF ME?
Aren't you supposed to be "grounded"?
I'm playing from home right now.
Yup.
BWA HA HA HA HA HA HA HA!
A joke!
It's a joke!
Don't do that!
You made the right choice, letting Shugo and the others go.
If you hadn't, I would have had to come out and MAKE you.
RIDICULOUS.
YOU MAKE IT SOUND AS IF I'M SOME KIND OF EVIL MINION.

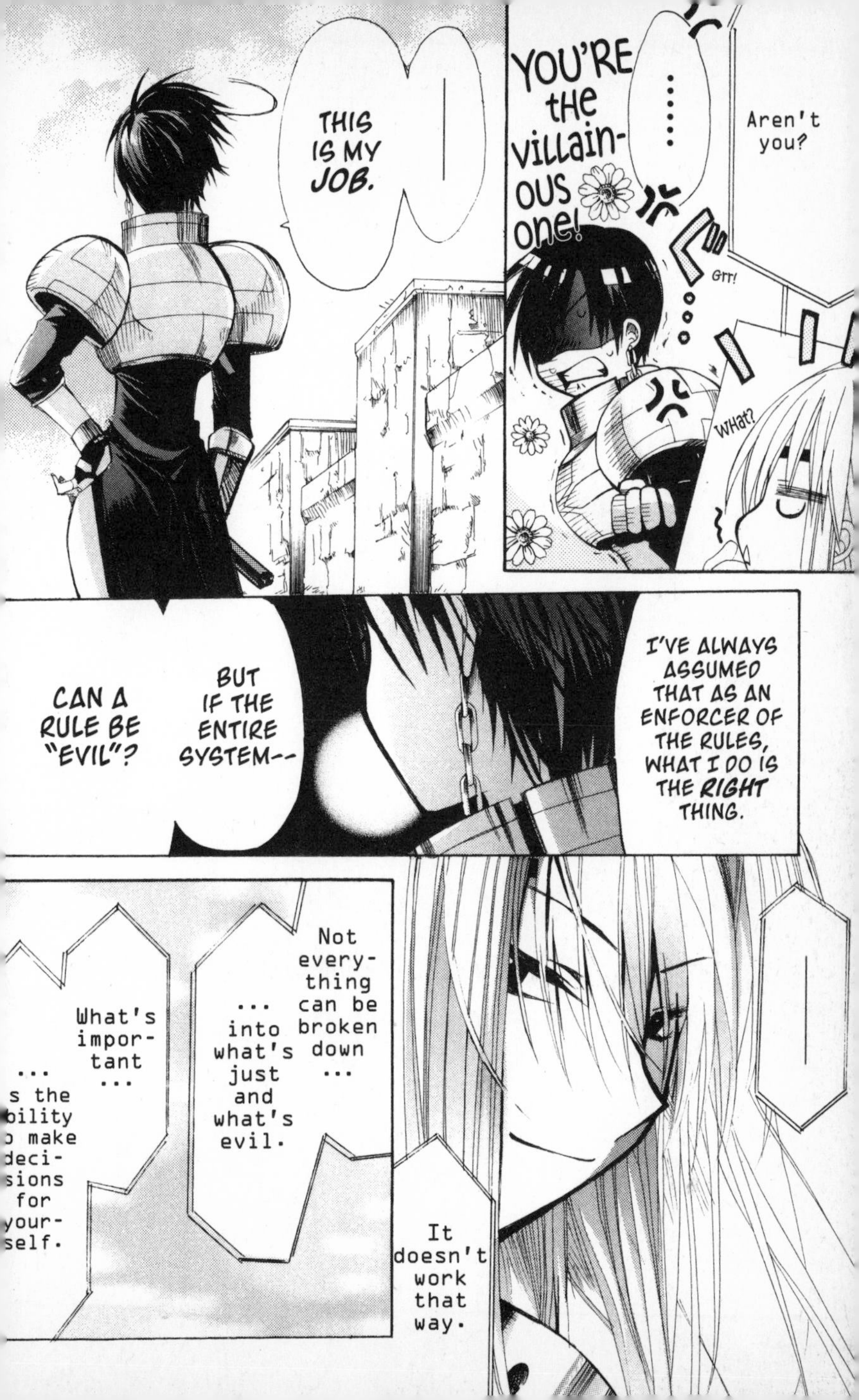
Aren't you?
......
YOU'RE the villainous one!
Grr!
What?
THIS IS MY JOB.
I'VE ALWAYS ASSUMED THAT AS AN ENFORCER OF THE RULES, WHAT I DO IS THE RIGHT THING.
BUT IF THE ENTIRE SYSTEM--
CAN A RULE BE "EVIL"?
Not everything can be broken down ...
... into what's just and what's evil.
What's important ...
... s the bility o make decisions for yourself.
It doesn't work that way.

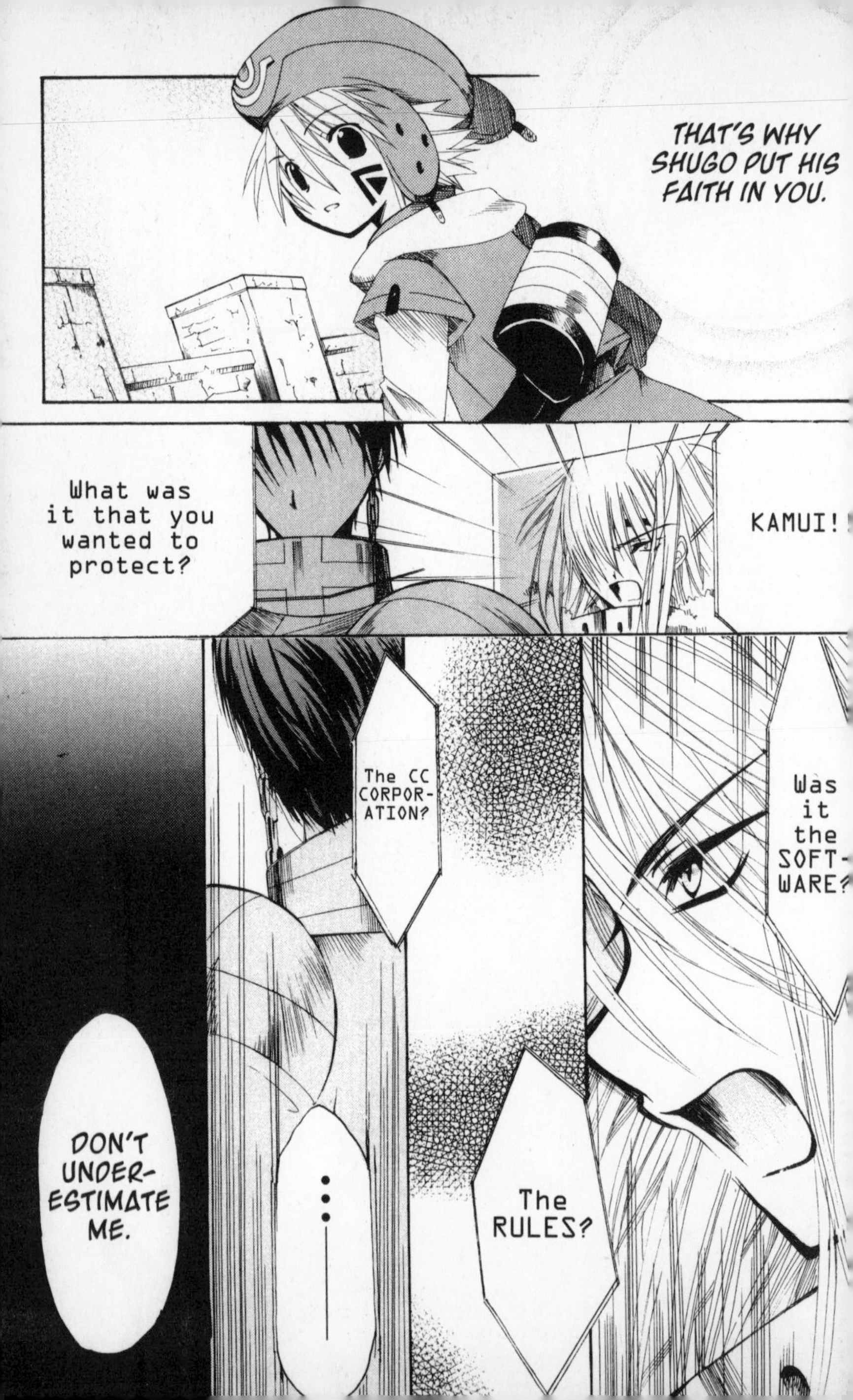
THAT'S WHY SHUGO PUT HIS FAITH IN YOU.
KAMUI!
What was it that you wanted to protect?
Was it the SOFT-WARE?
The CC CORPOR-ATION?
The RULES?
...
DON'T UNDER-ESTIMATE ME.

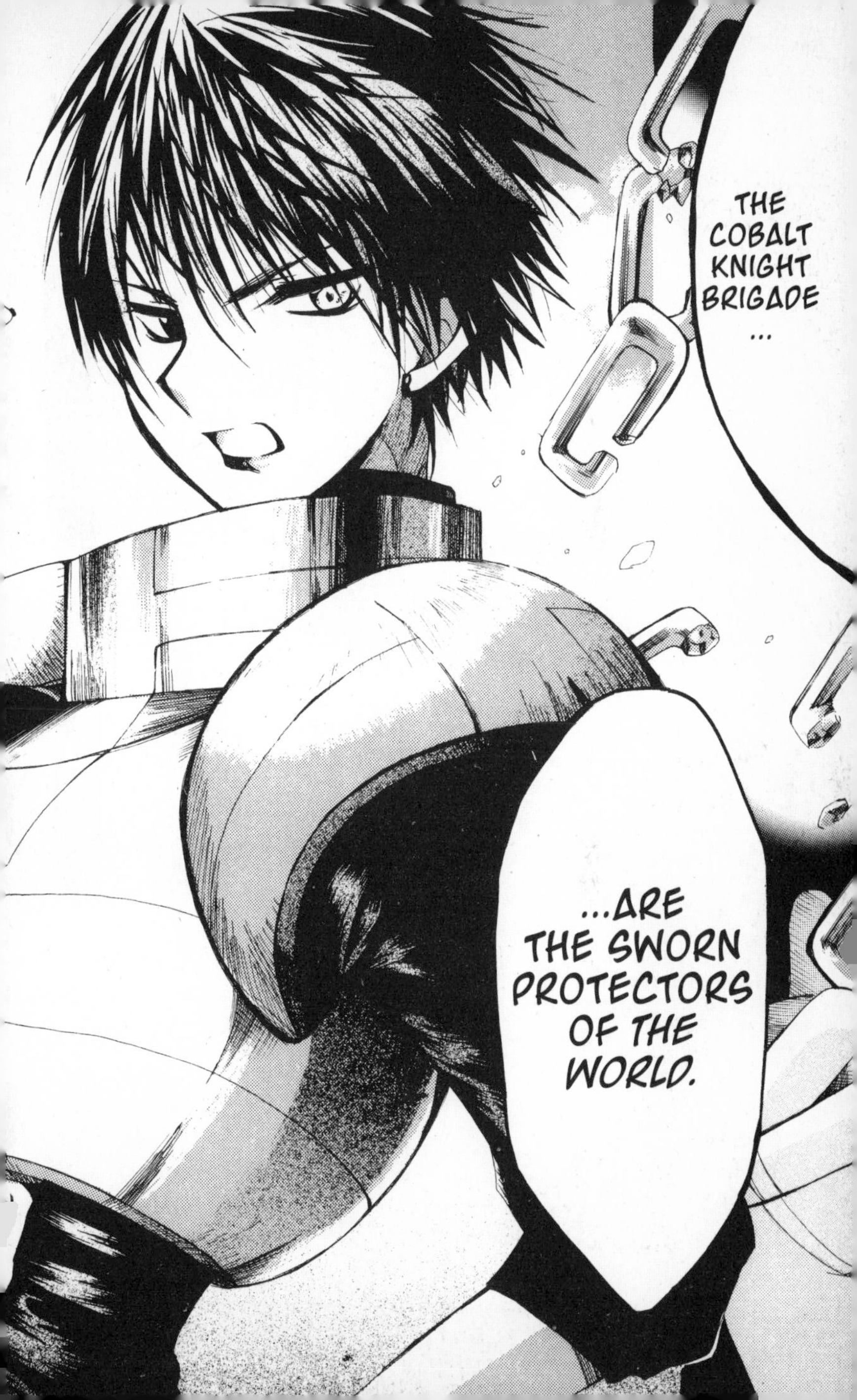
THE COBALT KNIGHT BRIGADE ...
...ARE THE SWORN PROTECTORS OF THE WORLD.

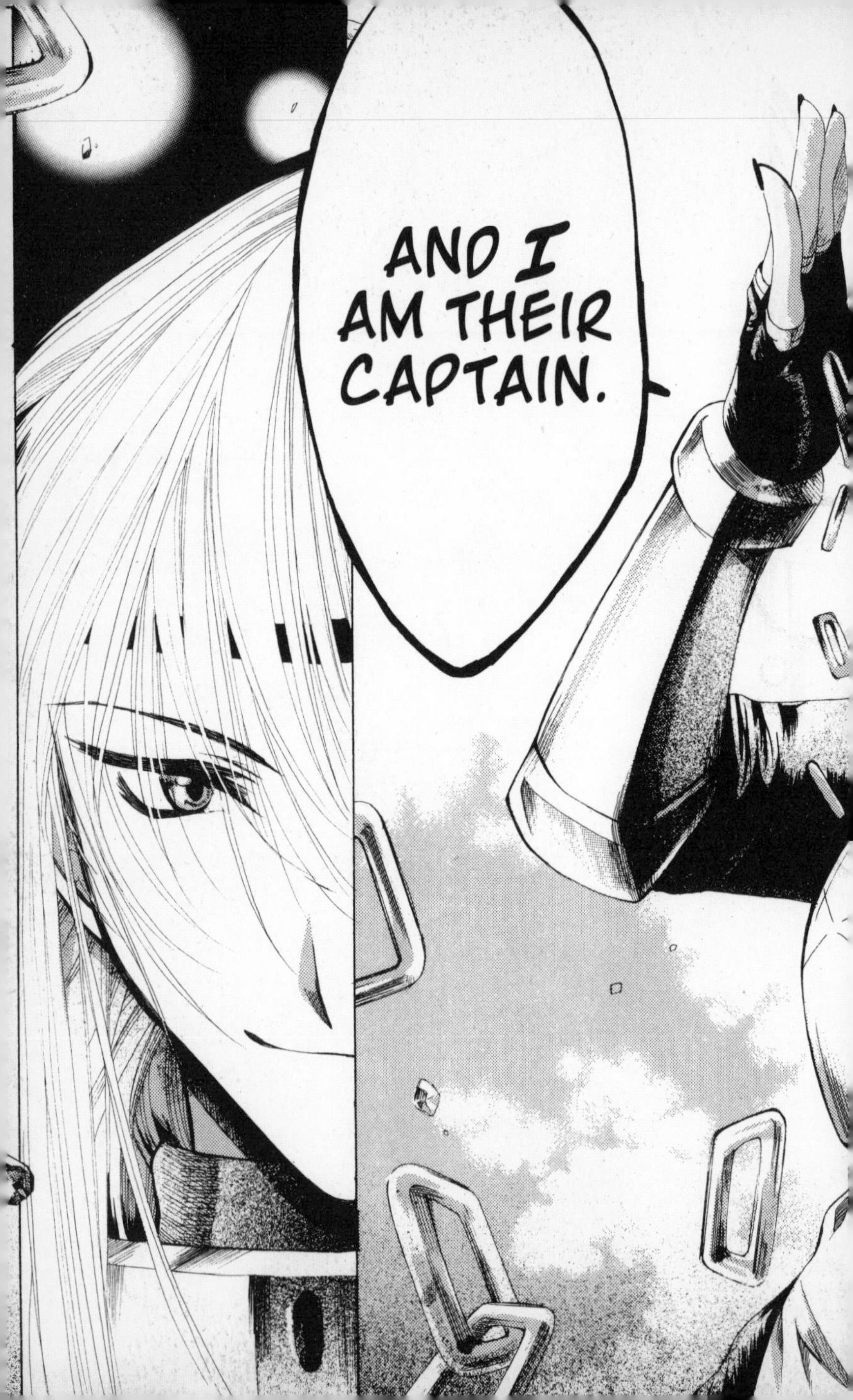
AND I AM THEIR CAPTAIN.

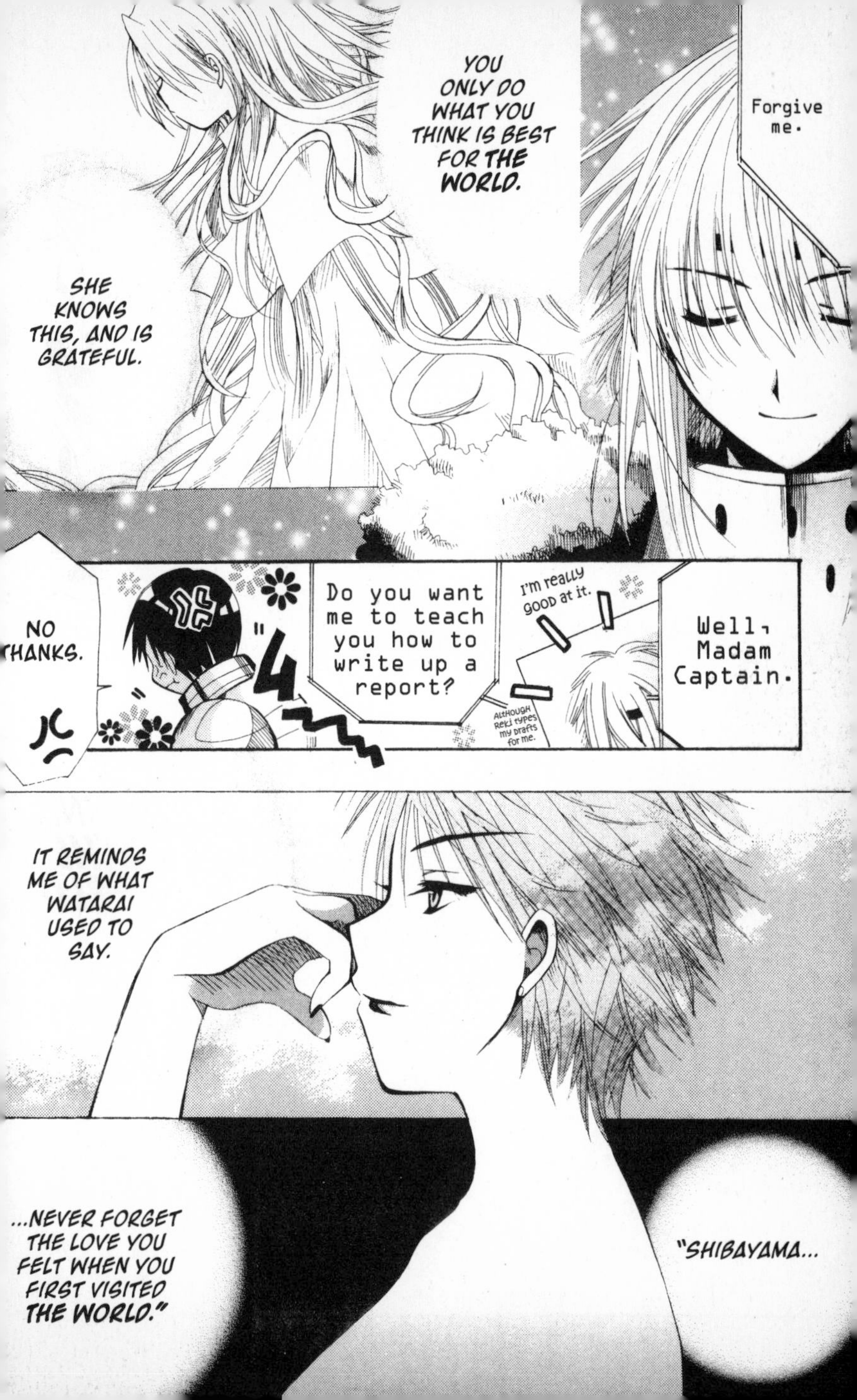
Forgive me.
YOU ONLY DO WHAT YOU THINK IS BEST FOR THE WORLD.
SHE KNOWS THIS, AND IS GRATEFUL.
Well, Madam Captain.
Do you want me to teach you how to write up a report?
I'm really GOOD at it.
Although Reki types my drafts for me.
NO THANKS.
IT REMINDS ME OF WHAT WATARAI USED TO SAY.
"SHIBAYAMA...
...NEVER FORGET THE LOVE YOU FELT WHEN YOU FIRST VISITED THE WORLD."

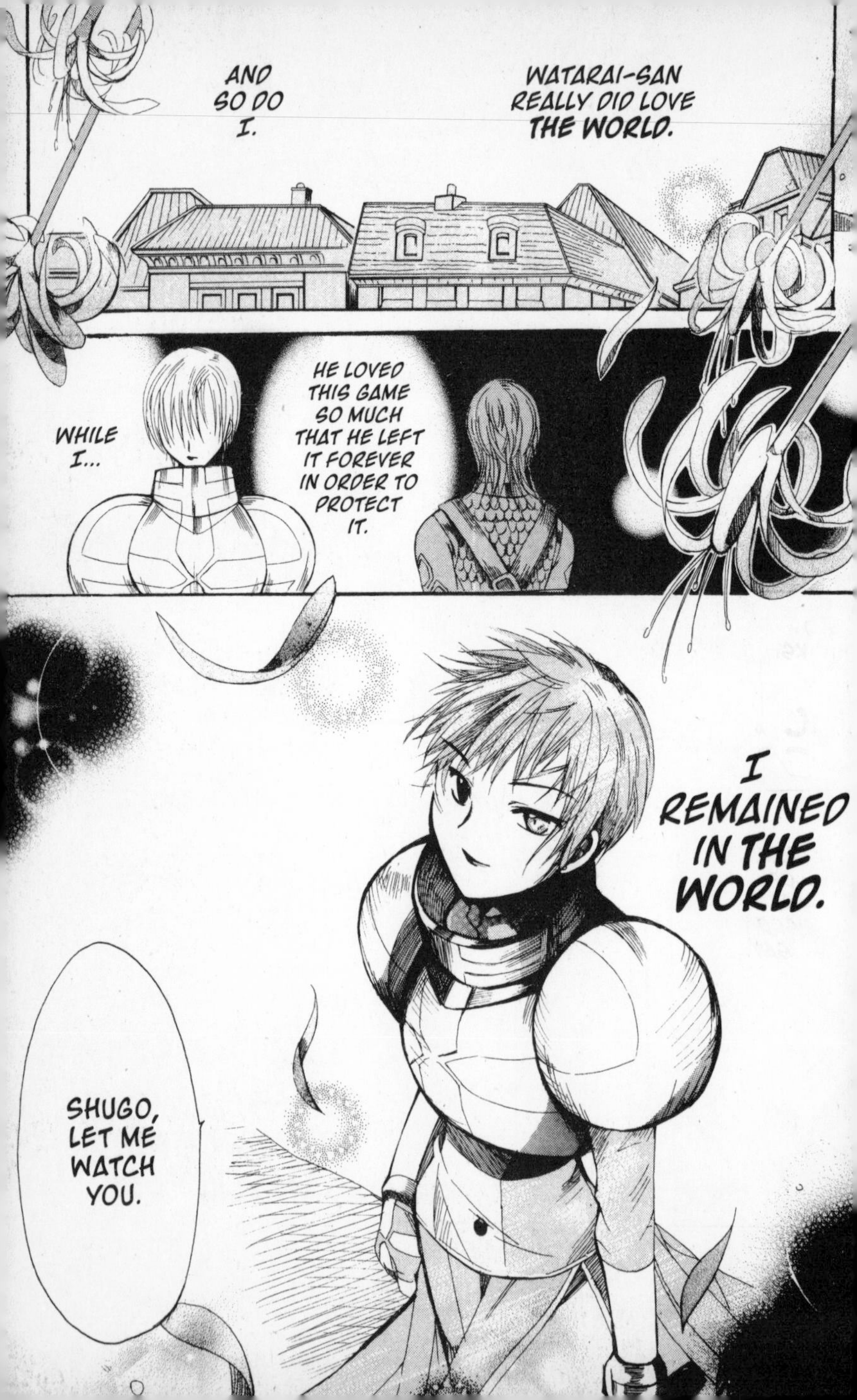
WATARAI-SAN REALLY DID LOVE THE WORLD.
AND SO DO I.
HE LOVED THIS GAME SO MUCH THAT HE LEFT IT FOREVER IN ORDER TO PROTECT IT.
WHILE I...
I REMAINED IN THE WORLD.
SHUGO, LET ME WATCH YOU.

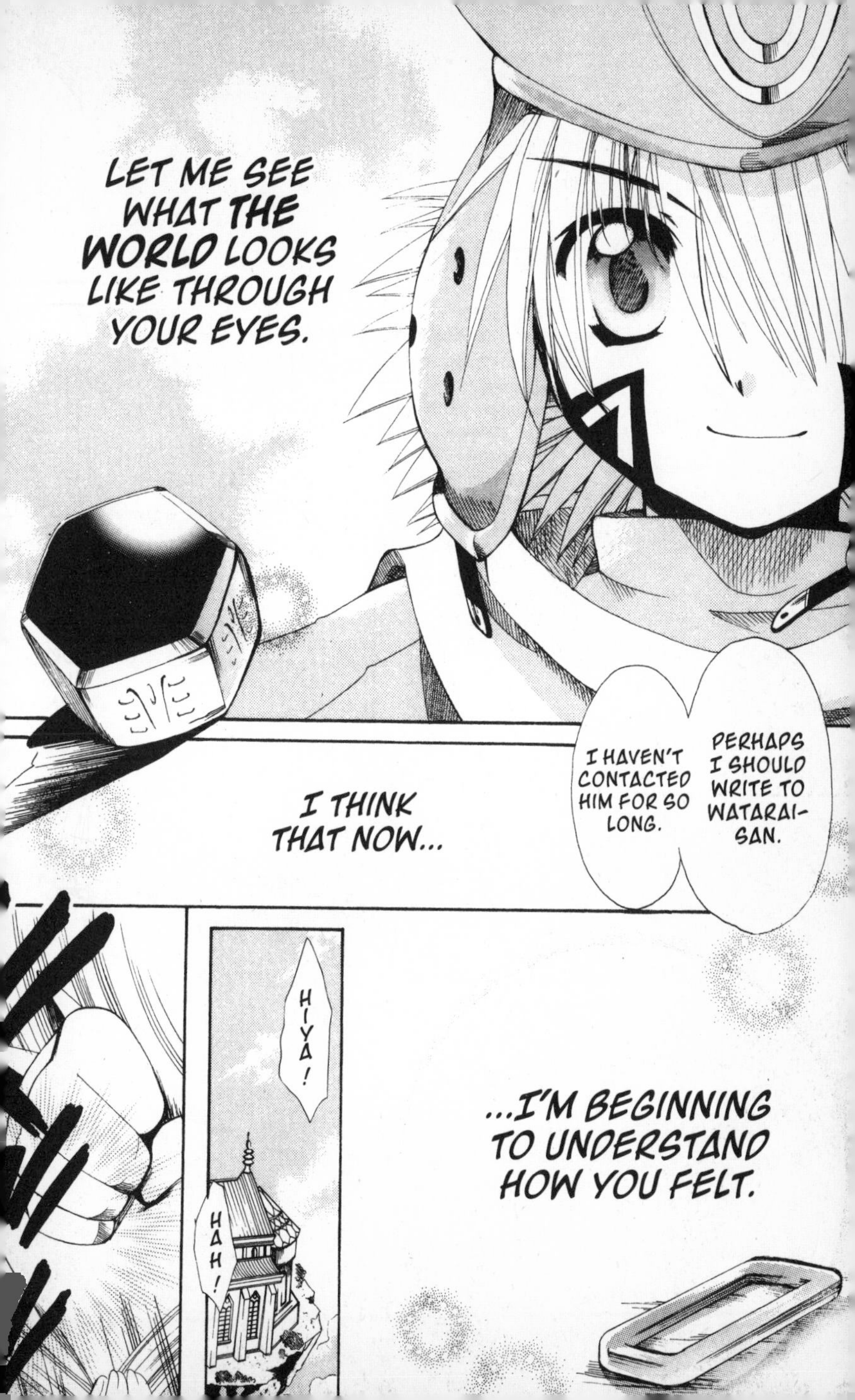
LET ME SEE WHAT THE WORLD LOOKS LIKE THROUGH YOUR EYES.
PERHAPS I SHOULD WRITE TO WATARAI-SAN.
I HAVEN'T CONTACTED HIM FOR SO LONG.
I THINK THAT NOW...
...I'M BEGINNING TO UNDERSTAND HOW YOU FELT.
HIYA!
HAH!

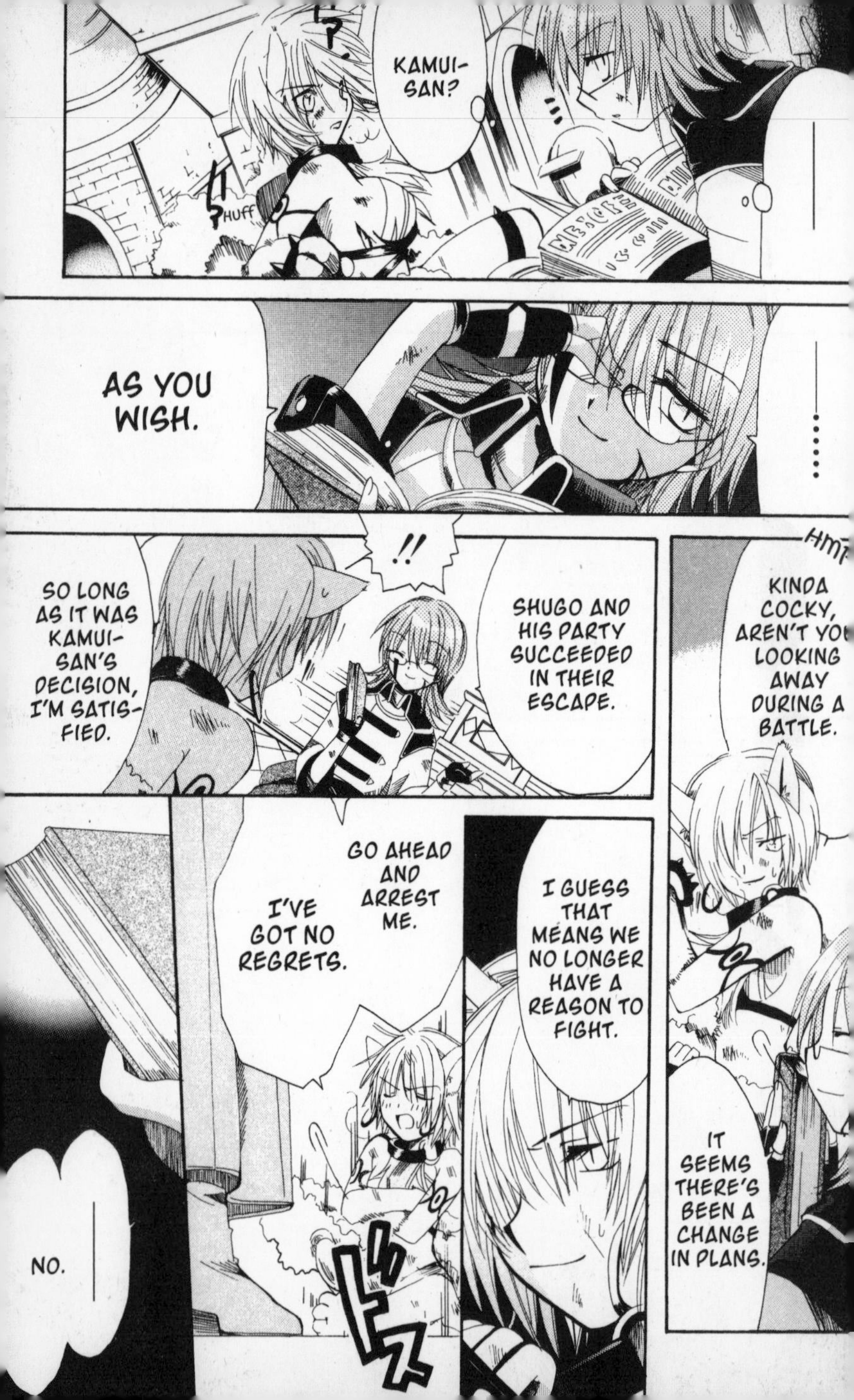
KAMUI-SAN?
HUFF
AS YOU WISH.
KINDA COCKY, AREN'T YOU LOOKING AWAY DURING A BATTLE.
!!
SHUGO AND HIS PARTY SUCCEEDED IN THEIR ESCAPE.
SO LONG AS IT WAS KAMUI-SAN'S DECISION, I'M SATISFIED.
IT SEEMS THERE'S BEEN A CHANGE IN PLANS.
I GUESS THAT MEANS WE NO LONGER HAVE A REASON TO FIGHT.
GO AHEAD AND ARREST ME.
I'VE GOT NO REGRETS.
NO.

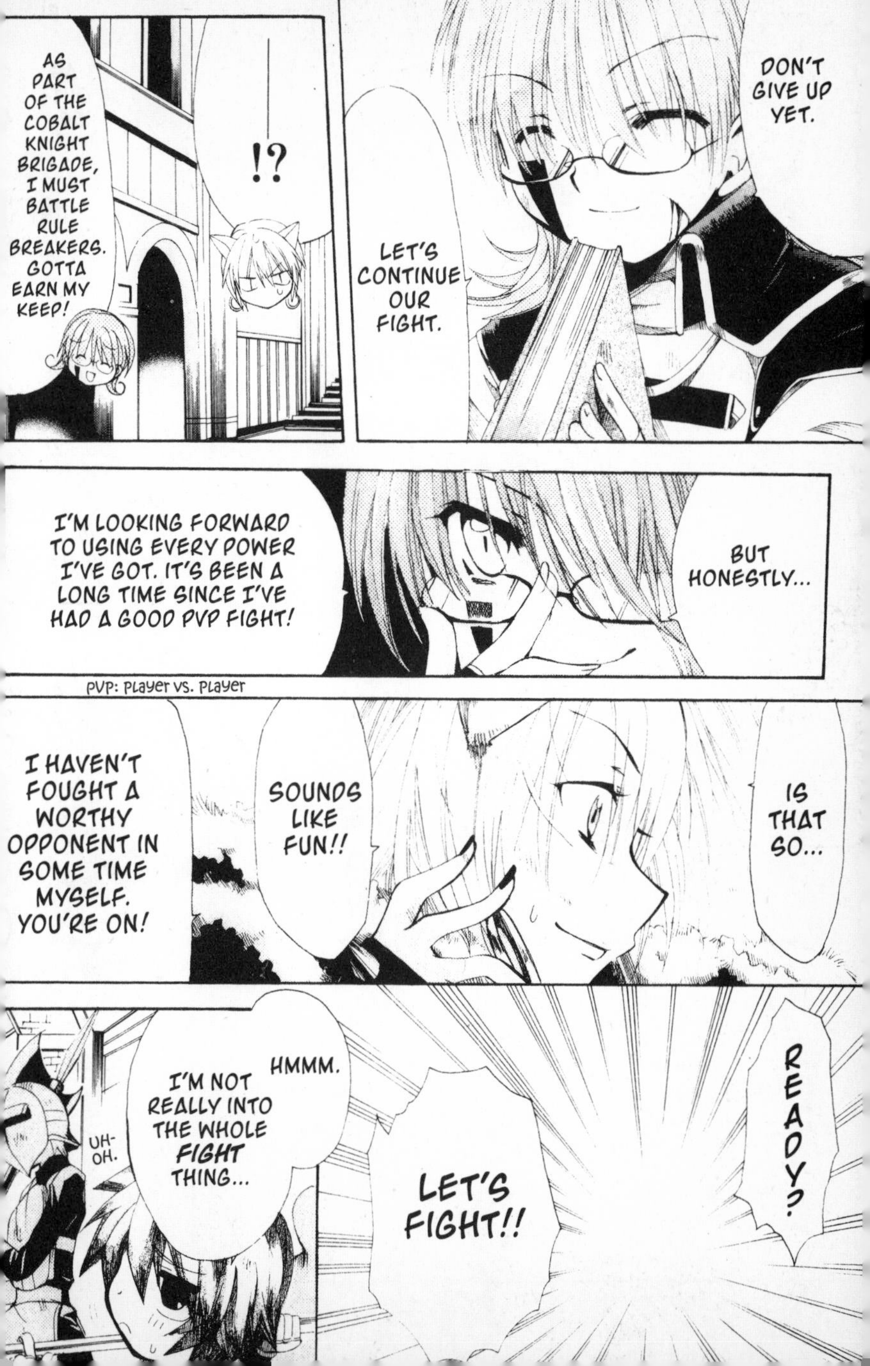
DON'T GIVE UP YET.
LET'S CONTINUE OUR FIGHT.
!?
AS PART OF THE COBALT KNIGHT BRIGADE, I MUST BATTLE RULE BREAKERS. GOTTA EARN MY KEEP!
BUT HONESTLY...
I'M LOOKING FORWARD TO USING EVERY POWER I'VE GOT. IT'S BEEN A LONG TIME SINCE I'VE HAD A GOOD PVP FIGHT!
IS THAT SO...
SOUNDS LIKE FUN!!
I HAVEN'T FOUGHT A WORTHY OPPONENT IN SOME TIME MYSELF. YOU'RE ON!
READY?
LET'S FIGHT!!
HMMM.
I'M NOT REALLY INTO THE WHOLE *FIGHT* THING...
UH-OH.
PVP: Player vs. Player

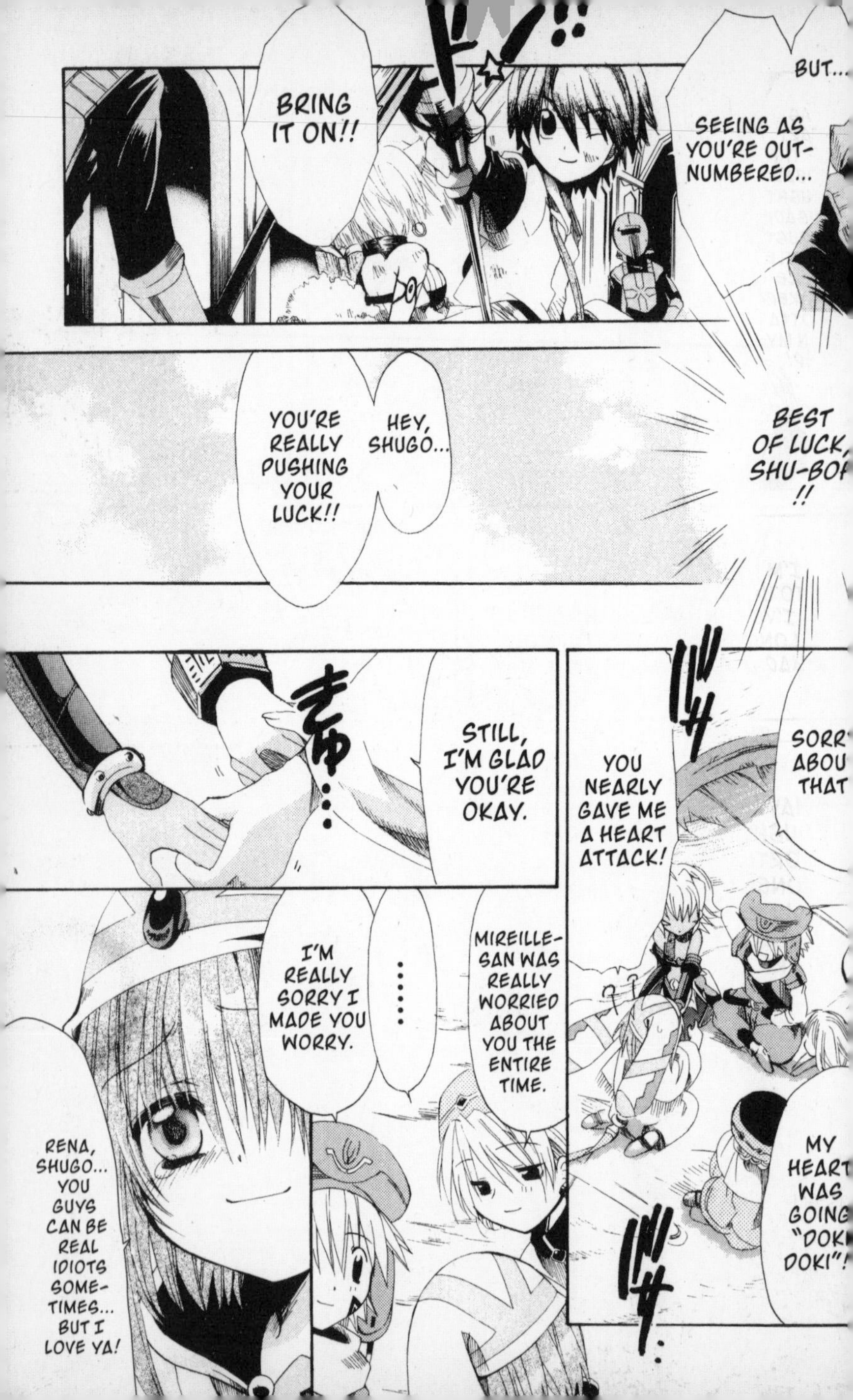
BUT...
SEEING AS YOU'RE OUT-NUMBERED...
BRING IT ON!!
BEST OF LUCK, SHU-BO !!
HEY, SHUGO...
YOU'RE REALLY PUSHING YOUR LUCK!!
SORR ABOU THAT
YOU NEARLY GAVE ME A HEART ATTACK!
MY HEART WAS GOING "DOK DOKI"!
STILL, I'M GLAD YOU'RE OKAY.
MIREILLE-SAN WAS REALLY WORRIED ABOUT YOU THE ENTIRE TIME.
......
I'M REALLY SORRY I MADE YOU WORRY.
RENA, SHUGO... YOU GUYS CAN BE REAL IDIOTS SOME-TIMES... BUT I LOVE YA!

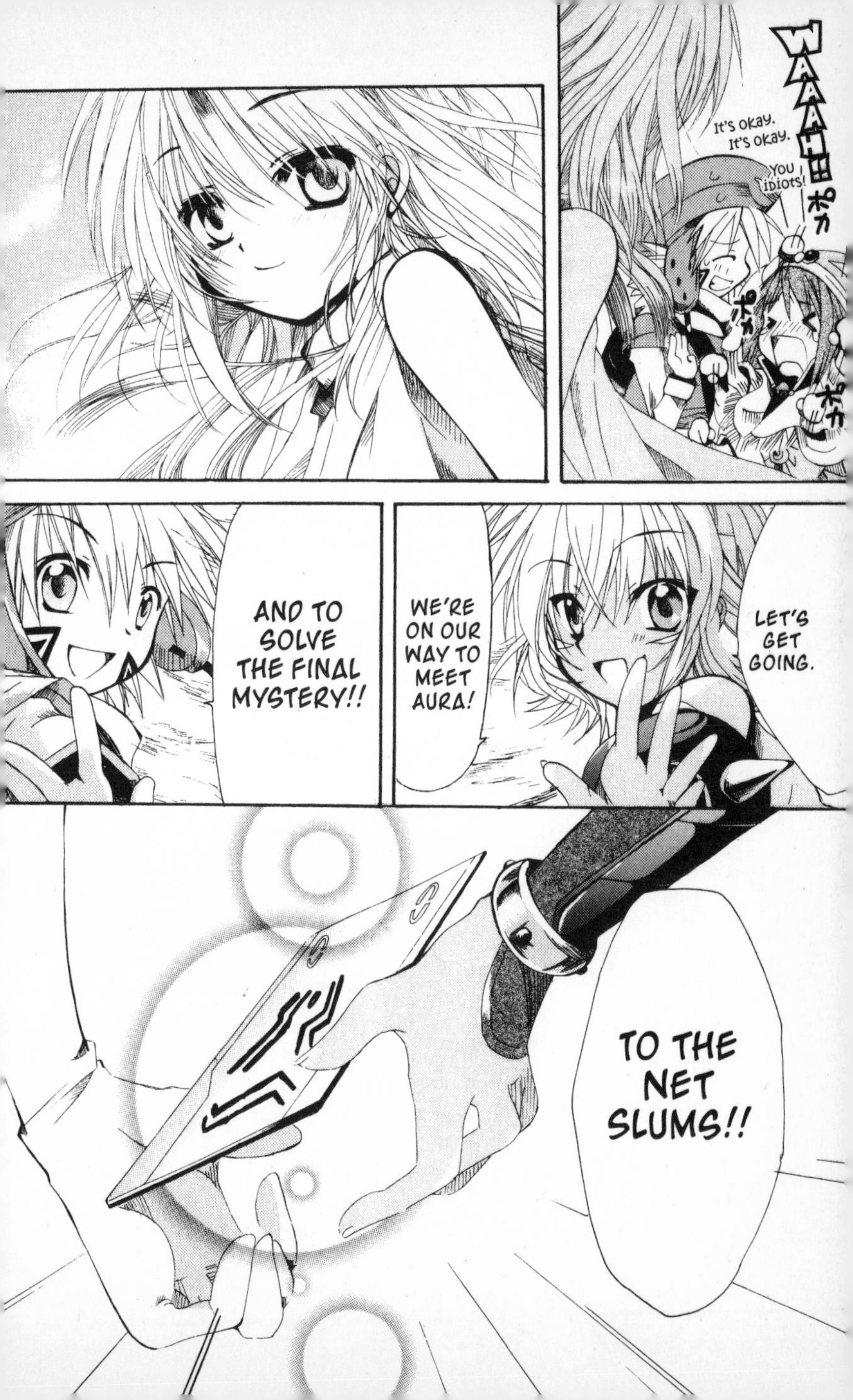
WAAAH!!
It's okay. It's okay.
You idiots!
ポカ
ポカ
ポカ
LET'S GET GOING.
WE'RE ON OUR WAY TO MEET AURA!
AND TO SOLVE THE FINAL MYSTERY!!
TO THE NET SLUMS!!

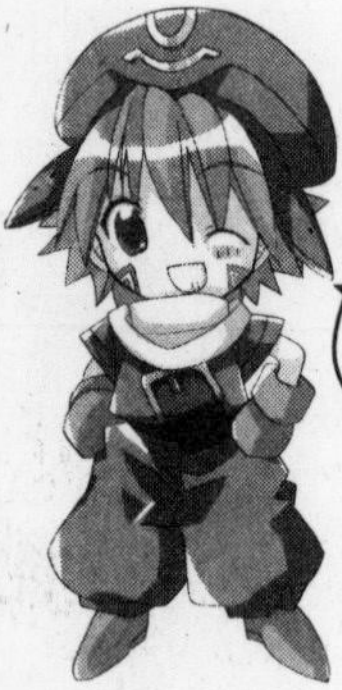

NEW GENERATION ONLINE
THE WORLD

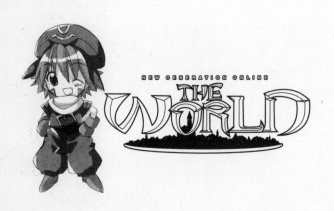

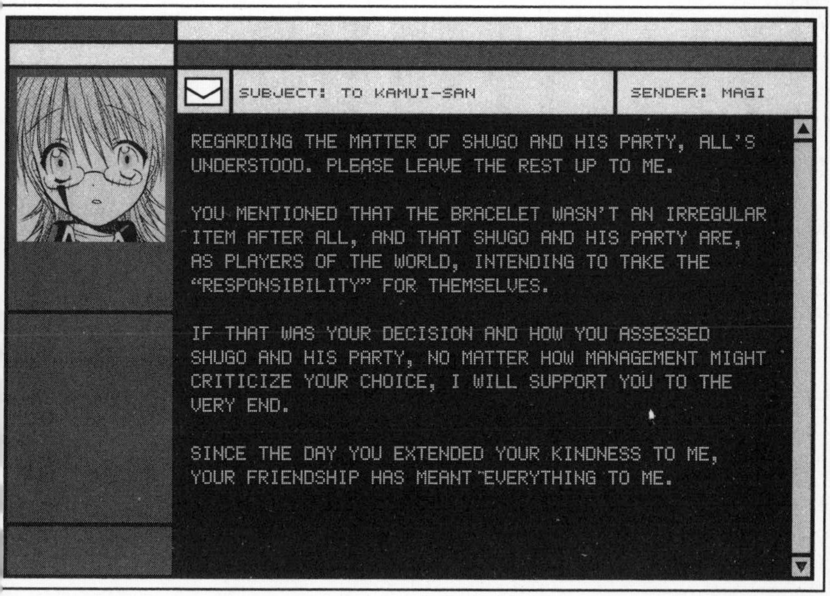
SUBJECT: TO KAMUI-SAN
SENDER: MAGI
REGARDING THE MATTER OF SHUGO AND HIS PARTY, ALL'S UNDERSTOOD. PLEASE LEAVE THE REST UP TO ME.
YOU MENTIONED THAT THE BRACELET WASN'T AN IRREGULAR ITEM AFTER ALL, AND THAT SHUGO AND HIS PARTY ARE, AS PLAYERS OF THE WORLD, INTENDING TO TAKE THE "RESPONSIBILITY" FOR THEMSELVES.
IF THAT WAS YOUR DECISION AND HOW YOU ASSESSED SHUGO AND HIS PARTY, NO MATTER HOW MANAGEMENT MIGHT CRITICIZE YOUR CHOICE, I WILL SUPPORT YOU TO THE VERY END.
SINCE THE DAY YOU EXTENDED YOUR KINDNESS TO ME, YOUR FRIENDSHIP HAS MEANT EVERYTHING TO ME.

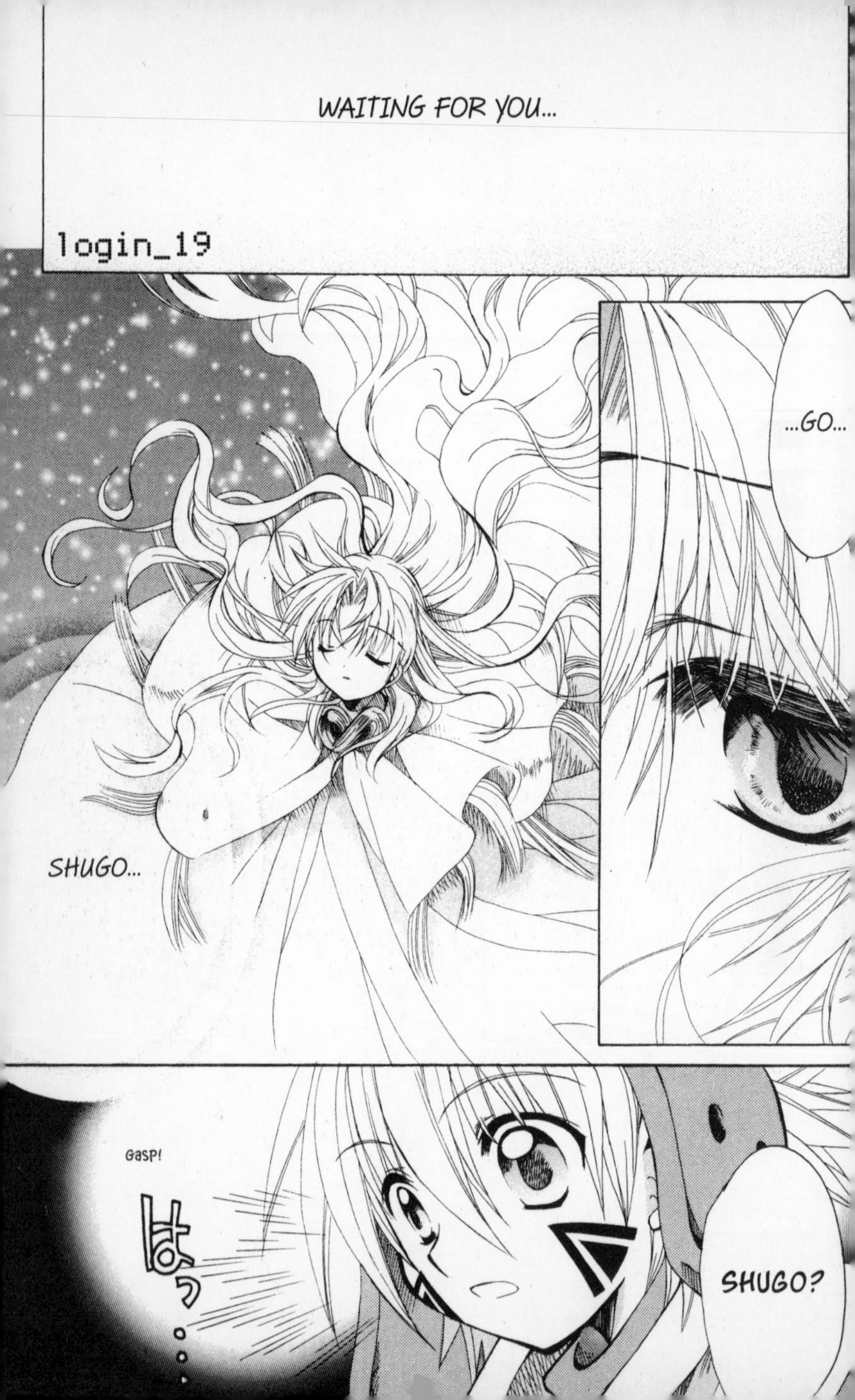
WAITING FOR YOU...
login_19
...GO...
SHUGO...
SHUGO?
GASP!
はっ…

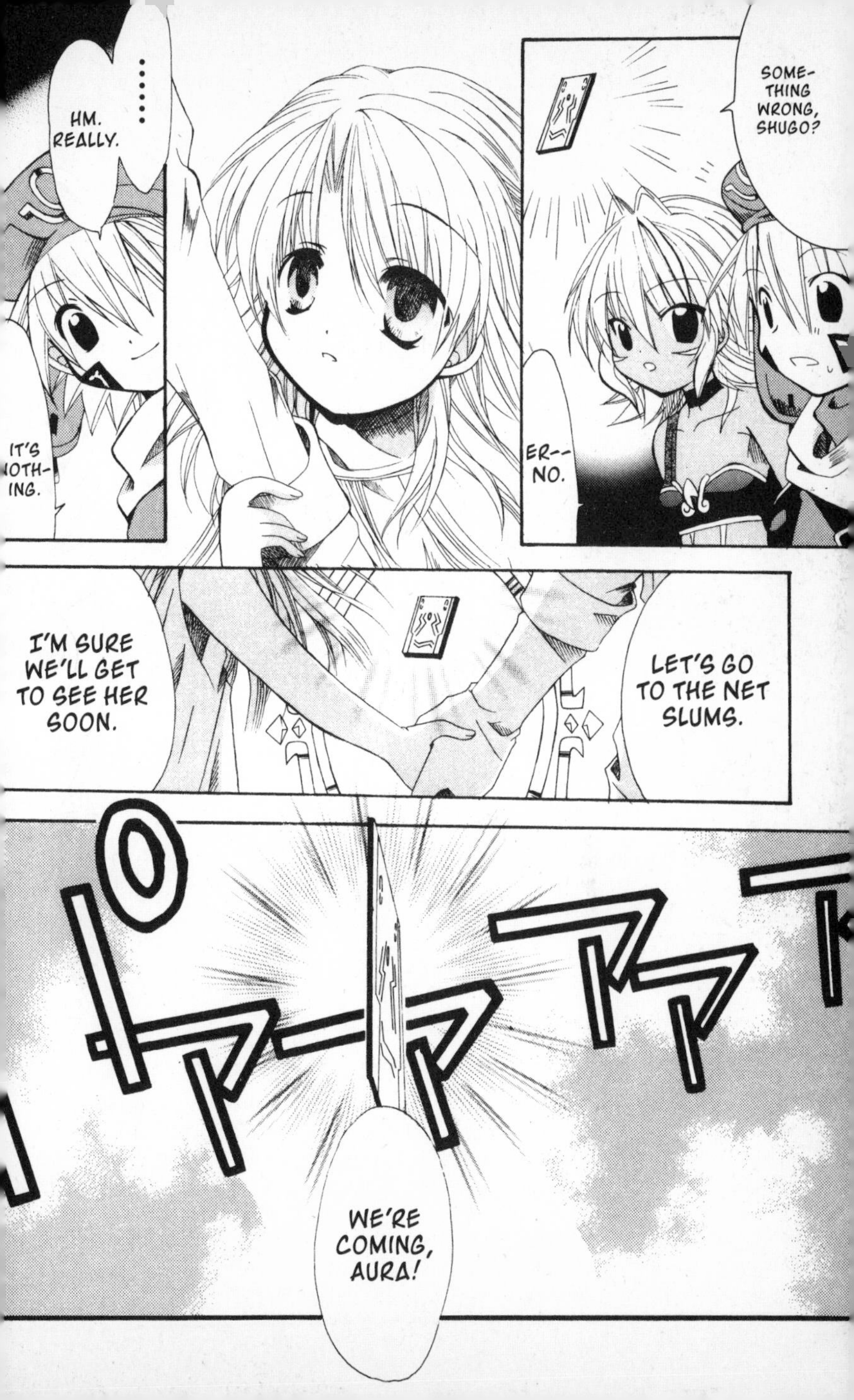
SOME-THING WRONG, SHUGO?
ER--NO.
......
HM. REALLY.
IT'S NOTHING.
LET'S GO TO THE NET SLUMS.
I'M SURE WE'LL GET TO SEE HER SOON.
WE'RE COMING, AURA!

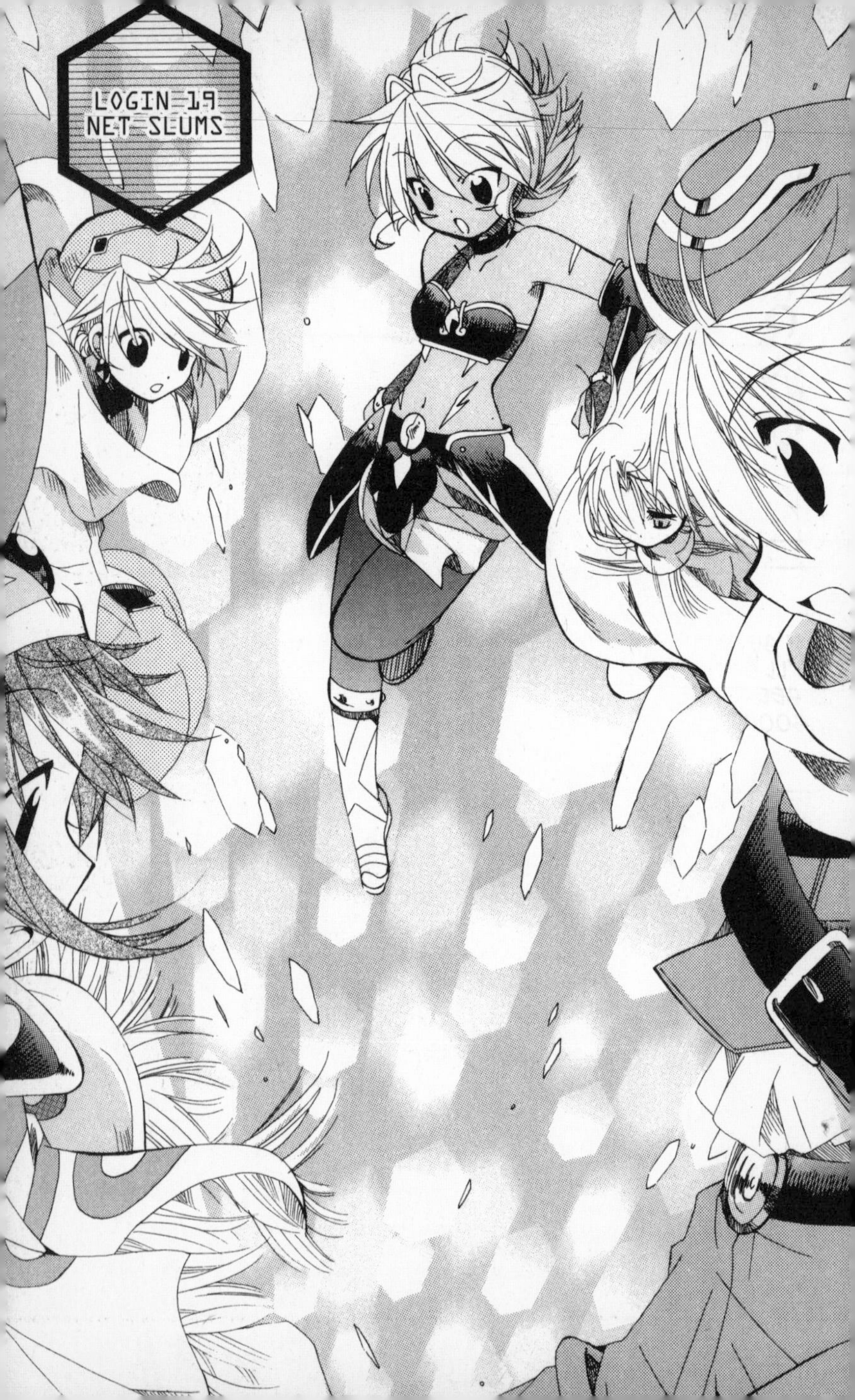
LOGIN 19
NET SLUMS

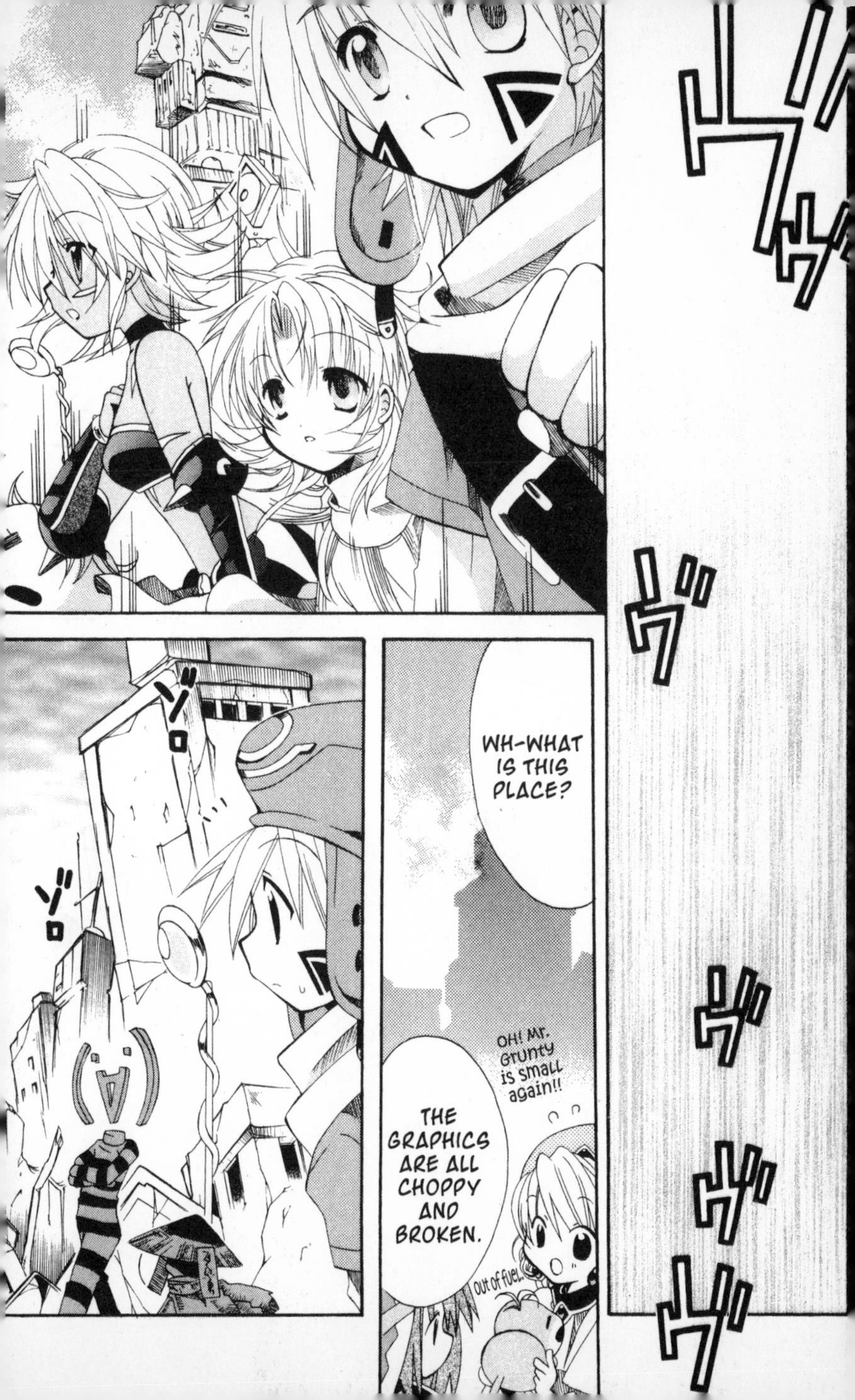
WH-WHAT IS THIS PLACE?
OH! Mr. Grunty is small again!!
THE GRAPHICS ARE ALL CHOPPY AND BROKEN.
Out of fuel.
ゾロ
ゾロ

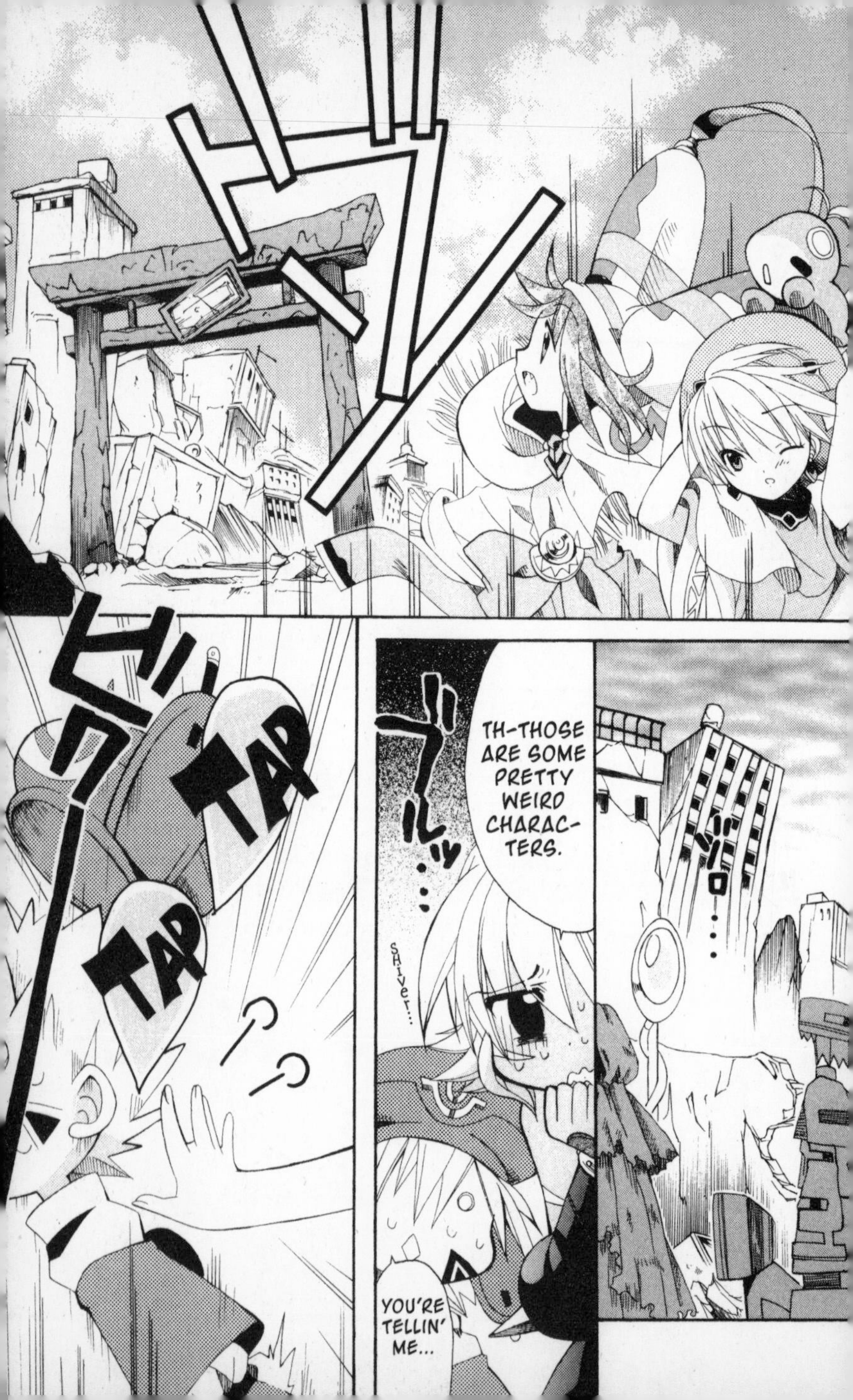
TH-THOSE ARE SOME PRETTY WEIRD CHARAC-TERS.
Shiver...
YOU'RE TELLIN' ME...
TAP
TAP

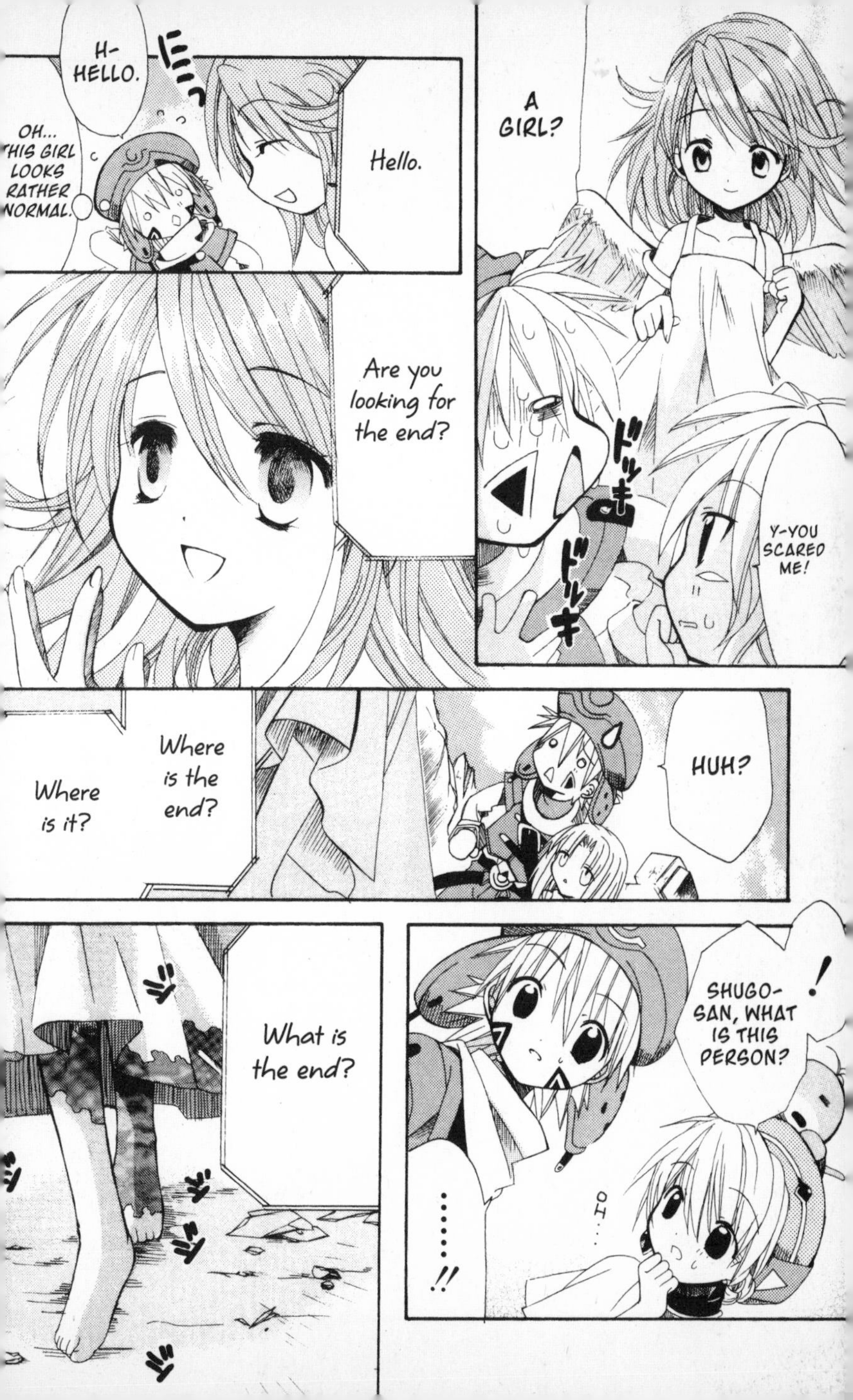
A GIRL?
ドッキ ドッキ
Y-YOU SCARED ME!
Hello.
H-HELLO.
OH... THIS GIRL LOOKS RATHER NORMAL.
Are you looking for the end?
HUH?
Where is the end?
Where is it?
SHUGO-SAN, WHAT IS THIS PERSON?
!
OH...
......!!
What is the end?

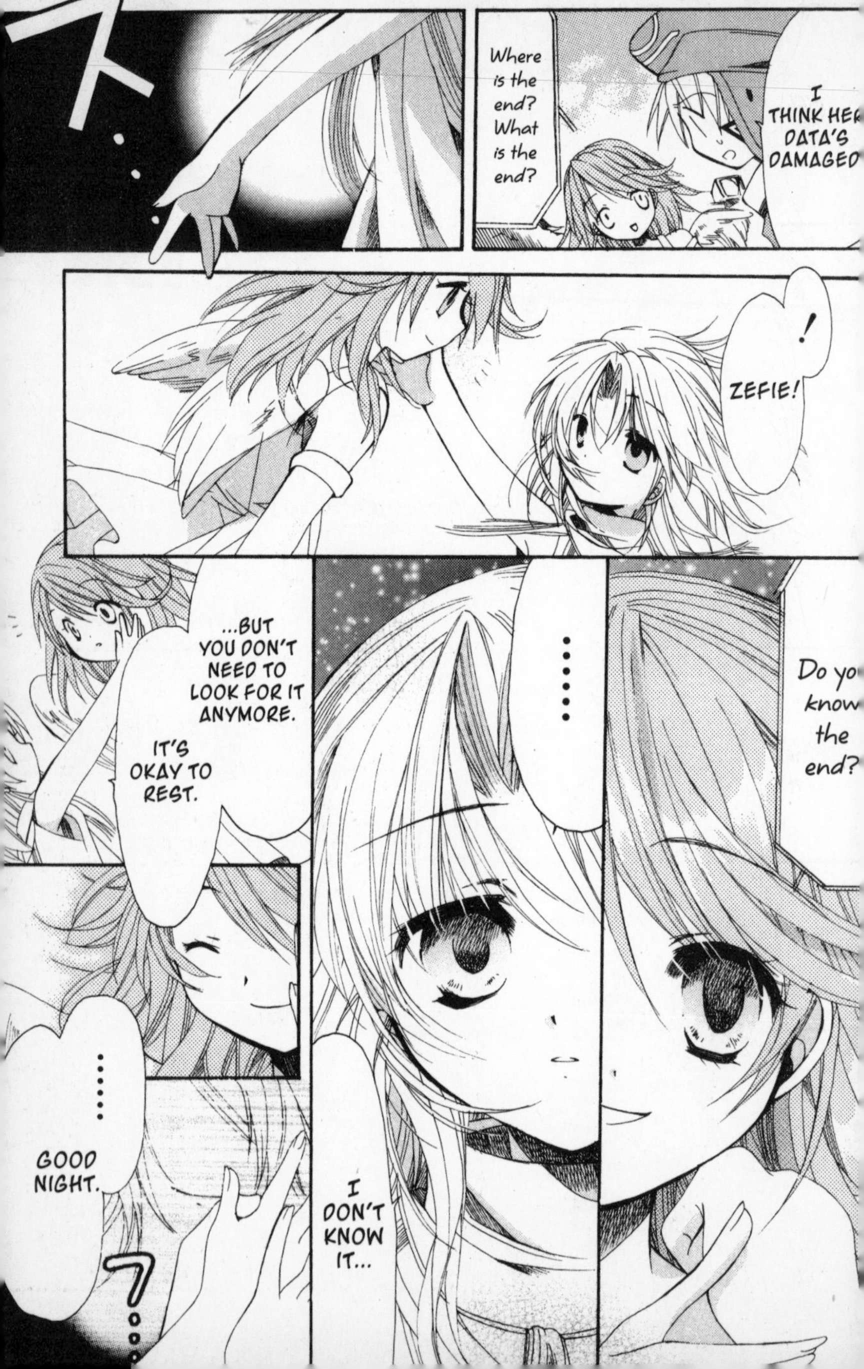
I THINK HER DATA'S DAMAGED
Where is the end? What is the end?
ス…
!
ZEFIE!
Do you know the end?
……
I DON'T KNOW IT…
…BUT YOU DON'T NEED TO LOOK FOR IT ANYMORE.
IT'S OKAY TO REST.
……
GOOD NIGHT.
フ…

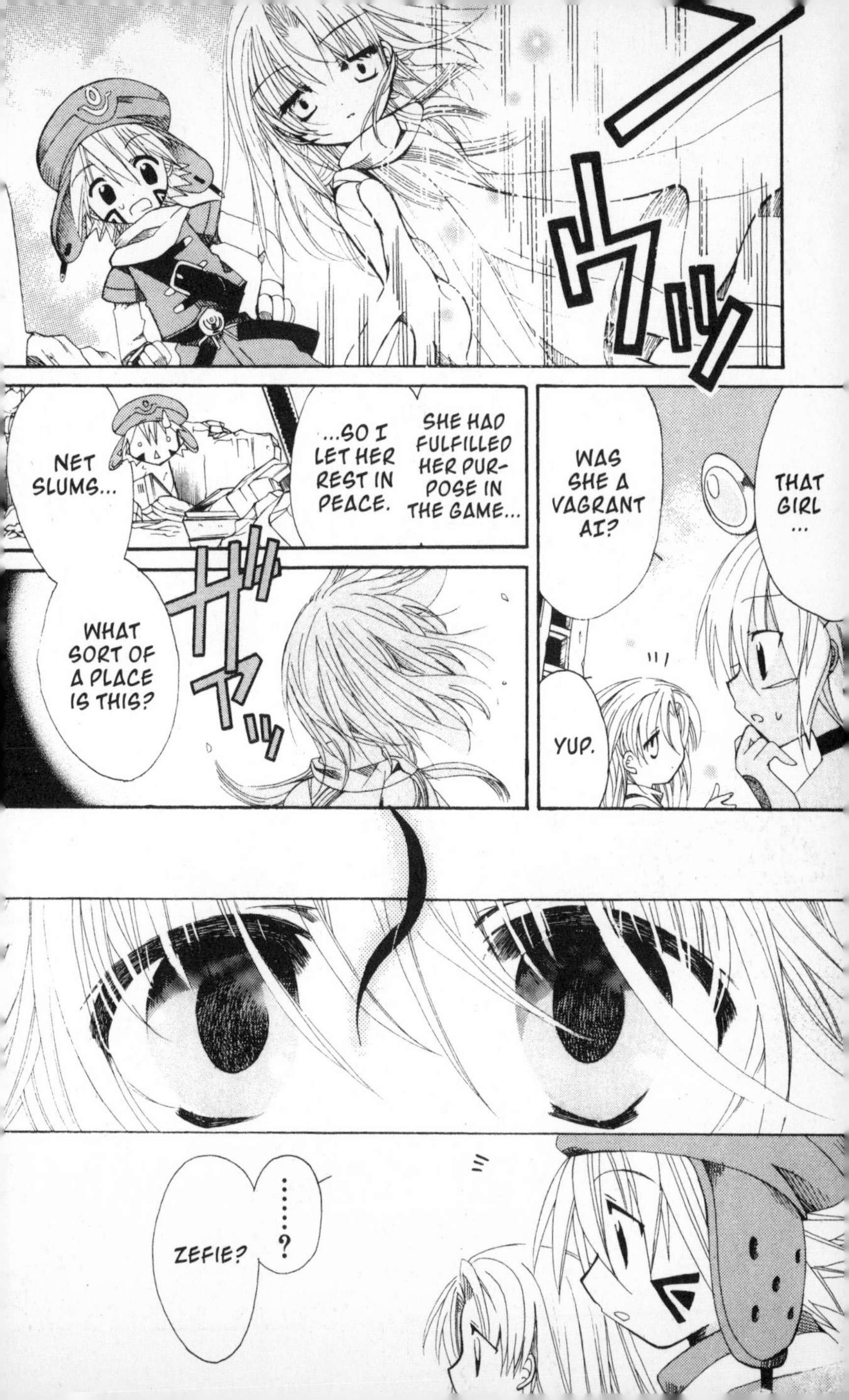
THAT GIRL ...
WAS SHE A VAGRANT AI?
YUP.
SHE HAD FULFILLED HER PURPOSE IN THE GAME...
...SO I LET HER REST IN PEACE.
NET SLUMS...
WHAT SORT OF A PLACE IS THIS?
......?
ZEFIE?

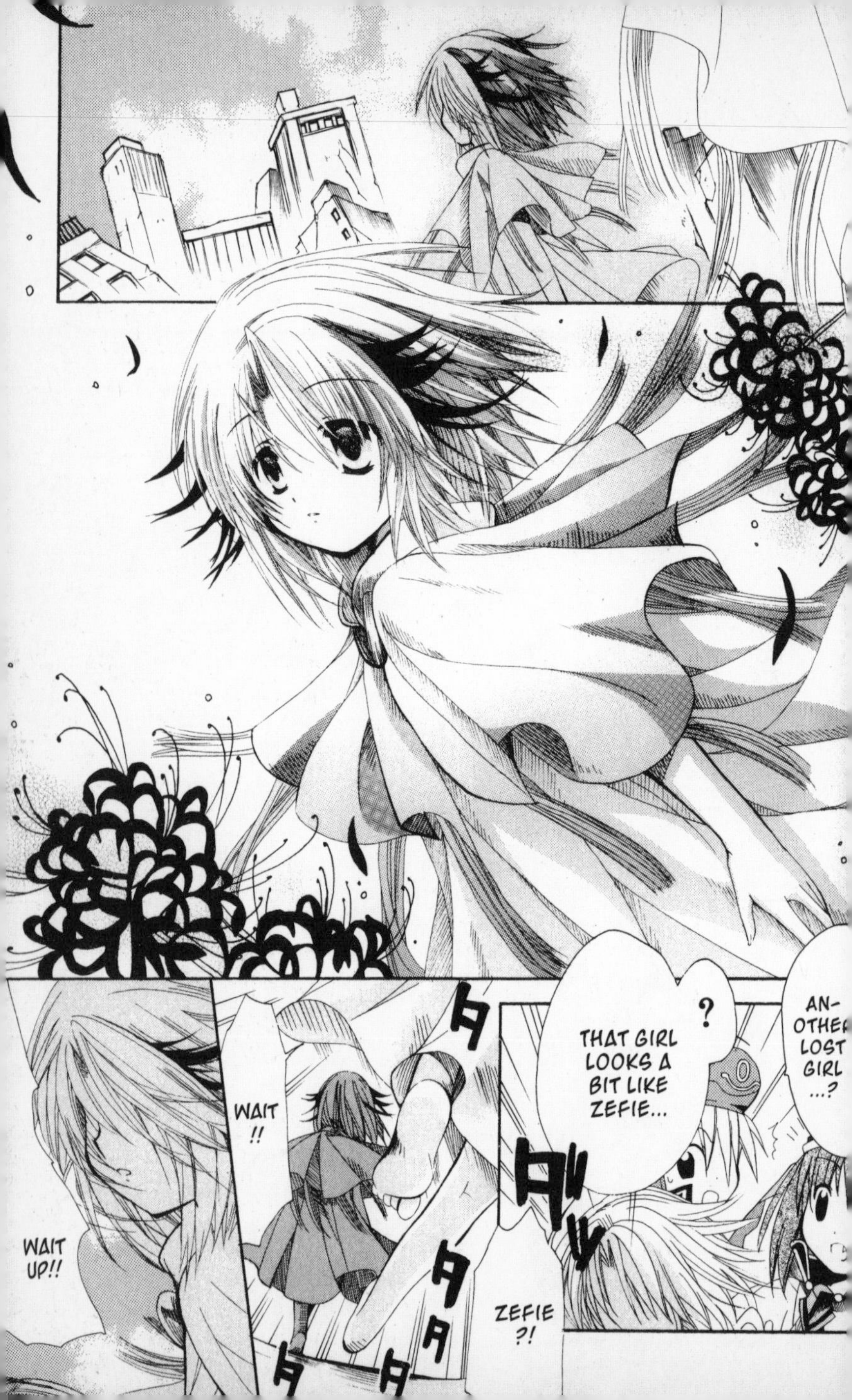

AN-OTHER LOST GIRL ...?
?
THAT GIRL LOOKS A BIT LIKE ZEFIE...
ZEFIE ?!
WAIT !!
WAIT UP!!

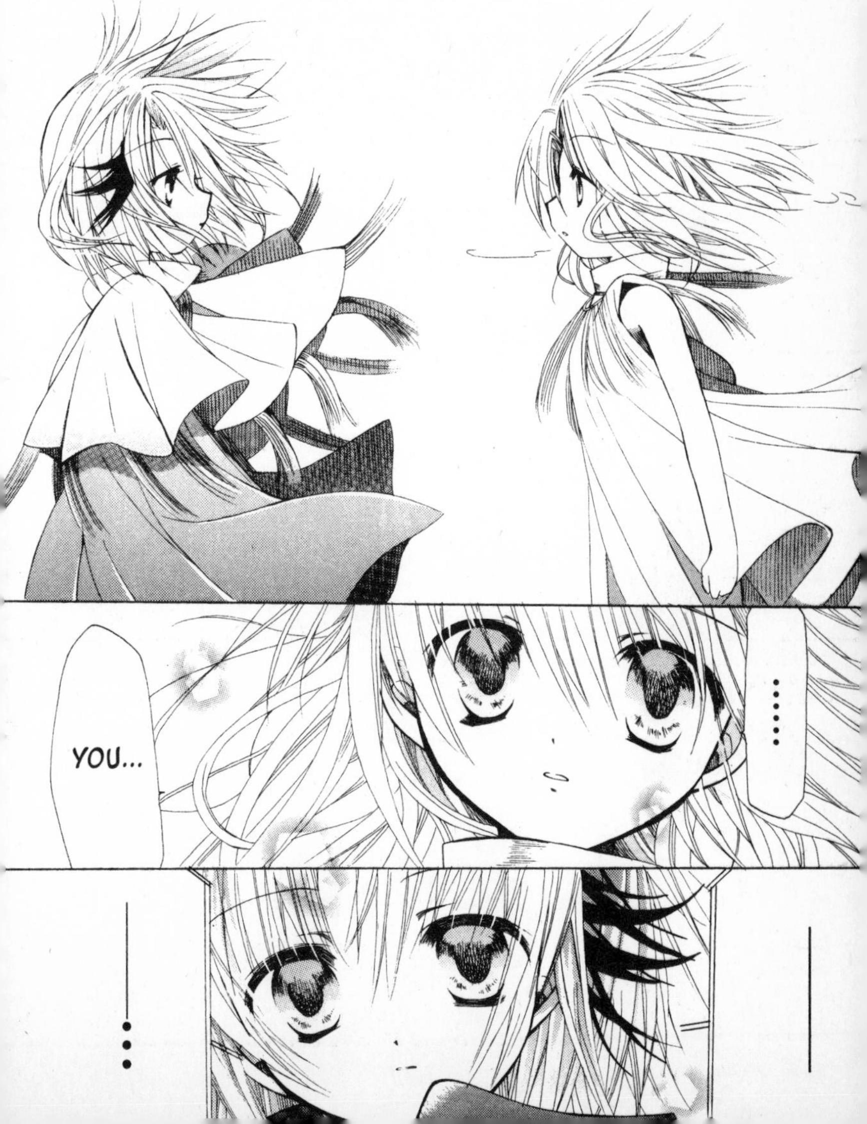
......
YOU...

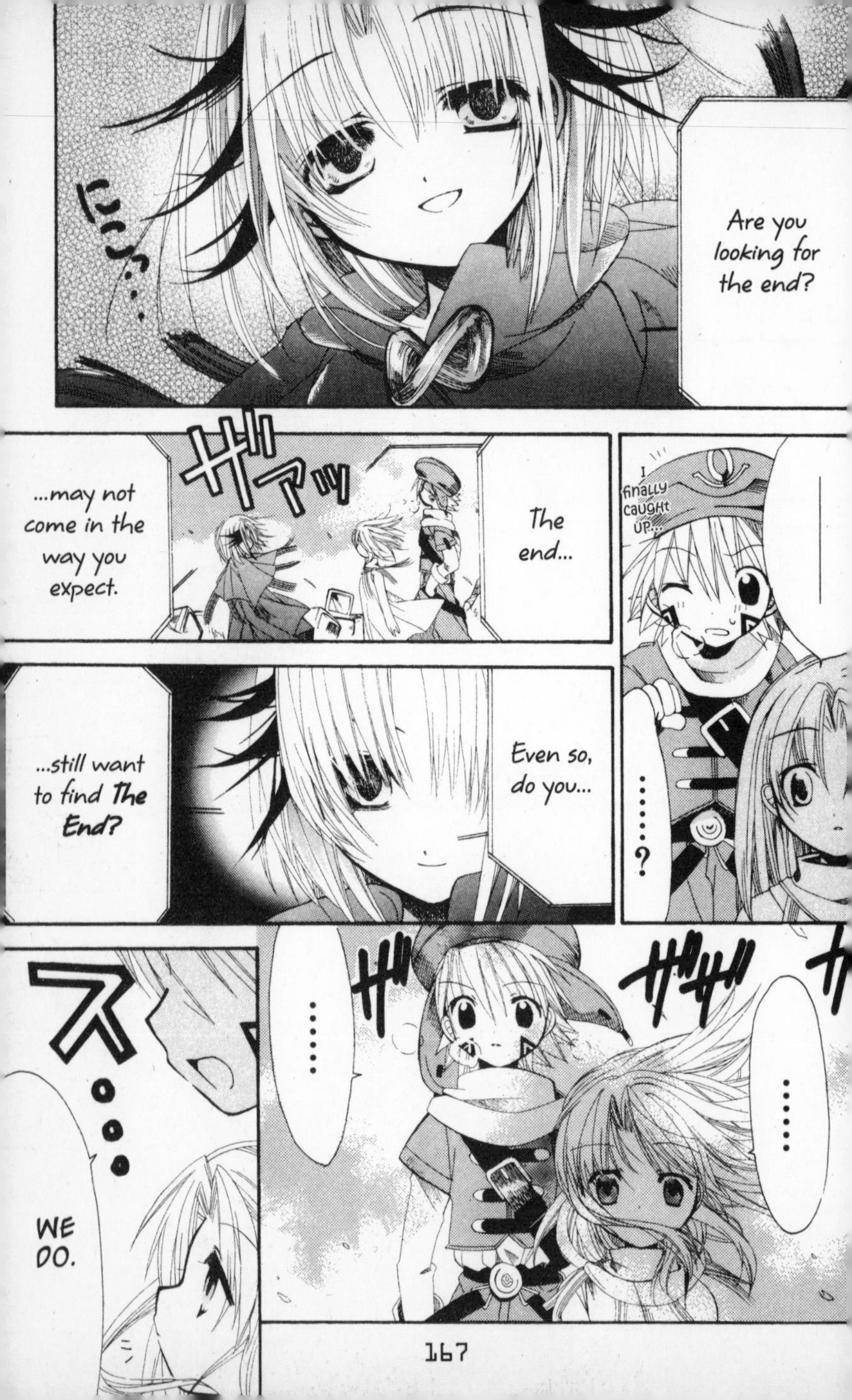

にこ…
Are you looking for the end?
I finally caught up...
......?
The end...
ザアッ
...may not come in the way you expect.
Even so, do you...
...still want to find The End?
ザザ
......
ザ
......
ス
...
WE DO.

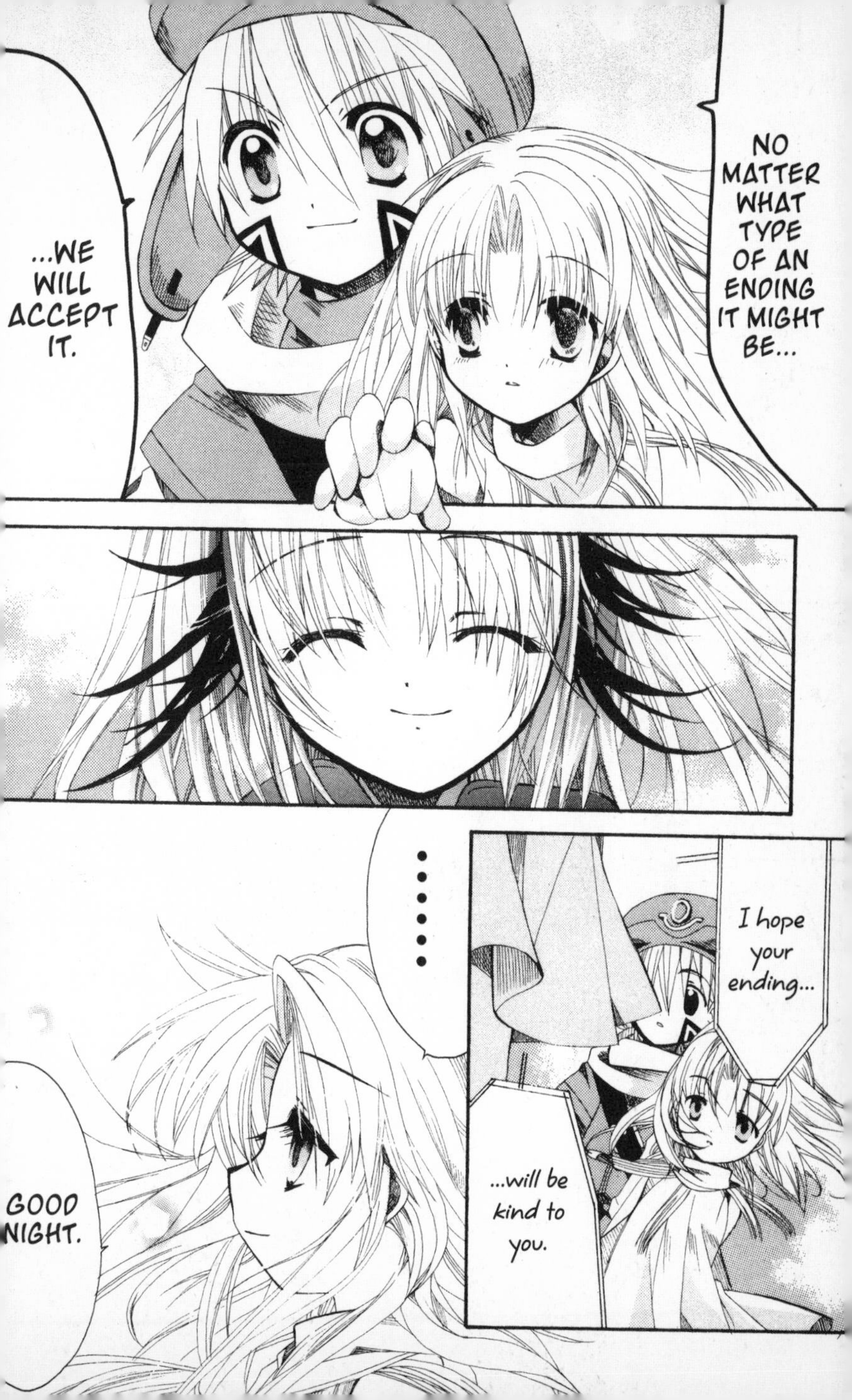
NO MATTER WHAT TYPE OF AN ENDING IT MIGHT BE...
...WE WILL ACCEPT IT.
I hope your ending...
...will be kind to you.
......
GOOD NIGHT.

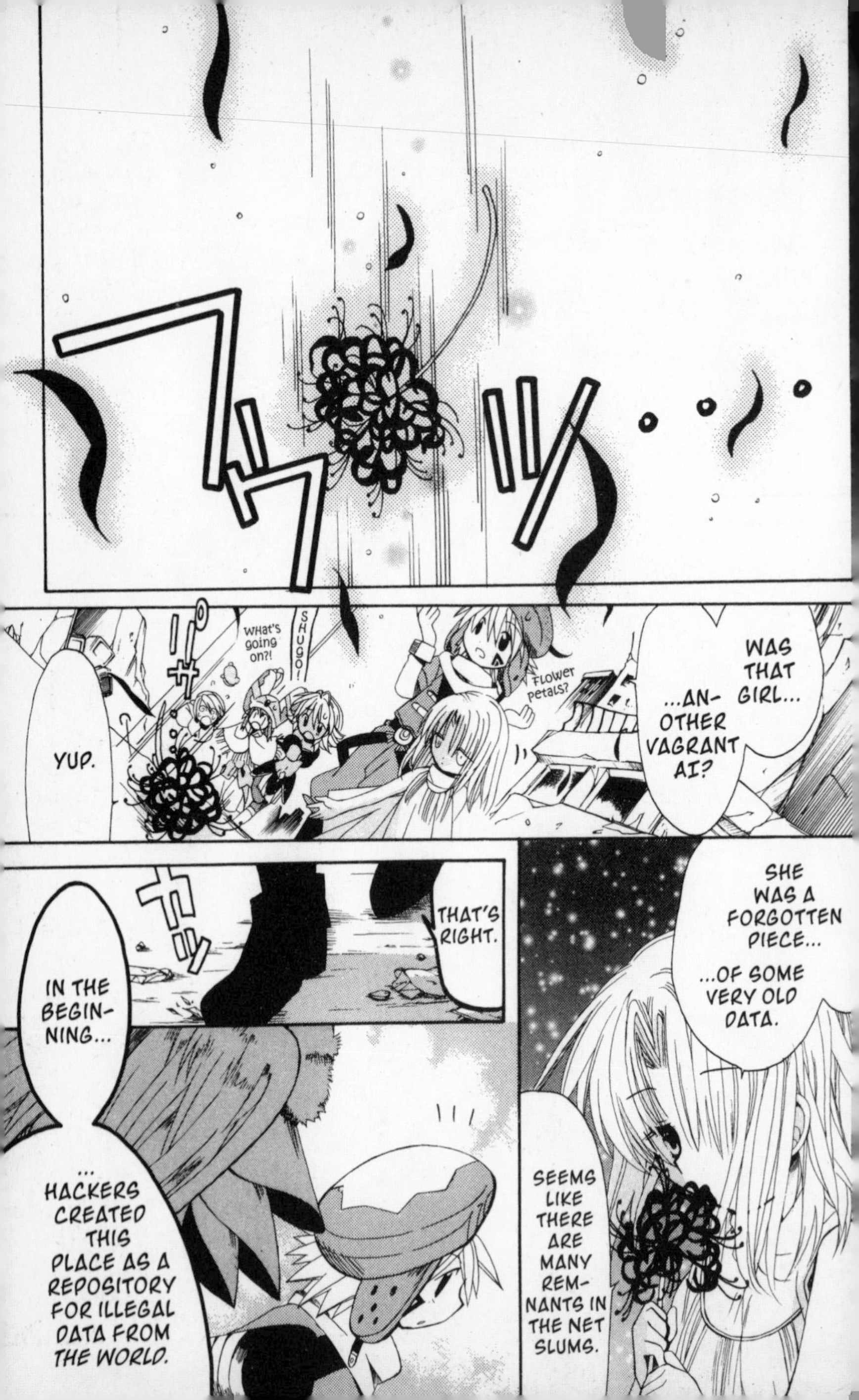

WAS THAT GIRL... ...AN-OTHER VAGRANT AI?
Flower petals?
SHUGO!
What's going on?!
YUP.
SHE WAS A FORGOTTEN PIECE...
...OF SOME VERY OLD DATA.
SEEMS LIKE THERE ARE MANY REM-NANTS IN THE NET SLUMS.
THAT'S RIGHT.
IN THE BEGIN-NING...
... HACKERS CREATED THIS PLACE AS A REPOSITORY FOR ILLEGAL DATA FROM THE WORLD.

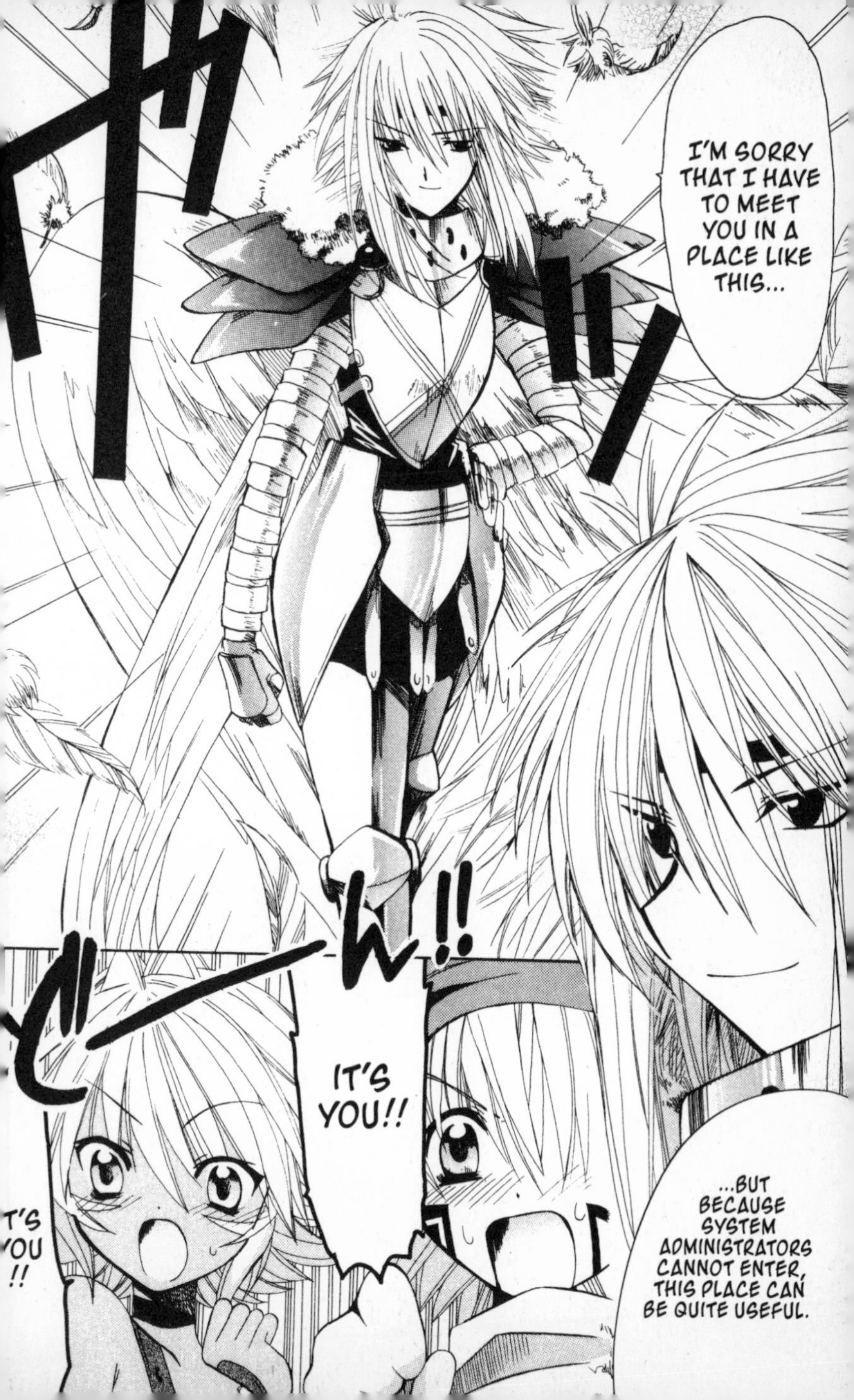
I'M SORRY THAT I HAVE TO MEET YOU IN A PLACE LIKE THIS...
...BUT BECAUSE SYSTEM ADMINISTRATORS CANNOT ENTER, THIS PLACE CAN BE QUITE USEFUL.
IT'S YOU!!

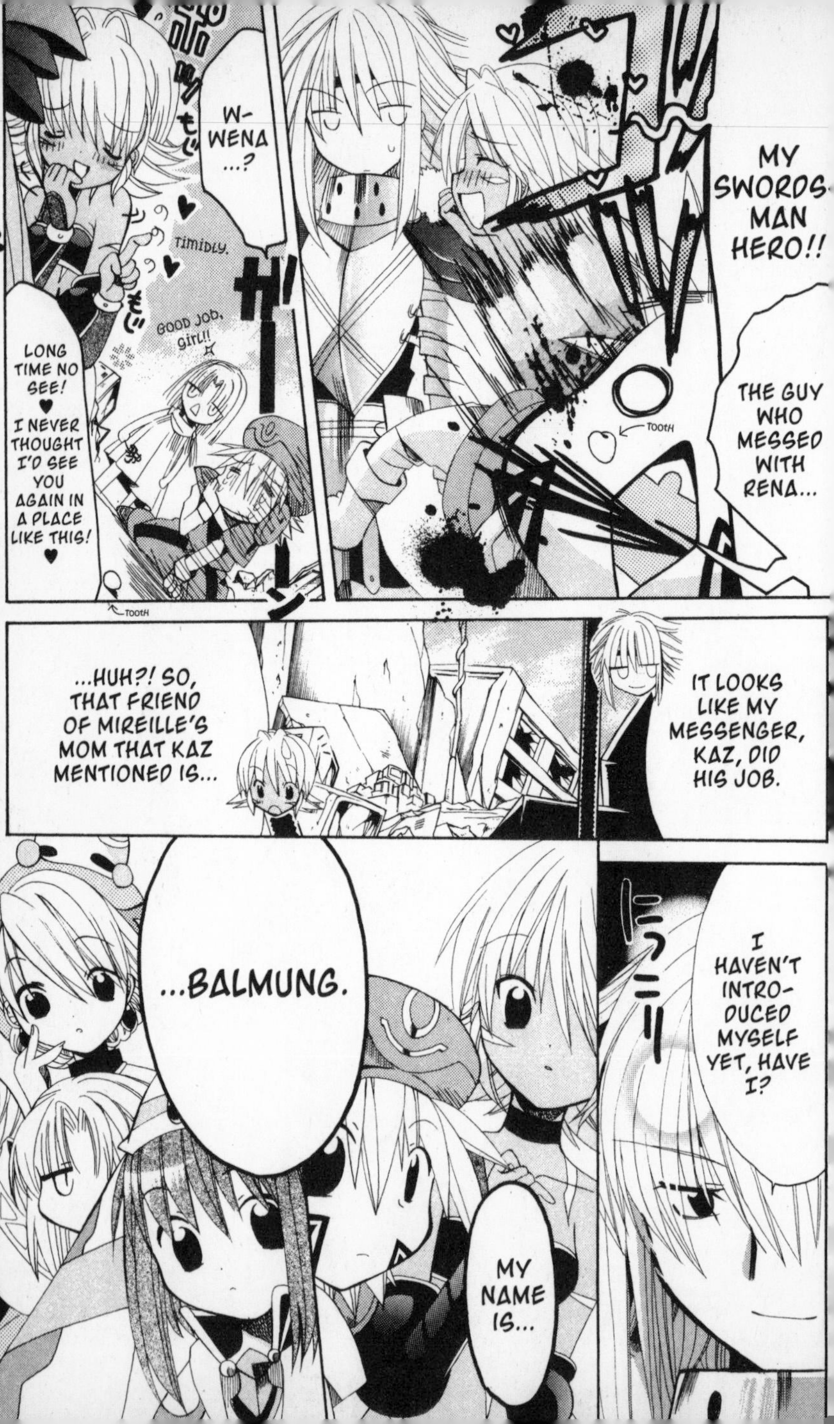
MY SWORDSMAN HERO!!
THE GUY WHO MESSED WITH RENA...
TOOTH
W-WENA ...?
TIMIDLY.
GOOD JOB, GIRL!!
LONG TIME NO SEE! ♥ I NEVER THOUGHT I'D SEE YOU AGAIN IN A PLACE LIKE THIS! ♥
TOOTH
IT LOOKS LIKE MY MESSENGER, KAZ, DID HIS JOB.
...HUH?! SO, THAT FRIEND OF MIREILLE'S MOM THAT KAZ MENTIONED IS...
I HAVEN'T INTRODUCED MYSELF YET, HAVE I?
MY NAME IS...
...BALMUNG.

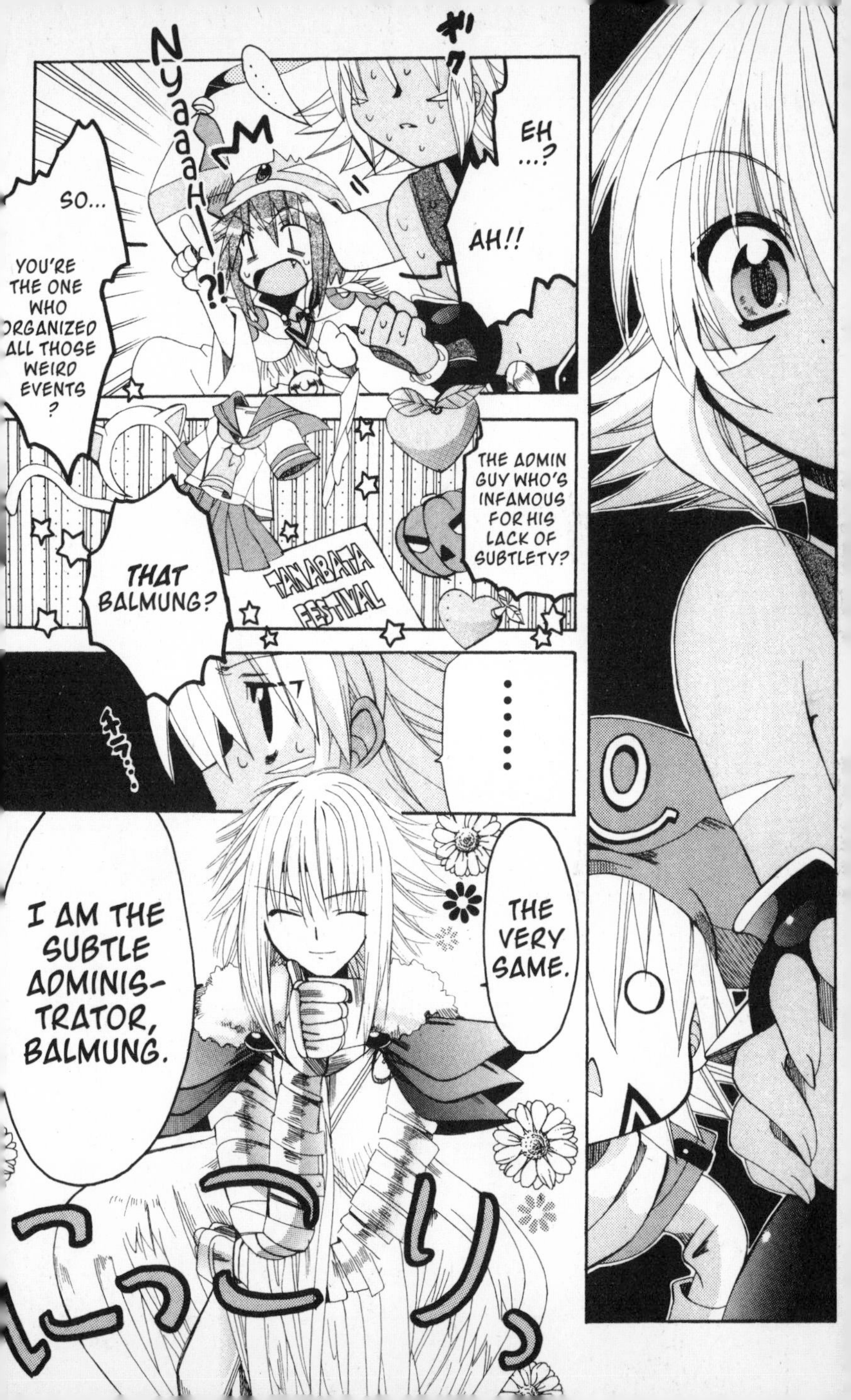
ギク
EH ...?
AH!!
NYAAAAH!!?!
SO...
YOU'RE THE ONE WHO ORGANIZED ALL THOSE WEIRD EVENTS?
THE ADMIN GUY WHO'S INFAMOUS FOR HIS LACK OF SUBTLETY?
THAT BALMUNG?
TANABATA FESTIVAL
......
THE VERY SAME.
I AM THE SUBTLE ADMINIS-TRATOR, BALMUNG.
にっこり

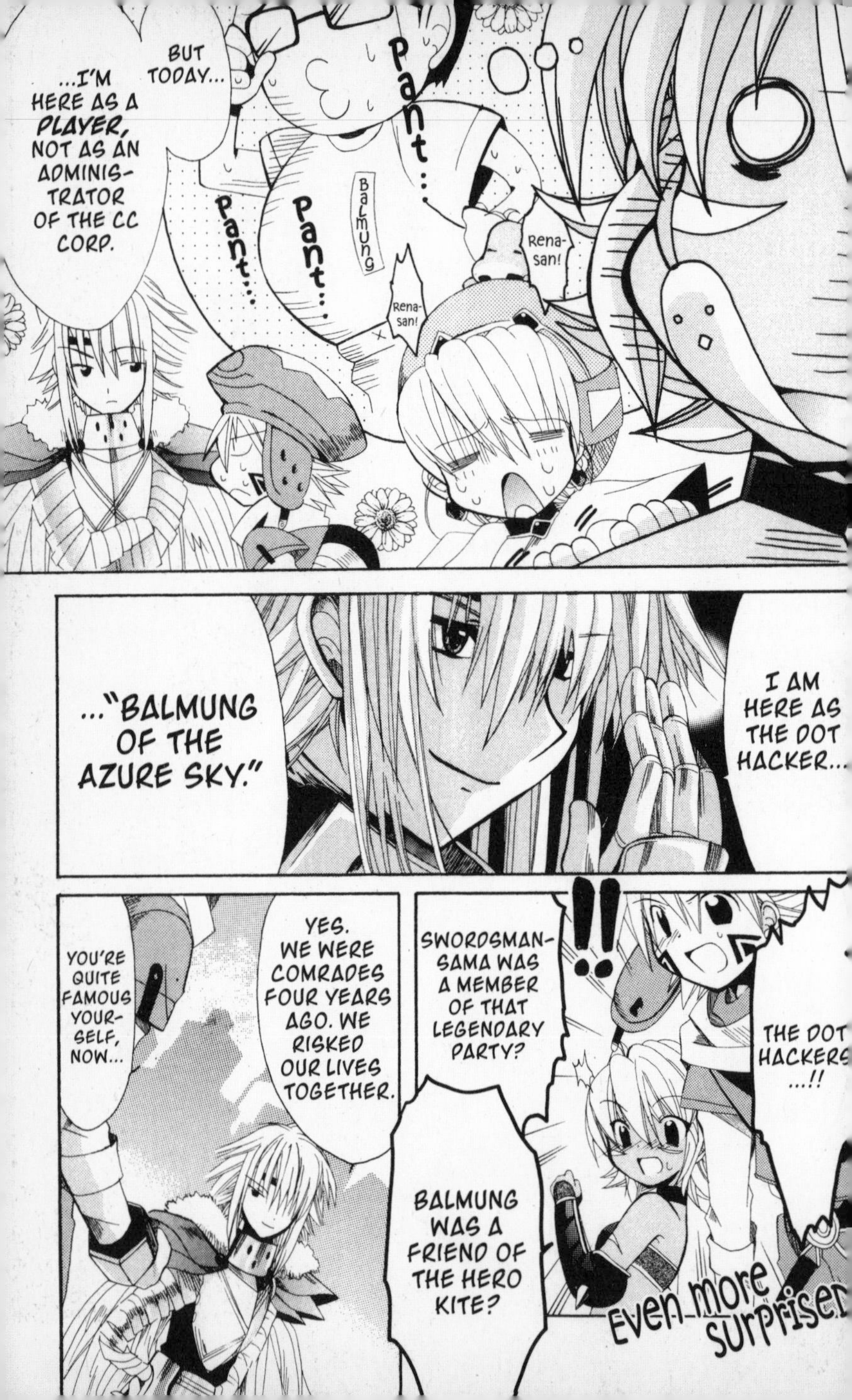

Rena-san!
Rena-san!
Pant...
Balmung
Pant...
Pant...
BUT TODAY...
...I'M HERE AS A PLAYER, NOT AS AN ADMINISTRATOR OF THE CC CORP.
I AM HERE AS THE DOT HACKER...
..."BALMUNG OF THE AZURE SKY."
!!
THE DOT HACKERS ...!!
SWORDSMAN-SAMA WAS A MEMBER OF THAT LEGENDARY PARTY?
BALMUNG WAS A FRIEND OF THE HERO KITE?
Even more surprised
YES. WE WERE COMRADES FOUR YEARS AGO. WE RISKED OUR LIVES TOGETHER.
YOU'RE QUITE FAMOUS YOURSELF, NOW...

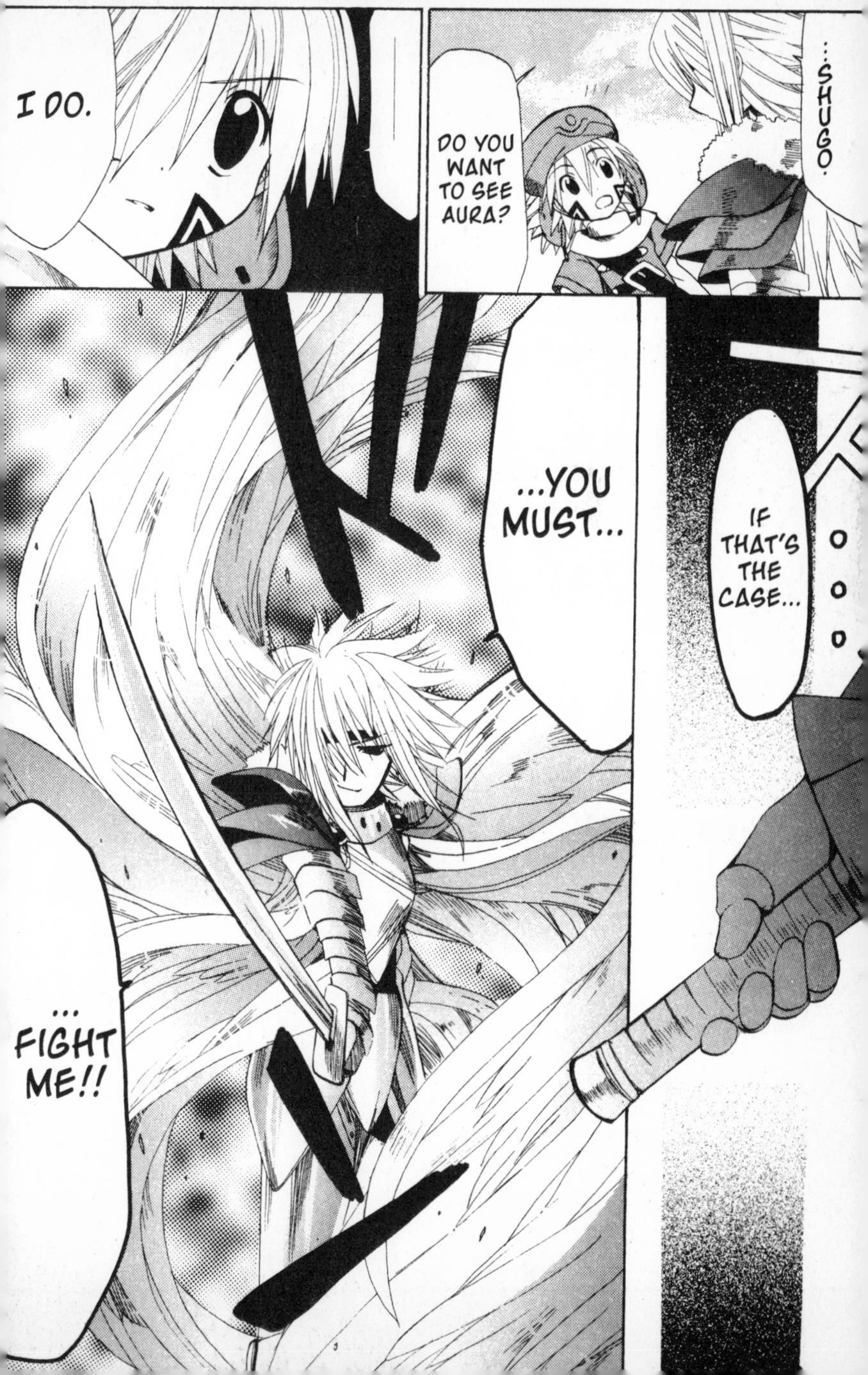
...SHUGO.
DO YOU WANT TO SEE AURA?
I DO.
IF THAT'S THE CASE...
...YOU MUST...
...FIGHT ME!!

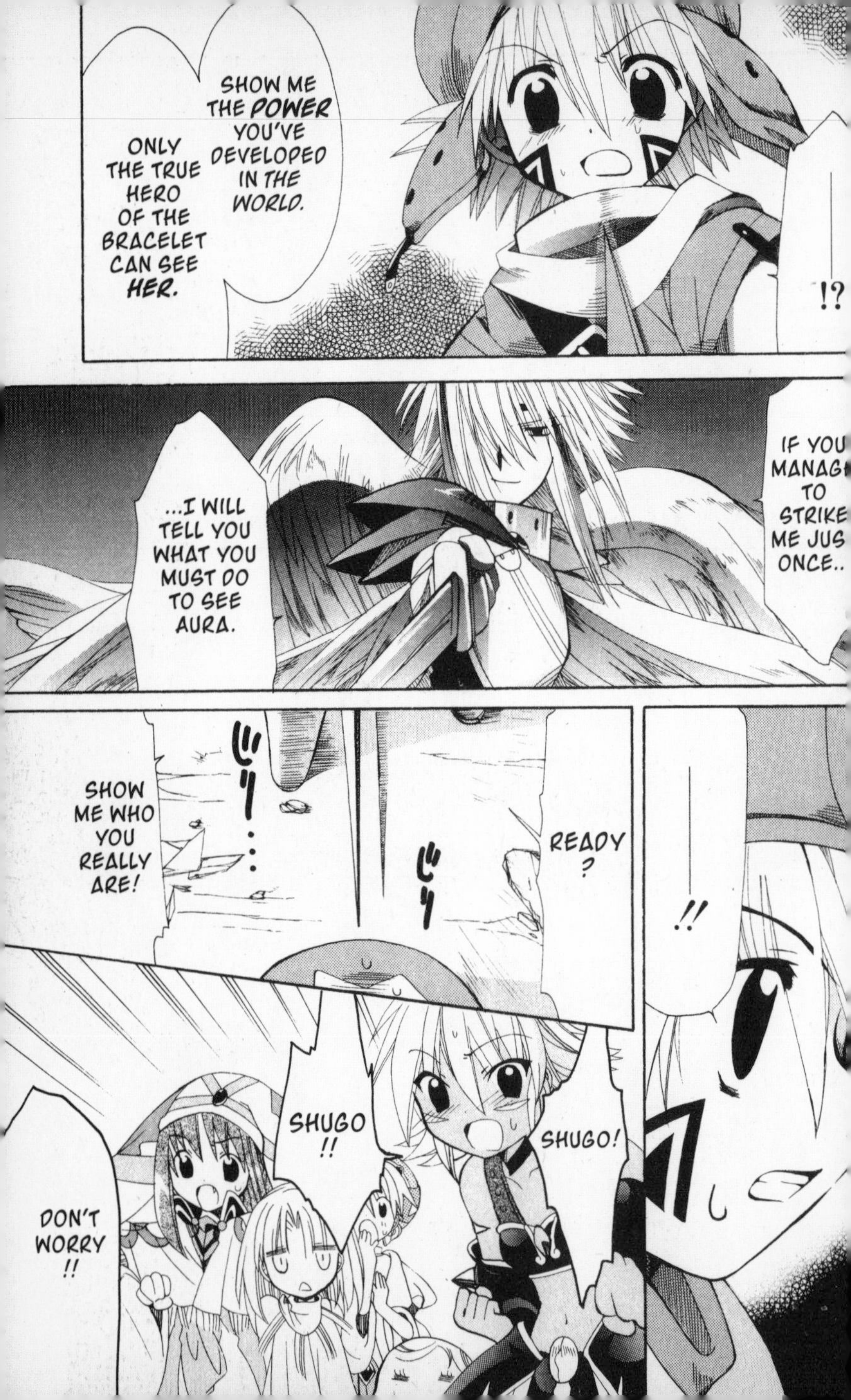
!?
SHOW ME THE POWER YOU'VE DEVELOPED IN THE WORLD.
ONLY THE TRUE HERO OF THE BRACELET CAN SEE HER.
IF YOU MANAG TO STRIKE ME JUS ONCE..
...I WILL TELL YOU WHAT YOU MUST DO TO SEE AURA.
!!
READY ?
ジリ
ジリ…
SHOW ME WHO YOU REALLY ARE!
SHUGO!
SHUGO !!
DON'T WORRY !!

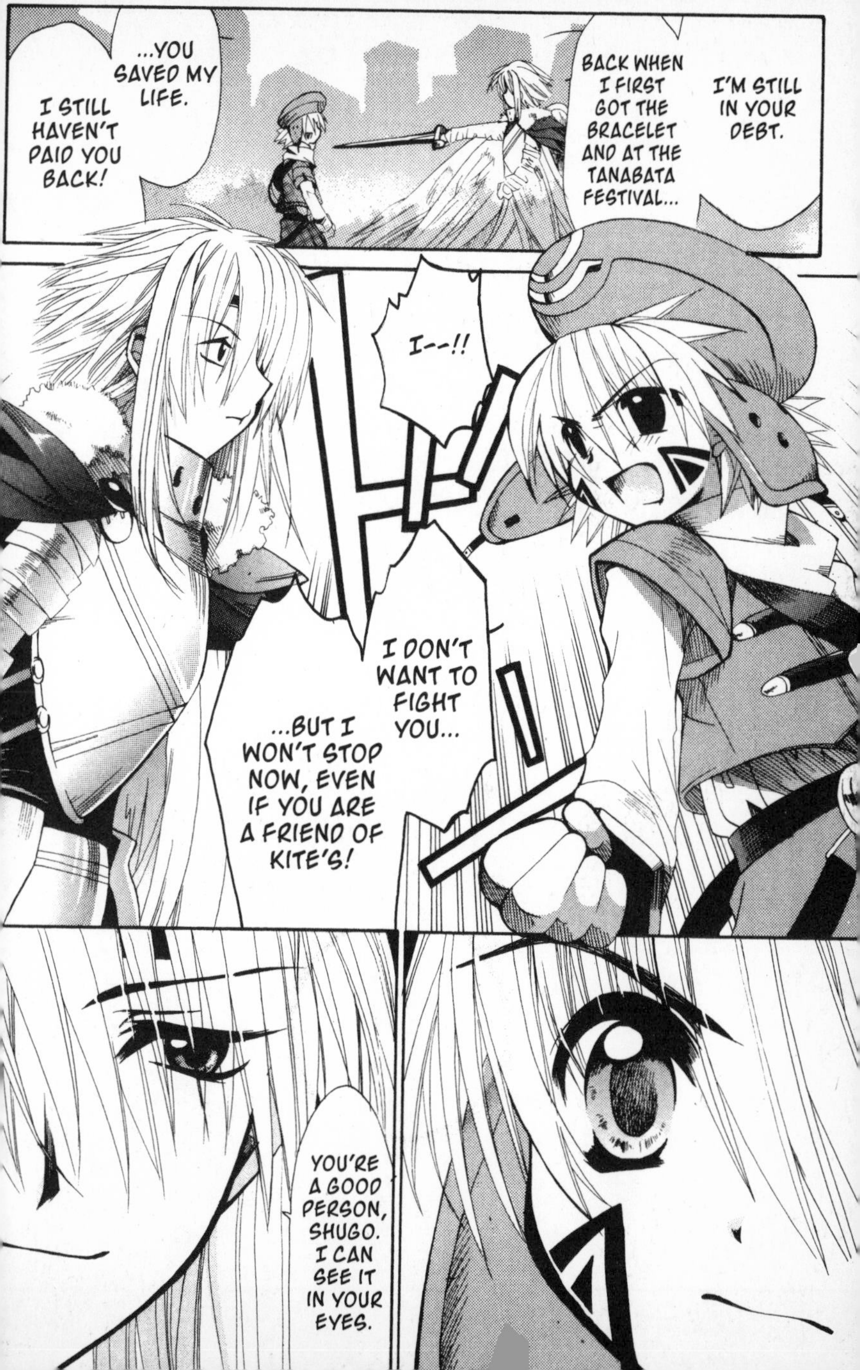
I'M STILL IN YOUR DEBT.
BACK WHEN I FIRST GOT THE BRACELET AND AT THE TANABATA FESTIVAL...
...YOU SAVED MY LIFE.
I STILL HAVEN'T PAID YOU BACK!
I--!!
I DON'T WANT TO FIGHT YOU...
...BUT I WON'T STOP NOW, EVEN IF YOU ARE A FRIEND OF KITE'S!
YOU'RE A GOOD PERSON, SHUGO. I CAN SEE IT IN YOUR EYES.

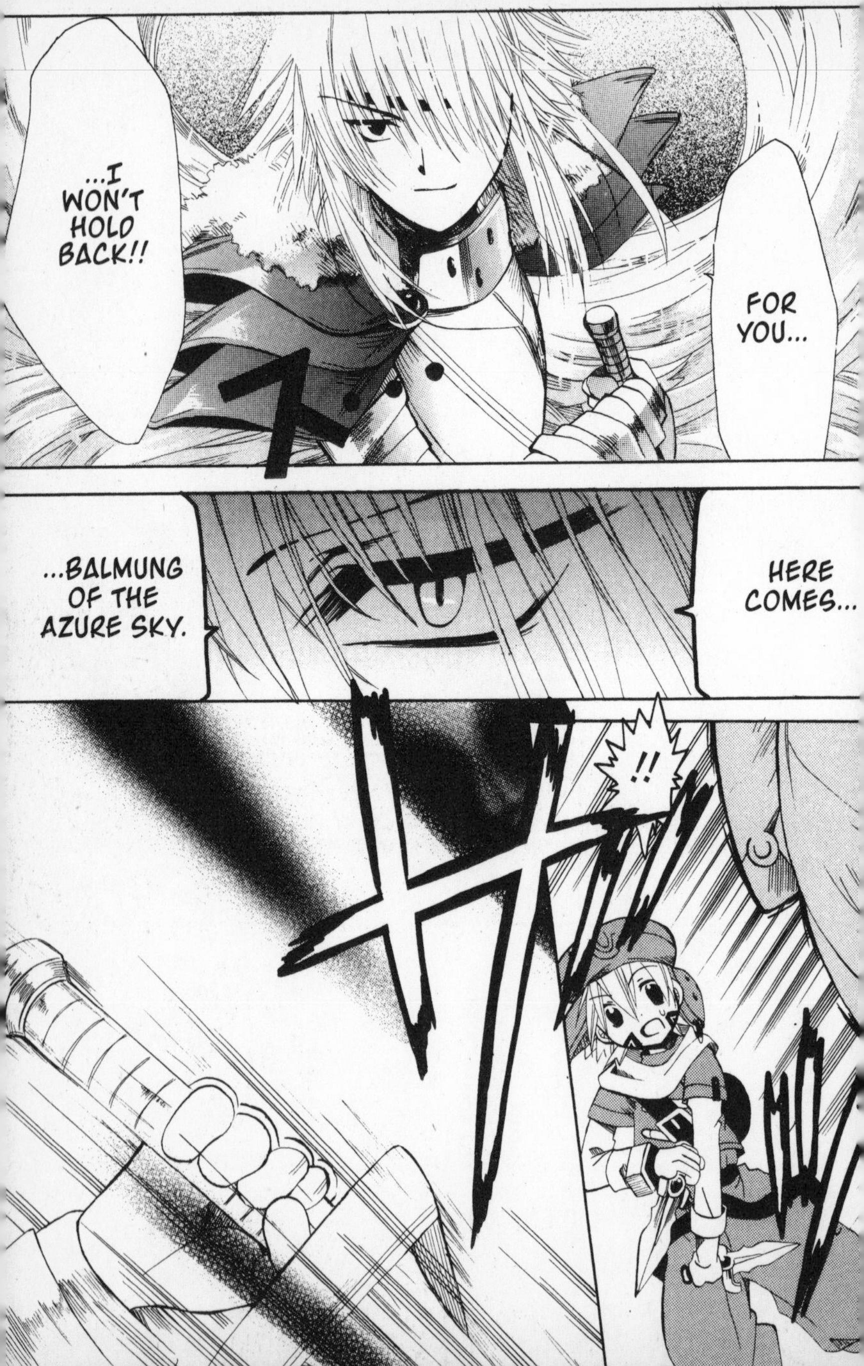
FOR YOU...
...I WON'T HOLD BACK!!
HERE COMES...
...BALMUNG OF THE AZURE SKY.
!!

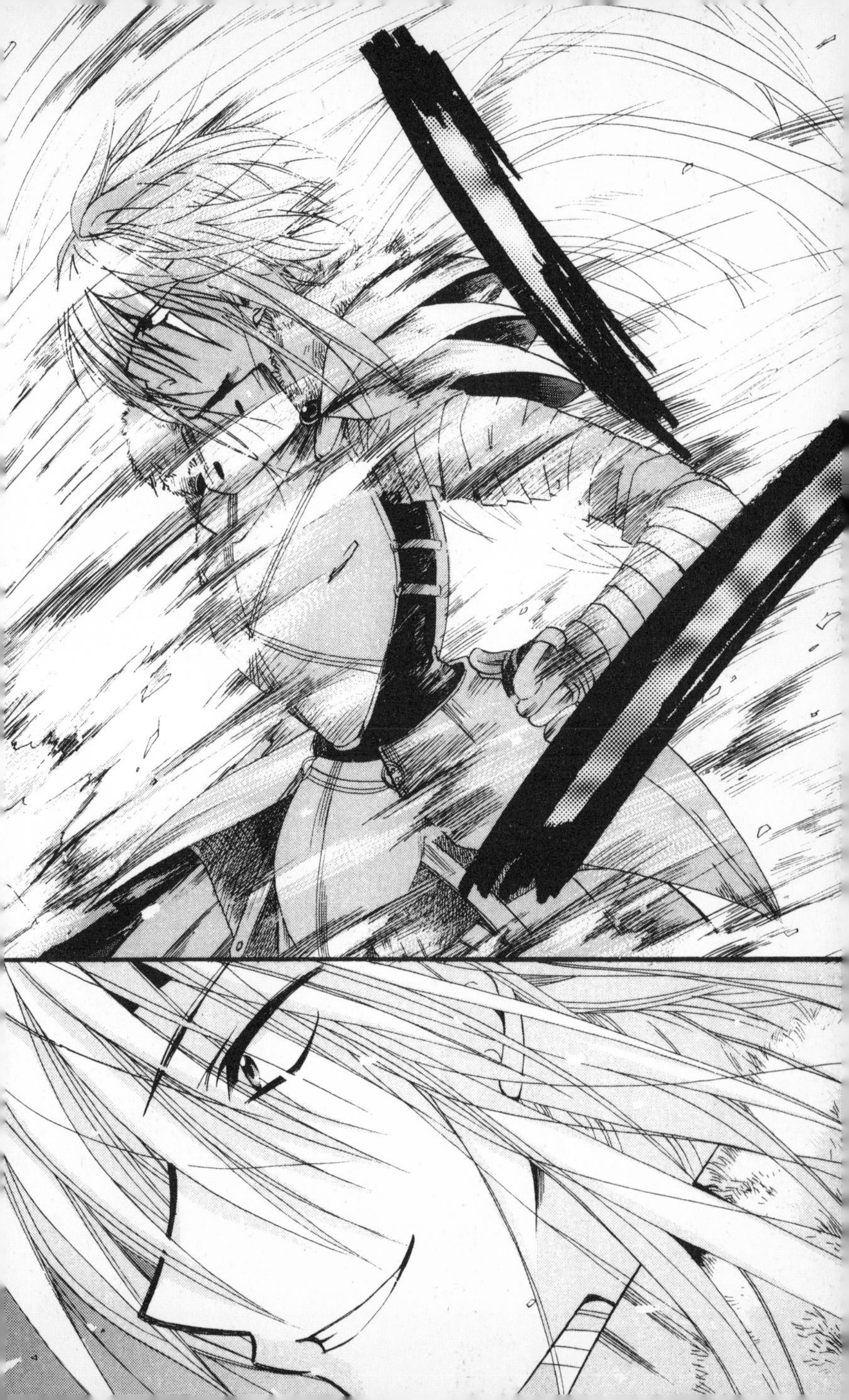

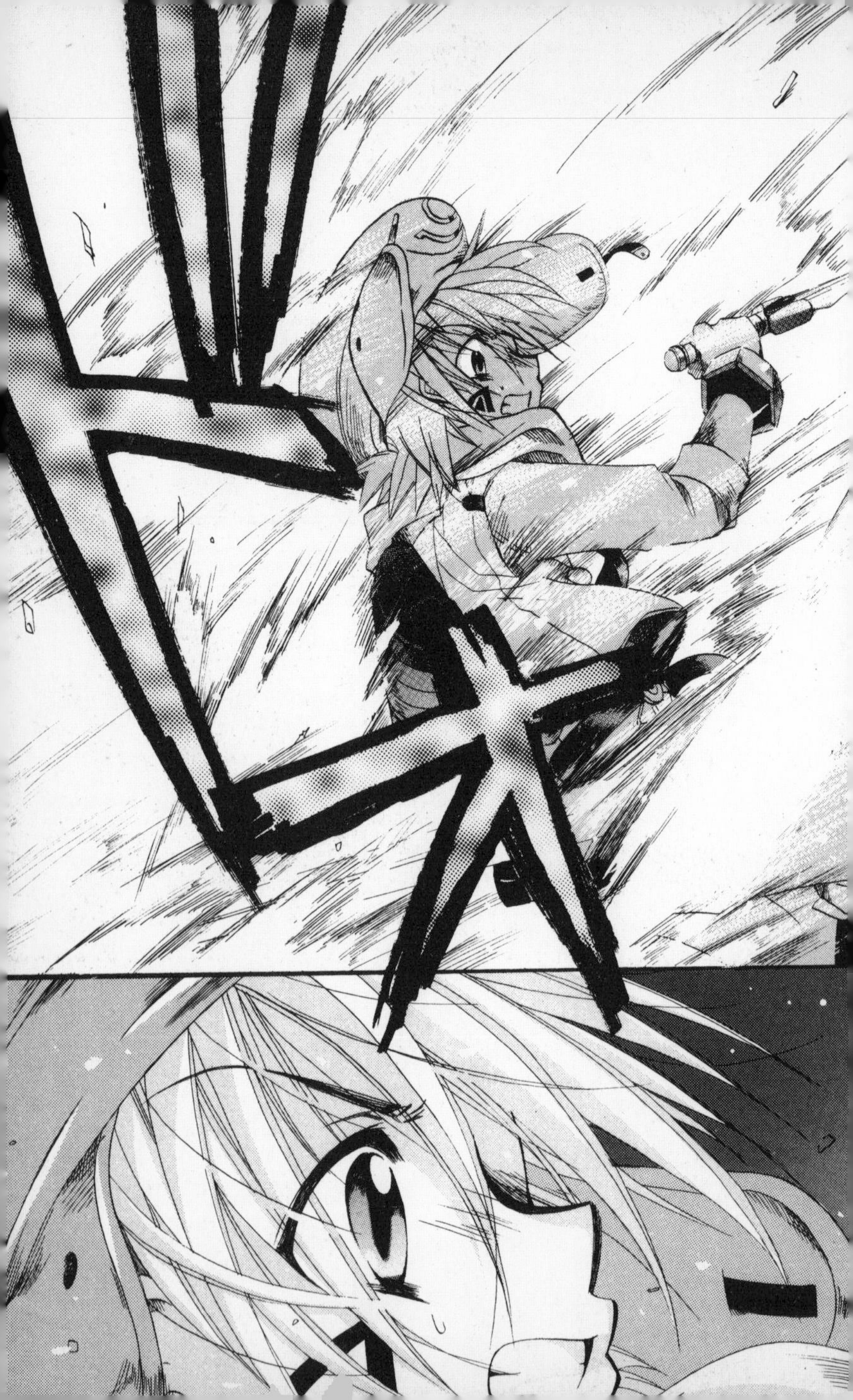

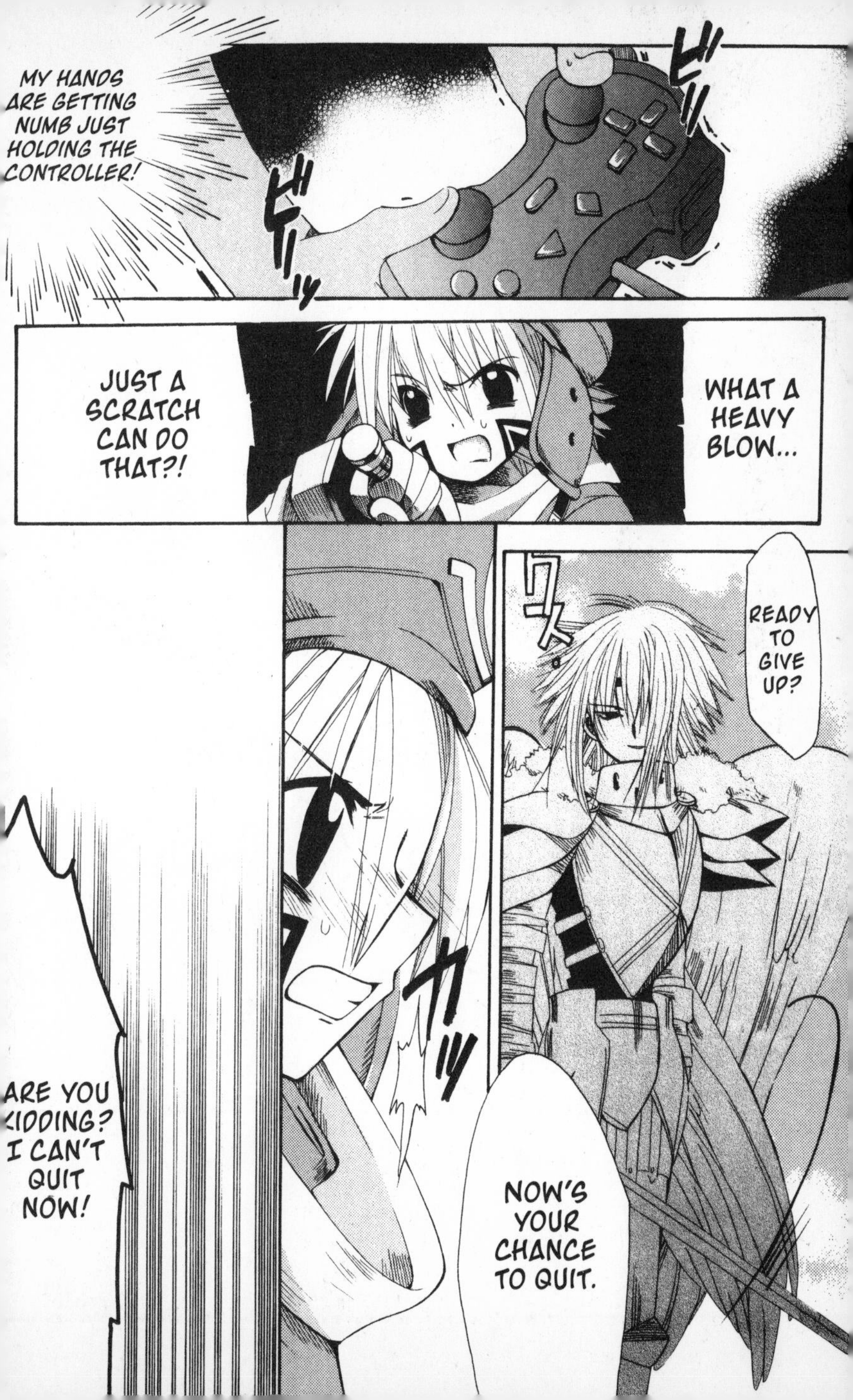
MY HANDS ARE GETTING NUMB JUST HOLDING THE CONTROLLER!
WHAT A HEAVY BLOW...
JUST A SCRATCH CAN DO THAT?!
READY TO GIVE UP?
NOW'S YOUR CHANCE TO QUIT.
ARE YOU KIDDING? I CAN'T QUIT NOW!

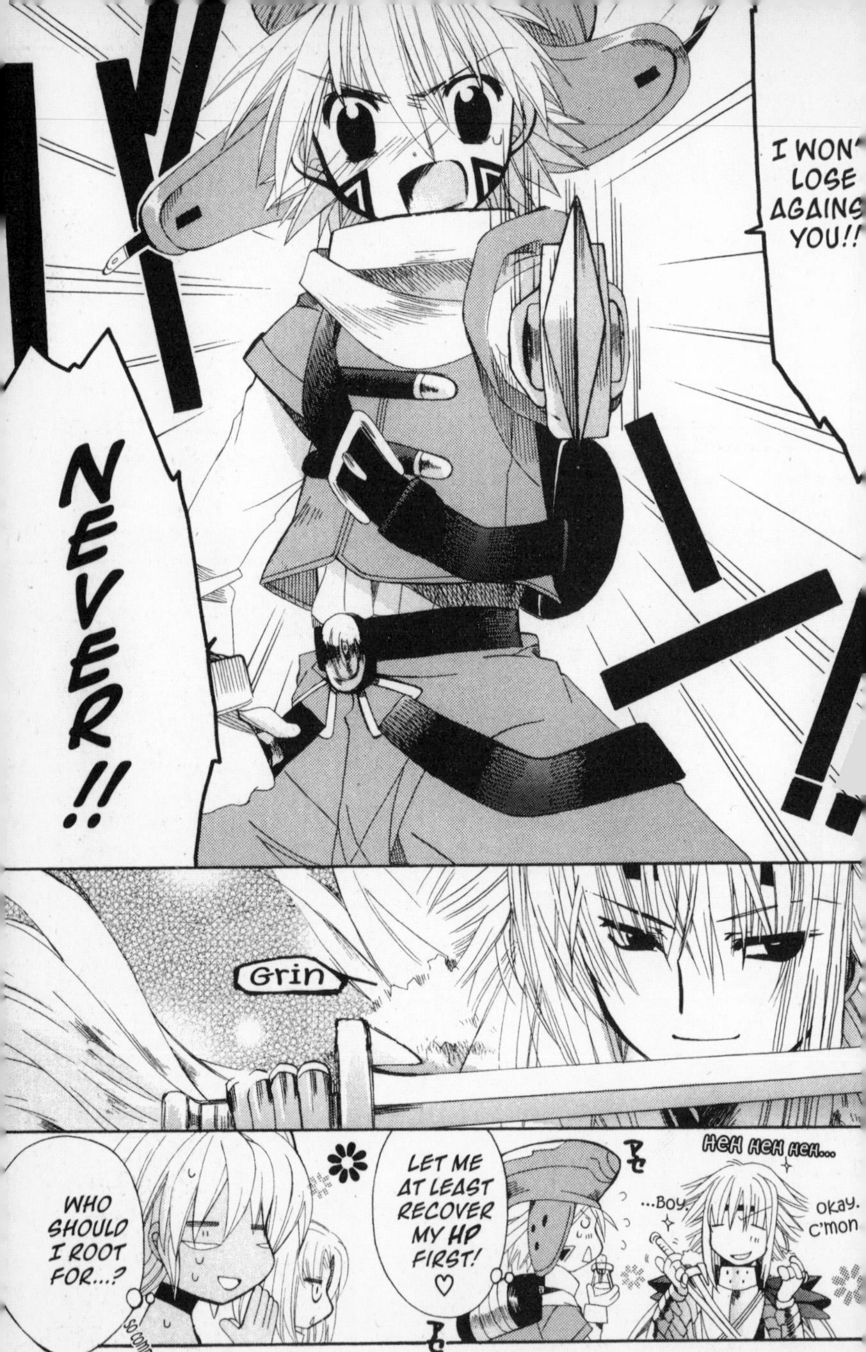
I WON' LOSE AGAINS YOU!!
NEVER!!
Grin
HEH HEH HEH...
Okay. C'mon
...Boy.
LET ME AT LEAST RECOVER MY HP FIRST! ♡
WHO SHOULD I ROOT FOR...?
so complicated...

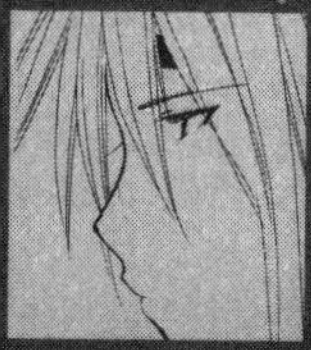

SUBJECT: TO: ORCA OF AZURE SEA

FROM: BALMUNG

JUST LIKE FOUR YEARS AGO, IT WAS A TERRIBLE BATTLE. WITHOUT AN ENEMY, WITHOUT A QUEST TO SOLVE, THEY SIMPLY STARTED AN ADVENTURE WITHOUT A QUESTION.

DESPITE THAT, THEY CREATED THEIR OWN ADVENTURE, ENJOYED PLAYING ON THEIR OWN, WILLINGLY SHARED DIFFICULT SCENARIOS, AND REACHED THE DOOR TO THE CORE. THEY ARE TRULY WONDERFUL PLAYERS.

BY THE TIME THE CHERRY BLOSSOMS BLOOM AGAIN, WHEN YOU AND KITE WILL RETURN, THIS WORLD WILL BECOME A MUCH BETTER PLACE. I'M SURE OF IT. WHEN THAT TIME COMES, THERE'S SOMEONE I WANT TO INTRODUCE YOU TO. AND, FOR THAT REASON, PLEASE MAKE SURE THAT YOU RETURN.

AURA WILL THINK IT FUNNY, I'M SURE.

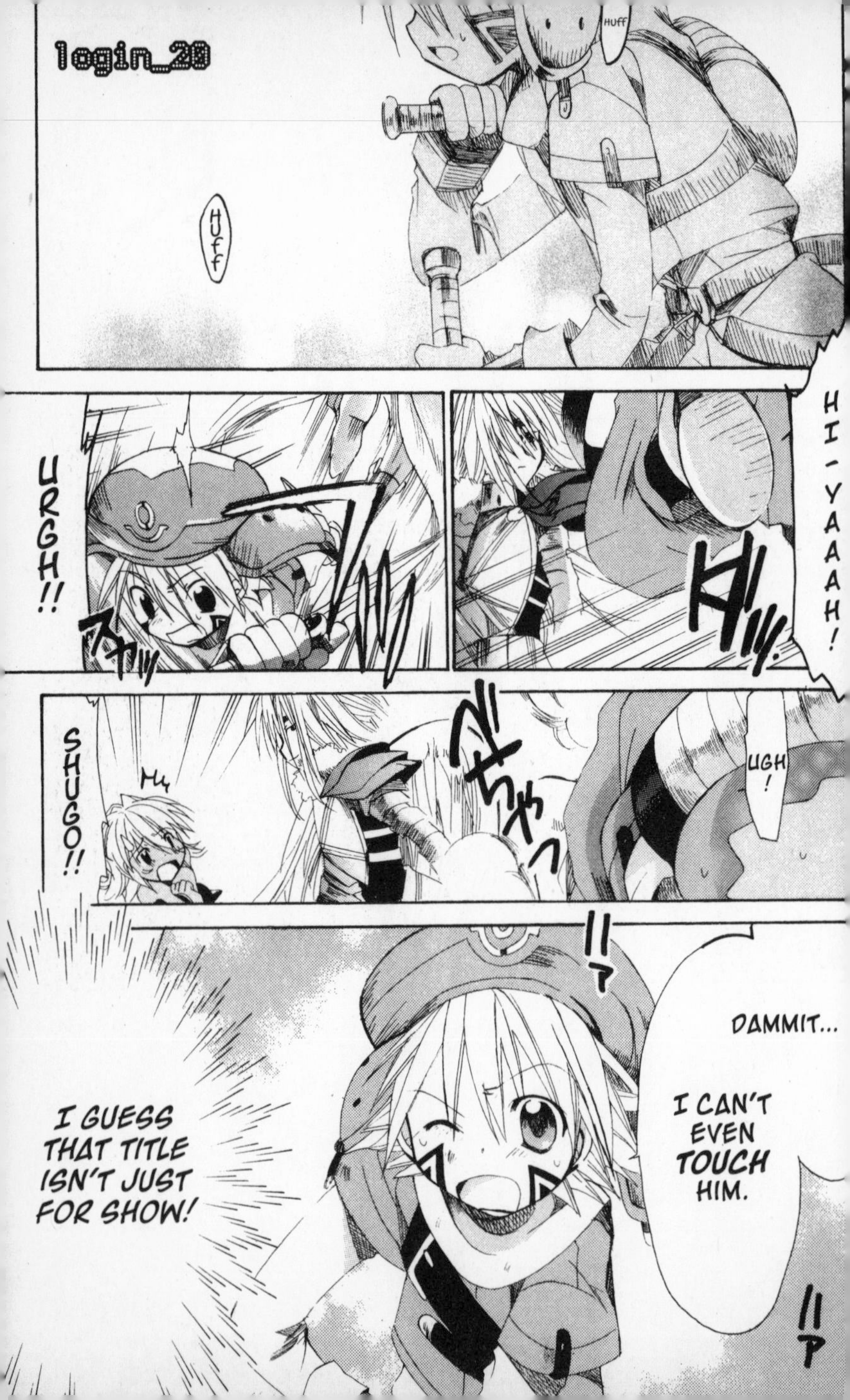
login_20
HUFF
HUFF
HI-YAAAH!
URGH!!
UGH!
SHUGO!!
DAMMIT...
I CAN'T EVEN TOUCH HIM.
I GUESS THAT TITLE ISN'T JUST FOR SHOW!

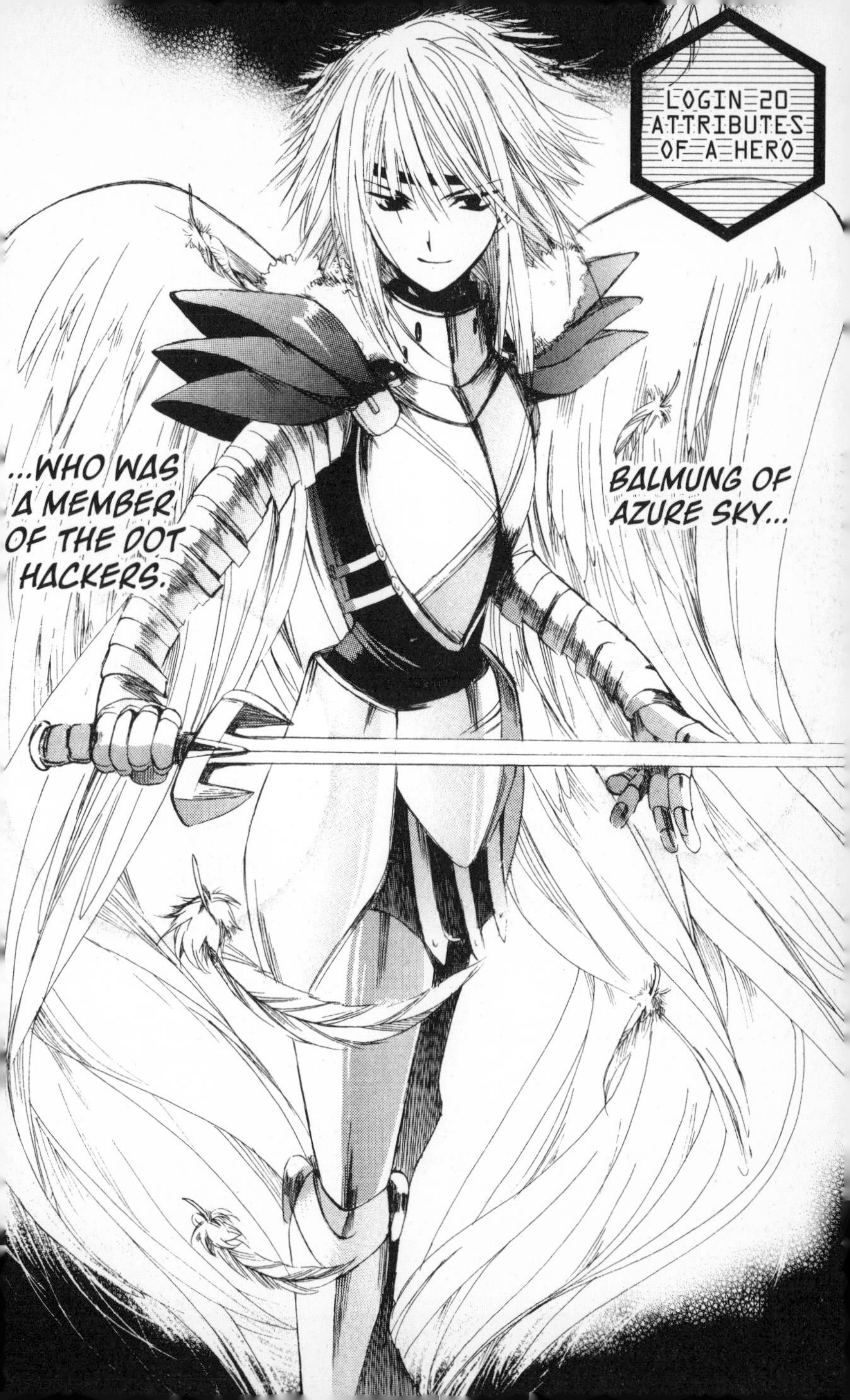
LOGIN 20
ATTRIBUTES OF A HERO
BALMUNG OF AZURE SKY...
...WHO WAS A MEMBER OF THE DOT HACKERS.

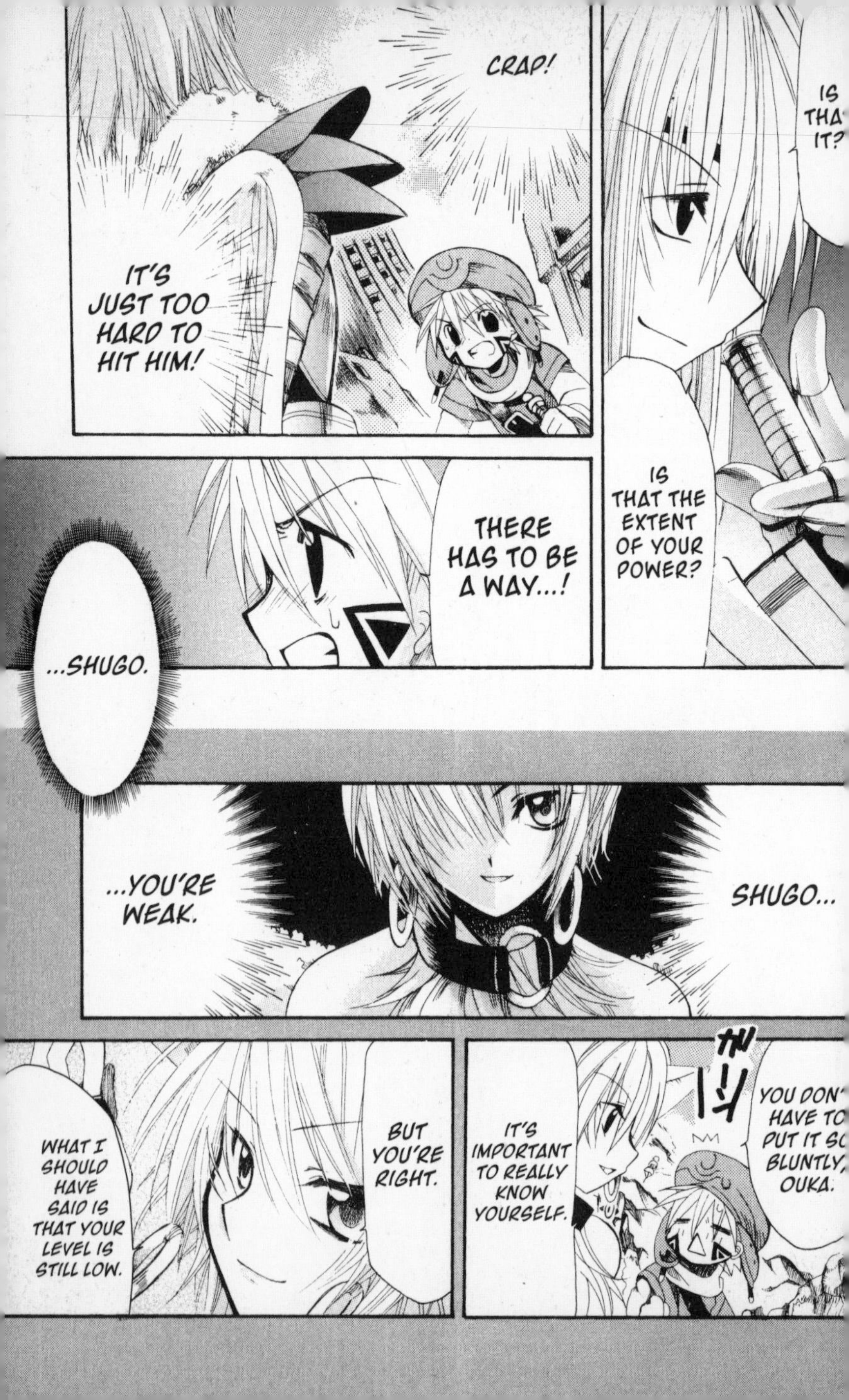
IS THA IT?
CRAP!
IT'S JUST TOO HARD TO HIT HIM!
IS THAT THE EXTENT OF YOUR POWER?
THERE HAS TO BE A WAY...!
...SHUGO.
SHUGO...
...YOU'RE WEAK.
YOU DON'T HAVE TO PUT IT SO BLUNTLY, OUKA.
IT'S IMPORTANT TO REALLY KNOW YOURSELF.
BUT YOU'RE RIGHT.
WHAT I SHOULD HAVE SAID IS THAT YOUR LEVEL IS STILL LOW.

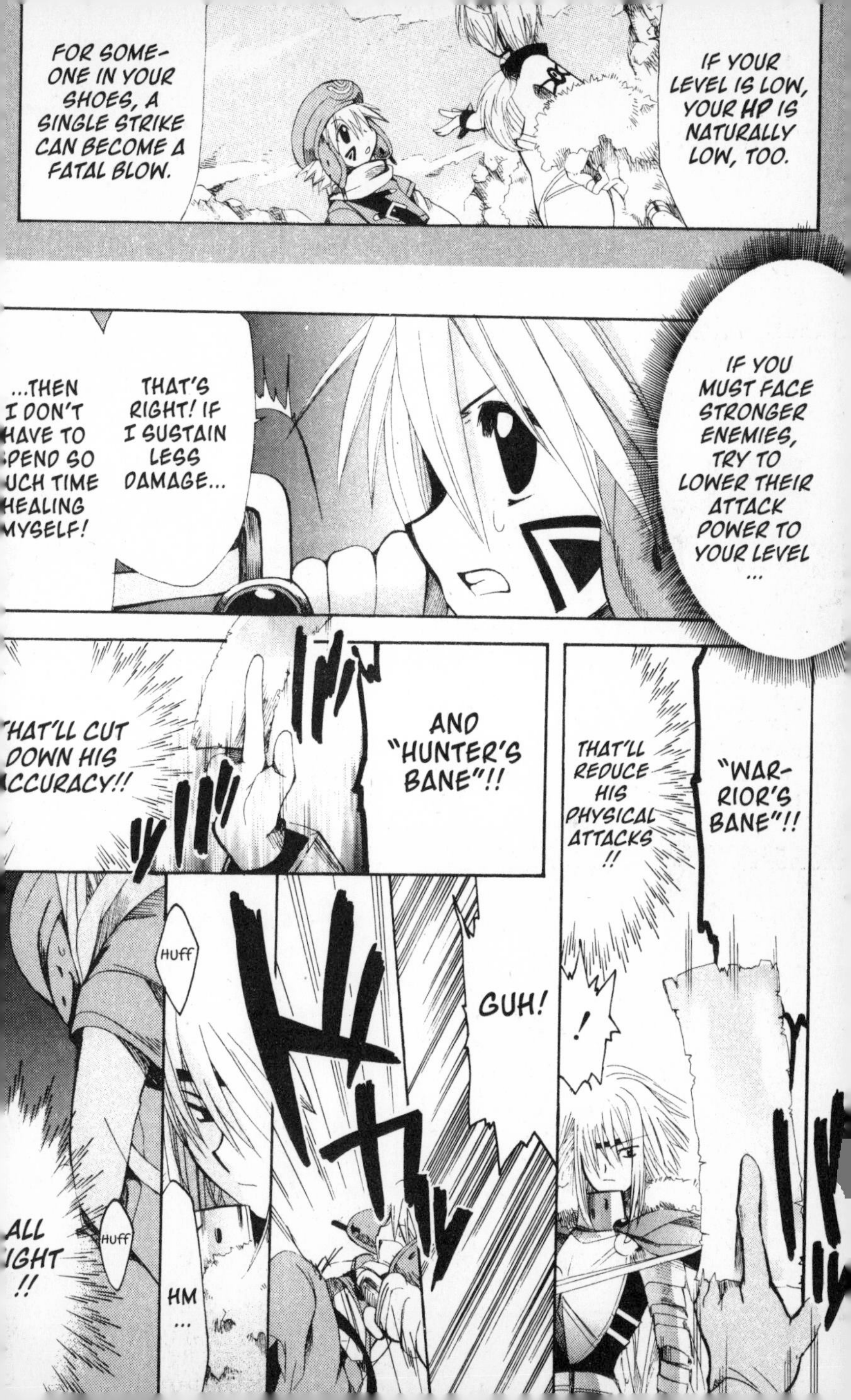
IF YOUR LEVEL IS LOW, YOUR HP IS NATURALLY LOW, TOO.
FOR SOME-ONE IN YOUR SHOES, A SINGLE STRIKE CAN BECOME A FATAL BLOW.
IF YOU MUST FACE STRONGER ENEMIES, TRY TO LOWER THEIR ATTACK POWER TO YOUR LEVEL ...
THAT'S RIGHT! IF I SUSTAIN LESS DAMAGE...
...THEN I DON'T HAVE TO PEND SO UCH TIME HEALING MYSELF!
"WAR-RIOR'S BANE"!!
THAT'LL REDUCE HIS PHYSICAL ATTACKS !!
AND "HUNTER'S BANE"!!
HAT'LL CUT DOWN HIS CCURACY!!
!
GUH!
HM ...
HUFF
HUFF
ALL IGHT !!

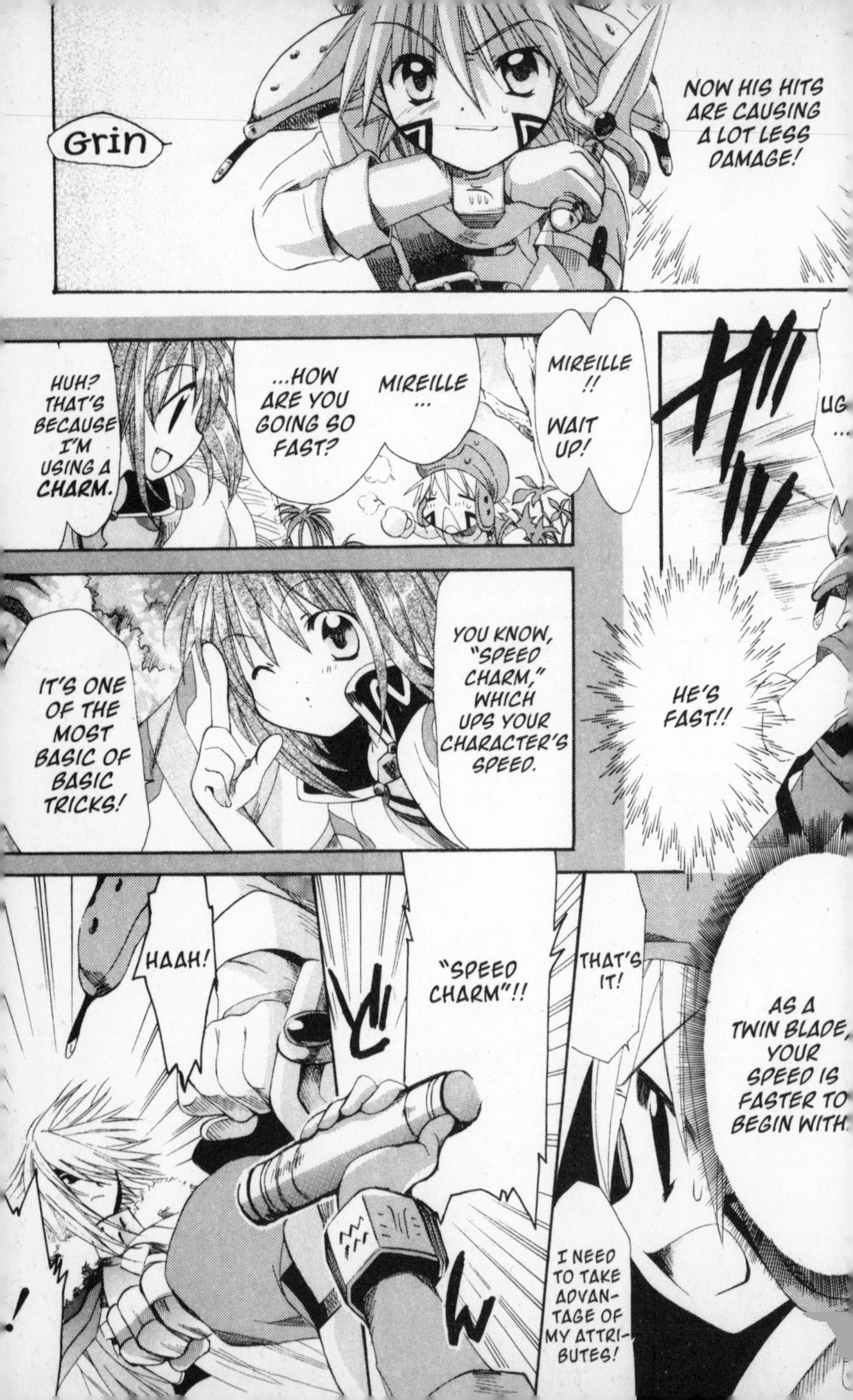
NOW HIS HITS ARE CAUSING A LOT LESS DAMAGE!
Grin
UG ...
HE'S FAST!!
MIREILLE !! WAIT UP!
MIREILLE ...
...HOW ARE YOU GOING SO FAST?
HUH? THAT'S BECAUSE I'M USING A CHARM.
YOU KNOW, "SPEED CHARM," WHICH UPS YOUR CHARACTER'S SPEED.
IT'S ONE OF THE MOST BASIC OF BASIC TRICKS!
AS A TWIN BLADE, YOUR SPEED IS FASTER TO BEGIN WITH.
THAT'S IT!
I NEED TO TAKE ADVANTAGE OF MY ATTRIBUTES!
"SPEED CHARM"!!
HAAH!
!

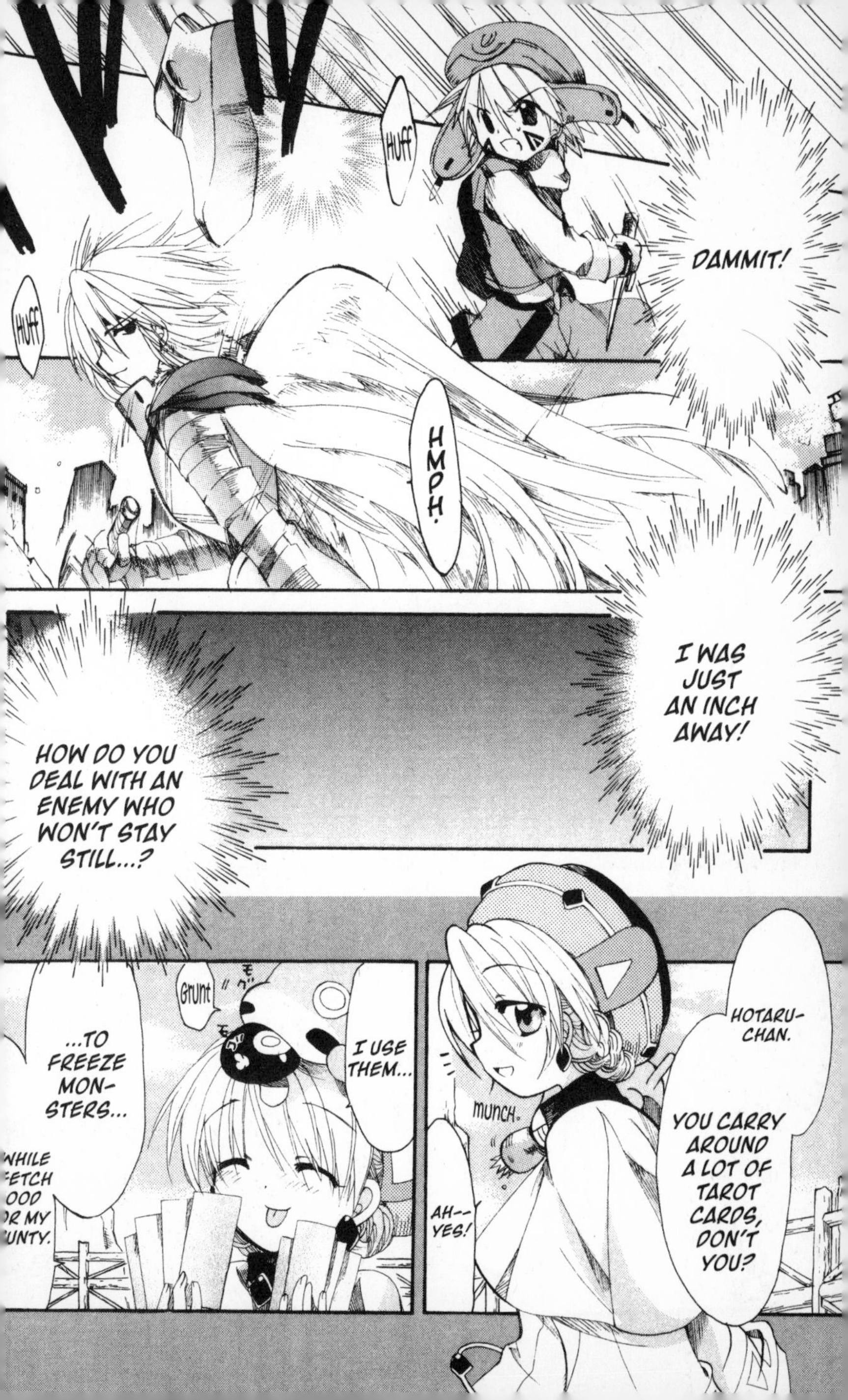

DAMMIT!
HUFF
HMPH.
HUFF
I WAS JUST AN INCH AWAY!
HOW DO YOU DEAL WITH AN ENEMY WHO WON'T STAY STILL...?
HOTARU-CHAN.
YOU CARRY AROUND A LOT OF TAROT CARDS, DON'T YOU?
munch.
AH-- YES!
I USE THEM...
Grunt
...TO FREEZE MONSTERS...
WHILE FETCH OOD OR MY UNTY.

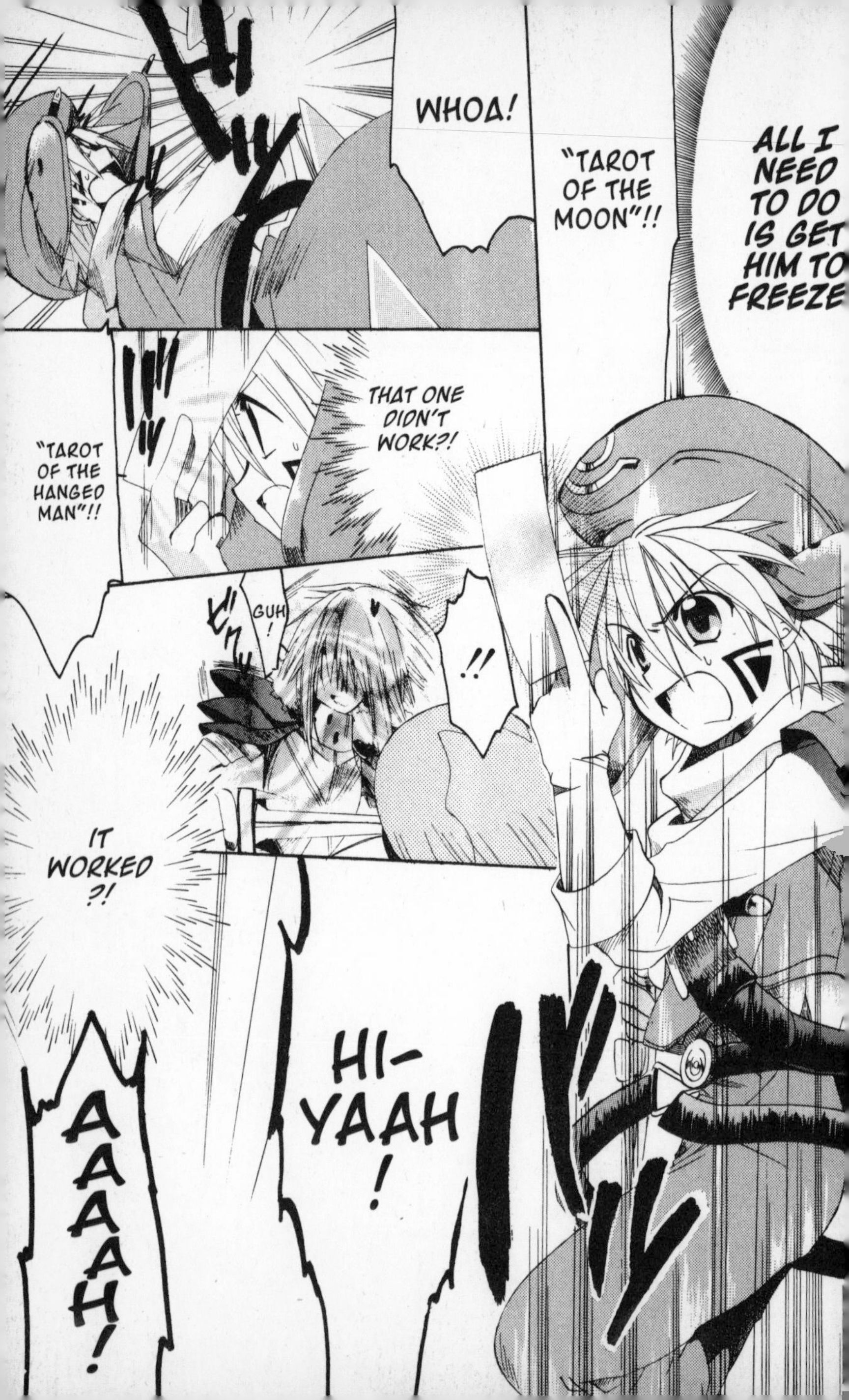
ALL I NEED TO DO IS GET HIM TO FREEZE
"TAROT OF THE MOON"!!
WHOA!
THAT ONE DIDN'T WORK?!
"TAROT OF THE HANGED MAN"!!
GUH!
!!
IT WORKED ?!
HI-YAAH!
AAAAH!

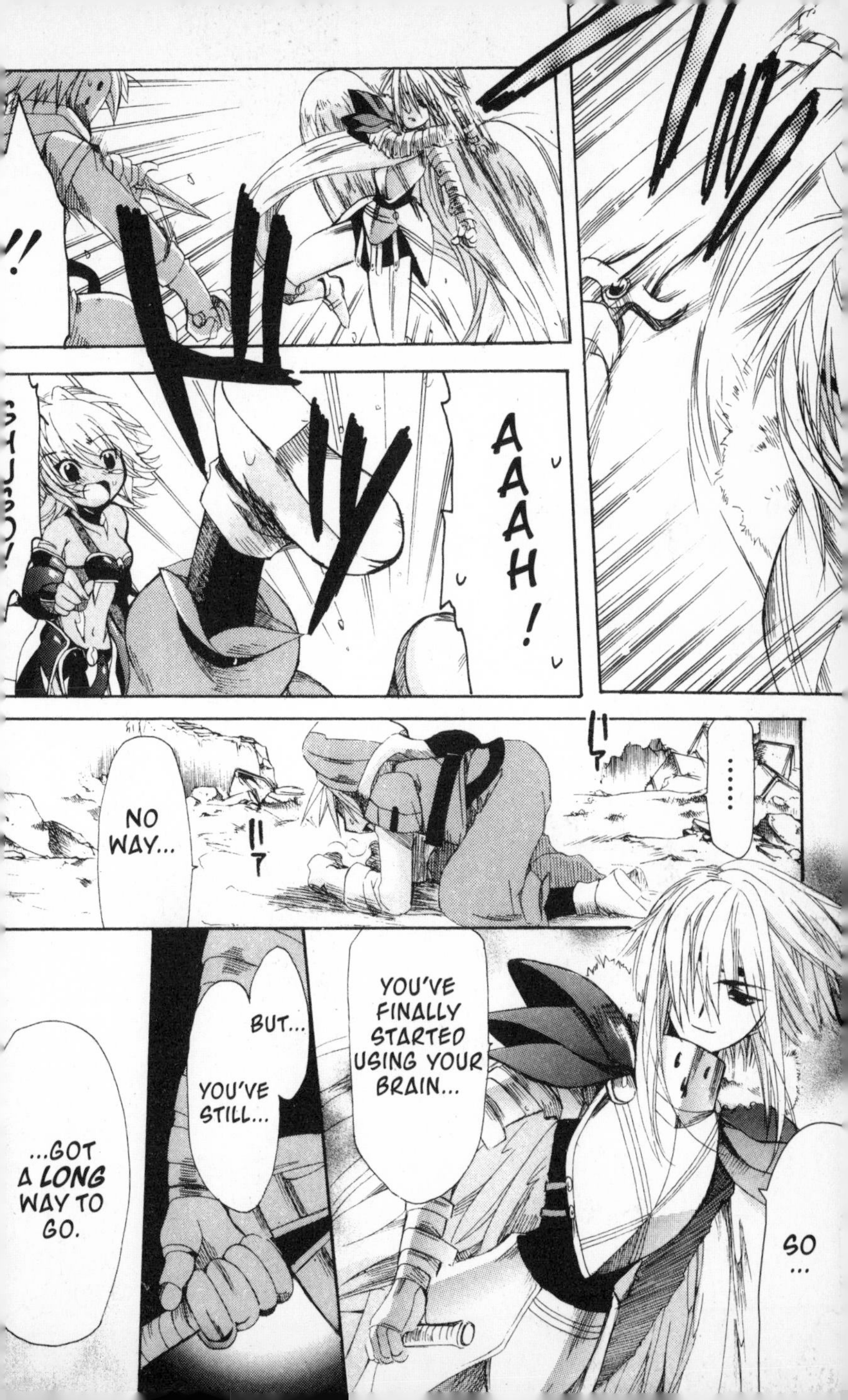

!!
AAAH!
......
NO WAY...
SO...
YOU'VE FINALLY STARTED USING YOUR BRAIN...
BUT...
YOU'VE STILL...
...GOT A LONG WAY TO GO.

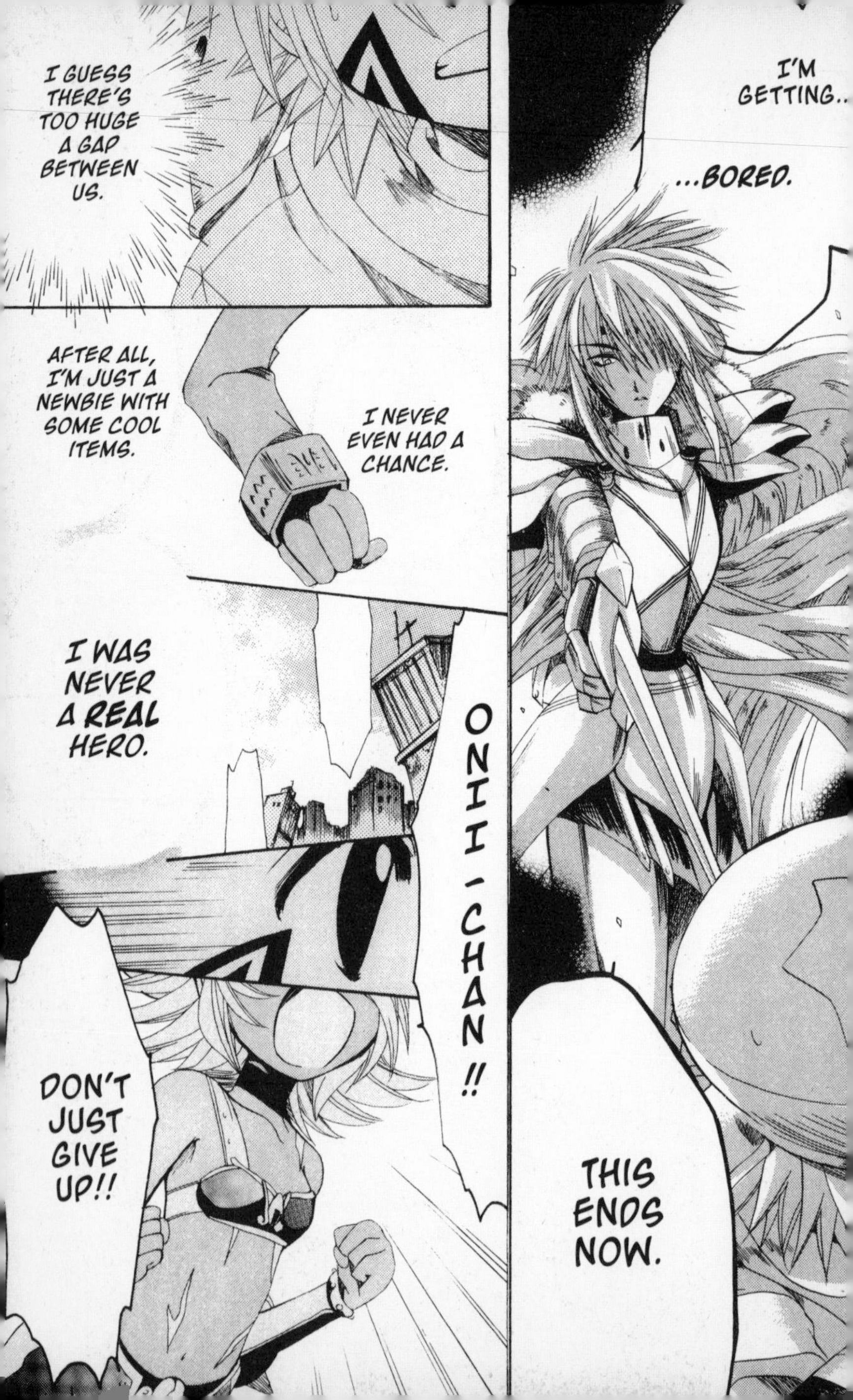
I'M GETTING..
...BORED.
THIS ENDS NOW.
I GUESS THERE'S TOO HUGE A GAP BETWEEN US.
AFTER ALL, I'M JUST A NEWBIE WITH SOME COOL ITEMS.
I NEVER EVEN HAD A CHANCE.
I WAS NEVER A **REAL** HERO.
ONIII-CHAN!!
DON'T JUST GIVE UP!!

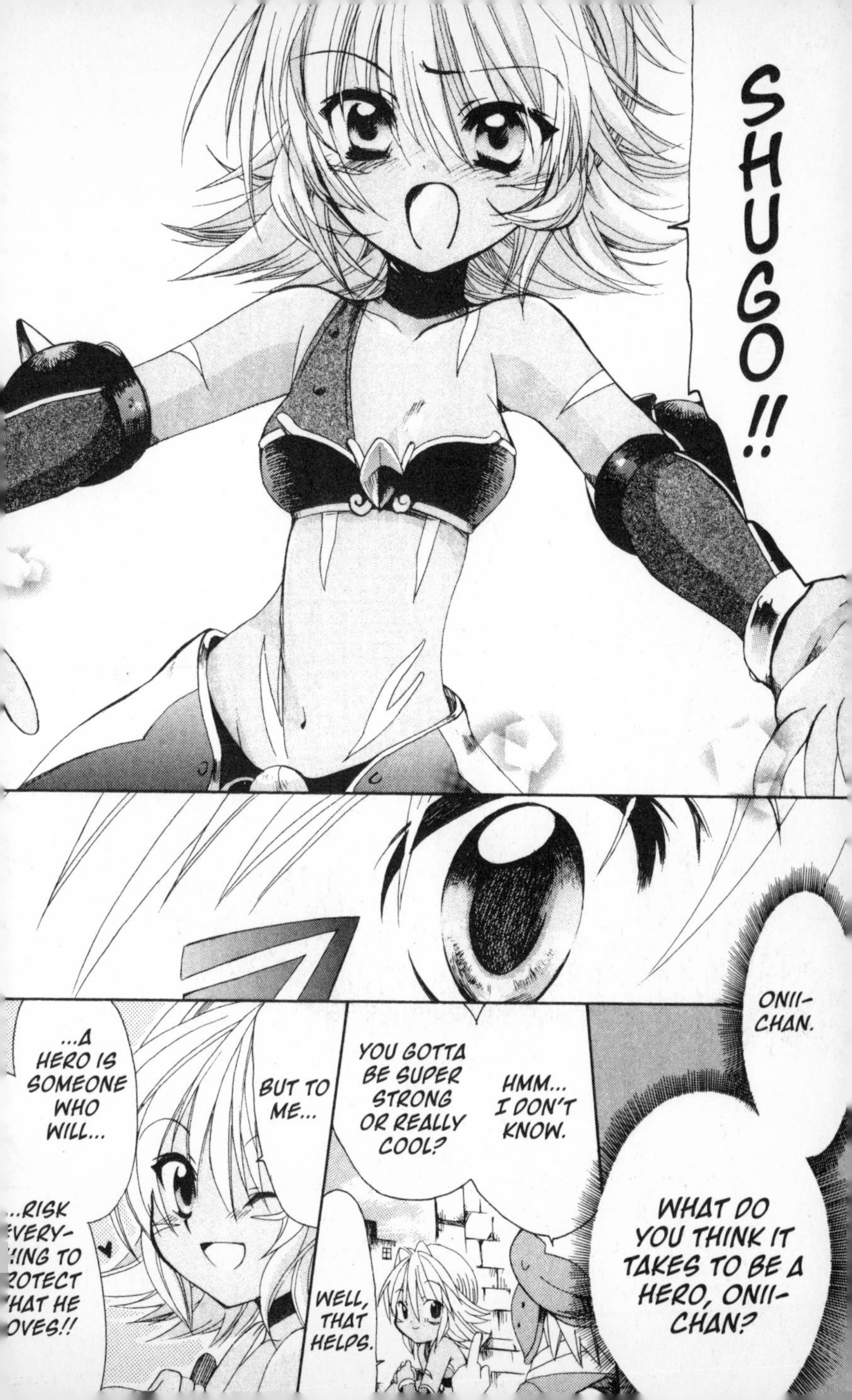
SHUGO!!
ONII-CHAN.
WHAT DO YOU THINK IT TAKES TO BE A HERO, ONII-CHAN?
HMM... I DON'T KNOW.
YOU GOTTA BE SUPER STRONG OR REALLY COOL?
WELL, THAT HELPS.
BUT TO ME...
...A HERO IS SOMEONE WHO WILL...
...RISK EVERYTHING TO PROTECT WHAT HE LOVES!!

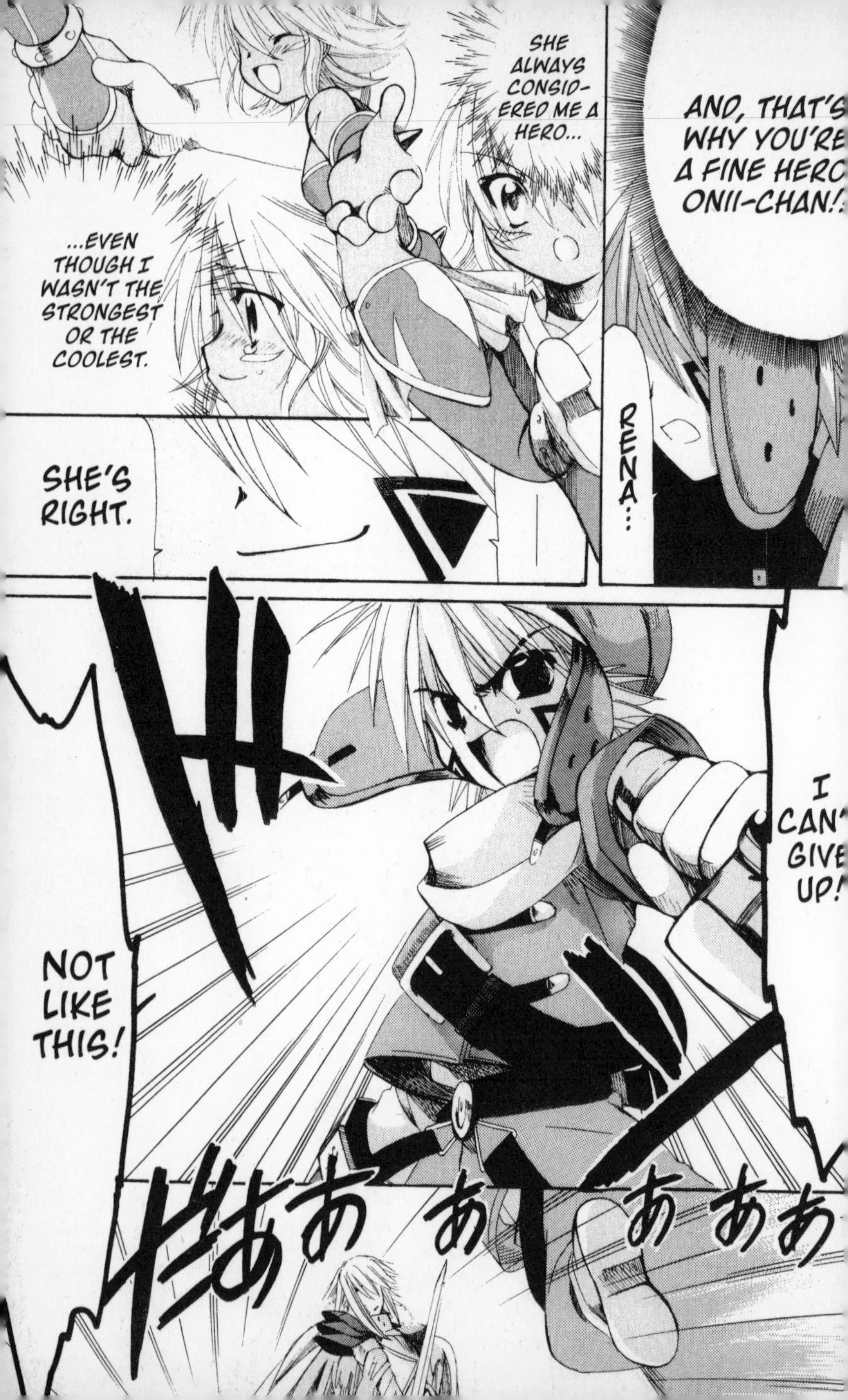
AND, THAT'S WHY YOU'RE A FINE HERO ONII-CHAN!
SHE ALWAYS CONSIDERED ME A HERO...
...EVEN THOUGH I WASN'T THE STRONGEST OR THE COOLEST.
RENA...
SHE'S RIGHT.
I CAN'T GIVE UP!
NOT LIKE THIS!
ダあああああ

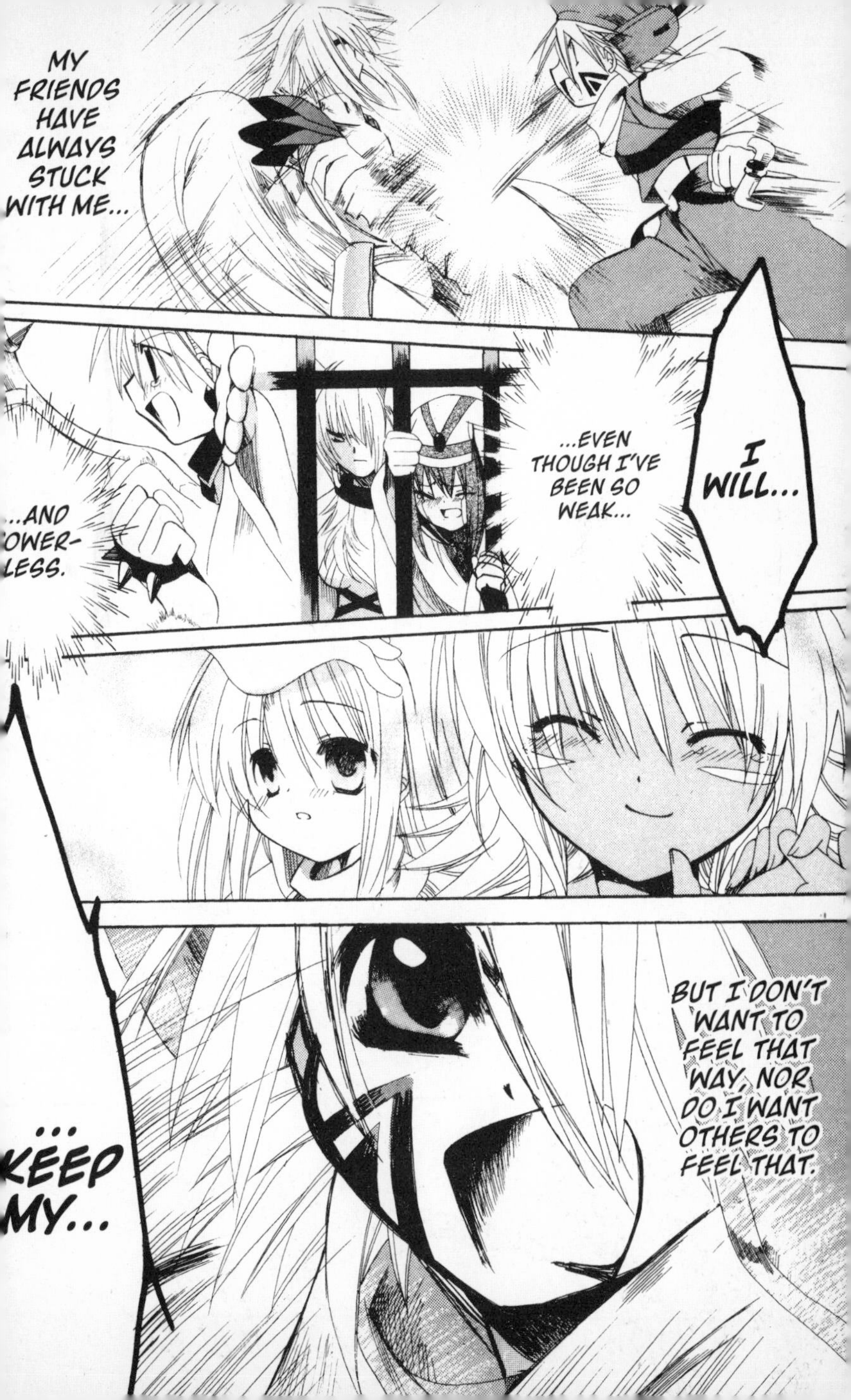
MY FRIENDS HAVE ALWAYS STUCK WITH ME...
I WILL...
...EVEN THOUGH I'VE BEEN SO WEAK...
...AND OWER-LESS.
BUT I DON'T WANT TO FEEL THAT WAY, NOR DO I WANT OTHERS TO FEEL THAT.
... KEEP MY...

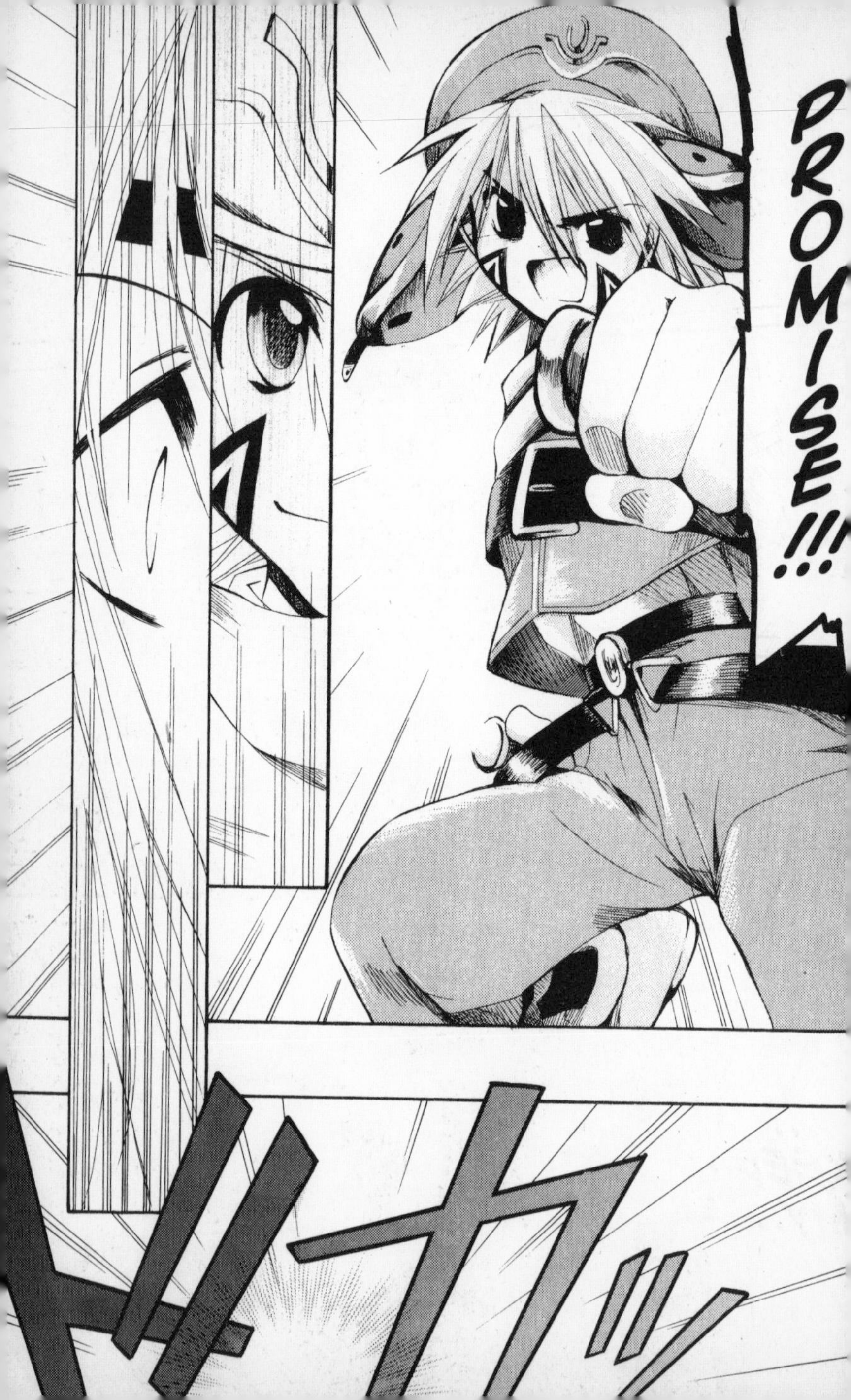
PROMISE!!!

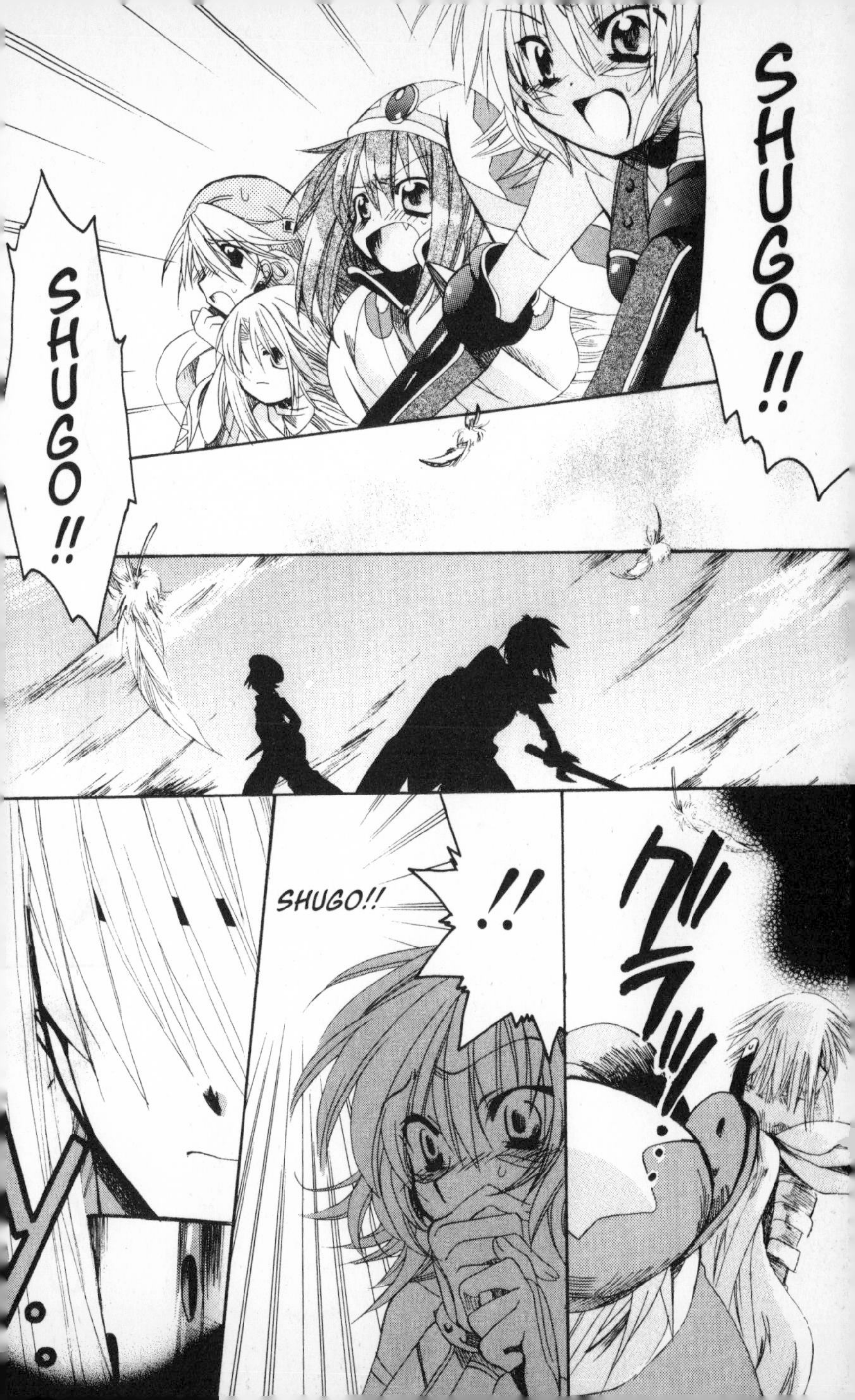
SHUGO!!
SHUGO!!
グラッ!!
SHUGO!!
!!

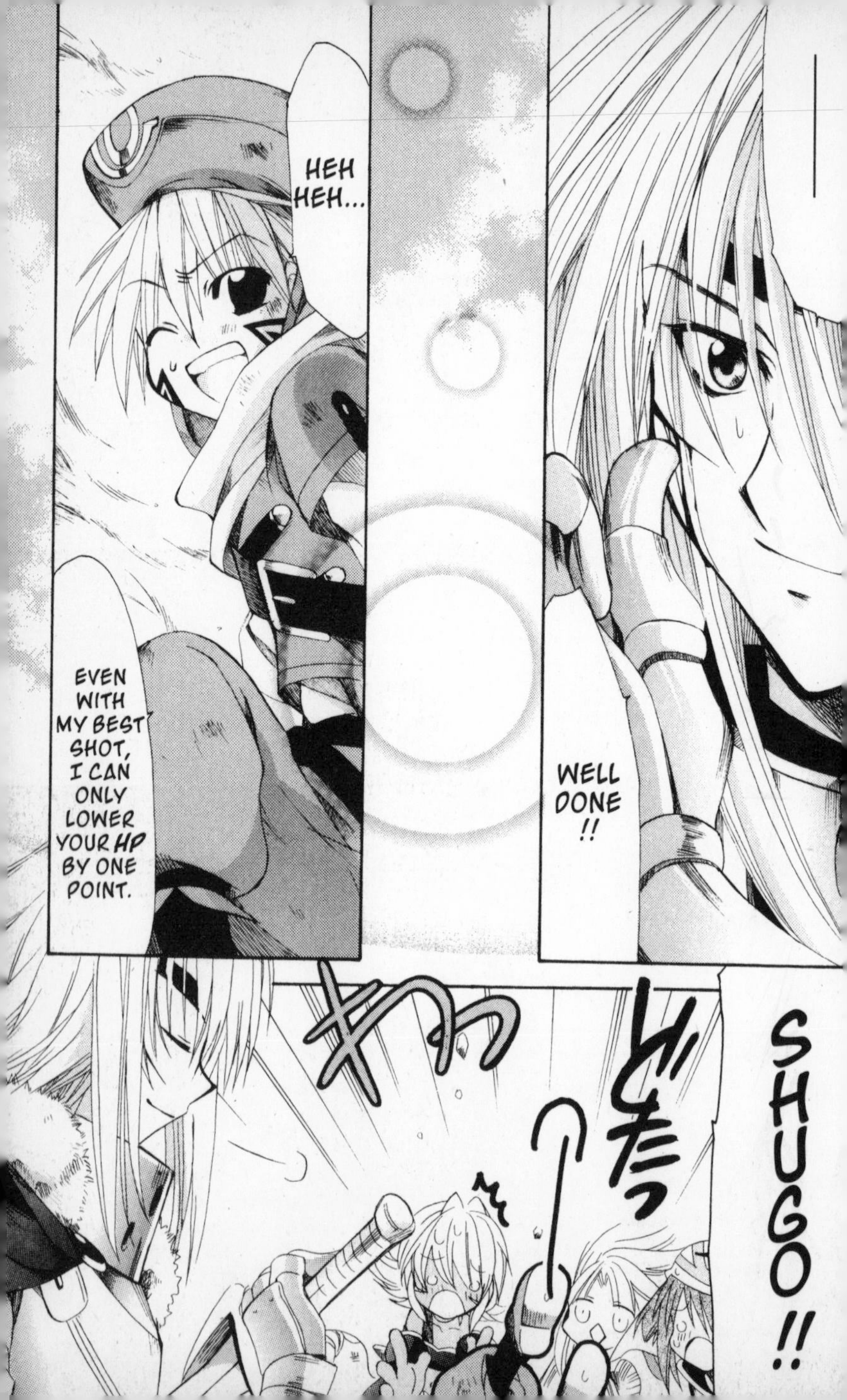
WELL DONE!!
HEH HEH...
EVEN WITH MY BEST SHOT, I CAN ONLY LOWER YOUR HP BY ONE POINT.
SHUGO!!
どたっ

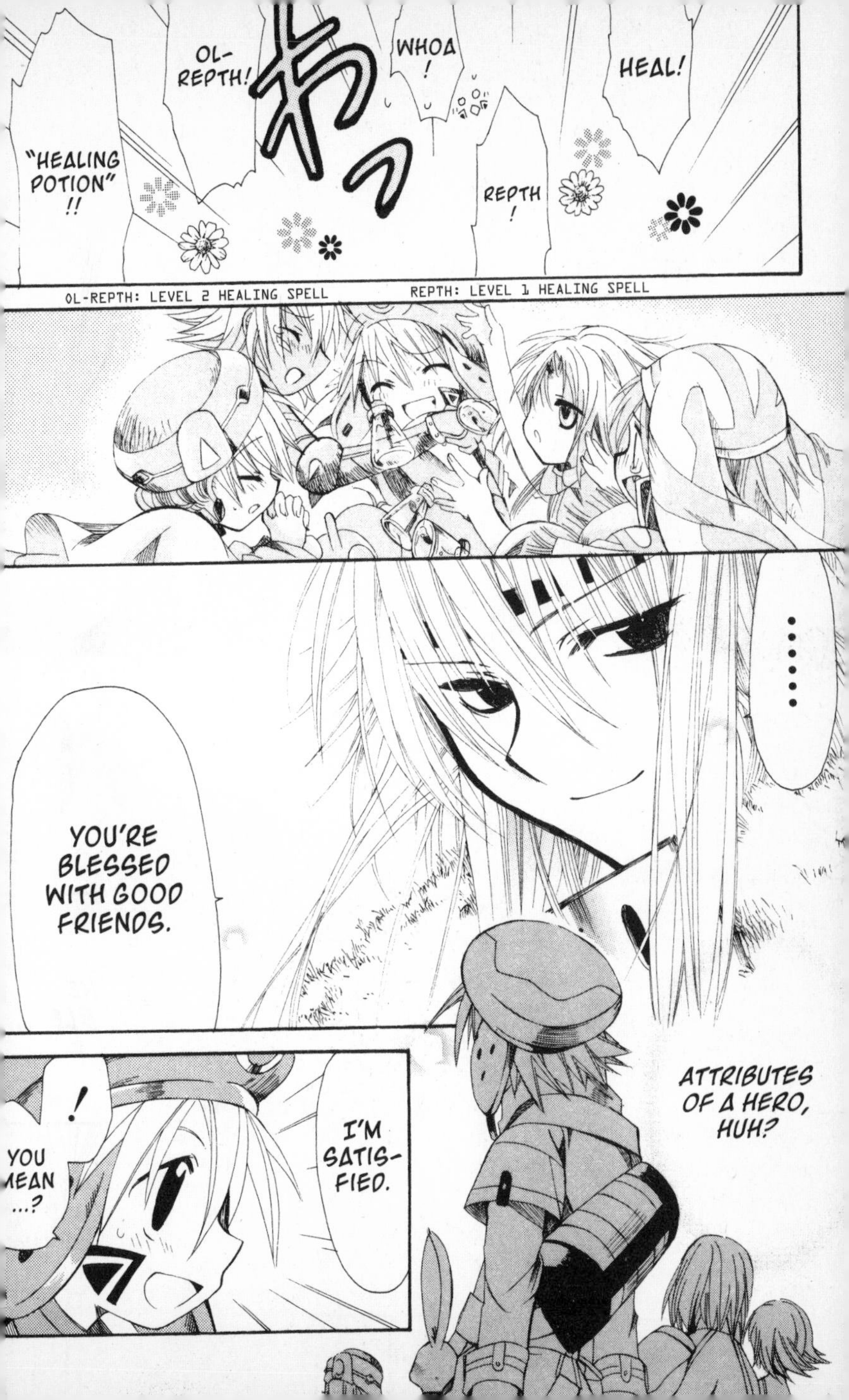
HEAL!
REPTH!
WHOA!
わっ
OL-REPTH!
"HEALING POTION"!!
OL-REPTH: LEVEL 2 HEALING SPELL
REPTH: LEVEL 1 HEALING SPELL
......
YOU'RE BLESSED WITH GOOD FRIENDS.
ATTRIBUTES OF A HERO, HUH?
I'M SATIS-FIED.
!
YOU MEAN ...?

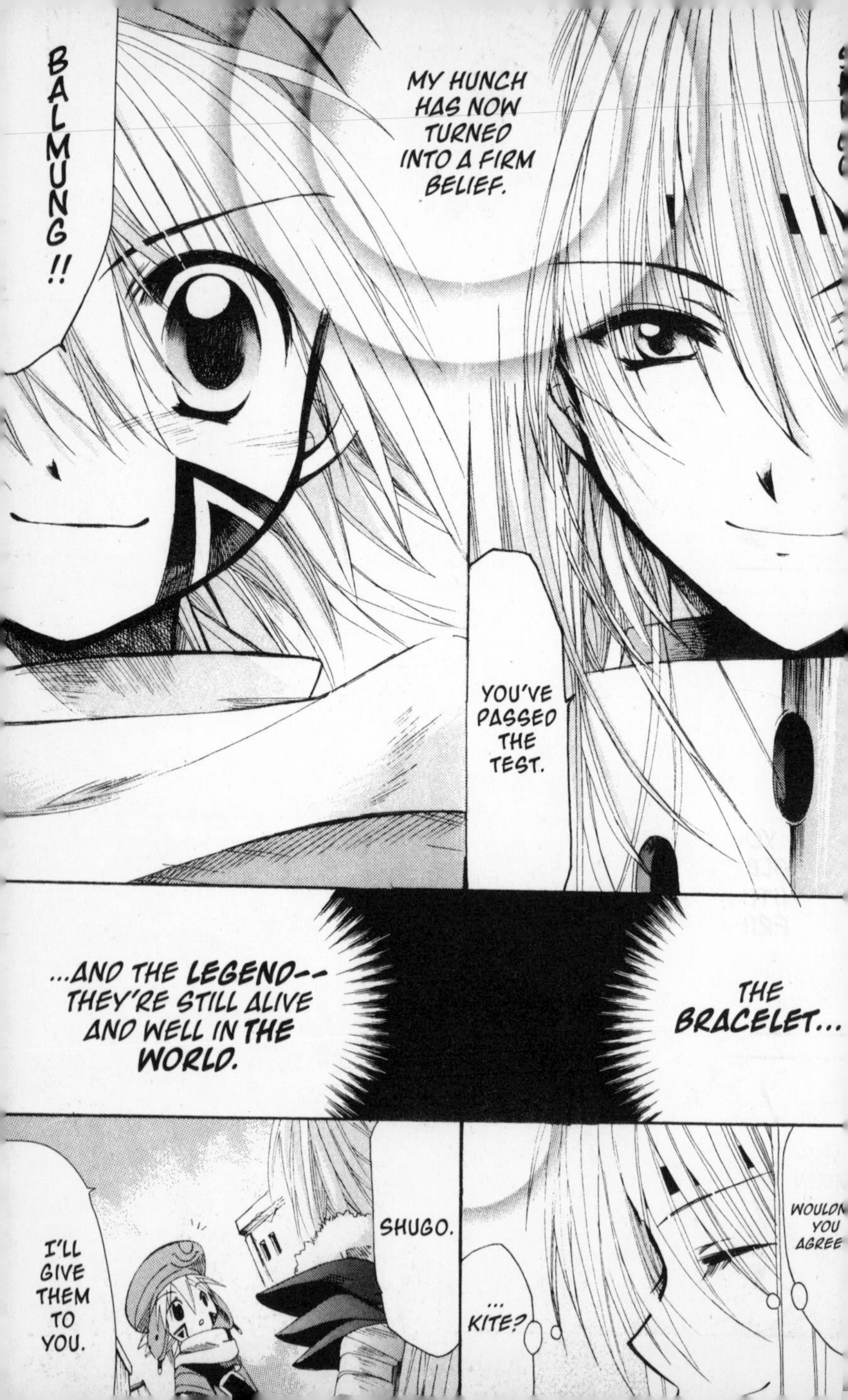
MY HUNCH HAS NOW TURNED INTO A FIRM BELIEF.
BALMUNG!!
YOU'VE PASSED THE TEST.
THE BRACELET...
...AND THE LEGEND--THEY'RE STILL ALIVE AND WELL IN THE WORLD.
WOULDN YOU AGREE
...KITE?
SHUGO.
I'LL GIVE THEM TO YOU.

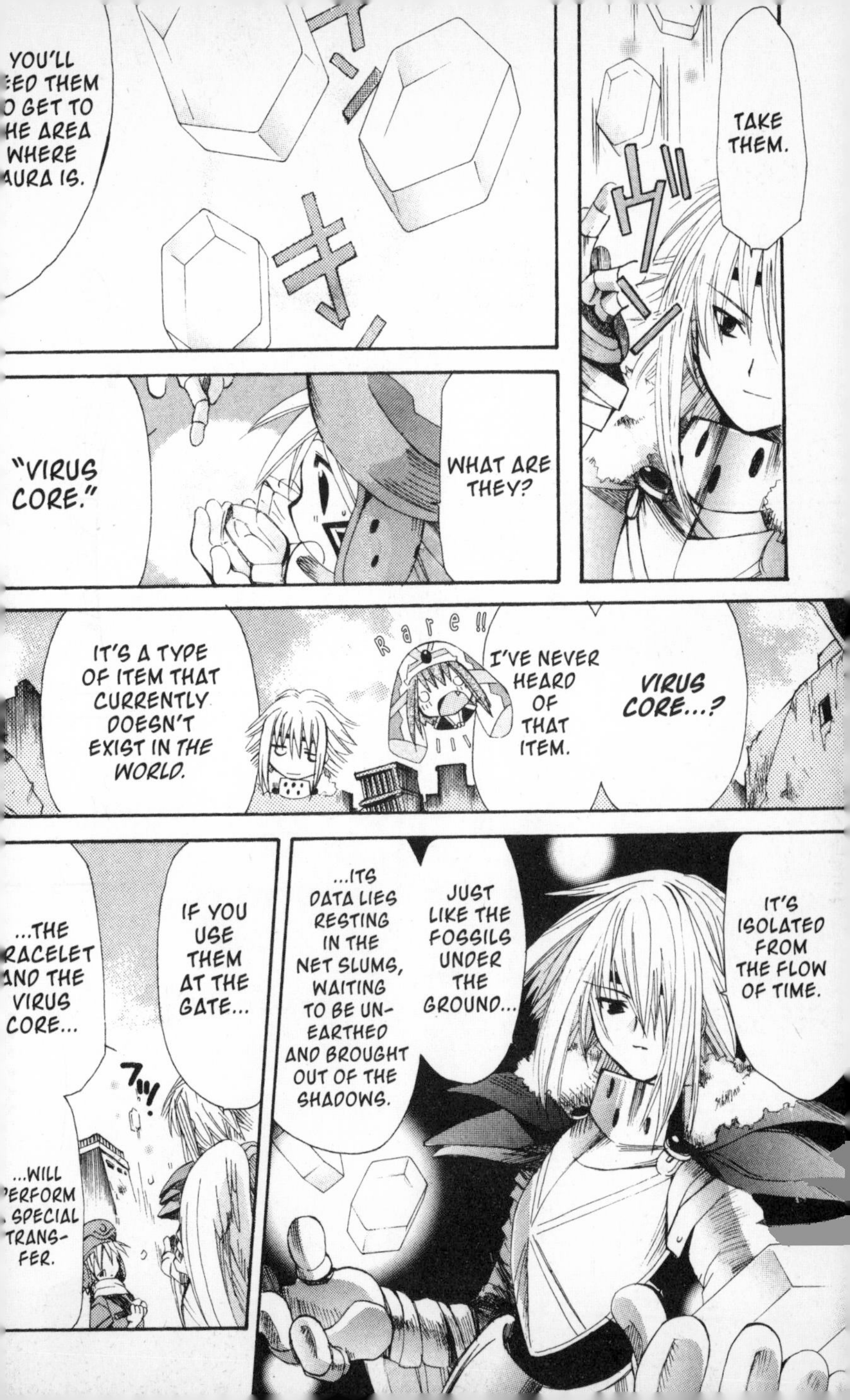
TAKE THEM.
YOU'LL EED THEM O GET TO HE AREA WHERE AURA IS.
WHAT ARE THEY?
"VIRUS CORE."
VIRUS CORE...?
I'VE NEVER HEARD OF THAT ITEM.
Rare!!
IT'S A TYPE OF ITEM THAT CURRENTLY DOESN'T EXIST IN THE WORLD.
IT'S ISOLATED FROM THE FLOW OF TIME.
JUST LIKE THE FOSSILS UNDER THE GROUND...
...ITS DATA LIES RESTING IN THE NET SLUMS, WAITING TO BE UNEARTHED AND BROUGHT OUT OF THE SHADOWS.
IF YOU USE THEM AT THE GATE...
...THE RACELET AND THE VIRUS CORE...
...WILL ERFORM SPECIAL TRANSFER.

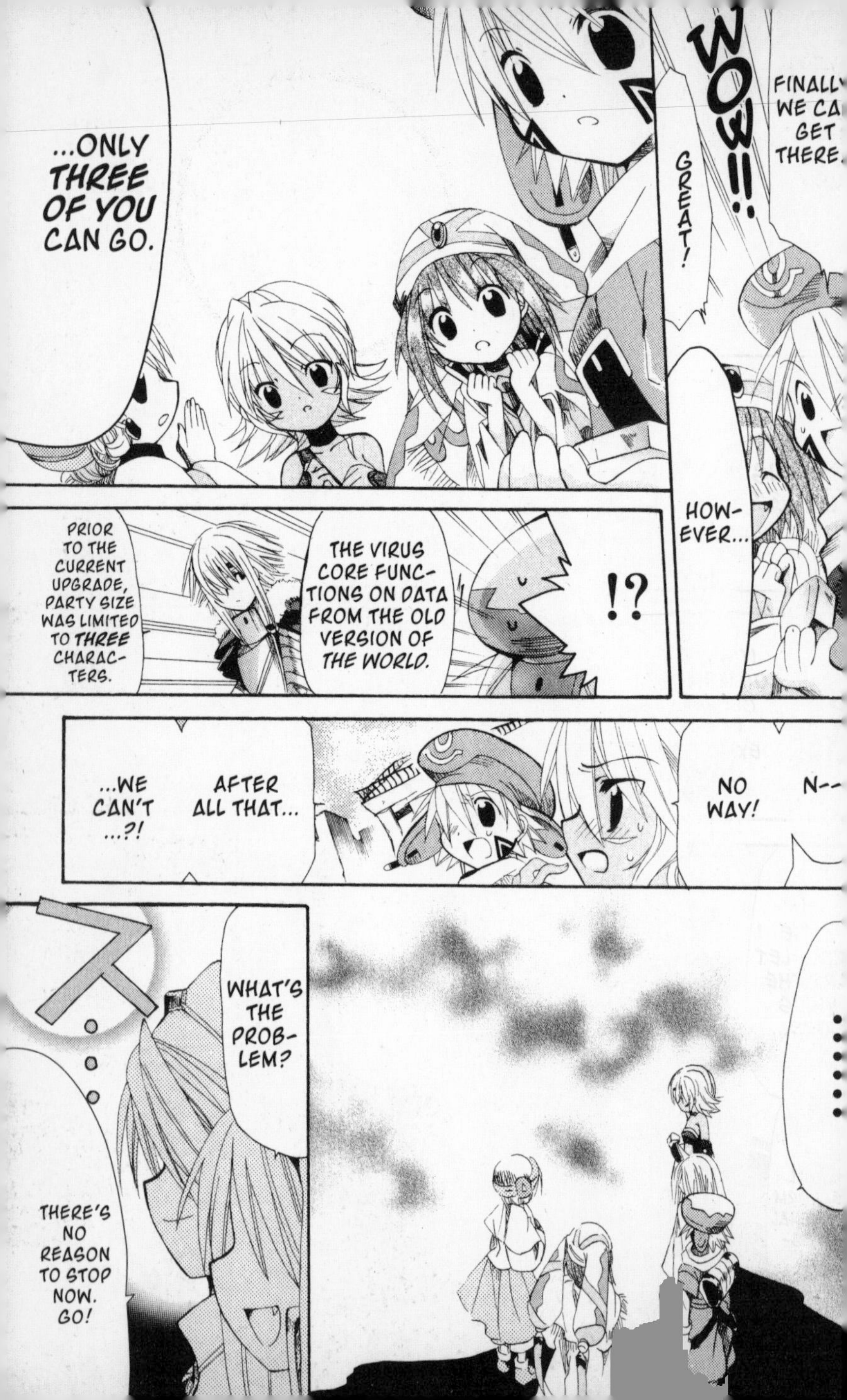

FINALLY WE CAN GET THERE.
WOW!!
GREAT!
HOW-EVER...
...ONLY THREE OF YOU CAN GO.
!?
THE VIRUS CORE FUNCTIONS ON DATA FROM THE OLD VERSION OF THE WORLD.
PRIOR TO THE CURRENT UPGRADE, PARTY SIZE WAS LIMITED TO THREE CHARACTERS.
N--
NO WAY!
AFTER ALL THAT...
...WE CAN'T ...?!
......
WHAT'S THE PROBLEM?
ス...
THERE'S NO REASON TO STOP NOW. GO!

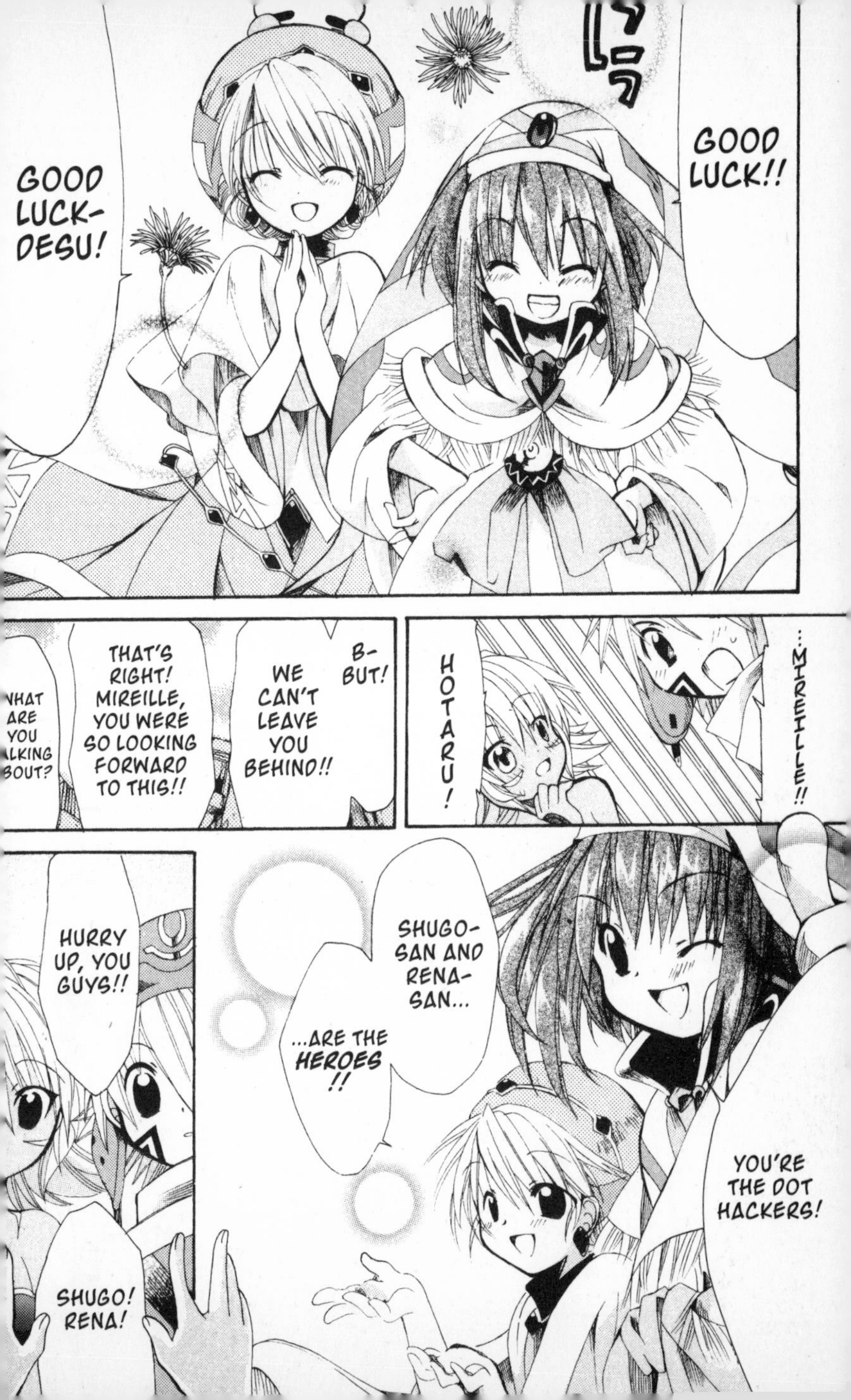
GOOD LUCK!!
GOOD LUCK-DESU!
...MIREILLE!!
HOTARU!
B-BUT!
WE CAN'T LEAVE YOU BEHIND!!
THAT'S RIGHT! MIREILLE, YOU WERE SO LOOKING FORWARD TO THIS!!
WHAT ARE YOU ALKING BOUT?
YOU'RE THE DOT HACKERS!
SHUGO-SAN AND RENA-SAN...
...ARE THE HEROES!!
HURRY UP, YOU GUYS!!
SHUGO! RENA!

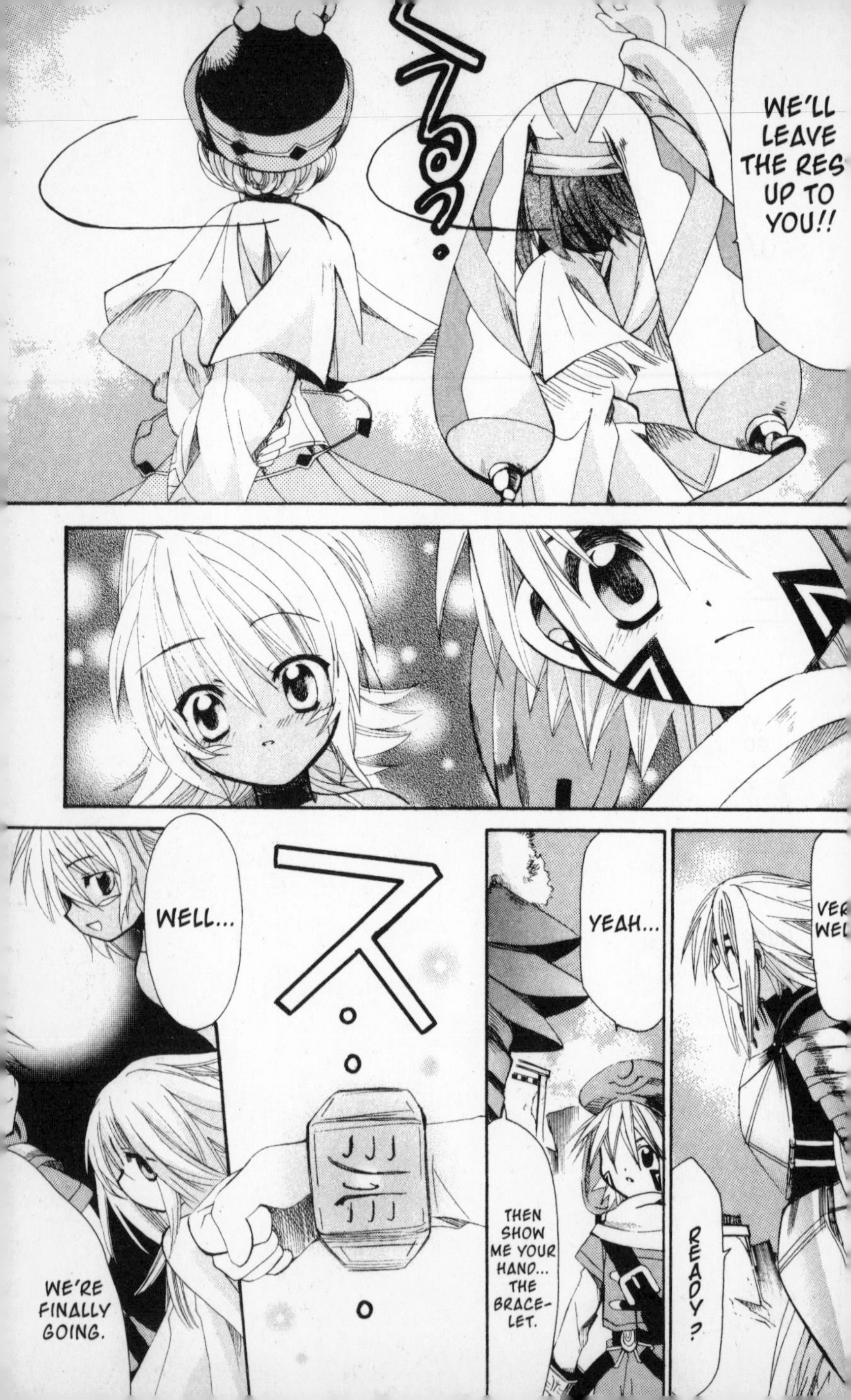
WE'LL LEAVE THE RES UP TO YOU!!
VER WEL
READY?
YEAH...
THEN SHOW ME YOUR HAND... THE BRACE-LET.
WELL...
WE'RE FINALLY GOING.

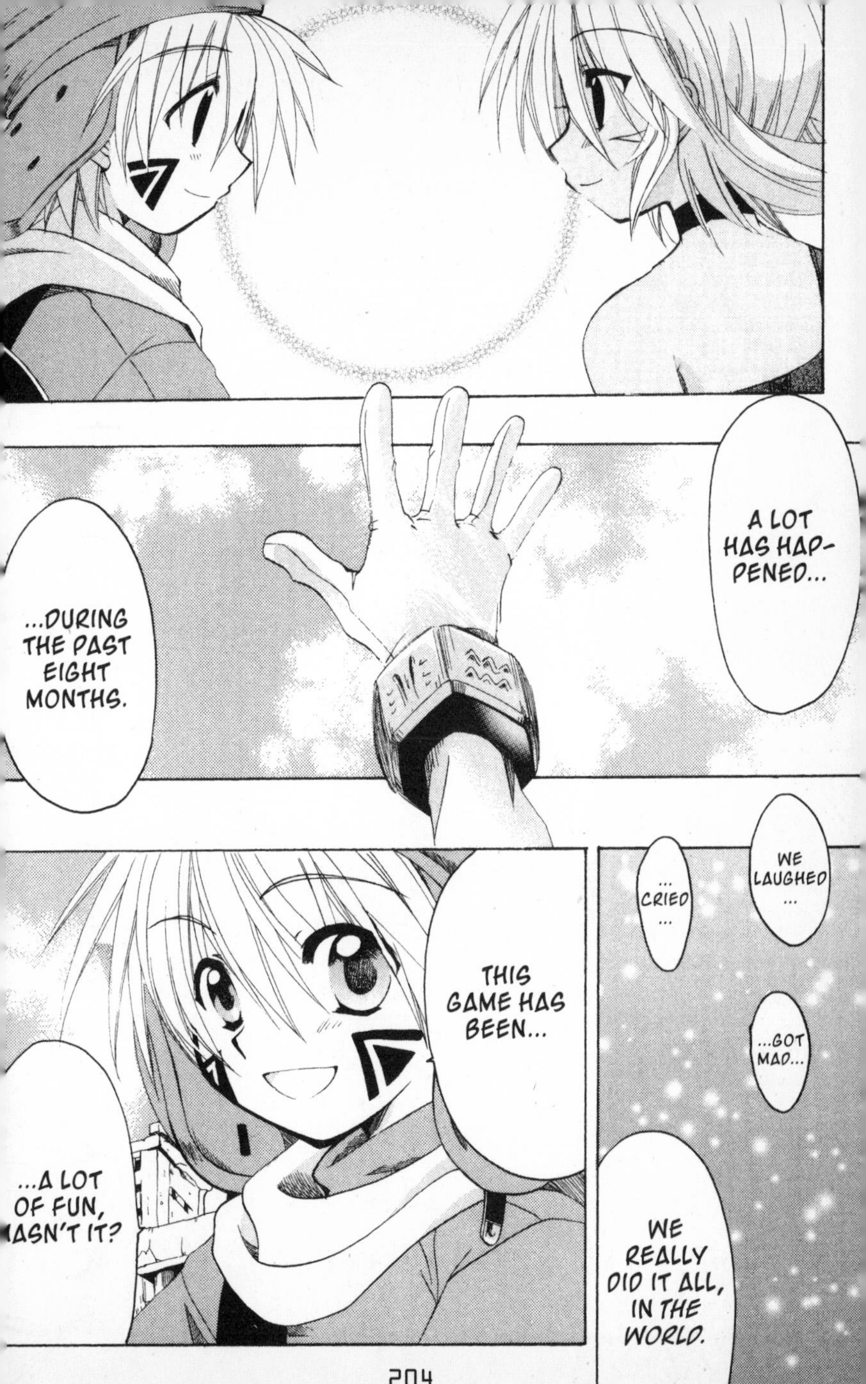
A LOT HAS HAP-PENED...
...DURING THE PAST EIGHT MONTHS.
WE LAUGHED ...
... CRIED ...
...GOT MAD...
WE REALLY DID IT ALL, IN THE WORLD.
THIS GAME HAS BEEN...
...A LOT OF FUN, ASN'T IT?

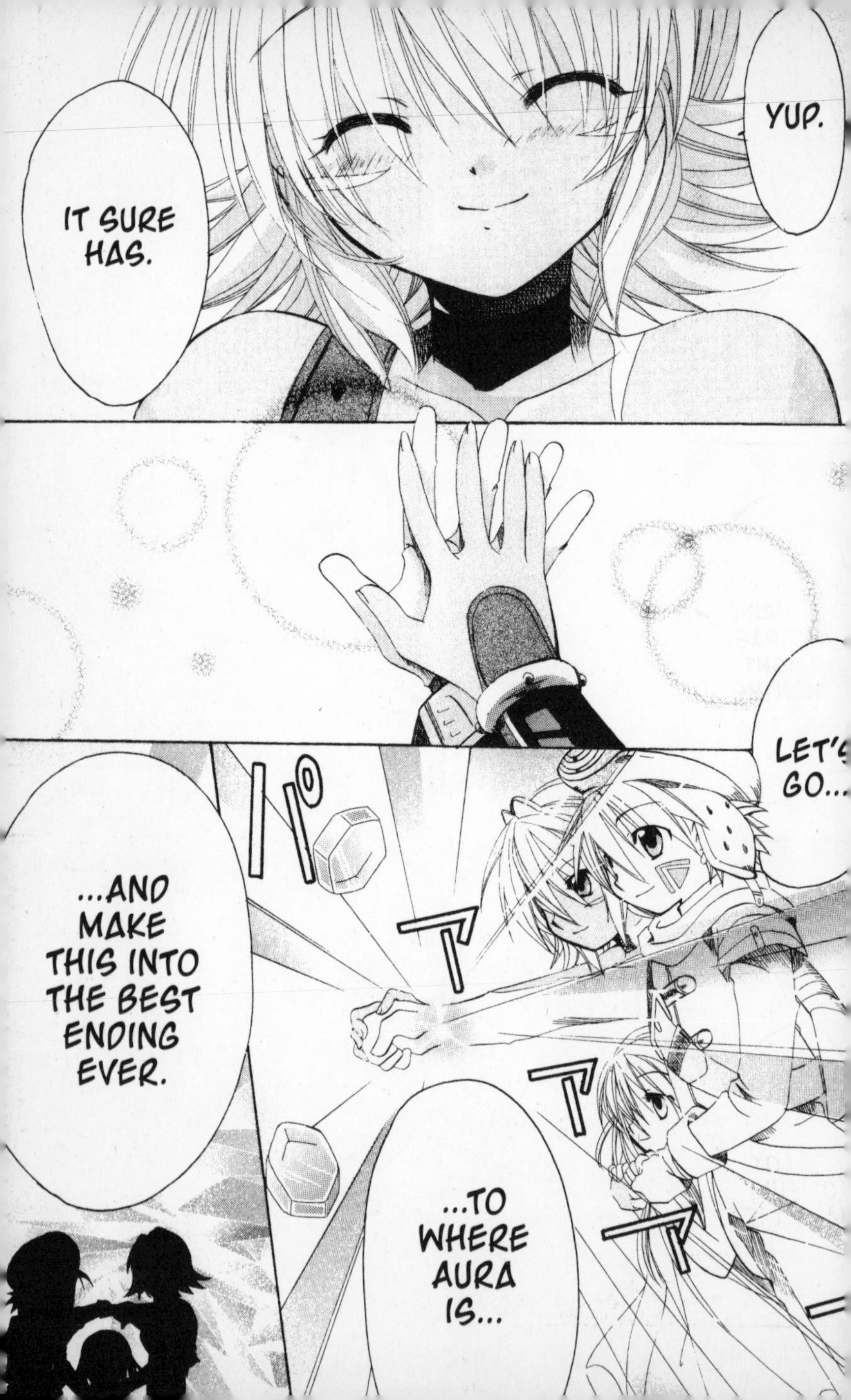
YUP.
IT SURE HAS.
LET'S GO...
...TO WHERE AURA IS...
...AND MAKE THIS INTO THE BEST ENDING EVER.

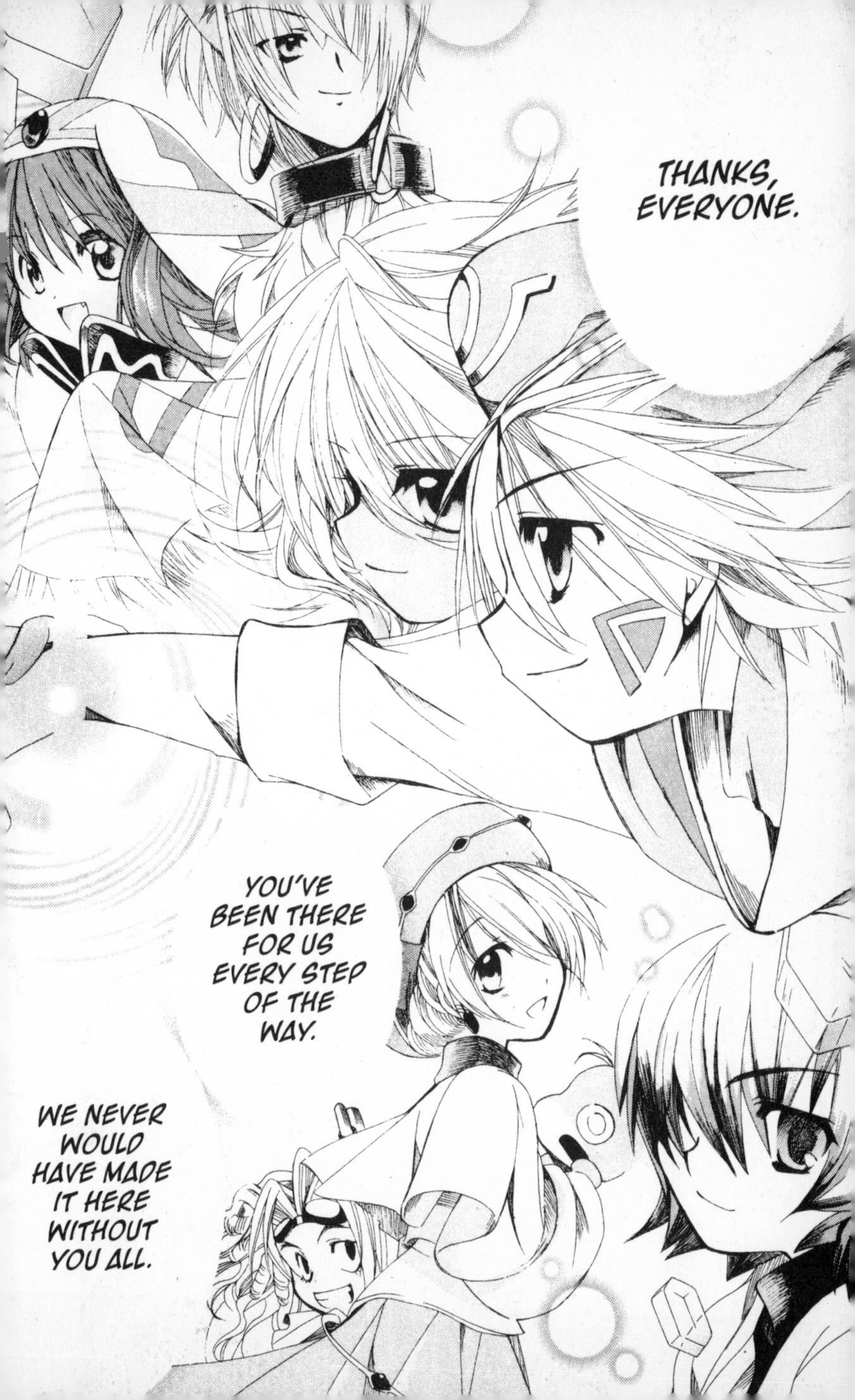
THANKS, EVERYONE.
YOU'VE BEEN THERE FOR US EVERY STEP OF THE WAY.
WE NEVER WOULD HAVE MADE IT HERE WITHOUT YOU ALL.

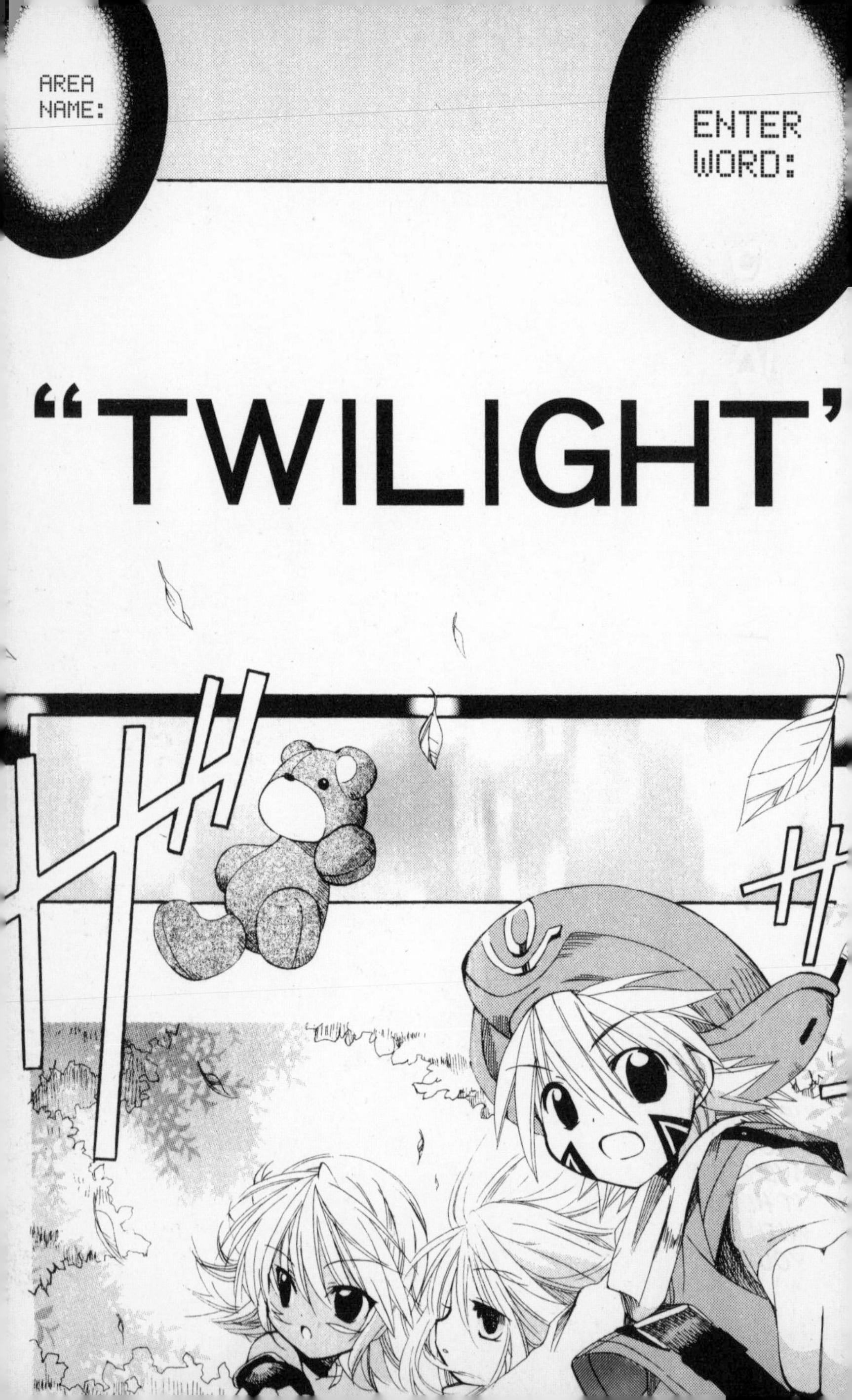
ENTER WORD:
AREA NAME:
"TWILIGHT'

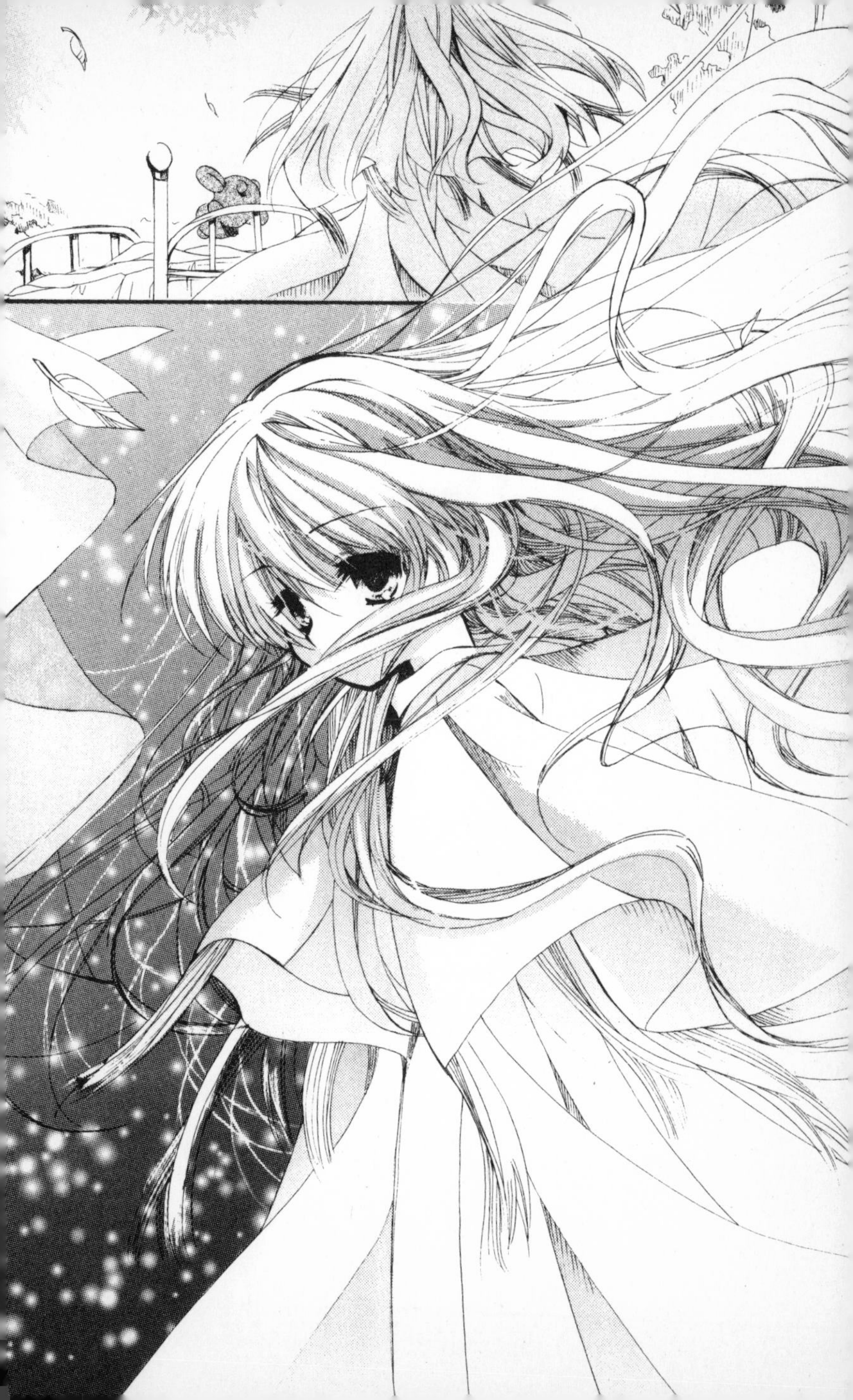

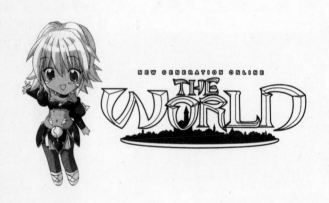

NEW GENERATION ONLINE

THE WORLD

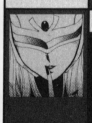

SUBJECT: TO ALL. SENDER: HELBA

THE MEANING OF THE TWILIGHT EVENT FOUR YEARS AGO;
THE MEANING OF THE BRACELET WHICH AURA BROUGHT BACK
FOUR YEARS LATER;
THE REASON WHY THE THE SHAPELESS "WILL" OF THE
WORLD RESURRECTED TWO LEGENDARY HEROES;
THE REASON WHY THIS WORLD EXISTS AT ALL;

THE REASON BEHIND THE DOT HACKERS...

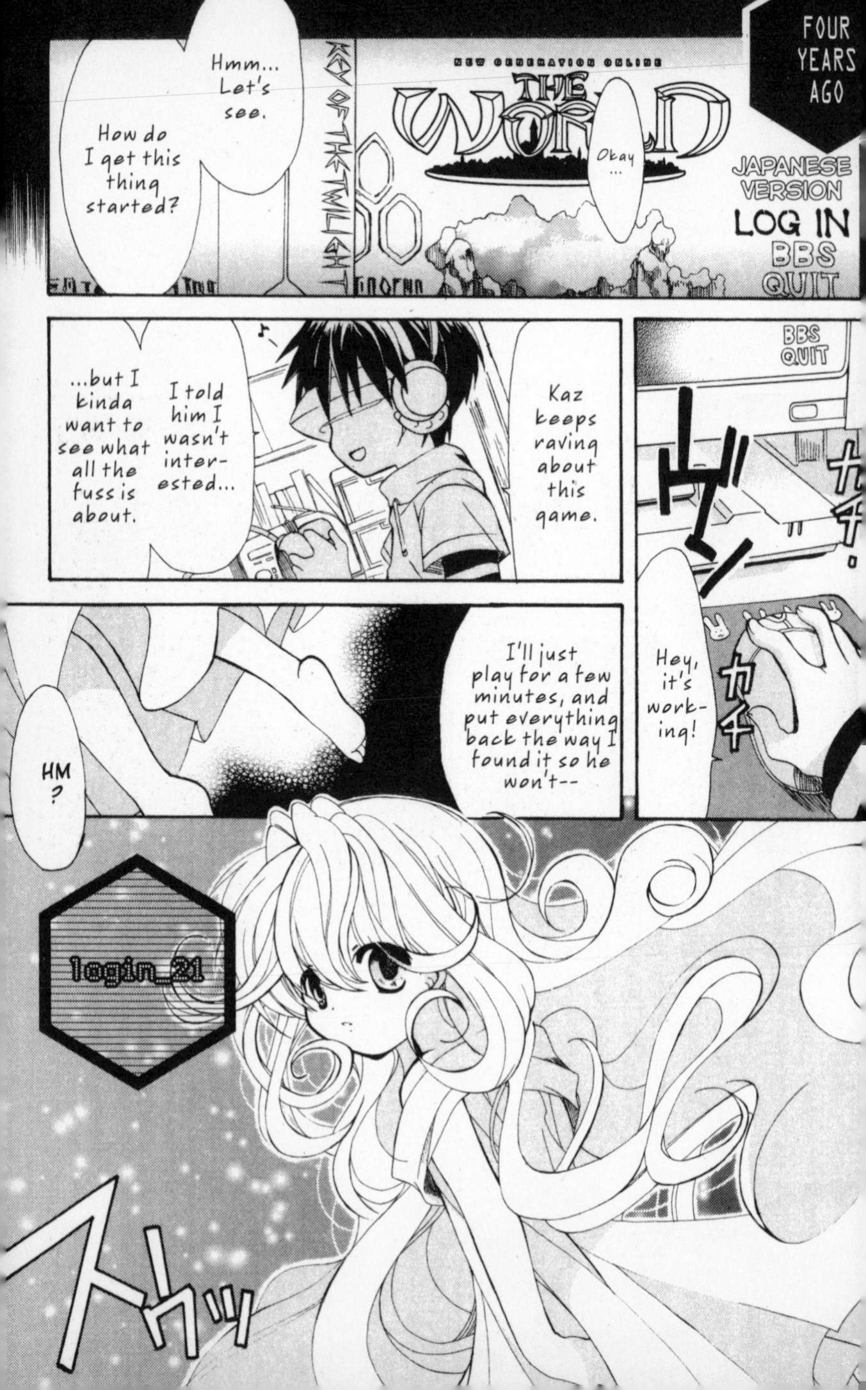
FOUR YEARS AGO
NEW GENERATION ONLINE
THE WORLD
JAPANESE VERSION
LOG IN
BBS
QUIT
Okay ...
KEY OF THE TWILIGHT
Hmm... Let's see.
How do I get this thing started?
BBS
QUIT
Kaz keeps raving about this game.
I told him I wasn't inter-ested...
...but I kinda want to see what all the fuss is about.
Hey, it's work-ing!
I'll just play for a few minutes, and put everything back the way I found it so he won't--
HM ?
login_21

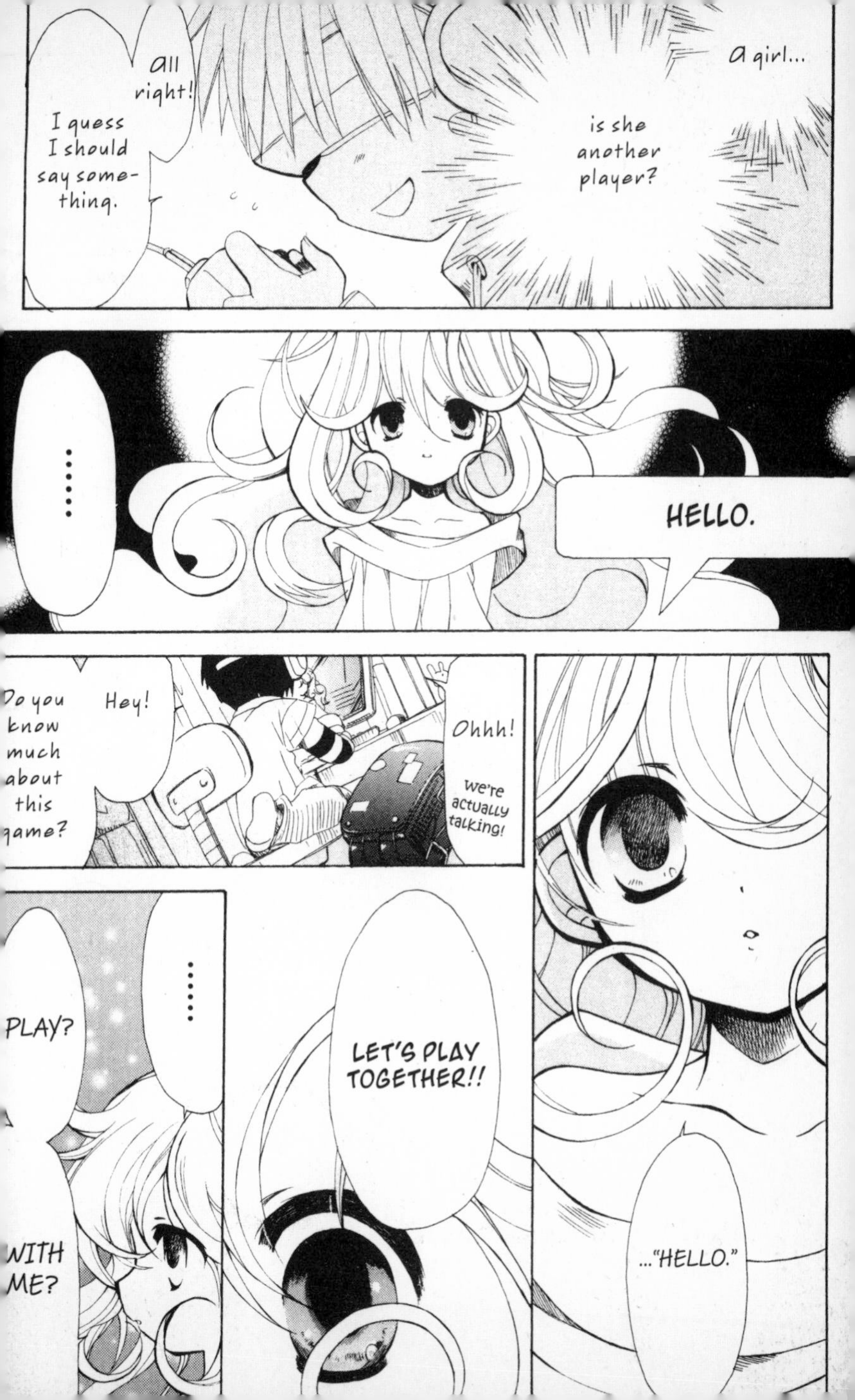
a girl...
is she another player?
all right! I guess I should say some-thing.
HELLO.
......
..."HELLO."
Ohhh!
we're actually talking!
Hey!
Do you know much about this game?
LET'S PLAY TOGETHER!!
......
PLAY? WITH ME?

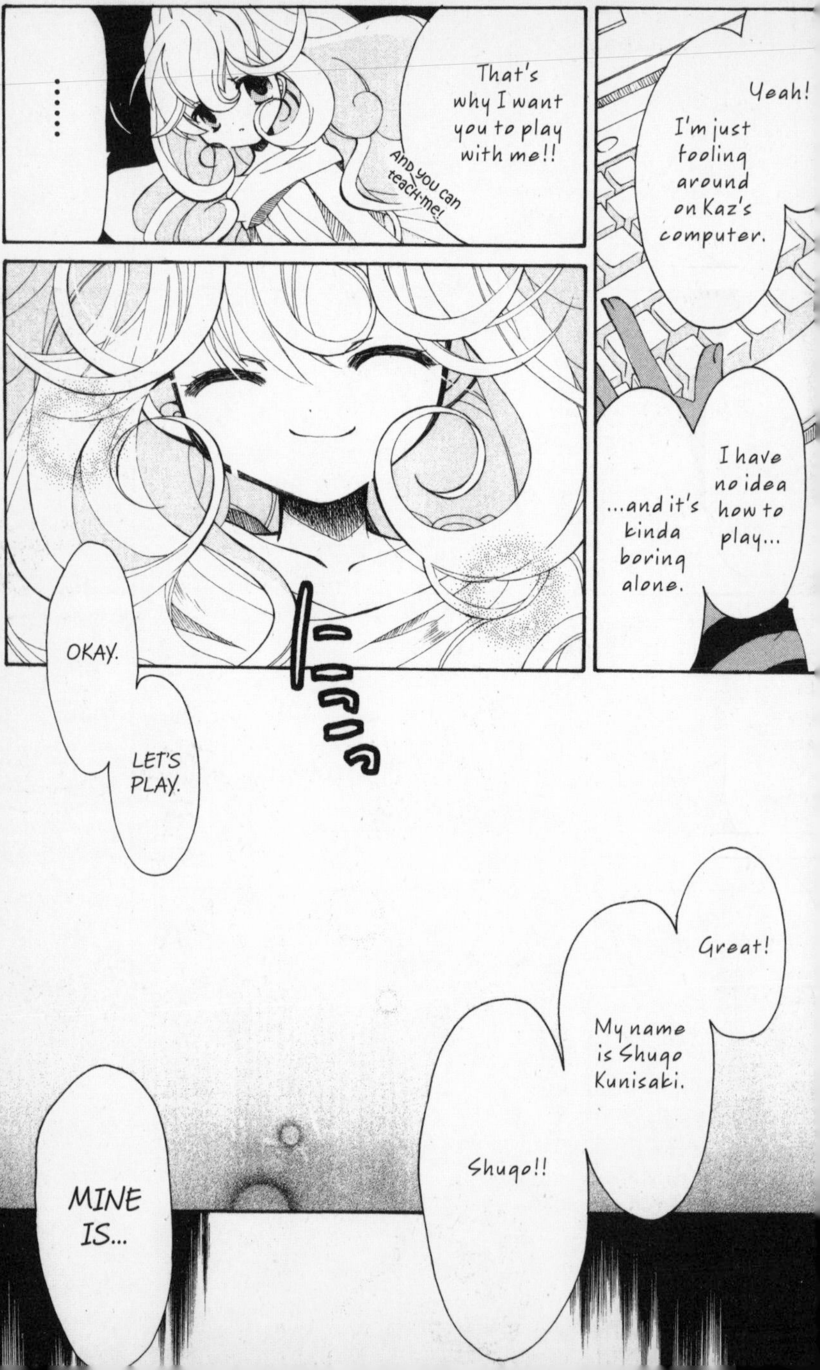
Yeah! I'm just fooling around on Kaz's computer.
I have no idea how to play...
...and it's kinda boring alone.
That's why I want you to play with me!!
And you can teach me!
......
OKAY.
LET'S PLAY.
Great!
My name is Shugo Kunisaki.
Shugo!!
MINE IS...

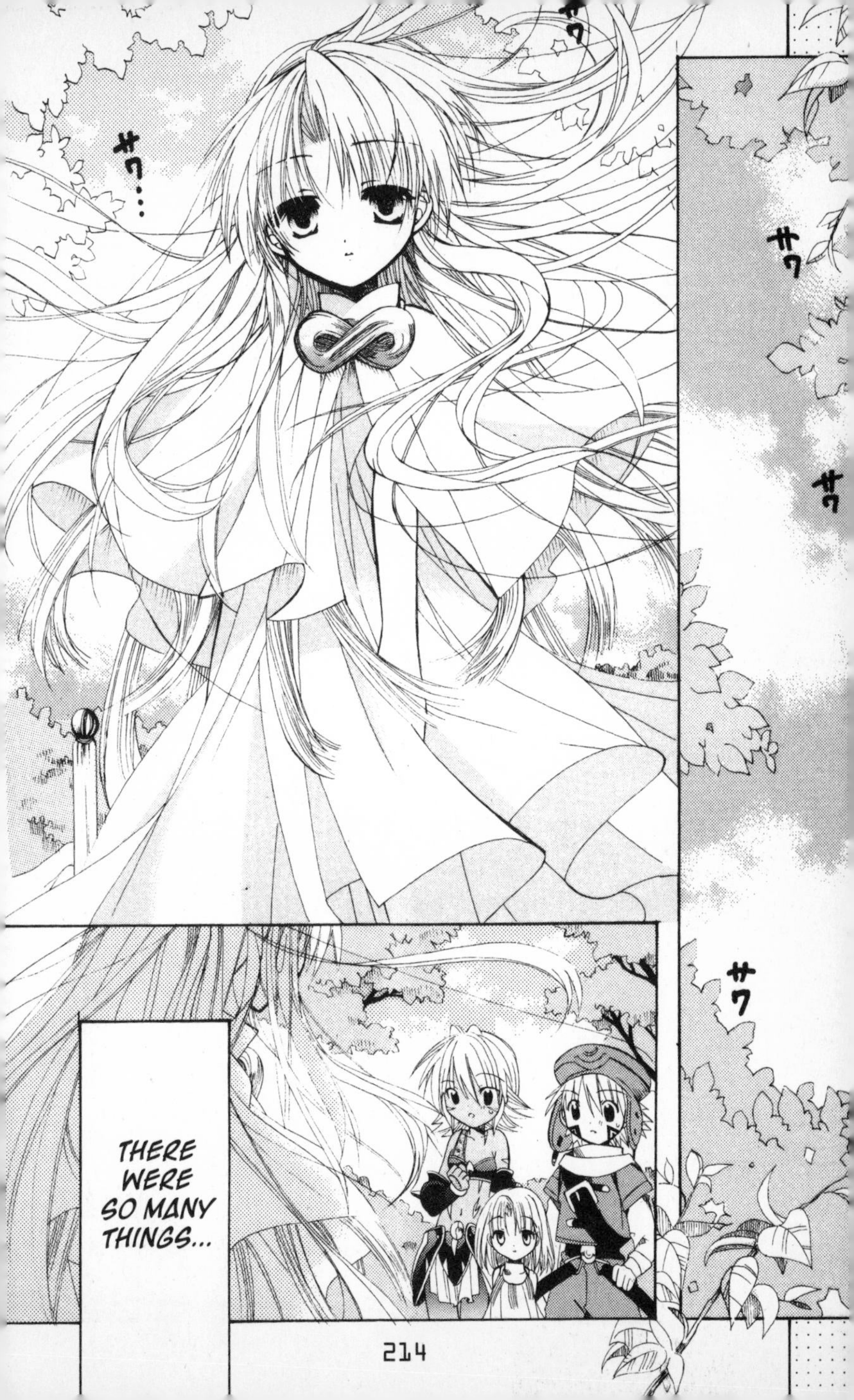
サク
サク
サク
サク
サク…
THERE WERE SO MANY THINGS...

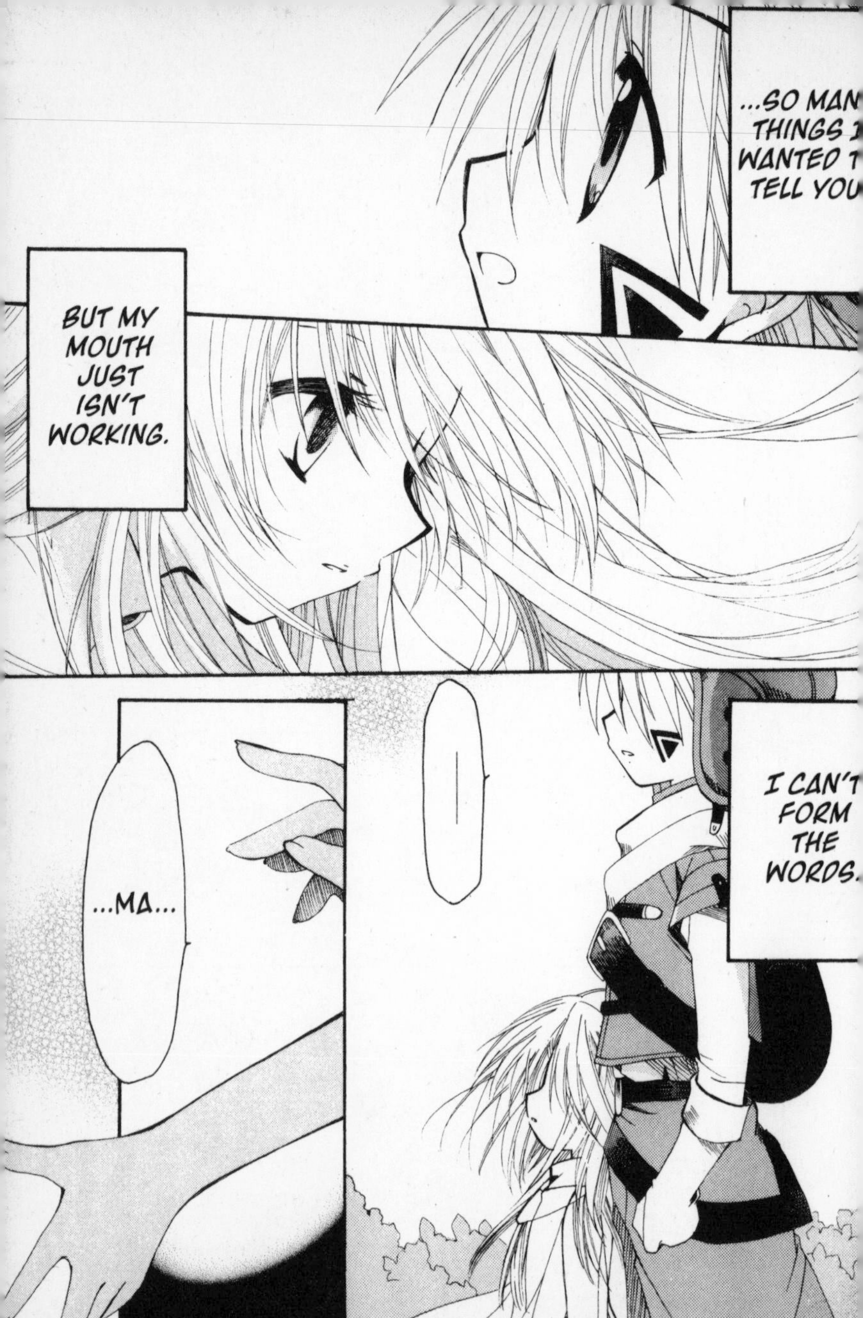
...SO MAN THINGS I WANTED T TELL YOU
BUT MY MOUTH JUST ISN'T WORKING.
I CAN'T FORM THE WORDS.
—
...MA...

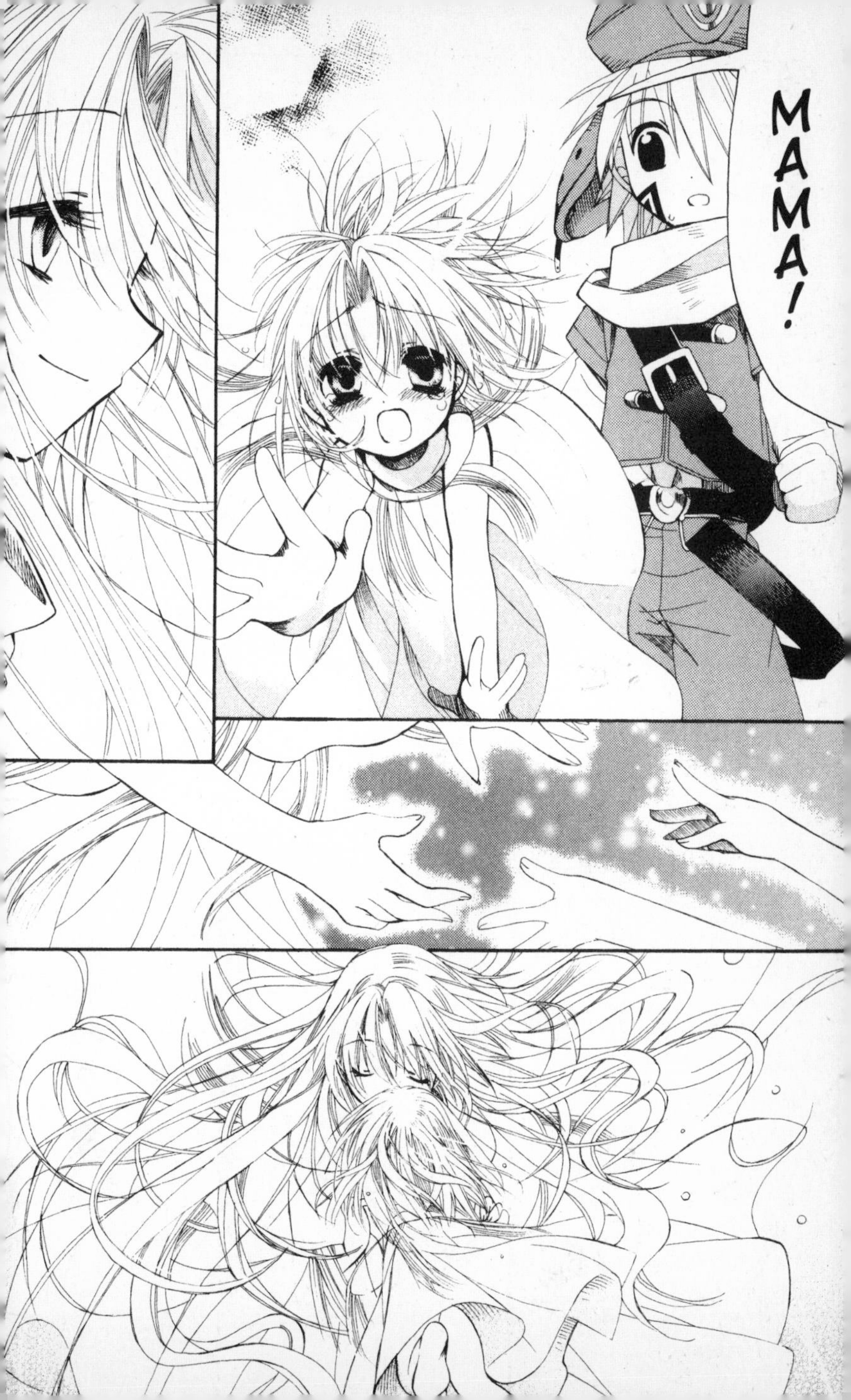
MAMA!

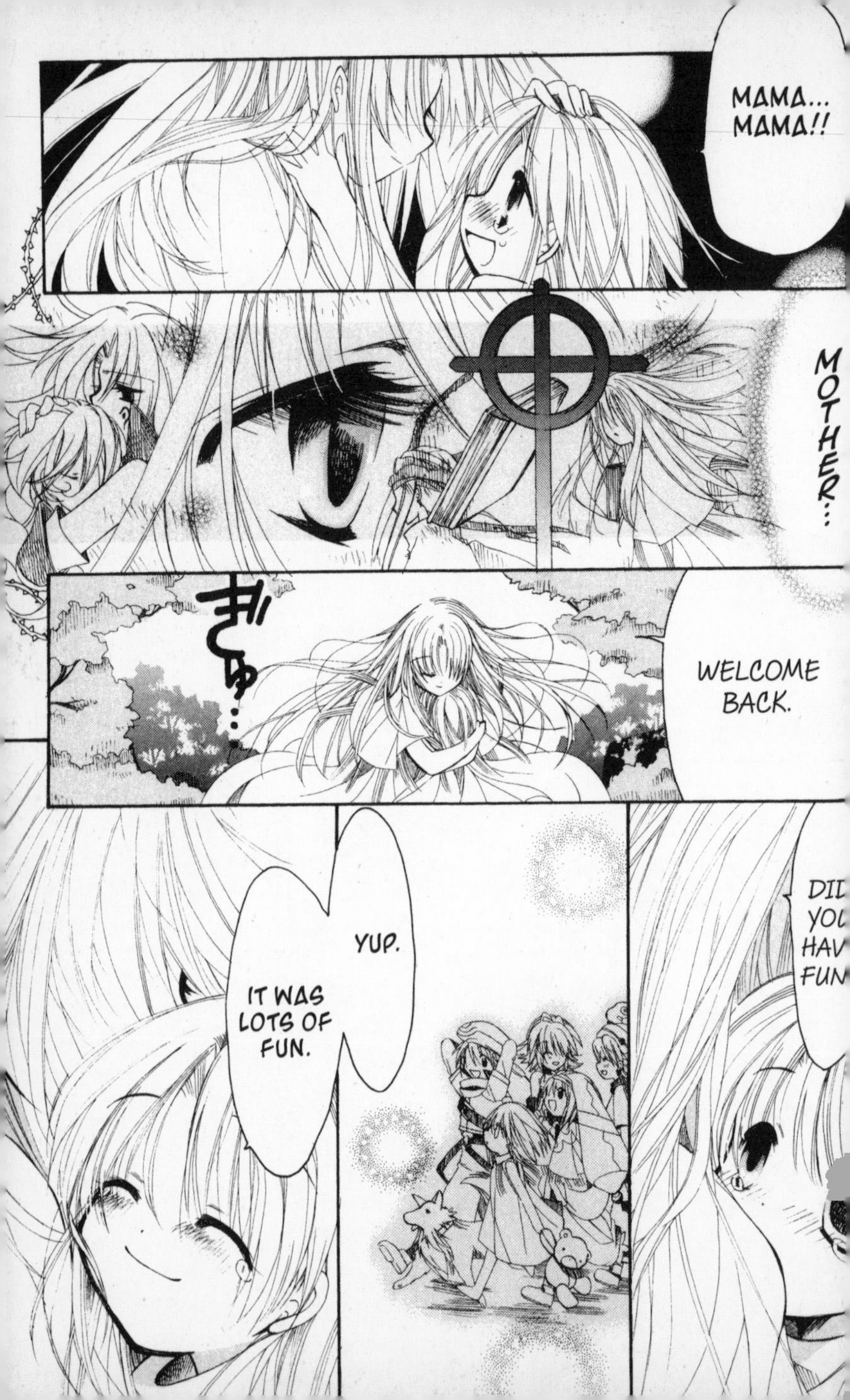
MAMA... MAMA!!
MOTHER...
ぎゅ...
WELCOME BACK.
DID YOU HAVE FUN?
YUP.
IT WAS LOTS OF FUN.

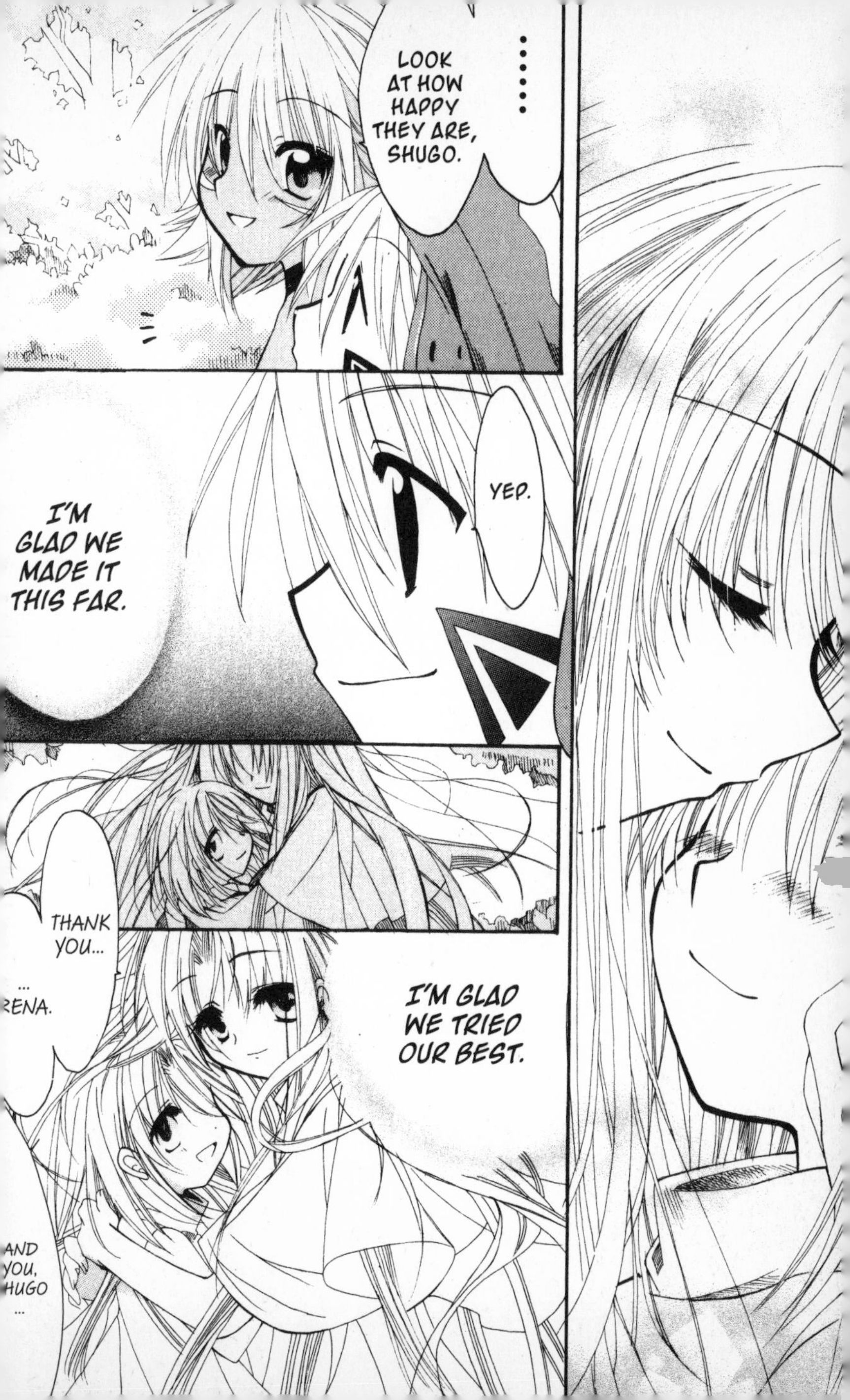
......
LOOK AT HOW HAPPY THEY ARE, SHUGO.
YEP.
I'M GLAD WE MADE IT THIS FAR.
I'M GLAD WE TRIED OUR BEST.
THANK YOU...
... ENA.
AND YOU, HUGO ...

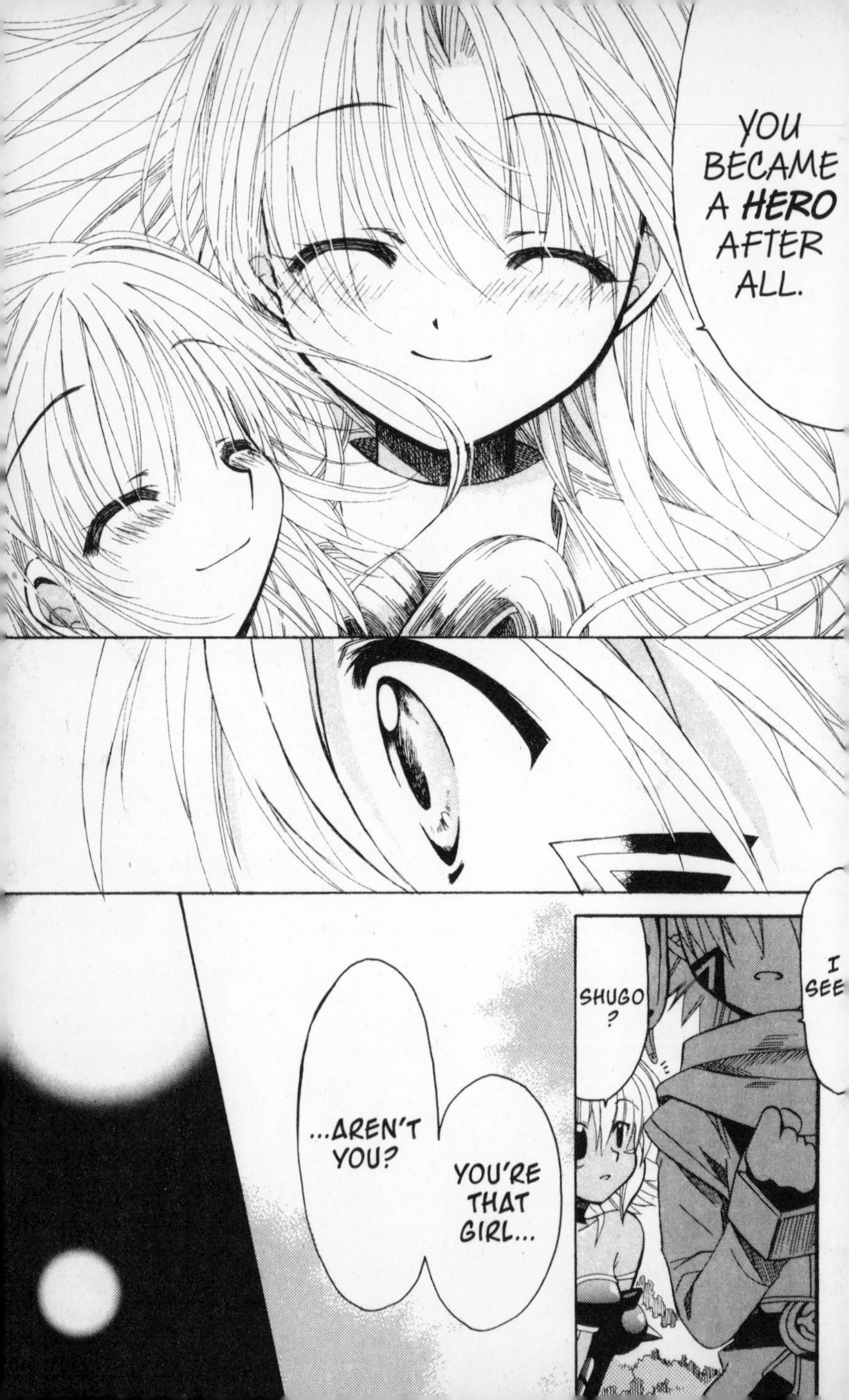
YOU BECAME A **HERO** AFTER ALL.
I SEE
SHUGO ?
YOU'RE THAT GIRL...
...AREN'T YOU?

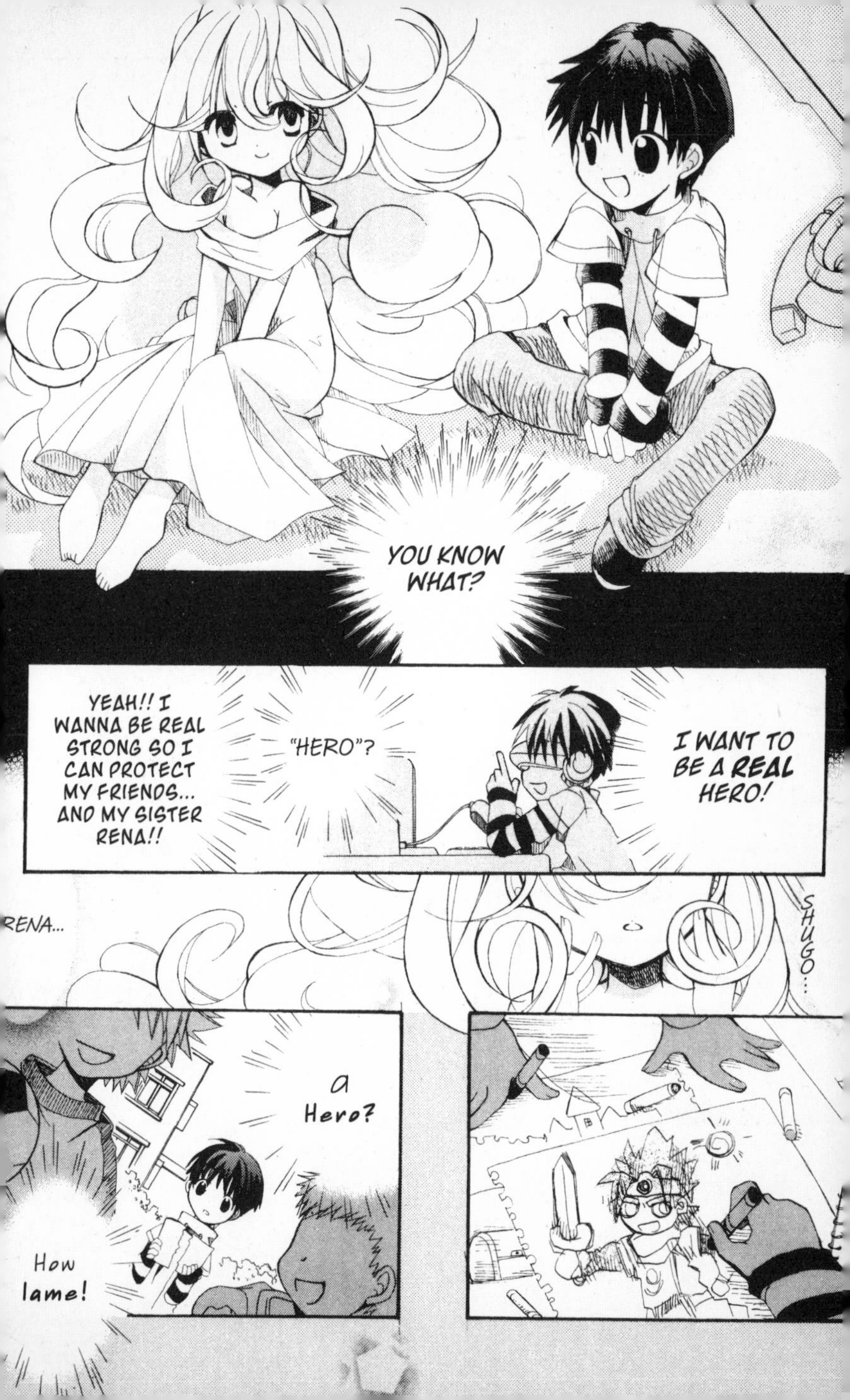
YOU KNOW WHAT?
I WANT TO BE A **REAL** HERO!
"HERO"?
YEAH!! I WANNA BE REAL STRONG SO I CAN PROTECT MY FRIENDS... AND MY SISTER RENA!!
SHUGO...
RENA...
a Hero?
How lame!

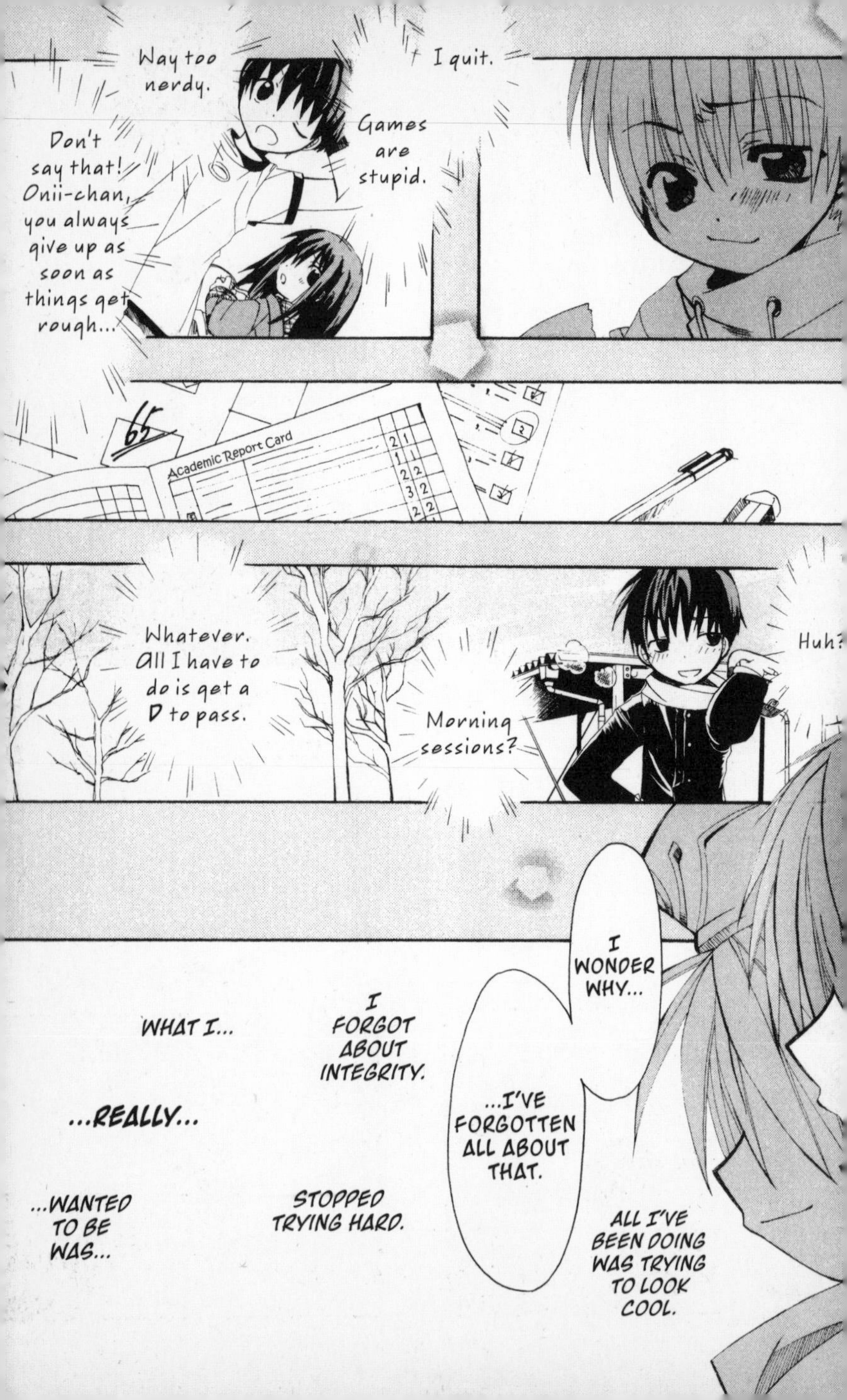
I quit.
Way too nerdy.
Games are stupid.
Don't say that! Onii-chan, you always give up as soon as things get rough...
65
Academic Report Card
Huh?
Morning sessions?
Whatever. All I have to do is get a D to pass.
I WONDER WHY... ...I'VE FORGOTTEN ALL ABOUT THAT.
ALL I'VE BEEN DOING WAS TRYING TO LOOK COOL.
I FORGOT ABOUT INTEGRITY.
STOPPED TRYING HARD.
WHAT I...
...REALLY...
...WANTED TO BE WAS...

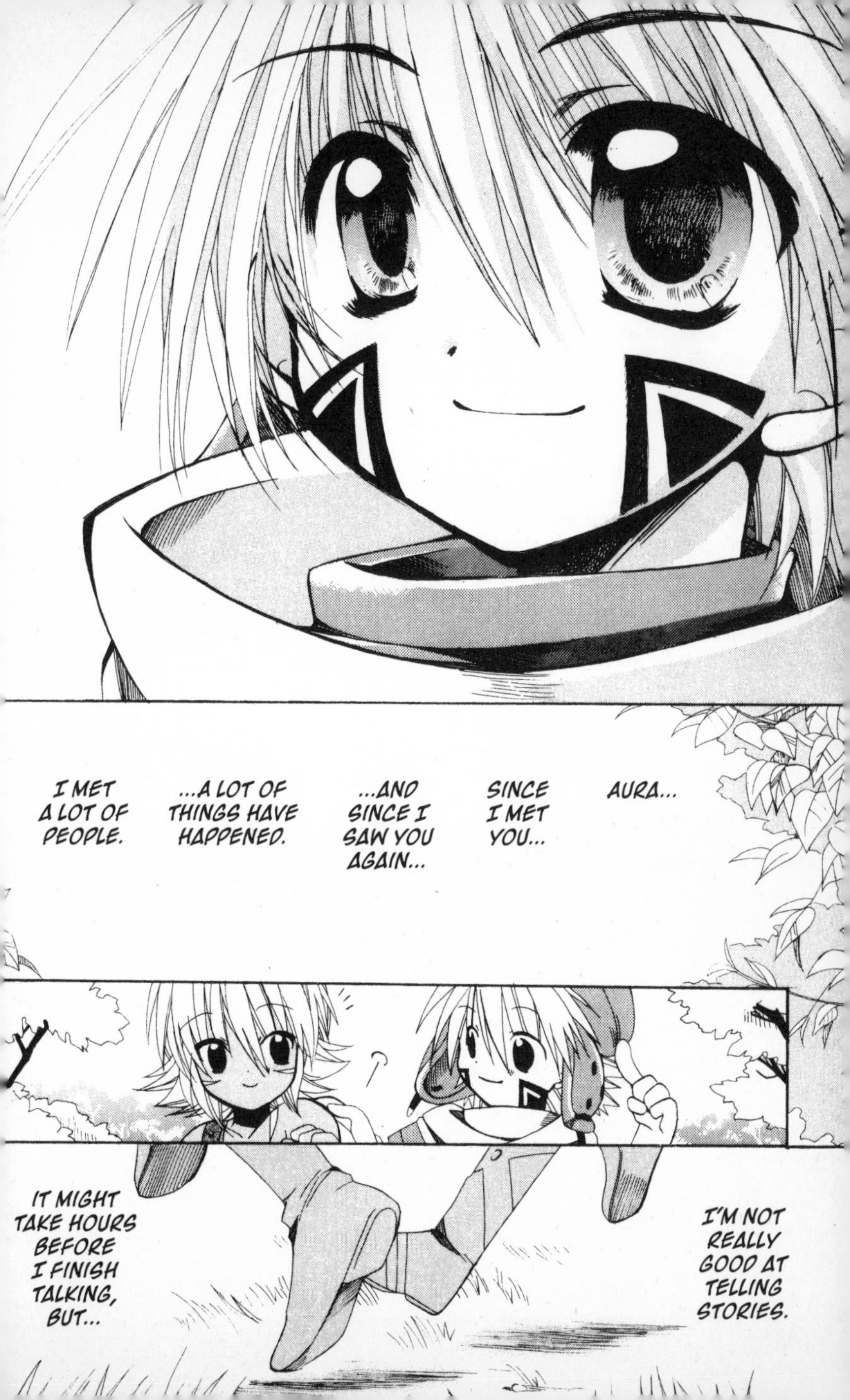
AURA...
SINCE I MET YOU...
...AND SINCE I SAW YOU AGAIN...
...A LOT OF THINGS HAVE HAPPENED.
I MET A LOT OF PEOPLE.
I'M NOT REALLY GOOD AT TELLING STORIES.
IT MIGHT TAKE HOURS BEFORE I FINISH TALKING, BUT...

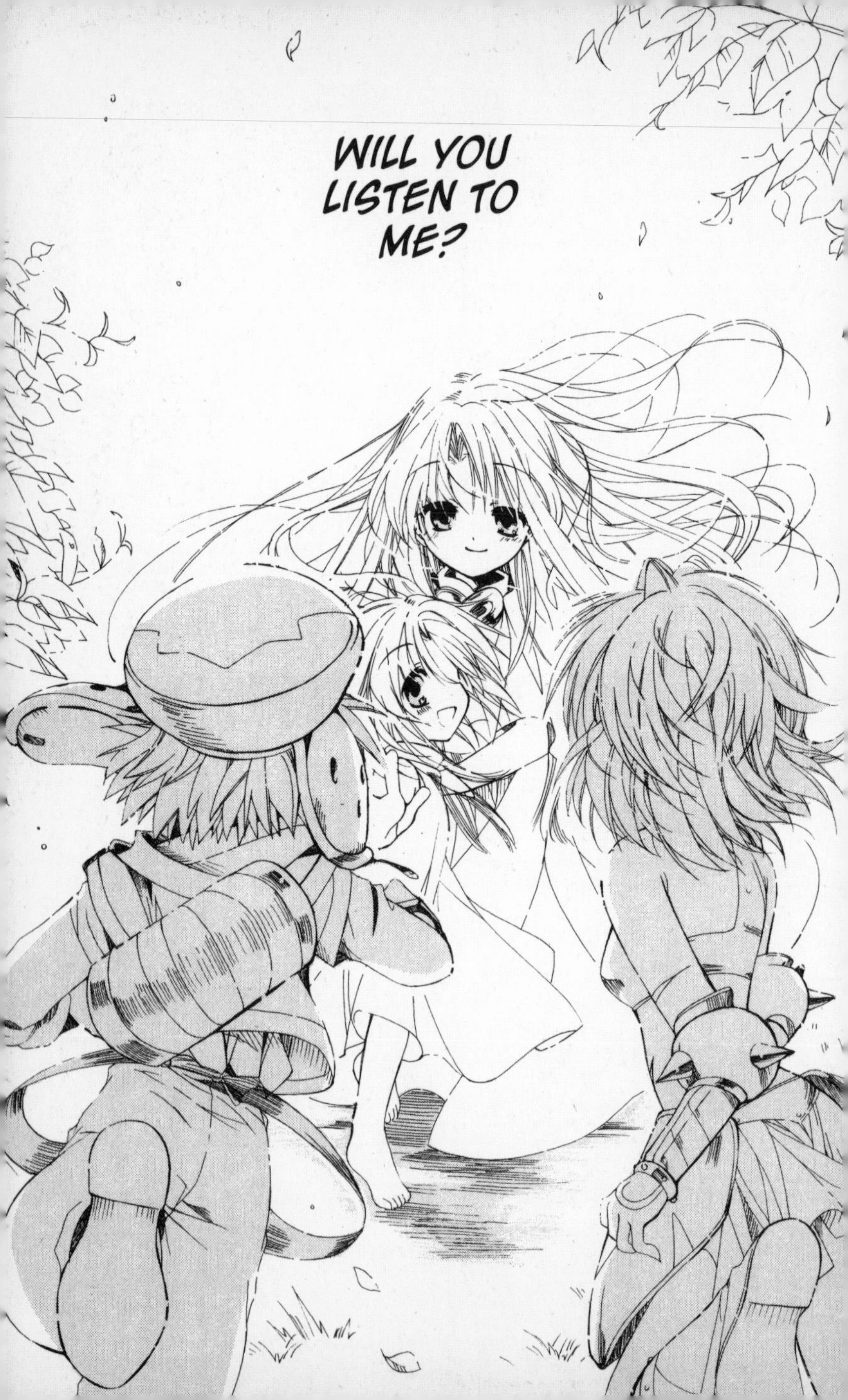
WILL YOU LISTEN TO ME?

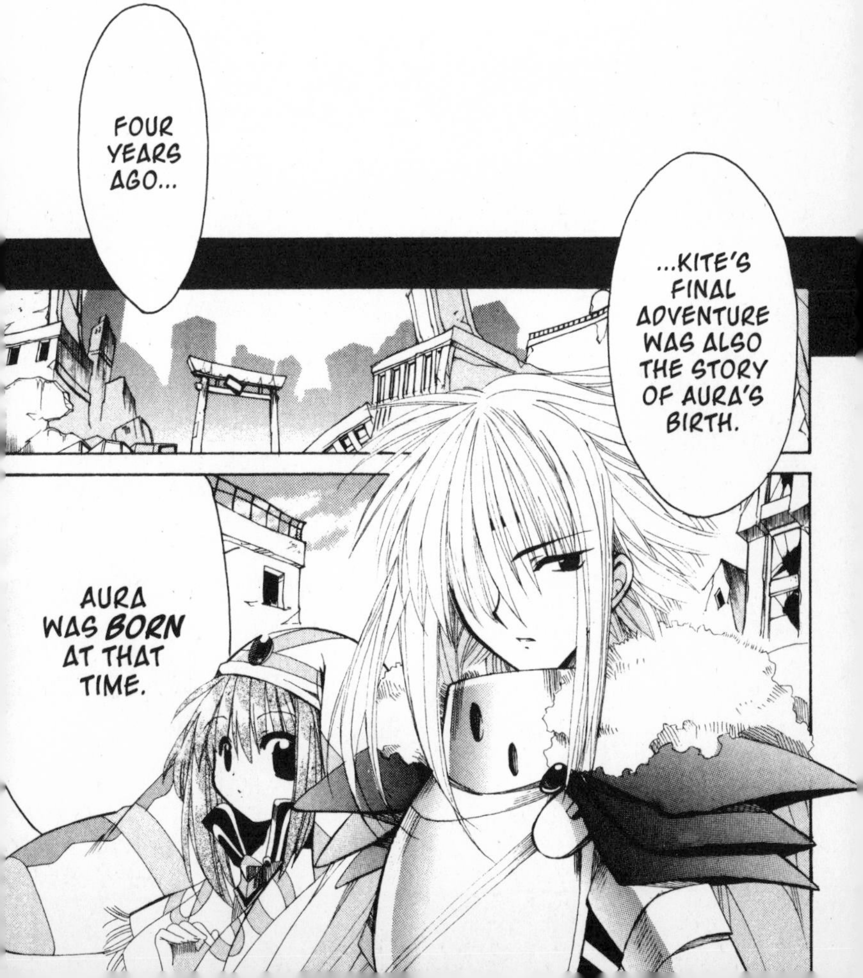
FOUR YEARS AGO...
...KITE'S FINAL ADVENTURE WAS ALSO THE STORY OF AURA'S BIRTH.
AURA WAS **BORN** AT THAT TIME.

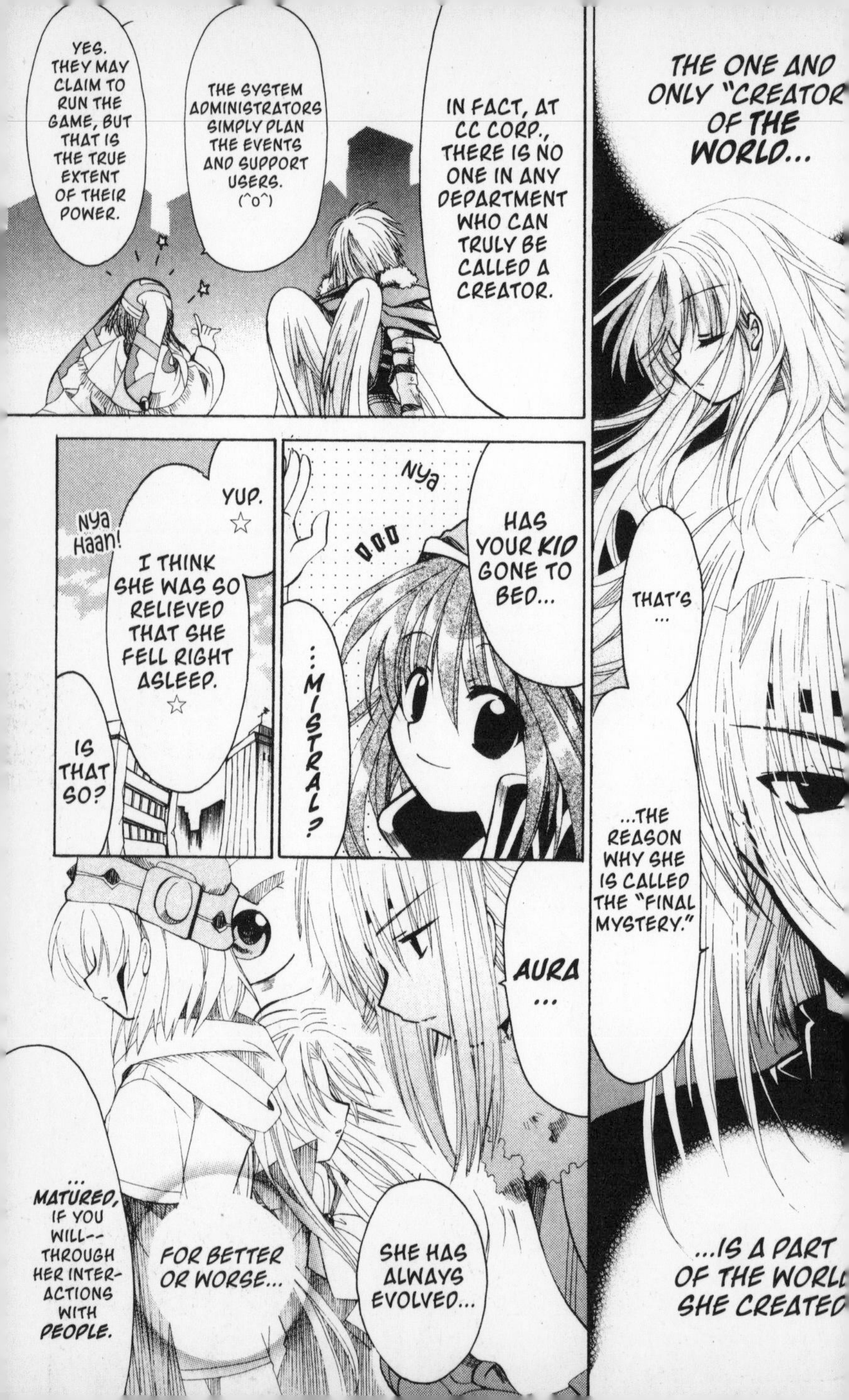
THE ONE AND ONLY "CREATOR OF THE WORLD...
THAT'S...
...THE REASON WHY SHE IS CALLED THE "FINAL MYSTERY."
...IS A PART OF THE WORLD SHE CREATED
IN FACT, AT CC CORP., THERE IS NO ONE IN ANY DEPARTMENT WHO CAN TRULY BE CALLED A CREATOR.
THE SYSTEM ADMINISTRATORS SIMPLY PLAN THE EVENTS AND SUPPORT USERS. (^o^)
YES. THEY MAY CLAIM TO RUN THE GAME, BUT THAT IS THE TRUE EXTENT OF THEIR POWER.
Nya
HAS YOUR KID GONE TO BED...
...MISTRAL?
YUP. ☆
I THINK SHE WAS SO RELIEVED THAT SHE FELL RIGHT ASLEEP. ☆
Nya Haan!
IS THAT SO?
AURA...
SHE HAS ALWAYS EVOLVED...
FOR BETTER OR WORSE...
...MATURED, IF YOU WILL--THROUGH HER INTERACTIONS WITH PEOPLE.

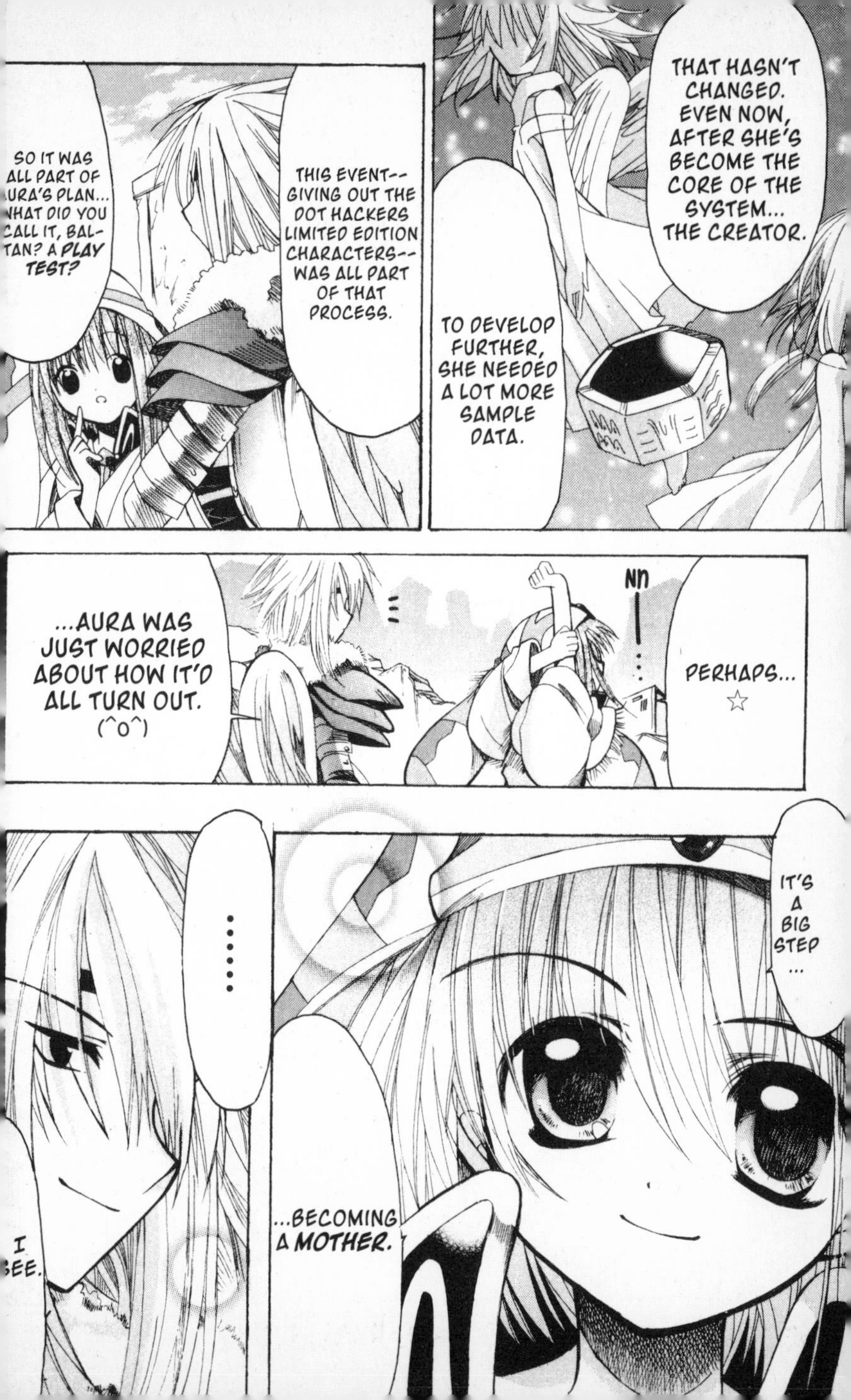
THAT HASN'T CHANGED. EVEN NOW, AFTER SHE'S BECOME THE CORE OF THE SYSTEM... THE CREATOR.
TO DEVELOP FURTHER, SHE NEEDED A LOT MORE SAMPLE DATA.
THIS EVENT--GIVING OUT THE DOT HACKERS LIMITED EDITION CHARACTERS--WAS ALL PART OF THAT PROCESS.
SO IT WAS ALL PART OF URA'S PLAN... HAT DID YOU CALL IT, BAL-TAN? A *PLAY TEST?*
PERHAPS... ☆
NN...!
...AURA WAS JUST WORRIED ABOUT HOW IT'D ALL TURN OUT. (^o^)
IT'S A BIG STEP...
...BECOMING A **MOTHER.**
......
I SEE.

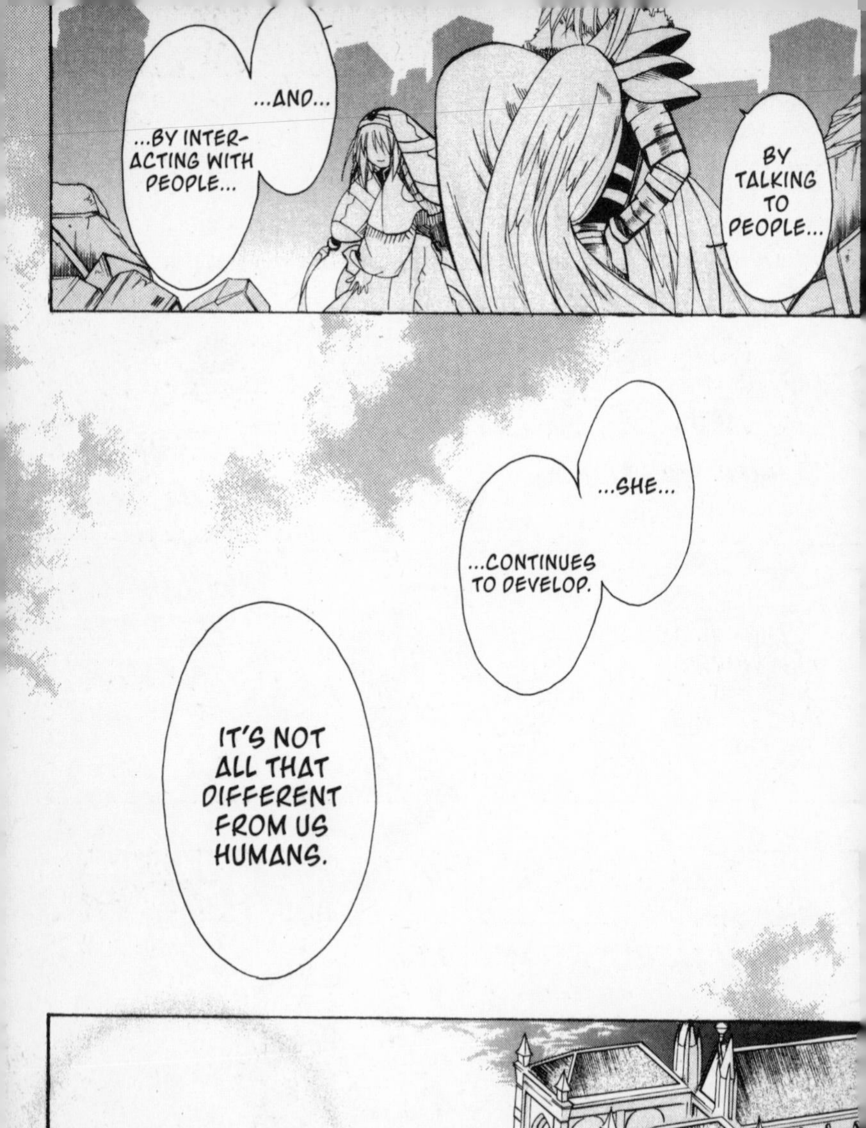
BY TALKING TO PEOPLE...
...AND...
...BY INTER-ACTING WITH PEOPLE...
...SHE...
...CONTINUES TO DEVELOP.
IT'S NOT ALL THAT DIFFERENT FROM US HUMANS.
I WONDER...

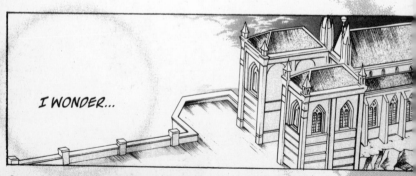

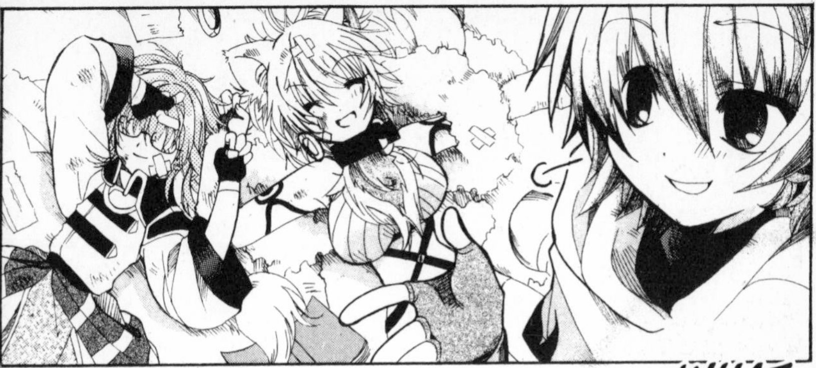

...WHAT KIND OF "WORLD" WILL SHE CREATE NEXT?

Manga // REI IZUMI

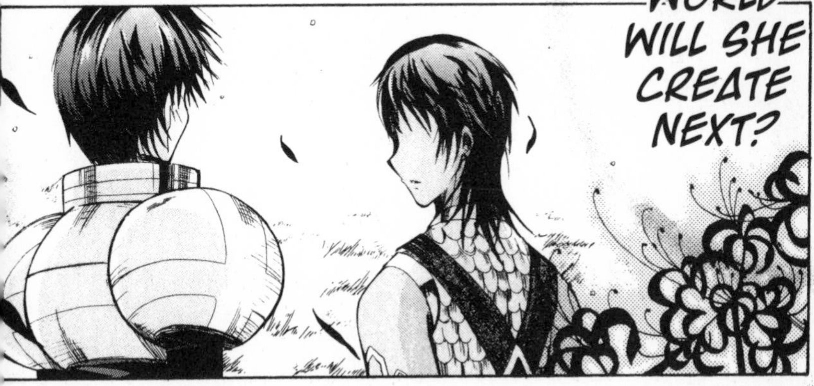

Story // TATSUYA HAMAZAKI

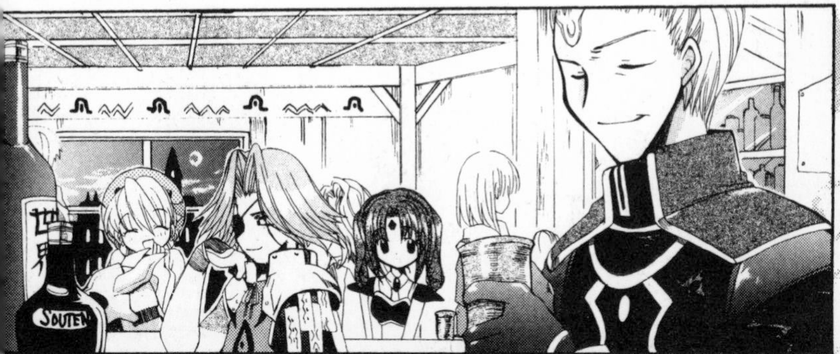
SOUTEN

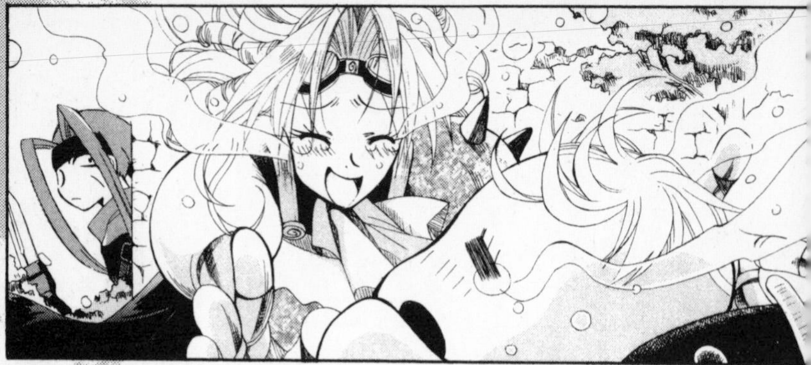

Managing Editor // HIROSHI MATSUYAMA
(Cyber Connect 2)

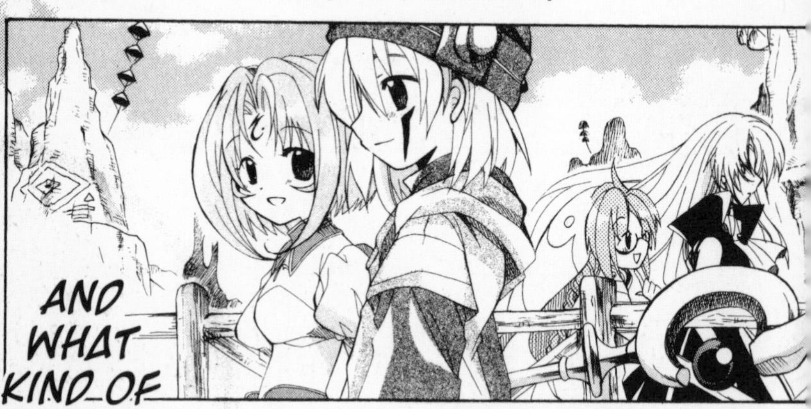
AND WHAT KIND OF STORIES WILL BE TOLD?

DAISUKE UCHIYAMA
(Bandai, Video Game Department)

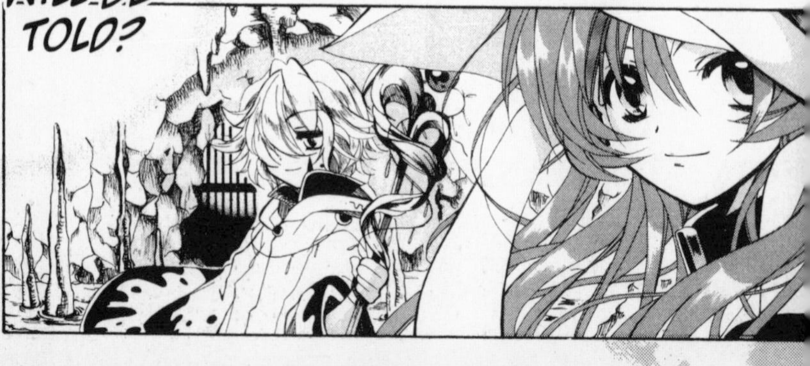

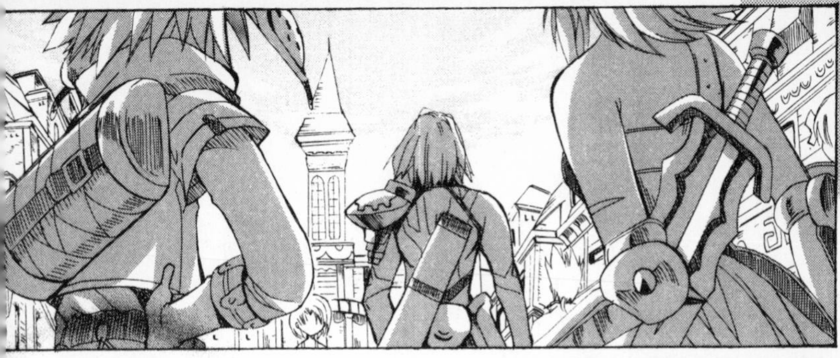

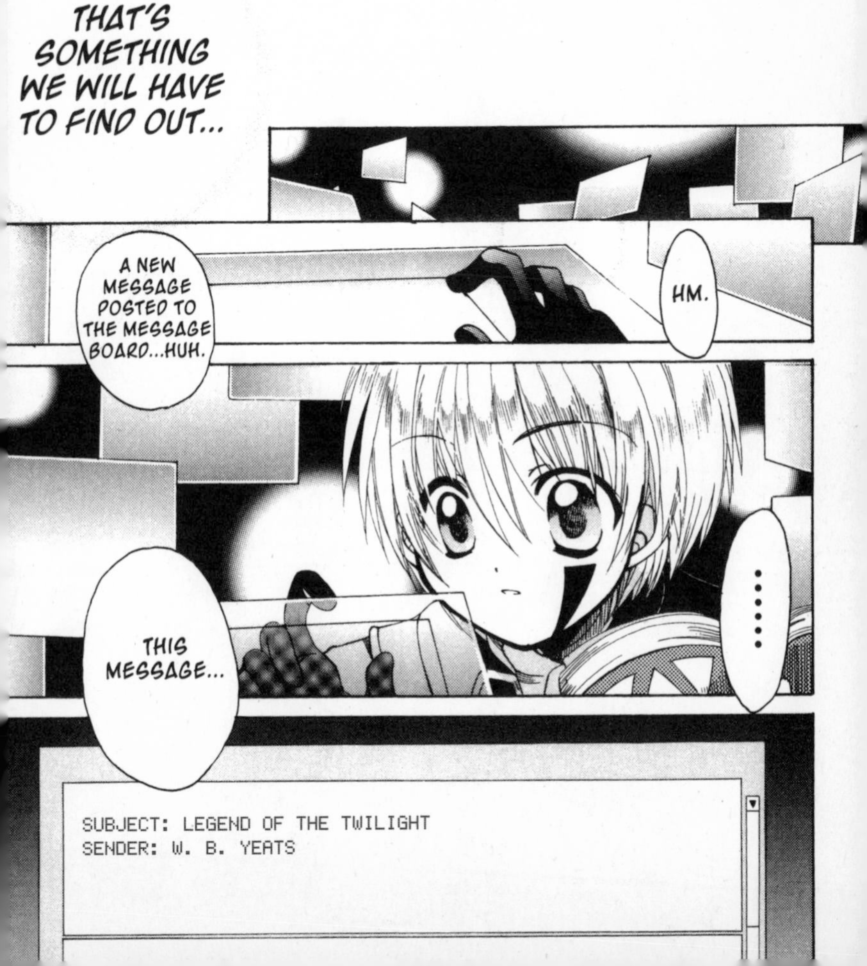
THAT'S SOMETHING WE WILL HAVE TO FIND OUT...
HM.
A NEW MESSAGE POSTED TO THE MESSAGE BOARD...HUH.
......
THIS MESSAGE...
SUBJECT: LEGEND OF THE TWILIGHT
SENDER: W. B. YEATS

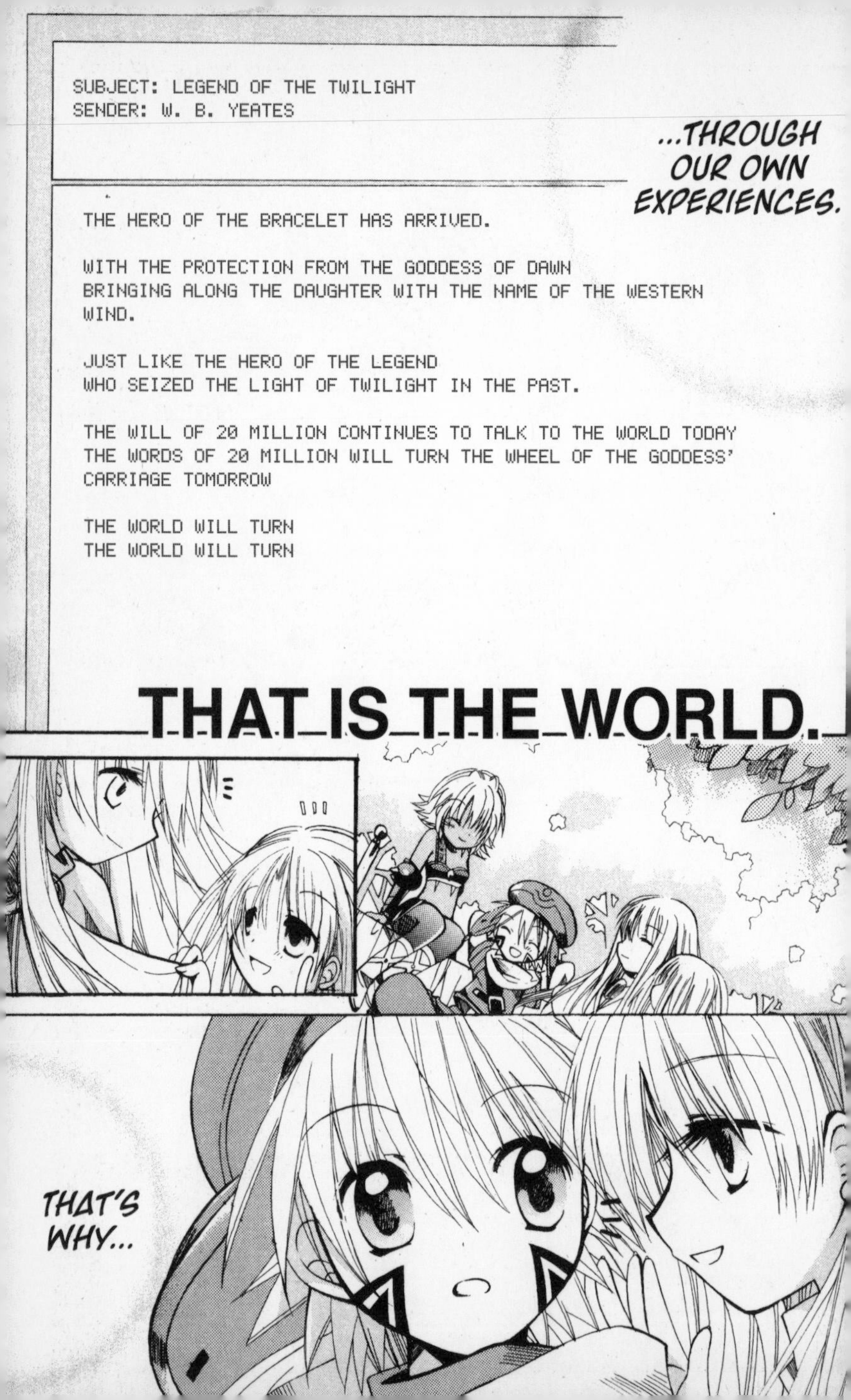
...THROUGH OUR OWN EXPERIENCES.
SUBJECT: LEGEND OF THE TWILIGHT
SENDER: W. B. YEATES
THE HERO OF THE BRACELET HAS ARRIVED.
WITH THE PROTECTION FROM THE GODDESS OF DAWN
BRINGING ALONG THE DAUGHTER WITH THE NAME OF THE WESTERN WIND.
JUST LIKE THE HERO OF THE LEGEND
WHO SEIZED THE LIGHT OF TWILIGHT IN THE PAST.
THE WILL OF 20 MILLION CONTINUES TO TALK TO THE WORLD TODAY
THE WORDS OF 20 MILLION WILL TURN THE WHEEL OF THE GODDESS' CARRIAGE TOMORROW
THE WORLD WILL TURN
THE WORLD WILL TURN
THAT IS THE WORLD.
THAT'S WHY...

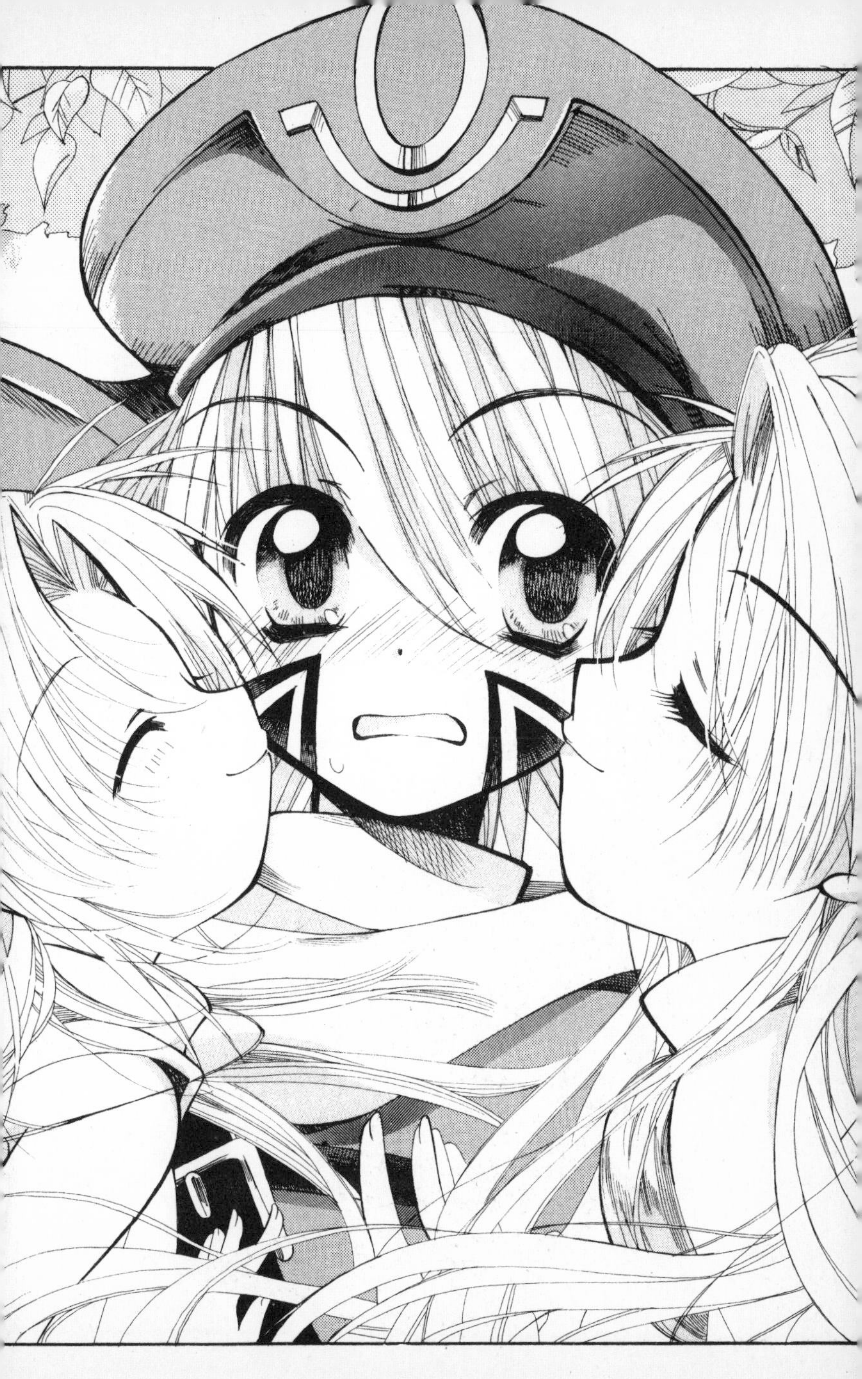

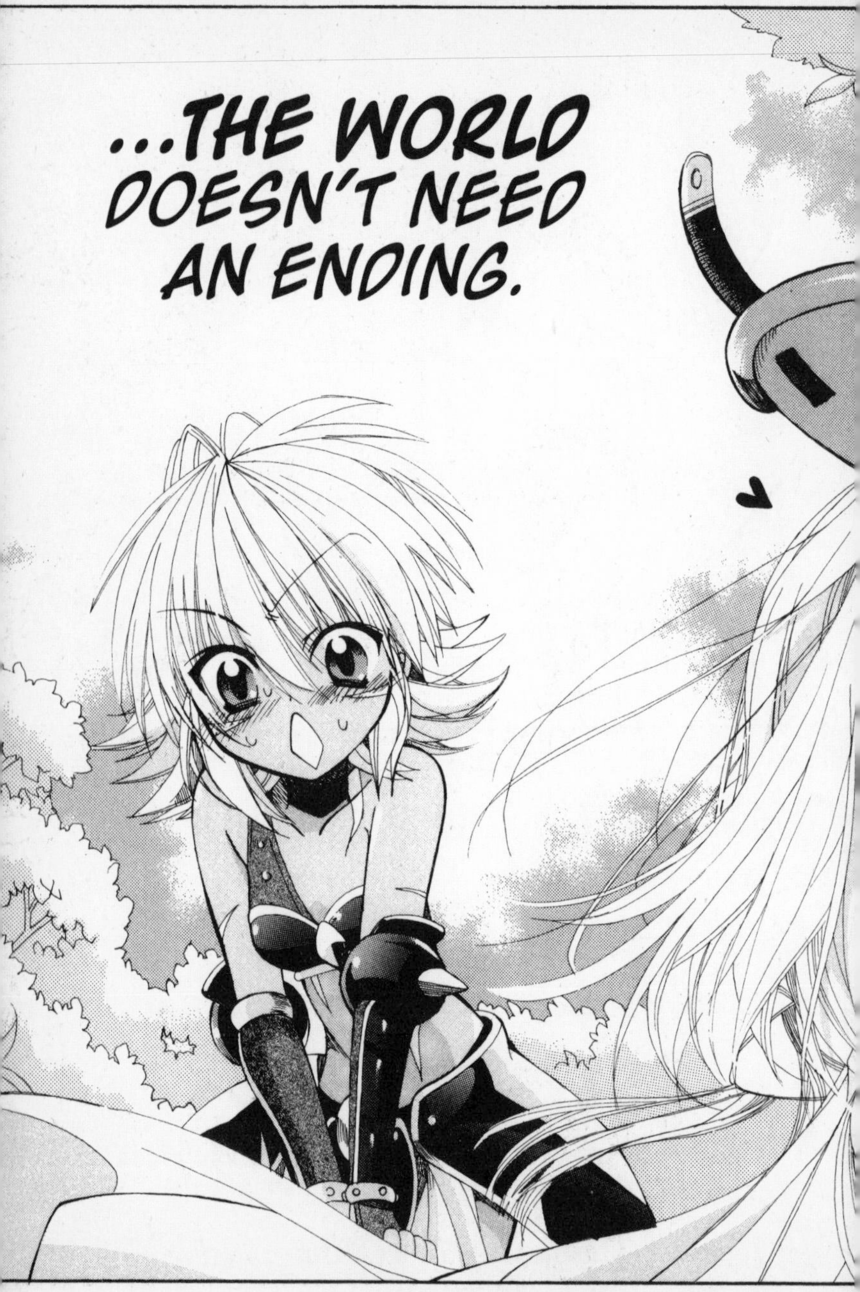
...THE WORLD DOESN'T NEED AN ENDING.

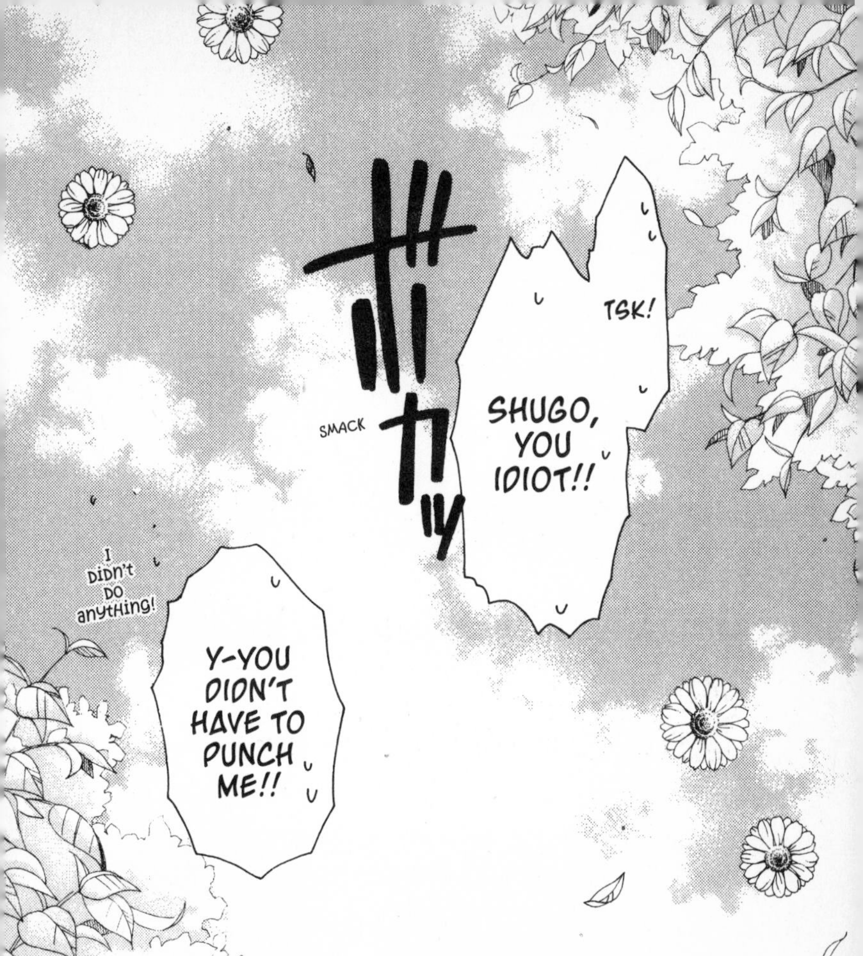
TSK!
SHUGO, YOU IDIOT!!
SMACK
I DIDN'T DO ANYTHING!
Y-YOU DIDN'T HAVE TO PUNCH ME!!
TEE HEE HEE...

.hack//LEGEND OF THE TWILIGHT

Thank you for reading
Never End...

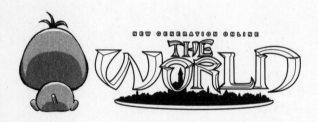

NEW GENERATION ONLINE
THE WORLD

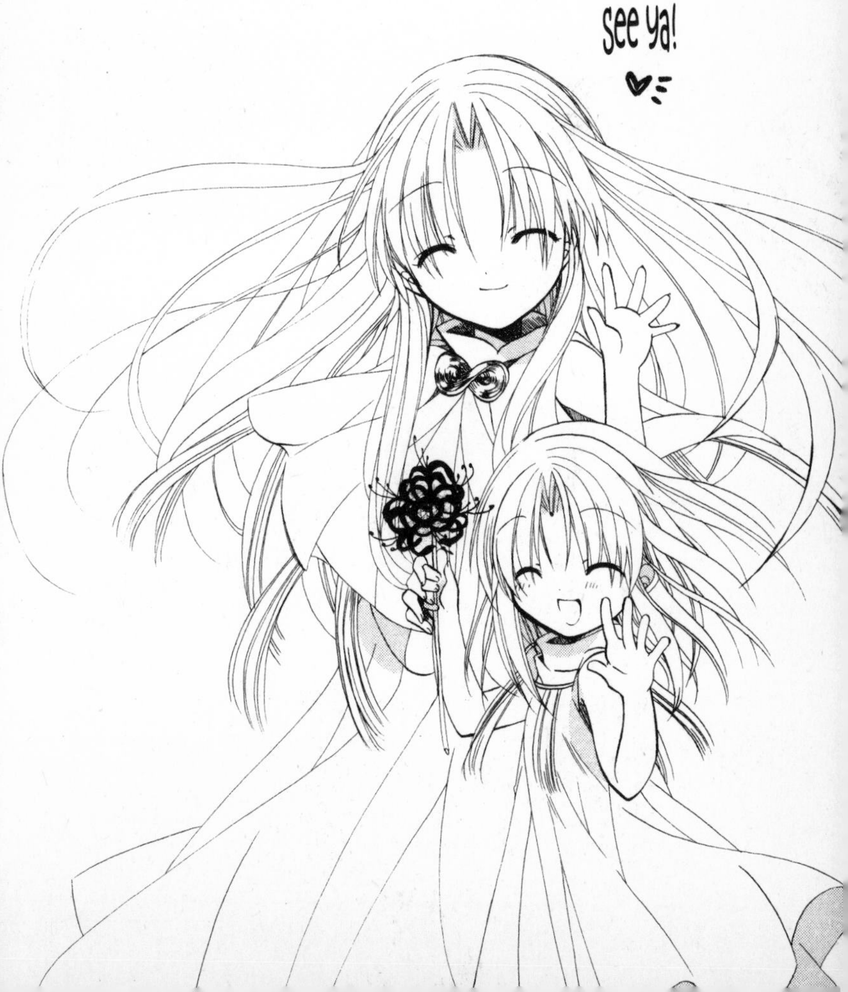
see ya!

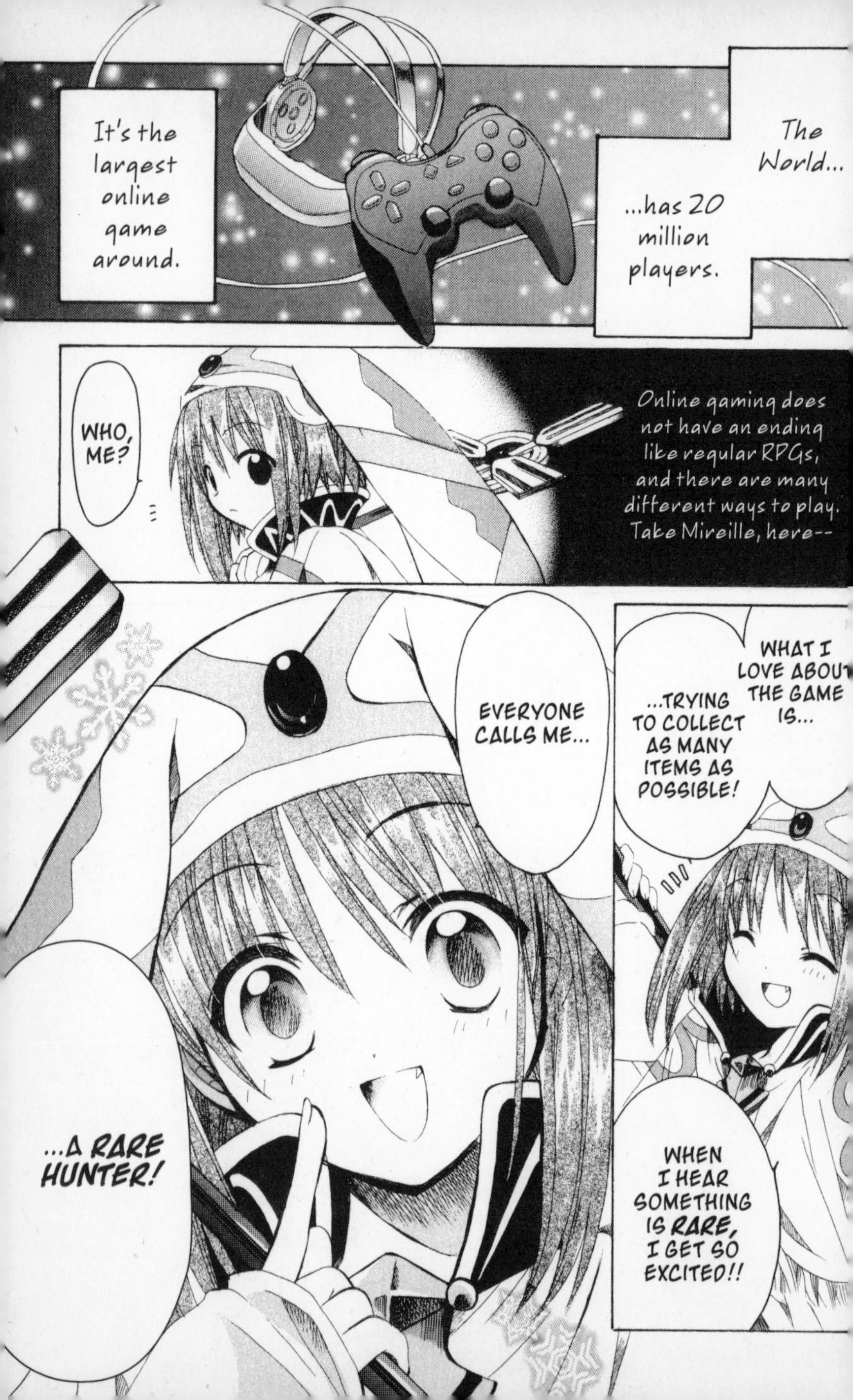
The World...
...has 20 million players.
It's the largest online game around.
Online gaming does not have an ending like regular RPGs, and there are many different ways to play. Take Mireille, here--
WHO, ME?
WHAT I LOVE ABOUT THE GAME IS...
...TRYING TO COLLECT AS MANY ITEMS AS POSSIBLE!
WHEN I HEAR SOMETHING IS RARE, I GET SO EXCITED!!
EVERYONE CALLS ME...
...A RARE HUNTER!

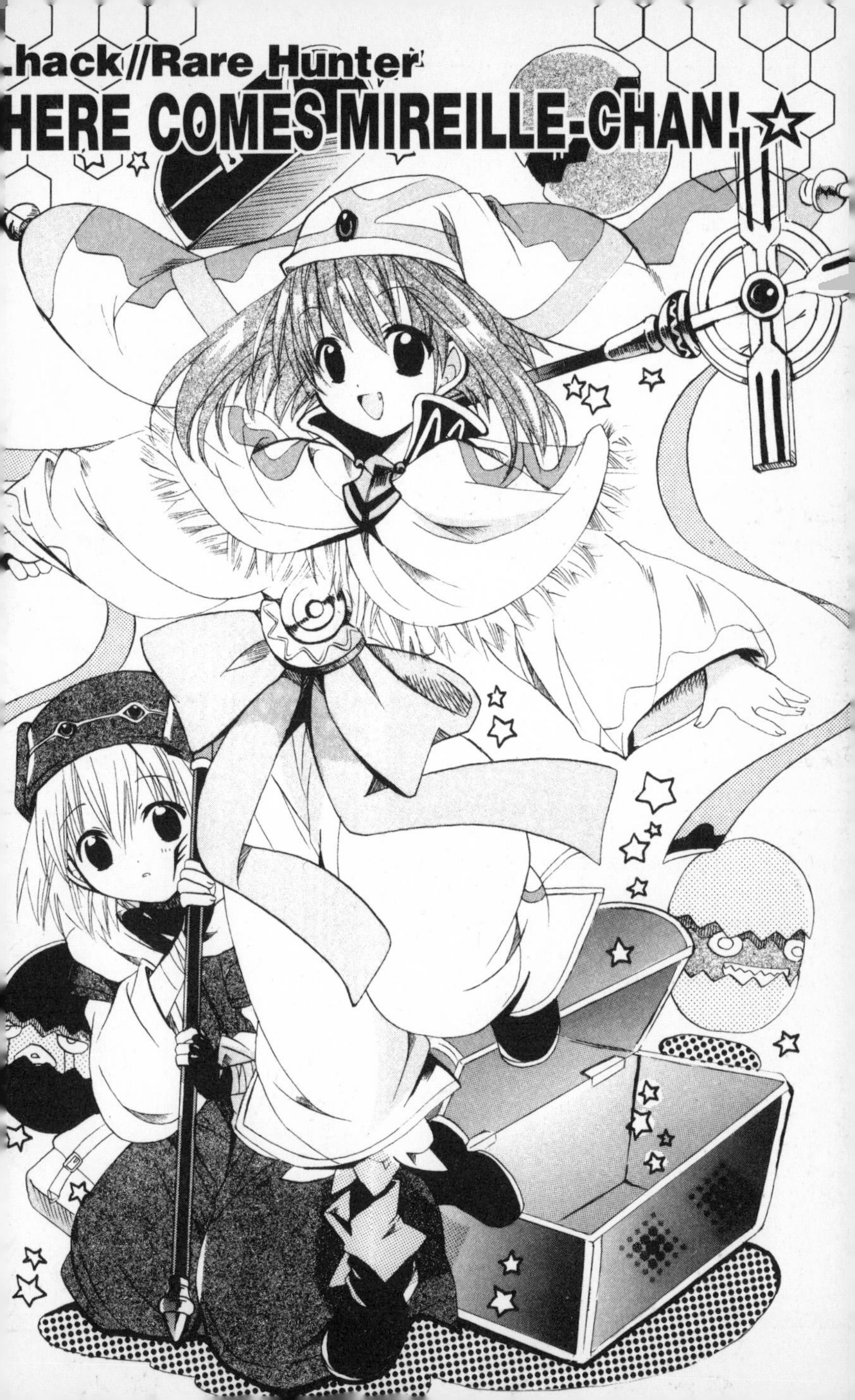
.hack//Rare Hunter
HERE COMES MIREILLE-CHAN! ☆

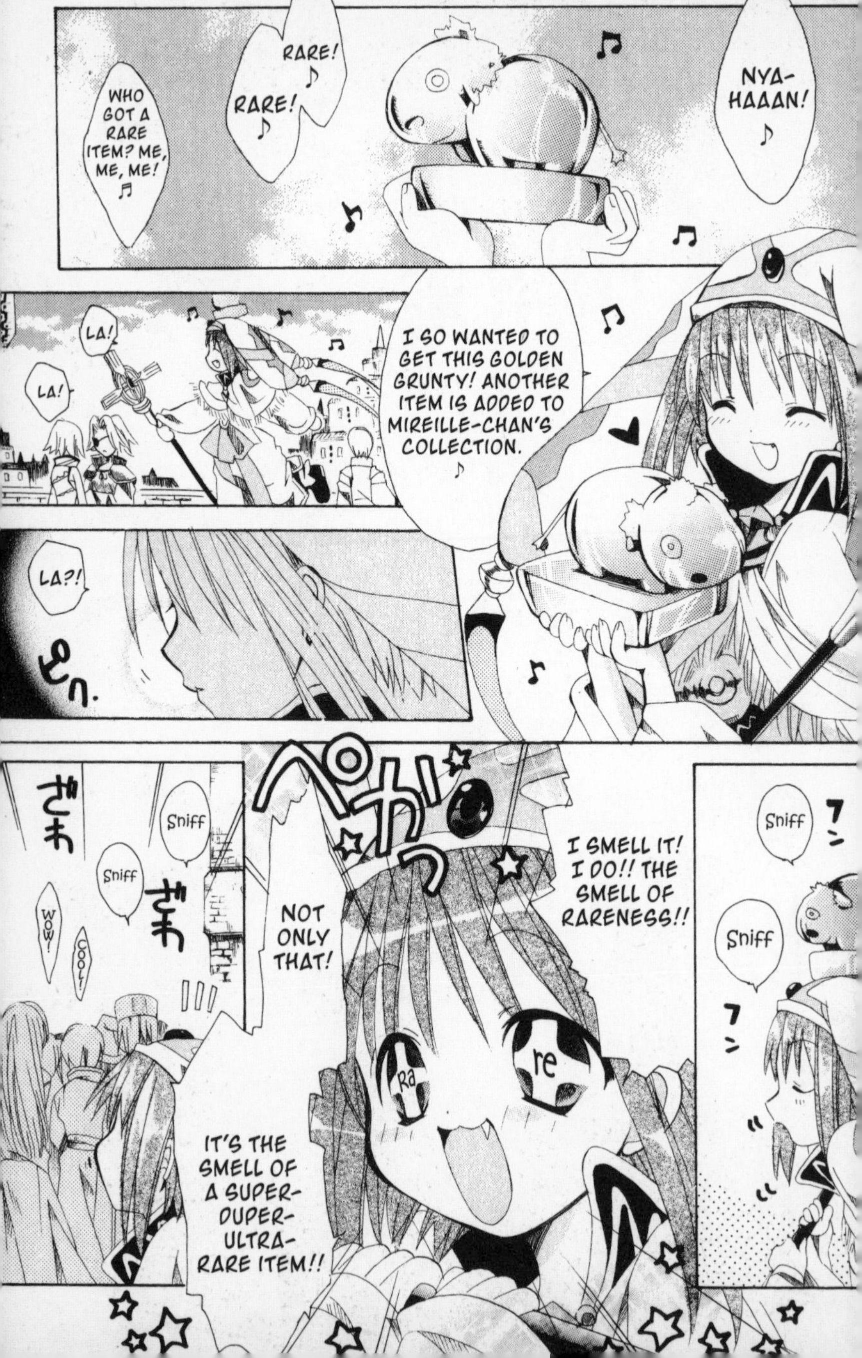
NYA-HAAAN! ♪
RARE! ♪
RARE! ♪
WHO GOT A RARE ITEM? ME, ME, ME! ♬
I SO WANTED TO GET THIS GOLDEN GRUNTY! ANOTHER ITEM IS ADDED TO MIREILLE-CHAN'S COLLECTION. ♪
LA!
LA!
LA?!
ぴく.
Sniff
Sniff
フン
フン
ぺかっ
I SMELL IT! I DO!! THE SMELL OF RARENESS!!
NOT ONLY THAT!
Ra
re
IT'S THE SMELL OF A SUPER-DUPER-ULTRA-RARE ITEM!!
ざわ
ざわ
Sniff
Sniff
WOW!
COOL!

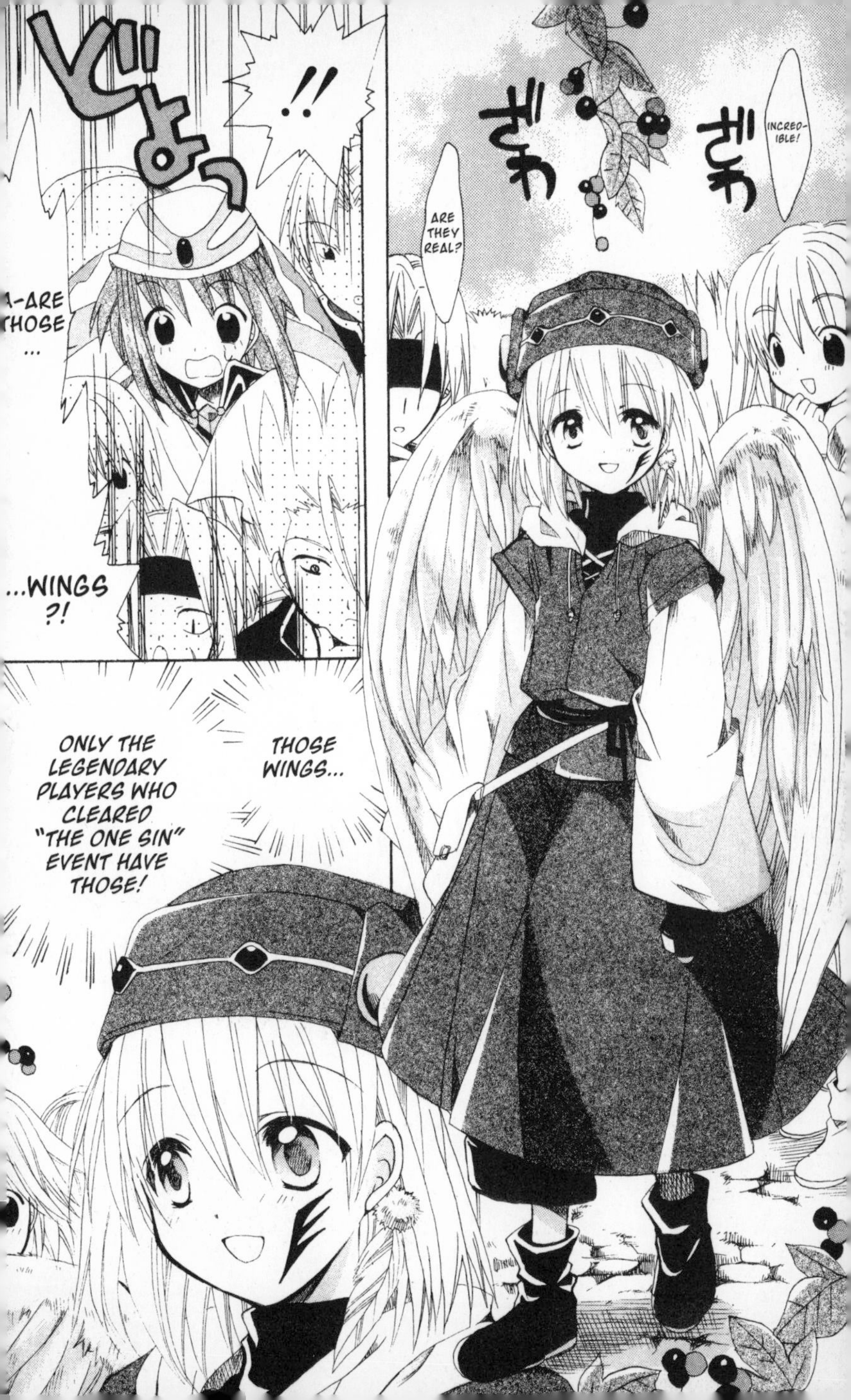
ざわ
ざわ
INCREDIBLE!
ARE THEY REAL?
どよっ
!!
A-ARE THOSE ...
...WINGS ?!
THOSE WINGS...
ONLY THE LEGENDARY PLAYERS WHO CLEARED "THE ONE SIN" EVENT HAVE THOSE!

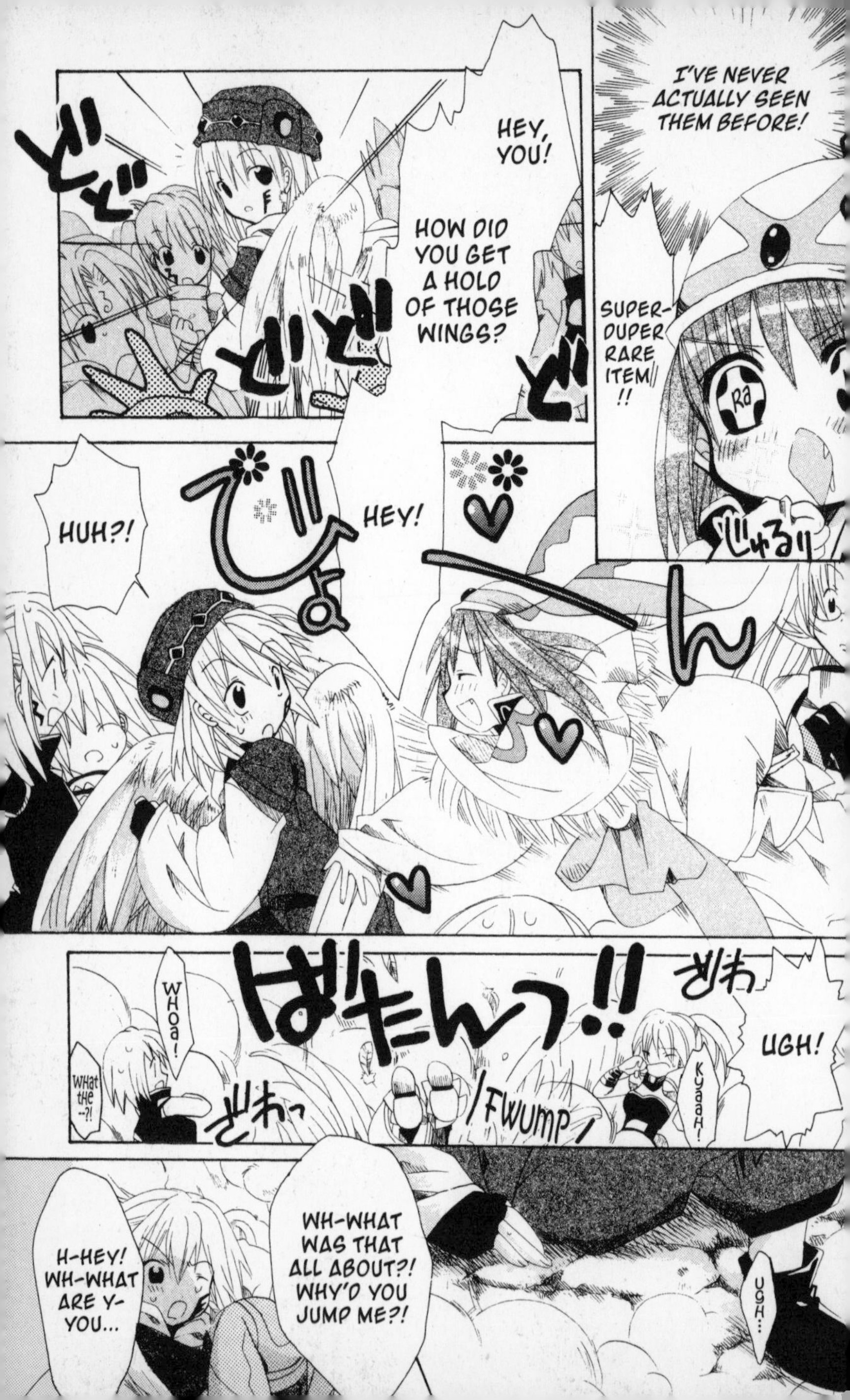
I'VE NEVER ACTUALLY SEEN THEM BEFORE!
SUPER-DUPER RARE ITEM!!
じゅるり
HEY, YOU!
HOW DID YOU GET A HOLD OF THOSE WINGS?
HEY!
HUH?!
ばたんっ!!
ざわ
UGH!
Kyaaah!
FWUMP
ざわっ
Whoa!
What the--?!
Ugh...
WH-WHAT WAS THAT ALL ABOUT?! WHY'D YOU JUMP ME?!
H-HEY! WH-WHAT ARE Y-YOU...

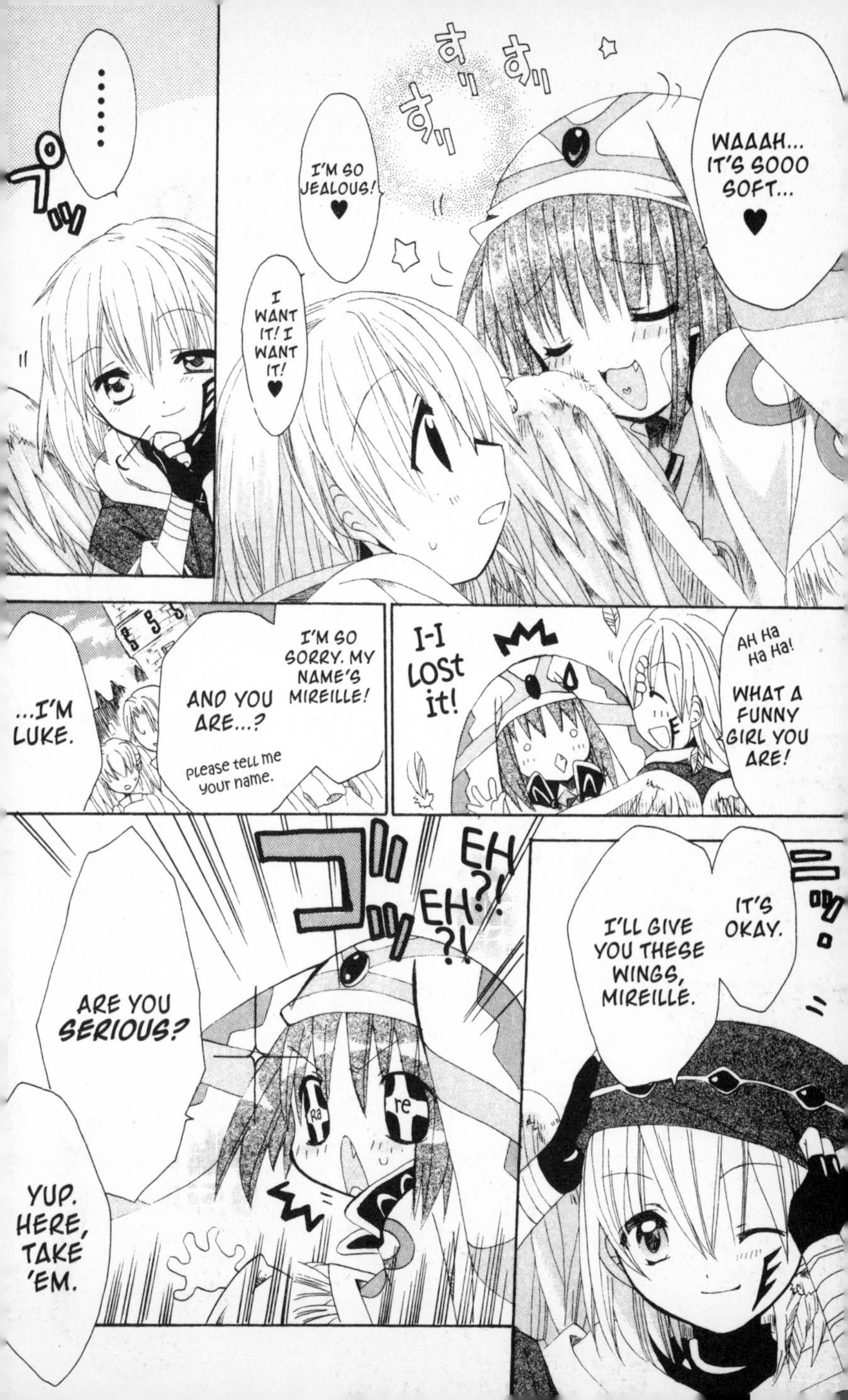
WAAAH... IT'S SOOO SOFT... ♥
I'M SO JEALOUS! ♥
I WANT IT! I WANT IT! ♥
......
AH HA HA HA! WHAT A FUNNY GIRL YOU ARE!
I-I LOST it!
I'M SO SORRY. MY NAME'S MIREILLE!
AND YOU ARE...?
Please tell me your name.
...I'M LUKE.
IT'S OKAY.
I'LL GIVE YOU THESE WINGS, MIREILLE.
EH?! EH?!
ARE YOU SERIOUS?
YUP. HERE, TAKE 'EM.

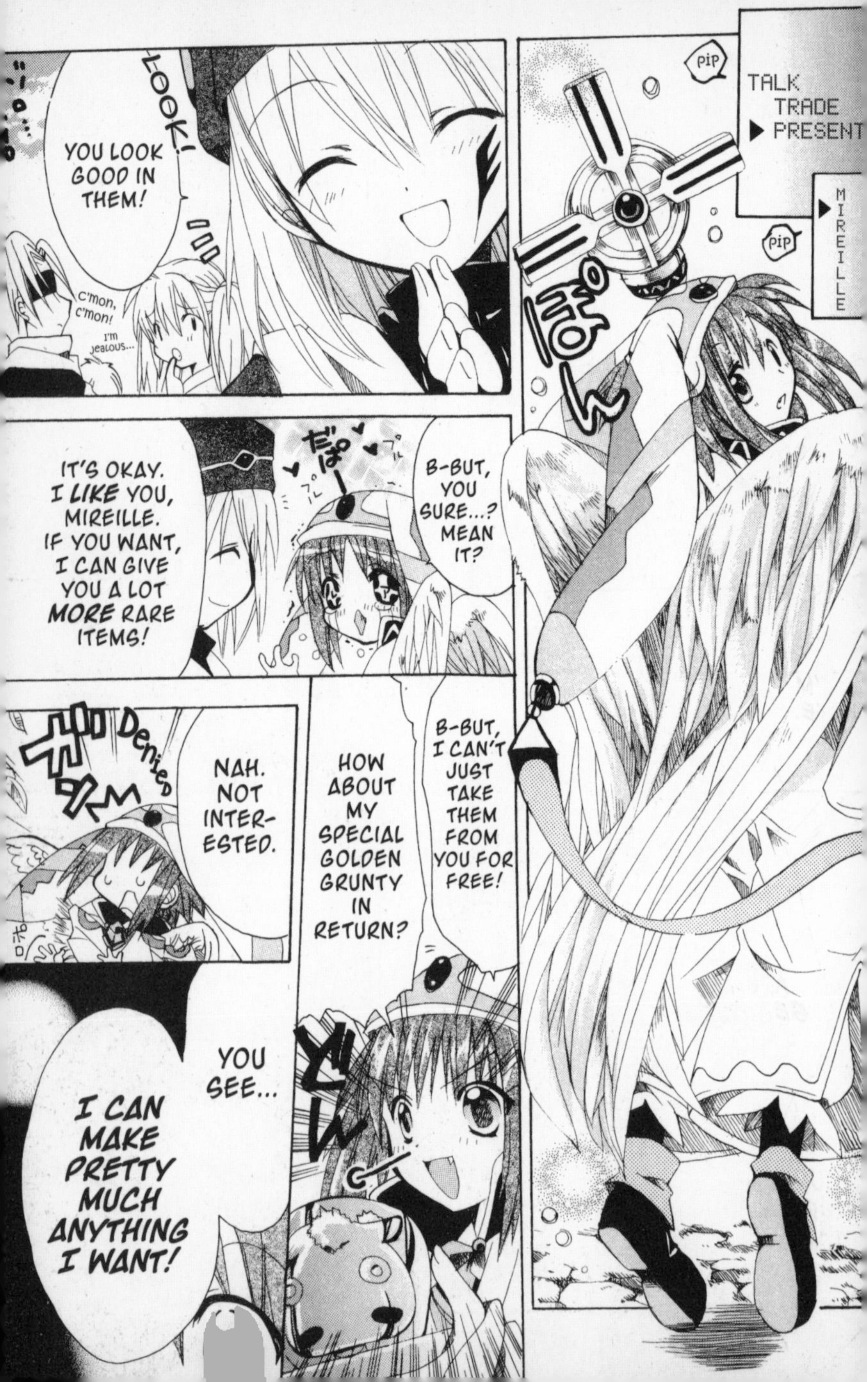

TALK
TRADE
▶ PRESENT
pip
▶ MIREILLE
pip
ぽん
LOOK!
YOU LOOK GOOD IN THEM!
C'mon, c'mon!
I'm jealous...
B-BUT, YOU SURE...? MEAN IT?
IT'S OKAY. I LIKE YOU, MIREILLE. IF YOU WANT, I CAN GIVE YOU A LOT MORE RARE ITEMS!
B-BUT, I CAN'T JUST TAKE THEM FROM YOU FOR FREE!
HOW ABOUT MY SPECIAL GOLDEN GRUNTY IN RETURN?
NAH. NOT INTERESTED.
Denied
YOU SEE...
I CAN MAKE PRETTY MUCH ANYTHING I WANT!

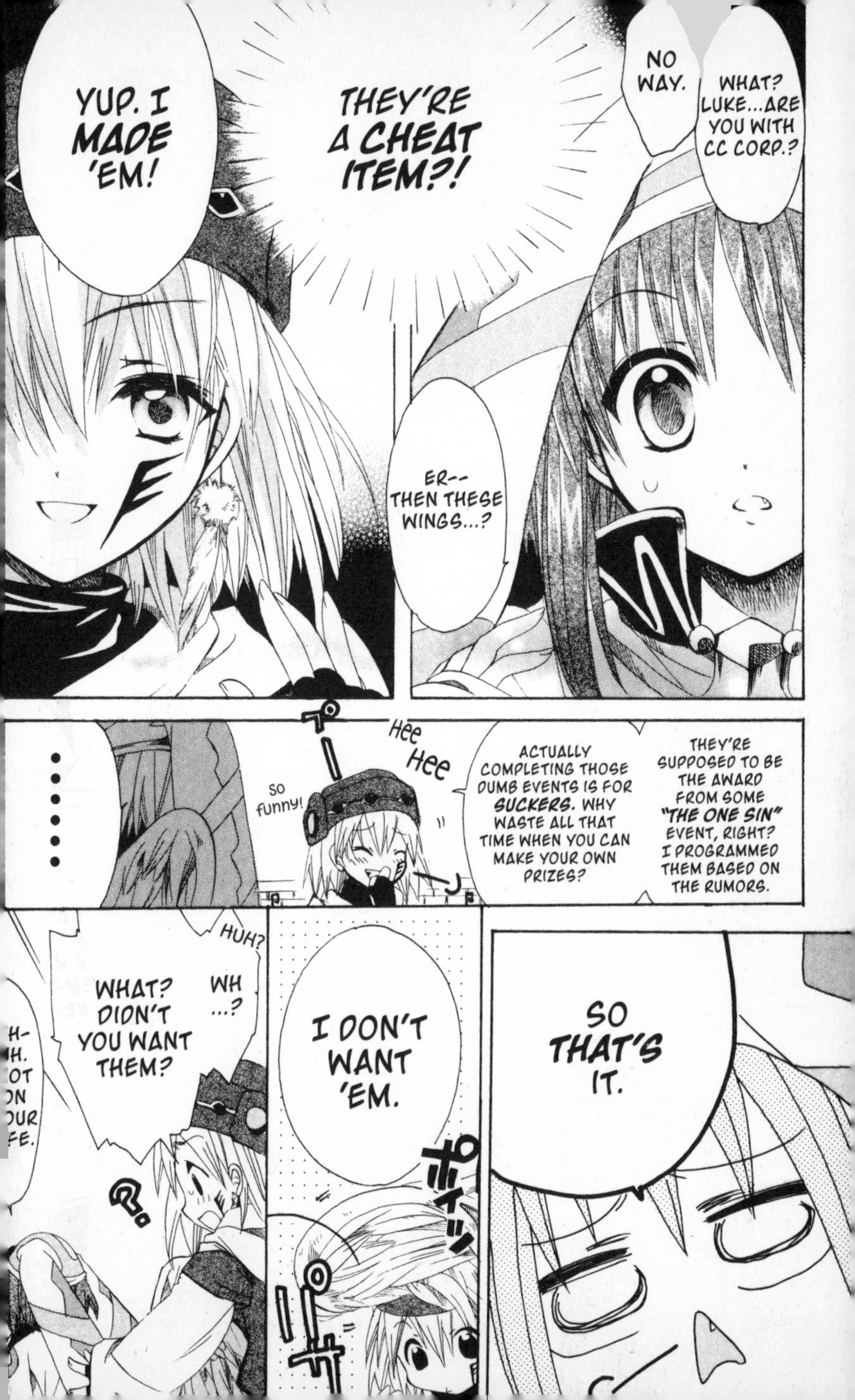
WHAT? LUKE...ARE YOU WITH CC CORP.?
NO WAY.
ER-- THEN THESE WINGS...?
THEY'RE A CHEAT ITEM?!
YUP. I MADE 'EM!
THEY'RE SUPPOSED TO BE THE AWARD FROM SOME "THE ONE SIN" EVENT, RIGHT? I PROGRAMMED THEM BASED ON THE RUMORS.
ACTUALLY COMPLETING THOSE DUMB EVENTS IS FOR SUCKERS. WHY WASTE ALL THAT TIME WHEN YOU CAN MAKE YOUR OWN PRIZES?
Hee Hee
so funny!
......
SO THAT'S IT.
I DON'T WANT 'EM.
HUH?
WH ...?
WHAT? DIDN'T YOU WANT THEM?

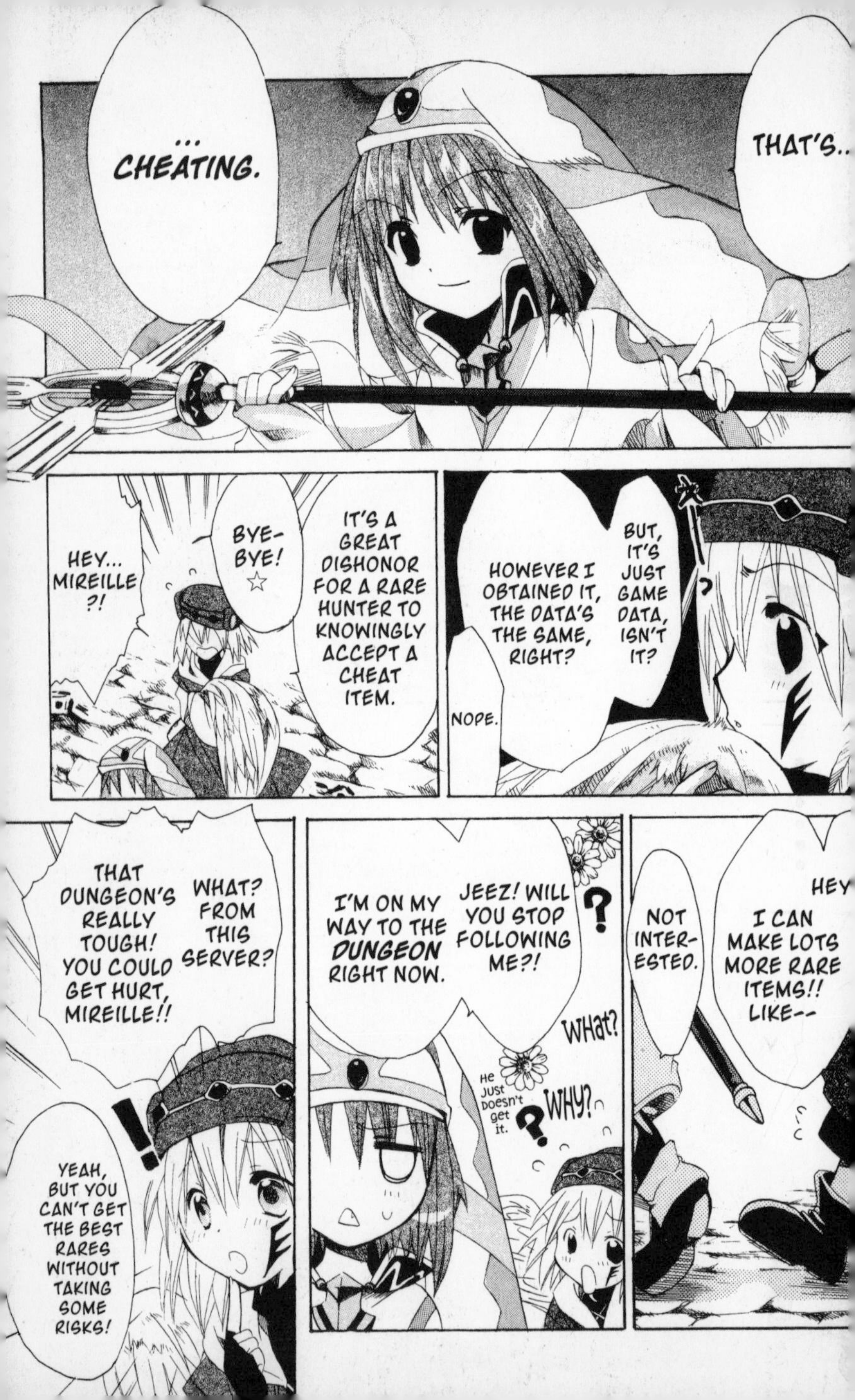
THAT'S...
...CHEATING.
BUT, IT'S JUST GAME DATA, ISN'T IT?
HOWEVER I OBTAINED IT, THE DATA'S THE SAME, RIGHT?
NOPE.
IT'S A GREAT DISHONOR FOR A RARE HUNTER TO KNOWINGLY ACCEPT A CHEAT ITEM.
BYE-BYE! ☆
HEY... MIREILLE?!
HEY I CAN MAKE LOTS MORE RARE ITEMS!! LIKE--
NOT INTER-ESTED.
JEEZ! WILL YOU STOP FOLLOWING ME?!
I'M ON MY WAY TO THE DUNGEON RIGHT NOW.
WHAT?
He just doesn't get it.
WHY?
WHAT? FROM THIS SERVER?
THAT DUNGEON'S REALLY TOUGH! YOU COULD GET HURT, MIREILLE!!
YEAH, BUT YOU CAN'T GET THE BEST RARES WITHOUT TAKING SOME RISKS!

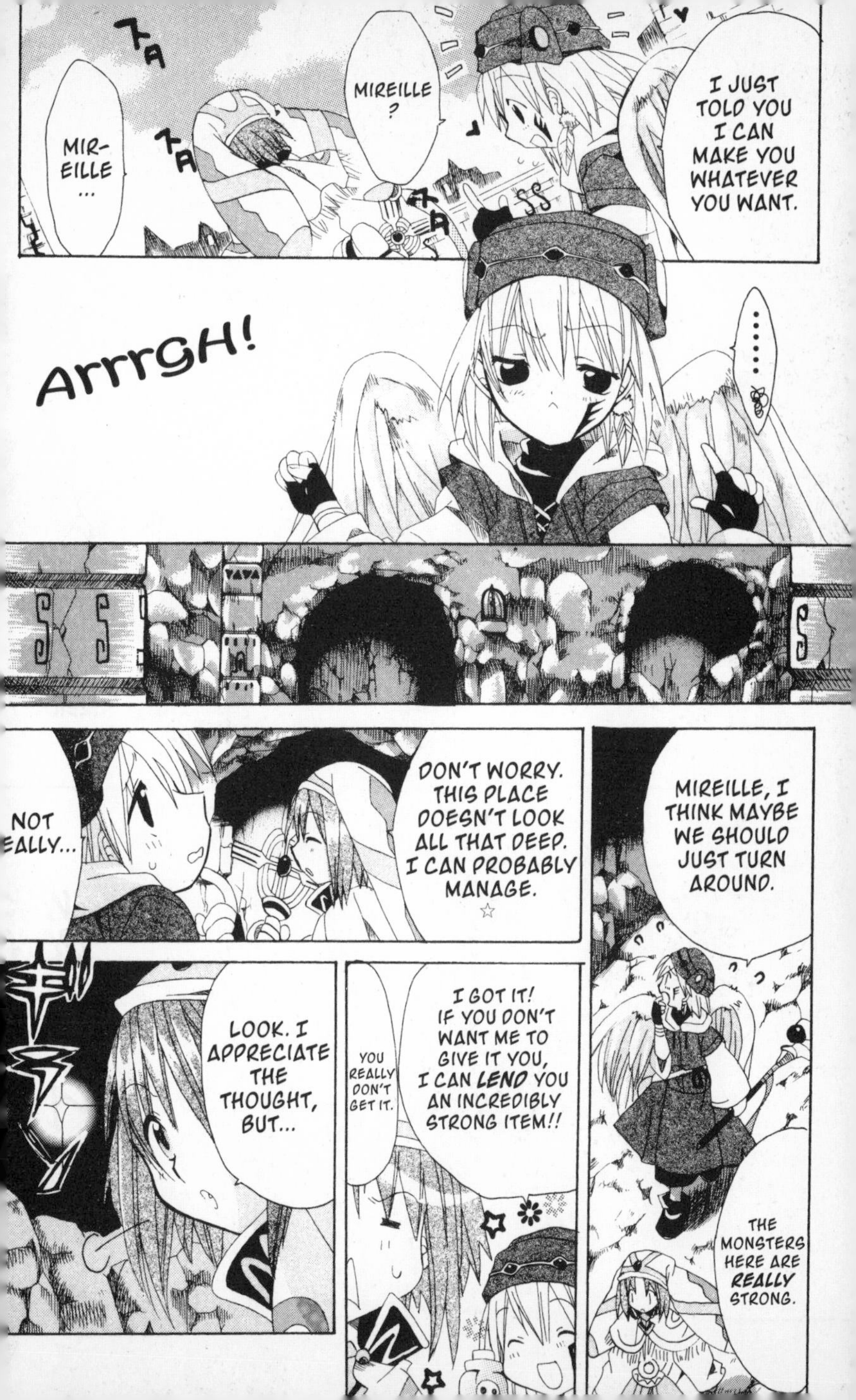
I JUST TOLD YOU I CAN MAKE YOU WHATEVER YOU WANT.
MIREILLE?
MIR-EILLE...
......
ArrrgH!
MIREILLE, I THINK MAYBE WE SHOULD JUST TURN AROUND.
THE MONSTERS HERE ARE *REALLY* STRONG.
DON'T WORRY. THIS PLACE DOESN'T LOOK ALL THAT DEEP. I CAN PROBABLY MANAGE. ☆
NOT EALLY...
I GOT IT! IF YOU DON'T WANT ME TO GIVE IT YOU, I CAN *LEND* YOU AN INCREDIBLY STRONG ITEM!!
YOU REALLY DON'T GET IT.
LOOK. I APPRECIATE THE THOUGHT, BUT...

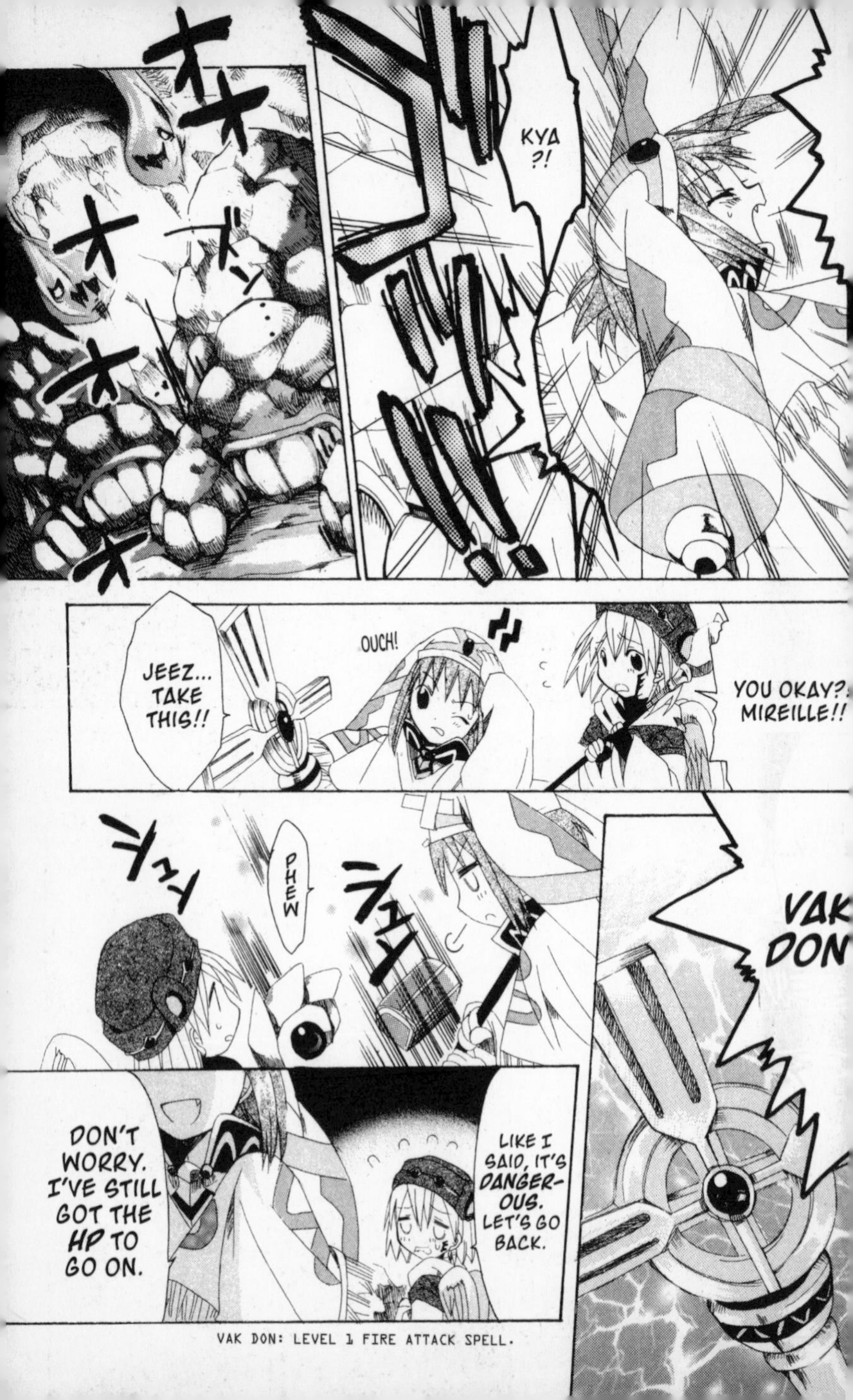
KYA ?!
YOU OKAY?! MIREILLE!!
OUCH!
JEEZ... TAKE THIS!!
VAK DON
PHEW
LIKE I SAID, IT'S DANGER-OUS. LET'S GO BACK.
DON'T WORRY. I'VE STILL GOT THE HP TO GO ON.

VAK DON: LEVEL 1 FIRE ATTACK SPELL.

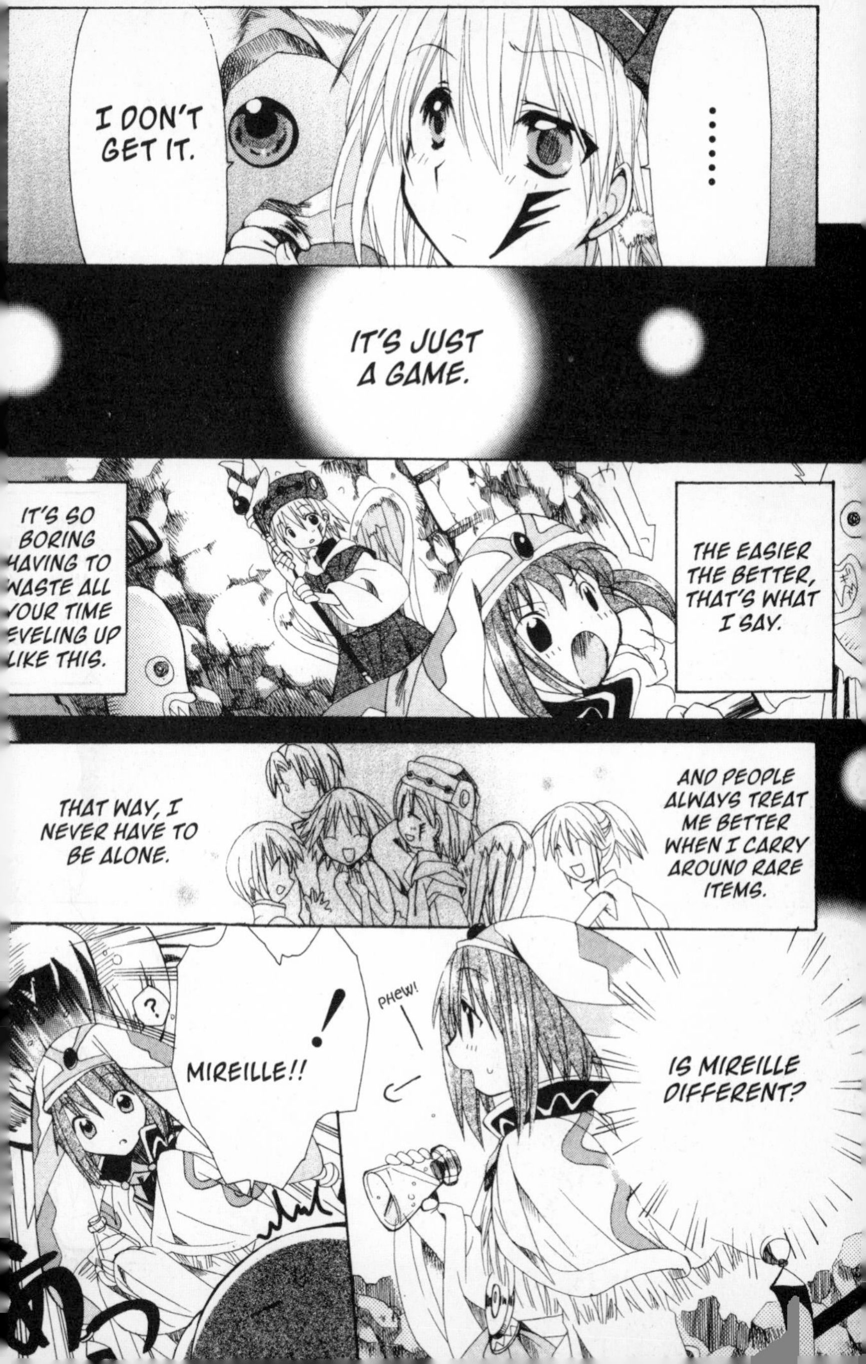
......
I DON'T GET IT.
IT'S JUST A GAME.
THE EASIER THE BETTER, THAT'S WHAT I SAY.
IT'S SO BORING HAVING TO WASTE ALL YOUR TIME LEVELING UP LIKE THIS.
AND PEOPLE ALWAYS TREAT ME BETTER WHEN I CARRY AROUND RARE ITEMS.
THAT WAY, I NEVER HAVE TO BE ALONE.
IS MIREILLE DIFFERENT?
PHEW!
!
MIREILLE!!
?

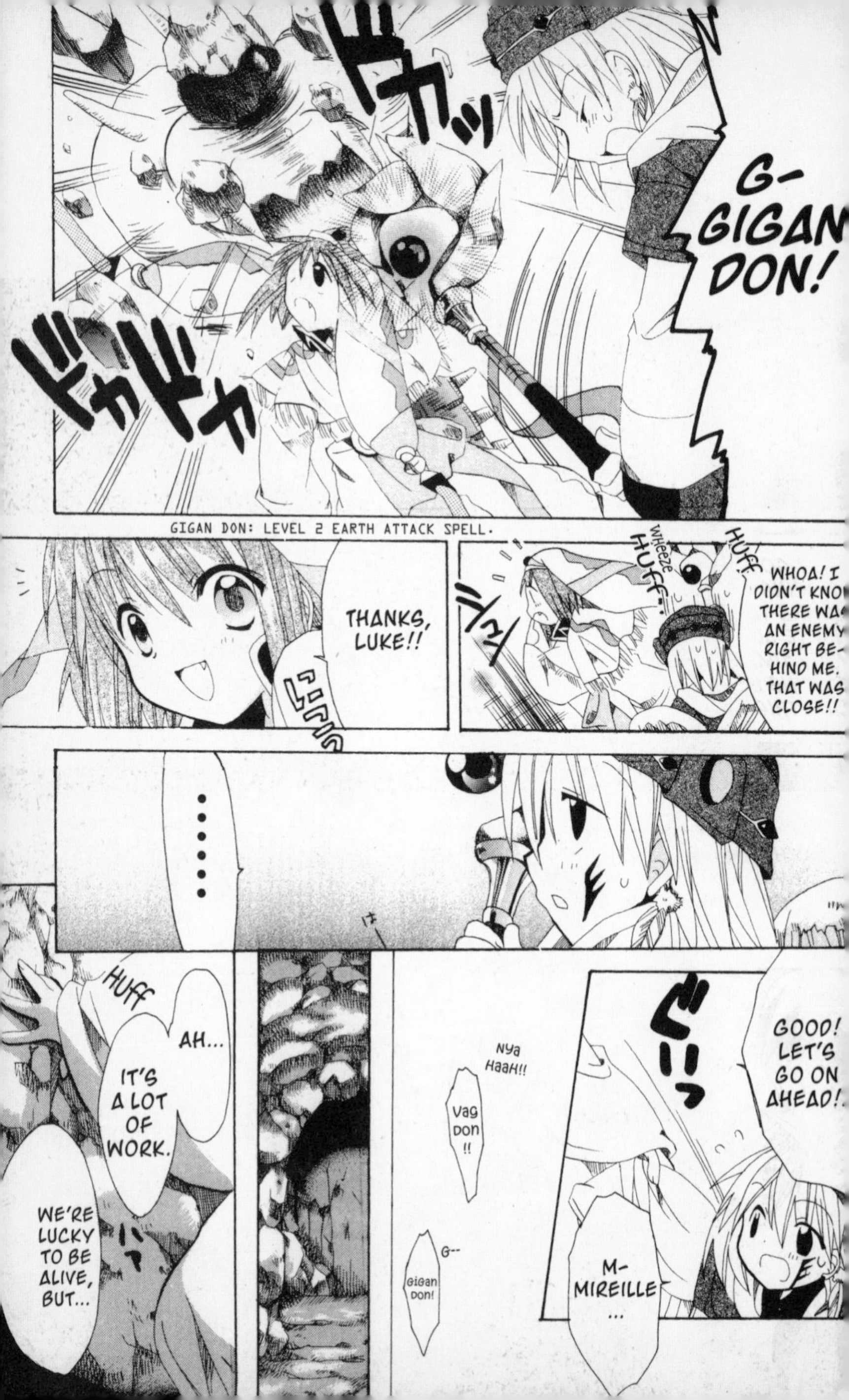
G-GIGAN DON!
GIGAN DON: LEVEL 2 EARTH ATTACK SPELL.
HUFF
WHEEZE HUFF...
WHOA! I DIDN'T KNO THERE WA AN ENEMY RIGHT BE-HIND ME. THAT WAS CLOSE!!
THANKS, LUKE!!
......
GOOD! LET'S GO ON AHEAD!
NYA HAAH!!
VAG DON!!
M-MIREILLE ...
G--
GIGAN DON!
HUFF
AH...
IT'S A LOT OF WORK.
WE'RE LUCKY TO BE ALIVE, BUT...

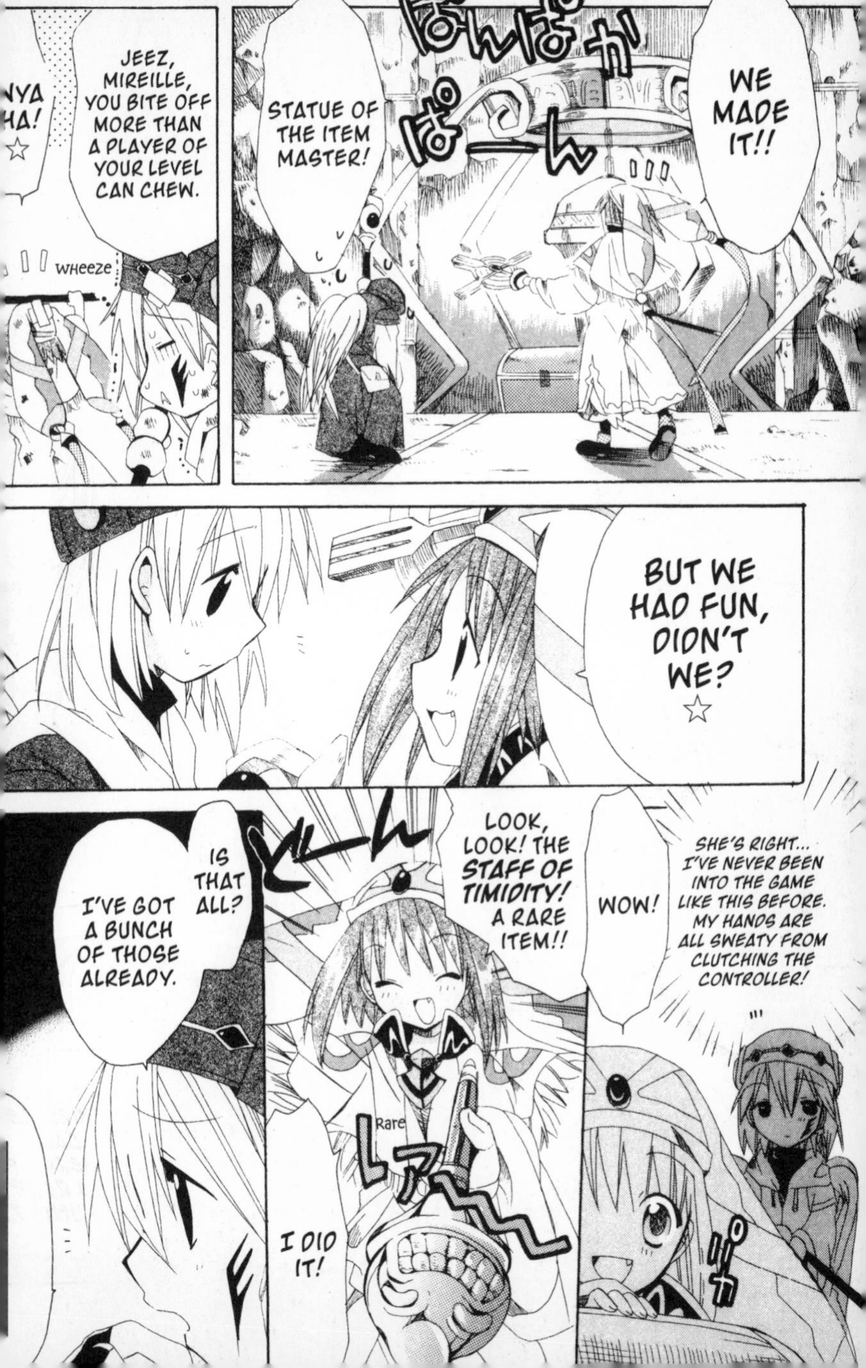
WE MADE IT!!
ぱんぱかぱーん
STATUE OF THE ITEM MASTER!
JEEZ, MIREILLE, YOU BITE OFF MORE THAN A PLAYER OF YOUR LEVEL CAN CHEW.
NYA HA! ☆
wheeze
BUT WE HAD FUN, DIDN'T WE? ☆
SHE'S RIGHT... I'VE NEVER BEEN INTO THE GAME LIKE THIS BEFORE. MY HANDS ARE ALL SWEATY FROM CLUTCHING THE CONTROLLER!
WOW!
LOOK, LOOK! THE STAFF OF TIMIDITY! A RARE ITEM!!
Rare
I DID IT!
IS THAT ALL?
I'VE GOT A BUNCH OF THOSE ALREADY.

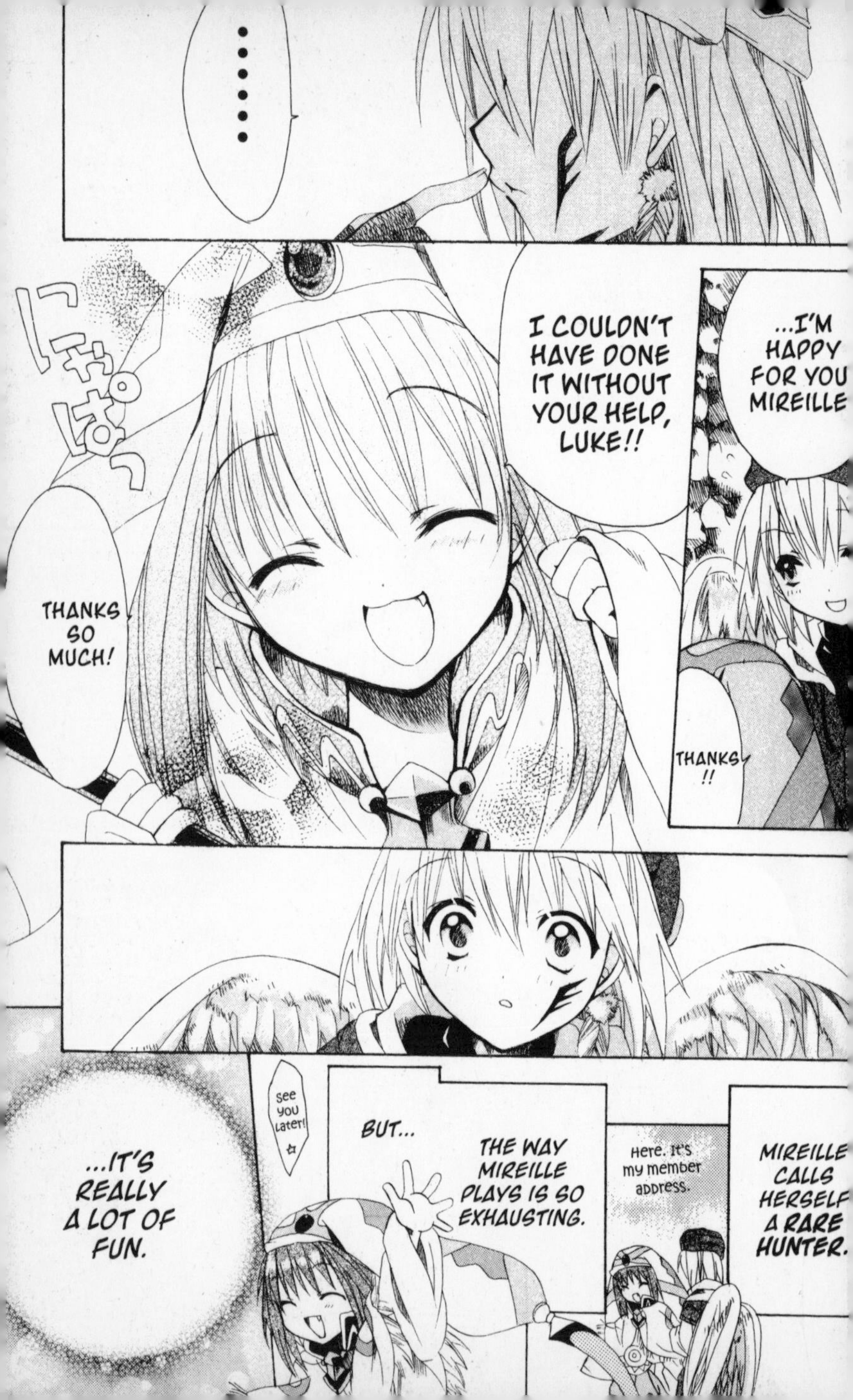
......
...I'M HAPPY FOR YOU MIREILLE
THANKS !!
I COULDN'T HAVE DONE IT WITHOUT YOUR HELP, LUKE!!
にぱっ
THANKS SO MUCH!
MIREILLE CALLS HERSELF A RARE HUNTER.
Here. It's my member address.
BUT...
THE WAY MIREILLE PLAYS IS SO EXHAUSTING.
see you later! ☆
...IT'S REALLY A LOT OF FUN.

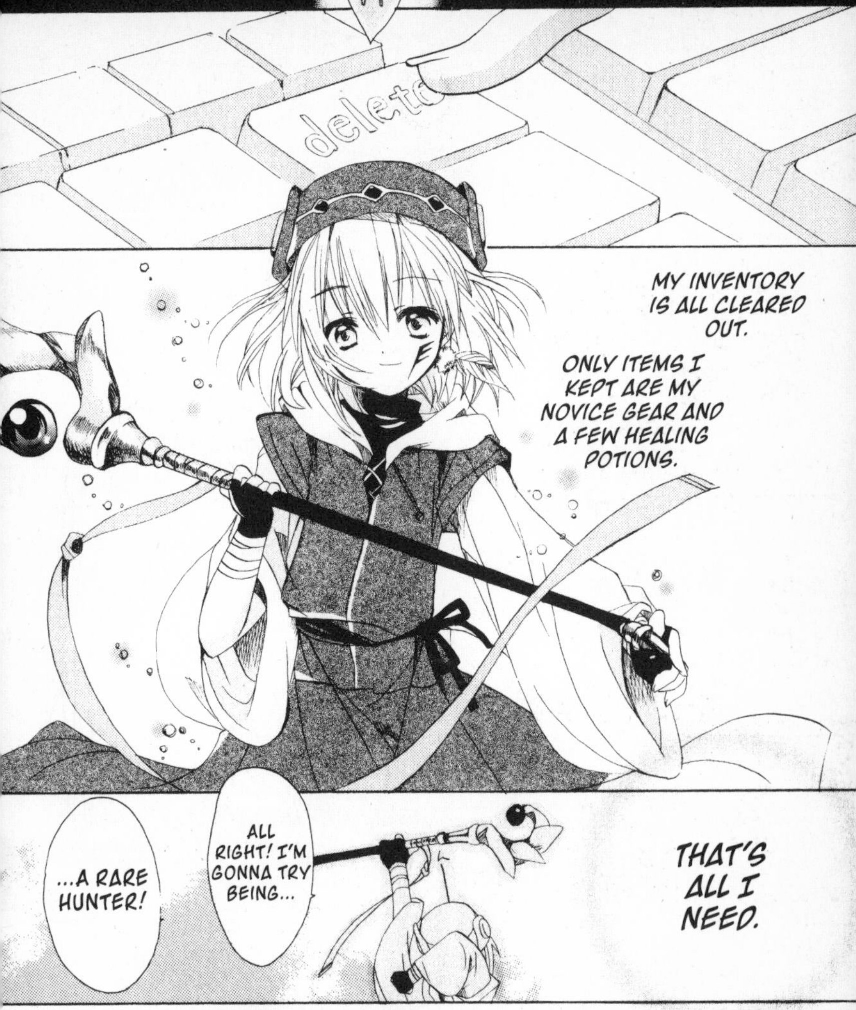
Pi
MY INVENTORY IS ALL CLEARED OUT.
ONLY ITEMS I KEPT ARE MY NOVICE GEAR AND A FEW HEALING POTIONS.
THAT'S ALL I NEED.
ALL RIGHT! I'M GONNA TRY BEING...
...A RARE HUNTER!

Omake = Bonus

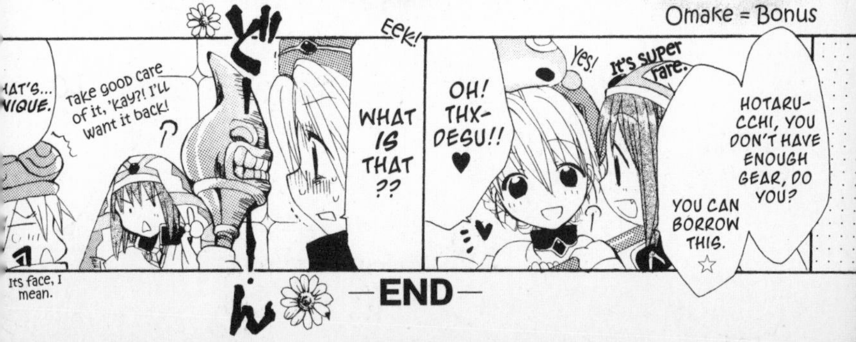
HOTARU-CCHI, YOU DON'T HAVE ENOUGH GEAR, DO YOU?
YOU CAN BORROW THIS. ☆
It's super rare.
Yes!
OH! THX-DESU!! ♥
EEK!
WHAT IS THAT ??
どーん
Take good care of it, 'kay?! I'll want it back!
AT'S... NIQUE.

Its face, I mean.

—END—

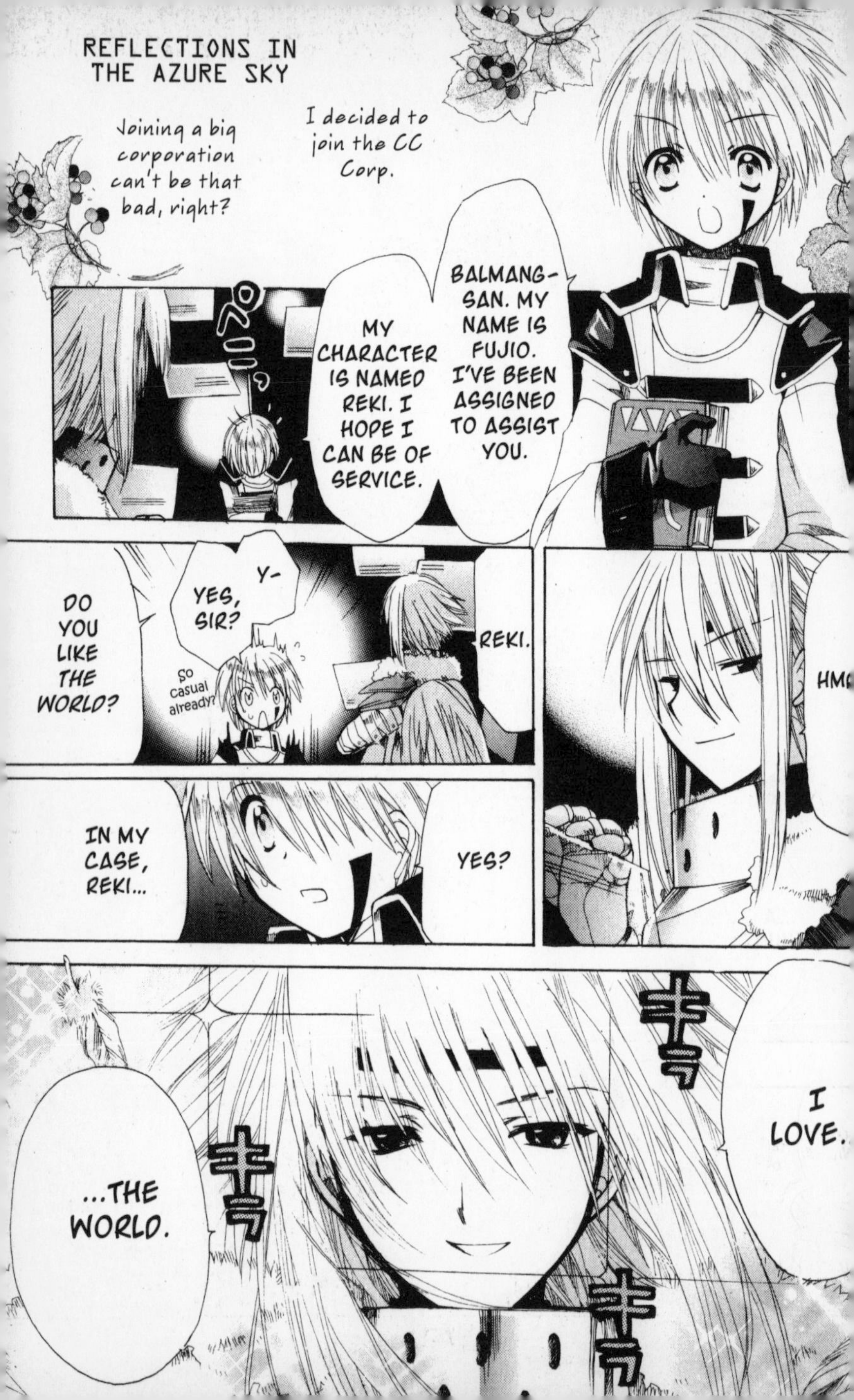
REFLECTIONS IN THE AZURE SKY
I decided to join the CC Corp.
Joining a big corporation can't be that bad, right?
BALMANG-SAN. MY NAME IS FUJIO. I'VE BEEN ASSIGNED TO ASSIST YOU.
MY CHARACTER IS NAMED REKI. I HOPE I CAN BE OF SERVICE.
HM
REKI.
Y-
YES, SIR?
So casual already?
DO YOU LIKE THE WORLD?
YES?
IN MY CASE, REKI...
I LOVE.
...THE WORLD.

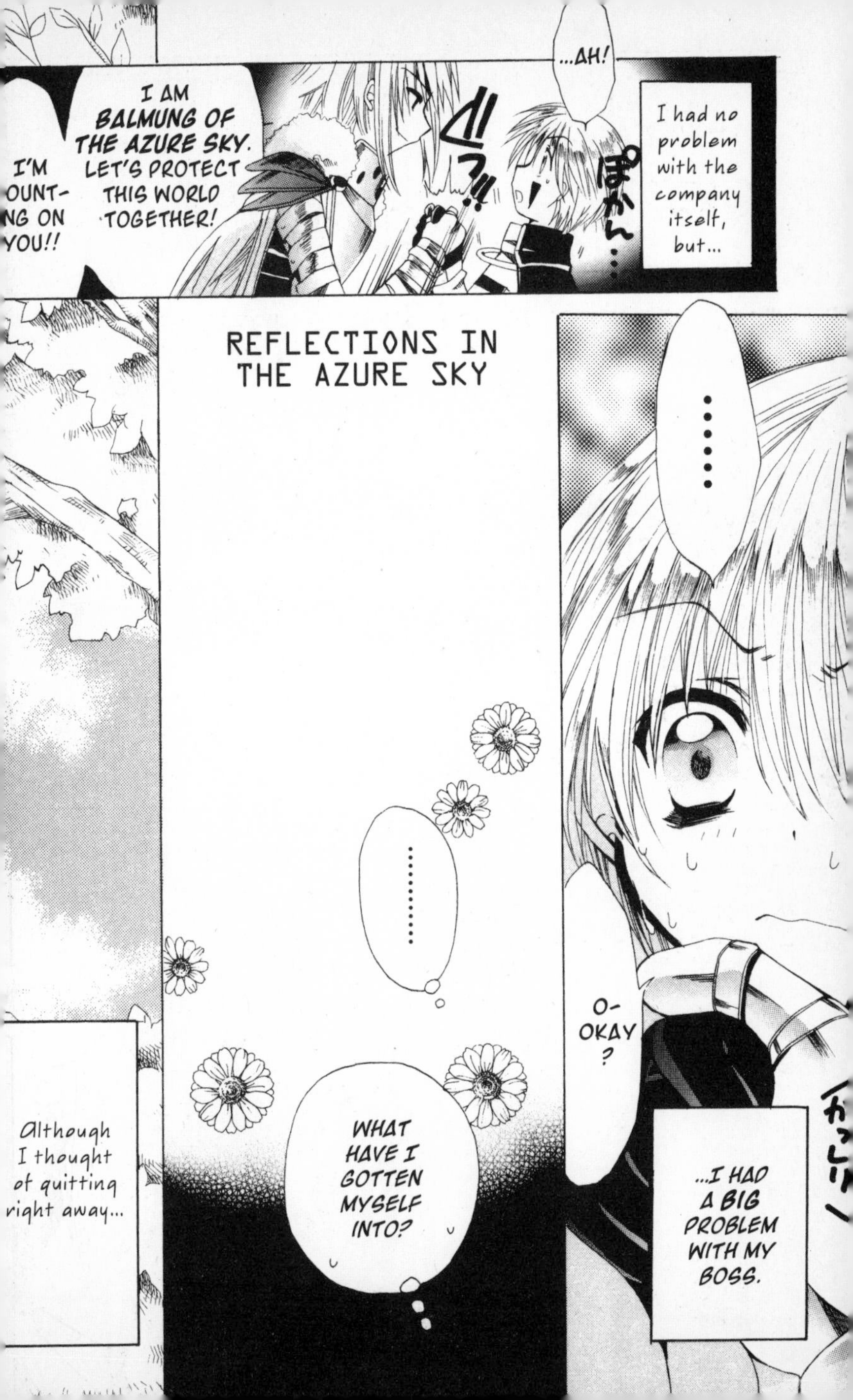
I had no problem with the company itself, but...
...AH!
ぽかん…
I AM BALMUNG OF THE AZURE SKY. LET'S PROTECT THIS WORLD TOGETHER!
I'M OUNT- NG ON YOU!!
......
O-OKAY?
...I HAD A BIG PROBLEM WITH MY BOSS.
REFLECTIONS IN THE AZURE SKY
......
WHAT HAVE I GOTTEN MYSELF INTO?
Although I thought of quitting right away...

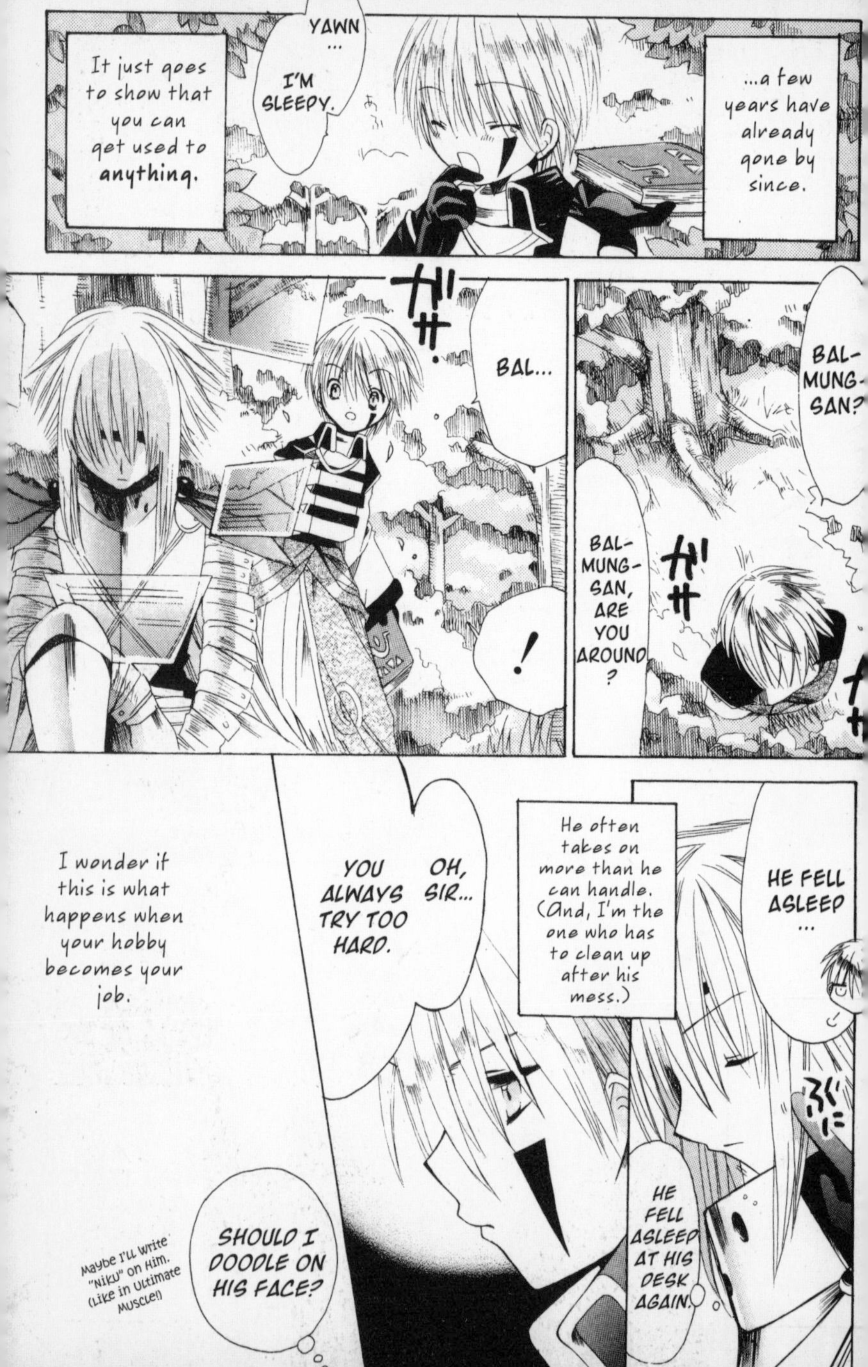
...a few years have already gone by since.
YAWN... I'M SLEEPY.
It just goes to show that you can get used to anything.
BAL-MUNG-SAN?
ガサ
BAL-MUNG-SAN, ARE YOU AROUND?
ガサ
BAL...
ガサ
!
HE FELL ASLEEP...
He often takes on more than he can handle. (And, I'm the one who has to clean up after his mess.)
HE FELL ASLEEP AT HIS DESK AGAIN.
OH, SIR... YOU ALWAYS TRY TOO HARD.
I wonder if this is what happens when your hobby becomes your job.
SHOULD I DOODLE ON HIS FACE?
Maybe I'll write "Niku" on him. (Like in Ultimate Muscle!)

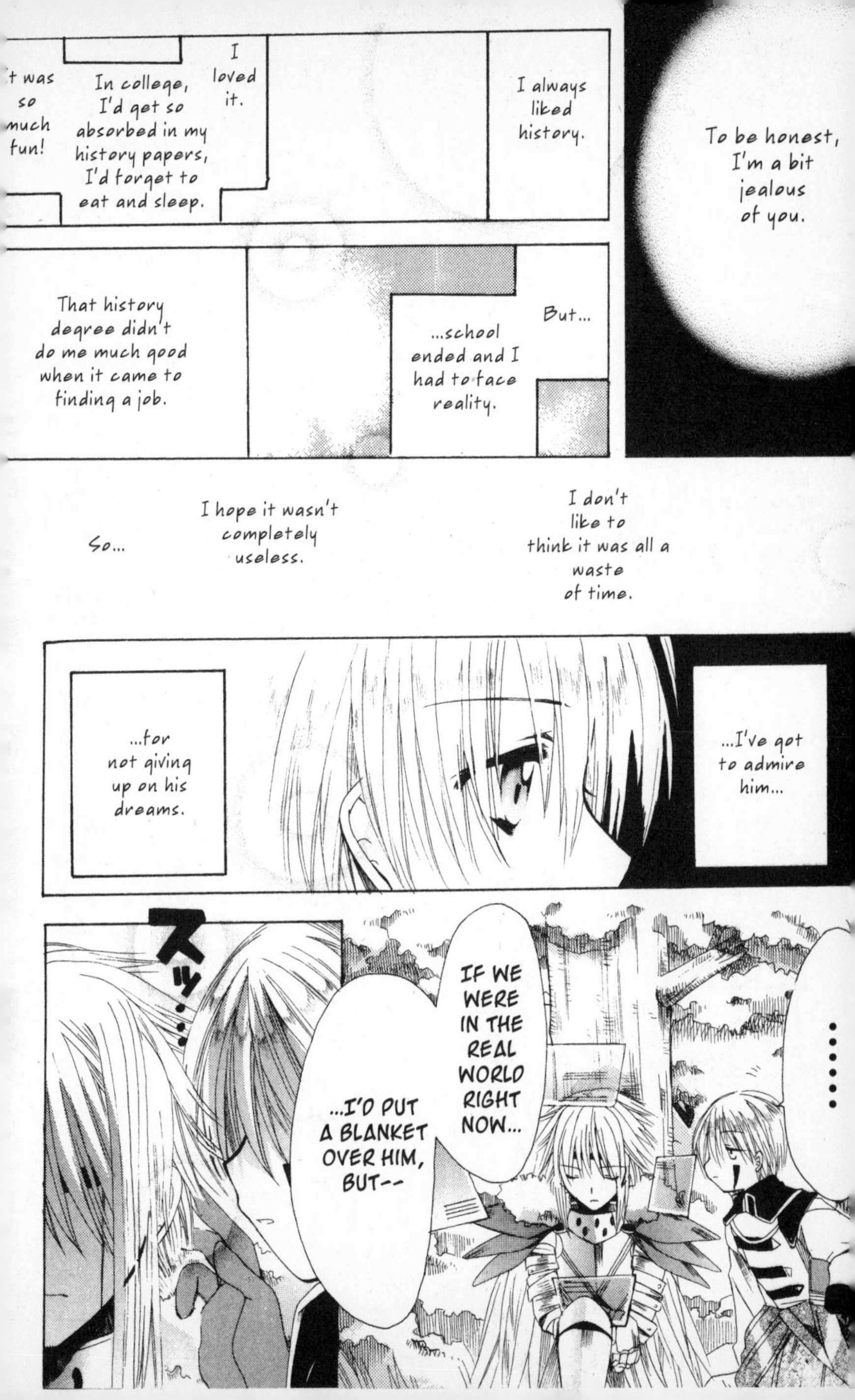
To be honest, I'm a bit jealous of you.
I always liked history.
I loved it.
In college, I'd get so absorbed in my history papers, I'd forget to eat and sleep.
t was so much fun!
But...
...school ended and I had to face reality.
That history degree didn't do me much good when it came to finding a job.
I don't like to think it was all a waste of time.
I hope it wasn't completely useless.
So...
...I've got to admire him...
...for not giving up on his dreams.
......
IF WE WERE IN THE REAL WORLD RIGHT NOW...
...I'D PUT A BLANKET OVER HIM, BUT--
スッ...

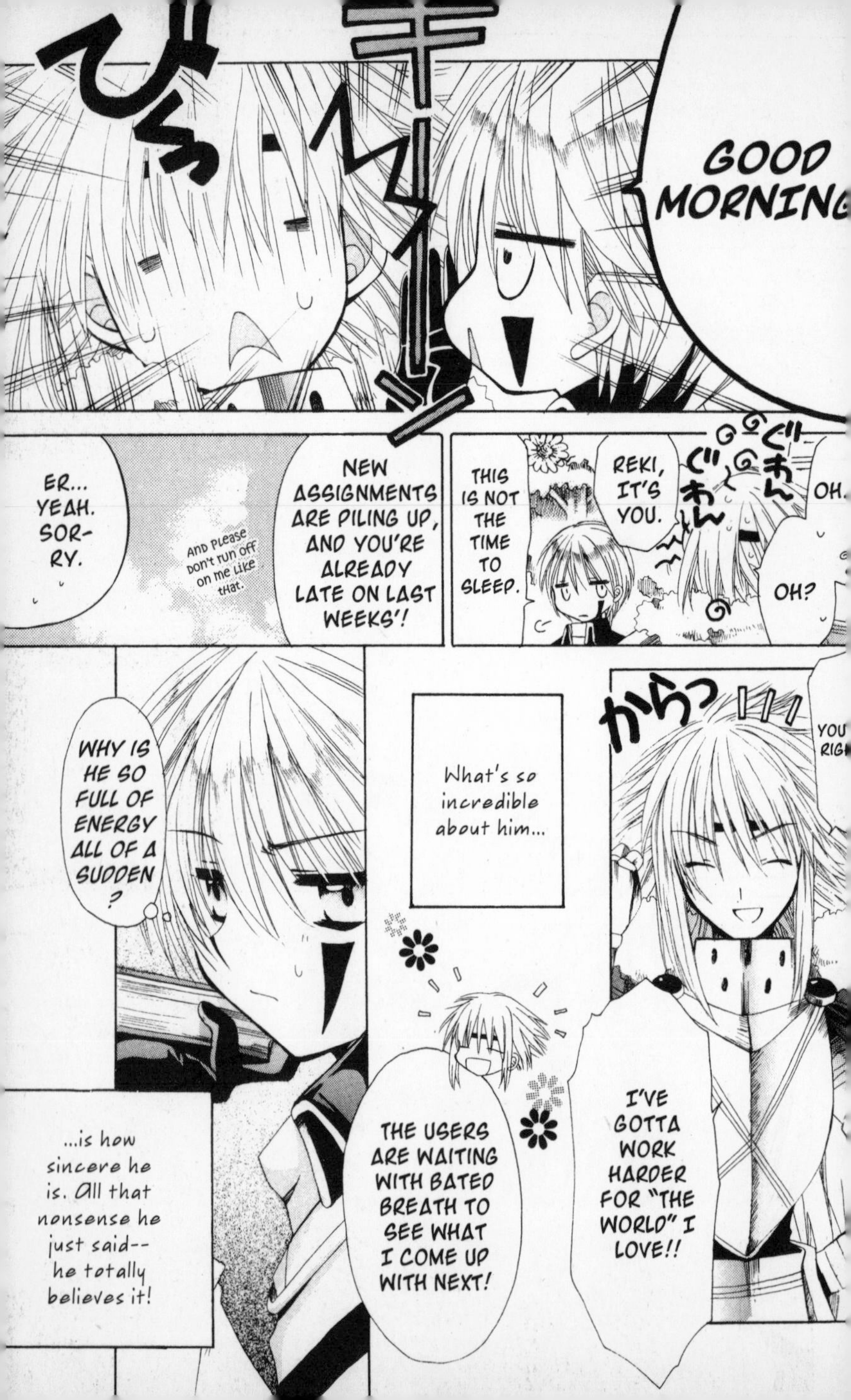
GOOD MORNING
OH.
OH?
ぐわん ぐわん
REKI, IT'S YOU.
THIS IS NOT THE TIME TO SLEEP.
NEW ASSIGNMENTS ARE PILING UP, AND YOU'RE ALREADY LATE ON LAST WEEKS'!
And please don't run off on me like that.
ER... YEAH. SOR-RY.
YOU RIG
からっ!!!
I'VE GOTTA WORK HARDER FOR "THE WORLD" I LOVE!!
THE USERS ARE WAITING WITH BATED BREATH TO SEE WHAT I COME UP WITH NEXT!
What's so incredible about him...
WHY IS HE SO FULL OF ENERGY ALL OF A SUDDEN?
...is how sincere he is. All that nonsense he just said--he totally believes it!

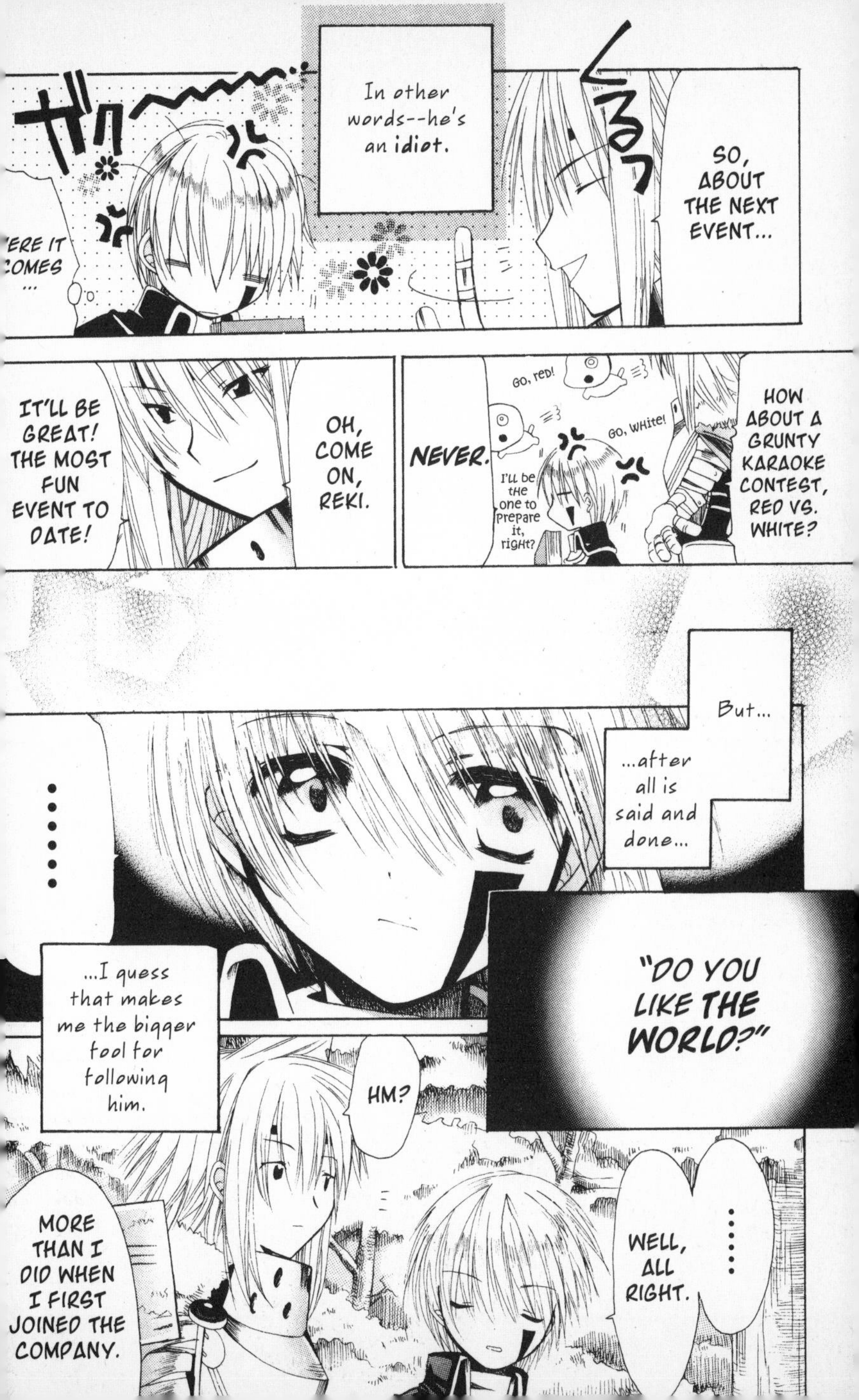
くるっ
SO, ABOUT THE NEXT EVENT...
In other words--he's an idiot.
ガク〜
ERE IT COMES ...
HOW ABOUT A GRUNTY KARAOKE CONTEST, RED VS. WHITE?
GO, RED!
GO, WHITE!
I'll be the one to prepare it, right?
NEVER.
OH, COME ON, REKI.
IT'LL BE GREAT! THE MOST FUN EVENT TO DATE!
But...
...after all is said and done...
......
"DO YOU LIKE THE WORLD?"
...I guess that makes me the bigger fool for following him.
......
WELL, ALL RIGHT.
HM?
MORE THAN I DID WHEN I FIRST JOINED THE COMPANY.

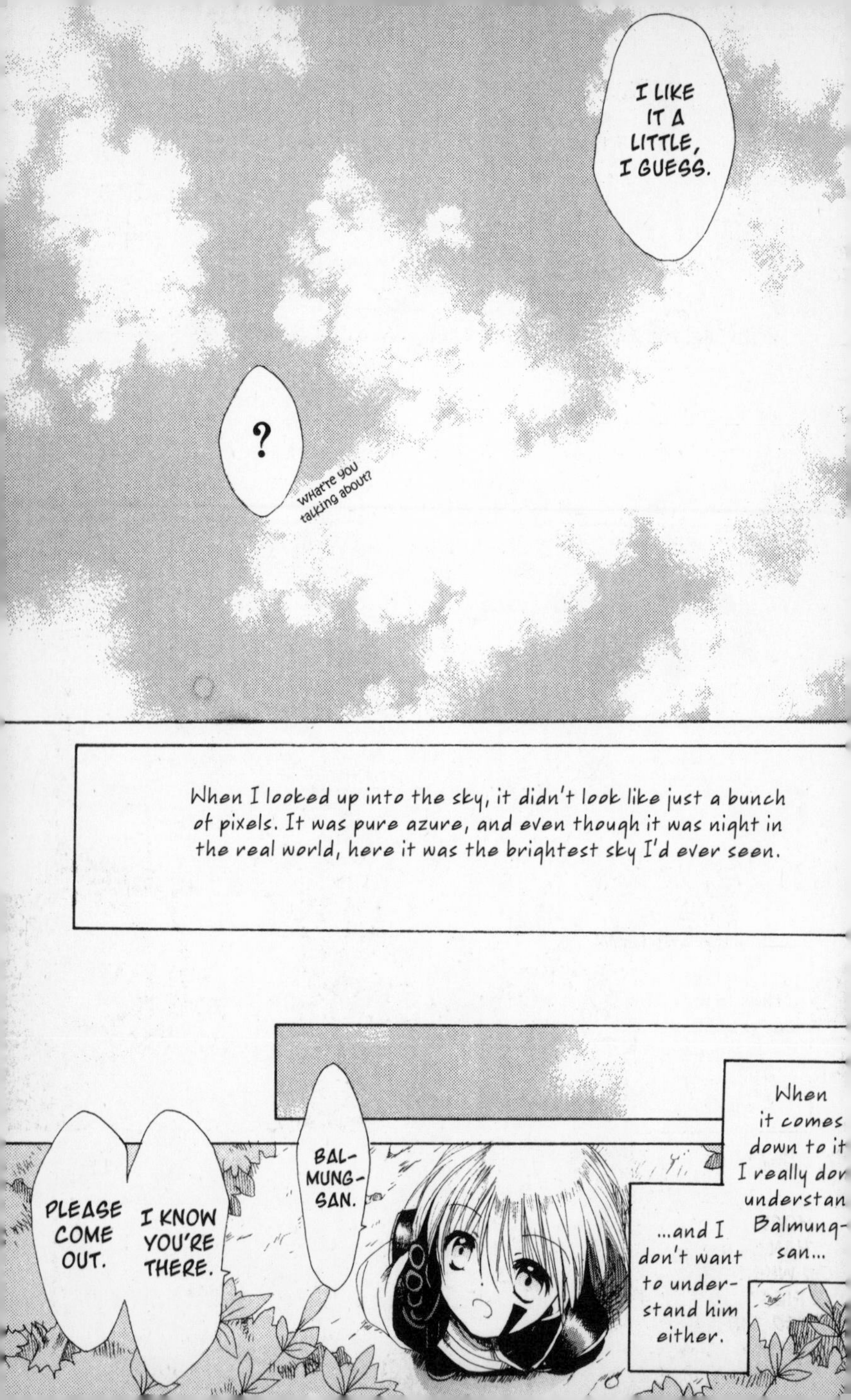

I LIKE IT A LITTLE, I GUESS.
?
What're you talking about?
When I looked up into the sky, it didn't look like just a bunch of pixels. It was pure azure, and even though it was night in the real world, here it was the brightest sky I'd ever seen.
When it comes down to it I really don understan Balmung-san...
...and I don't want to under-stand him either.
BAL-MUNG-SAN.
I KNOW YOU'RE THERE.
PLEASE COME OUT.

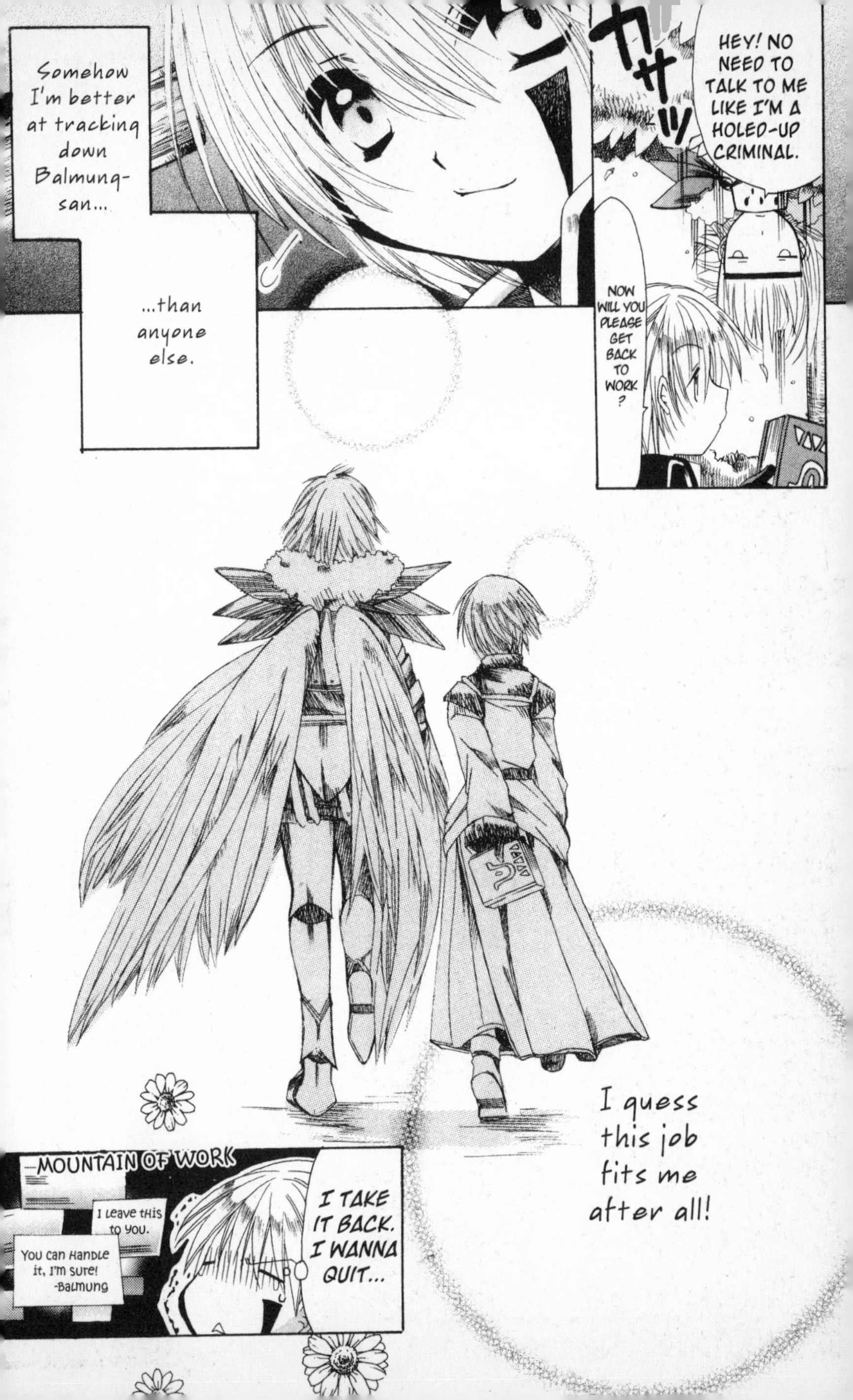

HEY! NO NEED TO TALK TO ME LIKE I'M A HOLED-UP CRIMINAL.
NOW WILL YOU PLEASE GET BACK TO WORK?
Somehow I'm better at tracking down Balmung-san...
...than anyone else.
I guess this job fits me after all!
—MOUNTAIN OF WORK
I TAKE IT BACK. I WANNA QUIT...
I leave this to you.
You can handle it, I'm sure!
-Balmung

Super-hot game version, .hack Volume 3 Cyber Connect 2 (Piroshi Matsuyama

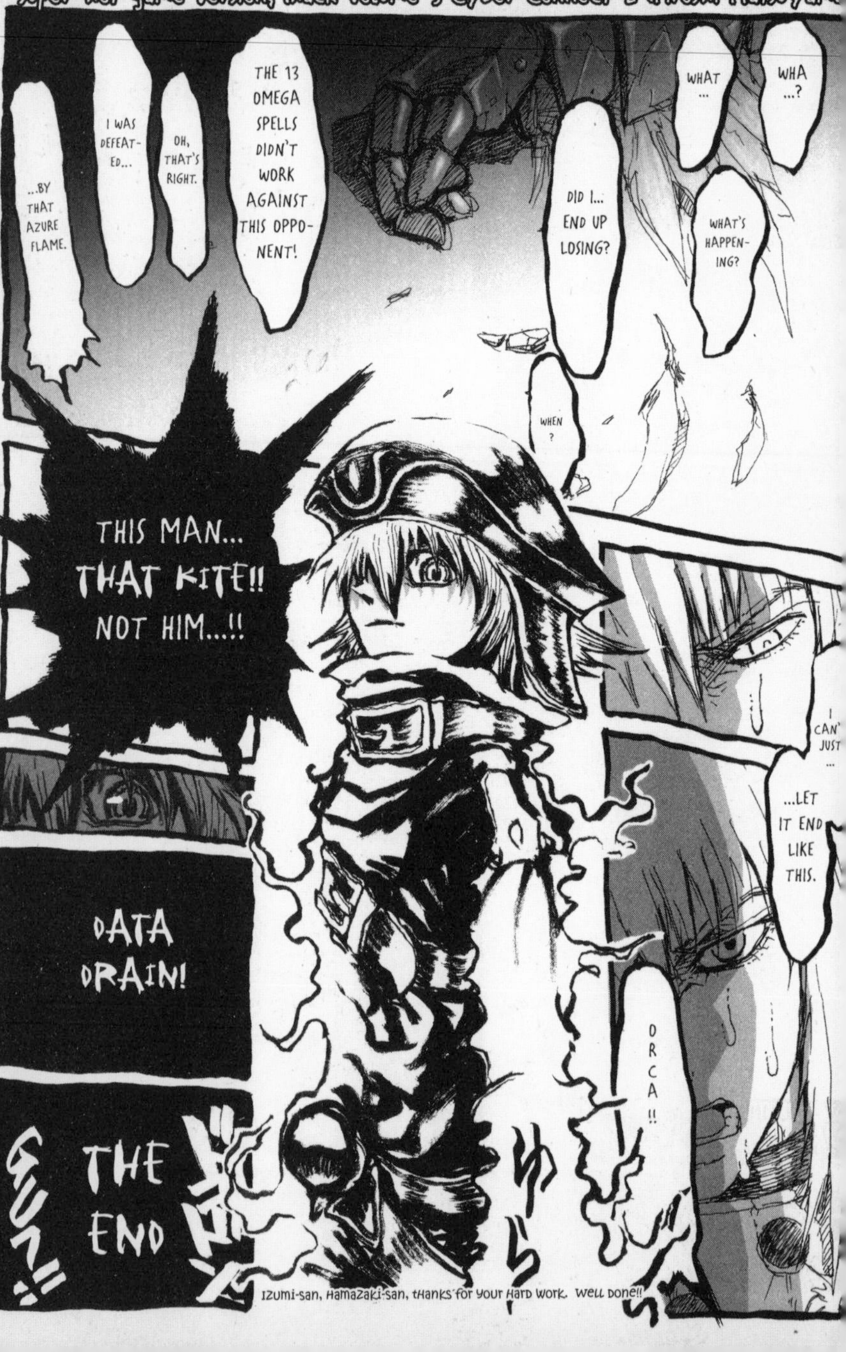
WHA...?
WHAT...
WHAT'S HAPPENING?
DID I... END UP LOSING?
WHEN ?
THE 13 OMEGA SPELLS DIDN'T WORK AGAINST THIS OPPONENT!
OH, THAT'S RIGHT.
I WAS DEFEATED...
...BY THAT AZURE FLAME.
I CAN'T JUST ...
...LET IT END LIKE THIS.
ORCA!!
THIS MAN... THAT KITE!! NOT HIM...!!
DATA DRAIN!
THE END
GUN!!
ゆら
Izumi-san, Hamazaki-san, thanks for your hard work. Well done!!

Record of Rei Izumi's visit to CC2

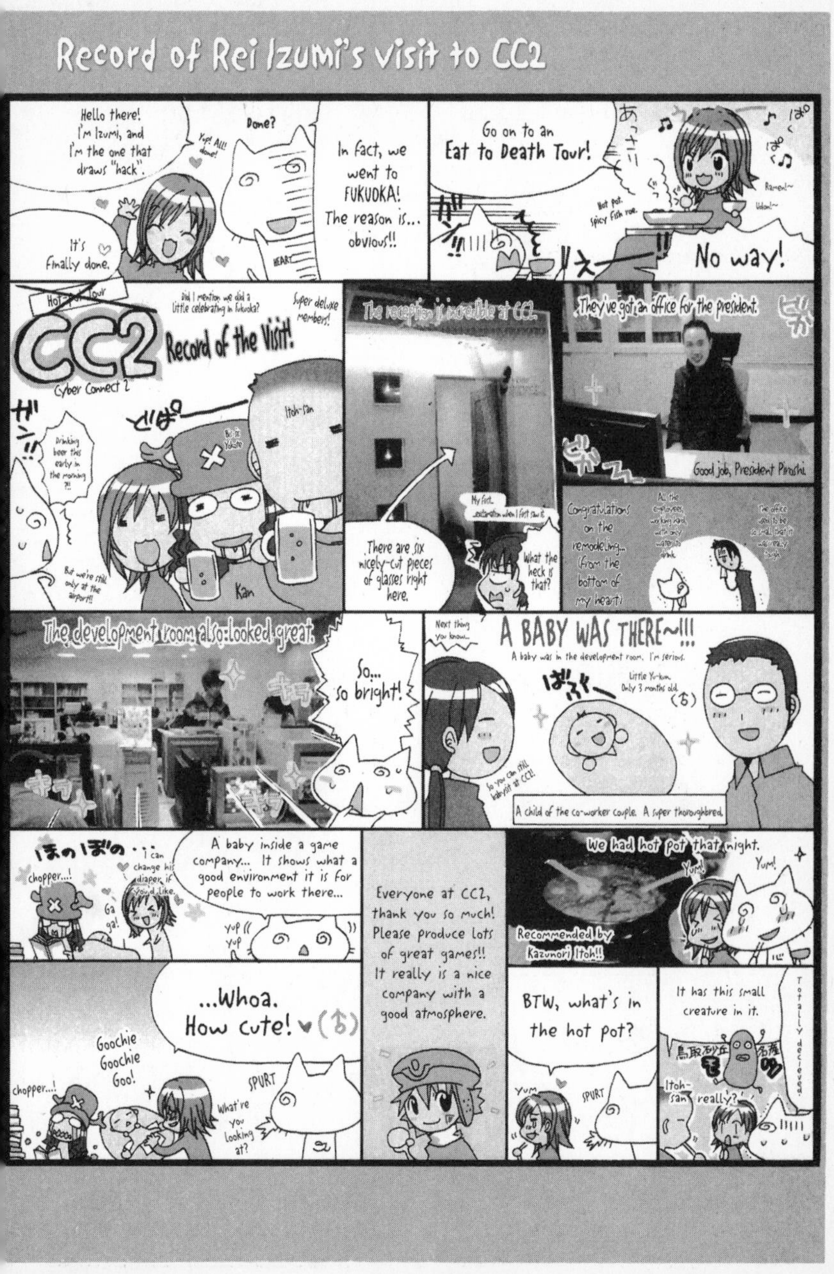

Hello there! I'm Izumi, and I'm the one that draws "hack".
Yup! All! done!
Done?
It's finally done.
HEART
In fact, we went to FUKUOKA! The reason is... obvious!!
Go on to an Eat to Death Tour!
Hot pot. Spicy fish roe.
Ramen!~ Udon!~
No way!
Hot Pot Tour
Did I mention we did a little celebrating in Fukuoka?
Super deluxe members!
CC2 Record of the Visit!
Cyber Connect 2
Itoh-san
Drinking beer this early in the morning?!!
But we're still only at the airport!!
Kan
The reception is incredible at CC2.
My first... exclamation when I first saw it.
There are six nicely-cut pieces of glasses right here.
What the heck is that?
They've got an office for the president.
Good job, President Piroshi.
Congratulations on the remodeling... (From the bottom of my heart)
All the employees working hard, with only water to drink.
The office used to be so small that it was really tough.
The development room also looked great.
So... so bright!
Next thing you know...
A BABY WAS THERE~!!!
A baby was in the development room. I'm serious.
Little Yu-kun. Only 3 months old.
So you can still babysit at CC2!
A child of the co-worker couple. A super thoroughbred.
ほのぼの・・・
chopper...!
I can change his diaper if you'd like.
Ga ga!
A baby inside a game company... It shows what a good environment it is for people to work there...
Yup Yup
Everyone at CC2, thank you so much! Please produce lots of great games!! It really is a nice company with a good atmosphere.
We had hot pot that night.
Yum!
Yum!
Recommended by Kazunori Itoh!!
...Whoa. How cute!
Goochie Goochie Goo!
chopper...!
SPURT
What're you looking at?
BTW, what's in the hot pot?
Yum
SPURT
It has this small creature in it.
鳥取砂丘名産
Itoh-san really?
Totally decieved.

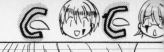

Hooray Cyber Connect Corporation

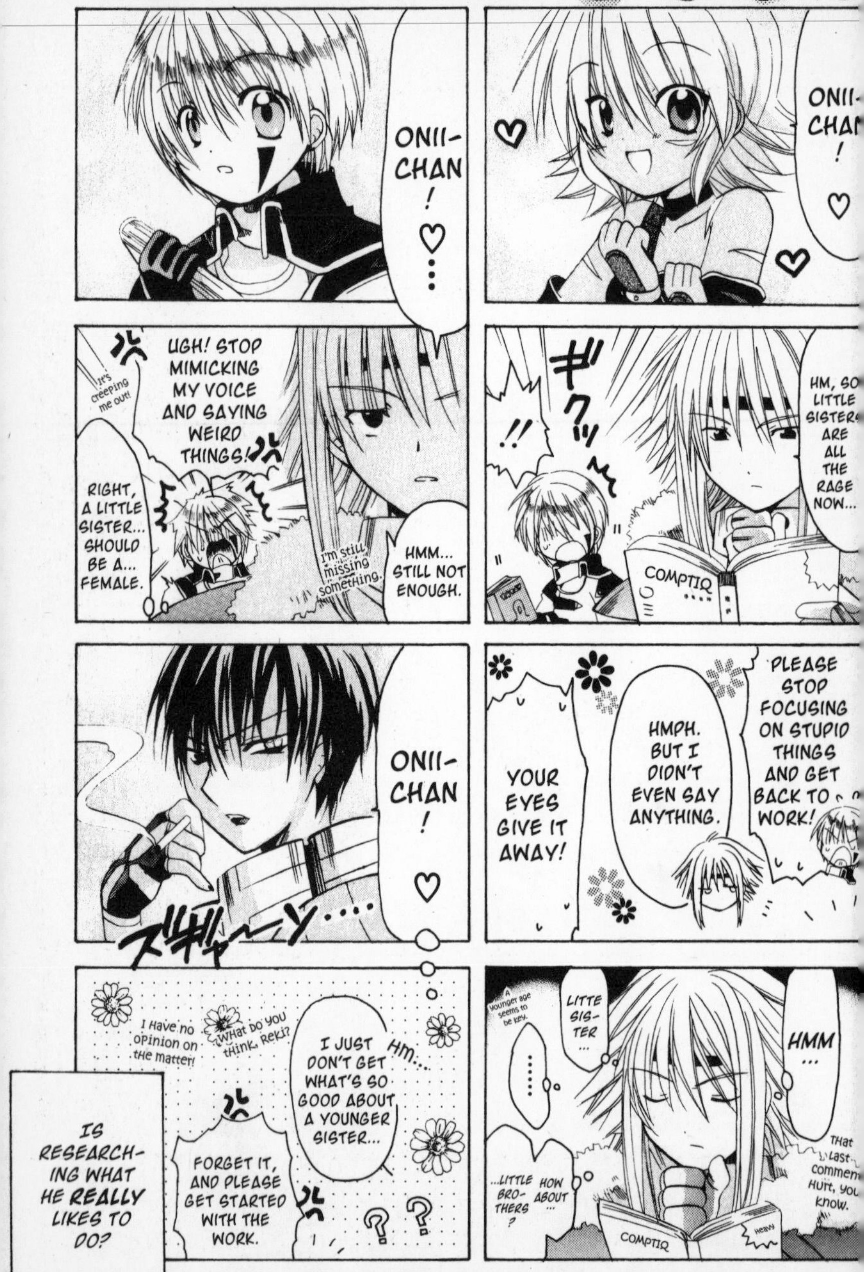
ONII-CHAN! ♡
HM, SO LITTLE SISTERS ARE ALL THE RAGE NOW...
!!
COMPTIQ
....
PLEASE STOP FOCUSING ON STUPID THINGS AND GET BACK TO WORK!
HMPH. BUT I DIDN'T EVEN SAY ANYTHING.
YOUR EYES GIVE IT AWAY!
HMM...
That last comment hurt, you know.
LITTE SISTER...
A younger age seems to be key.
......
HOW ABOUT... ...LITTLE BROTHERS?
COMPTIQ
Heavy
ONII-CHAN! ♡...
HMM... STILL NOT ENOUGH.
I'm still missing something.
UGH! STOP MIMICKING MY VOICE AND SAYING WEIRD THINGS!
It's creeping me out!
RIGHT, A LITTLE SISTER... SHOULD BE A... FEMALE.
ONII-CHAN! ♡
....
HM...
I JUST DON'T GET WHAT'S SO GOOD ABOUT A YOUNGER SISTER...
What do you think, Reki?
I have no opinion on the matter!
FORGET IT, AND PLEASE GET STARTED WITH THE WORK.
?
?
IS RESEARCHING WHAT HE REALLY LIKES TO DO?

Let's Go Cyber Connect Corporation

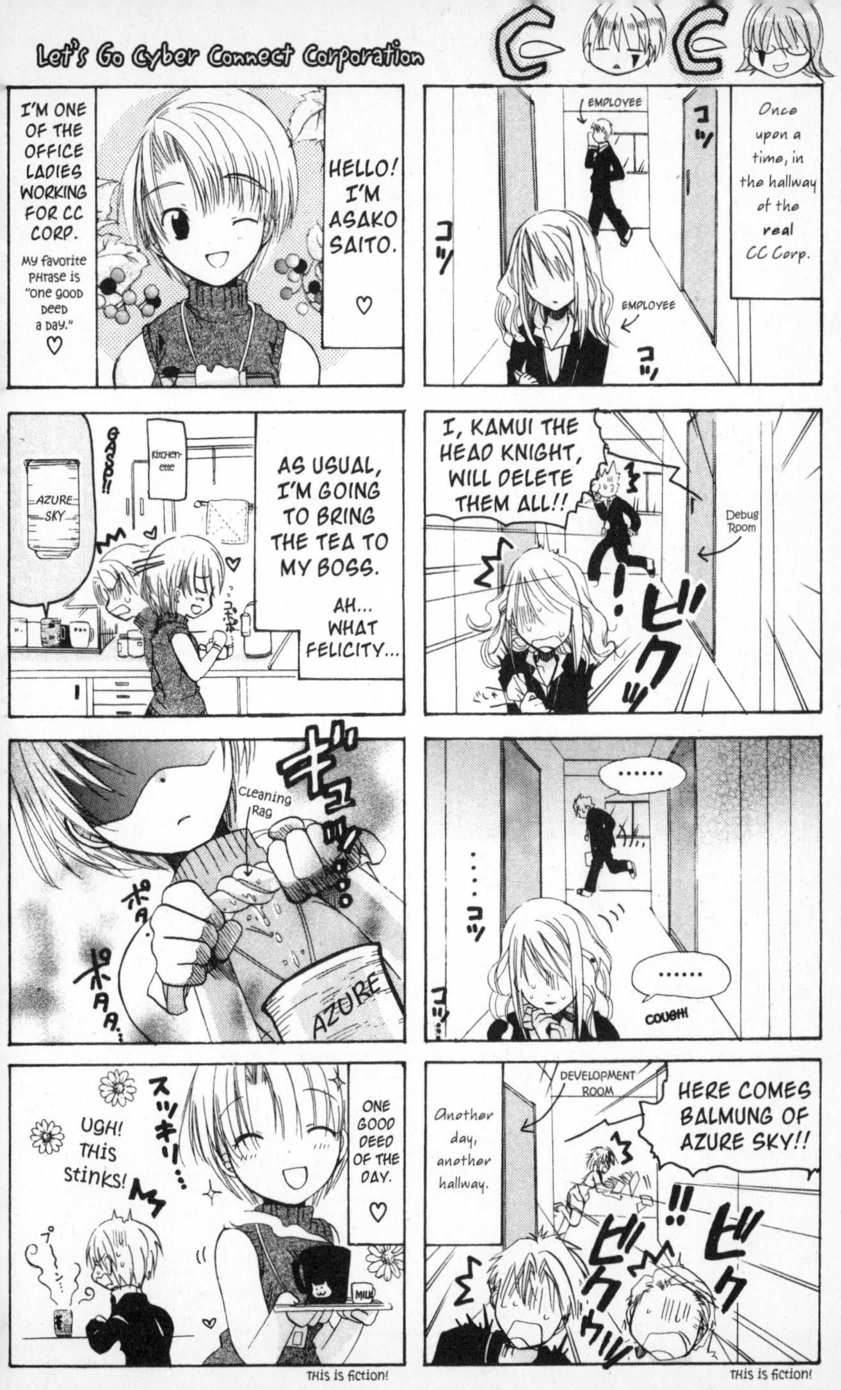

Once upon a time, in the hallway of the **real** CC Corp.
EMPLOYEE
EMPLOYEE
コツ
コツ
コツ
I, KAMUI THE HEAD KNIGHT, WILL DELETE THEM ALL!!
Debug Room
ビクッ
!
......
......
COUGH!
コツ…コツ
コツ…
Another day, another hallway.
DEVELOPMENT ROOM
HERE COMES BALMUNG OF AZURE SKY!!
ビクッ
ビクゥ!!
!!
THIS is fiction!
I'M ONE OF THE OFFICE LADIES WORKING FOR CC CORP.
My favorite PHrase is "one good deed a Day." ♡
HELLO! I'M ASAKO SAITO. ♡
AS USUAL, I'M GOING TO BRING THE TEA TO MY BOSS.
AH... WHAT FELICITY...
GASP!!
Kitchen-ette
AZURE SKY
Cleaning Rag
ギュッ
ポタ
ポタ…
AZURE
ONE GOOD DEED OF THE DAY. ♡
UGH! THIS stinks!
スッキリ…
MILK
THIS is fiction!

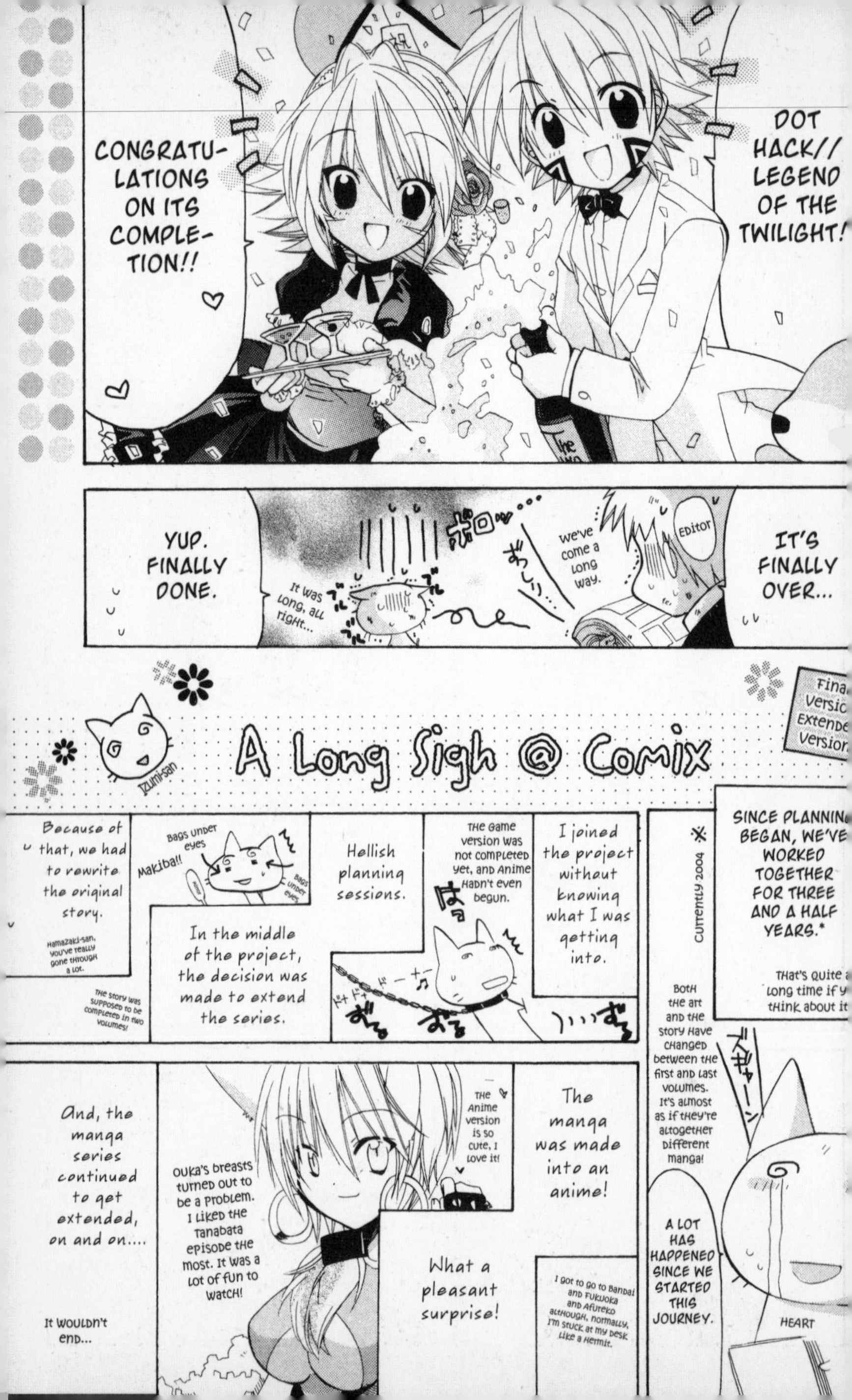

DOT HACK// LEGEND OF THE TWILIGHT!
CONGRATULATIONS ON ITS COMPLETION!!
IT'S FINALLY OVER...
Editor
We've come a long way.
It was long, all right...
YUP. FINALLY DONE.
A Long Sigh @ Comix
Izumi-san
SINCE PLANNING BEGAN, WE'VE WORKED TOGETHER FOR THREE AND A HALF YEARS.*
※ currently 2004
I joined the project without knowing what I was getting into.
The game version was not completed yet, and anime hadn't even begun.
Hellish planning sessions.
Bags under eyes
Makiba!!
Bags under eyes
Because of that, we had to rewrite the original story.
Hamazaki-san, you've really gone through a lot.
In the middle of the project, the decision was made to extend the series.
The story was supposed to be completed in two volumes!
Both the art and the story have changed between the first and last volumes. It's almost as if they're altogether different manga!
A LOT HAS HAPPENED SINCE WE STARTED THIS JOURNEY.
HEART
The manga was made into an anime!
The anime version is so cute, I love it!
What a pleasant surprise!
I got to go to Bandai and Fukuoka and Afureko although, normally, I'm stuck at my desk like a hermit.
Ouka's breasts turned out to be a problem. I liked the Tanabata episode the most. It was a lot of fun to watch!
And, the manga series continued to get extended, on and on....
It wouldn't end...

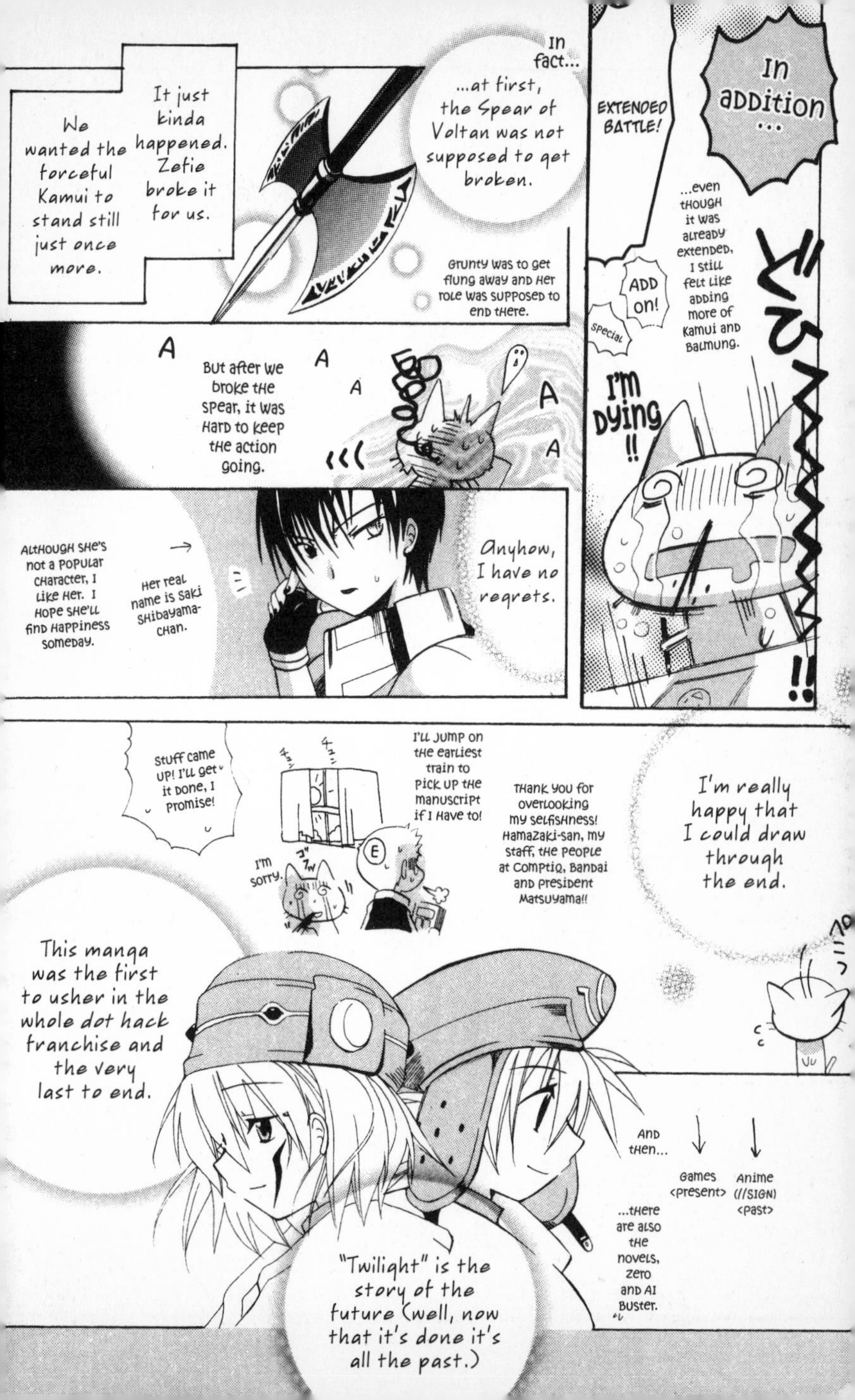
In addition...
EXTENDED BATTLE!
...even though it was already extended, I still felt like adding more of Kamui and Balmung.
ADD on!
Special
I'm Dying!!
In fact...
...at first, the Spear of Voltan was not supposed to get broken.
Grunty was to get flung away and her role was supposed to end there.
It just kinda happened. Zefie broke it for us.
We wanted the forceful Kamui to stand still just once more.
A
But after we broke the spear, it was hard to keep the action going.
A
A
A
A
Anyhow, I have no regrets.
Her real name is Saki Shibayama-chan.
Although she's not a popular character, I like her. I hope she'll find happiness someday.
I'm really happy that I could draw through the end.
Thank you for overlooking my selfishness! Hamazaki-san, my staff, the people at Comptiq, Bandai and President Matsuyama!!
I'll jump on the earliest train to pick up the manuscript if I have to!
Stuff came up! I'll get it done, I promise!
I'm sorry.
And then...
Games <present>
Anime (//SIGN) <past>
...there are also the novels, Zero and AI Buster.
"Twilight" is the story of the future (well, now that it's done it's all the past.)
This manga was the first to usher in the whole dot hack franchise and the very last to end.

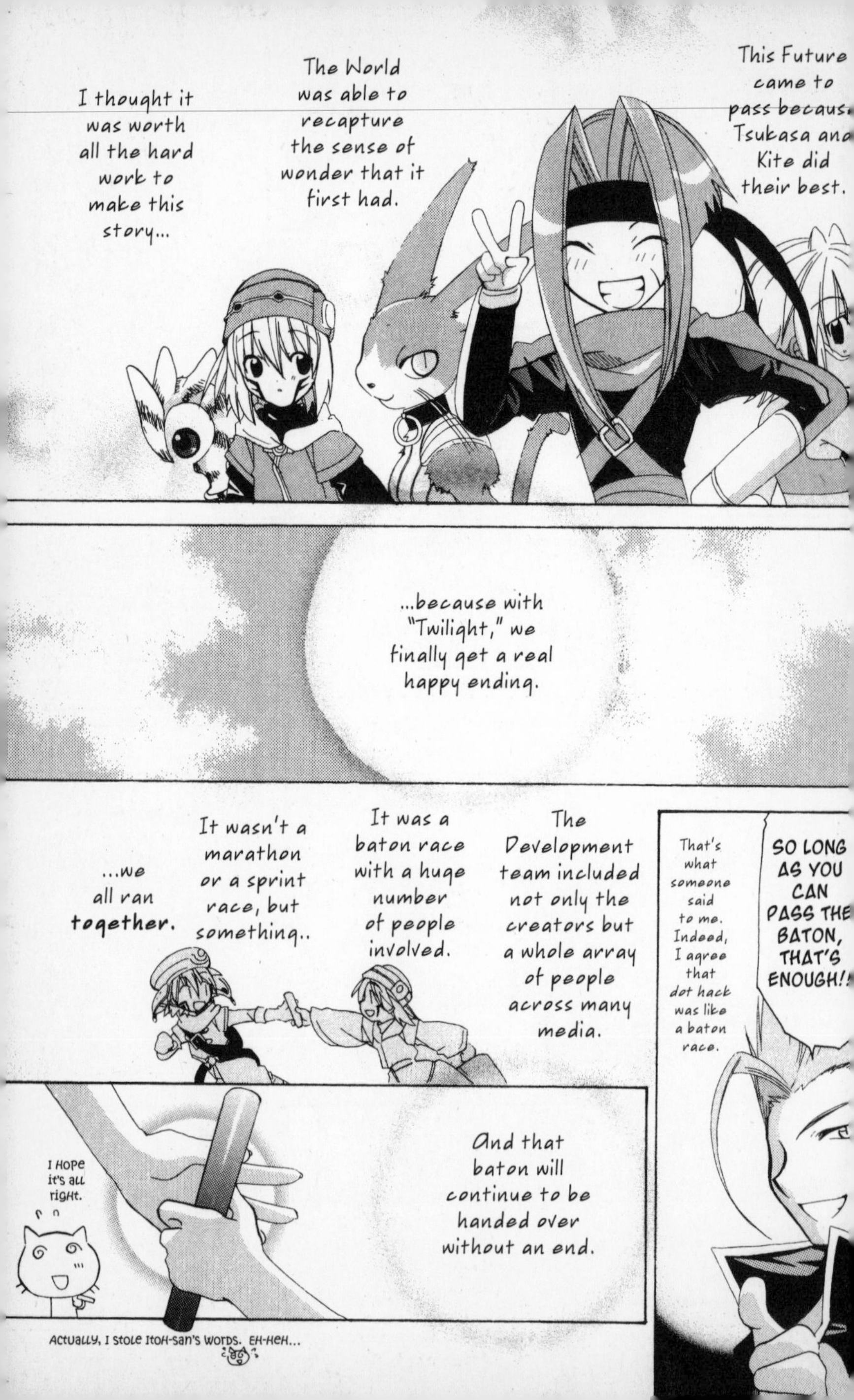
This Future came to pass becaus Tsukasa an Kite did their best.
The World was able to recapture the sense of wonder that it first had.
I thought it was worth all the hard work to make this story...
...because with "Twilight," we finally get a real happy ending.
SO LONG AS YOU CAN PASS THE BATON, THAT'S ENOUGH!!
That's what someone said to me. Indeed, I agree that dot hack was like a baton race.
The Development team included not only the creators but a whole array of people across many media.
It was a baton race with a huge number of people involved.
It wasn't a marathon or a sprint race, but something..
...we all ran **together.**
And that baton will continue to be handed over without an end.
I HOPE it's all right.
Actually, I stole Itoh-san's words. EH-HEH...

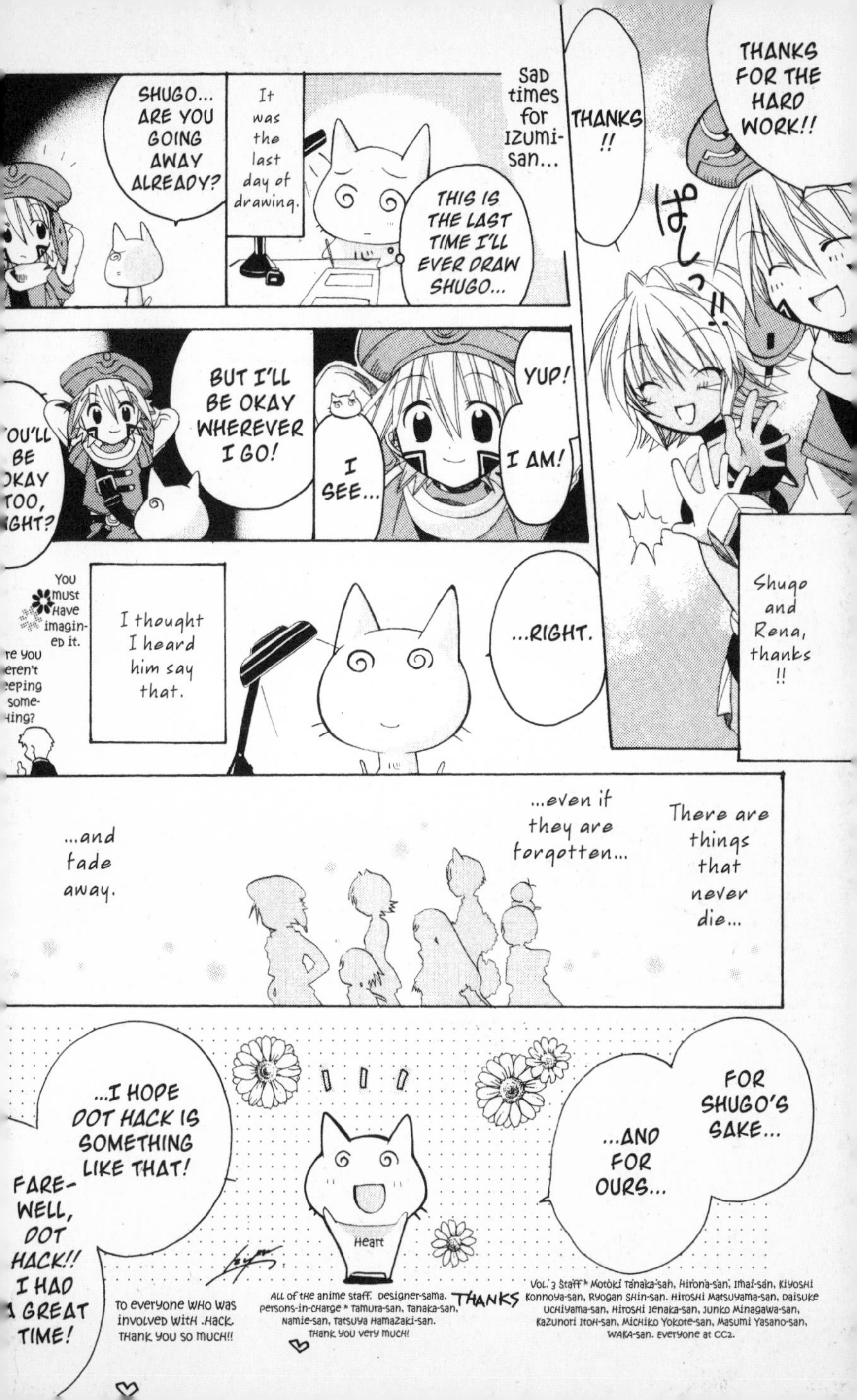
THANKS FOR THE HARD WORK!!
THANKS !!
ぱしっ!!
Shugo and Rena, thanks !!
Sad times for IZUMI-san...
It was the last day of drawing.
THIS IS THE LAST TIME I'LL EVER DRAW SHUGO...
SHUGO... ARE YOU GOING AWAY ALREADY?
YUP! I AM!
I SEE...
BUT I'LL BE OKAY WHEREVER I GO!
OU'LL BE KAY TOO, GHT?
...RIGHT.
I thought I heard him say that.
You must Have imagin-ed it.
re you eren't eeping some-hing?
There are things that never die...
...even if they are forgotten...
...and fade away.
FOR SHUGO'S SAKE...
...AND FOR OURS...
...I HOPE DOT HACK IS SOMETHING LIKE THAT!
FARE-WELL, DOT HACK!! I HAD A GREAT TIME!
Heart
Vol. 3 Staff * Motoki Tanaka-san, Hirona-san, Imai-san, Kiyoshi Konnoya-san, Ryogan Shin-san. Hiroshi Matsuyama-san, Daisuke Uchiyama-san, Hiroshi Ienaka-san, Junko Minagawa-san, Kazunori Itoh-san, Michiko Yokote-san, Masumi Yasano-san, Waka-san. Everyone at CC2.
THANKS
All of the anime staff. Designer-sama. persons-in-charge * Tamura-san, Tanaka-san, Namie-san, Tatsuya Hamazaki-san. Thank you very much!
To everyone who was involved with .Hack. Thank you so much!!

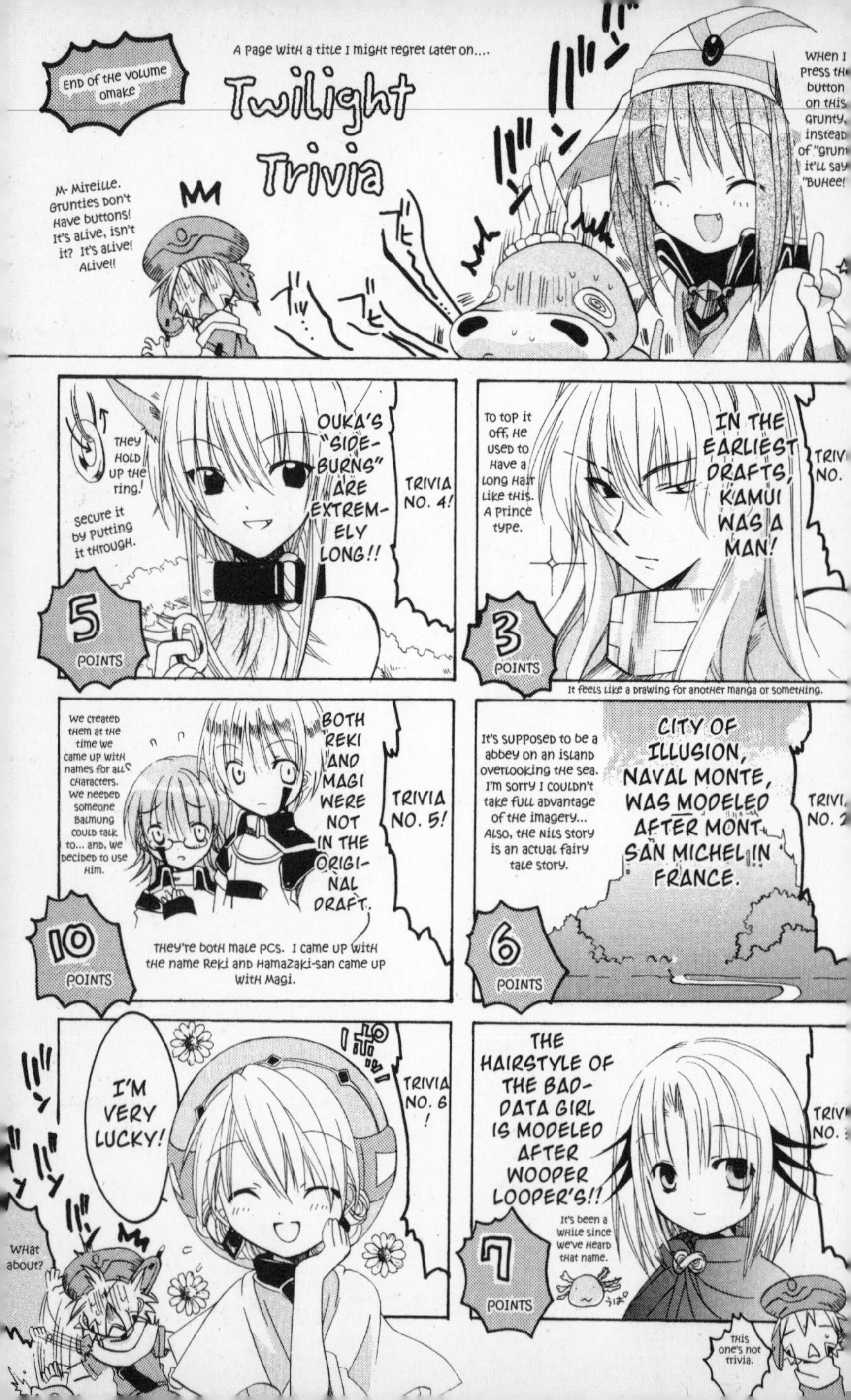
End of the volume omake
A page with a title I might regret later on....
Twilight Trivia
When I press th button on this grunty, instead of "grun it'll say "Buhee!
M- Mireille. Grunties don't have buttons! It's alive, isn't it? It's alive! Alive!!
Triv No.
In the earliest drafts, Kamui was a man!
To top it off, he used to have a long hair like this. A prince type.
3 points
It feels like a drawing for another manga or something.
Trivia No. 4!
Ouka's "sideburns" are extremely long!!
They hold up the ring!
Secure it by putting it through.
5 points
Trivi No. 2
City of Illusion, Naval Monte, was modeled after Mont San Michel in France.
It's supposed to be a abbey on an island overlooking the sea. I'm sorry I couldn't take full advantage of the imagery... Also, the Nils story is an actual fairy tale story.
6 points
Trivia No. 5!
Both Reki and Magi were not in the original draft.
We created them at the time we came up with names for all characters. We needed someone Balmung could talk to... and, we decided to use him.
They're both male PCs. I came up with the name Reki and Hamazaki-san came up with Magi.
10 points
Triv No.
The hairstyle of the bad-data girl is modeled after Wooper Looper's!!
It's been a while since we've heard that name.
7 points
This one's not trivia.
Trivia No. 6 !
I'm very lucky!
What about?

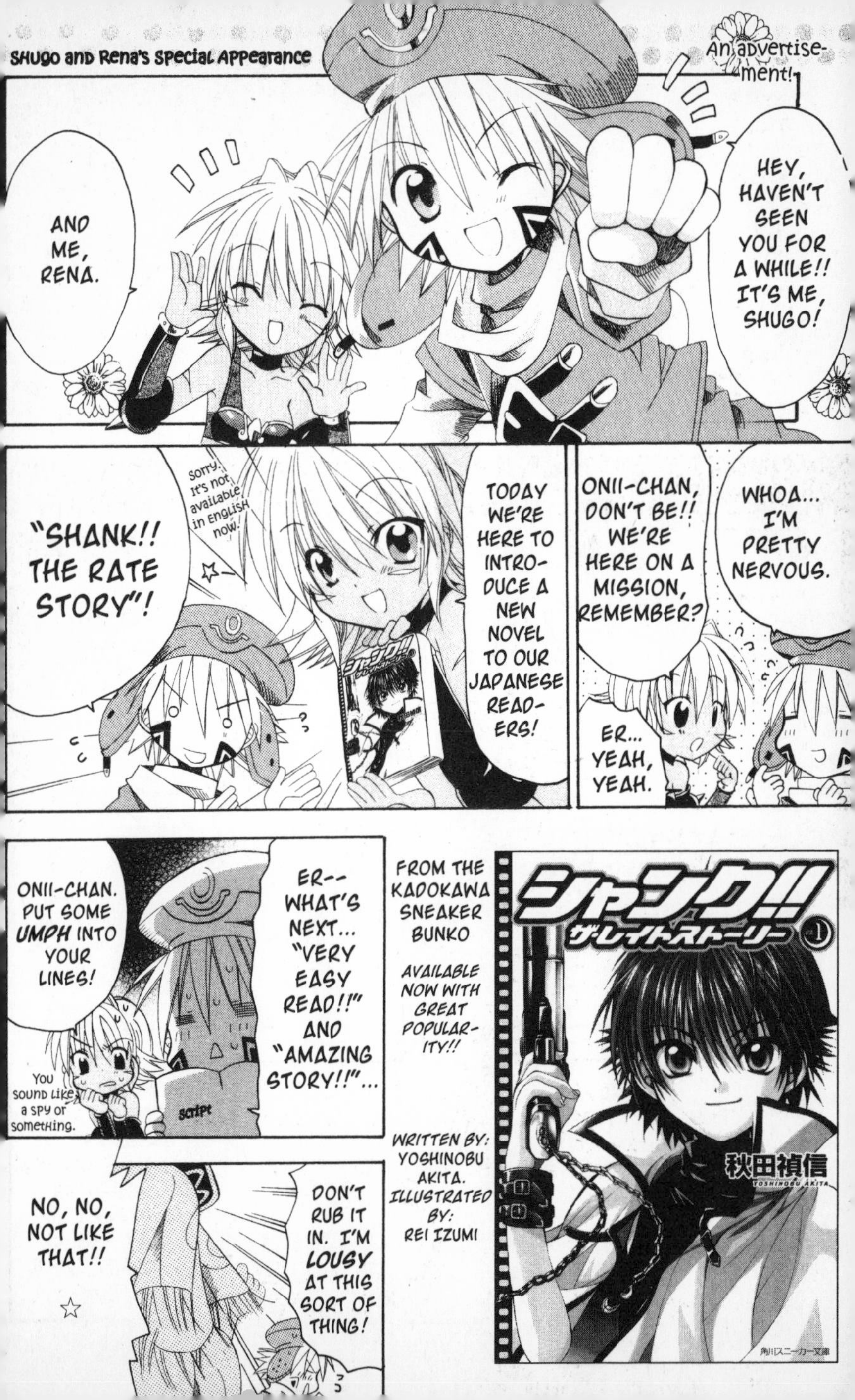
Shugo and Rena's Special Appearance
An advertisement!
HEY, HAVEN'T SEEN YOU FOR A WHILE!! IT'S ME, SHUGO!
AND ME, RENA.
WHOA... I'M PRETTY NERVOUS.
ONII-CHAN, DON'T BE!! WE'RE HERE ON A MISSION, REMEMBER?
ER... YEAH, YEAH.
TODAY WE'RE HERE TO INTRO-DUCE A NEW NOVEL TO OUR JAPANESE READ-ERS!
Sorry. It's not available in English now.
"SHANK!! THE RATE STORY"!
シャンク!!
ザ・レイトストーリー ①
秋田禎信
YOSHINOBU AKITA
角川スニーカー文庫
FROM THE KADOKAWA SNEAKER BUNKO
AVAILABLE NOW WITH GREAT POPULAR-ITY!!
WRITTEN BY: YOSHINOBU AKITA. ILLUSTRATED BY: REI IZUMI
ER-- WHAT'S NEXT... "VERY EASY READ!!" AND "AMAZING STORY!!"...
ONII-CHAN. PUT SOME UMPH INTO YOUR LINES!
You sound like a spy or something.
Script
DON'T RUB IT IN. I'M LOUSY AT THIS SORT OF THING!
NO, NO, NOT LIKE THAT!!

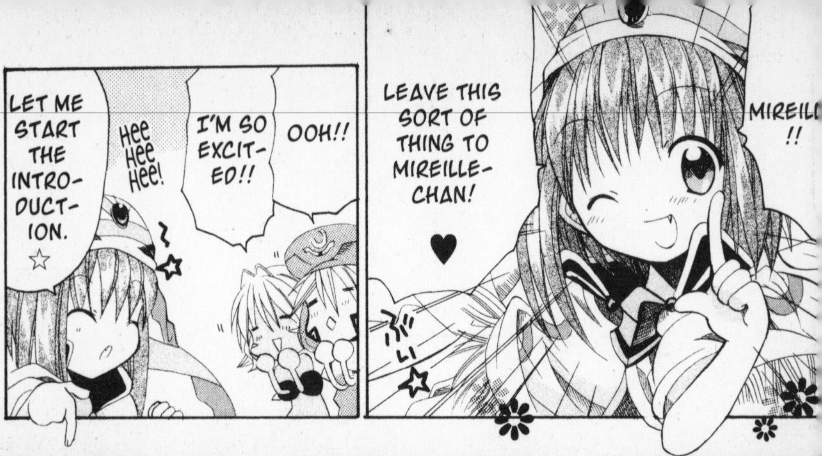
MIREILL
!!
LEAVE THIS SORT OF THING TO MIREILLE-CHAN! ♥
ぶい
OOH!!
I'M SO EXCIT-ED!!
Hee Hee Hee!
LET ME START THE INTRO-DUCT-ION. ☆

SHank!! THE Rate Story

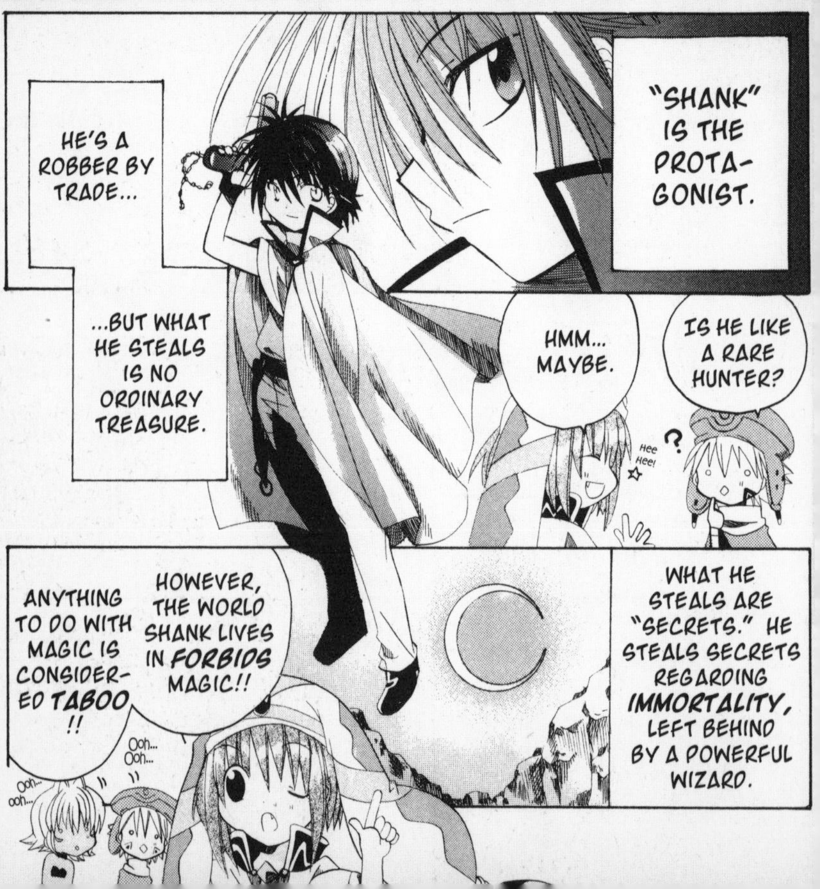
"SHANK" IS THE PROTA-GONIST.
HE'S A ROBBER BY TRADE...
IS HE LIKE A RARE HUNTER?
HMM... MAYBE.
Hee Hee!
...BUT WHAT HE STEALS IS NO ORDINARY TREASURE.
WHAT HE STEALS ARE "SECRETS." HE STEALS SECRETS REGARDING IMMORTALITY, LEFT BEHIND BY A POWERFUL WIZARD.
HOWEVER, THE WORLD SHANK LIVES IN FORBIDS MAGIC!!
ANYTHING TO DO WITH MAGIC IS CONSIDER-ED TABOO !!
Ooh... Ooh...
Ooh... ooh...

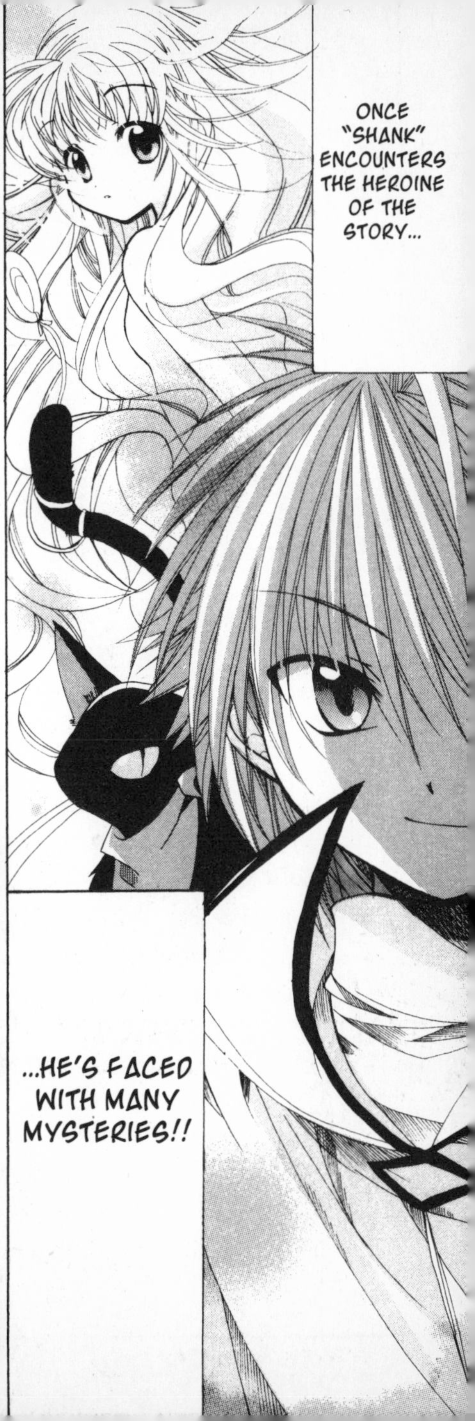
ONCE "SHANK" ENCOUNTERS THE HEROINE OF THE STORY...
...HE'S FACED WITH MANY MYSTERIES!!
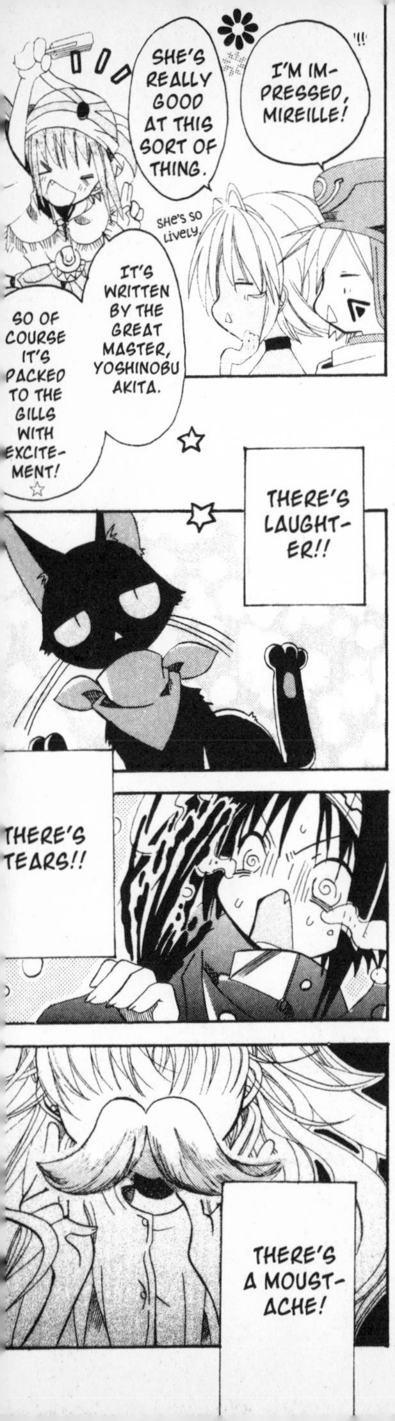
!!
I'M IM-PRESSED, MIREILLE!
SHE'S REALLY GOOD AT THIS SORT OF THING.
SHE'S SO LIVELY.
IT'S WRITTEN BY THE GREAT MASTER, YOSHINOBU AKITA.
SO OF COURSE IT'S PACKED TO THE GILLS WITH EXCITE-MENT!
THERE'S LAUGHT-ER!!
THERE'S TEARS!!
THERE'S A MOUST-ACHE!

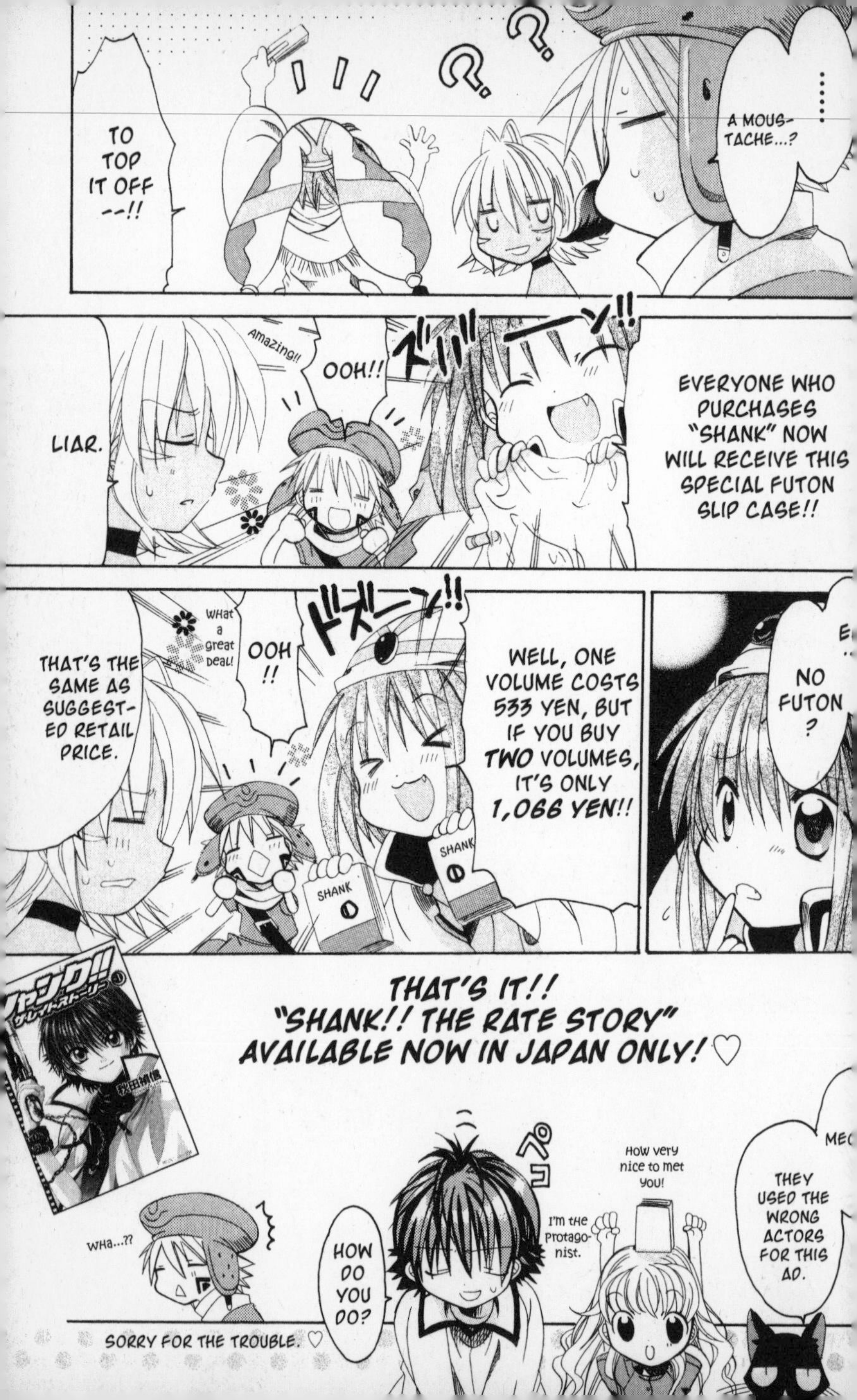

......
A MOUS-TACHE...?
? ?
TO TOP IT OFF--!!
ズバーン!!
EVERYONE WHO PURCHASES "SHANK" NOW WILL RECEIVE THIS SPECIAL FUTON SLIP CASE!!
OOH!!
Amazing!!
LIAR.
NO FUTON?
ドズーン!!
WELL, ONE VOLUME COSTS 533 YEN, BUT IF YOU BUY TWO VOLUMES, IT'S ONLY 1,066 YEN!!
SHANK
SHANK
OOH!!
What a great deal!
THAT'S THE SAME AS SUGGEST-ED RETAIL PRICE.
THAT'S IT!! "SHANK!! THE RATE STORY" AVAILABLE NOW IN JAPAN ONLY! ♡
THEY USED THE WRONG ACTORS FOR THIS AD.
How very nice to met you!
I'm the Protago-nist.
HOW DO YOU DO?
WHA...??
SORRY FOR THE TROUBLE. ♡

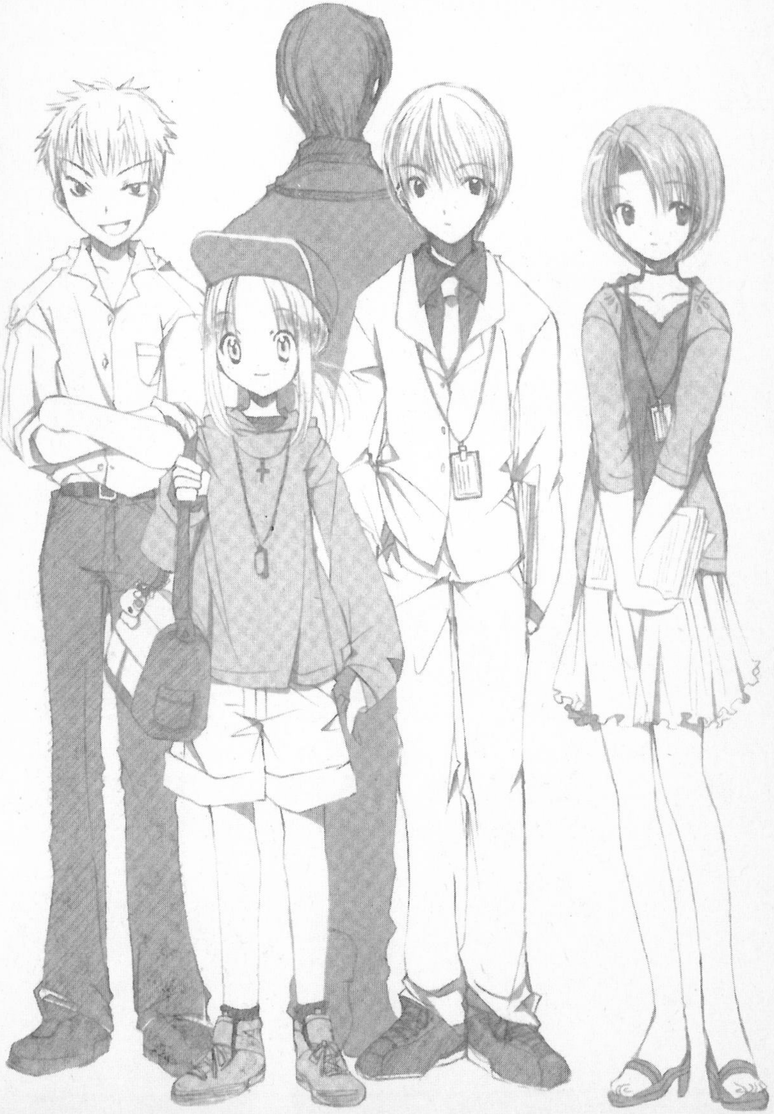

.hack//UNPLUGGED

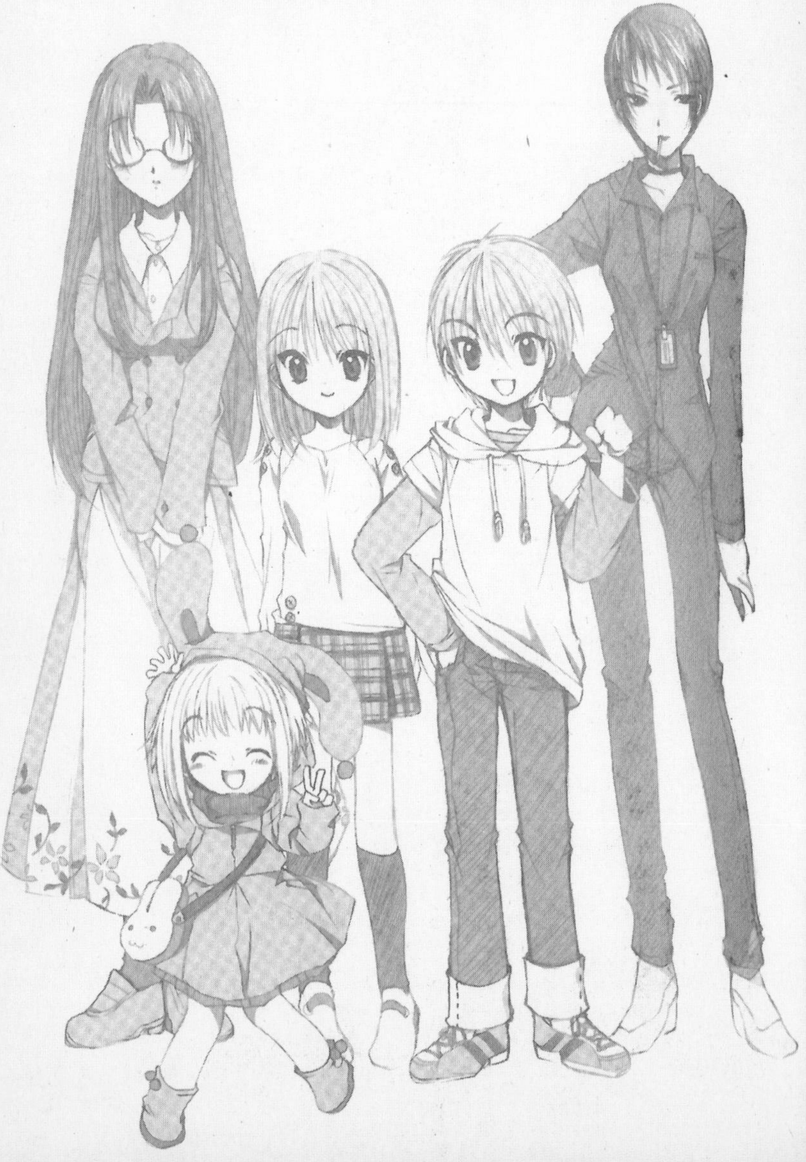

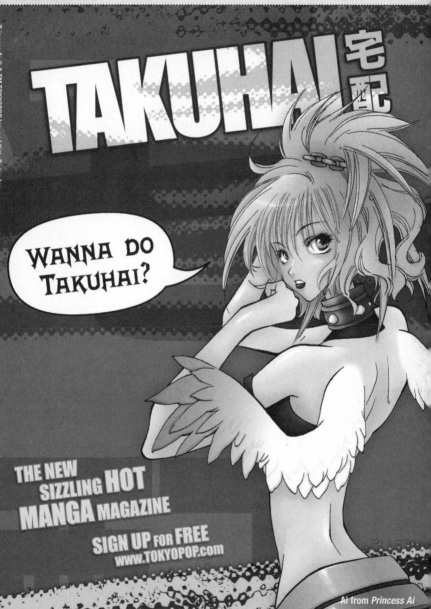

TOKYOPOP SHOP

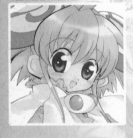

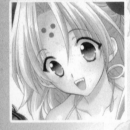
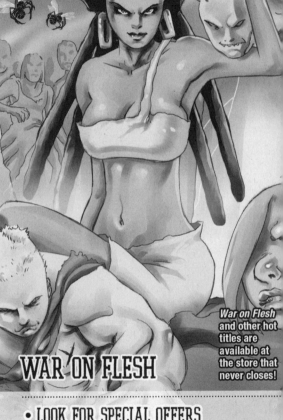

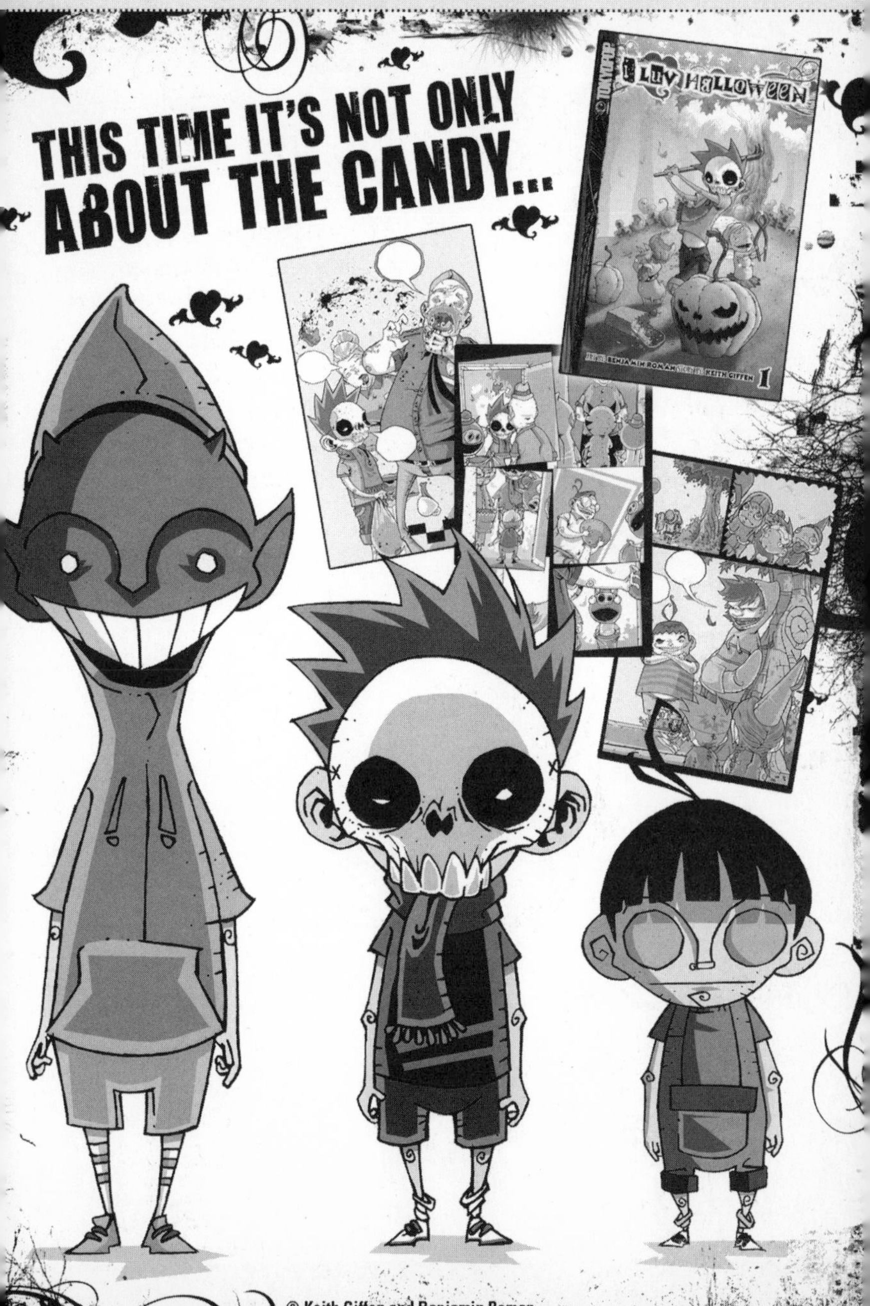
THIS TIME IT'S NOT ONLY
ABOUT THE CANDY...
I LUV HALLOWEEN
TOKYOPOP
BENJAMIN ROMAN
KEITH GIFFEN
1

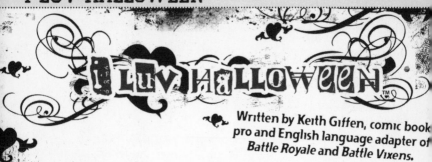

Written by Keith Giffen, comic book pro and English language adapter of *Battle Royale* and *Battle Vixens*.

Join the misadventures of a group of particularly disturbing trick-or-treaters as they go about their macabre business on Halloween night. Blaming the apples they got from the first house of the evening for the bad candy they've been receiving all night, the kids plot revenge on the old bag who handed out the funky fruit. Riotously funny and always wickedly shocking— who doesn't *love* Halloween?

OT
OLDER TEEN
AGE 16+

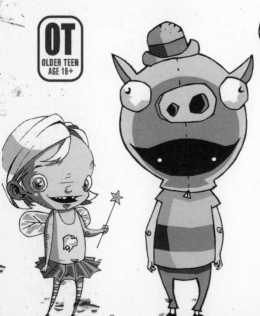

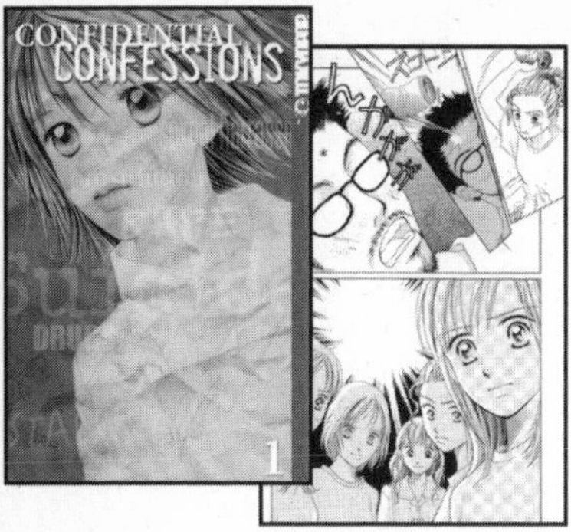
CONFIDENTIAL CONFESSIONS
1

BY REIKO MOMOCHI

CONFIDENTIAL CONFESSIONS

If you're looking for a happy, rosy, zit-free look at high school life, skip this manga. But if you're jonesing for a real-life view of what high school's truly like, *Confidential Confessions* offers a gritty, unflinching look at what really happens in those hallowed halls. Rape, sexual harassment, anorexia, cutting, suicide...no subject is too hardcore for *Confidential Confessions*. While you're at it, don't expect a happy ending.

~Julie Taylor, Sr. Editor

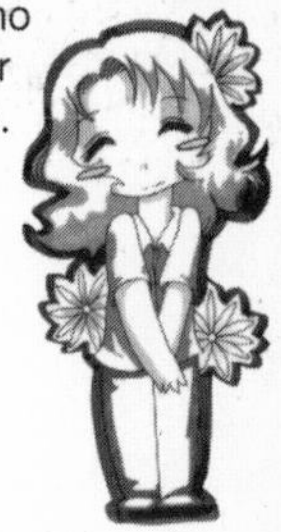

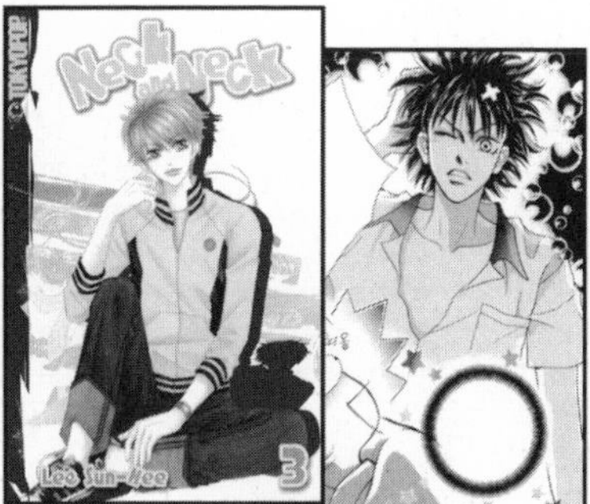
Neck and Neck
Lee Sun-Hee
3

BY LEE SUN-HEE

NECK AND NECK

Competition can bring out the best or the worst in people...but in *Neck and Neck*, it does both! Dabin Choi and Shihu Myoung are both high school students, both children of mob bosses, and each is out to totally humiliate the other. Dabin and Shihu are very creative in their mutual tortures and there's more than a hint of romantic tension behind their attacks. This book's art may look somewhat shojo, but I found the story to be very accessible and very entertaining!

~Rob Tokar, Sr. Editor

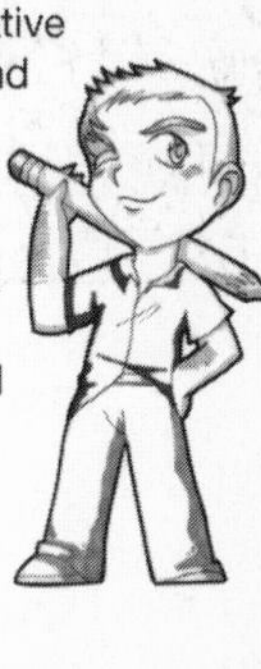

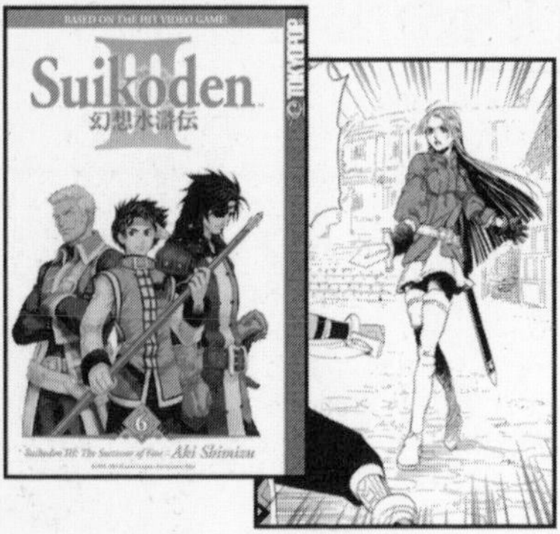
BASED ON THE HIT VIDEO GAME!
Suikoden
幻想水滸伝
III
6
Aki Shimizu

BY AKI SHIMIZU

SUIKODEN III

I'm one of those people who likes to watch others play video games (I tend to run into walls and get stuck), so here comes the perfect manga for me! All the neat plot of a great RPG game, without any effort on my part! Aki Shimizu, creator of the delightful series *Qwan*, has done a lovely, lovely job of bringing the world of Suikoden to life. There are great creatures (Fighting ducks! Giant lizard people!), great character designs, and an engaging story full of conflict, drama and intrigue. I picked up one volume while I was eating lunch at my desk one day, and was totally hooked. I can't wait for the next one to come out!

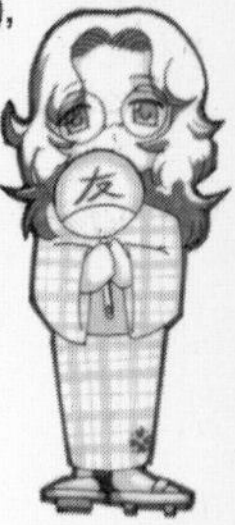

~Lillian Diaz-Przybyl, Editor

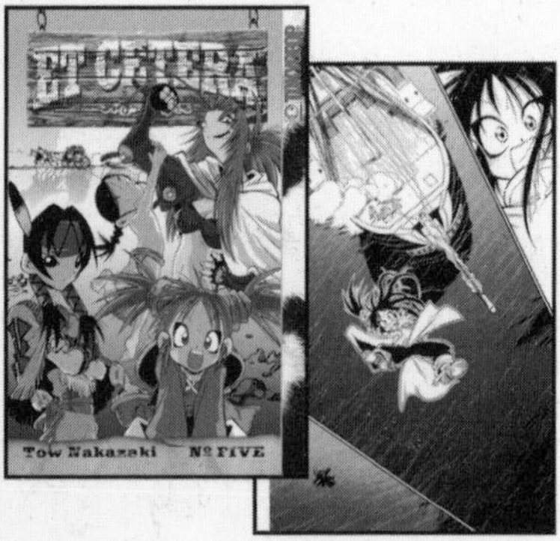
Tow Nakazaki
№ FIVE

BY TOW NAKAZAKI

ET CETERA

Meet Mingchao, an energetic girl from China who now travels the deserts of the old west. She dreams of becoming a star in Hollywood, eager for fame and fortune. She was given the Eto Gun—a magical weapon that fires bullets with properties of the 12 zodiac signs—as a keepsake from her grandfather before he died. On her journey to Hollywood, she meets a number of zany characters...some who want to help, and others who are after the power of the Eto Gun. Chock full of gun fights, train hijackings, collapsing mineshafts...this East-meets-wild-West tale has it all!

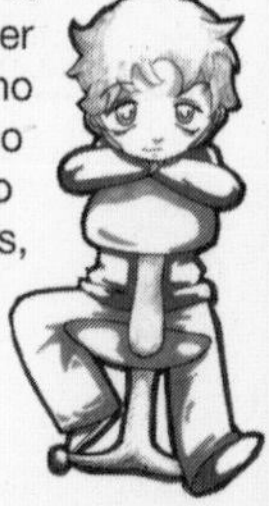

~Aaron Suhr, Sr. Editor

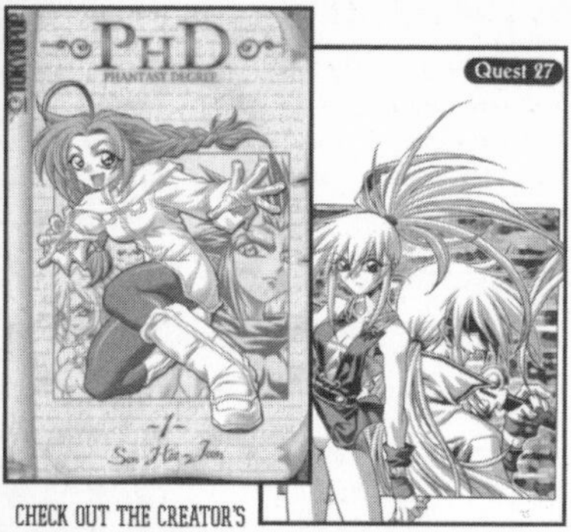
PhD
PHANTASY DEGREE
Quest 27

CHECK OUT THE CREATOR'S *iD_eNTITY*

BY SON HEE-JOON

PhD: PHANTASY DEGREE

So you think you've got it rough at *your* school? Try attending classes at Demon School Hades! When sassy, young Sang makes her monster matriculation to this arcane academy, all hell breaks loose—literally! But what would you expect when the graduating class consists of a werewolf, a mummy and demons by the score? Son Hee-Joon's underworld adventure is pure escapist fun. Always packed with action and often silly in the best sense, *PhD* never takes itself too seriously or lets the reader stop to catch his breath.

~Bryce P. Coleman, Editor

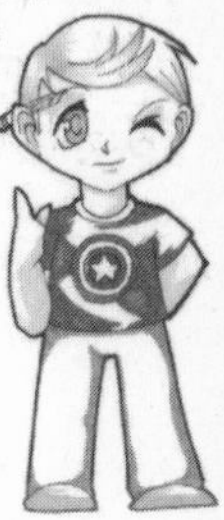

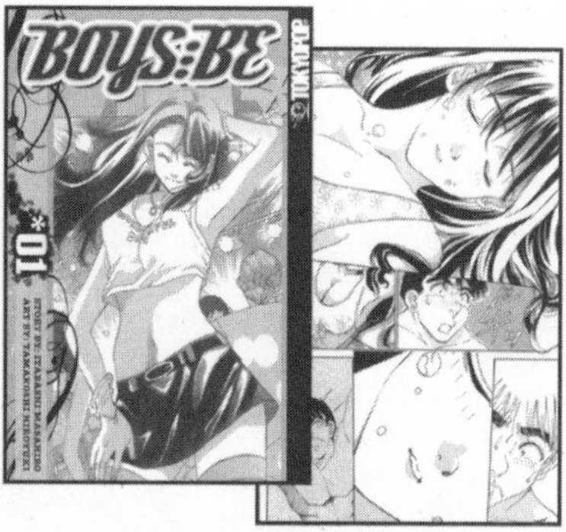
BOYS BE

BY MASAHIRO ITABASHI & HIROYUKI TAMAKOSHI

BOYS BE...

Boys Be... is a series of short stories. But although the hero's name changes from tale to tale, he remains Everyboy—that dorky high school guy who'll do anything to score with the girl of his dreams. You know him. Perhaps you *are* him. He is a dirty mind with the soul of a poet, a stumblebum with a heart of sterling. We follow this guy on quest after quest to woo his lady loves. We savor his victory; we reel with his defeat...and the experience is touching, funny and above all human.

Still not convinced? I have two words for you: fan service.

~Carol Fox, Editor

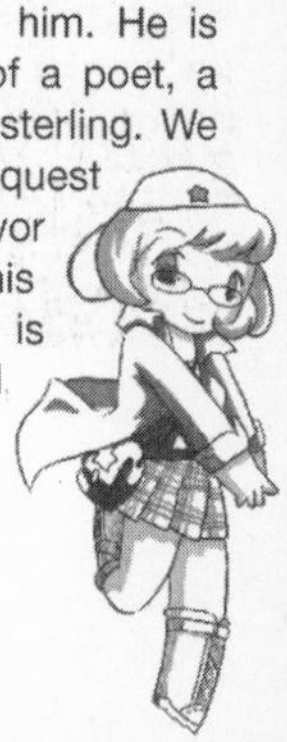

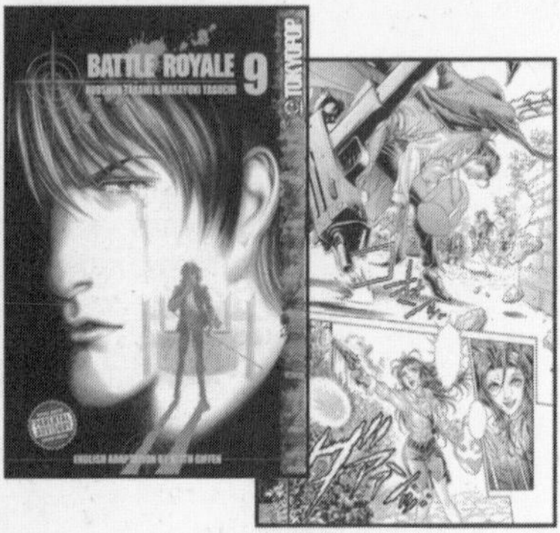
BATTLE ROYALE 9
KOUSHUN TAKAMI & MASAYUKI TAGUCHI
TOKYOPOP

BY KOUSHUN TAKAMI & MASAYUKI TAGUCHI

BATTLE ROYALE

As far as cautionary tales go, you couldn't get any timelier than *Battle Royale*. Telling the bleak story of a class of middle school students who are forced to fight one another to the death on national television, Koushun Takami and Masayuki Taguchi have created a dark satire that's sickening, yet undeniably exciting as well. And if we have that reaction reading it, it becomes alarmingly clear how the students could be so easily swayed into *doing* it.

~Tim Beedle, Editor

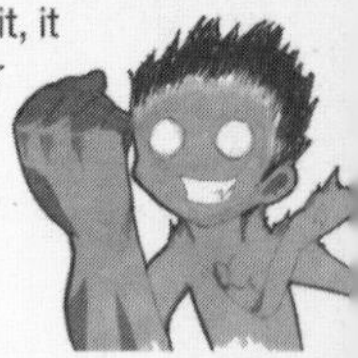

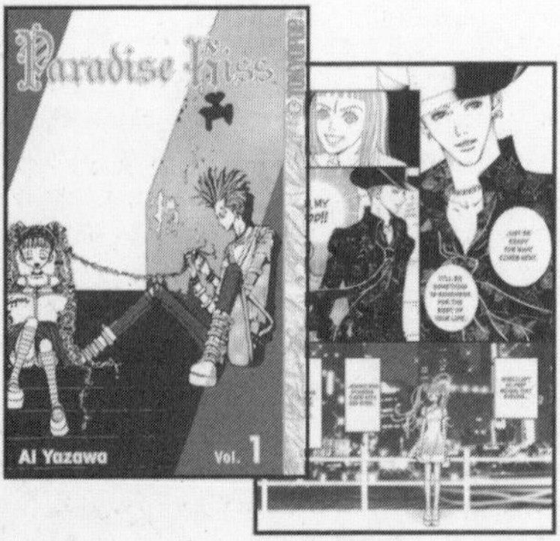
Paradise Kiss
Ai Yazawa
Vol. 1

BY AI YAZAWA

PARADISE KISS

The clothes! The romance! The clothes! The intrigue! And did I mention the clothes?! *Paradise Kiss* is the best fashion manga ever written, from one of the hottest shojo artists in Japan. Ai Yazawa is the coolest. Not only did she create the character designs for *Princess Ai*, which were amazing, but she also produced five fab volumes of *Paradise Kiss*, a manga series bursting with fashion and passion. Read it and be inspired.

~Julie Taylor, Sr. Editor

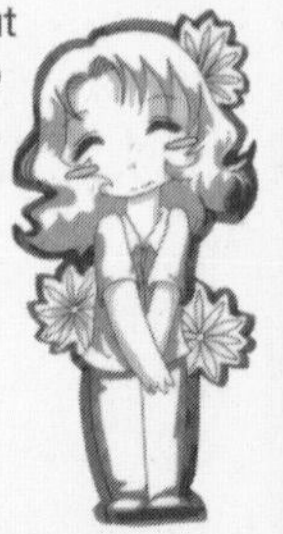

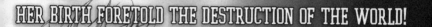

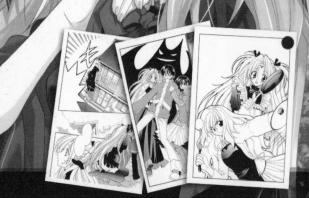

SHOWCASE TOKYOPOP MANGA SUPPLEMENT

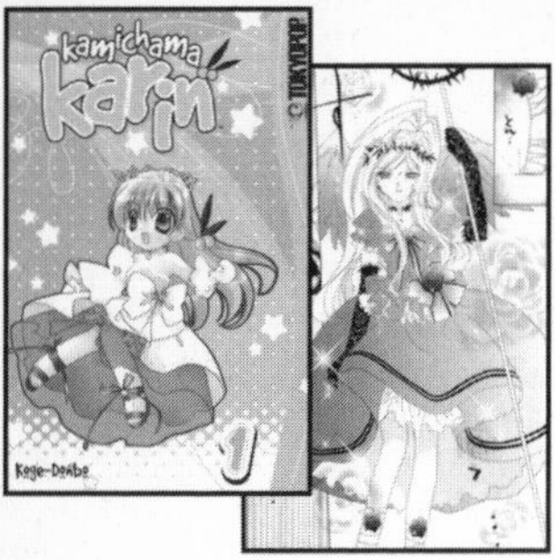
kamichama karin
TOKYOPOP
Koge-Donbo
1

KAMICHAMA KARIN

BY KOGE-DONBO

Karin is an average girl...at best. She's not good at sports and gets terrible grades. On top of all that, her parents are dead and her beloved cat Shi-chan just died, too. She is miserable. But everything is about to change—little does Karin know that her mother's ring has the power to make her a goddess!

From the creator of *Pita-Ten* and *Digi-Charat!*

Y YOUTH AGE 10+

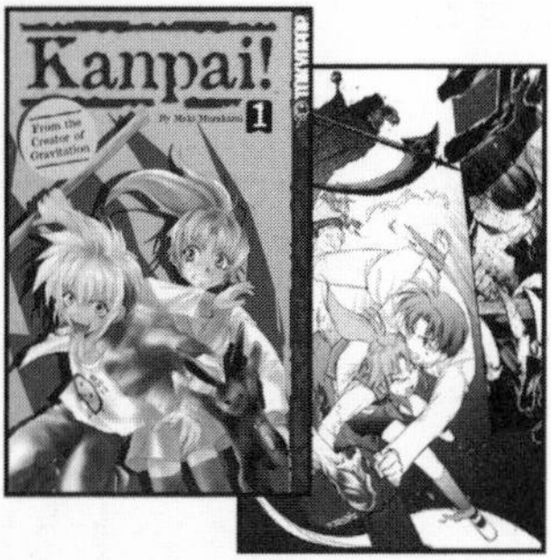
Kanpai!
1
TOKYOPOP

KANPAI!

BY MAKI MURAKAMI

Yamada Shintaro is a monster guardian in training—his job is to protect the monsters from harm. But when he meets Nao, a girl from his middle school, he suddenly falls in love...with her neckline! Shintaro will go to any lengths to prevent disruption to her peaceful life—and preserve his choice view of her neck!

A wild and wonderful adventure from the creator of *Gravitation!*

T TEEN AGE 13+

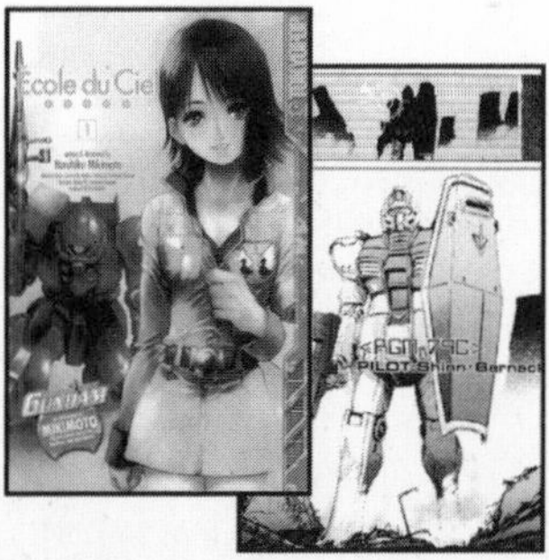
École du Ciel
1
GUNDAM
MIKIMOTO

MOBILE SUIT GUNDAM ÉCOLE DU CIEL

BY HARUHIKO MIKIMOTO

École du Ciel—where aspiring pilots train to become Top Gundam! Asuna, daughter of a brilliant professor, is a below-average student at École du Ciel. But the world is spiraling toward war, and Asuna is headed for a crash course in danger, battle, and most of all, love.

From the artist of the phenomenally successful *Macross* and *Baby Birth!*

T TEEN AGE 13+

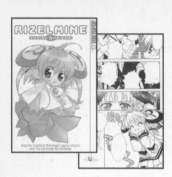

RIZELMINE
BY YUKIRU SUGISAKI

Tomonori Iwaki is a hapless fifteen-year-old whose life is turned upside down when the government announces that he's a married man! His blushing bride is Rizel, apparently the adorable product of an experiment. She does her best to win her new man's heart in this wacky romantic comedy from the creator of *D•N•Angel*!

Inspiration for the hit anime!

T TEEN AGE 13+

© YUKIRU SUGISAKI / KADOKAWA SHOTEN.

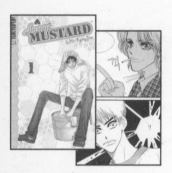

HONEY MUSTARD
BY HO-KYUNG YEO

When Ara works up the nerve to ask out the guy she has a crush on, she ends up kissing the wrong boy! The juicy smooch is witnessed by the school's puritanical chaperone, who tells their strict families. With everyone in an uproar, the only way everyone will be appeased is if the two get married—and have kids!

T TEEN AGE 13+

© Ho-Kyung Yeo, HAKSAN PUBLISHING CO., LTD.

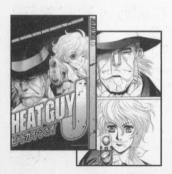

HEAT GUY J
BY CHIAKI OGISHIMA, KAZUKI AKANE, NOBUTERU YUKI & SATELIGHT

Daisuke Aurora and his android partner, Heat Guy J, work with a special division of peacekeepers to keep anything illegal off the streets. However, that doesn't sit too well with the new ruthless and well-armed mob leader. In the city that never sleeps, will Daisuke and Heat Guy J end up sleeping with the fishes?

The anime favorite as seen on MTV is now an action-packed manga!

T TEEN AGE 13+

© Satelight/Heatguy-J Project.

STOP!

This is the back of the book.
You wouldn't want to spoil a great ending

This book is printed "manga-style," in the authentic Japanese right-to-le format. Since none of the artwork has been flipped or altered, readers get to experience the story just as the creator intended. You've been asking for it, so TOKYOPOP® delivered: authentic, hot-off-the-press, and far more fun!

DIRECTIONS

If this is your first time reading manga-style, here's a quick guide to help you understand how it works.

It's eas the top
he
look fo
nga

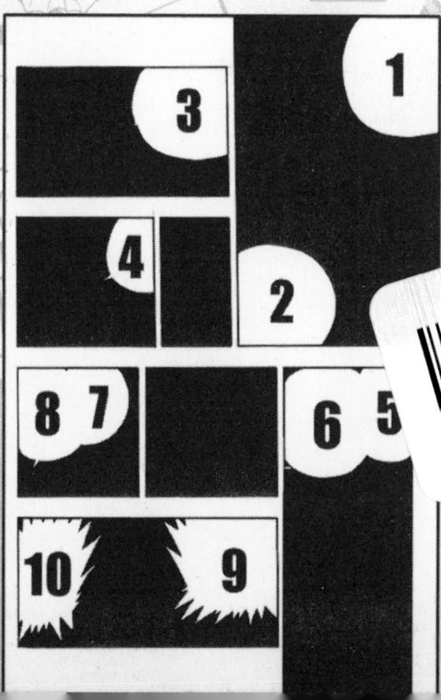
1
2
3
4
5
6
7
8
9
10

100% AUTHENTIC MANGA

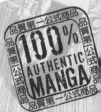